Myths & Legends

Classical Greek, Celtic, Norse, Chinese, African, Native American & More

Myths & Legends

Classical Greek, Celtic, Norse, Chinese, African, Native American & More

Foreword by William G. Doty

General Editor: Jake Jackson

METRO BOOKS
New York

METRO BOOKS
New York

An Imprint of Sterling Publishing
387 Park Avenue South
New York, NY 10016

ISBN: 978-1-4351-5023-2

For information about custom editions, special sales, and premium and corporate purchases, please contact Sterling Special Sales at 800-805-5489 or specialsales@sterlingpublishing.com.

Printed and bound by
CPI Group (UK) Ltd, Croydon, CR0 4YY

1 3 5 7 9 8 6 4 2

www.sterlingpublishing.com

Myths & Legends

Contents

Celtic

Chinese

Classical Greek

Indian

Native American

Norse

Scottish

Acknowledgements

Professor William G. Doty (Foreword)
Doty is a professor emeritus of humanities and religious studies at the University of Alabama. He is perhaps best known for his writings about myth and mythology. His many other works include studies about anthropology, psychology, classics, and art criticism. Doty has published fourteen books and over seventy essays. He also served as lecturer, translator and editor.

Jake Jackson (General Editor)
Jake Jackson has written, edited and contributed to over 20 books. Related works include studies of Babylonian creation myths, the philosophy of time and William Blake's use of mythology in his visionary literature.

Writers of each myth include the following:

O.B. Duane (African; Celtic; co-author of Chinese; Native American)

N. Hutchison (co-author of Chinese)

Judith John (co-author of Greek & Roman)

Christopher McNab (co-author of Greek & Roman)

K.E. Sullivan (co-author of Greek & Roman; Indian; Norse; Scottish)

Foreword

Myths & Legends presents a terrific collection of myths, fables, tales and legends from ancient sources from a range of cultures (Celtic, Greek, Scottish, Norse, Indian and Native American, African and Chinese) in such a way that they can be accessed readily by a contemporary reader. The authorial mode is a skillful retelling of mythical accounts, and the scope is widespread – the work becomes a very useful vade mecum indeed, a handbook that distills important aspects of the cultures included.

While the study of mythology has long been taught in schools as referring to primarily Greek and Roman examples, we must remember that it can encompass many more international cultures and, indeed, mythography today reaches into the mythologization of the singer Madonna, or the sports-lore of baseball – the basis for such analyses can be seen in the ways each of the chapters includes socio-historical introductions and discussion of primary resources. Much as in comparative literature, knowledge of the various genres or literary types and themes gives the reader sensitivity towards examples from various cultures beyond one's own. There truly are 'world myths' or at least themes and archetypes that reappear repeatedly, and a volume such as this introduces some of the many shared motifs and themes and even specific structures that surface across many of the cultures represented.

Our world is vastly larger than it was when I was a beginning student in the 1950s – world-scope is now upon us, whether through advertisements or in the mostly-early materials retold here. Think for instance of the importance of Indian and Native American thought: even the casual historian or student of religious myths can bring insights and observations that would not have appeared in previous decades. This volume sends us to primary sources by the careful retellings of the authors and introductions to the cultural wealth represented in the traditional materials, be they religious myths or folklore or legend.

William G. Doty
Professor Emeritus
University of Alabama

African Myths

Introduction

AFRICA IS A VAST CONTINENT, over three times the size of the United States of America, incorporating a huge expanse of desert and scrubland, mountains, valleys, rain forests, swamps, rivers and lakes. For much of its history, however, a large part of southern Africa has remained cut off from the outside world. The Sahara Desert, which divides the north from the south, covers nearly one-third of the continent, presenting an almost impossible obstacle for even the most resilient traveller.

North Africa stretches from Morocco to Egypt, and down through the Nile valley as far as Ethiopia. This rich and fertile region nurtures a distinctly Mediterranean culture dominated by Muslim and Christian religions. Africa south of the Sahara – the area known as 'Negro' or 'Black' Africa from which the myths and legends of this book have been selected – extends from the east and west Sudan, down through the savannas and central rain forests right into South Africa.

Sub-Saharan Africa is a land of colourful contrasts and diverse cultures, many of which have existed for hundreds and even thousands of years. Europeans remained ignorant of the region's rich history until the fifteenth century when the Portuguese arrived on the west coast, landing at the Cape of Good Hope. Before long, they were transporting thousands of African slaves to Europe and the Americas, a lucrative trade that continued until the mid-nineteenth century.

During the late nineteenth century, white settlers, among them the French, English and Dutch, began to explore further inland, and throughout the 1880s and 1890s they competed furiously for ownership of territories rich in natural resources, carving up the continent between them. By 1900, almost all of Africa was in European hands, remaining under European control until the 1950s, when the colonies began to demand their independence.

Archaeological research has revealed that by about 1200 BC, rich and powerful civilizations, such as that of Ancient Egypt, had developed in the northern part of Africa. Nothing now remains of these impressive empires, but their customs and beliefs are well recorded. Relatively little is known, on the other hand, of the earliest history of the peoples living south of the Sahara. Geographical isolation dictated that these peoples developed largely by themselves. Written culture became widespread only in the nineteenth century; before that time, the art of writing was completely unknown to Africans in the equatorial forests and the south.

The radical changes forced on the African continent as a result of colonialism and the slave trade led to the destruction of many traditional societies which had evolved over the centuries. Much information on Africa's cultural heritage remains buried forever, since there are no ancient books or documents to enlighten us. But Africa has always had a powerful tradition of storytelling. Before a European way of life prevailed, the old religions, rules and customs provided the raw material for those tribesmen who first promoted this extremely colourful oral culture. African people have persevered with their storytelling and continue to leave records of their history in songs and stories they pass down from parent to child through the generations. Stories are commonly told in the evening when the day's work is done, accompanied by mime and frequently music. They are an important medium of entertainment and instruction woven out of the substance of human experience and are very often realistic and down-to-earth.

The first African stories to reach western ears were written down only at the turn of the century when a number of missionaries, anthropologists and colonial officials arrived in Africa and made a concerted effort to record descriptions of the rituals and ceremonies they witnessed, and to transcribe as faithfully as possible tales told to them by old and young Africans before they had disappeared altogether. Some of these committed scholars wrote down what the elders told them about their gods, and man's understanding of his relationship with the gods, while others transcribed narrative myths, fables, poems, proverbs, riddles and even magic spells.

No real unified mythology exists in Africa, however. The migration of its peoples, the political fragmentation, and the sheer size of the continent have resulted in a huge diversity of lifestyles and traditions. Literally thousands of completely different languages are spoken, 2,000 in West Africa alone between the Senegal River and the headwaters of the Congo River. A complete collection of all myths of the African peoples would fill countless volumes, even if we were to ignore the fact that the collection is being added to all the time by modern-day enthusiasts.

To give a useful summary of the main characteristics of African mythology is therefore an extremely difficult task but, broadly speaking, a number of beliefs, ideas and themes are shared by African peoples, embellished by a creative spirit unique to a tribe, village or region. Nearly every tribe has its own set of cosmological myths – tales which attempt to explore the origin of the universe, the unseen forces of nature, the existence of God or a supreme being, the creation of mankind and the coming of mortality. Other stories, detailing the outrageous adventures and anti-social behaviour of one or another trickster figure are also common to nearly every tribe. Moral stories abound and animal fables, in particular, are some of the most popular of all African tales.

This chapter is divided into three sections containing only a cross-section of African tales. It is intended to provide an introduction to African mythology and is in no way a comprehensive study of its subject. A selection of creation stories, animal fables and stories which amuse and teach has been made with the aim of providing as interesting and entertaining an overview as possible.

Myths of Creation, Death and the Afterlife

MOST AFRICAN PEOPLES RECOGNIZE some sort of all-powerful, omniscient god, but the sheer size of the African continent has not allowed a uniform system of beliefs to develop. Innumerable myths on the origin and evolution of the universe exist as a result. The Fon of Dahomey speak of a supreme God, Mawu-Lisa, the 'twins' from whom all the gods and demigods are descended. The Zulu of South Africa call their deity uKqili, the wise one, and believe he raised mankind out of 'beds of grass'. The Hottentots refer to their god as Utixo, a benevolent deity who inhabits the sky and speaks with the voice of thunder.

The creation myth retold at the beginning of this chapter comes from the Yoruba tribe in west Africa, whose pantheon alone contains over 1,700 deities. The most important Yoruban gods feature in the stories. Olorun, the supreme being, is capable of seeing both 'the inside and the outside of man', while the other gods are depicted as sensitive to human problems and particularly receptive to human prayers.

Again, nearly every tribe has its own story on the creation of mankind, the origin of death and darkness, and its own unique descriptions of the Otherworld. Only a selection of these tales is retold here, chosen from among the Krachi, Kikuyu and Kono peoples of Africa.

Creation Myth: The Creation of the Universe
(From the Yoruba people, west Africa)

BEFORE THE UNIVERSE WAS CREATED, there existed only a vast expanse of sky above and an endless stretch of water and uninhabited marshland below. Olorun, the wisest of the gods, was supreme ruler of the sky, while Olokun, the most powerful goddess, ruled the seas and marshes. Both kingdoms were quite separate at that time and there was never any conflict between the two deities. Olorun was more than satisfied with his domain in the sky and hardly noticed what took place below him. Olokun was content with the kingdom she occupied, even though it contained neither living creatures nor vegetation of any kind.

But the young god Obatala was not entirely satisfied with this state of affairs, and one day, as he looked down from the sky upon the dull, grey terrain ruled by Olokun, he thought to himself:

'The kingdom below is a pitiful, barren place. Something must be done to improve its murky appearance. Now if only there were mountains and forests to brighten it up, it would make a perfect home for all sorts of living creatures.'

Obatala decided that he must visit Olorun, who was always prepared to listen to him.

'It is a good scheme, but also a very ambitious one,' Olorun said to Obatala. 'I have no doubt that the hills and valleys you describe would be far better than grey ocean, but who will create this new world, and how will they go about it?'

'If you will give me your blessing,' Obatala replied, 'I myself will undertake to do this work.'

'Then it is settled,' said Olorun. 'I cannot help you myself, but I will arrange for you to visit my son Orunmila. He will be able to guide you.'

Next day, Obatala called upon Orunmila, the eldest son of Olorun, who had been given the power to read the future and to understand the secret of existence. Orunmila produced his divining tray, and when he had placed sixteen palm nuts on it, he shook the tray and cast its contents high into the air. As the nuts dropped to the ground, he read their meaning aloud:

'First, Obatala,' he announced, 'you must find a chain of gold long enough for you to climb down from the sky to the watery wastes below. Then, as you descend, take with you a snail shell filled with sand, a white hen, a black cat and a palm nut. This is how you should begin your quest.'

Obatala listened attentively to his friend's advice and immediately set off to find a goldsmith who would make him the chain he needed to descend from the sky to the surface of the water below.

'I would be happy to make you the chain you ask for,' said the goldsmith, 'provided you can give me all the gold I need. But I doubt that you will find enough here for me to complete my task.'

Obatala would not be dissuaded, however, and having instructed the goldsmith to go ahead with his work, he approached the other sky gods and one by one explained to them his purpose, requesting that they contribute whatever gold they possessed. The response was generous. Some of the gods gave gold dust, others gave rings, bracelets or pendants, and before long a huge, glittering mound had been collected. The goldsmith examined all the gold that was brought before him, but still he complained that there was not enough.

'It is the best I can do,' Obatala told him. 'I have asked all of the other gods to help out and there is no more gold left in the sky. Make the chain as long as you possibly can and fix a hook to one end. Even if it fails to reach the water below, I am determined to climb down on it.'

The goldsmith worked hard to complete the chain and when it was finished, the hook was fastened to the edge of the sky and the chain lowered far below. Orunmila appeared and handed Obatala a bag containing the sand-filled snail's shell, the white hen, the black cat and the palm nut, and as soon as he had slung it over his shoulder, the young god began climbing down the golden chain, lower and lower until he saw that he was leaving the world of light and entering a world of twilight.

Before long, Obatala could feel the damp mists rising up off the surface of the water, but at the same time, he realized that he had just about reached the end of his golden chain.

'I cannot jump from here,' he thought. 'If I let go of the chain I will fall into the sea and almost certainly drown.'

And while he looked around him rather helplessly, he suddenly heard a familiar voice calling to him from up above.

'Make use of the sand I gave you,' Orunmila instructed him, 'toss it into the water below.'

Obatala obeyed, and after he had poured out the sand, he heard Orunmila calling to him a second time:

'Release the white hen,' Orunmila cried.

Obatala reached into his bag and pulled out the white hen, dropping her on to the waters beneath where he had sprinkled the sand. As soon as she had landed, the hen began to scratch in the sand, scattering it in all directions. Wherever the grains fell, dry land instantly appeared. The larger heaps of sand became hills, while the smaller heaps became valleys.

Obatala let go of his chain and jumped on to the solid earth. As he walked he smiled with pleasure, for the land now extended a great many miles in all directions. But he was proudest of the spot where his feet had first landed, and decided to name this place Ife. Stooping to the ground, he began digging a hole, and buried his palm nut in the soil. Immediately, a palm tree sprang up from the earth, shedding its seeds as it stretched to its full height so that other trees soon shot up around it. Obatala felled some of these trees and built for himself a sturdy house thatched with palm leaves. And here, in this place, he settled down, separated from the other sky gods, with only his black cat for company.

Creation Myth: Obatala Creates Mankind

(From the Yoruba people, west Africa)

OBATALA LIVED QUITE CONTENTEDLY in his new home beneath the skies, quite forgetting that Olorun might wish to know how his plans were progressing. The supreme god soon grew impatient for news and ordered Agemo, the chameleon, to go down the golden chain to investigate. The chameleon descended and when he arrived at Ife, he knocked timidly on Obatala's door.

'Olorun has sent me here,' he said, 'to discover whether or not you have been successful in your quest.'

'Certainly I have,' replied Obatala, 'look around you and you will see the land I have created and the plants I have raised from the soil. Tell Olorun that it is now a far more pleasant kingdom than it was before, and that I would be more than willing to spend the rest of my time here, except that I am growing increasingly weary of the twilight and long to see brightness once more.'

Agemo returned home and reported to Olorun all that he had seen and heard. Olorun smiled, for it pleased him greatly that Obatala had achieved what he had set out to do. The young god, who was among his favourites, had earned a special reward, and so Olorun fashioned with his own hands a dazzling golden orb and tossed it into the sky.

'For you, Obatala, I have created the sun,' said Olorun, 'it will shed warmth and light on the new world you have brought to life below.'

Obatala very gladly received this gift, and as soon as he felt the first rays of the sun shining down on him, his restless spirit grew calmer. He remained quite satisfied for a time, but then, as the weeks turned to months, he became unsettled once more and began to dream of spending time in the company of other beings, not unlike himself, who could move and speak and with whom he could share his thoughts and feelings.

Obatala sat down and began to claw at the soil as he attempted to picture the little creatures who would keep him company. He found that the clay was soft and pliable, so he began to shape tiny figures in his own image. He laid the first of them in the sun to dry and worked on with great enthusiasm until he had produced several more.

He had been sitting for a long time in the hot sunshine before he realized how tired and thirsty he felt.

'What I need is some palm wine to revive me,' he thought to himself, and he stood up and headed off towards the nearest palm tree.

He placed his bowl underneath it and drew off the palm juice, leaving it to ferment in the heat until it had turned to wine. When the wine was ready, Obatala helped himself to a very long drink, and as he gulped down bowl after bowl of the refreshing liquid, he failed to realize that the wine was making him quite drunk.

Obatala had swallowed so much of the wine that his fingers grew clumsy, but he continued to work energetically, too drunk to notice that the clay figures he now produced were no longer perfectly formed. Some had crooked backs or crooked limbs, others had arms and legs of uneven length. Obatala was so pleased with himself he raised his head and called out jubilantly to the skies:

'I have created beings from the soil, but only you, Olorun, can breathe life into them. Grant me this request so that I will always have human beings to keep me company here in Ife.'

Olorun heard Obatala's plea and did not hesitate to breathe life into the clay figures, watching with interest as they rose up from the ground and began to obey the commands of their creator. Soon they had built wooden shelters for themselves next to the god's own house, creating the first Yoruba village in Ife where before only one solitary house had stood. Obatala was filled with admiration and pride, but now, as the effects of the palm wine started to wear off, he began to notice that some of the humans he had created were contorted and misshapen. The sight of the little creatures struggling as they went about their chores filled him with sadness and remorse.

'My drunkenness has caused these people to suffer,' he proclaimed solemnly, 'and I swear that I will never drink palm wine again. From this day forward, I will be the special protector of all humans who are born with deformities.'

Obatala remained faithful to his pledge and dedicated himself to the welfare of the human beings he had created, making sure that he always had a moment to spare for the lame and the blind. He saw to it that the people prospered and, before long, the Yoruba village of Ife had grown into an impressive city. Obatala also made certain that his people had all the tools they needed to clear and cultivate the land. He presented each man with a copper bush knife and a wooden hoe and taught them to grow millet, yams and a whole variety of other crops, ensuring that mankind had a plentiful supply of food for its survival.

Creation Myth: Olokun's Revenge
(From the Yoruba people, west Africa)

AFTER HE HAD LIVED among the human race for a long period of time, Obatala came to the decision that he had done all he could for his people. The day had arrived for him to retire, he believed, and so he climbed up the golden chain and returned to his home in the sky once more, promising to visit the earth as frequently as possible. The other gods never tired of hearing Obatala describe the kingdom he had created below. Many were so captivated by the image he presented of the newly created human beings, that they decided to depart from the sky and go down to live among them. And as they prepared to leave, Olorun took them aside and counselled them:

'Each of you shall have a special role while you are down there, and I ask that you never forget your duty to the human race. Always listen to the prayers of the people and offer help when they are in need.'

One deity, however, was not at all pleased with Obatala's work or the praise he had received from Olorun. The goddess Olokun, ruler of the sea, watched with increasing fury as, one by one, the other gods arrived in her domain and began dividing up the land amongst themselves.

'Obatala has never once consulted me about any of this,' she announced angrily, 'but he shall pay for the insult to my honour.'

The goddess commanded the great waves of her ocean to rise up, for it was her intention to destroy the land Obatala had created and replace it with water once more. The terrible flood began, and soon the fields were completely submerged. Crops were destroyed and thousands of people were swept away by the roaring tide.

Those who survived the deluge fled to the hills and called to Obatala for help, but he could not hear them from his home high above in the sky.

In desperation, the people turned to Eshu, one of the gods recently descended to earth.

'Please return to the sky,' they begged, 'and tell the great gods of the flood that threatens to destroy everything.'

'First you must show that you revere the gods,' replied Eshu. 'You must offer up a sacrifice and pray hard that you will be saved.'

The people went away and returned with a goat which they sacrificed as food for Obatala. But still Eshu refused to carry the message.

'You ask me to perform this great service,' he told them, 'and yet you do not offer to reward me. If I am to be your messenger, I too deserve a gift.'

The people offered up more sacrifices to Eshu and only when he was content that they had shown him appropriate respect did he begin to climb the golden chain back to the sky to deliver his message.

Obatala was deeply upset by the news and extremely anxious for the safety of his people, for he was uncertain how best to deal with so powerful a goddess as Olokun. Once more, he approached Orunmila and asked for advice. Orunmila consulted his divining nuts, and at last he said to Obatala:

'Rest here in the sky while I descend below. I will use my gifts to turn back the water and make the land rise again.'

Orunmila went down and, using his special powers, brought the waves under control so that the marshes began to dry up and land became visible again. But although the people greeted the god as their saviour and pleaded with him to act as their protector, Orunmila confessed that he had no desire to remain among them. Before he departed, however, he passed on a great many of his gifts to the people, teaching them how to divine the future and to control the unseen forces of nature. What he taught the people was never lost and it was passed on like a precious heirloom from one generation to another.

Creation Myth: Agemo Outwits Olokun

(From the Yoruba people, west Africa)

BUT EVEN AFTER Orunmila had returned to his home in the sky, all was not yet settled between Olokun and the other sky gods. More embittered than ever before by her defeat, Olokun began to consider ways in which she might humiliate Olorun, the god who had allowed Obatala to usurp her kingdom.

Now the goddess was a highly skilled weaver, but she was also expert in dyeing the cloths she had woven. And knowing that no other sky god possessed greater knowledge of clothmaking, she sent a message to Olorun challenging him to a weaving contest. Olorun received her message rather worriedly and said to himself:

'Olokun knows far more about making cloth that I will ever know, but I cannot allow her to think that she is superior to me in anything. Somehow I must appear to meet her challenge and yet avoid taking part in the contest. But how can I possibly do this?'

He pondered the problem a very long time until, at last, he was struck by a worthwhile thought. Smiling broadly, he summoned Agemo, the chameleon, to his side, and instructed him to carry an important message to Olokun.

Agemo climbed down the golden chain and went in search of Olokun's dwelling.

'The ruler of the sky, Olorun, greets you,' he announced. 'He says that if your cloth is as magnificent as you say it is, then the ruler of the sky will be happy to compete with you in the contest you have suggested. But he thinks it only fair to see some of your cloth in advance, and has asked me to examine it on his behalf so that I may report to him on its quality.'

Olokun was happy to accommodate Olorun's request. She retired to a backroom and having put on a skirt of radiant green cloth, she stood confidently before the chameleon. But as the chameleon looked at the garment, his skin began to change colour until it was exactly the same brilliant shade as the skirt. Next Olokun put on an orange-hued cloth. But again, to her astonishment, the chameleon turned a beautiful shade of bright orange.

One by one, the goddess put on skirts of various bright colours, but on each occasion the chameleon perfectly matched the colour of her robe. Finally the goddess thought to herself:

'This person is only a messenger, and if Olorun's servants can reproduce the exact colours of my very finest cloth, what hope will I have in a contest against the supreme god himself?'

The goddess conceded defeat and spoke earnestly to the chameleon:

'Tell your master that the ruler of the seas sends her greetings to the ruler of the sky. Say to him that I acknowledge his supremacy in weaving and in all other things as well.'

And so it came to pass that Olorun and Olokun resumed their friendship and that peace was restored to the whole of the universe once more.

The Gods Descend from the Sky
(From the Dahomean people, west Africa)

NANA BALUKU, the mother of all creation, fell pregnant before she finally retired from the universe. Her offspring was androgynous, a being with one body and two faces. The face that resembled a woman was called Mawu and her eyes were the moon. She took control of the night and all territories to the west. The male face was called Lisa and his eyes were the sun. Lisa controlled the east and took charge of the daylight.

At the beginning of the present world, Mawu-Lisa was the only being in existence, but eventually the moon was eclipsed by the sun and many children were conceived. The first fruits of the union were a pair of twins, a male called Da Zodji and a female called Nyohwè Ananu. Another child followed shortly afterwards, a male and female form joined in one body, and this child was named Sogbo. The third birth again produced twins, a male, Agbè, and a female, Naètè. The fourth and fifth children were both male and were named Agè and Gu. Gu's torso was made of stone and a giant sword protruded from the hole in his neck where his head would otherwise have been. The sixth offspring was not made of flesh and blood. He was given the name Djo, meaning air, or atmosphere. Finally, the seventh child born was named Legba, and because he was the youngest, he became Mawu-Lisa's particular favourite.

When these children had grown to adulthood and the appropriate time had arrived to divide up the kingdoms of the universe among them, Mawu-Lisa gathered them together. To their first-born, the twins Da Zodji and Nyohwè Ananu, the parents gave the earth below and sent them, laden with heavenly riches, down from the sky to inhabit their new home. To Sogbo, who was both man and woman, they gave the sky, commanding him to rule over thunder and lightning. The twins Agbè and Naètè were sent to take command of the waters and the creatures of the deep, while Agè was ordered to live in the bush as a hunter where he could take control of all the birds and beasts of the earth.

To Gu, whom Mawu-Lisa considered their strength, they gave the forests and vast stretches of fertile soil, supplying him also with the tools and weapons mankind would need to cultivate the land. Mawu-Lisa ordered Djo to occupy the space between the earth and the sky and entrusted him with the life-span of human beings. It was also Djo's role to clothe the other sky gods, making them invisible to man.

To each of their offspring, Mawu-Lisa then gave a special language. These are the languages still spoken by the priests and mediums of the gods in their songs and oracles. To Da Zodji and Nyohwè Ananu, Mawu-Lisa gave the language of the earth and took from them all memory of the sky language. They gave to Sogbo, Agbè and Naètè, Agè and Gu the languages they would speak. But to Djo, they gave the language of men.

Then Mawu-Lisa said to Legba: 'Because you are my youngest child, I will keep you with me always. Your work will be to visit all the kingdoms ruled over by your brothers and sisters and report to me on their progress.'

And that is why Legba knows all the languages of his siblings, and he alone knows the language of Mawu-Lisa. You will find Legba everywhere, because all beings, human and gods, must first approach Legba before Mawu-Lisa, the supreme deity, will answer their prayers.

God Abandons the Earth
(From Ghana, west Africa)

IN THE BEGINNING, God was very proud of the human beings he had created and wanted to live as close as possible to them. So he made certain that the sky was low enough for the people to touch and built for himself a home directly above their heads. God was so near that everyone on earth became familiar with his face and every day he would stop to make conversation with the people, offering a helping hand if they were ever in trouble.

This arrangement worked very well at first, but soon God observed that the people had started to take advantage of his closeness. Children began to wipe their greasy hands on the sky when they had finished their meals and often, if a woman was in search of an extra ingredient for dinner, she would simply reach up, tear a piece off the sky and add it to her cooking pot. God remained tolerant through all of this, but he knew his patience would not last forever and hoped that his people would not test its limit much further.

Then one afternoon, just as he had lain down to rest, a group of women gathered underneath the sky to pound the corn they had harvested. One old woman among them had a particularly large wooden bowl and a very long pestle, and as she thumped down on the grains, she knocked violently against the sky. God arose indignantly from his bed and descended below, but as he approached the woman to chastise her, she suddenly jerked back her arm and hit him in the eye with her very long pestle.

God gave a great shout, his voice booming like thunder through the air, and as he shouted, he raised his powerful arms above his head and pushed upwards against the sky with all his strength, flinging it far into the distance.

As soon as they realized that the earth and the sky were separated, the people became angry with the old woman who had injured God and pestered her day and night to bring him back to them. The woman went away and although she was not very clever, she thought long and hard about the problem until she believed she had found the solution. Returning to her village, she ordered her children to collect all the wooden mortars that they could find. These she piled one on top of the other until they had almost bridged the gap between the earth and the heavens. Only one more mortar was needed to complete the job, but although her children searched high and low, they could not find the missing object. In desperation, the old woman told them to remove the lowest mortar from the bottom of the pile and place it on the top. But as soon as they did this, all the mortars came crashing down, killing the old woman, her children and the crowd who had gathered to admire the towering structure.

Ever since that day, God has remained in the heavens where mankind can no longer approach him as easily as before. There are some, however, who say they have caught a glimpse of him and others who offer up sacrifices calling for his forgiveness and asking him to make his home among them once more.

The Coming of Darkness
(From the Kono people, Sierra Leone)

WHEN GOD FIRST MADE THE WORLD, there was never any darkness or cold. The sun always shone brightly during the day, and at night, the moon bathed the earth in a softer light, ensuring that everything could still be seen quite clearly.

But one day God sent for the Bat and handed him a mysterious parcel to take to the moon. He told the Bat it contained darkness, but as he did not have the time to explain precisely what darkness was, the Bat went on his way without fully realizing the importance of his mission.

He flew at a leisurely pace with the parcel strapped on his back until he began to feel rather tired and hungry. He was in no great hurry he decided, and so he put down his load by the roadside and wandered off in search of something to eat.

But while he was away, a group of mischievous animals approached the spot where he had paused to rest and, seeing the parcel, began to open it, thinking there might be something of value inside of it. The Bat returned just as they were untying the last piece of string and rushed forward to stop them. But too late! The darkness forced its way through the opening and rose up into the sky before anyone had a chance to catch it.

Quickly the Bat gave chase, flying about everywhere, trying to grab hold of the darkness and return it to the parcel before God discovered what had happened. But the harder he tried, the more the darkness eluded him, so that eventually he fell into an exhausted sleep lasting several hours.

When the Bat awoke, he found himself in a strange twilight world and once again, he began chasing about in every direction, hoping he would succeed where he had failed before.

But the Bat has never managed to catch the darkness, although you will see him every evening just after the sun has set, trying to trap it and deliver it safely to the moon as God first commanded him.

The Sun and the Moon
(From the Krachi people, west Africa)

THE SUN AND THE MOON fell in love and decided to marry. For a time they were very happy together and produced many children whom they christened 'stars'. But it was not long before the moon grew weary of her husband and decided to take a lover, refusing to conceal the fact that she greatly enjoyed the variety.

Of course, the sun soon came to hear of his wife's brazen infidelity and the news made him extremely unhappy. He attempted to reason with the moon, but when he saw that his efforts were entirely fruitless, he decided to drive his wife out of his house. Some of the children sided with their mother, while others supported their father. But the sun was never too hard on his wife, in spite of their differences, and saw to it that their possessions were equally divided up.

The moon was always too proud to accept her husband's kindness, however, and even to this day, she continues to make a habit of trespassing on his lands, often taking her children with her and encouraging them to fight the siblings who remain behind with their father.

The constant battles between the star-children of the sun and the star-children of the moon produce great storms of thunder and lightning and it is only when she becomes bored of these confrontations that the moon sends her messenger, the rainbow, into the field, instructing him to wave a cloth of many colours as a signal for her children to retreat.

Sometimes the moon herself is caught by the sun attempting to steal crops from his fields. Whenever this happens, he chases after his estranged wife and if he catches her he begins to flog her or even tries to eat her.

So whenever a man sees an eclipse, he knows that things have come to blows once again between husband and wife up above. At this time, he must be certain to beat his drum and threaten the sun very loudly, for if he does not, the sun might finish the job, and we should certainly lose the moon forever.

How Death First Entered the World
(From the Krachi people, west Africa)

MANY YEARS AGO, a great famine spread throughout the land, and at that time, the eldest son of every household was sent out in search of food and instructed not to return until he had found something for the family to eat and drink.

There was a certain young man among the Krachi whose responsibility it was to provide for the family, and so he wandered off in search of food, moving deeper and deeper into the bush every day until he finally came to a spot he did not recognize. Just up ahead of him, he noticed a large form lying on the ground. He approached it cautiously, hoping that if the creature were dead, it might be a good source of food, but he had taken only a few steps forward when the mound began to stir, revealing that it was not an animal at all, but a ferocious-looking giant with flowing white hair stretched out for miles on the ground around him, all the way from Krachi to Salaga.

The giant opened one eye and shouted at the young man to explain his presence. The boy stood absolutely terrified, yet after some minutes, he managed to blurt out that he had never intended to disturb the giant's rest, but had come a great distance in search of food.

'I am Owuo,' said the giant, 'but people also call me Death. You, my friend, have caught me in a good mood and so I will give you some food and water if you will fetch and carry for me in return.'

The young man could scarcely believe his luck, and readily agreed to serve the giant in exchange for a few regular meals. Owuo arose and walked towards his cave where he began roasting some meat on a spit over the fire. Never before had the boy tasted such a fine meal, and after he had washed it down with a bowl of fresh water, he sat back and smiled, well pleased that he had made the acquaintance of the giant.

For a long time afterwards, the young man happily served Owuo, and every evening, in return for his work, he was presented with a plate of the most delicious meat for his supper.

But one day the boy awoke feeling terribly homesick and begged his master to allow him to visit his family, if only for a few days.

'You may visit your family for as long as you wish,' said the giant, 'on the condition that you bring another boy to replace you.'

So the young man returned to his village where he told his family the whole story of his meeting with the giant. Eventually he managed to persuade his younger brother to go with him into the bush and here he handed him over to Owuo, promising that he would himself return before too long.

Several months had passed, and soon the young man grew hungry again and began to yearn for a taste of the meat the giant had cooked for him. Finally, he made up his mind to return to his master, and leaving his family behind, he returned to Owuo's hut and knocked boldly on the door.

The giant himself answered, and asked the young man what he wanted.

'I would like some more of the good meat you were once so generous to share with me,' said the boy, hoping the giant would remember his face.

'Very well,' replied Owuo, 'you can have as much of it as you want, but you will have to work hard for me, as you did before.'

The young man consented, and after he had eaten as much as he could, he went about his chores enthusiastically. The work lasted many weeks and every day the boy ate his fill of roasted meat. But to his surprise he never saw anything of his brother, and whenever he asked about him, the giant told him, rather aloofly, that the lad had simply gone away on business.

Once more, however, the young man grew homesick and asked Owuo for permission to visit his village. The giant agreed on condition that this time, he bring back a girl to carry out his duties while he was away. The young man hurried home and there he pleaded with his sister to go into the bush and keep the giant company for a few months. The girl agreed, and after she had waved goodbye to her brother, she entered the giant's cave quite merrily, accompanied by a slave companion her own age.

Only a short time had passed before the boy began to dream of the meat again, longing for even a small morsel of it. So he followed the familiar path through the bush until he found Owuo's cave. The giant did not seem particularly pleased to see him and grumbled loudly at the disturbance. But he pointed the way to a room at the back and told the boy to help himself to as much meat as he wanted.

The young man took up a juicy bone which he began to devour. But to his horror, he recognized it at once as his sister's thigh and as he looked more closely at all the rest of the meat, he was appalled to discover that he had been sitting there, happily chewing on the body of his sister and her slave girl.

As fast as his legs could carry him, he raced back to the village and immediately confessed to the elders what he had done and the awful things he had seen. At once, the alarm was sounded and all the people hurried out into the bush to investigate the giant's dwelling for themselves. But as they drew nearer, they became fearful of what he might do to them and scurried back to the village to consult among themselves what steps should be taken. Eventually, it was agreed to go to Salaga, where they knew the giant's long hair came to an end, and set it alight. The chief of the village carried the torch, and when they were certain that the giant's hair was burning well, they returned to the bush, hid themselves in the undergrowth, and awaited the giant's reaction.

Presently, Owuo began to sweat and toss about inside his cave. The closer the flames moved towards him, the more he thrashed about and grumbled until, at last, he rushed outside, his head on fire, and fell down screaming in agony.

The villagers approached him warily and only the young man had the courage to venture close enough to see whether the giant was still breathing. And as he bent over the huge form, he noticed a bundle of medicine concealed in the roots of Owuo's hair. Quickly he seized it and called to the others to come and see what he had found.

The chief of the village examined the bundle, but no one could say what power the peculiar medicine might have. Then one old man among the crowd suggested that no harm could be done if they took some of the medicine and sprinkled it on the bones and meat in the giant's hut. This was done, and to the delight of everyone gathered, the slave girl, her mistress and the boy's brother returned to life at once.

A small quantity of the medicine-dust remained, but when the young man proposed that he should put it on the giant and restore him to life, there was a great uproar among the people. Yet the boy insisted that he should help the giant who had once helped him, and so the chief, by way of compromise, allowed him to sprinkle the left-over dust into the eye of the dead giant.

The young man had no sooner done this when the giant's eye opened wide, causing the people to flee in great terror.

But it is from this eye that death comes. For every time that Owuo shuts that eye, a man dies, and unfortunately for mankind, he is forever blinking and winking, trying to clear the dust from his eye.

Wanjiru, Sacrificed by Her Family
(From the Kikuyu people, Kenya)

THE SUN BEAT DOWN MERCILESSLY and there was no sign of any rain. This happened one year, and it happened again a second year, and even a third year, so that the crops died and the men, women and children found themselves close to starvation. Finally, the elders of the village called all the people together, and they assembled on the scorched grass at the foot of the hill where they had sung and danced in happier times.

Sick and weary of their miserable plight, they turned to each other and asked helplessly:

'Why is it that the rains do not come?'

Not one among them could find an answer, and so they went to the house of the witch-doctor and put to him the same question:

'Tell us why there is no rain,' they wept. 'Our crops have failed for a third season and we shall soon die of hunger if things do not change.'

The witch-doctor took hold of his gourd, shook it hard, and poured its contents on the ground. After he had done this three times, he spoke gravely:

'There is a young maiden called Wanjiru living among you. If you want the rain to fall, she must be bought by the people of the village. In two days time you should all return to this place, and every one of you, from the eldest to the youngest, must bring with him a goat for the purchase of the maiden.'

And so, on the appointed day, the people gathered together again, each one of them leading a goat to the foot of the hill where the witch-doctor waited to receive them. He ordered the crowd to form a circle and called for Wanjiru to come forward and stand in the middle with her relations to one side of her.

One by one, the people began to move towards Wanjiru's family, leading the goats in payment, and as they approached, the feet of the young girl began to sink into the ground. In an instant, she had sunk up to her knees and she screamed in terror as the soil tugged at her limbs, pulling her closer towards the earth.

Her father and mother saw what was happening and they, too, cried out in fear:

'Our daughter is lost! Our daughter is lost! We must do something to save her.'

But the villagers continued to close in around them, each of them handing over their goat until Wanjiru sank deeper to her waist.

'I am lost!' the girl called out, 'but much rain will come.'

She sank to her breast, and as she did so, heavy black clouds began to gather overhead. She sank even lower, up to her neck, and now the rain started to fall from above in huge drops.

Again, Wanjiru's family attempted to move forward to save her, but yet more people came towards them, pressing them to take goats in payment, and so they stood still, watching as the girl wailed:

'My people have forsaken me! I am undone.'

Soon she had vanished from sight. The earth closed over her, the rain poured down in a great deluge and the villagers ran to their huts for shelter without pausing to look back.

Now there was a particular young warrior of fearless reputation among the people who had been in love with Wanjiru ever since childhood. Several weeks had passed since her disappearance, but still he could not reconcile himself to her loss and repeated continually to himself:

'Wanjiru is gone from me and her own people have done this thing to her. But I will find her. I will go to the same place and bring her back.'

Taking up his shield and his spear, the young warrior departed his home in search of the girl he loved. For almost a year, he roamed the countryside, but still he could find no trace of her. Weary and dejected, he returned home to the village and stood on the spot where Wanjiru had vanished, allowing his tears to flow freely for the first time.

Suddenly, his feet began to sink into the soil and he sank lower and lower until the ground closed over him and he found himself standing in the middle of a long, winding road beneath the earth's surface. He did not hesitate to follow this road, and after a time, he spotted a figure up ahead of him. He ran towards the figure and saw that it was Wanjiru, even though she was scarcely recognizable in her filthy, tattered clothing.

'You were sacrificed to bring the rain,' he spoke tenderly to her, 'but now that the rain has come, I shall take you back where you belong.'

And he lifted Wanjiru carefully onto his back and carried her, as if she were his own beloved child, along the road he had come by, until they rose together to the open air and their feet touched the ground once more.

'You shall not return to the house of your people,' the warrior told Wanjiru, 'they have treated you shamefully. I will look after you instead.'

So they waited until nightfall, and under cover of darkness, the young warrior took Wanjiru to his mother's house, instructing the old woman to tell no one that the girl had returned.

The months passed by, and Wanjiru lived happily with mother and son. Every day a goat was slaughtered and the meat served to her. The old woman made clothes from the skins and hung beads in the girl's hair so that soon she had regained the healthy glow she once had.

Harvest time was now fast approaching, and a great feast was to be held among the people of the village. The young warrior was one of the first to arrive but Wanjiru waited until the rest of the guests had assembled before she came out of the house to join the festivities. At first, she was not recognized by anyone, but after a time, one of her brothers approached her and cried out:

'Surely that is Wanjiru, the sister we lost when the rains came.'

The girl hung her head and gave no answer.

'You sold Wanjiru shamefully,' the young warrior intervened, 'you do not deserve to have her back.'

And he beat off her relatives and took Wanjiru back to his mother's house.

But the next day, her family knocked on his door asking to see the young girl. The warrior refused them once more, but still they came, again and again, until, on the fourth day, the young man relented and said to himself:

'Those are real tears her family shed. Surely now they have proven that they care.'

So he invited her father and her mother and her brothers into his home and sat down to fix the bride-price for Wanjiru. And when he had paid it, the young warrior married Wanjiru who had returned to him from the land of shadows beneath the earth.

Animal Fables

A FABLE IS A SHORT MORAL STORY, and the African storyteller has shown a particular fondness for this sort of tale in which the actions and escapades of the characters are described not merely for our entertainment, but also for us to reflect on and from which to learn lessons.

Many African fables revolve entirely around animals, and the stories which follow are a selection of some of the most well-known. In all of the fables, animals have the ability to speak and they generally behave like humans. Some, like the chameleon in the last story, even marry human beings.

Two of the most outstanding characters of the animal fables are the spider and the tortoise. The first three stories of this section centre on the adventures of the shrewd and designing spider Anansi, who usually manages to outwit all of his opponents, yet whose behaviour is not always intended to reflect the correct moral course. The stories chosen originate in west Africa, although similar fables are told throughout the whole of the African continent.

Equally shrewd and clever, despite his slow-moving body and wrinkled skin, is the tortoise who, again and again, triumphs over his adversaries. In the four tales which follow, it is his uncanny wisdom that shines through, ensuring that he is never defeated, even by those who are much larger and stronger.

Tales of Anansi, the Spider Trickster

How Anansi Became a Spider
(From the Dagomba people, west Africa)

A VERY LONG TIME AGO, there lived a king who had amongst his possessions a very magnificent ram, larger and taller than any other specimen in the entire country. The ram was more precious to him than anything else he owned and he made it quite clear to his subjects that the animal must be allowed to roam wherever it chose, and be allowed to eat as much food as it desired, even if the people themselves were forced to go hungry. If anyone should ever hit or injure the king's ram, that man should certainly die.

Every citizen of the kingdom obeyed the king's orders without a great deal of complaint, but there was one among them, a wealthy farmer named Anansi, who was particularly proud of the crops he raised. Everyone suspected that he would not tolerate a visit from the king's ram and they prayed amongst themselves that such an event might never happen.

One day, however, when the rains had begun to fall, and his crops were already as tall as his waist, Anansi went out to make a final inspection of his fields. He was very pleased with what he saw and was just about to return to his farmhouse when he noticed in the distance an area of land where the corn had been trampled underfoot and the young shoots eaten away. There in the middle of the field, still munching away quite happily, stood the king's ram. Anansi was so furious he hurled a large pebble at the animal intending only to frighten him away. But the stone hit the ram right between the eyes and before he had quite realized what he had done, the animal lay dead at his feet.

Anansi did not know what he should do. Like everybody else in the village, he was only too familiar with the king's orders and knew he would face certain death if his crime was discovered. He leaned back against a shea-butter tree wondering how to resolve the dreadful mess. Suddenly a nut fell on his head from one of the branches above. Anansi picked it up and ate it. He liked the taste of it very much and so he shook the tree until several more nuts fell to the ground. Then the most fantastic idea entered his head. He picked up the nuts and put them in his pocket. He quickly lifted the ram and climbed the tree with him. As soon as he had tied the animal to a strong bough he descended once more and headed off towards the house of his friend, Kusumbuli, the spider.

Anansi found his friend at home and the two sat down and began to chat. After a few moments, Anansi took one of the shea-nuts from his pocket and handed it to his friend.

'This nut has an excellent flavour,' said Kusumbuli, as he sat chomping on the ripe flesh, 'tell me, where did you come across such a fine crop?'

Anansi promised to show the spider the exact spot and led him to the tree where the nuts were growing in large clusters.

'You'll have to shake quite hard to loosen them,' Anansi advised Kusumbuli, 'don't be afraid, the trunk is a strong one.'

So the spider began shaking the tree violently and as he did so, the dead ram fell to the ground.

'Oh, my friend,' cried Anansi at once, 'what have you done? Look, the king's ram is lying at your feet and you have killed him.'

Kusumbuli turned pale as a wave of panic swept over him.

'There is only one thing you can do now,' Anansi urged the spider, 'go and unburden your conscience at once. Tell the king precisely what has happened and with any luck he will understand that the whole affair was a most unfortunate accident.'

Kusumbuli thought that this was good advice, so he picked up the dead ram and set off to confess his crime, hoping the king would be in a good mood.

The road towards the king's palace brought him past his own home and the spider went indoors to bid a sad farewell to his wife and children, believing that he might never set eyes on them again. Anansi stood at the entrance while Kusumbuli went into the back room and told his wife everything that had happened. She listened attentively to what he said and immediately saw that there was some trick involved.

'I have never seen a ram climb a tree before, Kusumbuli,' she said to him. 'Use your head. Anansi has something to do with this and you are taking the blame for him. Hear me now and do exactly as I say.'

So she advised her husband that he must leave Anansi behind and pretend to go alone in search of the king. After he had gone some distance, she told him, he was to rest and then return home and announce that all had turned out well in the end. The spider agreed to do this and asked Anansi if he would be so good as to look after his wife and children. His friend promised to watch over them faithfully and the spider set off on his travels winking at his wife as he moved away.

Several hours later, Kusumbuli returned to his home, smiling from ear to ear as he embraced his family.

'Come and celebrate with us, Anansi,' he cried excitedly, 'I have been to see the king and he was not at all angry with me. In fact, he said he had no use for a dead ram and insisted that I help myself to as much of the meat as I wanted.'

At this, Anansi became enraged and shouted out:

'What! You have been given all that meat when it was I who took the trouble to kill that ram. I should have been given my fair share, you deserved none of it.'

Kusumbuli and his wife now leaped upon Anansi and bound his hands and legs. Then they dragged him to the king's palace and reported to their ruler the whole unpleasant affair.

Anansi squirmed on the floor and begged for the king's mercy. But the king could not control his fury and he raised his foot to kick Anansi as he lay on the ground. The king kicked so hard that Anansi broke into a thousand pieces that scattered themselves all over the room.

And that is how Anansi came to be such a small spider. And that is why you will find him in every corner of the house, awaiting the day when someone will put all the pieces together again.

Anansi Obtains the Sky-God's Stories
(From the Ashanti people, west Africa)

KWAKU ANANSI had one great wish. He longed to be the owner of all the stories known in the world, but these were kept by the Sky-God, Nyame [The Ashanti refer to God as 'Nyame'. The Dagomba call him 'Wuni', while the Krachi refer to him as 'Wulbari'.], in a safe hiding-place high above the clouds.

One day, Anansi decided to pay the Sky-God a visit to see if he could persuade Nyame to sell him the stories.

'I am flattered you have come so far, little creature,' the Sky-God told Anansi, 'but many rich and powerful men have preceded you and none has been able to purchase what they came here for. I am willing to part with my stories, but the price is very high. What makes you think that you can succeed where they have all failed?'

'I feel sure I will be able to buy them,' answered Anansi bravely, 'if you will only tell me what the price is.'

'You are very determined, I see,' replied Nyame, 'but I must warn you that the price is no ordinary one. Listen carefully now to what I demand of you.

'First of all, you must capture Onini, the wise old python, and present him to me. When you have done this, you must go in search of the Mmoboro, the largest nest of hornets in the forest, and bring them here also. Finally, look for Osebo, the fastest of all leopards and set a suitable trap for him. Bring him to me either dead or alive.

'When you have delivered me these three things, all the stories of the world will be handed over to you.'

'I shall bring you everything you ask for,' Anansi declared firmly, and he hastened towards his home where he began making plans for the tasks ahead.

That afternoon, he sat down with his wife, Aso, and told her all about his visit to the Sky-God.

'How will I go about trapping the great python, Onini?' he asked her.

His wife, who was a very clever woman, instructed her husband to make a special trip to the centre of the woods:

'Go and cut yourself a long bamboo pole,' she ordered him, 'and gather some strong creeper-vines as well. As soon as you have done this, return here to me and I will tell you what to do with these things.'

Anansi gathered these objects as his wife had commanded and after they had spent some hours consulting further, he set off enthusiastically towards the house of Onini.

As he approached closer, he suddenly began arguing with himself in a loud and angry voice:

'My wife is a stupid woman,' he pronounced, 'she says it is longer and stronger. I say it is shorter and weaker. She has no respect. I have a great deal. She is stupid. I am right.'

'What's all this about?' asked the python, suddenly appearing at the door of his hut. 'Why are you having this angry conversation with yourself?'

'Oh! Please ignore me,' answered the spider. 'It's just that my wife has put me in such a bad mood. For she says this bamboo pole is longer and stronger than you are, and I say she is a liar.'

'There is no need for the two of you to argue so bitterly on my account,' replied the python, 'bring that pole over here and we will soon find out who is right.'

So Anansi laid the bamboo pole on the earth and the python stretched himself out alongside it.

'I'm still not certain about this,' said Anansi after a few moments. 'When you stretch at one end, you appear to shrink at the other end. Perhaps if I tied you to the pole I would have a clearer idea of your size.'

'Very well,' answered the python, 'just so long as we can sort this out properly.'

Anansi then took the creeper-vine and wrapped it round and round the length of the python's body until the great creature was unable to move.

'Onini,' said Anansi, 'it appears my wife was right. You are shorter and weaker than this pole and more foolish into the bargain. Now you are my prisoner and I must take you to the Sky-God, as I have promised.'

The great python lowered his head in defeat as Anansi tugged on the pole, dragging him along towards the home of Nyame.

'You have done well, spider,' said the god, 'but remember, there are two more, equally difficult quests ahead. You have much to accomplish yet, and it would not be wise to delay here any longer.'

So Anansi returned home once more and sat down to discuss the next task with his wife.

'There are still hornets to catch,' he told her, 'and I cannot think of a way to capture an entire swarm all at once.'

'Look for a gourd,' his wife suggested, 'and after you have filled it with water, go out in search of the hornets.'

Anansi found a suitable gourd and filled it to the brim. Fortunately, he knew exactly the tree where the hornets had built their nest. But before he approached too close, he poured some of the water from the gourd over himself so that his clothes were dripping wet. Then, he began sprinkling the nest with the remaining water while shouting out to the hornets:

'Why do you remain in such a flimsy shelter Mmoboro, when the great rains have already begun? You will soon be swept away, you foolish people. Here, take cover in this dry gourd of mine and it will protect you from the storms.'

The hornets thanked the spider for this most timely warning and disappeared one by one into the gourd. As soon as the last of them had entered, Anansi plugged the mouth of the vessel with some grass and chuckled to himself:

'Fools! I have outwitted you as well. Now you can join Onini, the python. I'm certain Nyame will be very pleased to see you.'

Anansi was delighted with himself. It had not escaped his notice that even the Sky-God appeared rather astonished by his success and it filled him with great excitement to think that very soon he would own all the stories of the world.

Only Osebo, the leopard, stood between the spider and his great wish, but Anansi was confident that with the help of his wife he could easily ensnare the creature as he had done all the others.

'You must go and look for the leopard's tracks,' his wife told him, 'and then dig a hole where you know he is certain to walk.'

Anansi went away and dug a very deep pit in the earth, covering it with branches and leaves so that it was well-hidden from the naked eye. Night-time closed in around him and soon afterwards, Osebo came prowling as usual and fell right into the deep hole, snarling furiously as he hit the bottom.

At dawn on the following morning, Anansi approached the giant pit and called to the leopard:

'What has happened here? Have you been drinking, leopard? How on earth will you manage to escape from this great hole?'

'I have fallen into a silly man-trap,' said the leopard impatiently. 'Help me out at once. I am almost starving to death in this wretched place.'

'And if I help you out, how can I be sure you won't eat me?' asked Anansi. 'You say you are very hungry, after all.'

'I wouldn't do a thing like that,' Osebo reassured him. 'I beg you, just this once, to trust me. Nothing bad will happen to you, I promise.'

Anansi hurried away from the opening of the pit and soon returned with a long, thick rope. Glancing around him, he spotted a tall green tree and bent it towards the ground, securing it with a length of the rope so that the top branches hung over the pit. Then he tied another piece of rope to these branches, dropping the loose end into the pit for the leopard to tie to his tail.

'As soon as you have tied a large knot, let me know and I will haul you up,' shouted Anansi.

Osebo obeyed the spider's every word, and as soon as he gave the signal that he was ready, Anansi cut the rope pinning the tree to the ground. It sprung upright at once, pulling the leopard out of the hole in one swift motion. Osebo hung upside down, wriggling and twisting helplessly, trying with every ounce of his strength to loosen his tail from the rope. But Anansi was not about to take any chances and he plunged his knife deep into the leopard's chest, killing him instantly. Then he lifted the leopard's body from the earth and carried it all the way to the Sky-God.

Nyame now called together all the elders of the skies, among them the Adonten, the Oyoko, the Kontire and Akwam chiefs, and informed them of the great exploits of Anansi, the spider:

'Many great warriors and chiefs have tried before,' the Sky-God told the congregation, 'but none has been able to pay the price I have asked of them. Kwaku Anansi has brought me Onini the python, the Mmoboro nest and the body of the mighty Osebo. The time has come to repay him as he deserves. He has won the right to tell my stories. From today, they will no longer be called stories of the Sky-God, but stories of Anansi, the spider.'

And so, with Nyame's blessing, Anansi became the treasurer of all the stories that have ever been told. And even now, whenever a man wishes to tell a story for the entertainment of his people, he must acknowledge first of all that the tale is a great gift, given to him by Anansi, the spider.

Anansi and the Corn Cob
(From the Krachi people, west Africa)

ANANSI WAS BY FAR THE CLEVEREST of Wulbari's heavenly creatures. He was also the most ambitious among them and was always on the look-out for an opportunity to impress the supreme god with his intelligence and cunning.

One day he appeared before Wulbari and asked if he might borrow from him a corn cob.

'Certainly,' said Wulbari, 'but what a strange thing to ask for! Why do you wish to borrow a corn cob?'

'I know it is an unusual request,' replied Anansi, 'but Master, if you will give me the corn cob I will bring you a hundred slaves in exchange for it.'

Wulbari laughed aloud at this response, but he handed Anansi the cob and declared that he looked forward to the day when the spider might deliver such a prize. Anansi meant every word he had spoken, however, and without further delay he set off on the road leading down from the sky to the earth.

It was nightfall by the time he completed his long journey and because he felt very weary, he went straightaway in search of a night's lodging. He soon happened upon the home of the village chief and having requested a bed, he was shown to a comfortable mattress in the corner of the room. But before he lay down to sleep he asked the chief where he might put the corn cob for safe-keeping:

'It is the corn of Wulbari,' Anansi explained. 'Our great Creator has instructed me to carry it to the people of Yendi, and I must not lose it along the way.'

The chief pointed to a hiding place in the roof and Anansi climbed up and placed the cob amongst the straw. Then he retired to his bed and pretended to be asleep. But as soon as the sound of the chief's snoring filled the room, Anansi arose again and removed the corn from its hiding place. He crept quickly out of doors and threw the corn to the fowls, making certain that the greedy birds helped themselves to every last kernel.

On the following morning, when Anansi asked for his corn, the chief climbed to the roof, but could not find any trace of it. Anansi stared at his host accusingly and began to create the most appalling scene, screaming and shouting and stamping his feet until, at last, each of the villagers was ordered to present him with a whole basket of corn each. This appeared to pacify Anansi only slightly, and very soon afterwards he took his leave of the chief declaring that he would never again visit such dishonest people.

He continued on his journey, carrying with him the great sack of corn he had collected. After a time he sat down by the roadside to rest and soon he spotted a man heading towards him carrying a chicken. Anansi greeted the man warmly and before long they had struck up a lively conversation.

'That's a nice, plump bird you have there,' Anansi said to the man. 'Nothing would please me more right now than to exchange my sack of corn for your fowl, for I am sick and weary of carrying my load from place to place.'

The man could scarcely believe his luck. There was enough corn in the bag to feed his entire family for several months and he very readily agreed to the exchange. The two shook hands and then went their separate ways, Anansi carrying the chicken under one arm, the man dragging the heavy sack behind him.

Later that day, Anansi arrived at the next village, and having asked the way to the chief's house, he knocked upon the door to beg a night's lodging. As before, the chief of the village welcomed him with open arms, and when Anansi showed him the fowl of Wulbari he had his people prepare a nice, quiet out-house where the bird could be placed out of harm's way overnight. But again, Anansi arose when he was certain everyone else had fallen asleep and killed the fowl, leaving the corpse in the bush and smearing some of the blood and feathers on the chief's own doorstep.

The next morning Anansi awoke and began shouting and thrashing about wildly.

'You have killed my precious fowl,' he shrieked as he pointed to the blood and the feathers. 'Wulbari will never forgive such a crime.'

The chief and all his people begged Anansi to forgive them and tried desperately to think of something that might appease him. At long last Anansi announced that perhaps there was something they could give him to take to the people of Yendi instead, and he pointed to a flock of sheep grazing in a nearby field.

'We will give you any number of these sheep if you will only pardon us,' said the chief.

So Anansi accepted the ten best sheep from the flock and went on his way once more.

It was not long before he reached the outskirts of Yendi, but before he entered the village he decided to allow his sheep to graze for a few minutes. And while he was seated on the grass watching them eat, he noticed a group of people approach, weeping and wailing as they returned home to their village bearing the body of a young man.

'Where are you taking the corpse?' Anansi asked them.

'We have a long way to go yet,' they told him, 'beyond those mountains to the west towards the dead boy's home.'

'But you look worn out,' said Anansi, 'I would be only too delighted to help you in any way. Here, take my sheep and lead them to your village and I will follow behind with the body on my shoulders.'

But Anansi allowed himself to fall further and further behind the men until finally they drifted out of sight. Then he retraced his steps and walked into the village of Yendi carrying with him the corpse. There he knocked on the door of the chief's house, explaining that he had with him the favourite son of Wulbari who was very weary from travelling and in desperate need of a bed for the night.

The chief and his people were delighted to have such an important guest among them and a comfortable hut was soon made ready for the favourite son of Wulbari. Anansi laid the body down inside the hut, covering it with a cloth before joining the chief for a splendid celebratory feast.

'I'm so sorry that our guest of honour is unable to join us,' said Anansi to the chief, 'but we have journeyed so far today, he has collapsed with exhaustion.'

The chief insisted that some of the best food be set aside for the son of Wulbari, and at the end of the evening he presented it to Anansi who promised to feed it to his companion as soon as he awoke. But Anansi finished the entire meal himself and sat cross-legged on the floor of the hut, chortling away to himself in the darkness.

At dawn, he called to the chief's own children to go in and wake the son of Wulbari.

'If he does not stir,' Anansi told them, 'you will have to flog him, for nothing else appears to wake him when he has slept so soundly.'

So the children did as they were instructed, but Wulbari's son did not wake.

'Beat him harder, beat him harder,' Anansi encouraged them, and the children did as he told them. But still Wulbari's son did not wake. So Anansi announced that he would go and wake the boy himself.

Soon there was a great wailing from inside the hut as Anansi cried out that the children of the chief had beaten to death the favourite son of Wulbari. The chief himself rushed forward and examined all the evidence. He was convinced that Anansi had spoken the truth and immediately offered to have his children sacrificed to the supreme god for what they had done to the unfortunate boy. But Anansi continued to wail aloud. Then the chief offered to kill himself, but still Anansi refused and said that nothing he could think of would ever undo such a great loss.

'Please just bury the body, I can't bear to look upon him any longer' he told the people. 'Perhaps when my mind is clearer I will think of some plan to appease Wulbari's anger.'

It was much later that same evening when Anansi reappeared, his eyes red and puffy from squeezing out the tears, his body stooped in mock-anguish.

'I have been thinking long and hard,' he said to the chief, 'and I have decided that I will take all the blame on myself for this dreadful deed, for I know you would never survive the wrath of Wulbari. I will say that his son's death was a terrible accident, but you must allow one hundred of your men to accompany me, for I will need them to support my testimony.'

The chief, who was more than pleased with this solution, immediately chose a hundred of the best young men and ordered them to prepare themselves for the long journey back to the kingdom of Wulbari. By midday they had departed the village and were well on the road leading upwards from the earth to the heavens.

Wulbari observed the crowd of youths approach and came out to greet them personally, anxious to discover their business, for he had forgotten all about Anansi and the bold promise he had made many weeks before.

'I told you it was possible, Master,' Anansi piped up from amongst the crowd. 'Do you not remember giving me that single corn cob? Now you have a hundred excellent slaves in exchange. They are yours to keep and I have kept my promise.'

Wulbari smiled broadly and was so pleased with Anansi he confirmed his appointment as Chief of his Host there and then, ordering him to change his name from Anyankon to Anansi, which is the name he has kept to the present day.

Tortoise Fables

Tortoise and the Wisdom of the World

(From Nigeria, west Africa)

TORTOISE WAS VERY ANGRY when he awoke one day to discover that other people around him had started to behave just as wisely as himself. He was angry because he was an ambitious fellow and wanted to keep all the wisdom of the world for his own personal use. If he succeeded in his ambition, he felt he would be so wise that everyone, including the great chiefs and elders of the people, would have to seek his advice before making any decision, no matter how small. He intended to charge a great deal of money for the privilege, and was adamant that nothing would upset his great plan.

And so he set out to collect all the wisdom of the world before anyone else decided to help himself to it. He hollowed out an enormous gourd for the purpose and began crawling along on his stomach through the bush, collecting the wisdom piece by piece and dropping it carefully into the large vessel. After several hours, when he was happy he had gathered every last scrap, he plugged the gourd with a roll of leaves and made his way slowly homewards.

But now that he had all the wisdom of the world in his possession, he grew fearful that it might be stolen from him. So he decided straight away that it would be best to hide the gourd in a safe place at the centre of the forest. He soon found a very tall palm tree which seemed suitable enough and prepared himself to climb to the top. First of all he took a rope and made a loop around the neck of the gourd. When he had done this, he hung the vessel from his neck so that it rested on his stomach. Then he took a very deep breath and began to climb the tree.

But he found that after several minutes he had not made any progress, for the gourd was so large it kept getting in his way. He slung it to one side and tried again. Still he could not move forward even an inch. He slung the gourd impatiently to the other side, but the same thing happened. Finally, he tried to stretch past it, but all these efforts came to nothing and he beat the tree with his fists in exasperation.

Suddenly he heard someone sniggering behind him. He turned around and came face to face with a hunter who had been watching him with great amusement for some time.

'Tortoise,' said the hunter eventually, 'why don't you hang the gourd over your back if you insist on climbing that tree?'

'What a good idea,' replied the tortoise, 'I'd never have thought of that on my own.'

But he had no sooner spoken these words when it dawned on him that the hunter must have helped himself to some of the precious wisdom.

Tortoise now grew even more angry and frustrated and began scuttling up the tree to get away from the thieving hunter. He moved so fast, however, that the rope holding the gourd slipped from around his neck causing the vessel to drop to the ground where it broke into hundreds of little pieces.

All the wisdom of the world was now scattered everywhere. And ever since that time nobody else has attempted to gather it all together in one place.

But whenever he feels the need, Tortoise makes a special journey to the palm tree at the centre of the forest, for he knows that the little pieces are still there on the ground, waiting to be discovered by anyone who cares to search hard enough.

The Tortoise and the Baboon

(From the Swahili speaking peoples, west Africa)

THE TORTOISE AND THE BABOON had been friends for a very long time and so it was only natural that they should invite each other to their wedding feasts when they both decided to get married.

The Baboon was the first to celebrate his wedding and he insisted that the feast be as elaborate as possible. The most delicious food was prepared by a team of twelve cooks, and the finest palm wine was provided for every guest.

Tortoise arrived punctually on the day and was most impressed by what he saw. He was extremely hungry after his very long journey, and more than anything he looked forward to tucking into the food in the company of the other guests.

At last the dinner gong was sounded and all the baboons began climbing the trees where they sat waiting to be served. Tortoise, of course, could not climb at all well and struggled very hard to make it even to the lowest branch. By the time he eventually reached the party, the first half of the meal had been served and cleared and he found that he was ignored by the other guests who chatted loudly among themselves.

Finally, he thought it best to mention to his friend the slight problem he was having keeping his balance on the branch.

'But you must sit like the rest of us,' the baboon told Tortoise, 'it is our custom. When my people eat, they always sit this way. It would be so rude to lie on the ground when everyone else is upright.'

And so Tortoise tried a little harder to make himself comfortable, but as soon as he reached forward to grab hold of some food, he fell flat on his belly. All the baboons roared with laughter at the sight of him and he hung his head in shame, feeling hungry and frustrated, knowing that he would never get to eat any of the delicious food.

When the day arrived for the Tortoise to marry, he had no wish to provide a lavish banquet for his guests, but prepared a small dinner-party for his closest friends. Before any of the guests was due to arrive, however, Tortoise went outdoors and lit a torch. Holding the flame to the earth, he began to burn the dry grass around his house and all the scrubland nearby.

Baboon and his new wife soon appeared in the distance and Tortoise slipped indoors again to resume the preparations. He embraced the couple warmly when they arrived and made sure that they were given one of the best seats at his table. The food was set down before them, and all were about to tuck in when Tortoise suddenly stood up and raised both arms in the air:

'Let's just make sure that we all have clean hands,' he said. 'Nothing upsets me more than people who eat their food with dirty hands.'

One by one his guests began to examine their hands, quite confident that they were clean. But when Baboon stared at his, he was shocked to see that they were a filthy black colour.

'But I scrubbed them before I left my house,' he protested.

'None the less,' replied Tortoise, 'they are very dirty indeed and it would be offensive to my people if you did not make an effort to clean them one more time. Go back to the river across the bush and try again. We promise to eat slowly so that you do not miss the meal.'

Baboon set off to do as his host suggested, walking on all fours through the charred grass and soot until he reached the river. Here he washed his hands thoroughly and returned by the same path to Tortoise's house.

'But there is no improvement. You must go again,' said Tortoise, munching on a delicious yam. 'What a shame! We will have eaten everything if this keeps up.'

Again the Baboon returned and again the Tortoise sent him away, a third and a fourth and a fifth time, until all the splendid dishes had been gobbled up.

So in the end, Tortoise had his revenge, and for many years afterwards he took great delight in telling his friends the story of how he managed to outwit Baboon on his wedding day.

Tortoise and the Hot-water Test
(From the Yoruba people, west Africa)

EVERY YEAR AT HARVEST TIME, the chief called upon his people to help him gather in the crops. And every year, just as the work was about to commence, Tortoise disappeared to the country for a few weeks, for he was never very interested in lending a hand.

But there came a season when his own crops failed him and he began to worry about how he might survive the harsh winter ahead. Looking out through the window of his hut, he saw that the chief's fields were full of sweet yams and decided he would have to get his hands on enough of them to fill his empty storehouse.

Finally he came up with a plan. In the middle of the night, when nobody was looking, he took a large shovel and made his way to the chief's fields. He began to dig a very deep hole, broad at the base and narrow at the top. Then he scattered leaves and branches over the hole to hide it and crept back to his bed.

Early the next morning, Tortoise knocked upon the door of the chief's house.

'I have come to help you in the fields,' he told the chief, 'and I am prepared to stay as long as it takes, until every single yam has been harvested.'

Although very surprised, the chief was delighted with the extra pair of hands and sent Tortoise to join the others already hard at work filling their baskets. Opolo the frog had come to do his share, as had Ekun the leopard, Ekute the bush rat, Ewure the goat, and a great many more of the chief's people.

Tortoise watched for a few moments as each dug a yam, placed it in his basket and carried it to the chief's storehouse. He stooped and did the same for a while, making sure that his digging brought him closer and closer to the large hole he had made the night before. Then for every yam he placed in his basket, he began dropping one into the opening of the hole, slowly building a stockpile for himself and mopping his brow from time to time as if he were quite exhausted.

But some of the workers began to notice how little progress he was actually making and challenged Tortoise to increase his speed.

'Unlike the rest of you,' he answered them shortly, 'I have the greatest respect for the chief's yams and believe in handling them very gently so as not to bruise them.'

And so the work continued until at last all the yams were harvested and the people drifted home wearily to their supper.

That night, as soon as darkness fell, Tortoise led his wife and children to the spot where he had buried the yams. They tiptoed back and forth across the field many times, each carrying an armful of yams, until the hole was empty and the family storehouse was full. Tortoise was very pleased with himself. Everything had been taken care of, and he felt certain that he had more than enough food to last him through the winter months.

But when morning came, a group of the chief's servants, who had been touring the empty fields, stumbled upon the large hole Tortoise had dug. They also found footprints made by Tortoise and his family as they scurried to and fro during the night, and followed the footprints to Tortoise's storehouse. Carefully, they opened the door so as not to disturb the sleeping household, and there, piled high to the ceiling, they came face to face with an impressive mound of freshly harvested yams.

The servants immediately rushed back to the chief's house and reported to him their discovery. The chief was enraged to have been deceived in such a manner and ordered Tortoise to be brought before him at once.

'It has been reported to me that you have stolen yams from my field,' he challenged Tortoise, 'what have you got to say for yourself?'

'It really saddens me to think you have such a poor opinion of me,' replied Tortoise innocently, 'when I have gone out of my way to be of service to you. I went to your fields to work for you, I stooped and sweated and carried yams to your storehouse all day long. Now you reproach me and call me a thief.'

'Tortoise, your shrewd character is well known to me,' replied the chief, 'and you cannot argue your way out of this one as easily as you think. I have been told about the footprints leading from my fields to your storehouse.'

'Yes, I'm sure you have,' answered Tortoise confidently, 'but I could easily have made them when I returned home from my work. And besides, there were a lot of other people in the fields as well as myself.'

'There are no paths leading from my fields to their houses,' continued the chief, 'only to your house. But if you still insist you are innocent, I know of a way to prove it. Tomorrow you will take the hot-water test. Then we can put the matter to rest once and for all.'

The next day, the people gathered together in front of the chief's house where a large cauldron of water stood heating over a fire. As soon as the water had come to the boil, the chief appeared and began to address the crowd:

'You are assembled here to witness Tortoise take the hot-water test. He denies that he is guilty of theft. Therefore, he must drink a bowl of the boiling water. If he is innocent, he will feel nothing at all. But if he is guilty, the water will burn his throat and cause him great pain. Let us begin at once.'

But before the servants had ladled the water into the bowl, Tortoise spoke up:

'Sir, this test will only prove how faithful I have been to you and you will still be at a loss to know who has taken your yams. Don't you agree that it makes sense for everyone who worked alongside me in the fields to be tested as well?'

The chief considered this proposal a moment.

'Very well,' he said. 'Let everyone else who was in the fields come forward. I am sure they have nothing to hide and absolutely nothing to fear.'

And now Tortoise became very helpful, behaving as though he were the chief's special assistant. He ordered the pot to be removed from the fire and placed it in a spot where the chief would have a better view of the proceedings. Then he insisted, that because he was the youngest, he should respectfully serve the others before himself.

The chief agreed, and Tortoise took the bowl, filled it with boiling water and served it first of all to Opolo the frog. Opolo cried out in pain as the hot water burned his insides. Next came the bush rat and he too cried out in agony as the liquid scorched his throat.

Tortoise refilled the bowl and handed it to Ewure the goat. Tears came to his eyes also and he writhed on the ground as the pain consumed his entire body. Last of all, Ekun the leopard came forward and let out a piercing scream as he swallowed and suffered the same dreadful pain.

'You disappoint me, my friends,' said the chief, 'for I see that you all share a portion of the blame. But let us turn now to the Tortoise and see whether he is guilty or innocent.'

And so Tortoise stepped forward and filled his bowl to the brim. But before he held it to his lips he pushed it towards the chief:

'See how full it is, Sir,' he announced, 'I have taken more than anyone else.'

'I see it,' replied the chief, 'the amount is a good one.'

Tortoise carried the bowl towards the chief's wife.

'I see it also,' she cried, 'you have acted more than fairly, Tortoise.'

Tortoise walked slowly into the crowd and tilted the bowl so the men of the village could see it more clearly.

'We see it,' they said, 'the bowl is very full.'

He showed it to the women of the village.

'We see it,' they chanted, 'you are very brave indeed, Tortoise.'

He turned and called to all the children of the village.

'We see it,' they answered him, 'you do well, Tortoise.'

And as Tortoise presented the bowl for inspection to each group in turn, the water grew cooler and cooler until, at last, the chief called for him to get on with the drinking.

So Tortoise gulped down the water, but because it had grown so cool as he passed it around, it did not cause him any pain as it slid down his throat.

'You have seen it,' shouted Tortoise triumphantly, 'I did not cry out as the others did. How can I possibly be guilty?'

And as additional proof of his innocence, he poured the water over his entire body and rubbed it into his skin without showing any sign of discomfort.

'You can see it was not I who committed the crime,' he added. 'It must have been Opolo, Ekute, Ewure and Ekun. They should be taken away and punished severely.'

The chief nodded in agreement and sentenced the other animals to two years' hard labour on his farm for having stolen his yams.

But although Tortoise was victorious, there were some among the crowd who still held him in suspicion and ever since that day, whenever a person tries to point the finger at others for a crime he has committed himself, you will hear the people say:

'When Tortoise accuses the whole community,
He himself must have a great deal to hide.'

The Tortoise and the Elephant
(From the Akamba people, Kenya)

ONE DAY THE ELEPHANT WAS BOASTING as usual about his great size and strength.

'Have you ever come across a more impressive figure in the whole of the land?' he asked Tortoise, as he stared admiringly at his reflection in the lake. 'There is not one creature I know of that could outshine me. It wouldn't matter what sort of contest we were engaged in.'

'You can't be absolutely certain of that,' replied the Tortoise. 'Size isn't everything you know, and I'm sure there is someone out there who would put you in your place given half a chance.'

'I suppose you consider yourself worthy of that role,' mocked the Elephant. 'Come on then, prove to me that you are a greater athlete than myself.'

'That won't be so difficult,' answered the Tortoise defiantly. 'I bet I could jump as high as your trunk and land twenty feet beyond it without putting in too much effort.'

'Then meet me here later this afternoon,' the Elephant chuckled, 'and in the meantime go and work on your muscles! I can hardly wait to see you make a fool of yourself.'

So the Tortoise went home where he found his wife preparing their midday meal.

'The Elephant has challenged me to a trial of strength,' he told her, 'and I think it's time somebody taught him a lesson, but I will need your help.'

Leading his wife to the lakeside, Tortoise hid her among the bushes at exactly the spot where he judged he would land after making his miraculous leap. Soon afterwards, the Elephant arrived, still smirking to himself, and stood as he was instructed in the middle of a clear space where tortoise could get a good run at him.

'Jump high now, Tortoise,' cried the Elephant sarcastically, 'give it your best shot.'

'I'm coming now, hold your trunk up high,' called the Tortoise, pretending he was almost ready for his high jump.

The Elephant lifted his head towards the sky, and as he did so, the tortoise slipped into the grass, shouting 'Hi-i!' as he went. 'Eh-e!' came the reply from his wife who suddenly appeared on the other side of the grass, exactly twenty feet from the Elephant.

The Elephant now glanced to his right and found the Tortoise on the far side of his trunk. He was utterly astonished to see him there and suspected nothing, believing that the leap had been so masterfully executed, his eyes had not been quick enough to take it in.

'You have beaten me, Tortoise,' he said, shaking his head in bewilderment, 'I still can't quite believe it, however. Do you think you could convince me one more time, for I feel certain that you would never be able to outrun me in a foot-race.'

'If you insist then,' answered the Tortoise quite casually, 'but not today. I need my rest after all that exertion. I will meet you tomorrow morning by the great tree in the forest, and to make things easier, I suggest we run a circular course through the woods, finishing up in the same place where we started from.'

'That sounds ideal,' replied the Elephant and he tramped his way homewards, confident that he would achieve his victory on the following day.

Before the sun had risen the next morning, Tortoise had gathered together his wife and children and spent several hours placing them along the course, instructing them what to do once the race had started. Shortly afterwards, he spotted the Elephant pushing his way through the thick undergrowth as he headed towards the appointed tree. Tortoise went forward to greet him and without further delay the two took up their starting positions, anxious to begin the race.

Smiling happily to himself, the Elephant trotted off at an easy pace and was soon well ahead of the Tortoise who began to puff and pant under the strain. The Elephant laughed loudly at the sight of him, well pleased with himself for having chosen such a punishing contest.

When he had been running for quite some time he shouted back, 'Tortoise!', believing he had left his opponent far behind. But to his horror he heard a voice saying :

'Why are you looking behind you? I am here in front of you. Can't you move any faster?'

Shocked by the sight of Tortoise, the Elephant broke into a gallop, putting as much energy into his stride as he could possibly manage. But he had only moved on a short distance when he spotted Tortoise up ahead of him once more. This happened again and again, all the way along the course, until the Elephant arrived back at the great tree where he found Tortoise calmly waiting for him, not a drop of sweat on his brow.

'Here I am, what kept you?' said the tortoise.

'I didn't believe you could ever beat me,' replied the defeated Elephant, 'but it seems you are right about size.'

Tortoise turned away to hide his smile, but he never felt bad about cheating the Elephant, for he felt certain he had taught him an invaluable lesson.

Other Animal Stories

How the Leopard Got His Spots
(From Sierra Leone, west Africa)

LONG AGO, Leopard and Fire were the best of friends. Every morning, without fail, Leopard made a special effort to visit his friend even though the journey took him quite a distance from his own home. It had never before bothered him that Fire did not visit him in return, until the day his wife began to mock and tease him on the subject.

'He must be a very poor friend indeed,' she jeered, 'if he won't come and see you even once in your own house.'

Day and night, Leopard was forced to listen to his wife taunt him, until finally he began to believe that his house was somehow unworthy of his friend.

'I will prove my wife wrong,' he thought to himself, and set off before dawn on the following day to beg Fire to come and visit his home.

At first, Fire presented him with every possible excuse. He never liked to travel too far, he explained to Leopard. He always felt uncomfortable leaving his family behind. But Leopard pleaded and pleaded so that eventually Fire agreed to the visit on the condition that his friend construct a path of dry leaves leading from one house to the other.

As he walked homewards, Leopard gathered as many leaves as he could find and laid them in a long line between the two houses just as Fire had instructed him. He brought his wife the good news and immediately she began to prepare the finest food to welcome their guest.

When the meal was ready and the house sparkled as if it were new, the couple sat down to await the arrival of their friend. They had been seated only a moment when suddenly they felt a strong gust of wind and heard a loud crackling noise outside their front door. Leopard jumped up in alarm and pulled open the door, anxious to discover who could be making such a dreadful commotion. He was astonished to see Fire standing before him, crackling and sparking in a haze of intense heat, his body a mass of flames that leapt menacingly in every direction.

Soon the entire house had caught fire and the smell of burning skin filled the air. Leopard grabbed hold of his squealing wife and sprang, panic-stricken, through the window, rolling in the grass to put out the flames on his back.

The two lay there exhausted, grateful to be alive. But ever since that day, their bodies were covered all over with black spots where the fingers of Fire, their reluctant house-guest, had touched them.

The Donkey Who Sinned
(From Ethiopia, north-east Africa)

ONE HOT AND SUNNY AFTERNOON, the Lion, the Leopard, the Hyena and the Donkey met together at the bottom of the field. At once, they began to discuss the drought visiting the country and the dreadful conditions that had become widespread throughout the region. No rain had fallen now for several months, the crops had shrivelled beyond recognition, and there was very little food or water to be had anywhere.

'How can this have happened to us?' they repeated over and over again, shaking their heads in disbelief. 'Someone among us must have sinned very badly, or God would not be punishing us in this way.'

'Perhaps we should confess our sins,' the Donkey suddenly suggested, 'maybe if we repent, we will be forgiven and the land will become fertile and bear healthy crops again.'

They all agreed that this was a very sensible idea, and so the Lion, the most powerful of the group, immediately stood up to make his confession:

'I once committed an unforgivable crime,' he told the gathering. 'One day I found a young calf roaming close to a village, and even though I knew it belonged to the people, I attacked it and ate every morsel.'

The other animals looked towards the Lion, whom they feared and admired for his daring and strength, and began to protest his innocence loudly:

'No, no,' they reassured him. 'That was no great sin! You shouldn't worry about that at all.'

Next the Leopard stood up to make a clean breast of things:

'I have committed a much more dreadful sin,' he announced. 'One morning as I prowled through the valley, I happened upon a goat who had strayed from the rest of the herd. As soon as his back was turned, I leaped on him and devoured him.'

The rest of the animals looked at the Leopard, whom they admired as a most ruthless hunter, and once again they dismissed this crime:

'No, no!' they insisted. 'That is no sin! God would never hold such a thing against you.'

The Hyena then spoke his piece:

'Oh, I have committed a most wicked deed,' he cried. 'I was so greedy one evening, I stole into the village, caught a chicken and swallowed it down in one gulp.'

But again the other animals protested, judging the Hyena to be the most cunning among their friends:

'No, no! Let your conscience be at rest,' they answered him. 'That is no sin!'

Last of all, the Donkey came forward and began to confess:

'One day when my master was leading me along the road he met an old friend and started talking with him. While the two were deep in conversation, I crept silently to the edge of the road and began nibbling on a tuft of grass.'

The Lion, the Leopard and the Hyena stared at the Donkey, whom they neither feared, nor admired. A grave silence filled the air. Slowly they formed a circle around him, shaking their heads in absolute disgust:

'That is the worst sin we have ever heard,' they pronounced. 'There can be no doubt now that you are the source of all our trouble.'

And with that, the three of them jumped upon the donkey's back and began ripping him to pieces.

The Two Suns
(From Kenya, east Africa)

MANY HUNDREDS OF YEARS AGO, in the land now known as Kenya, the animals could speak just as well as human beings. At that time, the two species lived in harmony and agreed on most things. They even shared the same grievances, and were equally fond of complaining about the darkness, although they readily admitted that they were more than satisfied with the daylight.

'We cannot see at night,' complained the men. 'It is impossible to look after our cattle in the dark and we are often afraid of the great shadows that appear out of nowhere.'

The animals agreed with the men and soon they arranged a meeting to decide what to do. The great elders of the people were the first to speak and they outlined various plans to defeat the darkness, some suggesting that huge fires should be lit at night throughout the land, others insisting that every man should carry his own torch. At length, however, the man considered wisest among the elders stood up and addressed the crowd:

'We must pray to God to give us two suns,' he announced. 'One that rises in the east and one that rises in the west. If he provides us with these, we will never have to tolerate night again.'

The people immediately shouted their approval and all were in agreement with this plan, except for one small hare at the back of the crowd who ventured to challenge the speaker a little further:

'How will we get any shade?' he asked in a tiny voice.

But his question met with an impatient roar from the wisest elder who demanded to know the identity of the creature who had dared to oppose him.

'It was the Hare who spoke,' said one of the warriors in the crowd, noticing that the Hare was trying to hide himself away under the bushes. Soon he was hauled out to the middle of the gathering, visibly shaking under the gaze of the people.

'How dare you disagree with me,' said the elder. 'What do you know of such matters anyway?'

The Hare bowed his head silently and began to whimper.

'Speak up, great prophet,' said another of the elders. 'Let us hear your wise words of counsel.'

The people and the animals laughed loudly at the spectacle before them, all except for the warrior who had first spotted the Hare.

'Don't be afraid of them,' he said gently. 'Go on! Speak! Be proud of what you have to say.'

The Hare stared into the eyes of the tall warrior and his courage began to return. Then, clearing his throat and raising himself up on his hind legs, he spoke the following words:

'I only wanted to say that if we had two suns there would never be any shade again. All the waters of the rivers and lakes will dry up. We shall never be able to sleep and our cattle will die of heat and thirst. There will be fires and hunger in the land and we shall all eventually perish.'

The people listened and a great silence descended upon them as they considered the words of the little Hare.

At last, the wisest of the elders arose and patted the Hare warmly on the shoulder.

'Indeed you have shown greater wisdom than any of us,' he said. 'We are fortunate to have you among us.'

Everyone agreed, and to this day the people of Kenya say that the hare is the cleverest of all animals. And they still have day and night; they still have only one sun and nobody has ever complained about it since that day.

Gihilihili: The Snake-man
(From the Tutsi people, Rwanda)

THERE WAS ONCE A MIDDLE-AGED WOMAN living in a small village who for many years had tried to conceive a child. At last, when she had almost abandoned all hope, she discovered she was pregnant. The news filled her with great joy and she longed for the day when she could sit proudly amongst the other women holding her new-born infant in her arms.

But when nine months had passed and the time arrived for the woman to deliver her child, there was no sign of it emerging, and for several more years the infant remained within her womb, refusing to show itself. Eventually however, the woman began to suffer labour pains and was taken to her bed where she gave birth after a long and painful ordeal. She was surprised that her husband did not bring the infant to her and when she looked in his direction she saw that his eyes were filled with horror. Then she searched for the child, but no child lay on the bed. Instead she saw a long, thick-necked snake coiled up beside her, its body warm and glistening, its head lifted affectionately towards her.

Suddenly her husband grabbed hold of a shovel from a corner of the hut and began striking the snake furiously. But the woman cried out for him to stop at once:

'Do not harm the creature,' she pleaded, 'treat it with respect and gentleness. No matter what you may think of it, that snake is still the fruit of my womb.'

The man lowered his shovel and went outdoors. Soon he returned to the hut accompanied by a group of village elders. They gathered around the bed and began to examine the snake more closely. At length, the wisest among them spoke to the husband and wife:

'We have no reason to treat this creature unkindly,' he told them. 'Take it to the forest and build a house for it there. Let it be free to do as it pleases. Let it grow to maturity unharmed so that it may shed its skin in the normal way.'

The husband carried the snake to the heart of the forest and left it there as the elders had ordered him, making certain that it had a comfortable home to live in and a plentiful supply of food to survive on.

The years passed by quickly, and the snake grew to an impressive size, ready for the day when its old skin would be replaced by a new one. And as it wandered deeper into the forest the most wonderful transformation began to occur. The old skin started to shrink away to reveal a young man, tall, strong and handsome. The young man stood up and glanced around him. Then, lifting the snakeskin from the ground, he took a deep breath and followed the path through the forest back towards his parents' home.

Both mother and father were overjoyed to discover that the snake-creature they had abandoned so many years before had changed into such a fine and handsome youth. All the other members of the family were invited to assemble at the hut to admire their beautiful son and a great feast was held to welcome him into the community.

After their son had been with them several weeks, the father sat down with him one evening to discuss who would make the best wife for him.

'I have already chosen the daughter of Bwenge to be my wife,' the young man told his father. 'Even while I crawled on my belly through the forests I knew I would one day marry her. Each time she came to gather wood, I sat and watched and my love went out to her. Each time she came to get water, my love went out to her. Each time she came to cut grass for the young cattle, my love went out to her.'

'You are not rich enough for such a match,' his father replied. 'We are poor people, and she is the daughter of a noble chief.'

But the son said nothing further on the subject and called for a great fire to be made. As soon as the flames had grown quite tall, he cast the snakeskin which once covered his body into the centre of the fire, calling for his father and mother to keep a careful watch on it. They looked on in amazement as the skin crackled noisily and transformed itself into an array of valuable objects. Cattle, sheep and fowls began to leap from the flames. Drums, calabashes and churns began to appear, together with all other kinds of wealthy possessions.

Next morning the father and his son went in search of the daughter of Bwenge and presented to the chief a selection of these goods. The chief was more than satisfied by all that he saw and arranged for his daughter to be married immediately. The young man led his new wife back to his village where he made a home for them both. They were very happy together and lived long and fruitful lives, enriched by the birth of many healthy children.

The Snake-man grew old among the people who came to regard him as a man of profound wisdom and courage. Whenever there was trouble they turned to him for advice, and even after he died, his words lived on in their memory and they often recounted the story of his birth, mindful of what he had told them.

'Never allow yourself to be destroyed by misfortune,' he had said.

'Never despair of yourself or of others. And above all, never condemn a person for his appearance.'

How the Dog Came to Live with Man

(From the Bushogo people, Congo)

THERE WAS A TIME, LONG AGO, when the Dog and the Jackal lived together in the wilderness as brothers. Every day they hunted together and every evening they laid out on the grass whatever they had caught, making sure to divide the meal equally between them. But there were evenings when they both returned from a day's hunting empty-handed, and on these occasions they would curl up side-by-side under the stars dreaming of the bush calf or the plump zebra they had come so close to killing.

They had never before gone without food for longer than two days, but then, without warning, they suffered a long spell of bad luck and for over a week they could find nothing at all to eat. On the eighth day, although they had both searched everywhere, they returned to their shelter without meat, feeling exhausted and extremely hungry. To add to their misery, a bitterly cold wind blew across the bush, scooping up the leaves they had gathered for warmth, leaving them shivering without any hope of comfort throughout the long night ahead. Curled up together, they attempted to sleep, but the wind continued to howl and they tossed and turned despairingly.

'Jackal,' said the Dog after a while. 'Isn't it a terrible thing to go to bed hungry after all the effort we have put in today, and isn't it an even worse thing to be both hungry and cold at the same time?'

'Yes, it is brother,' replied the Jackal, 'but there's very little we can do about it at the moment. Let's just curl up here and try to sleep now. Tomorrow, as soon as the sun rises, we will go out hunting again and with any luck we will be able to find some food to satisfy us.'

But even though he snuggled up closer to the Jackal, the Dog could not sleep, for his teeth had begun to chatter and his stomach rumbled more loudly than ever. He lay on the cold earth, his eyes open wide, trying to recall what it was like to be warm and well-fed.

'Jackal,' he piped up again, 'man has a village quite close to this spot, doesn't he?'

'Yes, that is true,' answered the Jackal wearily. 'But what difference can that make to us right now?'

'Well,' replied the Dog, 'most men know how to light a fire and fire would keep us warm if we crept near enough to one.'

'If you are suggesting that we take a closer look,' said the Jackal, 'you can forget about it. I'm not going anywhere near that village. Now go to sleep and leave me in peace.'

But the Dog could not let go of the idea and as he thought about it more and more he began to imagine the delicious meal he would make of the scraps and bones left lying around by the villagers.

'Please come with me,' he begged the Jackal, 'my fur is not as thick as yours and I am dying here from cold and hunger.'

'Go there yourself,' growled the Jackal, 'this was all your idea, I want nothing to do with it.'

At last, the Dog could stand it no longer. Forgetting his fear, he jumped up and announced boldly:

'Right, I'm off, nothing can be worse than this. I'm going to that village to sit by the fire and perhaps I'll even come across a tasty bone. If there's any food left over, I'll bring you some. But if I don't return, please come and look for me.'

So the Dog started off towards the village, slowing down when he had reached the outskirts and crawling on his belly so that nobody would notice him approach. He could see the red glow of a fire just up ahead and already he felt the warmth of its flames. Very cautiously he slid along the earth and had almost reached his goal when some fowls roosting in a tree overhead began to cackle a loud warning to their master.

At once, a man came rushing out from a nearby hut and lifting his spear high in the air, brought it down within an inch of where the dog lay.

'Please, please don't kill me,' whimpered the Dog. 'I haven't come here to steal your chickens or to harm you in any way. I am starving and almost frozen to death. I only wanted to lie down by the fire where I could warm myself for a short while.'

The man looked at the wretched, shivering creature and could not help feeling a bit sorry for him. It was such a cold night after all, and the Dog's request was not so unreasonable under the circumstances.

'Very well,' he said, withdrawing his spear. 'You can warm yourself here for a few minutes if you promise to go away again as soon as you feel better.'

The Dog crept forward and lay himself down by the fire, thanking the man over and over for his kindness. Soon he felt the blood begin to circulate in his limbs once more. Slowly uncurling himself, he stretched out before the flames and there, just in front of him, he noticed a fat and juicy bone, thrown there by the man at the end of his meal. He sidled up alongside it and began to devour it, feeling happier than he had done for a very long time.

He had just about finished eating when the man suddenly reappeared:

'Aren't you warm enough yet?' he asked, rather anxious to be rid of his visitor from the bush.

'No, not yet,' said the Dog, who had spotted another bone he wished to gnaw on.

'Just a few more minutes then,' said the man, as he disappeared inside his hut once more.

The Dog grabbed hold of the second bone and began crushing it in his strong jaws, feeling even more contented with himself. But soon the man came out of his hut and asked again:

'When are you going to get up and go? Surely you must be warm enough by now?'

But the Dog, feeling very reluctant to leave the comfort of his surroundings, pleaded with his host:

'Let me stay just a little while longer and I promise to leave you alone after that.'

This time the man disappeared and failed to return for several hours, for he had fallen asleep inside his hut, quite forgetting about his guest. But as soon as he awoke, he rushed out of doors to make certain that the Dog had left him as promised. Now he became angry to see the creature snoozing by the fire in exactly the same position as before. Prodding him with his spear, he called for the Dog to get up at once. The Dog rose slowly to his feet and summoning every ounce of his courage, he looked directly into the man's eyes and spoke the following words:

'I know that you want me to go away, but I wish you would let me stay here with you. I could teach you a great many things. I could pass on to you my knowledge of the wild, help you hunt the birds of the forests, keep watch over your house at night and frighten off any intruders. I would never harm your chickens or goats like my brother, the Jackal. I would look after your women and children while you were away. All I ask in return is that you provide me with a warm bed close to your fire and the scraps from your table to satisfy my hunger.'

The man now stared back into the Dog's eyes and saw that their expression was honest and trustworthy.

'I will agree to this,' he replied. 'You may have a home here among the villagers if you perform as you have promised.'

And from that day, the Dog has lived with man, guarding his property, protecting his livestock and helping him to hunt in the fields. At night when the Dog settles down to sleep, he hears a cry from the wilderness, 'Bo-ah, Bo-ah', and he knows that it is his brother, the Jackal, calling him back home. But he never answers the call, for the Dog is more than content in his new home, enjoying the comforts Jackal was once so happy to ignore.

The Truth about Cock's Comb

(From the Baganda people, central Africa)

THERE WAS A TIME, MANY YEARS AGO, when the wild cats of the forests were forced to live as servants of the fowls who frequently beat them and treated them with the utmost cruelty. The fowls, then the laziest of creatures, sat around preening their great feathers all day long, demanding that their servants supply them with food and anything else they might require. Whenever the cats caught flying ants, the fowls took four-fifths of them; whenever they had gathered millet seed, the fowls simply helped themselves to as much as they wanted. Of course, the cats did not like this arrangement, and often they considered rising up in rebellion. But one thing always held them back. They lived in fear of the scarlet combs the fowls wore on their heads, for they had been warned that if ever they came too close to them, they would be severely burnt and scarred for life.

One day, when it had turned bitterly cold, Mother Cat discovered that her fire had gone out, and knowing that her family would not survive very long without heat, she made a brave decision to send her youngest son to the fowls to beg for fire. When the young cat arrived at the home of the Head Cock he found him stretched out on the floor of his hut, quite alone, and apparently very drunk. The young cat approached the Head Cock cautiously and announced the purpose of his visit in a tiny, terrified voice. But he received no response whatsoever as the cock continued to snore very loudly. Once more he tried, raising his voice ever so slightly, but still there was no answer.

So the young cat went back home and told his mother that he had tried to wake the cock without any success.

'You must go back there again,' his mother told him. 'And this time, take some dry grass with you. If you find that the cock is still asleep, stick a blade of grass into his comb and bring me back the fire.'

The young cat set off once more to do as his mother had bid him. When he arrived at the Head Cock's hut, he found he had not moved an inch. Slowly he crept towards the sleeping figure and, ever so carefully, touched the comb with the grass. But surprisingly, there was no sign of any fire, not even a spark, and the blade of grass remained quite as cold as it had ever been.

Again, the young cat returned home and told his mother what had happened.

'You can't have tried hard enough,' she scolded. 'I suppose I will have to abandon the rest of the children and come along with you this time.'

And so for the third time, the young cat set off towards the Head Cock's hut, accompanied by his mother who was determined to have her fire at any price. Luckily, the cock continued to snore as before and it was not difficult for Mother Cat to approach him and touch his comb with the grass. Gently she blew on the stalk, expecting it to burst into flame. But the result was exactly as her son had described it – there was no fire, no spark, not even the slightest glimmer of heat.

Mother Cat was now rather perplexed, and even though she was afraid of being burnt, she decided to risk placing her hands on the cock's comb to see if it was hot. Slowly and carefully she stretched out her fingers, but as soon as they rested on the scarlet comb, she found that it was stone cold.

At first astonished by the discovery, Mother Cat became very angry as she contemplated the long years of suffering her family had endured under Head Cock and the rest of the fowls. She began shaking the drunken creature violently and as soon as he had awoken she dragged him to his feet.

'We don't fear you anymore,' she screamed at him. 'We tested your comb while you were asleep and we know that you have deceived us all. There is no fire in it and there never has been. Now, if you value your life, you had better leave this place as quickly as you can.'

The Head Cock saw that his empty boasting had been discovered and fled from his village as fast as his legs could carry him. And ever since that time, fowls have been forced to take refuge with man, squawking in fear whenever they think a cat is coming too close to them.

Chameleon Wins a Wife
(From the Kikuyu people, Kenya)

ONE DAY FROG SWAM TO THE SURFACE of a little pond and glanced around him for a place to rest:

'The water is cold today,' he complained, 'it would do me good to bask in the sun for a little while.'

And so he left the water and crouched on a warm, flat stone at the edge of the pond.

After some time a beautiful young girl from the local village named Ngema came to the pond to fetch some water. The Frog remained seated on the stone without moving a muscle so that the young woman eventually began to stare at him, asking herself aloud whether or not he might be ill.

'No, I am not ill,' Frog called to her irritably, 'why do you imagine such a thing? Can't you see how strong I am?'

'Other frogs usually leap back into the water as soon as they see the villagers approach,' replied the girl, 'but you don't seem at all frightened and that is why I thought perhaps you must be sick.'

The Frog turned his two big eyes towards Ngema, rose up on his hind legs and stretched himself impressively towards the sky.

'Underneath this body, I am really a fine young man,' he boasted.

'I have enough cattle and goats to buy any number of beautiful girls like yourself, but a curse rests on me and I must remain here until it is lifted.

'When my father lay on his death bed, he said to me: "My son, you will spend most of your time by the water until the day comes when you meet a girl there and ask her to marry you. If she accepts, it will mean happiness for you both, but if she refuses, she will die." So I ask you to marry me here and now, and it is entirely up to you whether you live or die.'

The girl sat down on the grass and began thinking hard. After a while she stood up again and answered the Frog worriedly:

'If that curse rests on you, then it rests on me as well. I have seen you and you have asked me to be your wife. I will not refuse you now, for I have no wish to die just yet.'

So Ngema reluctantly agreed to marry the Frog and led him home to her parents' hut on the outskirts of the village.

In the courtyard at the front of her parents' house there stood a very beautiful palm tree. Among its broad, leafy branches sat a Chameleon watching the approach of the young girl and the Frog. Ngema escorted her companion indoors and left him there to discuss the wedding arrangements with her father while she sat down at the base of the tree to grind some corn for the midday meal. The Chameleon now moved cautiously towards her, descending from branch to branch slowly and carefully, his eyes darting suspiciously from side to side, until at last he stood within a few feet of her. But before he had the opportunity to address the girl, she suddenly turned towards him:

'I have been watching you all this time,' she said, 'and I can scarcely believe how long it took you to move such a short distance. Do you know that it has taken you over an hour to reach this spot?'

'I won't apologise for that,' answered the Chameleon. 'I am a stranger to you, and had I rushed upon you, you would have been frightened and called out to your people. But in this way I haven't alarmed you and now we will be able to talk quietly without anyone disturbing us.'

'I have been so anxious to meet you, but wanted to choose my moment carefully. I came here early this morning to tell you I love you and my greatest wish is for you to become my wife.'

The young girl set aside her bowl of corn and fell silent for several moments. At length, she raised her head and answered the Chameleon rather indifferently:

'You are too late with your request, and besides, I could never marry anyone who moves as slowly as you do. People would laugh to see us together.'

'Our elders say that empty gourds make a great noise, but it amounts to very little in the end,' replied the Chameleon. 'Think again before you reject me.'

Ngema sighed deeply as she pondered these words.

'Well,' she said finally, 'Frog is inside the house asking my father's permission to marry me. Whichever of you can satisfy him will earn the right to become my husband.'

So Chameleon waited for Frog to emerge and then entered the house to see if he could reason with the young girl's father. Their conversation was not half so difficult as Chameleon had expected and before long he reappeared smiling to himself, having agreed with the old man that he would return to claim his bride within a few days.

As soon as he had put all his affairs in order, Chameleon returned as promised to the girl's home, anxious to get on with the wedding ceremony. But to his disgust, he found Frog still pleading for Ngema's hand, insisting that he was by far the richer of the two, and that he would make a much more suitable husband.

Chameleon stormed into the room and interrupted Frog in mid-stream:

'You call me a slow and worthless creature,' he yelled furiously, 'but I call you a slippery, boneless, hideous carbuncle.'

And the two continued to hurl abuse at each other for some time, each of them determined to prove their worth before the young girl's family.

At last, the old man called for them both to stop and when they were ready to listen he offered them the following solution:

'I will fix a bride-price,' he told the pair, 'which must be delivered before the end of six days. The first of you to arrive here with everything I demand will win my daughter's hand in marriage.'

Then the old man listed out the various goods he desired from each of them and without further discussion Frog and Chameleon went their separate ways, eager to assemble their respective cargoes as hastily as possible.

The Frog enlisted a great number of his friends to help him and overnight he had prepared a vast quantity of beer and food of every kind, including sweet potatoes, corn, dove-peas, shea-nuts and bananas, which he piled on to an enormous caravan ready to take to the girl's house.

Early the next morning, a long line of frogs began hopping down the road, travelling at great speed in order to ensure that they would reach their destination before the Chameleon. But as they moved along, they began to attract the sniggers of the roadside workers, for they failed to notice that at every hop, the beer spilt from the gourds, the bananas dropped from the baskets, and the food crumbled to pieces in the open bags and fell to the ground.

When the company approached Ngema's house, they received a very warm welcome from the large crowd who set off to meet them. Songs of praise were sung by the women of the village and a loud chorus of cheering could be heard for miles around. But when, later that same evening, the villagers eventually came to unfasten the loads, they were horrified to see that all the sacks were completely empty and not a drop of beer remained in the gourds. The villagers called the father of the girl and reported to him their discovery:

'Come and examine the gifts Frog has brought you,' they told him, 'he has arrived here with empty sacks and dry bowls.'

The old man looked at the Frog sternly and raised his voice in anger:

'Why have you come here to mock us? Do you think I would exchange my precious child for such a worthless cargo? Go and seek a wife elsewhere, for I have no time for a son-in-law who would attempt to trick me like this.'

The Frog did not pause to argue his case, for he knew that his impatience and arrogance had cost him his bride and that now the curse would never be reversed. He hung his head in shame and silently slunk away, hopping despondently down the road with the rest of his companions.

Three more days passed by and most of the villagers had abandoned all hope that Chameleon would ever show his face among them. But then, from the opposite direction on the fifth morning, the people spotted a caravan of carriers making very slow progress towards the village. It was mid-afternoon by the time it reached the outskirts, and as before, the villagers went forward to welcome their guests.

But this time, the women of the village were very anxious to inspect the loads before disturbing the father of the bride. They approached the caravan warily, but their fears were quickly laid to rest, for as soon as they began to unwrap the cargo, they found the sacks overflowing with food and the gourds full to the brim with beer.

Ngema smiled as she moved forward to greet the Chameleon, remembering how he had once described to her the hollow sound of an empty gourd. The celebrations now began in earnest and the satisfied father gave his daughter to the victorious Chameleon who took her for his wife the very next day.

Stories Of Wit And Wisdom

STORIES WHICH EXPLORE HUMAN EXPERIENCE – man's strengths and weaknesses, his relationship with his fellow beings and his correct place within society, form an intrinsic part of the African mythological tradition.

Many of the stories included in this chapter may be described as 'proverbial'. They offer instruction, often culminating in some form of moral punch line, which demonstrates well the African storyteller's use of tales as a vehicle to teach man correct social values, responsibility, humility, and a sense of justice.

The tales are chosen from different regions of Africa and are widely known. 'The Young Man and the Skull', for example, a story which recurs in several different versions all over the African continent, is characteristic of the group. It embodies a simple proverb, linked to the protagonist's unhappy fate, warning us that boastfulness is a sign of moral decadence which cannot go unpunished. Similarly, 'The Rich Man and the Poor Man' demonstrates the fact that greed will never be rewarded.

Other stories, among them 'How Walakuga Answered the King' and 'The Two Rogues', have a less serious intention and focus rather more light-heartedly on man's cunning, commending it as an essential tool for his survival.

The Rich Man and the Poor Man

(From the Akamba people, Kenya)

IN A CERTAIN VILLAGE OF THE AKAMBA there lived two men, one rich and one poor. Yet in spite of their different circumstances, they lived together as neighbours. The rich man always supported his poor friend in times of trouble and in return, the poor man worked hard on the rich man's farm, ploughing the fields and carrying out as many odd jobs as he could manage.

But there came a time when a severe famine spread throughout the land, causing widespread hardship and misery. Even the rich man could not escape the suffering, and as he watched his wealth decline, he grew hard-hearted towards his fellow men. Soon he had forgotten all about the poor man and when, one day, his old friend arrived on his doorstep to beg the scraps from his table, the rich man dismissed him as a common beggar and warned him never to trespass on his land again.

The poor man watched his children die of starvation one by one until only himself and his wife remained. But even though his spirit was almost broken, he was determined to keep his wife alive, and so he swallowed his pride and set off one evening towards the village where he began searching through other people's waste for even an old bone to chew on. Before long, he was approached by a well-dressed woman who took pity on him and presented him with a handful of maize. The poor man carried the maize home to his wife and she set a great pot of water over the fire to boil. She had intended to make a hot, nourishing soup for them both, but this proved an impossible task, since they had no meat to add to the broth and no salt with which to season it.

The poor man sat at his table trying to figure out how he might improve the flavour of his meal when suddenly an idea came to him he thought might be worth trying.

'I wonder if my rich friend is having a nice dinner tonight,' he said to himself, and he promptly arose from the table and set off in the direction of the rich man's farmhouse. He crept close enough to take a good look through the kitchen window and there, right in front of him, he saw a steaming-hot chicken lying on a plate of thick gravy. The delicious smell of the cooked meat wafted on the breeze towards him, causing the poor man's stomach to grumble loudly. Without wasting another second, he rushed back to his hut, grabbed his bowl of watery soup, and sat down against the outside wall of the rich man's house. Then, as he spooned the thin liquid down his throat, he breathed in the aroma of the meat and began to imagine that he was chewing on the most tender pieces of chicken flesh. When he had finished his meal, he felt very satisfied and hurried off home to tell his wife how clever he had been.

A few days later, the poor man saw the rich man and could not prevent himself boasting of his cleverness once again.

'I came to your house a few days ago,' he told the rich man, 'and while I drank my watery soup I breathed in the delicious smell rising up from your table. I might as well have sat alongside you sharing the same chicken. My own meal tasted equally good.'

'So that is why my food tasted so dull,' roared the rich man, 'you stole all its flavour from me. Well, you must pay for what you have taken. I order you to come with me to the judge. We will let him decide your punishment.'

The poor man was hauled that same day before the judge who ordered him to pay one goat to the rich man for having stolen the aroma from his food. But the poor man could not even afford to pay the rich man a single grain of wheat, let alone a goat, and he drifted slowly homewards, his head bowed in despair, wondering how he could possibly break the distressing news to his wife.

While he walked towards his hut, he met a wise old man hobbling along the road. And as the two were headed in the same direction, they soon struck up a conversation. The poor man revealed to his companion the whole sad story of what had happened and the wise man agreed with him that he had been most unfairly treated.

'I have a goat I will give you,' said the old man, 'I will go and fetch it for you. Take it home and look after it until the day you are called upon to make your payment. When that day arrives, I promise I will reappear to help you.'

And saying this, the wise man went off to fetch the goat, leaving the poor man a little bewildered, yet relieved to know that all was not entirely lost.

Less than a week later, the judge sent a message to the poor man telling him that he should appear before him to deliver the promised payment. By midday a large group of people had gathered in front of the judge's house to witness the proceedings. At the centre of the crowd stood the wise man, listening intently to all that was said. He behaved as if he knew nothing of the whole affair and began asking the people to explain to him what was happening.

'The poor man is supposed to pay the rich man a goat for having stolen the smell from his food,' they told him.

'But why make so much fuss over such a trivial incident?' the wise man asked.

'The poor man must pay the rich man his goat,' the people repeated, 'that is the judge's decision and we must stand by it.'

'And would you accept another judgement on this case?' the old man enquired politely.

'We would,' replied the people, 'if you can prove yourself a good enough judge.'

So the old man moved forward to the front of the crowd and addressed the people with the following words:

'A man who steals should be forced to repay only as much as he has taken. If the poor man had eaten the food, he should be made to pay back that food. But if he has only breathed the smell, he should only pay back the smell, nothing more, nothing less.'

'Yes, that is very true,' answered the people, 'but how can a man give back just the smell of the food?'

'I will show you a way,' answered the wise man. Then he turned to the rich man and said to him:

'The goat you have asked for has been brought to you. But you may not have it unless the poor man has taken your food. Beat this goat with your staff instead and when the animal bleats, take the sound of its bleating as payment for the smell of your food. Surely you will agree with me that this is a fair exchange!'

The rich man could not argue against this judgement and all around him the people began to clap their hands, delighted to have experienced such wisdom at first hand.

And so the poor man was saved from an unfair sentence and was allowed to go home. But the rich man was made to appear a selfish and greedy individual before the entire village. He slunk away silently and hoped that the whole affair would blow over, but whenever he appeared again in public, the people pointed at him and whispered among themselves:

'He who rides the horse of greed at a gallop will be forced to dismount at the door of shame.'

How Walukaga Answered the King
(From the Baganda people, central Africa)

WALUKAGA, THE BLACKSMITH, was by far the most gifted craftsman in the village, capable of turning his hand to all kinds of metalwork. Every morning a crowd usually gathered at his home, gasping in amazement at the speed with which he produced spears and axes, shovels and hoes, armlets and collars, and a whole variety of objects for the benefit of the villagers. The blacksmith's fame had spread far and wide so that even the king took a particular interest in his work and lined his courtyards with wonderful iron figures Walukaga had created specially for him.

One day a messenger from the palace arrived at the blacksmith's home to announce that the king wished him to perform a very special task. Walukaga was delighted by the news, for nothing pleased him more than to serve the king with his craft. He hurried off into a back room where he put on his finest crimson robe and a beautifully decorated head-dress. Then he followed the messenger to the palace, trying to imagine as he went along what kind of exciting work lay in store for him.

He was immediately shown to the king's private chamber and as soon as the king clapped his hands a group of servants appeared carrying several trays of iron pieces in various shapes.

'I have a very special job for you, Walukaga,' the king announced enthusiastically. 'I was staring at those fine figures you made for me just the other day when it occurred to me how nice it would be to have a life-size metal man for a companion. But I don't just mean a statue. What I want is an iron man who can walk and talk, who has blood in his veins, wisdom in his head and feelings in his heart.'

Walukaga almost collapsed with the shock. He stared long and hard into the king's eyes looking for a sign that the whole thing was some kind of joke, but the king's stern expression filled him with despair. From that moment onwards, the blacksmith had no peace of mind, for he well knew that failure to obey his sovereign's wishes would certainly mean death for himself and his family.

'I will do my very best to please you,' he answered mournfully and arranged for the iron to be delivered to his forge later that same day.

Next morning, Walukuga arose earlier than usual and made a tour of the neighbouring houses hoping that someone among his friends would be able to help him out of the terrible situation he now found himself in. But every last person he turned to for advice could only offer the most impractical suggestions. One friend recommended that he build a metal shell and put a real man inside it, refusing to believe that the king would ever notice the difference. Another suggested that he flee the country and remain in hiding until the whole affair had been forgotten, entirely overlooking the fact that Walukaga had a wife and children to think of. A third even advised him to persuade the palace cook to poison the king's food. Walukaga listened to each neighbour in turn and fell into a deep depression. He returned home in the afternoon and shut himself away in his room, knowing that his days were numbered and trying desperately hard to come to terms with that fact.

A few days later, as Walukaga walked through the bush deep in thought, he managed to stray from his usual path and found himself wandering through a deserted stretch in search of a familiar landmark. Suddenly he thought he heard voices up ahead and moving closer to investigate, discovered a filthy-looking man sitting cross-legged on the ground chatting away to himself. The blacksmith recognized the man as someone once well-known in the village who had suffered so much misfortune as a youth he had gone completely mad and taken refuge in the wilderness.

Although frightened at first, Walukaga soon realized that the madman was in fact perfectly harmless and decided to accept the cup of water offered him as a sign of friendship. Soon the pair began chatting, and as the conversation turned to more important things, the blacksmith felt he would have nothing to lose if he unburdened himself and told the madman all about the king's impossible command. His companion sat and listened quietly to the very end without interruption and when Walukaga, only half-seriously, asked him whether he had any advice to spare, he was surprised to see the madman's eyes narrow almost to a squint and his face take on a grave and purposeful expression.

'I will tell you precisely what you should do,' the madman spoke clearly and decidedly. 'I want you to go to the king and tell him if he really wants you to make this remarkable iron man, you must have only the very finest materials. Say to him that you will need a very special charcoal and a plentiful supply of water from a most unusual source. Let him send word to the people of the village that they must shave their heads and burn their hair until they have produced a thousand loads of charcoal, and let him order them to weep into their water-bowls until they have given him a hundred pots of tears.'

The blacksmith pondered this advice and rapidly concluded it was by far the best he had received to date. But when he turned to thank the madman, he saw that he had begun rocking back and forth, laughing hysterically and shaking his head uncontrollably. Walukaga felt he had no more time to lose, and in spite of the late hour, he hurried off towards the palace, anxious to say his piece before his courage failed him.

Bowing low before the king, he timidly listed off all the things he would need to complete the work requested of him. But the king listened patiently and agreed to everything demanded, promising that the materials would be collected as smoothly and swiftly as possible.

So the very next day, messengers were sent out to every part of the kingdom ordering the people to shave their heads and weep into their bowls. Nobody dared disobey the king's command and even the women and children came forward without complaint. The people did their very best to comply with the king's wishes, but after seven days, when all of them had shaved their heads and wept until their eyes were red and raw, there was still not enough charcoal to make up even a single load, or enough tears to fill half a water-pot.

The elders of the kingdom had little choice but to appear before their leader and confess to him their lack of success. But as they stood before the king, quaking at the thought of the punishment he would deal them, they were relieved to discover that his response was more than reasonable. The king accepted that the people's efforts had been sincere and he sighed deeply and sent for the blacksmith to appear before him.

'Walukaga,' he said, 'you may stop your work on the iron man I asked you to build me. You have requested something impossible and my people cannot deliver the materials you need. Go home now and continue on with the work you are best at.'

Walukaga approached the king and smiled a little nervously.

'I hope you will not be angry with me, Your Majesty,' he said, 'but because you asked the impossible of me, I knew I had to do the same in return. I could never have made you a living man of iron, no more than your people could have delivered the charcoal and the water I demanded.'

But the king was not in the least bit angry, for he was delighted to have such a clever and honest man among his subjects.

The Young Man and the Skull
(From the Mbundu people, south-west Africa)

ONE DAY A YOUNG HUNTER had journeyed far into the bush in search of antelope when he accidentally stumbled upon a skull lying in the earth. Drawing nearer, he stooped to the ground to examine the object and began muttering to himself:

'How did you manage to get here my friend? What can have brought you to this unhappy end?'

To the young man's absolute astonishment, the skull opened its jaws and began speaking:

'Talking brought me here, my friend. Talking brought me to this place.'

The hunter raced back towards his village to tell the people all about his discovery.

'Friends,' he cried excitedly, 'I have just come across a human skull in the bush and it has spoken to me. It must be a wonderful sign.'

'Nonsense,' they replied, 'how can you possibly hold a conversation with the head of a dead man?'

'But it really did speak to me,' the young man insisted, 'you only refuse to believe me because you are jealous.'

But still the people continued to jeer him.

'Why not go and tell the chief all about your discovery,' one mocked, 'I'm sure he'll be overjoyed by the news!'

'I will do precisely that,' retorted the young man angrily, and off he marched towards the chief's house to tell him all about the skull.

But the chief, who had been taking his afternoon nap, was extremely unhappy that he had been disturbed.

'Why have you come here with your tall stories?' he shouted. 'You had better be telling the truth or I will see to it that your own head comes off. Now, take me to this wretched place and let me hear the skull's message for myself.'

A small crowd set off from the village, arriving shortly afterwards at the place where the young man had made his discovery. And sure enough, they soon spotted the skull sitting in the earth.

'It looks perfectly ordinary,' complained the people after a time, 'when are we going to hear it speak?'

The young man crouched to the ground and repeated the words he had first spoken to the skull. But no answer came and the skull's jaws remained firmly shut. Again, the hunter spoke to it, raising his voice more loudly, but only silence followed.

Now the crowd began to grow restless and when a third and fourth attempt produced exactly the same result, they leapt on the young man and chopped off his head as the chief had ordered.

The head fell to the ground and rolled alongside the skull. For a long time afterwards all remained quiet as the villagers disappeared over the hill bearing the body homewards for burial. Then the skull opened its jaws and spoke up:

'How did you manage to get here my friend? What can have brought you to this unhappy end?'

'Talking brought me here,' replied the head. 'Talking brought me to this place.'

The Story of the Glutton
(From the Bantu speaking peoples, east Africa)

SEBGUGUGU WAS A POOR MAN who lived with his wife and children in one of the shabbiest huts in the village. He had very few possessions worth speaking of and certainly nothing of any great value to his name, apart from a white cow and calf he had inherited from his bride many years before on their wedding day.

One morning, as Sebgugugu sat outside his hut lazing in the warm sunshine, he observed a brightly coloured bird hopping towards him. The bird drew closer and, perching itself on the gate-post, began to chirp a little song. Sebgugugu listened attentively, and after a time he became convinced that the bird was speaking to him through the melody.

'Kill the White One,' he heard it say. 'Kill the white one and you will get a hundred in return.'

Sebgugugu stood up excitedly and called to his wife across the fields to come and hear the strange song. Obediently, she stopped her work and hurried back towards the hut. But after she had listened to the bird singing for a few minutes she turned and said to her husband:

'I cannot hear anything unusual. It is only a sweet little song. Perhaps you have had too much hot sun for one day.'

'That bird is definitely speaking to us,' her husband argued, 'and I'm certain he is trying to deliver a message from the great Imana. [*Imana is the name given to the High God of the Bantu people, who commands everything, even Death.*] He is telling us that we will get a hundred fat cows if only we kill the white one we own.'

'Surely you would never consider doing such a thing!' his wife cried out in alarm. 'We depend on that cow for milk to feed our children and if anything happens to it they will die of starvation.'

But Sebgugugu chose to ignore these words and marched off, axe in hand, towards the field to kill the white cow.

That evening, the family feasted on freshly roasted beef and for several weeks afterwards they had enough food to keep them satisfied. Soon, however, the meat began to run out and their stomachs felt very empty. There was still no sign of the hundred cows intended to replace the one they had slaughtered, but Sebgugugu would not accept any of the blame for this and carried on as before, basking lazily in the sun while his wife struggled to feed their children and keep the household together.

A few weeks later, the strange bird made a second visit to Sebgugugu's hut and this time he heard it advise him to kill the calf of the white cow. Though his wife pleaded with him, Sebgugugu went ahead as before and slaughtered the young animal, cutting up the carcass for food. But there was far less meat on this occasion, and it lasted only a few days. The children, thirsty without milk, and hungrier than ever, began to grow pale and thin. And when he saw that the hundred cows had still failed to appear, Sebgugugu became slightly fearful for the first time.

'The children are starving,' he said to his wife anxiously, 'there is nothing else here for them to eat.'

'Didn't I warn you this would happen when you slaughtered the first of our precious cattle,' his wife replied angrily. 'You have left us with little choice now but to abandon our home and roam the countryside in search of food.'

Next morning, the family gathered together what few belongings remained in their hut and started off in search of food. By midday, they had travelled a long distance and sat down by the roadside to recover their strength. Weary and footsore, Sebgugugu buried his head in his hands, ready to give up the fight:

'What can I do to save my children?' he cried out despondently. 'I have been a very foolish creature.'

But the Great Creator, Imana, who had been watching over the family from above, now appeared before the sobbing man and spoke to him encouragingly:

'What is your trouble, Sebgugugu?' he enquired. 'You should know by now that you have only to ask and I will do my best to help you.'

Sebgugugu raised his eyes and confessed to the High God every detail of his selfish behaviour.

'I can see that you are sorry,' Imana responded, 'and I will give you the chance to prove to me that you are a man of worth. Walk towards that cattle-kraal beyond the hill and there you will find an old crow guarding the herd. Say to him that I have given you permission to drink the milk. Do not forget to thank him for his hospitality and remember to treat him always with the utmost respect.'

Sebgugugu promised to do all this and headed off towards the kraal. He could not find any trace of the old crow when he arrived, but his eyes soon lit up at the sight of four large churns standing nearby, full to the brim with creamy, white milk. Sebgugugu bent over the milk and helped himself to as much as he wanted, leaving just about enough for his wife and children.

Suddenly, in the distance, he caught sight of the old crow driving the cattle homewards, flying back and forth and squawking over their heads to keep them together. Remembering what Imana had said, Sebgugugu ran forward to greet the herdsman, apologizing for the fact that his wife had drunk so much of the milk.

'But I will see to it that she repays you in some way,' he reassured the crow. And as the two of them sat down to chat for the evening, he ordered his wife to fetch a pail and begin milking the cows. When she had done this, he ordered her to build a fire to drive the mosquitoes away. Then, he instructed her to bring the crow a bowl full of milk for his supper. Although exhausted, his wife performed all of these tasks without complaint, grateful for the fact that her children had found a place of refuge where they could be restored to health under the crow's protection.

For a long time, things went on well in this way, but then, without warning, Sebgugugu began to grow restless and discontented.

'That old crow is beginning to annoy me,' he said to his wife one day. 'There really couldn't be a better time to do away with him, you know. Our own children are now old enough to herd the cattle for me, so we really have no use for him anymore.'

His wife was appalled to hear him say such a thing, but although she protested loudly, Sebgugugu took his bow and arrows and went outdoors to lie in wait for the crow as he returned home with the cattle that evening. When the crow came near enough, he took aim and shot an arrow in his direction. But the arrow missed its target and the startled crow took to the skies. As he did so, the cattle began to disappear into thin air one by one until there was not so much as a stray calf remaining to satisfy the needs of the family. Sebgugugu looked to his wife for comfort, but she could not give him any. Reduced to destitution once more, she led her children by the hand along the road away from the kraal, her head bowed in disappointment and misery.

They had not gone very far, however, before the benevolent Imana appeared before them once more.

'You have behaved very badly,' he chastised Sebgugugu, 'but I am prepared to give you another chance. If you walk a little deeper into the bush you will come across a long, twisted vine lying in the earth. Sprinkle a little water on the vine, and soon you will be able to gather from it not only the most succulent melons, but also delicious gourds and fruits of every variety and colour. But you must never attempt to prune the vine or do anything to it other than gather the produce it yields. Do exactly as I say and you will never be short of food.'

Again Sebgugugu thanked the High God and promised to behave as he had been commanded. He quickly found the vine, watered it, and ordered his wife to harvest the fruit and vegetables it yielded. That evening, Sebgugugu sat down to a large helping of the wholesome food, and while his wife and children stood by, waiting to take their share of whatever he left behind, he patted his stomach contentedly and smiled at his good fortune.

But after a few weeks the same pattern repeated itself, and for no good reason, Sebgugugu became fidgety and began looking around him for some sort of diversion. Stooping to examine the vine one morning, he decided that it would be a far more productive plant if only its branches were thinned out to produce healthier shoots. He took his knife and without consulting anyone, began hacking at the stalks. But almost immediately, the vine withered away into the earth like a sun-scorched seedling.

This time when Imana appeared before Sebgugugu, he was fuming with anger. Sebgugugu fell on his knees and begged for forgiveness, but the High God spoke sternly, his voice as loud as the fiercest thunder:

'I have watched you disobey me repeatedly without any show of remorse,' he yelled, 'and it is only for the sake of your honest wife and children that I am prepared to give you a third and final chance. Leave this place now and a little further down the road you will come across a large rock embedded in the soil. The rock will provide you with every kind of food – corn, milk, beans and other grains. Never attempt to force the food from the rock. Be patient and you will always be given as much as you need.'

Sebgugugu stood up, his heart pounding in his breast, and scuttled off in search of the rock, taking with him a basket and a jar. He soon reached the spot Imana had described and saw before him an enormous grey boulder. Moving closer to inspect it, he observed that its surface was covered in a number of small cracks. He held up his jar and at once, through the cracks, a thin stream of milk began to flow, followed by a long, steady line of corn. He carried this food back home to his family and they all sat down together to enjoy a very pleasant meal.

It seemed as if Sebgugugu had thoroughly mended his ways and for several months after the High God had admonished him, he remained an attentive and considerate husband and father. But one morning he awoke in a very bad mood, for his wife had taken ill, and now the responsibility of feeding and caring for the family fell on his shoulders alone. Sebgugugu set off towards the rock, but as he stood waiting for the milk to flow and the grain to appear, he became very impatient and kicked the rock furiously. By sunset, when he had finally gathered all he needed, his anger had multiplied tenfold, and he shouted in exasperation to his sick wife:

'I have wasted the entire day waiting for that rock to deliver the food. I can stand it no longer. I am going to find a way to widen those cracks no matter what it takes.'

And with his usual disregard for the welfare of his wife and family, Sebgugugu stormed outside where he cut some stout poles and hardened them in the fire.

Next morning, he returned to the rock, and using the great poles as levers, attempted to enlarge the cracks. The task was far easier than he had imagined and soon he had created a wide gap, large enough for him to pop his head through to take a closer look at the food.

He pushed his nose towards the opening, but as he did so he was sucked further and further inwards until, with a crash like thunder, the gap closed up and the cracks disappeared, leaving not even the slightest trace on the smooth surface of the rock.

Sebgugugu's wife did not mourn his disappearance for very long and within a few months she had married a modest and respectable man from a neighbouring village. And if ever her children asked about their father, she told them the story of the glutton, who had pushed Imana's patience to the limit and had met with his just reward.

The Feast

(From the Cameroon, west Africa)

ONCE THERE LIVED A KIND AND GENEROUS CHIEF who wished to repay his people for the long hours they had worked for him on his farm. An idea came to him that he should hold a great feast and so he sent messengers to all of the surrounding villages inviting the men, women and children to attend his home the following evening, asking only that each man bring a calabash of wine along to the celebrations.

Next day, there was great excitement among the people. They chatted noisily about the event as they worked in the fields and when they had finished their labour they returned home to bathe and dress themselves in their finest robes. By sunset, more than a hundred men and their families lined the roadside. They laughed happily as they moved along, beating their drums and dancing in time to the rhythm. When they arrived at the chief's compound, the head of every household emptied his calabash into a large earthenware pot that stood in the centre of the courtyard. Soon the pot was more than half full and they all looked forward to their fair share of the refreshing liquid.

Among the chief's subjects there was a poor man who very much wanted to attend the feast, but he had no wine to take to the festivities and was too proud to appear empty-handed before his friends.

'Why don't you buy some wine from our neighbour?' his wife asked him, 'he looks as though he has plenty to spare.'

'But why should we spend money on a feast that is free?' the poor man answered her. 'No, there must be another way.'

And after he had thought about it hard for a few minutes he turned to his wife and said:

'There will be a great many people attending this feast, each of them carrying a calabash of wine. I'm sure that if I added to the pot just one calabash of water, nobody would notice the difference.'

His wife was most impressed by this plan, and while her husband went and filled his calabash with water, she stepped indoors and put on her best tunic and what little jewellery she possessed, delighted at the prospect of a good meal and an evening's free entertainment.

When the couple arrived at the chief's house they saw all the other guests empty the wine they had brought into the large earthen pot. The poor man moved forward nervously and followed their example. Then he went to where the men were gathered and sat down with them to await the serving of the wine.

As soon as the chief was satisfied that all the guests had arrived, he gave the order for his servants to begin filling everyone's bowl. The vessels were filled and the men looked to their host for the signal to begin the drinking. The poor man grew impatient, for he was quite desperate to have the taste of the wine on his lips, and could scarcely remember when he had last enjoyed such a pleasant experience for free.

At length, the chief stood up and delivered a toast to his people. Then he called for his guests to raise their bowls to their lips. Each of them tasted their wine, swallowed it, and waited to feel a warm glow inside.

They swallowed some more of the wine, allowing it to trickle slowly over their tongues, and waited for the flavour to release itself. But the wine tasted as plain as any water. And now, all around the room, the guests began to shuffle their feet and cough with embarrassment.

'This is really very good wine,' one of the men spoke up eventually.

'Indeed it is the best I've ever tasted,' agreed another.

'Quite the finest harvest I've ever come across,' added his neighbour.

But the chief of the people knew precisely what had happened, and he smiled at the comical spectacle as each man tried to hide the fact that he had filled his calabash that morning from the village spring.

The enormous earthen pot contained nothing but water, and it was water that the people were given to drink at the chief's great feast. For the chief had very wisely decided in his own mind:

'When only water is brought to the feast, water is all that should be served.'

The Three Tests

(From the Swahili speaking peoples, east Africa)

THERE ONCE LIVED A KING who had seven strong sons. When the day arrived for the eldest of them to leave the family home, he explained to his father that he longed to travel to a distant land and requested a sailing boat, together with some food and money. The king provided him with these things and the young man set sail across the ocean, promising to return to his family as soon as he had completed his great adventure.

He had been on the seas for some weeks when he spotted an island up ahead, and as he wished to rest awhile on dry land, he moored his boat and swam ashore. He found it a very pleasant spot, and strolled happily among the fruit-trees, helping himself to large handfuls of the juicy berries hanging from almost every branch. The berries satisfied not only his hunger, but also his thirst, and when the young man spat out the seeds, he noticed that they transformed themselves instantly into new plants laden with deliciously ripe fruit. Delighted with this discovery, he collected several baskets of the berries and took them on board his boat. He drew up his anchor and set sail once more, hoping that the next stage of his voyage would prove just as rewarding.

After several more days at sea, he approached another strange land, this time populated by a race of tall and powerful men, and discovered that it was ruled by a great sultan. Wishing to make a favourable impression, the young man offered the sultan some of the wonderful berries he had gathered, explaining how the seeds could bear fruit as soon as they touched fertile soil. The sultan was immediately suspicious and refused to believe a word until he had seen the evidence with his own eyes.

'If what you say is true,' the sultan declared, 'I will reward you handsomely. But if I find that you are lying, I will throw you in prison for having wasted my time.'

So the young man brought a basket of fruit from his boat, ate some of it and spat the seeds upon the ground. But to his great disappointment, the seeds lay there without altering their shape in any way. The sultan gave the signal, and at once a group of guards seized the young man, bound him, and carried him away to prison, promising that he would never again see the light of day.

When six months had passed and the king had still not received word of his eldest son, he began to grow extremely worried.

His brothers were also very concerned for his safety and so it was agreed that the next eldest should go in search of him. It was not long before he, too, arrived on the island bearing the wonderful fruit-trees and when he had eaten some of the fruit and found that the seeds sprang to life as soon as they touched the soil, he gathered several baskets of the berries and took them on board his boat.

Shortly afterwards, the second son approached the sultan's kingdom and, as his brother had done before him, he began to boast of the miraculous fruit he had discovered, offering to demonstrate its remarkable magic to the sultan. He ate some of the berries and threw the seeds upon the ground. But the seeds failed to spring up, and the sultan, enraged that he had been made to look a fool a second time, immediately ordered him to be imprisoned in a chamber next to his eldest brother.

One by one, the king's sons set sail from the palace. Each landed on the island and gathered the enchanted berries. Each boasted of their wonderful magic when they arrived in the sultan's kingdom, and each was immediately thrown into prison when the seeds failed to sprout.

At last, only the youngest son remained. The boy's name was Sadaka, and although he was scarcely a youth, he could not be persuaded to abandon the thought of going in search of his brothers. The king eventually agreed to give him a boat and when he had loaded it with millet, rice and cattle, he embraced his mother and his father and took to the waves.

After a long, storm-tossed journey, Sadaka arrived on a cold, desolate island and climbed ashore hoping to find some trace of his brothers. But the first sight to greet him was a flock of weather-beaten birds, perilously close to starvation. Without any hesitation, the young boy hauled a sack of millet ashore and scattered it all around for the dying creatures to feed on. Soon the birds had recovered their strength, and in return for Sadaka's kindness, they begged him to accept from them an incense stick:

'Burn this stick if at any time you need us,' they told him, 'and we will smell it and come to help you.'

Sadaka accepted the gift and walked on towards the trees. He had not gone very far before he encountered a swarm of flies, weak with hunger and unable to take to the air. The boy immediately slaughtered the cattle he had on board and threw them on to the island. Soon the flies were buzzing around him gratefully. Their leader thanked Sadaka and gave him a second incense stick:

'If at any time you need us,' the flies told him, 'burn this stick and we will come to your aid.'

Sadaka explored a little further. Eventually he came upon a family of jinns who were also without food. He stopped to light a great fire and began cooking a large pot of rice for them to eat. The jinns marvelled at this generosity and when they had eaten their fill, they handed him an incense stick, identical to the other two, instructing him to burn it if ever he ran into trouble.

Sadaka sailed away and before he had even lost sight of the island, the sun began to shine, the sea grew calmer, and soon he had arrived at the place where his brothers had gathered the enchanted berries. He could not quite believe his eyes when the seeds he spat out blossomed into new trees, and so he decided to gather some of the fruit and take it to the jinns to show them.

'O yes,' said the sultan of the jinns, 'we have heard all about these berries and they are very real. But if you intend to show them to anyone else, it is important to know that the miracle will only happen when the seeds fall on special soil.'

The young boy considered this information for a time, then he thanked the jinns and returned to the island of the fruit trees. Here he gathered up enough of the precious soil to fill three wooden barrels. He rolled the barrels on to his boat, hoisted his sails and set out to sea once more.

After he had travelled only a short stretch of the ocean he came upon the sultan's kingdom and presented himself before the great ruler.

'I have journeyed here in search of my brothers,' he informed the sultan, 'and if any of your people can help me find them, I will reward them with a very special tree that will always bear more fruit than they can eat, and whose branches will always remain strong and productive even in times of famine.'

But the sultan laughed uproariously for some minutes at the young man's speech.

'Listen to this fool,' he called to his attendants. 'There are six men in my prison who came here boasting exactly the same thing. See to it that this one joins them.'

But Sadaka began to protest noisily:

'Give me a chance to prove myself,' he pleaded. 'Tomorrow I will show you this wonder, but please be patient with me until then.'

'So be it,' replied the sultan indifferently, 'but remember, if you fail, I will show no mercy and you will be cast into prison with the others.'

That night, when he was certain that everyone lay sleeping , Sadaka crept from his chamber and headed towards the shore. He dragged the first of the three barrels from his boat and began sprinkling the soil thinly and evenly upon the ground. The work took several long hours and he had only just emptied the last of the barrels when the first rays of sunshine peered over the horizon. Silently and carefully, he crawled back to his bed and waited there anxiously for the people to stir.

As soon as the sultan and the wise men of the kingdom had awoken, Sadaka was summoned to appear before him. He carried a small basket of fruit with him and set it down on the ground. Slowly he lifted a handful of the ripe berries and began chewing on them. The sultan yawned aloud and twisted in his seat. The wise men glanced around them and took very little notice. But when Sadaka spat the seeds upon the earth and they began to rise up before their eyes, the sultan and all the people on the island cried out in sheer delight. Again Sadaka performed his great miracle and soon he was joined by others who ate the fruit and spat out the seeds until the whole kingdom blossomed with the magic trees.

From that moment onwards, the sultan took Sadaka under his wing and saw to it that everything he needed was provided for him. Almost immediately, he arranged for his brothers to be released from prison and ordered a great feast to be held to celebrate their freedom. And as time moved on, the sultan grew very fond of the young man and wished that he had been blessed with an equally wise and generous son of his own.

The sultan possessed a daughter, however, whose extraordinary beauty and talent were famous throughout the land. It was not long before Sadaka came to hear of her many virtues and when, one day, he spotted her strolling through the palace gardens, his heart was filled with a deep desire to be with her. He went before the sultan and asked if he might make her his wife, but to his surprise, the sultan grew very angry and declared that he had yet to encounter a man even half good enough to marry his daughter.

'What would I have to do to prove my worth to you?' Sadaka asked him, 'I will do anything you ask, for now that I have seen her, my heart will never be at peace.'

The sultan led Sadaka to a very large storeroom and pointed to the hundreds of sacks containing all kinds of mixed grain.

'If you can separate these different kinds of grain and place each kind in its own sack by tomorrow morning, then you may marry the princess,' he announced.

Sadaka eyes widened in disbelief at the sight of the huge task facing him, but he so badly wanted the sultan's daughter, he agreed at least to try his hand. So he sat down on the floor and began sorting through the first sack. But after a very short time, he realized how hopeless the situation was and buried his head in his hands. Then he suddenly remembered the incense stick the birds on the lonely island had given him. He took the stick from beneath his robe, and as soon as the pungent odour filled the air, a flock of birds appeared out of nowhere asking what they might do to help him. After the birds had heard what the sultan had ordered, they flew around the room and began picking up the grain in their beaks, separating each kind into its own sack.

Next morning, when the sultan arrived at his storehouse, he saw that all the grain was separated as he had ordered. But he walked away, shaking his head and gathered his wise men around him. At length, he came and spoke to Sadaka:

'We cannot quite believe what we have seen,' he told the young man, 'and so you must prove yourself once more if you wish to marry my daughter. If you can cut through the trunk of that Baobab tree over there, with one stroke of your sword, you can take her.'

Sadaka saw that the tree was of an enormous size and knew that he could not possibly perform what was required of him without help. So he asked to be allowed to go back to his room to get his weapon and here he burned the second incense stick. At once the family of jinns appeared before him and when he told them what the sultan wanted him to do, they flew away and returned with an army of white ants that marched towards the tree. The ants gnawed at the trunk leaving only the bark so that when Sadaka approached and drew his sword, he easily cut the tree in half and it fell to the ground effortlessly.

But the sultan was still not satisfied:

'Tomorrow will be your final test,' he told Sadaka. 'In the afternoon all the maidens of the kingdom will pass in front of you one by one, each of them wearing identical veils over their faces. You must pick the princess from among them and if you choose correctly, you shall have her for your wife.'

Then Sadaka retired once more to his chamber and burnt his last incense stick. Immediately, the leader of the flies appeared and Sadaka explained what had been demanded of him.

'When the maidens of the city pass before you,' said the fly, 'I will stand in front of you and you must keep watch on me. When the princess draws near, I will drum my wings and alight on her shoulder as she passes by.'

So the next afternoon all the maidens of the kingdom passed in a procession before the sultan and his attendants and, as promised, the leader of the flies took to the air and landed on the shoulder of the princess as she walked past. Sadaka stood up and walked forward to where the princess stood, planting a kiss on her cheek for everyone around to see.

Sadaka had now passed his three tests and the sultan could not deny he was more than a fitting son-in-law. Proudly he took the princess by the arm and led her away. They were married the very next day and the sultan built for them a fine palace where they lived a long and happy life together.

The Two Rogues

(From the Hausa speaking peoples, west Africa)

AMONG THE HAUSA PEOPLE, there were two men, each as devious as the other, who spent most of their time plotting and planning how best to earn a living by dishonest means. One rogue lived in Kano, while the other lived in Katsina, and although they had never actually met, news of their trickery travelled back and forth between the villages, so that even with some distance between them, they considered themselves powerful rivals.

One morning, when the rogue from Kano had run rather short of money, he sat down by a palm tree to consider his next crooked scheme. Suddenly an idea came to him and, taking his hunting knife, he began peeling a long length of bark from the tree. After he had trimmed it carefully, he took it to one of the women at the dye-pit and asked her to dip it in blue ink for him. The wood looked impressive when it had been stained, but in order to improve it even more, the rogue from Kano painted it with a glaze, giving it the appearance of the finest blue broadcloth. Then he wrapped it up in paper, placed it in his leather bag and set out for market, confident that the cloth would fetch a very favourable price.

But while the rogue from Kano had been doing all of this, the rogue from Katsina had also kept himself busy, for he, too, had recently run short of funds and had only a couple of hundred cowries left to his name. So he took a goatskin, laid it flat on the ground and heaped several loads of pebbles on to it. Then he sprinkled the cowries on top, drew the four corners together and set off with his bundle to market.

Half way along the road, the two rogues happened to meet and soon fell into conversation as they walked along.

'Where are you off to, my friend?' asked the rogue from Kano.

'I'm on my way to market,' said the rogue from Katsina. 'I've got all my money here in cowries, twenty thousand of them, and I intend to purchase something very special for my wife.'

'Well, fancy that! I was just heading in the same direction myself,' said the rogue from Kano, 'and I have with me the very best blue broadcloth to sell to the highest bidder.'

'Wouldn't it be nice to avoid such a long journey in this heat,' said the rogue from Katsina. 'You look almost as weary as I feel and we still have exactly the same distance to go.'

And so the two men rapidly abandoned all thought of going to market. They struck a bargain on the spot and exchanged their wares before parting in great friendship, each one believing he had got the better of the other.

When they had moved off a short distance, each man stopped in his path to examine the bargain he had carried away. But, of course, the rogue from Kano discovered that he had been handed a bag of stones, while the rogue from Katsina found that he had purchased little more than a parcel of bark.

As soon as they discovered they had been duped, they each turned back and retraced their steps until eventually they came face to face once more. At first angry and belligerent, they soon realized they had much in common and grew calmer at the thought of putting this to lucrative use:

'We are each as crafty as the other,' they said, 'and it would be wisest from now on to join forces and seek our fortune together.'

Shaking hands on this arrangement, they took to the road without further hostility and walked on until they had arrived at a neighbouring town. Here they found an old woman who sold them water-bottles, staffs and begging-bowls, and when they had equipped themselves with these items, they set off once more, pretending to be blind beggars as they hobbled along in the afternoon sunshine.

They followed a dusty trail deep into the bush and before long stumbled upon a party of traders pitching camp among the trees. The traders had only just begun to unload their caravan and as the two rogues hid in the undergrowth feasting their eyes on the rich cargo, they began discussing a plan which would enable them to get their hands on as much of the goods as possible.

Later that evening, when darkness had descended upon the camp, the two rogues came out of hiding and moved slowly towards the fire where the traders had just gathered together for their evening meal, beating their staffs on the ground before them and squeezing their eyes tightly shut. The pitiful sight they presented earned them immediate sympathy and without delay they were handed platefuls of hot food and encouraged to spend the night at the camp.

Soon the traders retired to their beds accompanied by the blind men who complained aloud of the great weariness that had suddenly overtaken them. They pretended to be the very first to fall asleep, but as soon as they were certain everyone else had followed their example, they opened their eyes again and crept from their beds. Very quietly, they began to rummage through the traders' property, carrying off quantities of food, drink, precious jewellery and money to a dry well a short distance away into which they very carefully dropped them.

Next morning when the party awoke and found they had been robbed of everything, they were quite devastated and began an immediate search for the thieves. The two rogues did not escape suspicion, but having anticipated that their innocence might be questioned, they had already made certain that some of their own possessions had been carried off.

'Where are our water-bottles?' they cried out in mock-despair, 'and our staffs! They are missing also. How will we manage to walk without them?'

But the traders grew angry to hear them voice such petty concerns.

'Here we are,' they cried, 'robbed of everything we own, and all you miserable beggars can think about are your water-bottles and your walking sticks. Get out of here before we throw you out.'

But as they groped their way through the bush, the two rogues smiled at one another, knowing that as soon as the coast was clear, they would hurry off to the well and help themselves to the stolen goods.

'Why don't you go down into the well,' said the rogue from Kano to his companion. 'I have strong labourer's hands and I can use a rope to haul up the goods more skilfully than you.'

'No, you go down,' said the rogue from Katsina, 'I have much better eyesight and can keep a more careful watch up here in case any of the traders return.'

'No, you go,' said the rogue from Kano.

'No, you,' replied the rogue from Katsina.

And they continued to argue back and forth in this manner for several minutes until, finally, the rogue from Katsina reluctantly agreed to go down into the well. Soon his companion had lowered a strong rope to which he tied the goods, allowing them to be hauled to the top swiftly and smoothly. The rogue from Kano worked as quickly as possible above the surface, trying hard to conceal the fact that while he stacked the stolen goods, he was also gathering together a mound of boulders at the mouth of the well. But his companion below had a pretty shrewd idea of what the rogue from Kano intended for him and was resolved to keep his head about him at all times.

When, at long last, the work of retrieving the stolen property had almost come to an end, the rogue from Kano shouted into the well:

'My friend, when you have secured the last item to the rope and are ready to come up yourself, give me a shout. That way, I can haul you up very carefully so that you don't tear yourself on the jagged stones along the sides.'

But the rogue from Katsina did not trust this gesture of friendship and shouted back:

'The next load will be a pretty heavy one, but it is the only thing left down here.'

Then he crawled into the last of the bales of wheat and hid himself inside.

The rogue from Kano now hauled up the remaining bale and carried it over to where he had stacked the other goods, not suspecting for one moment that his companion lay concealed within it. He then walked to the mouth of the well and began hurling the boulders into the opening one by one until he was satisfied that he had completely covered the base and crushed anything resting at the bottom.

But while he was busy doing this, the rogue from Katsina crawled out of hiding and started to divide up the stolen property, placing some in the bushes, some underneath the rocks and some beneath his robes. The hoard had been reduced to little or nothing by the time he heard his companion walking back from the well. He had no wish to be discovered alive, and so he decided to retreat to the bush until nightfall, at which time he intended to return and gather up everything for himself alone.

The rogue from Kano scratched his head in dismay and sat down on the ground trying to solve the riddle of the missing goods he had so carefully stacked by the side of the well.

'Someone must have come in the last few minutes and taken the stuff away,' he exclaimed to himself, but then it occurred to him that the thief could not be very far away and that, in all probability, he would be in desperate need of a pack-horse to help him carry his load.

The thought had no sooner entered his head when he leaped into the shelter of the trees and began braying like a donkey. Sure enough, after a few minutes, he saw a figure hurrying towards him calling out:

'Steady there donkey! Hold on until I can get to you. Don't run away now, boy!'

The figure reached through the branches and seized him by the collar. Within seconds, the rogue from Kano found himself pinned to the ground staring into the eyes of the rogue from Katsina. The two men remained speechless for a time, but then they stood up, smiled knowingly at one another and began dusting down their clothes.

Silently, they gathered up their booty and continued on their travels once more. The road they now followed happened to take them past the rogue of Kano's house and here the two men sat down and finally divided up the stolen property fairly and squarely.

Some days later, however, the rogue of Katsina announced his wish to visit his own family.

'I cannot possibly carry my share of the goods with me,' he told his companion, 'but I will leave them here and in three months' time I will come back and collect what is mine.'

And so he set off, believing he had seen the last of his friend's trickery and that he had nothing more to fear.

Two months passed by and the rogue of Kano kept his word and never once laid a finger on his friend's share of the stolen property. But when the third month had almost come to an end, he ordered his family to dig a grave in the field close to their hut. Then, on the night before the rogue of Katsina was due to return, he gathered up all of the goods, including his friend's portion, crammed them into a sack, and threw them into the grave, instructing his family to bury him alive alongside them.

'Cover the grave over with fresh earth,' he told his family, 'and when Katsina returns, say that I have passed away and that you have buried the contents of the house with me.'

And so, next morning, as soon as the family saw the rogue from Katsina appear in the distance, they ran towards him weeping and wailing:

'You have arrived too late!' they cried. 'Our brother is dead. We buried him four days ago.'

'Really?' said the rogue from Katsina, rather taken aback by the news. 'So he has gone the way of all flesh and taken his most valuable possessions with him, I suppose.'

'O yes!' replied the family, 'everything was cast into the grave, for we were uncertain which items belonged to him.'

'Take me to the grave so that I may see this for myself,' said the rogue from Katsina, his suspicion increasing every moment. 'I must pay my last respects even if I have missed out on the burial.'

When he was taken to the grave the rogue from Katsina broke into loud lamentations, but after a few minutes, when he had recovered himself, he spoke to the family:

'You really ought to cut some thorn-bushes and cover the mound well,' he told them, 'otherwise the hyenas may come and dig up the body and scatter the bones.'

'We'll do it tomorrow,' promised the family, and saying this, they led the rogue of Katsina into their hut and provided him with supper and a comfortable bed for the night.

At the first sign of darkness, when the household had grown very quiet, the rogue from Katsina stole from his bed and walked to his friend's grave. He crouched to the ground and began to growl ferociously, dropping on his hands and knees and scrabbling at the earth as if he were a hyena trying to get at the corpse underneath.

Inside the grave the rogue from Kano awoke from his sleep, and as soon as he heard the loud scratching and growling sounds he screamed out in terror:

'Help, help! Someone save me! The hyenas have come for me. They are trying to eat me. Let me out of here!'

The rogue from Katsina continued to dig, until he caught sight of his friend's ghostly face, lifted towards the opening in sheer horror.

'All right,' he said, 'out you come, Kano. I think you have finally learned your lesson.'

The rogue from Kano seized his friend's hand and was lifted to the surface. He was more relieved to see the rogue from Katsina than he had ever believed possible and as it began to dawn on him, once and for all, that he had finally met his match, he suddenly burst into a fit of laughter:

'Katsina, you are a scoundrel,' he said as he tittered away to himself.

'Yes, and you are another!' Katsina replied smiling from ear to ear.

Celtic Myths

Introduction

THE ATTEMPT TO ASSIGN a precise date to the birth of Celtic civilization has proved a complicated and problematic task, leading to many differences of opinion among historians and archaeologists. A straightforward answer to this and a number of other questions arising from the study of Celtic culture is rendered almost impossible by the fact that the Celts cannot simply be catalogued as a geographically unified race. Their evolution, unlike that of the Romans, is not well documented, nor is there any evidence of an organized ancient civic structure which might reveal to us more information about these people.

What we do know however, largely as a result of archaeological research, is that the Celts were an extremely imaginative and accomplished race and certainly no other barbarian tribe before them had ever made such a significant contribution to European culture as a whole. Although the Celts were nomads who began life as simple tribesmen scattered across the Alps of northern Europe and along the Upper Danube river, they possessed a fierce conquering spirit which enabled them to dominate Mediterranean society from about 500 BC right up until the Roman Empire began to take shape, roughly in the mid-third century BC. During this era of supremacy, the Celts sacked Rome and Delphi and spread in substantial numbers throughout France, Belgium, Switzerland, the Balkans and Asia Minor. Yet they never managed to establish permanent kingdoms in any of the lands they conquered, nor did they display any aptitude for cultivating a centrally co-ordinated military strategy. The loyalties of the Celts remained tribal rather than imperial and it was surely as a direct consequence of this that by the middle of the first century AD, the Romans occupied most of the old Celtic strongholds of Europe and managed to drive the Celts westwards into Scotland and Ireland.

We are not certain when it was precisely that the Celts arrived in Ireland. Some historians have suggested that the first Celtic immigrants to the British Isles may have arrived as early as the late Bronze Age, in the sixth century BC, but the majority of opinion adheres to the view that the Celts were more firmly established in Ireland during the Iron Age which began around 500 BC. The great stone fort of Dun Aengus on the Aran island of Innismore is positive evidence of the presence of early Celtic barbarians in Ireland whom the natives described as Fir Bolg.

Ireland, unlike other European countries, was never invaded by the Romans and it therefore escaped the systematic oppression of native language and traditions Rome insisted upon. Ireland's culture as a result remained largely unchanged up until the spread of Christianity, in contrast to its neighbour Britain, which by the year AD 40 had completely succumbed to Roman authority. An indigenous Celtic civilization was preserved in Ireland and ancient traditions were allowed to flourish. The spectacular array of Celtic artefacts discovered in various locations throughout Europe, including jewellery, pottery, decorated weapons, stone carvings, High Crosses and stunning illuminated manuscripts, has left us in little doubt that the Celts were extremely gifted craftsmen, but Ireland, unique among other countries penetrated by this race, may boast an additional treasure to add to the vast hoard Celtic culture has bequeathed us. Ireland's ancient literature is unparalleled by any other western European literature of the early Middle Ages in its originality, historical insight, imaginative charm, and sheer lyrical beauty.

The earliest form of narrative the Celts indulged in was no doubt in the oral tradition and we know from later written descriptions of them that storytelling was a favourite pastime and that their men of poetry were highly esteemed figures. Of those nations remaining beyond the influence of Rome, Ireland's was one of the few ancient societies that learned to write. This unusual situation came about as a result of Christian missionary activity, instigated by the Romans, which became widespread throughout the country by the late fifth century. In the fullness of time, the Celts were Christianized, but to begin with, as soon as they had mastered the art of writing, they began to transcribe for posterity native tales in their own vernacular which embodied pre-Christian traditions of their pagan lifestyles handed down over countless generations.

The earliest Irish literary manuscripts now in existence are thought to have been copied from texts written down by the Celts as early as the seventh century, or possibly even earlier. Many of the original manuscripts were destroyed however, during the Viking raids of the ninth and tenth centuries and only a very few fragmentary texts have survived which were written before AD 1000. Modern organization of Ireland's ancient tales based on these manuscripts divides them into four main groups, or cycles – the Invasions Cycle, the Ulster Cycle, the Fenian Cycle and the Historical Cycle. This volume presents typical examples of the first three cycles, generally considered to be the most important.

The Book of Invasions (*Lebor Gábala*) is a twelfth-century manuscript in which historical and mythical elements are very obviously fused. We discover, for example, that Ireland has been subject to at least six different invasions during the pre-Christian, pagan era, each account documented in an authentic tone and style which, for all that, conflicts with the fairytale physical descriptions of a great many of the invaders and the impossible feats they achieve. Out of this mingled context emerges a group of very powerful and lyrical tales forming the Invasions Cycle which manifests the same constant tension between a reality and a fantasy world. What is reinforced, however, is the Celtic love and worship of natural objects such as rivers and trees and the Celtic belief in a fairy realm, or Otherworld. Central to these stories is a supernatural and highly significant race of people known as the Tuatha De Danann of which more is revealed in the chapters to follow.

The Ulster Cycle is set in the reign of Conchobar mac Nessa and the notorious Queen Medb of Connacht in the first century of the Christian era. The stories are preserved in various manuscripts which date from the twelfth to the fifteenth centuries and are more readily 'historical' in that they are less fanciful, moving towards a firmer exploration of a Celtic society displaying a more elaborate system of law and order. The task of separating fact from fiction is still a difficult one in these tales, but many eminent scholars are agreed that characters such as Cuchulainn, Medb and Conchobar mac Nessa really did exist, however much their exploits and personalities are exaggerated and enhanced by the storytellers. Most of the tales of the Ulster Cycle, including The Birth of Cuchulainn, The Intoxication of the Ulstermen and The Cattle Raid of Cooley are found in their most original form in *The Book of the Dun Cow* (*Lebor na Huidre*) which was written sometime around AD 1100. The book containing 134 folio pages is now housed in the Royal Irish Academy in Dublin.

The earliest tales of the Fenian, or Ossianic cycle, set in the third century of the Christian era during the reign of Conn Céadchathach and his grandson Cormac mac Art, are preserved in manuscripts of the eleventh and twelfth centuries but were almost certainly written several hundreds of years earlier, probably in the eighth century. The Fianna, who are portrayed in these stories as a highly skilled band of volunteer soldiers led by Finn mac Cumaill, have been one of the most popular subjects of Irish and also Scottish literature since the Celts first immortalized them. The tale of Finn's son Oisín in the Land of Youth belongs less to the heroic tradition of the original Fenian tales, however. The dialogue sequence between Oisín and St Patrick which appeared in the late twelfth century manuscript *The Colloquy of Old Men* (*Agallamh na Seanórach*) is the work of a Christianized storyteller who uses the character and the cycle's narrative framework as a vehicle to introduce a topical Christian theme. This practice of adding additional tales to the cycle was one which continued well into the eighteenth century.

The Historical Cycle, which unfortunately cannot be covered in a volume of this length, includes a colourful multitude of miscellaneous tales and legends including tales of Cormac mac Art, and later kings of ancient Ireland.

The Invasions Cycle: Tales of the Tuatha De Danann and the Early Milesians

THE THREE STORIES which introduce this volume are based on tales selected from the Book of Invasions, otherwise known as the Mythological Cycle. This chapter begins after the conquest of the Fir Bolg by the Tuatha De Danann, the god-like race, whose name translates as 'the people of the god whose mother is Dana'. Three of the most outstanding stories have been chosen for this section, each of which has an especially powerful narrative impact.

The Tuatha De Danann are recorded as having originally travelled to Erin from the northern islands of Greece around 2000 BC. They possessed great gifts of magic and druidism and they ruled the country until their defeat by the Milesians, when they were forced to establish an underground kingdom known as the Otherworld or the Sidhe, meaning Hollow Hills.

Lugh [*Pronounced Lu, gh is silent, as in English.*] of the Long Arm, who also appears later in the Ulster Cycle as Cuchulainn's divine father, emerges as one of the principal heroes of the Tuatha De Danann who rescues his people from the tyranny of the Fomorians. The Quest of the Children of Tuirenn, together with the sorrowful account of Lir's children, are undoubtedly two of the great epic tales of this cycle.

The Wooing of Etain which concludes the trio, was probably written sometime in the eighth century. The story unfolds after the People of Dana are dispossessed by the Children of Miled and for the first time the notion of a Land of Youth, or Otherworld, is introduced, a theme again returned to in the third and final Fenian Cycle.

The Quest of the Children of Tuirenn

NUADA OF THE SILVER HAND rose to become King of the Tuatha De Danann during the most savage days of the early invasions. The Fomorians, a repulsive band of sea-pirates, were the fiercest of opponents who swept through the country destroying cattle and property and imposing tribute on the people of the land. Every man of the Tuatha De Danann, no matter how rich or poor, was required to pay one ounce of gold to the Fomorians and those who neglected to pay this tax at the annual assembly on the Hill of Uisneach were maimed or murdered without compassion. Balor of the Evil Eye was leader of these brutal invaders, and it was well known that when he turned his one glaring eyeball on his foes they immediately fell dead as if struck by a thunderbolt. Everyone lived in mortal fear of Balor, for no weapon had yet been discovered that could slay or even injure him. Times were bleak for the Tuatha De Danann and the people had little faith in King Nuada who appeared powerless to resist Balor's tyranny and oppression. As the days passed by, they yearned for a courageous leader who would rescue them from their life of wretched servitude.

The appalling misery of the Tuatha De Danann became known far and wide and, after a time, it reached the ears of Lugh of the Long Arm of the fairymounds, whose father was Cian, son of Cainte. As soon as he had grown to manhood, Lugh had proven his reputation as one of the most fearless warriors and was so revered by the elders of Fairyland that they had placed in his charge the wondrous magical gifts of Manannan the sea-god which had protected their people for countless generations. Lugh rode the magnificent white steed of Manannan, known as Aenbarr, a horse as fleet of foot as the wailing gusts of winter whose charm was such that no rider was ever wounded while seated astride her. He had the boat of Manannan, which could read a man's thoughts and travel in whatever direction its keeper demanded. He also wore Manannan's breast-plate and body armour which no weapon could ever pierce, and he carried the mighty sword known as 'The Retaliator' that could cut through any battle shield.

The day approached once more for the People of Dana to pay their annual taxes to the Fomorians and they gathered together, as was customary, on the Hill of Uisneach to await the arrival of Balor's men. As they stood fearful and terrified in the chill morning air, several among them noticed a strange cavalry coming over the plain from the east towards them. At the head of this impressive group, seated high in command above the rest, was Lugh of the Long Arm, whose proud and noble countenance mirrored the splendour of the rising sun. The King was summoned to witness the spectacle and he rode forth to salute the leader of the strange army. The two had just begun to converse amiably when they were interrupted by the approach of a grimy-looking band of men, instantly known to all as Fomorian tax-collectors. King Nuada bowed respectfully towards them and instructed his subjects to deliver their tributes without delay. Such a sad sight angered and humiliated Lugh of the Long Arm and he drew the King aside and began to reproach him:

'Why do your subjects bow before such an evil-eyed brood,' he demanded, 'when they do not show you any mark of respect in return?'

'We are obliged to do this,' replied Nuada. 'If we refuse we would be killed instantly and our land has witnessed more than enough bloodshed at the hands of the Fomorians.'

'Then it is time for the Tuatha De Danann to avenge this great injustice,' replied Lugh, and with that, he began slaughtering Balor's emissaries single-handedly until all but one lay dead at his feet. Dragging the surviving creature before him, Lugh ordered him to deliver a stern warning to Balor:

'Return to your leader,' he thundered, 'and inform him that he no longer has any power over the People of Dana. Lugh of the Long Arm, the greatest of warriors, is more than eager to enter into combat with him if he possesses enough courage to meet the challenge.'

Knowing that these words would not fail to enrage Balor, Lugh lost little time preparing himself for battle. He enlisted the King's help in assembling the strongest men in the kingdom to add to his own powerful army. Shining new weapons of steel were provided and three thousand of the swiftest white horses were made ready for his men. A magnificent fleet of ships, designed to withstand the most venomous ocean waves, remained moored at port, awaiting the moment when Balor and his malicious crew would appear on the horizon.

The time finally arrived when the King received word that Balor's fierce army had landed at Eas Dara on the northwest coast of Connacht. Within hours, the Fomorians had pillaged the lands of Bodb the Red and plundered the homes of noblemen throughout the province. Hearing of this wanton destruction, Lugh of the Long Arm was more determined than ever to secure victory for the Tuatha De Danann. He rode across the plains of Erin back to his home to enlist the help of Cian, his father, who controlled all the armies of the fairymounds. His two uncles, Cu and Cethen, also offered their support and the three brothers set off in different directions to round up the remaining warriors of Fairyland.

Cian journeyed northwards and he did not rest until he reached Mag Muirthemne on the outskirts of Dundalk. As he crossed the plain, he observed three men, armed and mailed, riding towards him. At first he did not recognize them, but as they drew closer, he knew them to be the sons of Tuirenn whose names were Brian, Iucharba and Iuchar. A long-standing feud had existed for years between the sons of Cainte and the sons of Tuirenn and the hatred and enmity they felt towards each other was certain to provoke a deadly contest. Wishing to avoid an unequal clash of arms, Cian glanced around him for a place to hide and noticed a large herd of swine grazing nearby. He struck himself with a druidic wand and changed himself into a pig. Then he trotted off to join the herd and began to root up the ground like the rest of them.

The sons of Tuirenn were not slow to notice that the warrior who had been riding towards them had suddenly vanished into thin air. At first, they all appeared puzzled by his disappearance, but then Brian, the eldest of the three, began to question his younger brothers knowingly:

'Surely brothers you also saw the warrior on horseback,' he said to them. 'Have you no idea what became of him?'

'We do not know,' they replied.

'Then you are not fit to call yourselves warriors,' chided Brian, 'for that horseman can be no friend of ours if he is cowardly enough to change himself into one of these swine. The instruction you received in the City of Learning has been wasted on you if you cannot even tell an enchanted beast from a natural one.'

And as he was saying this, he struck Iucharba and Iuchar with his own druidic wand, transforming them into two sprightly hounds that howled and yelped impatiently to follow the trail of the enchanted pig.

Before long, the pig had been hunted down and driven into a small wood where Brian cast his spear at it, driving it clean through the animal's chest. Screaming in pain, the injured pig began to speak in a human voice and begged his captors for mercy:

'Allow me a dignified death,' the animal pleaded. 'I am originally a human being, so grant me permission to pass into my own shape before I die.'

'I will allow this,' answered Brian, 'since I am often less reluctant to kill a man than a pig.'

Then Cian, son of Cainte, stood before them with blood trickling down his cloak from the gaping wound in his chest.

'I have outwitted you,' he cried, 'for if you had killed me as a pig you would only be sentenced for killing an animal, but now you must kill me in my own human shape. And I must warn you that the penalty you will pay for this crime is far greater than any ever paid before on the death of a nobleman, for the weapons you shall use will cry out in anguish, proclaiming your wicked deed to my son, Lugh of the Long Arm'.

'We will not slay you with any weapons in that case,' replied Brian triumphantly, 'but with the stones that lie on the ground around us.' And the three brothers began to pelt Cian with jagged rocks and stones until his body was a mass of wounds and he fell to the earth battered and lifeless. The sons of Tuirenn then buried him where he had fallen in an unmarked grave and hurried off to join the war against the Fomorians.

With the great armies of Fairyland and the noble cavalcade of King Nuada at his side, Lugh of the Long Arm won battle after battle against Balor and his men. Spears shot savagely through the air and scabbards clashed furiously until at last, the Fomorians could hold out no longer. Retreating to the coast, the terrified survivors and their leader boarded their vessels and sailed as fast as the winds could carry them back through the northern mists towards their own depraved land. Lugh of the Long Arm became the hero of his people and they presented him with the finest trophies of valour the kingdom had to offer, including a golden war chariot, studded with precious jewels which was driven by four of the brawniest milk-white steeds.

When the festivities had died down somewhat, and the Tuatha De Danann had begun to lead normal lives once more, Lugh began to grow anxious for news of his father. He called several of his companions to him and appealed to them for information, but none among them had received tidings of Cian since the morning he had set off towards the north to muster the armies of the fairymounds.

'I know that he is no longer alive,' said Lugh, 'and I give you my word that I will not rest again, or allow food or drink to pass my lips, until I have knowledge of what happened to him.'

And so Lugh, together with a number of his kinsmen, rode forth to the place where he and his father had parted company. From here, the horse of Manannan guided him to the Plain of Muirthemne where Cian had met his tragic death. As soon as he entered the shaded wood, the stones of the ground began to cry out in despair and they told Lugh of how the sons of Tuirenn had murdered his father and buried him in the earth. Lugh wept bitterly when he heard this tale and implored his men to help him dig up the grave so that he might discover in what cruel manner Cian had been slain. The body was raised from the ground and the litter of wounds on his father's cold flesh was revealed to him. Lugh rose gravely to his feet and swore angry vengeance on the sons of Tuirenn:

'This death has so exhausted my spirit that I cannot hear through my ears, and I cannot see anything with my eyes, and there is not one pulse beating in my heart for grief of my father. Sorrow and destruction will fall on those that committed this crime and they shall suffer long when they are brought to justice.'

The body was returned to the ground and Lugh carved a headstone and placed it on the grave. Then, after a long period of mournful silence, he mounted his horse and headed back towards Tara where the last of the victory celebrations were taking place at the palace.

Lugh of the Long Arm sat calmly and nobly next to King Nuada at the banqueting table and looked around him until he caught sight of the three sons of Tuirenn. As soon as he had fixed his eye on them, he stood up and ordered the Chain of Attention of the Court to be shaken so that everyone present would fall silent and listen to what he had to say.

'I put to you all a question,' said Lugh. 'I ask each of you what punishment you would inflict upon the man that had murdered your father?'

The King and his warriors were astonished at these words, but finally Nuada spoke up and enquired whether it was Lugh's own father that had been killed.

'It is indeed my own father who lies slain,' replied Lugh 'and I see before me in this very room the men who carried out the foul deed.'

'Then it would be far too lenient a punishment to strike them down directly,' said the King. 'I myself would ensure that they died a lingering death and I would cut off a single limb each day until they fell down before me writhing in agony.'

Those who were assembled agreed with the King's verdict and even the sons of Tuirenn nodded their heads in approval. But Lugh declared that he did not wish to kill any of the Tuatha De Danann, since they were his own people. Instead, he would insist that the perpetrators pay a heavy fine, and as he spoke he stared accusingly towards Brian, Iuchar and Iucharba, so that the identity of the murderers was clearly exposed to all. Overcome with guilt and shame, the sons of Tuirenn could not bring themselves to deny their crime, but bowed their heads and stood prepared for the sentence Lugh was about to deliver.

'This is what I demand of you,' he announced.

Three ripened apples
The skin of a pig
A pointed spear
Two steeds and a chariot
Seven pigs
A whelping pup
A cooking spit
Three shouts on a hill.

'And,' Lugh added, 'if you think this fine too harsh, I will now reduce part of it. But if you think it acceptable, you must pay it in full, without variation, and pledge your loyalty to me before the royal guests gathered here.'

'We do not think it too great a fine,' said Brian, 'nor would it be too large a compensation if you multiplied it a hundredfold. Therefore, we will go out in search of all these things you have described and remain faithful to you until we have brought back every last one of these objects.'

'Well, now,' said Lugh, 'since you have bound yourselves before the court to the quest assigned you, perhaps you would like to learn more detail of what lies in store,' And he began to elaborate on the tasks that lay before the sons of Tuirenn.

'The apples I have requested of you,' Lugh continued, 'are the three apples of the Hesperides growing in the gardens of the Eastern World. They are the colour of burnished gold and have the power to cure the bloodiest wound or the most horrifying illness. To retrieve these apples, you will need great courage, for the people of the east have been forewarned that three young warriors will one day attempt to deprive them of their most cherished possessions.

'And the pig's skin I have asked you to bring me will not be easy to obtain either, for it belongs to the King of Greece who values it above everything else. It too has the power to heal all wounds and diseases.

'The spear I have demanded of you is the poisoned spear kept by Pisar, King of Persia. This spear is so keen to do battle that its blade must always be kept in a cauldron of freezing water to prevent its fiery heat melting the city in which it is kept.

'And do you know who keeps the chariot and the two steeds I wish to receive from you?' Lugh continued.

'We do not know,' answered the sons of Tuirenn.

'They belong to Dobar, King of Sicily,' said Lugh, 'and such is their unique charm that they are equally happy to ride over sea or land, and the chariot they pull is unrivalled in beauty and strength.

'And the seven pigs you must gather together are the pigs of Asal, King of the Golden Pillars. Every night they are slaughtered, but every morning they are found alive again, and any person who eats part of them is protected from ill-health for the rest of his life.

'Three further things I have demanded of you,' Lugh went on. 'The whelping hound you must bring me guards the palace of the King of Iruad. Failinis is her name and all the wild beasts of the world fall down in terror before her, for she is stronger and more splendid than any other creature known to man.

'The cooking-spit I have called for is housed in the kitchen of the fairywomen on Inis Findcuire, an island surrounded by the most perilous waters that no man has ever safely reached.

'Finally, you must give the three shouts requested of you on the Hill of Midcain where it is prohibited for any man other than the sons of Midcain to cry aloud. It was here that my father received his warrior training and here that his death will be hardest felt. Even if I should one day forgive you of my father's murder, it is certain that the sons of Midcain will not.'

As Lugh finished speaking, the children of Tuirenn were struck dumb by the terrifying prospect of all that had to be achieved by them and they went at once to where their father lived and told him of the dreadful sentence that had been pronounced on them.

'It is indeed a harsh fine,' said Tuirenn, 'but one that must be paid if you are guilty, though it may end tragically for all three of you.' Then he advised his sons to return to Lugh to beg the loan of the boat of Manannan that would carry them swiftly over the seas on their difficult quest. Lugh kindly agreed to give them the boat and they made their way towards the port accompanied by their father. With heavy hearts, they exchanged a sad farewell and wearily set sail on the first of many arduous journeys.

'We shall go in search of the apples to begin with,' said Brian, and his command was answered immediately by the boat of Manannan which steered a course towards the Eastern World and sailed without stopping until it came to rest in a sheltered harbour in the lands of the Hesperides. The brothers then considered how best they might remove the apples from the garden in which they were growing, and it was eventually decided among them that they should transform themselves into three screeching hawks.

'The tree is well guarded,' Brian declared, 'but we shall circle it, carefully avoiding the arrows that will be hurled at us until they have all been spent. Then we will swoop on the apples and carry them off in our beaks.'

The three performed this task without suffering the slightest injury and headed back towards the boat with the stolen fruit. The news of the theft had soon spread throughout the kingdom, however, and the king's three daughters quickly changed themselves into three-taloned ospreys and pursued the hawks over the sea. Shafts of lightning lit up the skies around them and struck the wings of the hawks, scorching their feathers and causing them to plummet towards the waters below. But Brian managed to take hold of his druidic wand and he transformed himself and his brothers into swans that darted below the waves until the ospreys had given up the chase and it was safe for them to return to the boat.

After they had rested awhile, it was decided that they should travel on to Greece in search of the skin of the pig.

'Let us visit this land in the shape of three bards of Erin,' said Brian, 'for if we appear as such, we will be honoured and respected as men of wit and wisdom.'

They dressed themselves appropriately and set sail for Greece composing some flattering verses in honour of King Tuis as they journeyed along. As soon as they had landed, they made their way to the palace and were enthusiastically welcomed as dedicated men of poetry who had travelled far in search of a worthy patron. An evening of drinking and merry-making followed; verses were read aloud by the King's poets and many ballads were sung by the court musicians. At length, Brian rose to his feet and began to recite the poem he had written for King Tuis. The King smiled rapturously to hear himself described as 'the oak among kings' and encouraged Brian to accept some reward for his pleasing composition.

'I will happily accept from you the pig's skin you possess,' said Brian, 'for I have heard that it can cure all wounds.'

'I would not give this most precious object to the finest poet in the world,' replied the King, 'but I shall fill the skin three times over with red gold, one skin for each of you, which you may take away with you as the price of your poem.'

The brothers agreed to this and the King's attendants escorted them to the treasure-house where the gold was to be measured out. They were about to weigh the very last share when Brian suddenly snatched the pig's skin and raced from the room, striking down several of the guards as he ran. He had just found his way to the outer courtyard when King Tuis appeared before him, his sword drawn in readiness to win back his most prized possession. Many bitter blows were exchanged and many deep wounds were inflicted by each man on the other until, at last, Brian dealt the King a fatal stroke and he fell to the ground never to rise again.

Armed with the pig's skin that could cure their battle wounds, and the apples that could restore them to health, the sons of Tuirenn grew more confident that they would succeed in their quest. They were determined to move on as quickly as possible to the next task Lugh had set them and instructed the boat of Manannan to take them to the land of Persia, to the court of King Pisar, where they appeared once more in the guise of poets. Here they were also made welcome and were treated with honour and distinction. After a time, Brian was called upon to deliver his poem and, as before, he recited some verses in praise of the King which won the approval of all who were gathered. Again, he was persuaded to accept some small reward for his poem and, on this occasion, he requested the magic spear of Persia. But the King grew very angry at this request and the benevolent attitude he had previously displayed soon turned to open hostility:

'It was most unwise of you to demand my beloved spear as a gift,' bellowed the King, 'the only reward you may expect now is to escape death for having made so insolent a request.'

When Brian heard these words he too was incensed and grabbing one of the three golden apples, he flung it at the King's head, dashing out his brains. Then the three brothers rushed from the court, slaughtering all they encountered along the way, and hurried towards the stables where the spear of Pisar lay resting in a cauldron of water. They quickly seized the spear and headed for the boat of Manannan, shouting out their next destination as they ran, so that the boat made itself ready and turned around in the direction of Sicily and the kingdom of Dobar.

'Let us strike up a friendship with the King,' said Brian, 'by offering him our services as soldiers of Erin.'

And when they arrived at Dobar's court they were well received and admitted at once to the King's great army where they won the admiration of all as the most valiant defenders of the realm. The brothers remained in the King's service for a month and two weeks, but during all this time they never once caught a glimpse of the two steeds and the chariot Lugh of the Long Arm had spoken of.

'We have waited long enough,' Brian announced impatiently. 'Let us go to the King and inform him that we will quit his service unless he shows us his famous steeds and his chariot.'

So they went before King Dobar who was not pleased to receive news of their departure, for he had grown to rely on the three brave warriors. He immediately sent for his steeds and ordered the chariot to be yoked to them and they were paraded before the sons of Tuirenn. Brian watched carefully as the charioteer drove the steeds around in a circle and as they came towards him a second time he sprung onto the nearest saddle and seized the reins. His two brothers fought a fierce battle against those who tried to prevent them escaping, but it was not long before they were at Brian's side, riding furiously through the palace gates, eager to pursue their fifth quest.

They sailed onwards without incident until they reached the land of King Asal of the Pillars of Gold. But their high spirits were quickly vanquished by the sight of a large army guarding the harbour in anticipation of their arrival. For the fame of the sons of Tuirenn was widespread by this time, and their success in carrying away with them the most coveted treasures of the world was well known to all. King Asal himself now came forward to greet them and demanded to know why they had pillaged the lands of other kings and murdered so many in their travels. Then Brian told King Asal of the sentence Lugh of the Long Arm had pronounced upon them and of the many hardships they had already suffered as a result.

'And what have you come here for?' the King enquired.

'We have come for the seven pigs which Lugh has also demanded as part of that compensation,' answered Brian, 'and it would be far better for all of us if you deliver them to us in good will.'

When the King heard these words, he took counsel with his people, and it was wisely decided that the seven pigs should be handed over peacefully, without bloodshed. The sons of Tuirenn expressed their gratitude to King Asal and pledged their services to him in all future battles. Then Asal questioned them on their next adventure, and when he discovered that they were journeying onwards to the land of Iruad in search of a puppy hound, he made the following request of them:

'Take me along with you,' he said 'for my daughter is married to the King of Iruad and I am desperate, for love of her, to persuade him to surrender what you desire of him without a show of arms.'

Brian and his brothers readily agreed to this and the boats were made ready for them to sail together for the land of Iruad.

When they reached the shores of the kingdom, Asal went ahead in search of his son-in-law and told him the tale of the sons of Tuirenn from beginning to end and of how he had rescued his people from a potentially bloody war. But Iruad was not disposed to listen to the King's advice and adamantly refused to give up his hound without a fight. Seizing his weapon, he gave the order for his men to begin their attack and went himself in search of Brian in order to challenge him to single combat. A furious contest ensued between the two and they struck each other viciously and angrily. Eventually, however, Brian succeeded in overpowering King Iruad and he hauled him before Asal, bound and gagged like a criminal.

'I have spared his life,' said Brian, 'perhaps he will now hand over the hound in recognition of my clemency.'

The King was untied and the hound was duly presented to the sons of Tuirenn who were more than pleased that the battle had come to a swift end. And there was no longer any bitterness between Iruad and the three brothers, for Iruad had been honestly defeated and had come to admire his opponents. They bid each other a friendly farewell and the sons of Tuirenn took their leave of the land of the Golden Pillars and set out to sea once again.

Far across the ocean in the land of Erin, Lugh of the Long Arm had made certain that news of every success achieved by the sons of Tuirenn had been brought to his attention. He was fully aware that the quest he had set them was almost drawing to a close and became increasingly anxious at the thought. But he desired above everything else to take possession of the valuable objects that had already been recovered, for Balor of the Evil Eye had again reared his ugly head and the threat of another Fomorian invasion was imminent. Seeking to lure the sons of Tuirenn back to Erin, Lugh sent a druidical spell after the brothers, causing them to forget that their sentence had not yet been fully completed. Under its influence, the sons of Tuirenn entertained visions of the heroic reception that awaited them on the shores of the Boyne and their hearts were filled with joy to think that they would soon be reunited with their father.

Within days, their feet had touched on Erin's soil again and they hastened to Tara to the Annual Assembly, presided over by the High King of Erin. Here, they were heartily welcomed by the royal family and the Tuatha De Danann who rejoiced alongside them and praised them for their great courage and valour. And it was agreed that they should submit the tokens of their quest to the High King himself who undertook to examine them and to inform Lugh of the triumphant return of the sons of Tuirenn. A messenger was despatched to Lugh's household and within an hour he had arrived at the palace of Tara, anxious to confront the men he still regarded as his enemies.

'We have paid the fine on your father's life,' said Brian, as he pointed towards the array of objects awaiting Lugh's inspection.

'This is indeed an impressive sight,' replied Lugh of the Long Arm, 'and would suffice as payment for any other murder. But you bound yourselves before the court to deliver everything asked for and I see that you have not done so. Where is the cooking-spit I was promised? And what is to be done about the three shouts on the hill which you have not yet given?'

When the sons of Tuirenn heard this, they realized that they had been deceived and they collapsed exhausted to the floor. Gloom and despair fell upon them as they faced once more the reality of long years of searching and wandering. Leaving behind the treasures that had hitherto protected them, they made their way wearily towards their ship which carried them swiftly away over the storm-tossed seas.

They had spent three months at sea and still they could not discover the smallest trace of the island known as Inis Findcurie. But when their hopes had almost faded, Brian suggested that they make one final search beneath the ocean waves and he put on his magical water-dress and dived over the side of the boat. After two long weeks of swimming in the salt water, he at last happened upon the island, tucked away in a dark hollow of the ocean bed. He immediately went in search of the court and found it occupied by a large group of women, their heads bent in concentration, as they each embroidered a cloth of gold. The women appeared not to notice Brian and he seized this opportunity to move forward to where the cooking-spit rested in a corner of the room. He had just lifted it from the hearth when the women broke into peals of laughter and they laughed long and heartily until finally the eldest of them condescended to address him:

'Take the spit with you, as a reward for your heroism,' she said mockingly, 'but even if your two brothers had attended you here, the weakest of us would have had little trouble preventing you from removing what you came for.'

And Brian took his leave of them knowing they had succeeded in humiliating him, yet he was grateful, nonetheless, that only one task remained to be completed.

They lost no time in directing the boat of Manannan towards their final destination and had reached the Hill of Midcain shortly afterwards, on whose summit they had pledged themselves to give three shouts. But as soon as they had begun to ascend to the top, the guardian of the hill, none other than Midcain himself, came forward to challenge the sons of Tuirenn:

'What is your business in my territory,' demanded Midcain.

'We have come to give three shouts on this hill,' said Brian, 'in fulfilment of the quest we have been forced to pursue in the name of Lugh of the Long Arm.'

'I knew his father well,' replied Midcain, 'and I am under oath not to permit anyone to cry aloud on my hill.'

'Then we have no option but to fight for that permission,' declared Brian, and he rushed at his opponent with his sword before Midcain had the opportunity to draw his own, killing him with a single thrust of his blade through the heart.

Then the three sons of Midcain came out to fight the sons of Tuirenn and the conflict that followed was one of the bitterest and bloodiest ever before fought by any group of warriors. They battled with the strength of wild bears and the ruthlessness of starving lions until they had carved each other to pieces and the grass beneath their feet ran crimson with blood. In the end, however, it was the sons of Tuirenn who were victorious, but their wounds were so deep that they fell to the ground one after the other and waited forlornly for death to come, wishing in vain that they still had the pig skin to cure them.

They had rested a long time before Brian had the strength to speak, and he reminded his brothers that they had not yet given the three shouts on the Hill of Midcain that Lugh had demanded of them. Then slowly they raised themselves up off the ground and did as they had been requested, satisfied at last that they had entirely fulfilled their quest. And after this, Brian lifted his wounded brothers into the boat, promising them a final glimpse of Erin if they would only struggle against death a brief while longer.

And on this occasion the boat of Manannan did not come to a halt on the shores of the Boyne, but moved speedily overland until it reached Dun Tuirenn where the dying brothers were delivered into their father's care. Then Brian, who knew that the end of his life was fast approaching, pleaded fretfully with Tuirenn:

'Go, beloved father,' he urged, 'and deliver this cooking-spit to Lugh, informing him that we have completed all the tasks assigned us. And beg him to allow us to cure our wounds with the pig skin he possesses, for we have suffered long and hard in the struggle to pay the fine on Cian's murder.'

Then Tuirenn rode towards Tara in all haste, fearful that his sons might pass away before his return. And he demanded an audience with Lugh of the Long Arm who came out to meet him at once and graciously received the cooking-spit presented to him.

'My sons are gravely ill and close to death,' Tuirenn exclaimed piteously. 'I beg you to part with the healing pig skin they brought you for one single night, so that I may place it upon their battle wounds and witness it restore them to full health.'

But Lugh of the Long Arm fell silent at this request and stared coldly into the distance towards the Plain of Muirthemne where his father had fallen. When at length he was ready to give Tuirenn his answer, the expression he wore was cruel and menacing and the tone of his voice was severe and merciless:

'I would rather give you the expanse of the earth in gold,' said Lugh, 'than hand over any object that would save the lives of your sons. Let them die in the knowledge that they have achieved something good because of me, and let them thank me for bringing them renown and glory through such a valorous death.'

On hearing these words, Tuirenn hung his head in defeat and accepted that it was useless to bargain with Lugh of the Long Arm. He made his way back despondently to where his sons lay dying and gave them his sad news. The brothers were overcome with grief and despair and were so utterly devastated by Lugh's decision that not one of them lived to see the sun set in the evening sky. Tuirenn's heart was broken in two and after he had placed the last of his sons in the earth, all life departed from him and he fell dead over the bodies of Brian, Iucharba and Iuchar. The Tuatha De Danann witnessed the souls of all four rise towards the heavens and the tragic tale of the sons of Tuirenn was recounted from that day onwards throughout the land, becoming known as one of the Three Sorrows of Story-Telling.

The Tragedy of the Children of Lir

DURING THE GREAT BATTLE of Tailtiu that raged on the plain of Moytura, the Tuatha De Danann were slain in vast numbers and finally defeated by a race of Gaelic invaders known as the Milesians. Following this time of wretched warring, Erin came to be divided into two separate kingdoms. The children of Miled claimed for themselves all the land above ground, while the Tuatha De Danann were banished to the dark regions below the earth's surface. The Danann gods did not suffer their defeat easily, and immediately set about re-building an impressive underground kingdom worthy of the divine stature they once possessed. Magnificent palaces, sparkling with jewels and precious stones, were soon erected and a world of wondrous beauty and light was created where once darkness had prevailed. Time had no meaning in this new domain and all who lived there remained eternally beautiful, never growing old as mortals did above ground.

The day approached for the Tuatha De Danann to choose for themselves a King who would safeguard their future peace and happiness. The principle deities and elders of the people gathered together at the Great Assembly and began deliberating on their choice of leader. Lir, father of the sea-god, Manannan mac Lir, had announced his desire to take the throne, but so too had Bodb the Red, son of the divinity Dagda, lord of perfect knowledge. It came to pass that the People of Dana chose Bodb the Red as their King and built for him a splendid castle on the banks of Loch Dearg. The new ruler made a solemn pledge to his people, promising to prove himself worthy of the great honour bestowed on him. Before long, the People of Dana began to applaud themselves on their choice. Their lives were happy and fulfilled and their kingdom flourished as never before.

Only one person in the entire land remained opposed to the new sovereign. Lir was highly offended that he had not been elected by the People of Dana. Retreating to his home at Sídh Fionnachaidh, he refused to acknowledge Bodb the Red, or show him any mark of respect. Several of the elders urged the King to gather his army together and march to Armagh where Lir could be punished for this insult, but Bodb the Red would not be persuaded. He desired more than anything to be reconciled to every last one of his subjects and his warm and generous spirit sought a more compassionate way of drawing Lir back into his circle.

One morning, the King received news that Lir's wife had recently passed away, leaving him grief-stricken and despondent. Many had tried, but none had yet managed to improve Lir's troubled heart and mind and it was said that he would never recover from his loss. Bodb the Red immediately sent a message to Lir, inviting him to attend the palace. Deeply moved by the King's forgiveness and concern, Lir graciously accepted the invitation to visit Loch Dearg. A large banquet was prepared in his honour and four shining knights on horseback were sent forth to escort the chariot through the palace gates. The King greeted Lir warmly and sat him at the royal table at his right hand. The two men began to converse as if they had always been the closest of friends, and as the evening wore on it was noticed by all that the cloud of sorrow had lifted from Lir's brow. Presently, the King began to speak more earnestly to his friend of the need to return to happier times.

'I am sorely grieved to hear of your loss,' he told Lir, 'but you must allow me to help you. Within this court reside three of the fairest maidens in the kingdom. They are none other than my foster-daughters and each is very dear to me. I give you leave to take the one you most admire as your bride, for I know that she will restore to your life the happiness you now lack.'

At the King's request, his three daughters entered the hall and stood before them. Their beauty was remarkable indeed, and each was as fair as the next. Lir's eyes travelled from one to the other in bewilderment. Finally, he settled on the daughter known as Aeb, for she was the eldest and deemed the wisest of the three. Bodb the Red gave the couple his blessing and it was agreed that they should be married without delay.

After seven days of glorious feasting and celebrating, Aeb and Lir set off from the royal palace to begin their new life together as husband and wife. Lir was no longer weighted down by sorrow and Aeb had grown to love and cherish the man who had chosen her as his bride. Many years of great joy followed for them both. Lir delighted in his new wife and in the twin children she bore him, a boy and a girl, whom they named Aed and Fionnguala. Within another year or two, Aeb again delivered of twins, two sons named Fiachra and Conn, but the second birth proved far more difficult and Aeb became gravely ill. Lir watched over her night and day. Yet despite his tender love and devotion, she could not be saved and his heart was again broken in two. The four beautiful children Aeb had borne him were his only solace in this great time of distress. During the worst moments, when he thought he would die of grief, he was rescued by their image and his love for them was immeasurable.

Hearing of Lir's dreadful misfortune, King Bodb offered him a second foster-daughter in marriage. Aeb's sister was named Aoife and she readily agreed to take charge of Lir's household and her sister's children. At first, Aoife loved her step-children as if they were her very own, but as she watched Lir's intense love for them increase daily, a feeling of jealousy began to take control of her. Often Lir would sleep in the same bed chamber with them and as soon as the children awoke, he devoted himself to their amusement, taking them on long hunting trips through the forest. At every opportunity, he kissed and embraced them and was more than delighted with the love he received in return. Believing that her husband no longer felt any affection for her, Aoife welcomed the poisonous and wicked thoughts that invaded her mind. Feigning a dreadful illness, she lay in bed for an entire year. She summoned a druid to her bedside and together they plotted a course to destroy Lir's children.

One day Aoife rose from her sickbed and ordered her chariot. Seeking out her husband in the palace gardens, she told him that she would like to take the children to visit her father, King Bodb. Lir was happy to see that his wife had recovered her health and was quick to encourage the outing. He gathered his children around him to kiss them goodbye, but Fionnguala refused her father's kiss and drew away from him, her eyes brimming with tears.

'Do not be troubled, child,' he spoke softly to her, 'your visit will bring the King great pleasure and he will prepare the most fleet-footed horses for your speedy return'.

Although her heart was in turmoil, Fionnguala mounted the chariot with her three brothers. She could not understand her sadness, and could not explain why it deepened with every turning of the chariot wheels as they moved forward, away from her father and her beloved home at Sídh Fionnachaidh.

When they had travelled some distance from Lir's palace, Aoife called the horses to a halt. Waking the children from their happy slumber, she ordered them out of the chariot and shouted harshly to her manservants:

'Kill these monstrous creatures before you, for they have stolen the love Lir once had for me. Do so quickly, and I shall reward you as you desire.'

But the servants recoiled in horror from her shameful request and replied resolutely:

'We cannot perform so terrible an evil. A curse will surely fall on you for even thinking such a vile thing.'

They journeyed on further until they approached the shores of Loch Dairbhreach. The evening was now almost upon them and a bank of deep crimson cloud hung lazily on the horizon above the shimmering lake. Weary starlings were settling in their nests and owls were preparing for their nocturnal watch. Aoife now sought to kill the children herself and drew from her cloak a long, pointed sabre. But as she raised her arm to slay the first of them, she was overcome by a feeling of maternal sympathy and it prevented her completing the task. Angry that she had been thwarted once more, she demanded that the children remove their garments and bathe in the lake. As each one them entered the water, she struck them with her druid's wand and they were instantly transformed into four milk-white swans. A death-like chill filled the air as she chanted over them the words the druid had taught her:

'Here on Dairbhreach's lonely wave
For years to come your watery home
Not Lir nor druid can now ye save
From endless wandering on the lonely foam.'

Stunned and saddened by their step-mother's cruel act of vengeance, the children of Lir bowed their heads and wept piteously for their fate. Fionnguala eventually found the courage to speak, and she uttered a plea for lenience, mindful of her three brothers and of the terrible tragedy Lir would again have to suffer:

'We have always loved you Aoife,' she urged, 'why have you treated us in this way when we have only ever shown you loyalty and kindness?'

So sad and helpless were Fionnguala's words, so soft and innocent was her childlike voice, that Aoife began to regret what she had done and she was suddenly filled with panic and despair. It was too late for her to undo her druid's spell, and it was all she could do to fix a term to the curse she had delivered upon the children:

'You will remain in the form of four white swans,' she told them, 'until a woman from the south shall be joined in marriage to a man from the north, and until the light of Christianity shines on Erin. For three hundred years you will be doomed to live on Loch Dairbhreach, followed by three hundred years on the raging Sea of Moyle, and a further three hundred years on Iorras Domhnann. I grant you the power of speech and the gift of singing, and no music in the world shall sound more beautiful and pleasing to the ear than that which you shall make.'

Then Aoife called for her horse to be harnessed once more and continued on her journey to the palace of Bodb the Red, abandoning the four white swans to their life of hardship on the grey and miserable moorland lake.

The King, who had been eagerly awaiting the arrival of his grandchildren, was deeply disappointed to discover that they had not accompanied his daughter.

'Lir will no longer entrust them to you,' Aoife told him, 'and I have not the will to disobey his wishes.'

Greatly disturbed by this news, the King sent a messenger to Lir's palace, demanding an explanation for his extraordinary behaviour. A strange sense of foreboding had already entered Lir's soul and, on receiving the King's message, he became tormented with worry for his children's safety. He immediately called for his horse to be saddled and galloped away into the night in the direction of Loch Dearg. Upon his arrival at Bodb's palace, he was met by one of Aoife's servants who could not keep from him the terrible tale of his wife's treachery. The King was now also informed and Aoife was ordered to appear before them both. The evil expression in his daughter's eye greatly enraged the King and his wand struck violently, changing Aoife into a demon, destined to wander the cold and windy air until the very end of time.

Before the sun had risen the next morning, an anguished party had set off from the palace in search of Lir's children. Through the fog and mist they rode at great speed until the murky waters of Loch Dairbhreach appeared before them in the distance. It was Lir who first caught a glimpse of the four majestic white swans, their slender necks arched forwards towards the pebbled shore, desperately seeking the warm and familiar face of their father. As the swans swam towards him, they began to speak with gentle voices and he instantly recognized his own children in the sad, snow-white creatures. How Lir's heart ached at this woeful sight, and how his eyes wished to disbelieve the sorrowful scene he was forced to witness. He began to sob loudly and it seemed that his grief would never again be silenced.

'Do not mourn us, father,' whispered Fiachra comfortingly, 'your love will give us strength in our plight and we shall all be together one day.'

A beautiful, soothing music now infused the air, miraculously lifting the spirits of all who heard it. After a time, Lir and his companions fell into a gentle, peaceful sleep and when they awoke they were no longer burdened by troubles. Every day, Lir came to visit his children and so too did the Men of Erin, journeying from every part to catch even a single note of the beautiful melody of the swans.

Three hundred years passed pleasantly in this way, until the time arrived for the Children of Lir to bid farewell to the People of Dana and to move on to the cold and stormy Sea of Moyle. As the stars faded and the first rays of sunlight peered through the heavens, Lir came forward to the shores of the lake and spoke to his children for the very last time. Fionnguala began to sing forlornly of the grim and bitter times which lay ahead and as she sang she spread her wings and rose from the water. Aed, Fiachra and Conn joined in her song and then took to the air as their sister had done, flying wearily over the velvet surface of Loch Dairbhreach towards the north-east and the raging ocean:

Arise, my brothers, from Dairbhreach's wave,
On the wings of the southern wind;
We leave our father and friends today
In measureless grief behind.
Ah! Sad the parting, and sad our flight.

To Moyle's tempestuous main;
For the day of woe
Shall come and go
Before we meet again!

Great was the suffering and hardship endured by the swans on the lonely Sea of Moyle, for they could find no rest or shelter from the hissing waves and the piercing cold of the wintry gales. During that first desolate winter, thick black clouds perpetually gathered in the sky, causing the sea to rise up in fury as they ruptured and spilled forth needles of icy rain and sleet. The swans were tossed and scattered by storms and often driven miles apart. There were countless nights when Fionnguala waited alone and terrified on the Rock of Seals, tortured with anxiety for the welfare of her brothers. The gods had so far answered her prayers and they had been returned to her on each occasion, drenched and battered. Tears of joy and relief flowed freely from her eyes at these times, and she would take her brothers under her wing and pull them to her breast for warmth.

Three hundred years of agony and misery on the Sea of Moyle were interrupted by only one happy event. It happened that one morning, the swans were approached by a group of horsemen while resting in the mouth of the river Bann. Two of the figures introduced themselves as Fergus and Aed, sons of Bodb the Red, and they were accompanied by a fairy host. They had been searching a good many years for the swans, desiring to bring them happy tidings of Lir and the King. The Tuatha De Danann were all now assembled at the annual Feast of Age, peaceful and happy, except for the deep sorrow they felt at the absence of the four children of Lir. Fionnguala and her brothers received great comfort from this visit and talked long into the evening with the visitors. When the time finally came for the men to depart, the swans felt that their courage had been restored and looked forward to being reunited with the People of Dana sometime in the future.

When at last their exile had come to an end on the Sea of Moyle, the children of Lir made ready for their voyage westwards to Iorras Domhnann. In their hearts they knew they were travelling from one bleak and wretched place to another, but they were soothed by the thought that their suffering would one day be over. The sea showed them no kindness during their stay at Iorras Domhnann, and remained frozen from Achill to Erris during the first hundred years. The bodies of the swans became wasted from thirst and hunger, but they weathered the angry blasts of the tempests and sought shelter from the driving snow under the black, unfriendly rocks, refusing to give up hope. Each new trial fired the desire within them to be at home once again, safe in the arms of their loving father.

It was a time of great rejoicing among Lir's children when the three hundred years on Iorras Domhnann finally came to an end. With hearts full of joy and elation, the four swans rose ecstatically into the air and flew southwards towards Sídh Fionnachaidh, their father's palace. But their misery and torment was not yet at an end. As they circled above the plains of Armagh, they could not discover any trace of their former home. Swooping closer to the ground, they recognized the familiar grassy slopes of their childhood, but these were now dotted with stones and rubble from the crumbling castle walls. A chorus of wailing and sorrow echoed through the ruins of Lir's palace as the swans flung themselves on the earth, utterly broken and defeated. For three days and three nights they remained here until they could bear it no longer. Fionnguala led her brothers back to the west and they alighted on a small, tranquil lake known as Inis Gluare. All that remained was for them to live out the rest of their lives in solitude, declaring their grief through the saddest of songs.

On the day after the children of Lir arrived at Inis Gluare, a Christian missionary known as Chaemóc was walking by the lakeside where he had built for himself a small church. Hearing the haunting strains floating towards him from the lake, he paused by the water's edge and prayed that he might know who it was that made such stirring music. The swans then revealed themselves to him and began to tell him their sorry tale. Chaemóc bade them come ashore and he joined the swans together with silver chains and took them into his home where he tended them and provided for them until they had forgotten all their suffering. The swans were his delight and they joined him in his prayers and religious devotions, learning of the One True God who had come to save all men.

It was not long afterwards that Deoch, daughter of the King of Munster, came to marry Lairgnéan, King of Connacht, and hearing of Chaemóc's four wonderful swans, she announced her desire to have them as her wedding-present. Lairgnéan set off for Inis Gluare intent on seizing the swans from Chaemóc. Arriving at the church where they were resting, their heads bowed in silent prayer, he began to drag them from the altar. But he had not gone more than four paces when the plumage dropped from the birds and they were changed back into their human form. Three withered old men and a white-faced old woman now stood before Lairgnéan and he turned and fled in horror at the sight of them.

For the children of Lir had now been released from Aoife's curse, having lived through almost a thousand years, to the time when her prophecy came to be fulfilled. Knowing that they had little time left to them, they called for Chaemóc to baptize them and as he did so they died peacefully and happily. The saint carried their bodies to a large tomb and Fionnguala was buried at the centre, surrounded by her three beloved brothers. Chaemóc placed a large headstone on the mound and he inscribed it in oghram. It read, 'Lir's children, who rest here in peace at long last'.

The Wooing of Etain

MIDHIR THE PROUD WAS KING of the Daoine Sidhe, the fairy people of the Tuatha De Danann, and he dwelt at the grand palace in the Hollow Hills of Brí Leíth. He had a wife named Fuamnach with whom he had lived quite contentedly for a good many years. One day, however, while Midhir was out hunting with a group of his companions, he stumbled across the fairest maiden he had ever before laid eyes on, resting by a mountain stream. She had begun to loosen her hair to wash it and her chestnut tresses fell about her feet, shimmering magnificently in the sunlight. The King was enraptured by her perfect beauty and grace and he could not prevent himself from instantly falling in love with her. Nothing could persuade him to abandon the thought of returning to the palace with the maiden and making her his new wife. He boldly confessed to her this desire, hopeful that his noble bearing and royal apparel would not fail to win her approval. The maiden told him that her name was Etain. She was both honoured and delighted that the fairy king had requested her hand in marriage and agreed at once to return with him to Brí Leíth.

Within a short time, Etain's beauty had won her great fame throughout the land and the words 'as fair as Etain' became the highest compliment any man could bestow on a woman. Midhir had soon forgotten about his former wife and spent his days in the company of his new bride whom he doted on and could not bear to be parted from. Fuamnach was distressed and enraged to see them together, but her desire to be comforted and loved once more was entirely overlooked by her husband. When she could bear her cruel treatment no longer, she sought the help of the druid, Bressal, who was well known to the royal palace. Bressal heard Fuamnach's story and took great pity on her. That evening, as Etain lay in bed, they both entered her chamber. A great tempest began to rage around them as the druid waved his wand over the sleeping woman and delivered his curse in grave, commanding tones. As soon as he had uttered his final words, the beautiful Etain was changed into a butterfly and swiftly carried off by the howling winds through the open window far beyond the palace of Midhir the Proud.

For seven long years, Etain lived a life of intolerable misery. She could find no relief from her endless flight and her delicate wings were tattered and torn by the fiery gusts that tossed and buffeted her throughout the length and breadth of the country. One day, when she had almost abandoned hope of ever finding rest again, a chance flurry thrust her through a window of the fairy palace of Aengus Óg, the Danann god of love. All deities of the Otherworld possessed the ability to recognize their own kind, and Etain was immediately revealed to Aengus, despite her winged appearance. He could not entirely undo the druid's sorcery, but he took Etain into his care and conjured up a spell to return her to her human form every day, from dusk until dawn. During the daytime, Aengus set aside the sunniest corner of the palace gardens for her private use and planted it with the most colourful, fragrant flowers and shrubs. In the evening, when Etain was transformed once again into a beautiful maiden, she gave Aengus her love and they grew to treasure each other's company, believing they would spend many happy years together.

It was not long, however, before Fuamnach came to discover Etain's place of refuge. Still bent on revenge, she appeared at the palace of Aengus Óg in the form of a raven and alighted on an apple tree in the centre of the garden. She soon caught sight of a dainty butterfly resting on some rose petals and with a sudden swoop she opened her beak and lifted the fragile creature into the air. Once they were outside of the palace walls, a magic tempest began to blow around Etain. She found herself being carried away from the fairy mounds during the fierce storm, to the unfamiliar plains of Erin above ground where very few of the fairy people had ever dared to emerge.

As soon as he discovered that Etain had been outwitted by Fuamnach, Aengus sprinkled a magic potion into the air and called upon the gods to end the beautiful maiden's torturous wanderings above the earth's surface. A short time afterwards, Etain became trapped in a terrible gale and was hurled through the castle windows of an Ulster Chieftain named Etar. A great feast was in progress and all the noblemen of the province were gathered together for an evening of merry-making and dancing. Etar's wife sat at his right hand and she held a goblet of wine to her lips. Weary and thirsty from her flight, Etain came to rest on the rim of the vessel intending to sip some of the refreshing liquid. But as she leaned forward, she fell into the drinking-cup and was passed down the throat of the noblewoman as soon as she swallowed her next draught.

Several weeks after the great feast, Etar's wife was overjoyed to discover that she was carrying a child. The gods had fulfilled their promise and had caused Etain to nestle in her womb until the time when she could be reborn as a mortal child. After nine months, the Chieftain and his wife were blessed with a daughter and they gave her the name of Etain. She grew to become one of the most beautiful maidens in Ulster and although she bore the same name as before, she could remember nothing of her former life with the Daoine Sidhe.

It was at about this time that a distinguished warrior known as Eochaid Airem was crowned High King of Erin. One of the first tasks he set himself was to organize a splendid annual feast, gathering together all of the kingdom's noblemen to the royal palace for a month of glorious festivity. But the king was soon disappointed to discover that a great number of his noblemen would not accept his generous invitation. Deeply puzzled by this turn of events, he ordered several of them to appear before him and demanded an explanation.

'We cannot attend such a feast,' they told him, 'since the absence of a queen by your side would make it unwholesome. The people of Erin have never before served a king who does not possess a queen. There are many among us with daughters young and fair who would be more than willing to help restore your honour.'

The King was now made to realize that his integrity rested on securing a wife, and he immediately sent out horsemen to the four corners of Erin in search of a maiden who would make for him a suitable queen. Within a few days, a group of his messengers returned with the news that they had found the fairest creature in the land. Eochaid set forth at once to view with his own eyes the maiden his men had found for him. He rode for some distance until at last he happened upon four nymph-like figures laughing and dancing in the sunshine at the edge of a small, meandering brook. One of them was indeed far more beautiful than the others. She was clothed in a mantel of bright purple which was clasped over her bosom with a brooch of bright, glittering gold. Underneath, she wore a tunic of the finest emerald silk, intricately decorated with silver fringes and sparkling jewels. Her skin was as white and smooth as snow, her eyes were as blue as hyacinths and her lips as red as the finest rubies. Two tresses of chestnut hair rested on her head. Each one was plaited into four strands and fastened at the ends with tiny spheres of gold. Eochaid shyly approached the maiden and began to question her softly:

'Who are you,' he inquired, 'and who was it created so rare and beautiful a vision as you?'

'I am Etain, daughter of Etar,' said the maiden. 'Your messengers warned me of your visit Eochaid and I have heard noble tales of you since I was a little child.'

'Will you allow me to woo you then, fair Etain,' asked the King, 'for I cannot conceive of any greater pleasure left to me.'

'It is you I have waited for,' replied Etain, 'and I will only be truly fulfilled if you take me with you to Tara where I will serve you well as queen.'

Overwhelmed with joy at these words, Eochaid grasped Etain's hand and lifted her onto the saddle next to him. They rode speedily towards the palace at Tara where news of the king's betrothal had already reached the ears of his subjects. A hearty welcome awaited the couple as they approached the great gates and they were married that same afternoon to the jubilant sounds of chiming bells and shouts of approval from the large crowd that had gathered to wish them well.

The Royal Assembly of Tara was now the grand occasion everybody looked forward to and preparations began in earnest for the series of lavish banquets and pageants that were to take place in the grounds of the palace. On the morning of first day of the Assembly, Etain made ready to welcome Eochaid's guests and she rode to the top of the hill beyond the gates to catch a glimpse of the first to arrive. After a time, a young warrior on horseback appeared in the distance making his way steadily towards her. He wore a robe of royal purple and his hair, which tumbled below his shoulders, was golden yellow in colour. His face was proud and radiant and his eyes lustrous and gentle. In his left hand, he held a five-pointed spear and in his right, a circular shield, laden with white gold and precious gems. The warrior came forward and Etain welcomed him zealously:

'We are honoured by your presence, young warrior,' said Etain. 'A warm reception awaits you at the palace where I shall be pleased to lead you.'

But the warrior hesitated to accompany her and began to speak in a pained, anxious voice.

'Do you not know me, Etain?' he asked. 'For years I have been searching every corner of the land for you. I am your husband, Midhir the Proud, from the fairy kingdom of the Ever Young.'

'My husband is Eochaid Airem, High King of Erin,' replied Etain. 'Are you not deceived by your own eyes? You are a stranger to me and I have never before heard of your kingdom.'

'Fuamnach is dead and it is now safe for you to return to your home,' Midhir told her. 'It was the sorcery of Fuamnach and Bressal that drove us apart, Etain. Will you come with me now to a land full of music, where men and women remain eternally fair and without blemish. There, in the land of your birth, we may again live happily as man and wife.'

'I will not readily abandon the King of Erin for a man unknown to me,' answered Etain. 'I would never seek to depart with you without the King's consent and I know he will not give it, since his love for me deepens with every passing day.'

Hearing these words, Midhir bowed his head in defeat. It was not in his nature to take Etain by force and he sadly bade her farewell, galloping furiously across the plains of Erin, his purple cloak billowing around him in the breeze.

Throughout the winter months that followed, Etain remained haunted by the image of the stranger who had visited her on the hill. She began to dream of a land filled with sunshine and laughter where she frequently appeared seated on a throne, smiling happily. She could not explain these dreams and did not dare to confide in her husband. Often, however, she would ride to the place where she had met with Midhir the Proud and gaze outwards towards the flat, green carpet of land, secretly entertaining the hope that a rider on a white horse might suddenly appear on the horizon.

One fair summer's morning as Eochaid Airem peered out of the palace window, he noticed a young warrior in a purple cloak riding towards the Hill of Tara. The King was intrigued by the sight and ordered his horse to be saddled so that he might personally greet the stranger and establish the purpose of his visit to the palace.

'I am known to all as Midhir,' said the warrior. 'I have journeyed here to meet with Eochaid Airem, for I am told he is the finest chess-player in the land. I have with me a chessboard with which to test his skill if he is willing to meet my challenge.'

The warrior then produced from beneath his mantel a solid gold chessboard with thirty-two silver pieces, each one encrusted with the finest sapphires and diamonds.

'I would be more than delighted to play a game of chess with you,' replied the King, and he led the way to a brightly-lit chamber where they placed the board on a sturdy round table and sat down to play the first game. The King was not long in proving his reputation as a champion player and, as the young warrior seemed disappointed with his own performance, it was decided that they should play a second game. Again, the King was victorious and the warrior appeared to become more and more agitated. But it was Midhir's intention all along to win Eochaid's sympathy and to lure him into a false sense of security.

'Perhaps it would be best,' suggested the King, 'if we decided on a wager for our third and final game. Name your stake, choose any treasure you desire, and it will be forfeited to you if you are triumphant over me.'

'That is very generous of you,' replied Midhir, 'but I have more than enough wealth and possessions to satisfy me. Perhaps you have a wife, however, who would not protest too loudly if I stole from her a single kiss as my prize?'

'I am sure she would not object,' answered Eochaid cheerfully, for he felt certain that Etain would never have to deliver such a trophy.

The two played on, but this time the King struggled to keep control of the game and at length he was beaten by the younger man. Eochaid now fell silent and began to regret that he had so carelessly offered his wife as prize. In desperation and despair, he begged his opponent to surrender his claim to the pledged kiss. But Midhir insisted firmly on the forfeit and the King was forced to honour his part of the bargain.

'Perhaps you will find it in your heart to show me a little kindness,' Eochaid pleaded, 'and allow me time to reconcile myself to the dispatch of such a precious reward. Return to this palace one month from today and what you have asked for will not be denied you.'

'Your request is not unreasonable,' replied Midhir, 'and it leads me to believe that a kiss from your wife must be worth the long wait.'

Then Eochaid Airem appointed a day at the end of the month when Midhir would return to collect his prize and the young warrior departed the palace, his heart lighter than it had been for a very long time.

As the days passed by and the time approached for Etain to deliver her kiss, the King became more and more protective of his beautiful wife. Fearing that his handsome rival would appear at any moment, he gave the order for the palace to be surrounded by a great host of armed men and instructed them not to allow any stranger to enter the grounds. Once he had made certain that the outer courtyards were protected and that the doors to the inner chambers were properly guarded, Eochaid began to feel more at ease and decided to invite his closest friends to dine with him later that evening in the banqueting hall. Etain appeared next to him in a gown of shimmering silver and a row of servants carried trays of the most exotic food and flagons of the finest wine through to the long table. While the queen poured the wine for her hosts, the hall began to fill with laughter and conversation and it was not long before Eochaid called for his musicians to begin playing.

In the midst of this happy atmosphere, nobody noticed the tall, elegant figure enter the room and make his way towards the King, his face noble and determined, his spear held proudly in his left hand. Etain suddenly raised her eyes and saw before her the young rider whose image had filled her sleeping hours since their meeting on the Hill of Tara. He appeared more beautiful and resplendent than ever, more eloquent and powerful than her memory had allowed for. A wonderful feeling of warmth and affection stirred within Etain's breast as Midhir gazed tenderly upon her and she felt that somehow she had always known and loved the man who stood before her. Then Midhir addressed the King and his words were purposeful and resolute:

'Let me collect what has been promised me,' he said to Eochaid, 'It is a debt that is due and the time is ripe for payment.'

The King and his party looked on helplessly as Midhir encircled the fair Etain in his arms. As their lips met, a thick veil of mist appeared around them, and they were lifted gracefully into the air and out into the night. Eochaid and his noblemen rushed from the banqueting hall in pursuit of the couple, but all they could see were two white swans circling the star-filled sky above the royal palace. Eochaid wept bitterly for his loss and swore solemnly that he would not rest a single moment until every fairy mound in the land had been dug up and destroyed in his search for Midhir the Proud.

The Ulster Cycle: Stories of Cuchulainn of the Red Guard

THE ULSTER CYCLE, also known as the Red Branch Cycle, is compiled of tales of Ulster's traditional heroes, chief among whom is Cuchulainn [*Pronounced Koo khul-in.*], arguably the most important war-champion in ancient Irish literature. An account of his birth dating from the ninth century is retold here, although a great many variations exist.

From the age of six, Cuchulainn displays his supernatural ancestry and astounding strength. While still a child, he slays the terrifying hound of Culann. As a mere youth he is sent to train with the Knights of the Red Guard under Scathach and he alone is entrusted with the diabolical weapon known as the Gae Bolg. Later, he single-handedly defends Ulster against Queen Medb [*Pronounced Maev.*] while the rest of the province sleeps under the charm of Macha. His most notable exploits spanning his hectic warrior's life up until his early death are recounted here.

Cuchulainn is said to have fallen at the battle of Muirthemne, circa 12 BC. He was finally overcome by his old enemy Lugaid, aided by the monstrous daughters of Calatin. As death approaches, Cuchulainn insists that he be allowed to bind himself upright to a pillar-stone. With his dying breath, he gives a loud, victorious laugh and when Lugaid attempts to behead his corpse, the enemy's right hand is severed as the sword of Cuchulainn falls heavily upon it. The hero's death is avenged by Conall the Victorious, but with the defeat of Cuchulainn, the end is sealed to the valiant reign of the Red Guard Knights in ancient Irish legend.

The Birth of Cuchulainn

KING CONCHOBAR MAC NESSA was ruler of Ulster at the time when Cuchulainn, the mightiest hero of the Red Guard, came to be born. It happened that one day, the King's sister Dechtire, whom he cherished above all others, disappeared from the palace without warning, taking fifty of her maidens and her most valuable possessions with her. Although Conchobar summoned every known person in the court before him for questioning, no explanation could be discovered for his sister's departure. For three long years, the King's messengers scoured the country in search of Dechtire, but not one among them ever brought him news of her whereabouts.

At last, one summer's morning, a strange flock of birds descended on the palace gardens of Emain Macha and began to gorge themselves on every fruit tree and vegetable patch in sight. Greatly disturbed by the greed and destruction he witnessed, the King immediately gathered together a party of his hunters, and they set off in pursuit of the birds, armed with powerful slings and the sharpest of arrows. Fergus mac Roig, Conchobar's chief huntsman and guide, was among the group, as were his trusted warriors Amergin and Bricriu. As the day wore on, they found themselves being lured a great distance southward by the birds, across Sliab Fuait, towards the Plain of Gossa, and with every step taken they grew more angry and frustrated that not one arrow had yet managed to ruffle a single feather.

Nightfall had overtaken them before they had even noticed the light begin to fade, and the King, realizing that they would never make it safely back to the palace, gave the order for Fergus and some of the others to go out in search of a place of lodging for the party. Before long, Fergus came upon a small hut whose firelight was extremely inviting, and he approached and knocked politely on the door. He received a warm and hearty welcome from the old married couple within, and they at once offered him food and a comfortable bed for the evening. But Fergus would not accept their kind hospitality, knowing that his companions were still abroad without shelter.

'Then they are all invited to join us,' said the old woman, and as she bustled about, preparing food and wine for her visitors, Fergus went off to deliver his good news to Conchobar and the rest of the group.

Bricriu had also set off in search of accommodation, and as he had walked to the opposite side of the woodlands, he was certain that he heard the gentle sound of harp music. Instinctively drawn towards the sweet melody, he followed the winding path through the trees until he came upon a regal mansion standing proudly on the banks of the river Boyne. He timidly approached the noble structure, but there was no need for him to knock, since the door was already ajar and a young maiden, dressed in a flowing gown of shimmering gold, stood in the entrance hall ready to greet him. She was accompanied by a young man of great stature and splendid appearance who smiled warmly at Bricriu and extended his hand in friendship:

'You are indeed welcome,' said the handsome warrior, 'we have been waiting patiently for your visit to our home this day.'

'Come inside, Bricriu,' said the beautiful maiden, 'why is it that you linger out of doors?'

'Can it be that you do not recognize the woman who appears before you?' asked the warrior.

'Her great beauty stirs a memory from the past,' replied Bricriu, 'but I cannot recall anything more at present.'

'You see before you Dechtire, sister of Conchobar mac Nessa,' said the warrior, 'and the fifty maidens you have been seeking these three years are also in this house. They have today visited Emain Macha in the form of birds in order to lure you here.'

'Then I must go at once to the King and inform him of what I have discovered,' answered Bricriu, 'for he will be overjoyed to know that Dechtire has been found and will be eager for her to accompany him back to the palace where there will be great feasting and celebration.'

He hurried back through the woods to rejoin the King and his companions. And when Conchobar heard the news of Bricriu's discovery, he could scarcely contain his delight and was immediately anxious to be reunited with his sister. A messenger was sent forth to invite Dechtire and the warrior to share in their evening meal, and a place was hurriedly prepared for the couple at the table inside the welcoming little hut. But Dechtire was already suffering the first pangs of childbirth by the time Conchobar's messenger arrived with his invitation. She excused herself by saying that she was tired and agreed instead to meet up with her brother at dawn on the following morning.

When the first rays of sunshine had brightened the heavens, Conchobar arose from his bed and began to prepare himself for Dechtire's arrival. He had passed a very peaceful night and went in search of Fergus and the others in the happiest of moods. Approaching the place where his men were sleeping, he became convinced that he had heard the stifled cries of an infant. Again, as he drew nearer, the sound was repeated. He stooped down and began to examine a small, strange bundle lying on the ground next to Bricriu. As he unwrapped it, the bundle began to wriggle in his arms and a tiny pink hand revealed itself from beneath the cloth covering.

Dechtire did not appear before her brother that morning, or on any morning to follow. But she had left the King a great gift – a newborn male child fathered by the noble warrior, Lugh of the Long Arm, a child destined to achieve great things for Ulster. Conchobar took the infant back to the palace with him and gave him to his sister Finnchoem to look after. Finnchoem reared the child alongside her own son Conall and grew to love him as if he had been born of her own womb. He was given the name of Setanta, a name he kept until the age of six, and the druid Morann made the following prophecy over him:

His praise will be sung by the most valorous knights,
And he will win the love of all
His deeds will be known throughout the land
For he will answer Ulster's call.

How Setanta Won the Name of Cuchulainn

WITHIN THE COURT of Emain Macha, there existed an élite group of boy athletes whose outstanding talents filled the King with an overwhelming sense of pride and joy. It had become a regular part of Conchobar's daily routine to watch these boys at their various games and exercises, for nothing brought him greater pleasure than to witness their development into some of the finest sportsmen in Erin. He had named the group the Boy-Corps, and the sons of the most powerful chieftains and princes of the land were among its members, having proven their skill and dexterity in a wide and highly challenging range of sporting events.

Before Setanta had grown to the age of six, he had already expressed his desire before the King to be enrolled in the Boy-Corps. At first, Conchobar refused to treat the request seriously, since his nephew was a great deal younger than any other member, but the boy persisted, and the King at last agreed to allow him to try his hand. It was decided that he should join in a game of hurling one morning, and when he had dressed himself in the martial uniform of the Boy-Corps, he was presented with a brass hurley almost his own height off the ground.

A team of twelve boys was assembled to play against him and they sneered mockingly at the young lad before them, imagining they would have little difficulty keeping the ball out of his reach. But as soon as the game started up, Setanta dived in among the boys and took hold of the ball, striking it with his hurley and driving it a powerful distance to the other end of the field where it sailed effortlessly through the goal-posts. And after this first onslaught, he made it impossible for his opponents to retrieve the ball from him, so that within a matter of minutes he had scored fifty goals against the twelve of them. The whole corps looked on in utter amazement and the King, who had been eagerly following the game, was flushed with excitement. His nephew's show of prowess was truly astonishing and he began to reproach himself for having originally set out to humour the boy.

'Have Setanta brought before me,' he said to his steward, 'for such an impressive display of heroic strength and impertinent courage deserves a very special reward.'

Now on that particular day, Conchobar had been invited to attend a great feast at the house of Culann, the most esteemed craftsman and smith in the kingdom. A thought had suddenly entered Conchobar's head that it would be a very fitting reward for Setanta to share in such a banquet, for no small boy had ever before accompanied the King and the Knights of the Red Guard on such a prestigious outing. It was indeed a great honour and one Setanta readily acknowledged. He desperately wanted to accept the invitation, but only one thing held him back. He could not suppress the desire of a true sportsman to conclude the game he had begun and pleaded with the King to allow him to do so:

'I have so thoroughly enjoyed the first half of my game with the Boy-Corps,' he told the King, 'that I am loathe to cut it short. I promise to follow when the game is over if you will allow me this great liberty.'

And seeing the excitement and keenness shining in the boy's eyes, Conchobar was more than happy to agree to this request. He instructed Setanta to follow on before nightfall and gave him directions to the house of Culann. Then he set off for the banquet, eager to relate the morning's stirring events to the rest of Culann's house guests.

It was early evening by the time the royal party arrived at the dwelling place of Culann. A hundred blazing torches guided them towards the walls of the fort and a carpet of fresh green rushes formed a mile-long path leading to the stately entrance. The great hall was already lavishly prepared for the banquet and the sumptuous aroma of fifty suckling pigs turning on the spit filled every room of the house. Culann himself came forward to greet each one of his guests and he bowed respectfully before the King and led him to his place of honour at the centre of the largest table. Once his royal guest had taken his seat, the order was given for the wine to be poured and the laughter and music followed soon afterwards. And when it was almost time for the food to be served, Culann glanced around him one last time to make certain that all his visitors had arrived.

'I think we need wait no longer,' he said to the King. 'My guests are all present and it will now be safe to untie the hound who keeps watch over my home each night. There is not a hound in Erin who could equal mine for fierceness and strength, and even if a hundred men should attempt to do battle with him, every last one would be torn to pieces in his powerful jaws.'

'Release him then, and let him guard this place,' said Conchobar, quite forgetting that his young nephew had not yet joined the party. 'My men are all present and our appetites have been whetted by our long journey here. Let us delay no longer and begin the feasting at once.'

And after the gong had been sounded, a procession of elegantly-clad attendants entered the room carrying gilded trays of roasted viands and freshly harvested fruit and vegetables, which they set down on the table before the King and the hungry warriors of the Red Guard.

It was just at this moment that the young Setanta came to the green of Culann's fort carrying with him the hurley and the ball that had brought him victory against the Boy-Corps. As the boy drew nearer to the entrance of the fort, the hound's ears pricked up warily and it began to growl and bark in such a way as to be heard throughout the entire countryside. The whole company within the great hall heard the animal snarling ferociously and raced outdoors to discover what exactly it was that had disturbed the creature. They saw before them a young boy, who showed little sign of fear as he stood facing the fierce dog with gaping jaws. The child was without any obvious weapon of defence against the animal, but as it charged at him, he thrust his playing ball forcefully down its throat causing it to choke for breath. Then he seized the hound by the hind legs and dashed its head against a rock until blood spewed from its mouth and the life had gone out of it.

Those who witnessed this extraordinary confrontation hoisted the lad triumphantly into the air and bore him on their shoulders to where Conchobar and Culann stood waiting. The King, although more than gratified by the boy's demonstration of courage, was also much relieved to know that Setanta was safe. Turning to his host, he began to express his joy, but it was immediately apparent that Culann could share none of Conchobar's happiness. He walked instead towards the body of his dead hound and fell into a mournful silence as he stroked the lifeless form, remembering the loyal and obedient animal who had given its life to protect its master's property. Seeing Culann bent over the body of his faithful dog, Setanta came forward without hesitation and spoke the following words of comfort to him:

'If in all of Erin there is a hound to replace the one you have lost, I will find it, nurture it and place it in your service when it is fit for action. But, in the meantime, I myself will perform the duty of that hound and will guard your land and your possessions with the utmost pride.'

There was not one among the gathering who remained unmoved by this gesture of contrition and friendship. Culann, for his part, was overcome with gratitude and appreciation and declared that Setanta should bear the name of Cuchulainn, 'Culann's Hound', in remembrance of his first great act of valour. And so, at the age of six, the boy Setanta was named Cuchulainn, a name by which he was known and feared until the end of his days.

The Tragedy of Cuchulainn and Connla

AS SOON AS CUCHULAINN had reached the appropriate age to begin his formal training as a Knight of the Red Guard, it was decided at the court of Conchobar mac Nessa that he should depart for the Land of Shadows, where Scathach, the wisest, strongest, most celebrated woman-warrior, had prepared the path of his instruction in the feats of war. The stronghold of Scathach lay in a mysterious land overseas, beyond the bounds of the Plain of Ill-luck. It could only be reached by crossing the Perilous Glen, a journey very few had survived, for the Glen teemed with the fiercest of goblins lying in wait to devour hopeful young pilgrims. But even if a youth managed to come through the Perilous Glen unharmed, he had then to cross the Bridge of Leaps, underneath which the sea boiled and hissed furiously. This bridge was the highest and narrowest ever built and it spanned the steepest gorge in the western world. Only a handful of people had ever crossed it, but those who did were privileged to become the highest ranking scholars of Scathach and the very finest of Erin's warriors.

Within a week of leaving the court of Emain Macha, Cuchulainn had arrived at the Plain of Ill-luck and although he had already suffered many trials along the way, he knew in his heart that the worst still lay ahead. As he gazed out over the vast stretch of barren land he was obliged to traverse, he grew despondent, for he could see that one half was covered in a porous clay which would certainly cause his feet to stick fast, while the other was overgrown with long, coarse, straw-coloured grass, whose pointed blades were designed to slash a man's limbs to pieces. And as he stood crestfallen, attempting to decide which of the two routes would prove less hazardous, he noticed a young man approaching on horseback from the east. The very appearance of the rider lifted Cuchulainn's spirits, but when he observed that the youth's countenance shone as splendidly as the golden orb of the sun (though he does not reveal himself, this is, of course, Cuchulainn's father, Lugh of the Long Arm), he immediately felt hopeful and reassured once more. The two began to converse together and Cuchulainn enquired of the young man which track he considered the best to follow across the Plain of Ill-luck. The youth pondered the question awhile and then, reaching beneath his mantel, he handed Cuchulainn a leather pouch containing a small golden wheel.

'Roll this before you as you cross the quagmire,' he told Cuchulainn, 'and it will scorch a path in the earth which you may follow safely to the stronghold of Scathach.'

Cuchulainn gratefully received the gift and bid farewell to the youth. And after he had set the wheel in motion, it led him safely, just as the young rider had promised, across the Plain of Ill-luck and through the Perilous Glen until he reached the outskirts of the Land of Shadows.

It was not long before he happened upon a small camp in the heart of the woodlands where the scholars of Scathach, the sons of the noblest princes and warriors of Erin, were busy at their training. He recognized at once his friend Ferdia, son of the Firbolg, Daman, and the two men embraced each other warmly. After Cuchulainn had told Ferdia all of the latest news from Ulster, he began to question his friend about the great woman-warrior who was set to educate him in arms.

'She dwells on the island beyond the Bridge of Leaps,' Ferdia told him, 'which no man, not even myself, has ever managed to cross. It is said that when we have achieved a certain level of valour, Scathach herself will teach us to cross the bridge, and she will also teach us to thrust the Gae Bolg, a weapon reserved for only the bravest of champions.'

'Then I must prove to her that I am already valorous,' replied Cuchulainn, 'by crossing that bridge without any assistance from her.'

'You are unlikely to succeed,' warned Ferdia, 'for if a man steps on one end of the bridge, the middle rises up and flings him into the waters below where the mouths of sea-monsters lie open, ready to swallow him whole.'

But these words of caution merely fired Cuchulainn's ambition to succeed in his quest. Retiring to a quiet place, he sat down to recover his strength from his long journey and waited anxiously for evening to fall.

The scholars of Scathach had all gathered to watch Cuchulainn attempt to cross the Bridge of Leaps and they began to jeer him loudly when after the third attempt he had failed to reach the far side. The mocking chorus that greeted his failure greatly infuriated the young warrior but prompted him at the same time to put all his strength and ability into one final, desperate leap. And at the fourth leap, which came to be known as 'the hero's salmon-leap', Cuchulainn landed on the ground of the island at the far side of the bridge. Lifting himself off the ground, he strode triumphantly to the fortress of Scathach and beat loudly on the entrance door with the shaft of his spear. Scathach appeared before him, wonder-struck that a boy so young and fresh of face had demonstrated such courage and vigour. She agreed at once to accept him as her pupil, promising to teach him all the feats of war if he would pledge himself to remain under her tuition and guidance for a period not less than a full year and a day.

During the time that Cuchulainn dwelt with Scathach, he grew to become her favourite pupil, for he acquired each new skill with the greatest of ease and approached every additional challenge set him with the utmost enthusiasm. Scathach had never before deemed any of her students good enough to be trained in the use of the Gae Bolg, but she now considered Cuchulainn a champion worthy of this special honour and presented him one morning with the terrible weapon. Then she instructed him on how to use it and explained that it should be hurled with the foot, and upon entering the enemy it would fill every inch of his body with deadly barbs, killing him almost instantly.

It was while Cuchulainn remained under Scathach's supervision that the Land of Shadows came under attack from the fiercest of tribal warriors, led by the Princess Aife. After several weeks of bloody battle, during which no solution to the conflict could be reached, it was agreed that Scathach and Aife should face each other in single combat. On hearing this news, Cuchulainn expressed the gravest concern and was adamant that he would accompany Scathach to the place where the contest was due to take place. Yet Scathach feared that something untoward might befall her young protégé, and she placed a sleeping-potion in Cuchulainn's drink with the power to prevent him waking until she was safely reached her meeting place with Aife. But the potion, which would have lasted twenty-four hours in any other man, held Cuchulainn in a slumber for less than one hour and when he awoke he seized his weapon and went forth to join the war against Aife.

And not only did he slay three of Aife's finest warriors in the blink of an eyelid, he insisted on trading places with Scathach and facing the tribal-leader by himself. But before going into battle against her, he asked Scathach what it was that Aife prized above all other things.

'What she most loves are her two horses, her chariot, and her charioteer,' she informed Cuchulainn. So he set off to meet Aife, forearmed with this knowledge.

The two opponents met on the Path of Feats and entered into a vicious combat there. They had only clashed swords three or four times however, before Aife delivered Cuchulainn a mighty blow, shattering his powerful sword to the hilt and leaving him defenceless. Seeing the damage to his weapon, Cuchulainn at once cried out:

'What a terrible fate that charioteer beyond has met with. Look, his chariot and his two beautiful horses have fallen down the glen.'

And as Aife glanced around, Cuchulainn managed to seize her by the waist, squeezing firmly with his hands until she could hardly breathe and had dropped her sword at his feet. Then he carried her over his shoulder back to the camp of Scathach and flung her on the ground where he placed his knife at her throat.

'Do not take my life from me, Cuchulainn,' Aife begged, 'and I will agree to whatever you demand.'

It was soon settled between Scathach and Cuchulainn that Aife should agree to a lasting peace and, as proof of her commitment, they pronounced that she should bind herself over to remain a full year as Cuchulainn's hostage in the Land of Shadows. And after nine months, Aife gave birth to a son whom she named Connla, for she and Cuchulainn had grown to become the best of friends and the closest of lovers with the passing of time.

Now sadly, the day arrived for Cuchulainn to depart the Land of Shadows, and knowing that Aife would not accompany him, he spoke the following wish for his son's future:

'I give you this golden ring for our child,' he told Aife. 'And when he has grown so that the ring fits his finger, send him away from here to seek out his father in Erin.

'Counsel him on my behalf to keep his identity secret,' he added, 'so that he may stand proud on his own merit and never refuse a combat, or turn out of his way for any man.'

Then after he had uttered these words, Cuchulainn took his leave of Aife and made his way back to his own land and his people.

Seven years had passed, during which time Cuchulainn had chosen Emer, daughter of Forgall, one of the finest maidens in Ulster, to become his wife, and the two lived a very happy life together. He rarely thought of Aife and the son he had left behind in the Land of Shadows, for he had also risen to become captain of the House of the Red Branch of Conchobar mac Nessa and was by far the busiest and most respected warrior in the kingdom.

It was at this time, however, that Connla, son of Cuchulainn, set out on his journey to be reunited with his father in Erin, approaching her shores on the precise day that all the great warriors and noble lords of Ulster were assembled for an annual ceremony on the Strand of Footprints. They were very much surprised to see a little boat of bronze appear on the crest of the waves, and in it a small boy clutching a pair of gilded oars, steering his way steadily towards them. The boy seemed not to notice them and every so often he stopped rowing and bent down to pick up a stone from the heap he had collected at the bottom of the boat. Then, putting one of these stones into a sling, he launched a splendid shot at the sea-birds above, bringing the creatures down, stunned, but unharmed, one after another, in a manner far too quick for the naked eye to perceive. The whole party looked on in amazement as the lad performed these wonderful feats, but the King soon grew uncomfortable at the spectacle he witnessed and called Condere, son of Eochaid, to him:

'This boy's arrival here does not bode well for us,' said the King. 'For if grown-up men of his kind were to follow in his wake, they would grind us all to dust. Let someone go to meet him and inform him that he is not welcome on Erin's soil.'

And as the boy came to moor his boat, Condere approached him and delivered Conchobar's message.

'Go and tell your King,' said the boy, 'that even if everyone among you here had the strength of a hundred men, and you all came forward to challenge me, you would not be able to persuade me to turn back from this place.'

Hearing these words, the King grew even more concerned and he called Conall the Victorious to him:

'This lad mocks us,' Conchobar told him, 'and it is now time for a show of force against him.'

So Conall was sent against the boy, but as he approached the lad put a stone in his sling and sent it whizzing with a noise like thunder through the air. It struck Conall on the forehead, knocking him backwards to the ground and before he could even think about rising to his feet, the boy had bound his arms and legs with the strap from his shield. And in this manner, the youth made a mockery of the host of Ulster, challenging man after man to confront him, and succeeding on every occasion to defeat his opponents with little or no effort.

At last, when King Conchobar could suffer this humiliation no longer, he sent a messenger to Dundalk to the house of Cuchulainn requesting that he come and do battle against the young boy whom Conall the Victorious could not even manage to overcome. And hearing that her husband was prepared to meet this challenge, Emer, his wife, went and pleaded with him not to go forward to the Strand of Footprints:

'Do not go against the boy,' she begged Cuchulainn, 'since the great courage he possesses has convinced me that he is Connla, son of Aife. Hear my voice, Cuchulainn, and do not go forward to murder your only child.'

'Even if he were my son,' replied Cuchulainn, 'I would slay him for the honour of Ulster.'

And he ordered his chariot to be yoked without further delay and set off in the direction of the strand.

Soon afterwards, he came upon the young boy sitting in his boat polishing stones and calmly awaiting his next opponent. Cuchulainn strode towards him, demanding to know his name and lineage. But the boy would not reveal his identity or the slightest detail of the land of his birth. Then Cuchulainn lost patience with him and they began to exchange blows. With one daring stroke, the boy cut off a lock of Cuchulainn's hair, and as he watched it fall to the ground, the older warrior became greatly enraged.

'Enough of this child's play,' he shouted and, dragging the boy from the boat, he began to wrestle with him in the water. But the boy's strength was astonishing and he managed twice to push Cuchulainn's head beneath the waves, almost causing him to drown. And it was on the third occasion that this occurred, when Cuchulainn gasped helplessly for air, that he remembered the Gae Bolg which Scathach had entrusted him with, and he flung it at the boy through the water. At once, the boy loosened his powerful hold and reached agonizingly towards his stomach, where the blood flowed freely from the vast gaping wound the weapon had made there.

'That is a weapon Scathach has not yet taught me to use,' said the boy. 'Carry me now from the water, for I am gravely injured.'

And as Cuchulainn bore the boy in his arms towards the shore he noticed a golden ring on his middle finger.

'It is true then,' he murmured sadly to himself, and set the boy down on the ground before the King and the men of Ulster.

'You see here before you my son,' Cuchulainn announced solemnly, 'the child I have mortally wounded for the good of Ulster.'

'Alas, it is so,' spoke Connla in a feeble voice, 'and I wish with all my heart that I could remain with you to the end of five years. For in that time, I would grow among you and conquer the world before you on every side, so that soon you would rule as far as Rome. But since this cannot be, let me now take my leave of the most famous among you before I die.'

So, one after another, the most courageous knights of the Red Guard were brought before Connla and he placed his arms around the neck of each of them and embraced them affectionately. Then Cuchulainn came forward and his son kissed his father tenderly before drawing his last breath. And as he closed his eyes, a great lament was raised among them and they dug a grave for the boy and set a splendid pillar-stone at its head. Connla, son of Aife, was the only son Cuchulainn ever had and he lived to regret for the rest of his days that he had destroyed so precious a gift.

The Combat of Ferdia and Cuchulainn

BEYOND THE BORDERS OF ULSTER in the province of Connacht, there ruled a spirited and domineering queen named Medb, daughter of Eochaid Fedlech, whose husband, King Ailill, was the meekest and gentlest of creatures. Medb's nature was such that whatever she desired she took for her own, and whatever law displeased her, she refused to obey, so that her husband gave her whatever she demanded and nothing was ever too great a task for him to complete on her behalf. Medb was also the strongest and mightiest of warriors and she had gathered together a powerful army, convinced that one day she would conquer the whole land of Erin.

One evening as Medb and her husband lay together, they began to count up and compare their numerous possessions, for it was one of Medb's favourite entertainments to ridicule Ailill by proving that she had acquired far more treasures and wealth than he had over the years. Weapons, rings and jewellery were counted out, as well as chariots, horses, mansions and plots of land, but each of them was found to possess precisely the same amount as the other. So they began to count the herds of cattle and sheep that roamed the pastures beyond the walls of the castle and it was then that Ailill remembered the Bull of Finnbennach and began to tease his wife about the animal, reminding her of how the bull had deserted her herd in favour of his because it refused to remain in the hands of a woman. As soon as Medb heard these words, all of her property lost its value for her, and she grew adamant that she would soon find a bull to equal the Bull of Finnbennach even if she had to scour the entire countryside for it and bring it back to Connacht by force.

Mac Roth, the King's steward, was summoned to appear before Medb and when she questioned him on the whereabouts of such a bull, he was able to tell her without any hesitation exactly where the best specimen in the country might be found:

'It belongs to Daire mac Fiachna in the province of Ulster,' he told the Queen. 'It is known as the Brown Bull of Cooley and is regarded as the finest beast in the whole of Erin.'

'Then you must go to the son of Fiachna and ask him for the loan of the bull for a year,' replied Medb, 'informing him that at the end of this time, the beast will be safely returned to him, together with fifty of the finest heifers my kingdom has to offer. And if Daire chooses to bring the bull here himself, he may add to his reward a measure of land equalling the size of his present domain in Ulster and a splendid war chariot worthy of the bravest of Connacht's warriors.'

On the following morning, a group of nine foot-messengers led by mac Roth set off in the direction of Ulster, carrying with them a number of gifts from Queen Medb to the owner of the bull, including an oak chest loaded with gold and silver ornaments and several decorated bronze flagons filled with the finest mead in the land. The mere sight of such a treasure-laden party approaching the fort of Daire mac Fiachna raised the spirits of all who set eyes on them and a very warm welcome was lavished on the men. Then Daire himself came forward to greet the party and enquired of them the purpose of their journey to his home. Mac Roth began to tell him of the squabble between Medb and Ailill and of how the Queen had decided that she must quickly find a bull to match the impressive Bull of Finnbennach. Flattered that his own beast had achieved such fame in Connacht, Daire was immediately disposed to help Queen Medb as best he could, but when he heard of the generous reward he would receive in return for the loan of his property, he was well pleased with himself and gave the order at once for the Bull of Cooley to be prepared for its journey to Connacht the next day.

The evening was spent feasting and drinking and a happy atmosphere prevailed for a time as the men of the two provinces exchanged friendly conversation. But as the wine flowed, the tongues of Queen Medb's messengers began to loosen and in the company of their hosts they began to brag of their army's great strength:

'It is just as well for Daire,' boasted one of Medb's envoys, 'that he has surrendered the beast willingly to us. For if he had refused to do so, the Queen's mighty army would have marched on Ulster and taken the bull from him without any trouble at all.'

When Daire's men heard these offensive remarks, they went straightaway to their master's quarters and demanded that he avenge such a dreadful insult. Mac Roth was immediately summoned to appear before Daire who angrily informed him of the conversation that had been overheard.

'Go back to your Queen,' said Daire, 'and tell her that she shall never take from me by foul means what she cannot win by fair. Let Medb and Ailill invade Ulster if they dare, for we are well equipped to meet the challenge.'

Before the break of day, Medb's messengers had set off for Connacht to deliver the unhappy tidings to their Queen. But when Medb saw that they had not returned with the Brown Bull of Cooley, she did not fly into the rage they had expected. Instead, she spoke calmly to mac Roth:

'I have foreseen this result,' she told him. 'Your dispute with the son of Fiachna is of little consequence, for I have always known that if the Brown Bull of Cooley was not given willingly, he would be taken by force. That time is now arrived, and taken he shall be!'

So began the Queen of Connacht's great war on Ulster, one of the bloodiest wars the country had ever before endured. From every corner of Erin came the allies of Medb and Ailill, including Fraech, son of Fidach, and Calatin, accompanied by his twenty-seven sons. Warriors of great renown from the provinces of Leinster and Munster swelled the numbers of Medb's armed legions, and they were joined by many heroic Ulstermen, among them Fergus mac Roy and Cormac, son of Conchobar, who had defected from their own army, unhappy with their King's leadership.

Not a day or a night passed without a fierce and fiery combat between the armies of Connacht and Ulster. Rivers and streams ran crimson with blood and the bodies of the slain littered the emerald hills and plains. Medb was not slow to display her true worth as a warrior in her own right and Fergus, her chief scout, proved himself a most loyal and courageous comrade in arms. Yet there was none among Medb's great army who could emulate the feats of one particular Ulster warrior, a youthful figure who seemed utterly invincible and who drove himself against them time and time again, bursting with renewed vitality and strength on each occasion.

Cuchulainn, leader of Ulster's Red Guard, was well known to both Fergus and Cormac, but he had grown stronger and more powerful than they had ever imagined possible during their brief time of exile. And as they observed his powers of command and his exceptional skill on the battlefield, they became increasingly alarmed and went before the Queen to warn her that she was faced with no ordinary opponent. Medb grew worried at this news and took counsel with the most prominent figures of her army. After some deliberation, it was decided that her most valiant warrior should be sent to do battle against Cuchulainn. The son of Daman, known as Ferdia, was nominated for this task, for he had been trained alongside Cuchulainn under the great woman-warrior Scathach in the Land of Shadows and had risen to become Connacht's champion warrior, a man feared and respected by all who encountered him.

Nothing had ever yet challenged the deep bond of friendship formed between Ferdia and Cuchulainn during their time together in the Land of Shadows. The love and respect the two men felt for each other had remained constant over the years, and whenever they found occasion to be together, it was not unusual for people to mistake them for brothers. When Ferdia discovered what Medb demanded of him, he was greatly disturbed, and though he was loathe to oppose the wishes of his sovereign, he immediately refused the Queen's request and dismissed her messengers. Then Medb sent her druids and men of poetry to Ferdia's tent, instructing them to recite the most savage and mocking verses in the loudest of voices for everybody to hear.

It was for the sake of his own honour that Ferdia agreed to meet with Medb and Ailill without any further delay. The King and Queen were more than delighted to receive him and Medb wasted no time reeling off the numerous rewards Ferdia could hope to receive if he would only obey her simple wish. But Ferdia showed no interest in the riches that were intended for him, so that Medb grew more and more angry and frustrated. She had little or nothing to lose by playing her one last card and with a tone of false resignation she addressed Ferdia once more:

'It must be true what Cuchulainn has said of you,' said Medb slyly. 'He said that you feared death by his hands and that you would be wise not to go against him. Perhaps it is just as well that the two of you do not meet.'

On hearing this, Ferdia could scarcely contain his anger:

'It was unjust of Cuchulainn to say such a thing,' he roared. 'He well knows that it is not cowardice, but love, that prevents me facing him. So it is settled then. Tomorrow I will go forth to his camp and raise my weapon against him.'

But even as he spoke these words, a mood of gloom and despair descended upon Ferdia and he walked out into the black night, his head bowed in sadness. His closest companions and servants were also overcome with grief to discover what it was that Ferdia was compelled to do, for each was troubled by the knowledge that one of the two great champion warriors of Erin would fail to return home alive.

Word had soon reached Cuchulainn that Medb had chosen his dearest friend to face him in combat and, as he watched Ferdia's war chariot approach, he was forced to acknowledge in his own mind that he would much rather fall by his friend's weapon than slay Ferdia with his own. Yet, at the same time, he could not fully understand why his fosterbrother had so easily given into the wishes of Queen Medb. The betrayal he felt could not be ignored and he prepared himself to greet Ferdia with a degree of caution and reserve. As Ferdia stood down from his chariot, Cuchulainn did not rush forward to embrace him as he would have done in the past, but remained at a distance, waiting for his friend to make the first gesture of friendship.

'I wish that we could have met again in more favourable circumstances,' said Ferdia. 'With all my heart I long to embrace you, old friend.'

'I once would have trusted such words,' answered Cuchulainn, 'but I no longer place any trust in what you say when I know that you have abandoned our friendship for the sake of a treacherous queen and the rewards she no doubt promised you.'

'I see that treason has overcome our love,' replied Ferdia sadly, 'but it is just as well that you think this way. It is best not to remember our friendship, but to meet each other as true enemies of war.'

And so they began to choose the weapons they would use against each other and it was agreed that they would begin the day's fighting with small javelins. They hurled these at each other, backwards and forwards through the air with great energy and speed, but by the close of day, not one spear had pierced the shield of either champion. As nightfall approached, they called a truce, and agreed to resume combat with different weapons at dawn on the following morning.

On the second day, Cuchulainn and Ferdia took up the fight once more, remaining seated in their chariots as they cast heavy, broad-bladed spears at each other across the ford from noon until sundown. But on this day, they both suffered many wounds that stained their flesh red with blood. When they had grown weary of the battle, they again agreed to stop fighting until morning and, placing their weapons in the hands of their servants, they moved towards each other and kissed and embraced warmly in remembrance of their friendship. Their horses shared the same paddock that evening and their charioteers gathered round the same fire. Healing herbs were laid on their wounds and they both rested until daybreak.

As the third day of combat was about to commence and the two men stood opposite each other once more, Cuchulainn was suddenly struck by the change which seemed to have occurred overnight in his friend. Ferdia's brow was now deeply furrowed and his eyes reflected a deep, dark sadness. He no longer held himself upright and he lurched forward wearily to meet his opponent. Filled with pity and sorrow, Cuchulainn pleaded with Ferdia to abandon the fighting, but his friend merely shook his head, insisting that he must fulfil his contract with Queen Medb and King Ailill. They proceeded to choose their weapons and armed themselves with full-length shields and hard-smiting swords. Then they began to strike each other savagely and viciously until they had each carved great wedges of flesh from the other's shoulder-blades and thighs. Still the combat could not be resolved and they decided to part once more for the evening, their bodies torn to shreds and their friendship shattered irreparably. And on this occasion, no kiss was exchanged between them, no curing herbs were exchanged, and their horses and charioteers slept in separate quarters.

As the sun was about to rise on the fourth morning, Ferdia arose and walked out alone to the ford of combat. He wore the jaded, sorrowful expression of a man who senses death close at hand and he began to arm himself with particular care and attention. He knew instinctively that the decisive day of the battle had arrived and that one of them would certainly fall before the evening had drawn to a close. Next to his skin he wore a tunic of silk, speckled with gold and over this he placed a thick leather smock. He then laid a huge, flat stone, which he had carried all the way from Africa, across his torso and covered it with a solid iron apron. On his head he placed a crested war-helmet, adorned with crystals and rubies. He carried in his left hand a massive shield with fifty bosses of bronze and in his right, he clutched his mighty battle-sword. And when at last he was satisfied that he had protected himself against injury as best he could, he remained by the ford, performing many impressive feats with his sword while he awaited the arrival of Cuchulainn.

It was decided between the two warriors on this fourth day that they should use whatever weapons they had to hand and once they had gathered these together the fighting began in earnest. So wild was their rage on that morning, so bitter and violent the clashing of their swords, even the goblins and demons of the air fled in fear. Every creature of the forest shrieked in terror and ran for cover, while the waters themselves changed course, recoiling from the horror and ruthlessness of the combat. And as the afternoon came and went, the wounds inflicted were now deeper and more savage. Each man, although staggering with exhaustion, sought to outdo the other and remained watchful of just such an opportunity. Then, at last, in a moment of acute weariness, Cuchulainn lowered his heavy shield and as soon as he had done so, Ferdia thrust at him with his blade, driving it cleanly through his breast, causing the blood to flow freely down the battle-warrior's tunic. Again, Ferdia struck with his sword and this time it entered Cuchulainn's stomach so that he curled over in agony and began writhing on the earth. And knowing that he must save himself before it was too late, Cuchulainn reached for the Gae Bolg, a weapon he was resolved to use only as a last resort. Taking careful aim, he let fly the instrument with his right foot so that it passed through Ferdia's protective iron apron, through to the flat stone which it broke in three pieces and into the body of his friend filling every joint and every limb with its deadly barbs.

Cuchulainn hastened towards where his friend lay and pulled him gently to his bosom.

'Death is almost upon me,' sighed Ferdia, 'and it is a sad day for us that our friendship should come to such an end. Do not forget the love we once had, Cuchulainn.'

And as Ferdia perished in his arms, Cuchulainn wept piteously, clasping his friend's cold hand lovingly in his own. Then he lifted the body from the damp earth and carried it northwards across the ford to a place where they would not be disturbed by the approaching armies of Ulster. Daylight faded and as Cuchulainn lay down next to Ferdia he fell into a death-like swoon from which he could not be roused for a full seven days.

The Fenian Cycle: Tales of Finn Mac Cumaill and the Fianna

THE CENTRAL CHARACTER OF THE FENIAN, or Ossianic Cycle is Finn mac Cumaill [*Pronounced Finn mac Cool.*], thought to be a real historical person who lived in Ireland some time in the third century AD. A myriad of stories now exists detailing the adventures of this distinguished warrior who rose to leadership of the Fianna and whose stronghold was situated on the Hill of Allen near Co. Kildare. The tales in this cycle generally take place in the Midlands of Ireland and describe a much later epoch when life was less turbulent and the climate of war had been replaced by a more harmonious and romantic atmosphere. The men of the Fianna were not merely military soldiers therefore, but highly accomplished hunter-fighters, often trained in the wilderness, and forced to submit to a number of rigourous tests before they were accepted into the Fianna. Alongside warrior attributes, members of the Fianna were also expected to know by heart the full poet's repertoire, numbering twelve books, and to possess the gift of poetic composition. Oisín [*Pronounced Usheen.*], son of Finn mac Cumaill, is traditionally regarded as the greatest poet of all ancient Irish tales.

The parentage of Finn and the cause of the feud between himself and the Clan of Morna are recounted in this chapter, followed by the story of The Pursuit of Diarmuid and Gráinne which is considered to be one of the most striking and inventive tales of the cycle. The visit of Oisín to Tir na N-Óg is a much later addition to the Fenian tales, and only made a first appearance in literary form in the mid-eighteenth century.

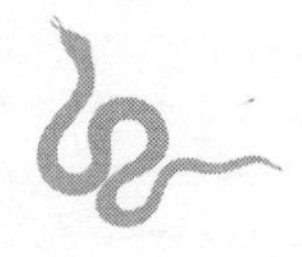

The Coming of Finn mac Cumaill

MANY HUNDREDS OF YEARS after the death of Cuchulainn and the Knights of the Red Guard, the Fianna of Erin reached the height of their fame under the leadership of Finn mac Cumaill. The great warriors of the Fianna were every bit as courageous as their forerunners and each was carefully chosen for his strength and fearlessness on the battlefield. They were also powerful hunters who loved the outdoor life, and many among them possessed the gift of poetry which led to the writing of beautiful tributes to the land of their birth, with its breathtaking mountain valleys and swift-flowing, silver streams. These noble Fenian fighters were above all champion protectors of Erin and during their reign no foreign invader ever dared to set foot on her illustrious shores.

Cumall, son of Trenmor of Clan Brascna, was the father of Finn mac Cumaill and he served as one of the bravest leaders of the Fianna until the day he was slain by his rival, Goll mac Morna, at the battle of Cnucha. Following his death, the Clan of Morna took control of the Fianna and the relatives and friends of Cumall were forced into hiding in the dense forests of the midlands where they built for themselves makeshift homes and yearned for the day when their household would again be restored to power. The Clan of Morna stole from the dead leader the Treasure Bag of the Fianna, filled with strange magical instruments from the Eastern World that had the power to heal all wounds and illnesses. It was placed in the charge of Lia, a chieftain of Connacht, for it was he who had dealt Cumall the first significant wound in the battle of Cnucha.

After the defeat of her husband, Muirne, wife of Cumall, hurriedly abandoned her home and fled to the west to the woodlands of Kerry, accompanied by two of her most trusted handmaidens. For she was carrying the child of the deceased warrior and wished to bring it safely into the world, out of the reach of the bloodthirsty sons of Morna. Within the month, Muirne had given birth to a son and she gave him the name of Demna. And as she gazed upon the infant's face, she was struck by its likeness to the face of Cumall, not yet cold in his grave. Tears of sorrow and anguish flooded down her cheeks and she grasped the child fiercely to her bosom, making a solemn promise to protect him from all harm and evil until he should grow to manhood.

But it was not long before Goll mac Morna received news of the birth of Cumall's heir and he rode forth in great haste through the forests of Erin towards Kerry, intent on destroying the infant. That evening, as she lay sleeping, Muirne had a disturbing vision of a war chariot with wheels of fire approaching her home and she arose at once and summoned her handmaidens to her.

'The sons of Morna have knowledge of our whereabouts,' she told them, 'and the child is unsafe while he remains here with me. Take him under cover of darkness to a safe retreat and do not rest until you are certain you have discovered the remotest dwelling in Erin where he may grow to adulthood unharmed and untroubled.'

The two handmaidens took the tiny bundle from Muirne's arms and set off in the piercingly cold night air towards the protection of the woods. They journeyed for fourteen days by secret paths until they reached the mountains of Slieve Bloom and here, under the shelter of the sprawling oak trees, they finally came to rest, satisfied at last that they had found a true place of sanctuary.

In the fullness of time, the boy Demna grew fair and strong and the two women who cared for him taught him how to hunt and how to spear fish and they marvelled at the speed and zealousness with which he learned to do these things. Before he had reached the age of ten, he could outrun the fastest wild deer of the forests and was so accomplished in the use of his various weapons that he could bring down a hawk with a single shot from his sling, or pin down a charging wild boar with one simple thrust of his spear. It was obvious too that he had the makings of a fine poet, for he was at one with nature and grew to love her fruits, whether listening for hours to the sound of a running brook, or gazing in awe and wonder at the delicate petals of mountain snowdrops. And his nursemaids were overjoyed with their charge and knew that Muirne would be proud of the son they had reared on her behalf, though she may never again lay eyes on the child.

One day, when Demna was in his fourteenth year and had grown more adventurous in spirit, he went out alone and journeyed deep into the mountains until he had reached the place known as Mag Life on the shores of the Liffey. Here, he came upon a chieftain's stronghold and, as he peered beyond the walls of the castle, he observed a group of young boys his own age engaged in a game of hurling. He boldly approached them and expressed his desire to join them in their sport, so they presented him with a hurley and invited him to play along. Though he was outnumbered by the rest of them and was unfamiliar with the rules of the game, Demna quickly proved that he could play as well as any of them and managed, on every occasion, to take the ball from the best players in the field. He was invited to join the group for another game on the following day and, this time, they put one half of their number against him. But again, he had little difficulty beating them off. On the third day, the group decided to test his ability even further and all twelve of them went against him. Demna was triumphant once more and his athletic skill was much admired and applauded. After this, the boys went before their chieftain and told him the story of the youth who had bravely defeated them. The chieftain asked for the young man to be brought before him and when he laid eyes on Demna's beautiful golden hair and saw the milky whiteness of his skin, he pronounced that he should be given the name of Finn, meaning 'fair one', and it was by this name that he was always known thereafter.

At the end of three months, there was not a living person in the land who had not heard rumours of the daring feats of Finn, the golden-haired youth. And it was not long before Goll mac Morna had dispatched his horsemen throughout the countryside to track down the son of Cumall, ordering them to bring him back dead or alive. Finn's two foster-mothers grew anxious that he would be found and they called Finn back home to them and advised him to leave his home in the mountains of Slieve Bloom:

'The champion warriors of the sons of Morna will arrive soon,' they told him, 'and they have been instructed to kill you if they find you here. It was Goll, son of Morna, who murdered your father Cumall. Go from us now, Finn, and keep your identity secret until you are strong enough to protect yourself, for the sons of Morna know that you are the rightful leader of the Fianna and they will stop at nothing until you are dead.'

And so Finn gathered together his belongings and set off in the direction of Loch Lein in the west where he lived for a time in the outdoors, safe from the attention of everyone. At length, however, he began to yearn for the company of other warriors and could not suppress his desire to volunteer himself in military service to the King of Bantry. Even though he did not make himself known to any of his companions, it was not long before their suspicions were aroused, for there was not a soldier more intrepid, nor a hunter more accomplished in the whole of the kingdom. The King himself was curious to learn more about the young warrior and invited him to visit the palace. The two men sat down to a game of chess and the King was greatly surprised to witness the ease with which the youth managed to defeat him. They decided to play on, and Finn won seven games, one after another. Then the King gave up the contest and began to question his opponent warily:

'Who are you,' he asked, 'and who are your people?'

'I am the son of a peasant of the Luagni of Tara,' replied Finn.

'I do not believe this to be the truth,' said the King, 'I am convinced that you are the son that Muirne bore to Cumall. You need not fear me if this is so and I advise you, as proof, to depart here without delay, since I do not wish you to be slain by the sons of Morna while under my poor protection.'

Then Finn realized that he had little choice but to continue his wanderings over the lonely plains of Erin. And it was always the case that whenever he came into contact with other people, his beauty and noble bearing betrayed him, so that the eyes of all were fixed upon him, and the news of his presence promptly spread throughout the region.

He journeyed onwards into Connacht, restricting himself to those areas of the wilderness where he felt certain he would not encounter another living soul. But as he was on his way one morning, he heard the unmistakable sound of a woman wailing and soon came upon her in a clearing of the woods, kneeling over the body of a dead youth.

'I have good cause to mourn in such a fashion,' said the woman looking up at Finn, 'for my only son has been struck down without mercy by the tall warrior who has just passed by here.'

'And what was your son's name who suffered this cruel, unwarranted fate?' enquired Finn.

'Glonda was his name,' replied the woman, 'and I ask you, under bond as a warrior, to avenge his death, since I know of no other who can help me.'

Without hesitating a moment longer, Finn set off in pursuit of the warrior, following the tracks through the woods until he came to the dwelling place of Lia Luachair on the outskirts of Connacht. Taking up the old woman's challenge, he drew his sword and began attacking Lia, striking him down with little effort. It was then that Finn noticed a strange bag on the floor at the older man's feet, and as he looked inside, the treasures of Cumall and the Fianna were revealed to him, and he was overcome with pride that he had unwittingly slain the man who had dealt his father the first wound at Cnucha.

It was at this time that Finn grew weary of his solitary life and began to gather around him all the young warriors of the country who had come to admire his courage and determination. And one of the first tasks he set himself was to go in search of his uncle Crimall and the rest of the Clan Brascna who were still in hiding from the sons of Morna. Accompanied by his followers, he crossed the River Shannon and marched into Connacht where he found his uncle and a number of the old Fianna lying low in the heart of the forest. Crimall stepped forwards and lovingly embraced his nephew, for it was apparent at once that the young stranger before him was the son of Cumall. Then Finn presented the old man with the Bag of Treasures and told him the story from beginning to end of how he had come upon it and slain its custodian. And as he spoke, Crimall laid out the treasures on the ground before them and all who gazed upon them grew fresh of face and strong in body and the burden of age and sorrow was instantly lifted from their brows.

'Our time of deliverance is close at hand,' shouted Crimall joyfully, 'for it has been foretold that he who recovers the Treasure Bag of the Fianna from the hands of the enemy is the one who will lead the Clan of Brascna to victory once more. Go now Finn,' he added, 'and seek out the ancient bard known as Finnegas, since he is the one destined to prepare you for the day when you will rise to your rightful position as head of the Fianna.'

Hearing these words, Finn bade the company farewell and set off alone towards the shores of the River Boyne in the east, eager to meet with the wise old druid who had schooled his father in the ways of poetry and story-telling, whose masterful instruction was deemed essential for any man aspiring to leadership of the Fianna.

For seven long years, Finnegas had lived on the banks of the Boyne, seeking to catch the

Salmon of Fec. The salmon, which swam in a deep pool overhung by hazel boughs, was famous throughout the land, for it was prophesied that the first person to eat of its flesh would enjoy all the wisdom of the world. And it happened one day that while Finn was sitting by the river with Finnegas at his side, the salmon swam boldly towards them, almost daring them to cast their rods into the water. Finnegas lost no time in doing so and was astounded when the fish got caught on his hook, struggling only very weakly to release itself. He hauled the salmon onto the shore and watched its silver body wriggle in the sand until all life had gone out of it. When it finally lay still, he gave the salmon over to Finn and ordered him to build a fire on which to cook it.

'But do not eat even the smallest morsel,' Finnegas told him, 'for it is my reward alone, having waited patiently for seven years.'

Finn placed a spit over the fire and began turning it as requested until the fish was cooked through. He then placed it on a plate and took it to Finnegas.

'And have you eaten any of the salmon?' asked the poet.

'No,' answered Finn, 'but I burned my thumb while cooking it and put it in my mouth to relieve the pain.'

'Then you are indeed Finn mac Cumaill,' said Finnegas, 'and I bear you no ill-will for having tasted the salmon, for in you the prophecy is come true.'

Then Finnegas gave Finn the rest of the salmon to eat and it brought him instant knowledge of all he desired to know. And that evening he composed the finest of verses, proving that he possessed a talent equal to the most gifted poets in Erin:

May-day! delightful day!
Bright colours play the vale along.
Now wakes at morning's slender ray
Wild and gay the Blackbird's song.

Now comes the bird of dusty hue,
The loud cuckoo, the summer-lover;
Branchy trees are thick with leaves;
The bitter, evil time is over.

Loaded bees with puny power
Goodly flower-harvest win;
Cattle roam with muddy flanks;
Busy ants go out and in.

Through the wild harp of the wood
Making music roars the gale–
Now it settles without motion,
On the ocean sleeps the sail.

Men grow mighty in the May,
Proud and gay the maidens grow;
Fair is every wooded height;
Fair and bright the plain below.

A bright shaft has smit the streams,
With gold gleams the water-flag;
Leaps the fish and on the hills
Ardour thrills the leaping stag.

Loudly carols the lark on high,
Small and shy his tireless lay,
Singing in wildest, merriest mood,
Delicate-hued, delightful May.
T.W. Rolleston, May-Day

The Rise of Finn to Leadership of the Fianna

AFTER FINN HAD EATEN of the Salmon of Fec which gave him all the gifts of wisdom, he had only to put his thumb in his mouth and whatever he wished to discover was immediately revealed to him. He knew beyond all doubt that he had been brought into the world to take the place of Cumall as head of the Fianna, and was confident at last that he had learned from Finnegas all that he would ever need to know. Turning his back on the valley of the Boyne, he set off to join Crimall and his followers in the forests of Connacht once more in order to plan in earnest for his future. He had by now become the most courageous of warriors, yet this quality was tempered by a remarkable generosity and gentleness of spirit that no man throughout the length and breath of the country could ever hope to rival. Finn was loved and admired by every last one of his comrades and they devoted their lives to him, never once slackening in their efforts to prove themselves worthy of his noble patronage.

It was decided among this loyal group that the time had come for Finn to assert his claim to the leadership of the Fianna and they went and pledged him their support and friendship in this bravest of quests. For it was well known that the Clan of Morna, who continued to rule the Fenian warriors, would not surrender their position without a bitter struggle. Finn now believed himself ready for such a confrontation and the day was chosen when he and his army would march to the Hill of Tara and plead their case before Conn Céadchathach, the High King of Erin.

As it was now the month of November and the Great Assembly of Tara was once more in progress, a period of festivity and good-will, when every man was under oath to lay aside his weapon. Chieftains, noblemen, kings and warriors all journeyed to Tara for the splendid event and old feuds were forgotten as the wine and mead flowed freely and the merry-making and dancing lasted well into the small hours. It was not long before Finn and his band of followers had arrived at Tara and they proceeded at once to the main banqueting hall where they were welcomed by the King's attendants and seated among the other Fenian warriors. As soon as he had walked into the hall, however, all eyes had been turned towards Finn, and a flurry of hushed enquiries circulated around the room as to the identity of the golden-haired youth. The King too, was quick to acknowledge that a stranger had entered his court, and he picked up a goblet of wine and instructed one of his servants to present it to the young warrior. At this gesture of friendship, Finn felt reassured in approaching the King, and he walked forward to the royal table and introduced himself to one and all.

'I am Finn, son of Cumall,' he declared, 'and I have come to take service with you, High King of Erin, just as my father did before me as head of the Fianna.'

And when he heard these words, Goll mac Morna, who sat at the King's right hand, grew pale in anger, and shuddered to hear the King respond favourably to the young warrior:

'I would be honoured to have you serve in my ranks,' replied Conn Céadchathach. 'If you are the son of Cumall, son of Trenmor, then you are also a friend of mine.'

After this, Finn bound himself in loyalty to the King, and his own band of men followed his example, and each was presented with a sword of the Fianna which they accepted with great pride and humility.

Everybody in the kingdom had either heard of Aillen the goblin or seen the creature with their own eyes. Every year during the Great Assembly, Conn Céadchathach increased the number of men guarding the royal city, but still the goblin managed to pass undetected through the outer gates, moving swiftly towards the palace and setting it alight with its flaming breath. Not even the bravest of warriors could prevent Aillen from reeking havoc on Tara, for he carried with him a magic harp and all who heard its fairy music were gently lulled to sleep. The King lived in hope however, that one day the goblin would be defeated and he adamantly refused to be held to ransom by the creature, insisting that the annual festivities take place as normal. A handsome reward awaited that warrior who could capture or destroy Aillen, but none had yet succeeded in doing so. It was at this time that Goll mac Morna conceived of his wicked plan to belittle his young rival before the King, for he could see that Conn Céadchathach secretly entertained the hope that Finn would rescue Tara from further destruction. He called the young warrior to him and told him of the one true way to win the King's favour, being careful not to mention the enchanting harp or the difficulty of the task that lay ahead:

'Go and bind yourself before the King to rid this city of the terrible goblin who every year burns it to the ground,' said Goll. 'You alone possess the courage to do this Finn, and you may name your price if you are successful.'

So Finn went before the King and swore that he would not rest in peace until he had slain Aillen the goblin.

'And what would you have as your reward?' asked the King.

'If I manage to rid you of the goblin,' Finn replied, 'I should like to take up my rightful position as captain of the Fianna. Will you agree, under oath, to such a reward?'

'If this is what you desire,' answered the King, 'then I bind myself to deliver such a prize.'

Satisfied with these words, Finn took up his weapon and ventured out into the darkness to begin his lonely vigil over the palace.

As night fell and the November mists began to thicken round the hill of Tara, Finn waited anxiously for the goblin to appear. After some time, he saw an older warrior enter the courtyard and make his way towards him. He noticed that the warrior held in his hand a long, pointed spear, protected by a case of the soft, shining leather.

'I am Fiacha,' said the warrior gently, 'and I was proud to serve under your father, Cumall, when he was leader of the Fianna. The spear I carry is the spear of enchantment which Cumall placed in my charge upon his death.

'Take this weapon,' he added, 'and as soon as you hear the fairy music, lay its blade against your forehead and you will not fall under the melody's spell.'

Finn thanked the warrior for his gift and turned it over to inspect it, admiring its shining handle of Arabian gold and the sharp steel body of the blade that glinted challengingly in the moonlight. Then he began to roam the ramparts once more, straining his ear to catch the first notes of the magic harp. He gazed out over the wide, frosty plains of Meath but still there was no sign of the evil goblin. He had almost given up hope that Aillen would appear and had sat down wearily on the hard, frozen earth, when he caught sight of a shadowy, phantom-like figure in the distance, floating eerily over the plain towards the royal palace. At first the strange music that wafted through the air was scarcely audible, but as the goblin drew nearer, the sweet sound of the harp strings filled the air like a potent fragrance, intoxicating the senses and inducing a warm, drowsy feeling. Finn was immediately enraptured by the sound and his eyelids slowly began to droop as the music weaved its magic spell over him. But something within him struggled against the opiate of the melody and his fingers searched for the spear of enchantment. Releasing the weapon from its leather shroud, he lay the cold steel blade against his forehead and drew a long, deep breath as he allowed its rejuvenating strength to flow through his tired limbs.

As soon as Aillen had reached the crest of the Hill of Tara he began to spit blazing fire-balls through the palace gates, unaware that Finn had escaped the enchantment of the harp. Now Aillen had never before come face to face with an alert and animate mortal, and the sudden appearance of the young warrior quenching the flames with the cloak off his back prompted a shriek of terror and alarm. Turning swiftly around in the direction he had come from, Aillen fled for his safety, hoping to reach the fairy mound at Sliabh Fuaid before Finn could overtake him. But the young warrior was far too fleet of foot and before the goblin had managed to glide through the entrance of the mound, Finn had cast his spear, striking down the goblin with a single fatal blow through the chest. Then Finn bent over the corpse and removed Aillen's head and carried it back to the palace so that all were made aware that he had put an end to the reign of destruction.

When the sun had risen on the following morning, the King was overjoyed to discover that his kingdom remained untouched by the goblin's flame. He knew at once that Finn must have fulfilled his promise and was eager to express his gratitude. He called together all the men of the Fianna and sent his messenger to Finn's chamber requesting him to appear before him. Then the King stood Finn at his right hand and addressed his audience slowly and solemnly with the following words:

'Men of Erin,' said the King, 'I have pledged my word to this young warrior that if he should ever destroy the goblin Aillen, he would be granted leadership of the Fianna. I urge you to embrace him as your new leader and to honour him with your loyalty and service. If any among you cannot agree to do this, let him now resign his membership of the Fianna.'

And turning to face Goll mac Morna, the King asked him:

'Do you swear service to Finn mac Cumaill, or is it your decision to quit the Fianna?'

'The young warrior has risen nobly to his position,' replied Goll, 'and I now bow to his superiority and accept him as my captain.'

Then Goll mac Morna swore allegiance to Finn and each warrior came forward after him and did the same in his turn. And from this day onwards it was deemed the highest honour to serve under Finn mac Cumaill, for only the best and bravest of Erin's warriors were privileged to stand alongside the most glorious leader the Fianna had ever known.

The Pursuit of Diarmuid and Gráinne

FOLLOWING THE DEATH OF HIS WIFE Maignes, Finn mac Cumaill had spent an unhappy year alone as a widower. The loss of his wife had come as a severe blow to the hero of the Fianna and even though he was surrounded by loved ones, including his beloved son Oisín and his grandson Oscar, who watched over and comforted him, he could not rid himself of thoughts of Maignes and was increasingly overwhelmed by deep feelings of loneliness and despair.

One morning, seeing his father in such a pitiful state of grief, Oisín called upon his most trusted friend, Diorruing O'Baoiscne, and together they agreed that something must be done to rescue Finn from his prolonged melancholy. It was Diorruing who suggested that perhaps the time had come for Finn to take a new wife and the two young men began to consider who best would fill this role. And as they pondered this question, Oisín suddenly remembered that the High King of Erin, Cormac mac Art, was said to possess one of the most beautiful daughters in the land. Her name was Gráinne, and although several suitors had sought her hand, it was known that she had not consented to marry any of them and was still in search of a husband.

Oisín and Diorruing went before Finn and expressed their concern that he had not yet recovered his good spirits. Finn listened attentively, and he could not deny that every word they spoke was the truth. But he had tried, he told them, to put aside all memory of his wife, and his attempts so far had been utterly futile.

'Will you let us help you then?' Oisín asked his father. 'For we feel certain that you would be better off with a strong woman by your side. The maiden you seek is named Gráinne, daughter of Cormac mac Art, and if you will allow it, we will journey to Tara on your behalf and request her hand in marriage.'

After they had persuaded Finn that he had little to lose by agreeing to such a venture, both Oisín and Doirruing set off for the royal residence at Tara. So impressive was their stature as warriors of the Fianna, that as soon as they arrived, they were respectfully escorted through the palace gates and permitted an immediate audience with the King. And when Cormac mac Art heard that Finn mac Cumaill desired to take his daughter for a wife, he was more than pleased at the prospect, yet at the same time, he felt it his duty to inform Oisín of the outcome of Gráinne's previous courtships:

'My daughter is a wilful and passionate woman,' the King told Oisín. 'She has refused the hand of some of the finest princes and battle-champions Erin has ever known. Let her be brought before us so that she may give you her own decision on the matter, for I would rather not incur your displeasure by saying yes, only to have her go against me.'

So Gráinne was brought before them and the question was put to her whether or not she would have Finn mac Cumaill for a husband. And it was without the slightest show of interest or enthusiasm that Gráinne made the following reply:

'If you consider this man a fitting son-in-law for you, father, then why shouldn't he be a suitable husband for me?'

But Oisín and Doirruing were satisfied with this answer and taking their leave of the King after having promised to visit as soon as possible in the company of Finn mac Cumaill, they hastened back to the Hill of Allen to deliver the good news.

Within a week, the royal household of Tara was busy preparing itself to welcome the leader of the Fianna and the captains of the seven battalions of his great army. An elaborate banquet was prepared in their honour and King Cormac mac Art received his visitors with great pride and excitement. Then he led the way to the vast dining hall and they all sat down to enjoy a merry evening of feasting and drinking. Seated at Cormac's left hand was his wife, Eitche, and next to her sat Gráinne, resplendent in a robe of emerald silk which perfectly enhanced her breathtaking beauty. Finn mac Cumaill took pride of place at the King's right hand and beside him were seated the most prominent warriors of the Fianna according to his rank and patrimony.

After a time, Gráinne struck up a conversation with her father's druid Daire who sat close by, demanding to know of him the cause of the great celebrations taking place.

'If you are not aware of the reason,' said the druid, 'then it will indeed be hard for me to explain it to you.'

But Gráinne continued to pester Daire with the same question until eventually he was forced to give her a more direct answer:

'That warrior next to your father is none other than Finn mac Cumaill,' said the druid, 'and he has come here tonight to ask you to be his wife.'

And so, for the first time, Gráinne scrutinized the figure she had so flippantly agreed to marry, and having studied his face at some length she fell silent for a time. Then she addressed the druid once more:

'It comes as a great surprise to me,' said Gráinne, 'that it is not for his own son Oisín, or even his grandson Oscar, that Finn seeks me as a wife, since it would be far more appropriate if I married one of these two than marry this man who must be three times my own age.'

'Do not say such things,' answered Daire worriedly, 'for if Finn were to hear you, he would certainly now refuse you and none among the Fianna would ever dare to look at you afterwards.'

But Gráinne merely laughed to hear these words and her eye began to wander in the direction of the young Fenian warriors at the banqueting table. As she surveyed each of them in turn, she questioned the druid as to their identity, desiring to know what exceptional qualities they each had to recommend them. And when her eyes came to rest upon one particularly handsome warrior with dusky-black hair, her interest was very keenly aroused.

'That is Diarmuid, son of Dubne,' the druid informed her, 'who is reputed to be the best lover of women and of maidens in all the world.'

As she continued to sip her wine, Gráinne stared even more closely at the black-haired youth until eventually she called her attendant to her and whispered in her ear:

'Bring me the jewelled goblet from my chamber closet that holds enough wine for nine times nine men.' she told her. 'Have it filled to the brim with wine, then set it down before me.'

When her servant returned with the heavy goblet Gráinne added to it the contents of a small phial she had secretly hidden in a fold of her gown.

'Take the goblet to Finn first of all,' she urged her handmaiden, 'and bid him swallow a draught of wine in honour of our courtship. After he has done so, pass the goblet to all of the company at the high table, but be careful not to allow any of the youthful warriors of the Fianna to drink from it.'

The servant did as she was requested and it was not long before all who swallowed the wine from Gráinne's cup had fallen into a deep and peaceful slumber. Then Gráinne rose quietly from her place at the table and made her way towards where Diarmuid was seated.

'Will you receive my love, Diarmuid,' Gráinne asked him, 'and escape with me tonight to a place far away from here?'

'It is Finn mac Cumaill you are set to wed,' answered the young warrior, stunned at her suggestion. 'I would not do such a thing for any woman who is betrothed to the leader of the Fianna.'

'Then I place you under bonds as a warrior of the King,' said Gráinne, 'to take me out of Tara tonight and to save me from an unhappy union with an old man.'

'These are evil bonds indeed,' said Diarmuid, 'and I beg you to withdraw them, for I cannot understand what it is I have done to deserve such unwarranted punishment.'

'You have done nothing except allow me to fall in love with you,' replied Gráinne, 'ever since the day, many years ago, when you visited the palace and joined in a game of hurling on the green of Tara. I turned the light of my eyes on you that day, and I never gave my love to any other man from that time until now, nor will I ever, Diarmuid.'

Torn between his loyalty to Finn, and an allegiance to the sacred bonds Gráinne had placed him under, Diarmuid turned to his Fenian friends for counsel and advice. But all of them, including Oisín, Oscar, Diorruing and Cailte, advised that he had little choice but to go with Gráinne:

'You have not invited Gráinne's love,' Oisín told him, 'and you are not responsible for the bonds she has laid upon you. But he is a miserable wretch who does not honour his warrior's oath. You must follow Gráinne therefore, and accept this destiny, though your own death may come of it.'

Filled with despair and sorrow at these words, Diarmuid gathered up his weapons and then moving towards his comrades, he embraced each of them sadly, knowing that his days with the Fianna had now come to an end, to be replaced by days of tortured exile, when Finn mac Cumaill would ruthlessly pursue the couple from one end of Erin to the next.

As soon as the flight of Diarmuid and Gráinne had been brought to his attention, the leader of the Fianna was consumed with violent jealousy and rage and swore the bitterest revenge on the pair. At once, Finn mac Cumaill called for his horses to be saddled and a great host of his men set off on the trail of the couple, journeying for days along the most secluded tracks through the densest forests of Erin until they had crossed the river Shannon and arrived near to the place known as Doire Da Both. On the outskirts of this forest, the Fenian trackers discovered a makeshift camp dusted with the ashes of a small fire, which although now cold, left them in little doubt that they were moving very closely behind their prey.

On the following evening, after they had travelled a lengthy distance deeper into the forest, Finn and his men came upon a form of wooden enclosure built of saplings, stones and mud, containing seven narrow doors. Climbing to one of the tallest trees, Finn's chief scout peered inside the structure and saw there Diarmuid and a woman lying next to him on a blanket of deer-skin. The men of the Fianna were ordered to stand guard at each of the seven exits and then Finn himself approached the hut and shouted loudly for Diarmuid to come forward and surrender himself to them. Diarmuid awoke abruptly from his sleep and taking Gráinne by the hand thrust his head through the smallest of the doors. But his eyes betrayed not the slightest glimmer of fear to see Finn and his great warriors surrounding the hut. Instead, he clasped Gráinne closer to him and planted three kisses on her lips for all the men of the Fianna to observe. Finn mac Cumaill was seized by a fury on seeing this, and proclaimed at once that the removal of Diarmuid's head by whatever method his men were forced to employ would alone prove fitting reprisal for so brazen a show of disrespect.

Now Aengus Óg, the god of love, was the foster-father of Diarmuid, son of Dubne, the deity who had protected and watched over the couple since the night they had fled the palace of Tara. And witnessing their plight at the hands of the Fianna, Aengus now took it upon himself to come to their aid, drifting invisibly towards them on the breeze.

'Come and take shelter under my cloak,' he appealed to them, 'and we will pass unseen by Finn and his people to a place of refuge and safety.'

But Diarmuid insisted that he would remain behind to face his former comrades as a true warrior, and requested that Aengus take only Gráinne with him. So Aengus drew Gráinne under his mantel for protection and they both rose up into the air, gliding towards the woodlands of the south where they felt certain Diarmuid would survive to meet up with them later.

After he had bid Aengus and Gráinne farewell, Diarmuid stood upright, tall and proud, and prepared himself for the task of fighting his way through the formidable band of Fenian warriors. Taking up his weapon, he approached the first of the seven doors and demanded to know which of his former comrades stood behind it waiting to do combat with him:

'I wish you no harm, Diarmuid,' replied the gentle voice of Oisín. 'Let me guide you out through this door, and I promise I will not raise a finger to hurt you.'

And on each of the other doors upon which he knocked, apart from the very last, Diarmuid met with the same response, for it appeared that not one among his old friends of the Fianna was prepared to meet him with hostility. Finally, however, Diarmuid arrived at the seventh door and this time when he knocked, the response was anything but warm and friendly:

'It is I, Finn mac Cumaill,' came the thundering reply, 'a man who bears you no love, as you well know. And if you should come out through this gate I would take great pleasure in striking you down and cleaving asunder every last bone in your body.'

'I will not go out by any other door in that case,' answered Diarmuid, 'for I would not wish such raw anger to be unleashed on any of my friends gathered here whose desire it is to let me go free.'

And then, having driven the shafts of his mighty spears firmly into the earth, Diarmuid used them to spring high into the air, leaping over the walls of the wooden hut, clean over the heads of Finn and his men. So swift was this manoeuvre, so light his descent on the grass beyond the warrior group, that none could trace the path of his escape and they stood looking on in amazement, deliberating a long time whether or not it was some goblin of the air who had helped carry Diarmuid so effortlessly to freedom.

It was not long before Diarmuid had arrived at the clearing in the woods where Aengus and Gráinne waited anxiously to see him. Great was their relief to know that he had escaped the Fianna unharmed and they both listened in admiration as he related to them the tale of his daring escape. When the excitement of the reunion had abated however, Aengus Óg grew more serious and spoke earnestly to his foster-son and Gráinne:

'I must now depart from you,' he said to them, 'but I leave you with these words of advice. Do not slacken in caution while Finn mac Cumaill remains in pursuit of you. Never enter a cave with only one opening; and never take refuge on an island with only one harbour. Always eat your meals in a place different to where you have cooked them; never rest your head where you eat your meal, and wherever you sleep tonight, make sure you choose a fresh bed on the following night.'

For many months afterwards, Diarmuid and Gráinne followed the advice of Aengus Óg and lived precisely as he had counselled them. But the time came when they grew weary once more of shifting from place to place and they longed for even two nights together when they might sleep under the same familiar oak tree or heather bush. They had by now reached the forests of the west and had entered a bower guarded by the fierce giant Searbhán.

'Surely we may rest awhile here, Diarmuid,' said Gráinne. 'Is it not the most unlikely thing in the world that Finn and his men would find us out in such a lonely and shaded part of the woods?'

And seeing the look of exhaustion on Gráinne's face, Diarmuid agreed to go in search of Searbhán to beg permission to shelter in the forest. The giant also took pity on Gráinne and it was soon settled that the couple were free to roam the forests and hunt for their food for up to three days provided neither of them touched the quicken tree of Dubros growing in its centre or ate any of its sweet-smelling berries. For this particular tree belonged to the people of the Fairymounds who did not wish that any mortal should eat of its fruit and share the gift of immortality. And so Diarmuid accepted responsibility for both himself and Gráinne and swore upon his sword that during their short stay the berries would remain the sacred property of the fairies.

As for Finn mac Cumaill and his loyal followers of the Fianna, they had not tired in their quest for revenge and were little more than half a day's journey away from the outskirts of Searbhán's forest. And it was while Finn awaited news from his scouts, sent forth to search for evidence of Diarmuid and Gráinne, that he observed a group of horsemen approaching the Fenian camp. He recognized these riders at once as the offspring of the sons of Morna who had murdered his father at the battle of Cnucha and with whom he still had a long-standing feud. But it soon became apparent that these young warriors had travelled a great distance to beg forgiveness for the sins of their fathers and to be reconciled to the Fianna.

Now when Finn's scouts returned to inform him that Diarmuid and Gráinne rested under the protection of Searbhán beneath the tree of Dubros, Finn made up his mind to test the commitment of the warriors of the Clan of Morna:

'If you truly seek forgiveness,' he told them, 'go forth into the woods and bring me one of two things, either the head of Diarmuid, son of Dubne, or a fistful of berries from the tree of Dubros.'

And when the offspring of Morna heard this request, they answered the leader of the Fianna innocently:

'We would be honoured to perform such a task. Point us in the direction of the woods and we shall soon return with one of these two prizes.'

When they were still quite a long way off however, Diarmuid spotted the warriors of Clan Morna approaching and he made ready his weapon for attack. And as they came closer he jumped to the earth from a tree above, blocking the path of their progress.

'Who are you,' Diarmuid asked them, 'and why have you come to the forest of Searbhán?'

'We are of the Clan of Morna,' they replied, 'and we have been sent here by Finn mac Cumaill to perform one of two tasks, either to recover the head of Diarmuid, son of Dubne, or to escape here with a fistful of berries from the tree of Dubros.'

'I am the man whose head you seek,' replied Diarmuid, 'and over there is the tree bearing the fruit you are required to remove. But it will be no easy task for you to accomplish either of these things. Choose now which of the two feats you would attempt to perform.'

'I would sooner fight for your head,' answered the eldest of the warriors, 'than go against the giant Searbhán.'

So the children of Morna began wrestling with Diarmuid who had little or no difficulty overcoming them and within minutes they had been bound hand and foot by him.

Then Gráinne, who had been watching the struggle with some amusement, came forward and began to question Diarmuid about the berries. And when she heard of their magic properties, and of how, in particular, they could make the old young and beautiful once more, she insisted that she must taste them before putting any other food in her mouth again. It was useless for Diarmuid to try and persuade her otherwise, and he began to sharpen his spear, resigned to the fact that he must soon confront the tree's ferocious guardian. Seeing that he was reluctant to break his bond of friendship with the giant, the children of Morna offered to go and get the berries for Gráinne. But although Diarmuid would not agree to this, he was nonetheless touched by their generosity and offered to loosen their bonds so that they might witness the combat.

And so Diarmuid, accompanied by the children of Morna, went forward and roused the giant from his sleep, demanding that he hand over some of the precious berries for Gráinne to eat. Furious at this request, the giant swung his mighty club over his shoulder and brought it down hard in Diarmuid's direction. But Diarmuid managed to leap aside, avoiding any injury, and then hurled himself at the giant forcing him to loosen his hold on the club so that it fell heavily to the ground. Seizing the weapon, Diarmuid delivered three strong blows to the giant's head, dashing his brains to pieces. And when he was certain that Searbhán was dead, he climbed the tree of Dubros and plucked the juiciest berries, handing one bunch to Gráinne and the other to the children of Morna.

'Take these berries to Finn,' he told the warriors, 'and do not pretend to him that you have seen me. Tell him instead that you have earned his forgiveness by slaying the giant with your own bare hands.'

The children of Morna were more than happy to do this, and they expressed their gratitude to Diarmuid that he had finally brought peace between the two clans. And having placed the berries carefully in their saddlebags, they made their way back towards Finn and the men of the Fianna.

As soon as he laid eyes on the berries, Finn mac Cumaill placed them under his nose and announced at once that it was Diarmuid, not the offspring of Morna, who had gathered them:

'For I can smell his skin on them,' roared Finn, 'and I will now go myself in search of him and remove his head with my own sword.'

And he tore through the forest as fast as his horse could carry him until he reached the tree of Dubros where he suspected Diarmuid and Gráinne must be hiding. Here he sat down and called for Oisín to bring his chess-board to him. The two began to play a long and complicated game, for they were each as skilled as the other, until eventually they reached a point where the victor of the game would be decided by Oisín's next move. And Diarmuid, who had been closely following the game from above, could not prevent himself from helping his friend. Impulsively, he threw a berry down from one of the branches where it landed on the board indicating to Oisín how the game should be won. At this, Finn rose rapidly to his feet and calling all the warriors of the Fianna together he ordered them to surround the tree. Then Garb of Sliab Cua announced that Diarmuid had slain his father and that nothing would make him happier than to avenge this death. So Finn agreed to this and Garb climbed the tree in pursuit of Diarmuid.

Again, however, Aengus Óg was watchful of his foster-son and rushed to his aid without the Fianna's knowledge. And as Diarmuid flung Garb backwards from the branches with one swift movement of his foot, Aengus put the form of his foster-son upon him so that his own warriors took off his head believing him to be Diarmuid, son of Dubne. After they had done this, Garb was again changed back into his own shape causing great distress to all who witnessed the transformation. And of the nine Fenian warriors Finn mac Cumaill ordered to ascend the tree in search of Diarmuid, the same fate befell each of them so that Finn fell into a heavy mood of anguish and grief. And when Diarmuid announced that he would descend the tree and slaughter every living person under Finn's protection, Finn at last could tolerate the killing no longer and begged for it to come to an end.

So Diarmuid and Aengus Óg appeared before Finn and it was agreed among the three of them that peace should be restored between Finn and Diarmuid. Then the leader of the Fianna and five of his captains went to the stronghold of the High King of Erin to secure a pardon for Diarmuid and Gráinne. Once this had been done, the couple were allowed to return to their native country of west Kerry where they built for themselves a fine home and lived in peace and harmony together for a great many years to follow.

Oisín in Tír na N-Óg (The Land of Youth)

FINN MAC CUMAILL, the mightiest warrior of the Fianna, had no equal among mortal men and his reputation as one of the fiercest fighters in Ireland spread with each glorious victory on the battlefield. His young son, Oisín, was a particular favourite with him, for the boy showed signs of remarkable courage at an early age and had clearly inherited his father's voracious thirst for adventure. Each time Finn gazed at his golden-haired son a memory of Blaí, the boy's mother, stirred within his breast, filling him with both joy and sorrow. Blaí was now lost to him, but the child she had borne him possessed her great beauty and gift of poetry. Oisín was a true warrior and the greatest of Fenian poets. Many women had fallen in love with him, but none had yet succeeded in winning his heart. The son of Finn mac Cumaill was happiest fighting alongside his father, or roaming the dense forests that chimed with birdsong in the company of his trusty hounds.

While hunting in the middle of the woods one summer's morning, just as the silver veil of mist was rising from the shores of Loch Lein, Oisín was struck by the most enchanting vision. A young maiden appeared before him, seated majestically on a milk-white steed. Oisín had never seen her kind before, but felt certain she must have come from the fairy world. Her luxuriant golden hair, adorned by an elaborate jewelled crown, cascaded over her shoulders and she was clothed in a mantle of the finest red silk. Her saddle was made of purple and gold and her horse's hooves were placed in four shoes of gold, studded with the most precious gems. She moved gracefully towards Oisín, who was immediately entranced by her radiance and perfection. The maiden's cheeks were as delicate as the satin petals of a rose; her eyes were as bright and pure as two drops of dew on a violet; her skin was as white and delicate as the first snows of winter.

'I am Niamh [*Pronounced Niav.*] daughter of the great King who rules the Land of Youth,' she spoke softly. 'Your name is well known to me, brave Oisín, son of the noble Finn mac Cumaill. I have hastened here for love's sake, to woo you.'

Oisín stood bewitched before the maiden as she began to sing to him of Tír na N-Óg, the Land of Youth. Her music drifted lightly towards him like a perfumed summer breeze, and it was the sweetest sound the young warrior had ever heard.

Delightful land of honey and wine
Beyond what seems to thee most fair –
Rich fruits abound the bright year round
And flowers are found of hues most rare.

Unfailing there the honey and wine
And draughts divine of mead there be,
No ache nor ailing night or day –
Death or decay thou ne'er shalt see!

A hundred swords of steel refined,
A hundred cloaks of kind full rare,
A hundred steeds of proudest breed,
A hundred hounds – thy meed when there!

The royal crown of the King of Youth
Shall shine in sooth on thy brow most fair,
All brilliant with gems of luster bright
Whose worth aright none might declare.

All things I've named thou shalt enjoy
And none shall cloy – to endless life –
Beauty and strength and power thou'lt see
And I'll e'er be thy own true wife!
Michael Comyn, Niamh sings to Oisin

'Niamh of the Golden Hair,' Oisín spoke to her. 'I have never before met a maiden so pleasing to the eye and I long to visit the kingdom of which you sing. I would be honoured to take you as my bride and will depart this land of mortals without delay to be with you.'

Before reaching up to grasp her hand, he looked around him only once, catching a final glimpse of his father's great palace and the beautiful woodlands he had now chosen to leave behind. Bidding a valiant farewell in his heart to the men of the Fianna, he mounted the powerful horse which carried them both away towards the cliffs of the west, and further on into the crashing waves.

For five days and five nights they rode, crossing the great plains of Erin and journeying on through various kingdoms of the Otherworld. The deep sea opened up to greet them and they passed underneath the bed of the ocean into a land of golden light. Regal citadels, surrounded by luscious green lawns and exotic, vibrantly coloured blooms, gleamed in the rays of sparkling sunshine. A youthful knight, clad in a magnificent raiment of purple and silver, suddenly appeared alongside them, riding a white mare. A fair young maiden sat next to him on the saddle holding a golden apple in the palm of her hand. Niamh again told Oisín of the beauty of Tír na N-Óg, a land even more beautiful than the splendid images now before them. They journeyed onwards, passing from this luminous world through a raging, violent tempest, moving as swiftly as the howling winds and driving rains would carry them across mountains, valleys and bottomless dark lakes until the bright orb of the sun emerged in all its splendour once more.

The kingdom now before them was far more breathtaking than Oisín had ever imagined possible. A silver-pebbled stream wound its way towards a gently undulating hill dotted with purple and yellow orchids which breathed a rich, opulent fragrance into the air. A magnificent castle stood on the hilltop, shaded by giant leafy trees laden with ripe golden pears. The sound of honey-bees buzzing from flower to flower united melodiously with the singing of birds, languidly pruning their feathers in the amber glow of early twilight. A large crowd moved forward to welcome the couple. Minstrels played soothing, magical airs and delicate blossoms were strewn at their feet creating a soft carpet for them to tread on. The happy pair were escorted to the palace where the King and Queen had prepared a large wedding banquet. The King warmly embraced his new son-in-law and ordered the seven days of feasting and celebrations to commence.

As each new day dawned in the Land of Youth it brought with it an abundance of joy for Oisín and Niamh. Time stood absolutely still in this perfect world and they had only to wish for something and it would instantly appear. Before long, the couple were blessed with three healthy children: two handsome sons, and a beautiful daughter. The son of Finn mac Cumaill had won the admiration and respect of every person in the kingdom and he enthralled each and every subject with tales of his Fenian friends and the splendid adventures they had survived together. Only one thing now threatened to destroy his happiness. At night, Oisín was tormented by dreams of Erin and of his people, the Fianna. These dreams became more and more powerful with the passing of time and he ached with the desire to visit his homeland once again. Such a dreadful anxiety could not be hidden from Niamh, for she knew what troubled her husband and could not bear to see him suffer this deep sadness and unrest.

'Go, Oisín,' she told him, 'though it breaks my heart, I will not hinder you. But you must promise me, in the name of our love for each other and for our children, that you will not dismount on Erin's soil, for time has autonomy in the land of Erin. Hear my warning that if you touch the earth, you will never again return to the Land of Youth.'

Having listened carefully to these words of caution, Oisín rode away, guided by his magical steed across the plains leading back to his beloved country. After five long days, he arrived in his native land and made his way to the home of his father. Cheered by memories of his youth and the joyous welcome home he knew he would soon receive, he rode to the far side of the forest and waited anxiously for the thick mist to clear so that the great house would be revealed in all its regal splendour. Yet when the drizzling clouds finally dispersed, Oisín was shocked to discover only a pile of crumbling stones where the stronghold of Finn mac Cumaill had once stood firm. Utterly distressed and bewildered, he turned his horse swiftly around and galloped away in search of any mortal creature who might bring him news of the Fianna.

After what seemed an eternity, he spotted on the horizon a strange band of men toiling and sweating in their efforts to lift a slab of granite from the ground. Oisín marvelled at their small frames and their lack of strength in lifting such a trifling load.

'I am searching for the dwelling place of Finn mac Cumaill and the Fianna,' he shouted to the men.

'We have often heard of Finn,' replied a stooped, wizened figure, the eldest of the group. 'But it has been many hundreds of years since the great battle of Gabra where he and the last of the Fianna lost their lives.'

'I can see you possess the blood of such mighty ancestors,' added another of the band. 'Can you lend us your strength to shift this stone?'

Niamh's words of counsel to Oisín had not been forgotten, but he was angered by these men of Erin who stood before him so weak and feeble. Filled with a great pride in his own strength and ability, he bent forward from his horse to assist in the lifting of the slab. But the angle at which he had leaned towards the men, added to the weight of the stone, caused the animal's saddle-girth to snap and Oisín could not save himself from falling to the ground. In an instant, his steed had disappeared into thin air, his royal garments had turned to grimy sackcloth and his youthful warrior's face had become creased and lined as the burden of three hundred years of mortal life fell on him. Withered and blind, he reached out with his bony arms, grasping in the dark for some form of comfort. A wretched, pitiful cry escaped his lips and he heard again Niamh's parting words to him. As he lay helpless on the cold, damp earth, he began to weep inconsolably for the wife and children to whom he could never now return in the Land of Eternal Youth.

Chinese Myths

Introduction

CHINA IS A VAST, SPRAWLING NATION, as geographically diverse as Europe and comparable to the European continent in size, containing at least one third of the world's population. It has always retained a mysterious and captivating appeal, and remains a country of rich contrasts and diverse cultural influences drawn from many different sources over the centuries.

Archaeologists and social historians trace the origin of Chinese civilization back to the twelfth century BC, which is roughly the same date that Greek civilization emerged. Some of the earliest objects uncovered from excavated sites support the existence of a race of simple agriculturalists, known as the Shang, occupying the basin of the Yellow River in the north of the country at about this time. Again, like their Greek counterparts, the Chinese evolved quickly into a sophisticated and efficient people, so that by the fourth century BC, they were able to boast a relatively civilized, structured society.

Unlike other European nations, China was not conquered by foreign invaders, with the result that she remained largely isolated from the West, and was able to preserve her own unique culture and traditions. That is not to say, however, that China remained immune to outside influences or that she was unduly possessive of her own traditions. More often than not, those invaders who landed on Chinese shores were surprised to encounter a society more developed than their own, and instead of wishing to subjugate it, ended up appropriating the country's values and practices. China, for her part, took what she considered worthwhile from foreign cultures and modified and assimilated it into her own. In this way, a mutually beneficial exchange was enacted.

The most significant external impact on the development of Chinese society was not made by would-be conquerors, however, but by tradesmen travelling the Rome-China Silk Road which was in commercial use by about 100 BC. At this time, India had cultivated an equally advanced society and the trade route allowed the two civilizations to meet without hostility. This encounter brought Buddhism to China, which of any other alien influence, had perhaps the most dramatic, long-term effect on her culture and literary heritage.

In common with many other nations, both Western and Eastern, the earliest mythology of the Chinese was in the oral tradition. Myths were very rare before 800 BC when fragments of tales with an astrological theme began to gain popularity. Subsequent Chinese myths and legends fall into several distinct groups. The myths presented in the first two sections of this chapter are all based on ancient tales arising from a highly fertile mythical period, up to and including the overthrow of the Yin dynasty and the establishment of the Zhou dynasty in 1122 BC. The third section offers a selection of popular, miscellaneous fables, spanning a number of later eras. It should be noted, however, that the period of antiquity in which these legends and fables are set is no indication of when they were actually first transcribed. The earliest myths, as we know them today, for example, the Creation Myths, have to be recognized as the reconstructions of a later, post-Confucian culture. These early tales, collected in different ancient books, such as the great historical annals, give only the most frugal biographical account of characters and events. In time, these tales were embellished with more detail, appearing in works like the Toaist Shanghaijing (The Classic of Mountains and Seas), where a deeper sense of mystery and fantasy is woven around an existing historical record.

The imaginative minds of the ancient Chinese were crowded with Gods, giants, fairies, mortal heroes and devils, all of which ultimately appeared in their literature. Before Buddhism, Chinese religious practices were similar to those of the ancient Greeks, incorporating a huge number of deities who represented every aspect of nature, and a whole system of beliefs which attempted to explain the complexities of the universe in simple, human terms. The most important school of thought dominating China for thousands of years, was Confucianism, which devoted itself principally to the regulation of human relationships with a view to creating a practical social structure which would enable people to live in greater harmony together. Confucius favoured a more rational approach to life than that which he saw around him and discouraged the belief in the supernatural.

Co-existing with this methodical outlook, however, was the school of thought known as Taoism, seeking out the essential laws of nature which govern our lives, and in the age of Lao Tzu, the reputed founder of the Taoist religion, fresh myths began to appear. The period of the Warring States, 500 to 100 BC, again brought new impetus and greater emotional depth to mythological creation.

This era was followed by the advent of Buddhism which introduced to China many tales adapted from Indian mythology. To combat this foreign influence, Taoists invented newer characters and legends, mixing fact and fiction to a degree where the worlds of myth and reality become indistinguishable.

Broadly speaking, the diverse influences of Confucianism, Taoism and Buddhism resulted in a literature which was firmly rooted in the concept that everything on earth was in some way subject to divine authority. Order and peace exist on earth when Heaven's authority is acknowledged, but when it is ignored, natural calamities, such as floods and drought, are set to occur. According to the Taoist view, the supreme power of Heaven is administered by celestial government officials. Compared to the other splendours of creation, the mountains and streams, the forests and flowers, man's importance is diminished. Never before, in any other culture or early literature, was the emphasis on nature and humanity's communion with it, so crucial. Man's good fortune depended on his ability to behave in accordance with the dictates of Heaven. From ancient times onwards, the highest ambition he could aspire to was to determine the natural law of things and to behave in sympathy with it.

The Chinese mythological tradition has furnished us with an extensive catalogue of ancient tales, several thousand in number. This volume is intended to provide an enjoyable and entertaining introduction to the most popular of those myths and fables and is in no way a comprehensive study of its subject. Nonetheless, it is hoped that the stories included will encourage the reader to explore further the fascinating world of Chinese mythology.

The Creation Myths

THE EARLIEST CHINESE MYTHS, believed to have evolved in the primitive society of what is now northern China, are very old indeed, some of them dating back to the eighth century BC. They were passed on by word of mouth, by a simple people attempting to explain the origins of the cosmos and other astronomical phenomena beyond their comprehension.

The story of Pan Gu, although generally considered one of China's earliest legends, is actually from a much later period. Some scholars of Chinese mythology suggest that this myth was imported from Indo-China shortly before the advent of Buddhism in the first century BC. Other scholars attribute the tale specifically to the fourth century Taoist philosopher Ko Hung, author of the Shen Hsien Chuan (Biographies of the Gods).

But whatever his precise origins, the tale of how Pan Gu fashioned the universe is now very firmly established in Chinese folklore and a great number of Chinese people still trace their ancestry back to this particular god and his successor, the goddess Nü Wa. Ancient Chinese tales which centre on these two characters are commonly known as 'Creation Myths'.

Nü Wa and her consort, Fu Xi, were created to embellish the mythological notion of the origin of things. Again, the concept of Nü Wa is a very ancient one, first mentioned by Lieh Tzu in the fifth century BC. Nü Wa and Fu Xi are the great gentle protectors of humanity, while the God of Water, Gong Gong, is depicted as the destroyer of the earth. In these stories an interesting tension is introduced between the opposing forces of creativity and destruction.

Pan Gu and the Creation of the Universe

AT THE VERY BEGINNING OF TIME, when only darkness and chaos existed and the heavens and the earth had not yet been properly divided up, the universe resembled the shape of a large egg. And at the centre of this egg, the first living creature one day came into being. After many thousands of years, when he had gathered sufficient strength and energy and had grown to the size of a giant, the creature, who gave himself the name of Pan Gu, awoke fully refreshed from his long rest and stood upright within his shell. He began to yawn very loudly and to stretch his enormous limbs, and as he did so, the walls of the egg were cracked open and separated into two even portions. The lighter, more fragile, part of the egg floated delicately upwards to form the white silken sheet of the sky, while the heavier, more substantial part, dropped downwards to form the earth's crusty surface.

Now when Pan Gu observed this, he was happy and proud to have created some light in place of the darkness and chaos out of which he had emerged. But at the same time, he began to fear that the skies and the earth might fuse once more, and he stood and scratched his huge head, pondering a solution to the problem. And after he had thought things through for quite a while, he decided that the only way to keep the two elements at a safe distance from each other was to place his own great bulk between them. So he took up his position, heaving and pushing upwards against the sky with his hands and pressing downwards into the earth with all the weight of his massive feet until a reasonable gap had been formed.

For the next eighteen thousand years, Pan Gu continued to push the earth and the sky apart, growing taller and taller every day until the gap measured some thirty thousand miles. And when this distance between them had been established, the sky grew firm and solid and the earth became securely fixed far beneath it. Pan Gu then looked around him and seeing that there was no longer any danger of darkness returning to the universe, he felt at last that he could lay down and rest, for his bones ached and he had grown old and frail over the years. Breathing a heavy sigh, he fell into an exhausted sleep from which he never awoke. But as he lay dying, the various parts of his vast body were miraculously transformed to create the world as we mortals know it today.

Pan Gu's head became the mountain ranges; his blood became the rivers and streams; the hairs on his head were changed into colourful and fragrant blossoms and his flesh was restored to become the trees and soil. His left eye was transformed into the sun and his right eye became the moon; his breath was revived in the winds and the clouds and his voice resounded anew as thunder and lightning. Even his sweat and tears were put to good use and were transformed into delicate droplets of rain and sweet-smelling morning dew.

And when people later came to inhabit the earth, they worshipped Pan Gu as a great creator and displayed the utmost respect for all the natural elements, believing them to be his sacred body spread out like a carpet before them beneath the blue arch of the heavens.

Nü Wa Peoples the Earth

WHEN THE UNIVERSE FIRST EMERGED from chaos, mankind had not yet been created and the firmament and all the territories beneath it were inhabited by Gods or giants who had sprung forth from the body of Pan Gu. At that time, one particularly powerful Goddess appeared on earth in the company of her chosen heavenly companion. The Goddess's name was Nü Wa and her companion's name was Fu Xi. Together these deities set out to bring an even greater sense of order and regulation to the world.

And of all the other Gods residing in the heavens, Nü Wa was the strangest and most unusual in appearance, for the upper half of her body was shaped like a human being, while the lower part took the form of a snake. Nü Wa also possessed the unique ability to change her shape up to seventy times a day and she frequently appeared on earth in several different guises.

Although Nü Wa took great pleasure in the wondrous beauty of the new-born world she occupied, deep within she felt it to be a little too silent and she yearned to create something that would fill the empty stillness. One day shortly afterwards, as she walked along the banks of the great Yellow River, she began to imagine spending time in the company of other beings not unlike herself, animated creatures who might talk and laugh with her and with whom she could share her thoughts and feelings. Sitting herself down on the earth, she allowed her fingers to explore its sandy texture and without quite realizing it, began to mould the surrounding clay into tiny figures. But instead of giving them the lower bodies of reptiles, the Goddess furnished her creatures with little legs so they would stand upright. Pleased with the result, she placed the first of them beside her on the earth and was most surprised and overjoyed to see it suddenly come to life, dancing around her and laughing excitedly. She placed another beside it and again the same thing happened. Nü Wa was delighted with herself and with her own bare hands she continued to make more and more of her little people as she rested by the river bank.

But as the day wore on, the Goddess grew tired and it was then that she decided to make use of her supernatural powers to complete the task she had begun. So breaking off a length of wood from a nearby mulberry tree, she dredged it through the water until it was coated in mud. Then she shook the branch furiously until several hundred drops of mud landed on the ground and as each drop landed it was instantly transformed into a human being. Then Nü Wa pronounced that the beings she had shaped with her own hands should live to become the rich and fortunate people of the world, while those created out of the drops of mud should lead ordinary and humble lives. And realizing that her little creatures should themselves be masters of their own survival, Nü Wa separated them into sons and daughters and declared that they should marry and multiply until the whole wide world had become their home and they were free once and for all from the threat of extinction.

The War Between the Gods of Fire and Water

FOR A GREAT MANY YEARS after Nü Wa had created human beings, the earth remained a peaceful and joyous place and it was not until the final years of the Goddess's reign that mankind first encountered pain and suffering. For Nü Wa was extremely protective of the race she had created and considered it her supreme duty to shelter it from all harm and evil. People depended on Nü Wa for her guardianship and she, in turn, enabled them to live in comfort and security.

One day, however, two of the Gods who dwelt in the heavens, known as Gong Gong and Zhurong, became entangled in a fierce and bitter dispute. No one knew precisely why the two Gods began to shout and threaten one another, but before long they were resolved to do battle against each other and to remain fighting to the bitter end. Gong Gong, who was the God of Water, was well known as a violent and ambitious character and his bright red wavy hair perfectly mirrored his fiery and riotous spirit. Zhurong, the God of Fire, was equally belligerent when provoked and his great height and bulk rendered him no less terrifying in appearance.

Several days of fierce fighting ensued between the two of them during which the skies buckled and shifted under the strain of the combat. An end to this savage battle seemed to be nowhere in sight, as each God thrust and lunged with increasing fury and rage, determined to prove himself more powerful than the other. But on the fourth day, Gong Gong began to weary and Zhurong gained the upper hand, felling his opponent to the ground and causing him to tumble right out of the heavens.

Crashing to the earth with a loud bang, Gong Gong soon became acutely aware of the shame and disgrace of his defeat and decided that he would never again have the courage to face any of his fellow Gods. He was now resolved to end his own life and looked around him for some means by which he might perform this task honourably and successfully. And seeing a large mountain range in the distance rising in the shape of a giant pillar to the skies, Gong Gong ran towards it with all the speed he could muster and rammed his head violently against its base.

As soon as he had done this, a terrifying noise erupted from within the mountain, and gazing upwards, Gong Gong saw that a great wedge of rock had broken away from the peak, leaving behind a large gaping hole in the sky. Without the support of the mountain, the sky began to collapse and plummet towards the earth's surface, causing great crevasses to appear on impact. Many of these crevasses released intensely hot flames which instantly engulfed the earth's vegetation, while others spouted streams of filthy water which merged to form a great ocean. And as the flood and destruction spread throughout the entire world, Nü Wa's people no longer knew where to turn to for help. Thousands of them drowned, while others wandered the earth in terror and fear, their homes consumed by the raging flames and their crops destroyed by the swift-flowing water.

Nü Wa witnessed all of this in great distress and could not bear to see the race she had created suffer such appalling misery and deprivation. Though she was now old and looking forward to her time of rest, she decided that she must quickly take action to save her people, and it seemed that the only way for her to do this was to repair the heavens as soon as she possibly could with her very own hands.

Nü Wa Repairs the Sky

NÜ WA RAPIDLY SET ABOUT gathering the materials she needed to mend the great hole in the sky. One of the first places she visited in her search was the river Yangtze where she stooped down and gathered up as many pebbles as she could hold in both arms. These were carefully chosen in a variety of colours and carried to a forge in the heavens where they were melted down into a thick, gravel-like paste. Once she had returned to earth, Nü Wa began to repair the damage, anxiously filling the gaping hole with the paste and smoothing whatever remained of it into the surrounding cracks in the firmament. Then she hurried once more to the river bank and, collecting together the tallest reeds, she built a large, smouldering fire and burnt the reeds until they formed a huge mound of ashes. With these ashes Nü Wa sealed the crevasses of the earth, so that water no longer gushed out from beneath its surface and the swollen rivers gradually began to subside.

After she had done this, Nü Wa surveyed her work, yet she was still not convinced that she had done enough to prevent the heavens collapsing again in the future. So she went out and captured one of the giant immortal tortoises which were known to swim among the jagged rocks at the deepest point of the ocean and brought it ashore to slaughter it. And when she had killed the creature, she chopped off its four sturdy legs and stood them upright at the four points of the compass as extra support for the heavens. Only now was the Goddess satisfied and she began to gather round her some of her frightened people in an attempt to reassure them that order had finally been restored.

To help them forget the terrible experiences they had been put through, Nü Wa made a flute for them out of thirteen sticks of bamboo and with it she began to play the sweetest, most soothing music. All who heard it grew calmer almost at once and the earth slowly began to emerge from the chaos and destruction to which it had been subjected. From that day forth, Nü Wa's people honoured her by calling her 'Goddess of music' and many among them took great pride in learning the instrument she had introduced them to.

But even though the heavens had been repaired, the earth was never quite the same again. Gong Gong's damage to the mountain had caused the skies to tilt permanently towards the north-west so that the Pole Star, around which the heavens revolved, was dislodged from its position directly overhead. The sun and the moon were also tilted, this time in the direction of the west, leaving a great depression in the south-east. And not only that, but the peak of the mountain which had crashed to the earth had left a huge hollow where it landed in the east into which the rivers and streams of the world flowed incessantly.

Nü Wa had done all she could to salvage the earth and shortly afterwards, she died. Her body was transformed into a thousand fairies who watched over the human race on her behalf. Her people believe that the reason China's rivers flow eastwards was because of Gong Gong's foolish collision with the mountain, a belief that is still shared by their ancestors today.

Tales of the Five Emperors

AFTER NÜ WA HAD PEOPLED THE EARTH, several of the heavenly gods began to take a greater interest in the world below them. The five most powerful of these gods descended to earth in due course and each was assigned various territories of the new world.

The Yellow Emperor (Huang Ti), the most important of the five sovereigns, is a part-mythical, part-historical figure who is reputed to have founded the Chinese nation around 4000 BC. During his 'historical' reign he is said to have developed a number of important astronomical instruments and mathematical theories, as well as introducing the first calendar to his people and a system for telling the time. He is always depicted as a figure who takes particular pride in humanity and one who consistently reveals a great love of nature and of peaceful existence.

Yet in order to achieve peace, the Yellow Emperor is forced, at one time or another, to battle against the other four gods. These include the Fiery or Red Emperor (Chih Ti), who is the Yellow Emperor's half-brother by the same mother, the White Emperor (Shao Hao), the Black Emperor (Zhuan Xu), and the Green Emperor (Tai Hou). The Yellow Emperor is victorious over all of these gods and he divides up the earth into four equal regions. The Red Emperor is placed in charge of the south, the White Emperor is in charge of the west, the Black Emperor rules the north, while the Green Emperor rules the east.

The Yellow Emperor's Earthly Kingdom

AFTER HE HAD GROWN for twenty-five months in his mother's womb, the infant God Huang Ti was safely delivered at last, bringing great joy to his celestial father, the God of Thunder. As soon as he appeared, Huang Ti had the gift of speech, and in each of his four faces the determination and energy of a born leader shone brightly for all to see. By the time the young God had grown to manhood, he alone among other deities had befriended every known spirit-bird, and a great many phoenixes travelled from afar simply to nest in his garden, or to perch themselves on the palace roof and terraces to serenade him with the sweetest of melodies.

When the five most powerful Gods decided to explore the earth, it was already in the minds of each that one among them should be assigned absolute and supreme control over the others. But the God of Fire, who was later known as the Red Emperor, was reluctant to share power with anyone, especially with his half-brother Huang Ti who seemed to be everyone else's natural choice. So when the time of the election came, the Red Emperor launched a vicious attack on the Yellow Emperor, instigating one of the fiercest battles the earth had ever witnessed. It was fought on the field of Banquan where the allies of Huang Ti, including wolves, leopards, bears and huge birds of prey, gathered together and rushed at the Red Emperor's troops until every last one of them lay slain.

Once this great battle was over and the Yellow Emperor had been acknowledged by all as supreme ruler, he set about building for himself a divine palace at the top of Mount Kunlun, which reached almost to the clouds. The magnificent royal residence, consisting of no less than five cities and twelve towers surrounded by solid walls of priceless jade, was flanked by nine fire-mountains which burnt day and night casting their warm red glow on the palace walls.

The front entrance faced eastwards and was guarded by the Kaiming, the loyal protector of the Gods, who had nine heads with human faces and the body of a giant panther. The exquisite gardens of the royal palace, where the Emperor's precious pearl trees and jade trees blossomed all year round, were protected by the three-headed God Li Zhu who sat underneath the branches never once allowing his three heads to sleep at the same time. This God was also guardian of the dan trees which bore five different exotic fruits once every five years, to be eaten exclusively by the Emperor himself.

From the largest garden, which was known as the Hanging Garden, a smooth path wound its way upwards to the heavens so that many of the most prestigious Gods and the rarest divine beasts chose to make the Emperor's wondrous kingdom their home, content that they had discovered earthly pleasures equal to their heavenly experience. And it was here, in this garden, that the supreme ruler particularly loved to sit each evening, taking time to admire his newly discovered world just as the setting sun bathed it in a gentle golden light. As he looked below him, he saw the reviving spring of Yaoshui flowing jubilantly into the crystal-clear waters of the Yaochi Lake. To the west he saw the great Emerald trees swaying delicately in the breeze, shedding a carpet of jewels on the earth beneath them. When he looked northwards his eyes were fixed upon the towering outline of Mount Zhupi where eagles and hawks soared merrily before their rest. The Yellow Emperor saw that all of this was good and knew that he would spend many happy years taking care of the earth.

The Fiery Emperor and the First Grain

THE FIERY EMPEROR, who ruled as God of the south, had the head of an ox and the body of a human being. He was also known as the God of the Sun and although in the past he had led his people in a disastrous rebellion against the Yellow Emperor, he was still much loved by his subjects and they held him in the highest esteem. The Fiery Emperor taught mankind how to control and make constructive use of fire through the art of forging, purifying and welding metals so that eventually his subjects were able to use it for cooking, lighting and for making domestic tools and hunting weapons. In those early times, the forests were filled with venomous reptiles and savage wild animals and the Fiery Emperor ordered his people to set fire to the undergrowth to drive away these dangerous and harmful creatures. He was also the first to teach them how to plant grain, together with a whole variety of medicinal herbs that could cure any ailment which might trouble them.

It was said that when the Fiery Emperor first appeared on earth he very wisely observed that there was not enough fruit on the trees, or vegetables in the ground to satisfy the appetite of his people. Knowing that mankind was forced to eat the flesh of other living creatures, the Emperor became unhappy and quickly set about instructing his subjects in the use of the plough and other tools of the land until they learned how to cultivate the soil around them. And when he saw that the soil was ready, the Emperor called for his people to pray aloud for a new and abundant food to rise up before them out of the ground.

As the people raised their faces to the heavens, a red bird carrying nine seedlings in its beak suddenly appeared through the clouds. As it swooped to the ground it began to scatter grains on to the upturned soil. After it had done this, the Fiery Emperor commanded the sun to warm the earth and from the seeds emerged five young cereal plants which began to multiply rapidly until a vast area of land was covered with luscious vegetation.

The fruits of these plants were harvested at the close of day to fill eight hundred wicker baskets. Then the Fiery Emperor showed his people how to set up market stalls and explained to them how to keep time according to the sun in order that they might barter among themselves in the future for whatever food they lacked. But even after having provided all of this, the Fiery Emperor was still not satisfied with his work. And so, taking his divine whip, he began to lash a number of the plants, which caused them to be endowed with healing properties, and he set them aside to be used by mankind whenever disease struck. The people, overjoyed that they were so well cared for, decided that the Fiery Emperor should henceforth go by the name of the Divine Peasant and they built in his honour a giant cauldron for boiling herbs and carried it to the summit of the Shenfu Mountains where it stands to this day.

The Bird and the Sea

THE FIERY EMPEROR had three daughters whom he loved and cared for very much, but it was his youngest daughter who had always occupied a special place in his heart. She was named Nü Wa, after the great Goddess who created mankind, and like her sisters she possessed a cheerful disposition and a powerful spirit of adventure.

One day Nü Wa went out in search of some amusement and seeing a little boat moored in the tiny harbour at a short distance from the palace gates, she went towards it, untied it and jumped aboard, allowing it to carry her out over the waves of the Eastern Sea. The young girl smiled happily to see the sun sparkle on the water and the graceful gulls circling overhead, but became so preoccupied in her joy that she failed to notice she had drifted out of sight, further and further towards the centre of the ocean. Suddenly, the wind picked up speed and the waves began to crash violently against the side of the boat. There was nothing Nü Wa could do to prevent herself being tossed overboard into the foaming spray and even though she struggled with every ounce of strength to save herself, she eventually lost the fight and was sadly drowned.

Just at that time, a small jingwei bird happened to approach the place where Nü Wa had fallen. And at that moment, her spirit, resentful of the fact that life had been cut short so unfairly, rose up in anger and entered the creature. Nü Wa now lived on in the form of a bird with a speckled head, white beak and red claws, and all day long she circled the skies angrily, vowing to take revenge on the sea which had deprived her of her life and left her father grieving for his beloved child.

It was not long before she conceived of a plan to fill up the sea with anything she could find, hoping that in time there would no longer be any room left for people to drown in it. So every day the little bird flew back and forth from the land out over the Eastern ocean until she grew weary with exhaustion. In her beak she carried pebbles, twigs, feathers and leaves which she dropped into the water below. But this was no easy task, and the sea laughed and jeered at the sight of the tiny bird labouring so strenuously:

'How do you imagine you will ever complete your work,' hissed the waves mockingly. 'Never in a million years will you be able to fill up the sea with twigs and stones, so why not amuse yourself somewhere else.'

But the little jingwei would not be deterred: 'If it takes me a hundred times a million years, I will not stop what I am doing. I will carry on filling you up until the end of the world, if necessary.'

And although the sea continued to laugh even more loudly over the years, the jingwei never ceased to drop into the ocean whatever she managed to collect. Later, after she had found herself a mate and they had produced children together, a flock of jingwei birds circled above the water, helping to fill up the sea. And they continue to do so to this day in China, where their persistent courage and strength have won the admiration and applause of each and every Chinese citizen.

Tai Hou, the Green Emperor

EVEN IN THE WORLD OF DEITIES, the birth of the Green Emperor, God of the East, was judged quite an extraordinary affair. The story handed down among the other Gods was that the Emperor's mother, a beautiful young mortal named Hua Xu, lived originally in the ancient kingdom of Huaxushi, a place so remote and inaccessible, that many people had begun to question its very existence. Those who believed in this land, however, knew that its inhabitants possessed unique powers and gifts and often they were referred to as partial-Gods. They could move underwater as freely as they did above the earth, for example, and it was said that they could pass through fire without suffering any injury to the flesh. They walked through the air as easily as they walked on the ground and could see through the clouds as clearly as they could through glass.

One day the young girl Hua Xu was out walking across the northern plain of Leize, a name which means 'marshes of thunder', when she happened upon a gigantic footprint in the earth. She had never before encountered an imprint of its size and stooped to the ground to inspect it more closely. Imagining that a strange and wonderful being must have passed through the marshes, she grew very excited and found that she could not suppress the urge to compare the size of the footprint with her own. Slowly and carefully, Hua Xu placed her tiny foot in the enormous hollow and as she did so a strange vibration travelled up from the ground through the entire length of her body.

Shortly afterwards, the young girl found that she was pregnant and she was more than happy to be carrying a child, for there was no doubt in her mind that the Gods had intervened on that strange day to bring about her condition. After nine months Hua Xu gave birth to a son who bore the face of a man and the body of a snake. The elders of the people of Huanxushi advised that he should be named Tai Hou, a name fit for a supreme being they were convinced had been fathered by the God of Thunder.

Shao Hao, Son of the Morning Star

THE EMPEROR OF THE WEST, Shao Hao, was also said to have come into being as the result of a strange and wonderful union. His mother, who was considered to be one of the most beautiful females in the firmament, worked as a weaver-girl in the Palace of Heaven. And it was always the case that after she had sat weaving the whole day, she preferred nothing better than to cruise through the Milky Way in a raft of silver that had been specially built for her use. On these occasions, she would pause for rest underneath the old mulberry tree which reached more than ten thousand feet into the skies. The branches of this tree were covered in huge clusters of shining berries, hidden from the naked eye by delicately spiced, scarlet-coloured leaves. It was a well-known fact that whoever ate the fruit of this tree would

immediately receive the gift of immortality and many had journeyed to the centre of the Milky Way with this purpose in mind.

At that time, a very handsome young star-God named Morning Star, who was also known as Prince of the White Emperor, regularly took it upon himself to watch over these berries. Often he came and sat under the Mulberry Tree where he played his stringed instrument and sang the most enchanting songs. One evening, however, Morning Star was surprised to find his usual place occupied by a strange and beautiful maiden. Timidly, he approached her, but there was hardly any need for such caution, for as the maiden raised her head, their eyes met and the two fell in love almost instantly.

The maiden invited the young God aboard her raft and together they floated off into the night sky, along the silver river of the Milky Way down towards the earth and the waves of the sea. And as Morning Star played his magical music, the maiden carved a turtledove from a precious piece of white jade and set it on the top of the mast where it stood as a joint symbol of their mutual love and their deep desire to be guided by each other through the various storms of life. The lovers drifted together over the earth's ocean as their immortal music echoed through the air. And from this joyful union a son was born whom the happy couple named Shao Hao, and it was the child's great destiny to become White Emperor of the western realms and to rule wisely over his people.

Zhuan Xu, Emperor of the North

THE YELLOW EMPEROR and his wife once had a son called Chang Yi who turned out to be a very disappointing and disobedient child. One day, Chang Yi committed a crime so terrible, even his own father could not bring himself to discuss it, and immediately banished his son to a remote corner of the world where he hoped he would never again set eyes on him. After a time, Chang Yi had a son of his own, a very foolish-looking creature it was said, with a long, thin neck, round, beady eyes, and a pig's snout where his mouth should have been. By some form of miracle, Chang Yi's son also managed to find a mate and eventually married a strong and wholesome woman named Ah Nu. From this marriage, the Yellow Emperor's great grandson, Zhuan Xu, was produced, a God who managed to redeem the family name and who, after a careful trial period, was appointed ruler of the earth's northern territories.

Following the Yellow Emperor's great battle against Chiyou, he began to look around for a successor, for he had grown extremely weary of the rebellion and discontent he had experienced during his long reign. His great-grandson had proven himself a faithful servant and everyone now agreed that Zhuan Xu should be the next God to ascend the divine throne.

Chiyou had brought widespread destruction and suffering to the earth which led Zhuan Xu to believe that the alliance between mortals and immortals must be dissolved to prevent an even greater disaster in the future. And so he set about the task of separating the people from the Gods and turned his attention first of all to the giant ladder which ran between heaven and earth. For in those days, it was not unusual for people to ascend the ladder to consult with the Gods when they were in trouble, and the Gods, in turn, often made regular visits to the earth's surface. Chiyou had made such a visit when he secretly plotted with the Maio tribe in the south to put an end to the Yellow Emperor's sovereignty. The bloodshed which followed would never again be tolerated by Zhaun Xu and he enlisted the aid of two Gods in his destruction of the ladder.

With their help, the world became an orderly place once more. The God Chong was assigned control of the heavens and his task was to ensure that immortals no longer descended to earth. The God Li, together with his son Yi, were put in charge of the earth. Yi had the face of a human but his feet grew out of his head to form a fan-shaped bridge to the heavens behind which the sun and the stars set each evening. Zhaun Xu supervised the work of the other Gods and took it upon himself to re-introduce discipline to a race which had become untamed. It was said that he banished all cruel instruments of war and taught mankind respect for his own kind once again. He forbade women to stand in the path of men and severely punished a sister and brother who lived together as husband and wife.

By the time Zhuan Xu died, the world was a much more peaceful place and on the day he passed away it was said that the elements rose up in a great lament. Jagged lightning lit up the skies and thunder clouds collided furiously with each other. The north wind howled fiercely and the underground streams burst to the surface in torrents of grief. Legend has it that Zhuan Xu was swept away by the water and his upper-half transformed into a fish so that he might remain on the earth in another form, ever watchful of mankind's progress.

Chiyou Challenges the Yellow Emperor

CHIYOU WAS A FEROCIOUS and ambitious God who had begun life as an aide and companion to the young deity, Huang Ti, in the days before he had risen to become Yellow Emperor on earth. During this time, the two had become firm friends and close confidants, but as soon as Huang Ti ascended the throne, this favourable relationship came to an abrupt end. For Chiyou could not bear to see his friend achieve the success he secretly longed for, and it became his obsession to find a way to reverse this situation and take the throne for himself.

Chiyou was the eldest of seventy-two brothers, all of them huge and powerful in stature. They each spoke the language of humans, but their bodies below the neckline were those of animals with cloven feet. Their heads were made of iron and their hideous copper faces contained four repulsive eyeballs protruding from mottled foreheads. These brothers ate all kinds of food, but they particularly liked to eat stones and chunks of metal, and their special skill was the manufacture of battle weapons, including sharp lances, spears, axes, shields and strong bows.

Now Chiyou had become convinced that he could easily overthrow the Yellow Emperor and so, gathering together his brothers and other minor Gods who were discontented with the Emperor's reign, he made an arrogant and boisterous descent to earth. First of all, however, he decided to establish a reputation for himself as a great warrior and immediately led a surprise attack on the ageing Fiery Emperor, knowing that he would seize power without a great deal of effort. The Fiery Emperor, who had witnessed his fair share of war, had no desire to lead his people into a climate of further suffering and torment, and soon fled from his home, leaving the way open for Chiyou to take control of the south. Shortly after this event, one of the largest barbarian tribes known as the Miao, who had been severely punished for their misdemeanours under the Fiery Emperor's authority, decided to take their revenge against the ruling monarchy and enthusiastically joined ranks of Chiyou and his brothers.

It was not long before the Yellow Emperor received word of the disturbances in the south, and hearing that it was his old friend who led the armies to rebellion, he at first tried to reason with him. But Chiyou refused to listen and insisted on war as the only path forward. The Yellow Emperor found that he had little choice but to lead his great army of Gods, ghosts, bears, leopards and tigers to the chosen battlefield of Zhuolu and here the terrible war began in earnest.

It was in Chiyou's nature to stop at nothing to secure victory against his opponent. Every subtle trick and sudden manoeuvre, no matter how underhanded, met with his approval and he had no hesitation in using his magic powers against the enemy. When he observed that his army had not made the progress he desired, he grew impatient and conjured up a thick fog which surrounded the Yellow Emperor and his men. The dense blanket of cloud swirled around them, completely obscuring their vision and they began to stab blindly with their weapons at the thin air. Then suddenly, the wild animals who made up a large part of the Emperor's forces started to panic and to flee in every direction straight into the arms of the enemy. The Yellow Emperor looked on desperately and, realizing that he was helpless to dispel the fog himself, he turned to his ministers and pleaded for help.

Fortunately, a little God named Feng Hou was among the Emperor's men, a deity renowned for his intelligence and inventiveness. And true to his reputation, Feng Hou began to puzzle a solution to the problem and within minutes he was able to offer a suggestion.

'I cannot banish from my mind an image of the Plough which appears in our skies at night-time and always points in the same direction,' he informed the Emperor. 'Now if only I could design something similar, we would be able to pinpoint our direction no matter which way we were forced to move through the mist.'

And so Feng Hou set to work at once, using his magic powers to assist him, and within a very short time he had constructed a device, rather like a compass, which continued to point southwards, regardless of its position. And with this incredible new instrument, the Yellow Emperor finally managed to make his way out of the fog, through to the clear skies once more.

But the battle was far from over, and the Emperor began to plan his revenge for the humiliation Chiyou had brought upon his men. At once, he summoned another of his Gods before him, a dragon-shaped deity named Ying Long, who possessed the ability to make rain at will, and commanded him to produce a great flood that would overwhelm the enemy. But Chiyou had already anticipated that the Yellow Emperor would not gladly suffer his defeat, and before the dragon had even begun to prepare himself for the task ahead, Chiyou had called upon the Master of Wind and the Master of Rain who together brought heavy rains and howling winds upon the Yellow Emperor's army, leaving them close to defeat once more.

As a last desperate measure, the Emperor introduced one of his own daughters into the battlefield. Ba was not a beautiful Goddess, but she had the power to generate tremendous heat in her body, enough heat to dry up the rain which now threatened to overcome her father's legions. So Ba stood among them and before long, the rains had evaporated from the earth and the sun began to shine brilliantly through the clouds. Its bright rays dazzled Chiyou's men which enabled Ying Long to charge forward unnoticed, and as he did so, hundreds of enemy bodies were crushed beneath his giant feet, lying scattered behind him on the plains.

And seeing this result, the Yellow Emperor managed to recover some of his dignity and pride, but his army lay exhausted and the morale of his men was very low. He was worried also that they would not be able to withstand another onslaught, for although Chiyou had retreated, the Emperor was certain he would soon return with reinforcements. He knew that he must quickly find something to lift the spirits of his men, and after much thought it suddenly came to him. What he needed most was to fill their ears with the sound of a victory drum, a drum which would resound with more power and volume than anyone had ever before imagined possible.

'With such a drum, I would bring fear to the enemy and hope to my own men,' the Emperor thought to himself. 'Two of my finest warriors must go out on my behalf and fetch a very special skin needed to produce this instrument.'

And having decided that the great beast from the Liubo Mountain possessed the only skin which would suffice, the Yellow Emperor dispatched two of his messengers to kill the strange creature. It resembled an ox without horns, he told them, and they would find it floating on the waves of the Eastern Sea. Sometimes the beast was known to open its mouth to spit out great tongues of lightning, and its roar, it was said, was worse than that of any wild cat of the forests.

But in spite of the creature's terrifying description, the Emperor's men found the courage to capture and skin it without coming to any great harm. After they had done so, they carried the hide back to the battlefield where it was stretched over an enormous bamboo frame to create an impressively large drum. At first, the Yellow Emperor was satisfied with the result, but when his men began to beat upon it with their hands, he decided that the sound was not loud enough to please him. So again, he sent two of his finest warriors on an expedition, and this time they went in search of the God of Thunder, Lei Shen. They found the God sleeping peacefully and crept up on him to remove both his thigh bones as the Emperor had commanded them to do. With these thigh bones a suitable pair of drumsticks was made and handed over to the principal drummer who stood awaiting his signal to beat on the giant instrument.

At last, the drum was struck nine times, releasing a noise louder than the fiercest thunder into the air. Chiyou's men stood paralysed with terror and fear as all around them the earth began to quake and the mountains to tremble. But this was the opportunity the Yellow Emperor's men had waited for and they rushed forward with furious energy, killing as many of Chiyou's brothers and the Miao warriors as they could lay their hands on. And when the battlefield was stained with blood and the casualties were too heavy for Chiyou to bear much longer, he called for his remaining men to withdraw from the fighting.

Refusing to surrender to the Yellow Emperor, the defeated leader fled to the north of the country to seek the help of a group of giants who took particular delight in warfare. These giants were from a tribe known as the Kua Fu and with their help Chiyou revived the strength of his army and prepared himself for the next attack.

The Yellow Emperor Returns to the Heavens

CHIYOU HAD SPENT THREE DAYS and three nights after his defeat at the battle of Zhuolu in the kingdom of the Kua Fu giants gathering rebel forces for his ongoing war against the Yellow Emperor. Both sides, it seemed, were now evenly matched once more and Chiyou relished the thought of a return to battle. But the Yellow Emperor saw that a renewal of conflict would only result in more loss of life and he was deeply disturbed and saddened by the prospect.

On the day before the second great battle was due to commence, the Emperor was sitting deep in thought in his favourite garden at the palace of Mount Kunlun when a strange Goddess suddenly appeared before him. She told him she was the Goddess of the Ninth Heaven and that she had been sent to help him in his plight.

'I fear for the lives of my men,' the Yellow Emperor told her, 'and I long for some new battle plan that will put an end to all this bloodshed.'

So the Goddess sat down on the soft grass and began to reveal to him a number of new strategies conceived by the highest, most powerful Gods of the heavens. And having reassured the Emperor that his trouble would soon be at an end, she presented him with a shining new sword furnished of red copper that had been mined in the sacred Kunwu Mountains.

'Treat this weapon with respect,' she told him as she disappeared back into the clouds, 'and its magic powers will never fail you.'

The next morning, the Emperor returned to the battlefield armed with his new strategies and the sacred weapon the Goddess had given him. And in battle after battle, he managed to overcome Chiyou's forces until at last they were all defeated and Chiyou himself was captured alive. The evil God was dragged in manacles and chains before the Yellow Emperor, but he showed no sign of remorse for the anguish he had caused and the destruction he had brought to the earth. The Yellow Emperor shook his head sadly, knowing that he now had little option but to order his prisoner's execution. The death sentence was duly announced, but Chiyou struggled so fiercely that the shackles around his ankles and wrists were stained crimson with blood.

When it was certain that he lay dead, Chiyou's manacles were cast into the wilderness where it is said they were transformed into a forest of maple trees whose leaves never failed to turn bright red each year, stained with the blood and anger of the fallen God.

And now that relative peace had been restored to the world once more, the Yellow Emperor spent his remaining time on earth re-building the environment around him. He taught the people how to construct houses for themselves where they could shelter from the rains; he brought them the gift of music and he also introduced them to the skill of writing. Mankind wanted to believe that the Yellow Emperor would always be with them on earth, but soon a divine dragon appeared in the skies, beckoning him back to the heavens. The time had arrived for the Yellow Emperor to answer this call and to acknowledge an end to the long reign of the Gods on earth. And so in the company of his fifty officials and all the other willing immortals whose stay had also run its course, he climbed on to the dragon's back and was carried up into the sky back to the heavens to take up his position again as crowned head of the celestial realms.

Giants in early Chinese Legend

IN CHINESE MYTHOLOGY, the earthly home, or 'Place of the Giant People', was said to have been in the region of the east sea, close to the Dayan Mountains. On top of Bogu Mountain lived the descendants of the dragons, giants who grew in the womb for thirty-six years before emerging fully matured and usually covered in long black hair. They could be up to fifty feet in height, with footprints six feet in length. Like their winged ancestors, they could fly before walking, and some lived as long as eighteen thousand years.

Xing Tian, the Headless Giant

ONCE THERE WAS A GIANT named Xing Tian who was full of ambition and great plans for his future. At one time, he had been an official of the Fiery Emperor, but when Chiyou had conquered the region, he had quickly switched loyalties and offered his services to the new, corrupt usurper of the south. It greatly disturbed the giant to hear reports of the bloody deaths of Chiyou's men at the hands of the Yellow Emperor and he wanted nothing less than to meet the Emperor face to face and challenge him to single combat until one of them lay dead.

So Xing Tian took up his axe and his shield and set off for the divine palace at the top of Mount Kunlun, seething with anger and rage as he thundered along. But the Yellow Emperor had received word of the giant's approach and seized his most precious sword ready to meet him head on. For days the two battled furiously, lashing out savagely with their weapons as they fought into the clouds and down the side of the mountain. They fought along all the great mountain ranges of northern China until eventually they reached the place known as the Long Sheep range in the north-east.

And it was here that the Yellow Emperor caught the giant off-guard and, raising his sword high into the air just at the level of the giant's shoulder, he slashed sideways with his blade until he had sliced off Xing Tian's head. A terrifying scream escaped the gaping, bloody mouth of the giant as his head began to topple forward, crashing with a loud thud to the ground and rolling down the hill like a massive boulder.

The giant stood frozen in absolute horror, and then he began feeling desperately with his hands around the hole above his shoulders where his head ought to have been. Soon panic had taken control of him and he thrashed about wildly with his weapon, carving up trees and tossing huge rocks into the air until the valleys began to shake and the sky began to cloud over with dust from the debris.

Seeing the giant's great fury, the Yellow Emperor grew fearful that Xing Tian might actually find his head and put it back on his shoulders again. So he swiftly drew his sword and sliced open the mountain underneath which the head had finally come to rest. Then he kicked the head into the chasm and sealed up the gap once more.

For ten thousand years afterwards the giant roamed the mountainside searching for his head. But in all that time he never found what he was looking for although he remained defiant that he would one day face the Yellow Emperor again. Some people say that the giant grew to be very resourceful, and to help him in his long search he used his two breasts for eyes and his navel for a mouth.

Kua Fu Chases the Sun

THE UNDERWORLD OF THE NORTH where the most ferocious giants had lived since the dawn of time was centred around a wild range of black mountains. And underneath the tallest of these mountains the giant Kua Fu, gatekeeper of the dark city, had built for himself a home. Kua Fu was an enormous creature with three eyeballs and a snake hanging from each ear, yet in spite of his intimidating appearance he was said to be a fairly good-natured giant, though not the most intelligent of his race.

Kua Fu took great pleasure in everything to do with the sun. He loved to feel its warm rays on his great body, and nothing delighted him more than to watch the golden orb rise from its bed in the east each morning. He was never too keen, however, to witness it disappear below the horizon in the evenings and longed for the day when the sun would not have to sleep at night.

And as he sat watching the sun descend in the sky one particular evening, Kua Fu began thinking to himself:

'Surely I can do something to rid the world of this depressing darkness. Perhaps I could follow the sun and find out where it hides itself at night. Or better still, I could use my great height to catch it just as it begins to slide towards the west and fix it firmly in the centre of the sky so that it never disappears again.'

So the following morning, Kua Fu set off in pursuit of the sun, stepping over mountains and rivers with his very long legs, all the time reaching upwards, attempting to grab hold of the shining sphere above him. Before long, however, evening had approached, and the sun began to glow a warm red, bathing the giant in a soothing, relaxing heat. Puffing and panting with exhaustion, Kua Fu stretched his huge frame to its full length in a last great effort to seize his prize. But as he did so, he was overcome by an unbearable thirst, the like of which he had never experienced before. He raced at once to a nearby stream and drank its entire contents down in one mouthful. Still his thirst had not been quenched, so he proceeded to the Weishui River and again gulped down the water until the river ran dry. But now he was even more thirsty and he felt as if he had only swallowed a single drop.

He began to chase all over the earth, pausing at every stream and lake, seeking to drown the fiery heat that raged within his body. Nothing seemed to have any effect on him, though he had by now covered a distance of eight thousand miles, draining the waters from every possible source he encountered. There was, however, one place that he had not yet visited where surely he would find enough water to satisfy him. That place was the great lake in the province of Henan where it was said the clearest, purest water flowed from the mountain streams into the lake's great cavern.

The giant summoned all his remaining strength and plodded along heavily in the direction of this last water hole. But he had only travelled a short distance before he collapsed to the ground, weak with thirst and exhaustion. The last golden rays of the sun curved towards his outstretched body, softening the creases on his weary forehead, and melting away his suffering. Kua Fu's eyelids began to droop freely and a smile spread its way across his face as he fell into a deep, deep, eternal sleep.

At dawn on the following morning, the sun rose as usual in the east, but the sleeping figure of the giant was no longer anywhere to be seen. In its place a great mountain had risen up towards the sky. And on the western side of the mountain a thick grove of trees had sprung up overnight. These trees were laden with the ripest, most succulent peaches whose sweet juices had the power to quench the most raging thirst of any passer-by. Many believe that the giant's body formed this beautiful site and that is why it is still named Kua Fu Mountain in his honour.

Myths of Other Gods and the Yin Nation

THE STORIES OF THIS CHAPTER centre on the adventures of some of the most popular heroes of the ancient Yin nation, from Dijun and Xihe, to Yi, the indomitable archer; from Yao, the wise and benevolent Emperor, to Yü, the saviour of the human race. The welfare of the people is the dominant concern of Yao's reign, and the struggle to maintain order on earth when it is threatened by the hasty intervention of angry gods, or the foolish behaviour of lesser deities, is a recurring theme in these tales.

As with the earlier stories, many of the figures presented here are reputed to be genuinely historical. More often than not, however, characters are endowed with superhuman strength and magical skills, typical of the Chinese mythological tradition of blending fact and fiction, myth and history. Yü, for example, who succeeds Yao to the throne after the brief reign of Emperor Shun (2205–2197 BC) is an outstanding legendary hero, who first appears in the shape of a giant dragon and controls the great floodwaters on earth. He is at the same time, however, the historical founder of the Xia Dynasty, a powerful leader of the Chinese nation, ultimately responsible for the division of China into nine provinces.

Aside from these great legends, the mythological world of the Chinese is peopled by a multitude of gods and immortals, too large in number to describe here. The end of this chapter offers a brief account of the most popular of this group, among them the Eight Immortals, the Kitchen God, the Goddess of Mercy and other lesser gods of distinction.

The Ten Suns of Dijun and Xihe

THE GOD OF THE EAST, Dijun, had married the Goddess of the Sun, Xihe, and they lived together on the far eastern side of the world just at the edge of the great Eastern Ocean. Shortly after their marriage, the Goddess gave birth to ten suns, each of them a fiery, energetic, golden globe, and she placed the children lovingly in the giant Fusang tree close to the sea where they could frolic and bathe whenever they became overheated.

Each morning before breakfast, the suns took it in turns to spring from the enormous tree into the ocean below in preparation for their mother's visit when one of them would be lifted into her chariot and driven across the sky to bring light and warmth to the world. Usually the two remained together all day until they had travelled as far as the western abyss known as the Yuyuan. Then, when her sun had grown weary and the light had begun to fade from his body, Xihe returned him to the Fusang tree where he slept the night peacefully with his nine brothers. On the following morning, the Goddess would collect another of her suns, sit him beside her in her chariot, and follow exactly the same route across the sky. In this way, the earth was evenly and regularly heated, crops grew tall and healthy, and the people rarely suffered from the cold.

But one night, the ten suns began to complain among themselves that they had not yet been allowed to spend an entire day playing together without at least one of them being absent. And realizing how unhappy this situation made them feel, they decided to rebel against their mother and to break free of the tedious routine she insisted they follow. So the next morning, before the Goddess had arrived, all ten of them leapt into the skies at once, dancing joyfully above the earth, intent on making the most of their forbidden freedom. They were more than pleased to see the great dazzling light they were able to generate as they shone together, and made a solemn vow that they would never again allow themselves to become separated during the daytime.

The ten suns had not once paused to consider the disastrous consequences of their rebellion on the world below. For with ten powerful beams directed at the earth, crops began to wilt, rivers began to dry up, food became scarce and people began to suffer burns and wretched hunger pangs. They prayed for rains to drive away the suns, but none appeared. They called upon the great sorceress Nu Chou to perform her acts of magic, but her spells had no effect. They hid beneath the great trees of the forests for shade, but these were stripped of leaves and offered little or no protection. And now great hungry beasts of prey and dreaded monsters emerged from the wilderness and began to devour the human beings they encountered, unable to satisfy their huge appetites any longer. The destruction spread to every corner of the earth and the people were utterly miserable and filled with despair. They turned to their Emperor for help, knowing he was at a loss to know what to do, but he was their only hope, and they prayed that he would soon be visited by the God of Wisdom.

Yi, the Archer, is Summoned

DIJUN AND XIHE WERE HORRIFIED to see the effect their unruly children were having upon the earth and pleaded with them to return to their home in the Fusang tree. But in spite of their entreaties, the ten suns continued on as before, adamant that they would not return to their former lifestyle. Emperor Yao now grew very impatient, and summoning Dijun to appear before him, he demanded that the God teach his suns to behave. Dijun heard the Emperor's plea but still he could not bring himself to raise a hand against the suns he loved so dearly. It was eventually settled between them, however, that one of Yao's officials in the heavens, known as Yi, should quickly descend to earth and do whatever he must to prevent any further catastrophe.

Yi was not a God of very impressive stature, but his fame as one of the most gifted archers in the heavens was widespread, for it was well known that he could shoot a sparrow down in full flight from a distance of fifty miles. Now Dijun went to meet with Yi to explain the problem his suns had created, and he handed the archer a new red bow and a quiver of white arrows and advised him what he must do.

'Try not to hurt my suns any more than you need to,' he told Yi, 'but take this bow and ensure that you bring them under control. See to it that the wicked beasts devouring mankind are also slain and that order and calm are restored once more to the earth.'

Yi readily accepted this challenge and, taking with him his wife Chang E, he departed the Heavenly Palace and made his descent to the world below. Emperor Yao was overjoyed to see the couple approach and immediately organized a tour of the land for them, where Yi witnessed for himself the devastation brought about by Dijun's children, as he came face to face with half-burnt, starving people roaming aimlessly over the scorched, cracked earth.

And witnessing all of this terrible suffering, Yi grew more and more furious with the suns of Dijun and it slipped his mind entirely that he had promised to treat them leniently. 'The time is now past for reasoning or persuasion,' Yi thought to himself, and he strode to the highest mountain, tightened the string of his powerful bow and took aim with the first of his arrows. The weapon shot up into the sky and travelled straight through the centre of one of the suns, causing it to erupt into a thousand sparks as it split open and spun out of control to the ground, transforming itself on impact into a strange three-legged raven.

Now there were only nine suns left in the sky and Yi fitted the next arrow to his bow. One after another the arrows flew through the air, expertly hitting their targets, until the earth slowly began to cool down. But when the Emperor saw that there were only two suns left in the sky and that Yi had already taken aim, he wisely remembered that at least one sun should survive to brighten the earth and so he crept up behind the archer and stole the last of the white arrows from his quiver.

Having fulfilled his undertaking to rid Emperor Yao of the nine suns, Yi turned his attention to the task of hunting down the various hideous monsters threatening the earth. Gathering a fresh supply of arrows, he made his way southwards to fight the man-eating monster of the marsh with six feet and a human head, known as Zao Chi. And with the help of his divine bow, he quickly overcame the creature, piercing his huge heart with an arrow of steel. Travelling northwards, he tackled a great many other ferocious beasts, including the nine-headed monster,

Jiu Ying, wading into a deep, black pool and throttling the fiend with his own bare hands. After that, he moved onwards to the Quingqiu marshes of the east where he came upon the terrible vulture Dafeng, a gigantic bird of unnatural strength with a wing span so enormous that whenever the bird took to the air, a great typhoon blew up around it. And on this occasion, Yi knew that his single remaining arrow would only wound the bird, so he tied a long black cord to the shaft of the arrow before taking aim. Then as the creature flew past, Yi shot him in the chest and even though the vulture pulled strongly on the cord as it attempted to make towards a place of safety, Yi dragged it to the ground, plunging his knife repeatedly into its breast until all life had gone from it.

All over the earth, people looked upon Yi as a great hero, the God who had single-handedly rescued them from destruction. Numerous banquets and ceremonial feasts were held in his honour, all of them attended by the Emperor himself, who could not do enough to thank Yi for his assistance. Emperor Yao invited Yi to make his home on earth, promising to build him the a very fine palace overlooking Jade Mountain, but Yi was anxious to return to the heavens in triumph where he felt he rightly belonged and where, in any event, Dijun eagerly awaited an account of his exploits.

Chang E's Betrayal

AFTER YI, THE GREAT ARCHER, had returned to the heavens with his wife, he immediately went in search of the God Dijun to report on the success of his mission on earth. He had managed to save mankind from the evil destruction of the ten suns, as Dijun had requested him, and was still basking in the glory of this mammoth achievement. Yi fully expected a reception similar to the one he had been given on earth, but instead he found an angry and unforgiving God waiting to receive him. Dijun did not welcome the archer with open arms, but walked forward and spoke only a few harsh words.

'I feel no warmth or gratitude in my heart towards you,' he said to Yi in the bitterest of voices, 'you have murdered all but one of my suns, and now I cannot bear to have you in my sight. So I have decided that from this day forth, you and your wife will be banished to the earth to live among the mortals you appear to have enjoyed serving so well. Because of the foul deed you have committed, it is my judgment that you no longer merit the status of Gods and neither of you will ever be permitted to enter the Heavens again.'

And although Yi argued against his sentence, Dijun would not listen to a single word of his plea. Slowly, the archer made his way homewards, shocked and saddened by the breach of friendship and weighted down by the certain knowledge that his wife would not react well to the news.

And as expected, when Chang E had been told that she and her husband had been exiled to the earth, she was absolutely furious. Much more so than Yi, she revelled in the pleasures and privileges the Gods alone enjoyed, and throughout their married life together, she had never attempted to hide the fact that she had little or no tolerance for the inferior company of mortals. Now she began to regret ever tying herself in matrimony to the archer, for she felt strongly that she was being unduly punished for his hot-headed behaviour. Surely her banishment was totally unjust! And why was it that she was being punished for her husband's foolish actions? These thoughts circled around her head as she reluctantly gathered up her things, and she promised herself that she would never cease to reproach Yi, or allow him a day's rest, until he had made amends for what he had done to her.

The couple's earthly home was as comfortable as Yi could make it and all day long he trudged through the forests in search of the luxuries his wife demanded – the tenderest deer-flesh, or the most exotic, sun-ripened berries. But often when he would return exhausted with these items, Chang E would fling them away, declaring that she had no appetite for unsophisticated mortal food. And then she would begin to bemoan their dreadful misfortune, over and over again, while Yi sat there gloomily, his head in his hands, wishing that he had never set eyes on the suns of Dijun.

One evening, when Chang E had been thinking particularly long and hard about her miserable existence on earth, she went and stood before her husband and announced that she had made firm plans for their future.

'I have had more than enough of this wretched place,' she told Yi, 'and I have no intention of dying here like a mortal and descending to the Underworld afterwards. If you want to keep me, Yi, you must do what I ask of you and go to the west, to the Mountain of Kunlun. For I have heard that the Queen Mother of the West, who lives there, keeps a very special substance. People call it the elixir of immortality and it is said that whoever takes this potion will be granted eternal life.'

Now Yi had also heard a report of this strange queen and her magic medicine, and noticing that some of the old sparkle danced in his wife's eyes as she spoke about it, he could not find it in his heart to refuse her this request even though he knew that the journey ahead would be a treacherous one. For the Queen Mother of the West lived close to the earthly palace of the Yellow Emperor, a region encircled by fire mountains and a deep moat filled with boiling, hissing water which no mortal had ever yet penetrated. The Queen herself may have had the human face of a woman, but her teeth, it was said, were those of a tiger and her hair was long and matted, covering her ugly, scaly body which ended in a leopard's tail.

It was fortunate for Yi that he still possessed some of his God-like powers, since these enabled him to pass through the scorching flames and to swim through the intense heat of the water without coming to any harm. And having reached the opening of the cave where the queen rested, he decided that the best way to approach her was to greet her openly and honestly and tell her his story from start to finish in the hope that she might help him.

To the archer's immense relief, the Queen Mother of the West listened to all he had to say with an open mind, and certainly the image he painted of his innocent wife forced to suffer equal hardship because of what he had done, invited a genuine heartfelt sympathy. The queen suddenly reached into a copper box close by and withdrew a small leather pouch which she handed to Yi.

'The magic medicine inside of this pouch is very precious indeed,' she told him. 'It has been collected from the immortal trees on Mount Kunlun which flower only every three thousand years and bear fruit only every six thousand years. If two people eat this amount, which is all I have to give you, they will both have eternal life in the world of men. But if only one person swallows it all, that person will have the complete immortality of the Gods. Now take the medicine away with you and guard it well, for its value is beyond all measure.'

And so Yi returned to his home and to his anxious wife, feeling as if a great burden had been lifted from his shoulders. For the first time in many years, his wife appeared happy to see him and she kissed his cheek as he presented her with the pouch and began to relate the entire story of his adventure, including everything the queen had told him about the magic potion. Chang E agreed with her husband that they should prepare a great feast to celebrate the end to their mortal lives and she took it upon herself to guard the medicine while her husband went in search of something very special for them to eat.

But as soon as Yi had disappeared into the trees, Chang E began to stare at the little pouch and her thoughts travelled to the days when she lived among the Gods in Heaven, breathing in the scent of beautiful flowers or reclining in the warm sunshine listening to the soothing tones of immortal music drifting gently on the breeze. A deep resentment against her husband rose up within her as she indulged this daydream of a divine kingdom she considered her rightful home and she knew that she would never be content simply with eternal life on earth. She could not let go of what Yi had trustingly told her, that there was only enough elixir to make one of them fully immortal again, and now she allowed her selfish desire to overcome her. Without hesitating a moment longer, Chang E quickly opened up the pouch and swallowed the entire contents all at once.

The effect of the medicine was almost immediate and Chang E felt her body become lighter and lighter until her feet began to lift themselves off the ground as they had done in the past so many times before.

'How glorious it is to be a Goddess again,' she thought to herself as she floated happily towards the flickering stars in the direction of the heavens. She rose higher and higher through the air until the earth below resembled a tiny egg and the skies around her were completely silent and still. But now a sudden fear told hold of the Goddess, for it began to dawn on her that she was entirely alone, cut off from her husband Yi and other earthly mortals, yet not safely arrived in the world of deities. And as she thought more about her return to the Heavens it occurred to her for the first time that she may not necessarily receive a warm welcome there.

'How can I confront these other Gods,' she said to herself, 'when they will certainly scorn me for taking all of the elixir myself and for abandoning my poor husband. Perhaps it is not such a good idea to return straight to Heaven.'

Chang E gazed around her and saw that she had must make an unhappy choice, either to return to the unwelcoming, grey earth, or move onwards towards the cold, silvery moon. 'It is probably quite lonely on the moon,' she thought, 'still, it seems the best place to go to for a short length of time until the Gods have forgotten my crime.' And so, she floated off towards the moon, determined that she would move on from here before too long.

But the moon was far more desolate and dispiriting than she had imagined possible, a cold, hostile place, totally uninhabited, apart from one rabbit who sat forlornly under a cassia tree. Chang E could not bear it a moment longer, and having decided that even a host of angry Gods presented a more desirable alternative, she attempted to rise again into the air. But she soon discovered that her powers had deserted her and that a strange metamorphosis was taking place in her body. Her back stiffened suddenly and then curved forwards. Her breasts separated and flattened, causing her stomach to bulge outwards. Small swellings began to appear all over her skin which lost its translucence and changed to a dull, murky green. Her mouth stretched wider and wider to the edge of her face where her ears once rested and her eyes grew larger and larger until they formed two ugly black rounds.

Once a beautiful and faithful wife, the greedy and disloyal Chang E had finally met with her punishment and was transformed into a giant toad. And in this form she remained until the end of time, doomed to keep a lonely watch over the earth below while yearning, every passing moment, to be with the husband she had so falsely deceived.

Hou-Ji, the Ice-Child

JIANG YUAN was one of four wives of Di Ku, God of the East. For many years the couple had tried to have a child together but they had not been successful and their marriage was not a very happy one as a result. One day, however, Jiang Yaun was walking along by the riverbank when she spotted a trail of large footprints in the earth. She was intrigued by them and began to follow where they led, placing her own tiny feet in the hollows of the ground. She was unaware that by doing this, she would conceive a child, and not long afterwards she gave birth to a son, an event which under normal circumstances would have brought her great joy.

But Jiang Yuan was filled with shame to see the tiny bundle wriggling in her arms, knowing that she had absolutely no knowledge of its father. And realizing that she would have great difficulty explaining the infant's birth to her husband, Jiang Yaun made up her mind to dispose of the child before she became a victim of scandalous gossip and derision. So she took the baby to a deserted country lane and left him to perish in the cold among the sheep and cattle. But then a strange thing happened. For instead of rejecting the baby and trampling him to death, the sheep and cattle treated him as one of their own, carrying him to a nearby barn where they nestled up close to him to keep him warm and suckled him with their own milk until he grew fit and strong.

Now Jiang Yuan had sent her scouts into the countryside to make sure that her unwanted child no longer lived. The news that he had survived and that he was being cared for by the animals of the pastures threw her into a fit of rage and she ordered her men to take the infant deep into the forests, to the most deserted spot they could find, where he was to be abandoned without any food or water. Jiang Yuan's messengers performed their duty exactly as they had been commanded, but again, fate intervened to save the child.

For one morning, a group of woodcutters who had travelled into the heart of the forest to find sturdier trees, spotted the child crawling through the undergrowth. Alarmed by his nakedness and grimy appearance, they immediately swept him up off the ground and carried him back to their village. Here, the woman Chingti, who was herself without child, took charge of the infant. She wrapped him in warm clothing and filled him with nourishing food until gradually he grew plump and healthy. His foster-mother doted on her son and it brought her great pleasure to see him thrive in her care.

But again, Jiang Yuan managed to track down the child and this time she was resolved to stop at nothing until she was certain of his destruction. And so, as a last resort, she carried him herself to a vast frozen river in the north where she stripped him naked and threw him on to the ice. For two years, the infant remained on the frozen waters, but from the very first day, he was protected from the piercing cold by a flock of birds who took it in turn to fly down with morsels of food and to shelter him under their feathered wings.

The people grew curious to know why the birds swooped on to the icy surface of the river every day when clearly there were no fish to be had. Eventually a group of them set off across the ice to investigate further and soon they came upon the young child, curled up against the warm breast of a motherly seagull. They were amazed at the sight and took it as a sign that the child they had discovered was no ordinary mortal, but a very precious gift from the Gods. They rescued the young boy and named him Hou-Ji and as they watched him grow among them, his outstanding talents began to manifest themselves one by one.

Hou-Ji became an excellent farmer in time, but he did not follow any conventional model. He was a born leader and from a very early age he had learned to distinguish between every type of cereal and edible grain. He made agricultural tools for the people, such as hoes and spades, and soon the land delivered up every variety of crop, including wheat, beans, rice and large, succulent wild melons. The people had a bountiful supply of food and when the Emperor himself heard of Hou-Ji's great work he appointed him a minister of the state so that his knowledge of agriculture would spread throughout the nation.

When Hou-Ji died he left behind a 'Five-Crop-Stone' which guaranteed the Chinese people a constant supply of food even in times of famine. He was buried on the Duguang Plain, a magnificent region of rolling hills and clear-flowing rivers where the land has always remained exceptionally fertile.

Gun Battles the Great Flood

KING YAO, the first mortal emperor of China, was judged an outstanding monarch by his subjects, one of the wisest, most devoted rulers that had ever risen to power. Humble and charitable almost to a fault, Yao never allowed himself luxuries of any kind. He wore sackcloth in summer and only a deerskin during the winter months and spent his entire life making sure that his people had everything they could possibly need to keep them satisfied. If the Emperor spotted a man without clothes, he would remove the shirt from his own back and hand it over to the unfortunate person. If his people were short of food, he blamed himself for their suffering. If they committed a crime, he was immediately understanding and took personal responsibility for the breach of law and order.

Yet in spite of Yao's remarkably warm and tolerant nature, he was destined to suffer repeated misfortunes during his lifetime and his reign was plagued by disasters of every kind, including drought, starvation, disease and floods. But perhaps the worst period of the Emperor's rule came immediately after he had rid the earth of the suns of Dijun, when he had just breathed a sigh of relief and had set to work restoring the shattered morale of his nation.

During these days immediately following the destruction of the suns, when chaos still ruled the earth and the world of mortals failed to communicate a peaceful and harmonious atmosphere, the High God, Tiandi, happened to peer down from the Heavens and began to shake his head disappointedly. Everywhere the God looked, he saw people living miserable and wretched lives. Flames had devoured the homes of many and now they squabbled bitterly among themselves, desperate to secure basic food and provisions even by the most dishonest means.

Now Tiandi was not a God renowned for his patience and he saw only that mankind had begun to tread a path of wickedness and corruption. And taking swift action, he sent the God of Water to the earth's surface, commanding him to create a flood that would punish mankind for its debauched behaviour. This flood, he announced, would last for a period of no less than twenty-two years, after which time, it was hoped that the world would be properly cleansed of all evil.

So day after day the rains beat down upon the soil, pulverizing the crops which remained, flooding the houses, swelling the rivers to bursting point, until eventually the whole of the earth resembled one vast ocean. Those who were fortunate enough to avoid drowning, floated on the treacherous waters in search of tall trees or high mountains where they might come to rest. But even if they managed to reach dry land, they were then forced to compete with the fiercest beasts of the earth for food, so that many were mercilessly devoured even as they celebrated the fact that they had been saved.

Only one God among the deities of the heavens appeared to feel any sympathy for the innocent people suffering such appalling misery on earth. The God's name was Gun and he was the grandson of the Yellow Emperor. Now Gun took it upon himself to plead with Tiandi to put an end to the heavy rains, but the High God would not listen to a word of what he had to say and so Gun was forced to continue roaming the heavens, powerless to help the drowning people.

One day, however, as the young God sat alone dejectedly, pondering the destruction caused by the ongoing flood, he was approached by two of his friends, an eagle and a tortoise. And seeing their companion so downcast, the two enquired what they might do to lift his spirits.

'The only thing that would make me happy right now,' Gun answered them, 'would be to stop this water pouring out of the skies. But I have no idea how I can bring this about.'

'It is not such a difficult task,' replied the eagle, 'if you feel you have courage enough to pay a visit to Tiandi's palace. For he is the keeper of the Shirang, a very precious substance which has exactly the same appearance of soil or clay. But if you can manage to drop some of this magical clay into the ocean, it will swell up to form a great dam that will hold back the flood waters.'

It remains a great mystery to this day precisely how Gun overcame every obstacle to retrieve a handful of the magic soil, but he managed this task successfully and immediately departed for the earth where he flung the clay into the ocean. Almost at once, mountains began to spring up from the water and soon great stretches of land appeared everywhere as the huge waves began to subside. Filled with gratitude, the gaunt-faced people crawled down from the trees and out of their remote hiding places and began to hail Gun as the saviour of mankind.

But the High God, Tiandi, was not at all pleased with Gun's theft of the Shirang and its subsequent healing effect on the world below. Enraged by this challenge to his authority, he ordered the God of Fire, Zhurong, to go down to earth to murder the God who had betrayed him. The two met in combat on Mount Yushan, but Gun was no match for Zhurong and the God of Fire quickly overcame his opponent, striking him down without difficulty after they had exchanged only a few blows. And now the flood waters burst through the dam Gun had created, crashing on to the dried-out earth which became completely submerged once again.

Gun had sacrificed his life on Mount Yushan for the good of mankind, but he had died without completing his work and so his spirit refused to rest within the shell of his dead body. For three years, his remains lay in a special vault in the mountains, watched over by the people who greatly mourned his loss. But in all this time, Gun's body showed no sign of decomposing, for a new life had begun to grow inside of him, waiting for the day when it would be mature enough to emerge.

After these three years had passed and Gun's body had still not wasted away, Tiandi grew very concerned, fearing that the dead God was being transformed into an evil spirit destined to plague him for the rest of his days. So Tiandi sent one of his most trusted officials down to earth to carve up Gun's remains, presenting him with a divine sword called the Wudao. But a fantastic thing occurred as soon as the official's blade had slashed open Gun's belly. For instead of the blood he had anticipated would emerge from the opening, a large and mighty golden dragon sprung forth in its place. This dragon was Yü, the son of Gun, who had inherited all the strength and courage of his father and who had entered the world in all his magnificent glory to complete Gun's unfinished work.

Yü Controls the Flood

THE APPEARANCE OF a great golden dragon in the skies, whose sole purpose it was to save mankind from destruction, encouraged the High God, Tiandi, to question whether or not the punishment he had meted out to the people below had been a little too severe. The mysterious creature was fiercely determined and persistent, he noticed, and to allow any further grievances between them was not the most prudent way forward. So Tiandi decided to yield to the dragon's wishes and put an end to the suffering on earth at long last.

Yü's mission so far had been an easy one. Tiandi not only ordered the God of Water to call a halt to the downpour, he also gave Yü enough Shirang to construct another great dam to hold back the flood waters. He sent the dragon Ying Long down to earth to assist him in repairing the widespread damage. Yü received this help gratefully and day and night channelled all his available energy into the task at hand.

Now all would have gone on smoothly, and the earth been restored to its original condition in little or no time, but for the God of Water, Gong Gong, who decided to cause as much trouble as possible for Yü. For it was Gong Gong who had originally created the flood and to see his great work undone by a mere boy-dragon was more than he could tolerate. No one had yet dared to disobey Yü's commands, but Gong Gong ignored every last one of them, entirely underestimating the dragon's strength and the powerful influence he exerted over his followers. And seeing that Gong Gong would not be reasoned with, Yü called together all the fairies, spirits and giants of the earth, so that not one remained to fight alongside Gong Gong. Then Yü challenged the God of Water to single combat, an encounter Gong Gong now wished he could avoid, for in no time, Yü had defeated him and skewered his ugly head upon his sword.

And after he had vanquished the God of Water, Yü went among the people handing them pieces of the magic clay so that they could decide for themselves where mountain ranges should appear and where stretches of land would flourish most. But it was not enough simply to rebuild the earth again, nor was the giant dam a permanent safeguard against flooding in the future. Yü realized that something more had to be done and so, dragging his great tail in the earth, he began to hollow out the soil, digging a long, tunnel-like structure through which the water could easily and swiftly flow, away from the land in the direction of the sea. Throughout the country, people followed his example and soon an entire network of shallow gullies began to appear, draining the surplus water from the plains. In this way, Yü brought the flood under control and created the great rivers of China that still flow eastwards towards the ocean to this very day.

The Marriage of Yü

YÜ HAD SPENT THIRTY YEARS on earth regulating the waters before it even occurred to him that he had earned a well-deserved rest and that perhaps the time had now arrived to make plans for his own future. Never in the past had he paused to consider the possibility that he might one day marry, but suddenly he felt lonely and in need of a wife who could love him and attend to him in old age. He had no idea how he might go about choosing a wife, however, and decided to put his trust in the Gods, waiting patiently for a sign from the divine powers above.

One morning, he observed a strange white fox with nine tails making its way towards him and he felt at once that the animal must be a heavenly messenger sent to help him in his quest. The fox approached and began to sing a strange little song which Yü listened to attentively, confident that its words would somehow enlighten him. The fox's song cheered him immensely and left him in little doubt that his search for a suitable wife was drawing to a close:

He who meets with the fox of nine tails
Will soon become king of the land.
He who weds the chief's daughter on Mount Tu
Will become a prosperous man.

Nu Jiao was reputed to be one of the most beautiful maidens in China and she dwelt in the distant valley of Tu on the summit of the great mountain. Ever since childhood, she had heard nothing but favourable reports of Yü and by now she was familiar with everything he had accomplished on earth. She had come to admire him from a distance as a God of legendary stature, and in her heart she had always entertained the hope that one day they would meet. And so when Yü appeared unexpectedly and asked for her hand in marriage, Nu Jiao could scarcely believe her good fortune and agreed at once to become his bride.

The two departed her father's kingdom and travelled southwards where they set up home and began a very happy married life together. It was not long before Nu Jiao became pregnant and the couple were overjoyed at the prospect of a son who would carry on his father's good work. For although the majority of the floods had been checked, the task of clearing the debris and ensuring that no similar disasters occurred in the future was still very much incomplete. And as the days passed by, the responsibility of overseeing more and more of this kind of work fell on Yü's experienced shoulders. Often he was forced to spend days away from home and occasionally he was away for several weeks at a time.

Now when the time was close at hand for Nu Jiao to deliver her child, Yü was unfortunately summoned to help restore the Huanyan Mountain which had begun to collapse and slide treacherously into the sea. And knowing that his wife would be anxious during his absence, Yü offered her the following words of comfort:

'If the task ahead were not so dangerous I would allow you to accompany me,' he told her. 'But I won't be very far away and I will take this drum with me and beat on it loudly when it is safe for you to join me.'

Nu Jiao was relieved to hear this and she bade her husband farewell and watched him disappear into the forest.

As soon as he was within range of the great mountain, Yü transformed himself into a giant black bear with mighty claws and powerful shoulders in preparation for the gruelling work ahead. Then, after he had tied the drum to a tree behind him, he stooped to the ground and tossed a boulder high into a crevice of the mountain where he could see it had originally broken loose. One after another he tossed the huge boulders in the same direction until almost all the gaps in the mountain had been filled in and the towering structure took on a more solid appearance again. But just as his work was coming to an end, Yü allowed one of the boulders to slip from his upraised arms and it slid over his shoulder, striking the drum that remained tied to the tree.

At once, Nu Jiao prepared a small parcel of food for her husband and set off in the direction of Huanyan Mountain. Arriving at the place where the drum dangled in the breeze, she looked around for Yü, but was confronted instead by a terrifying black bear. Screaming in fright, Nu Jiao ran as fast as her legs would carry her towards her home, pursued by Yü who failed to realize that he had not changed back into his human shape. The young woman ran onwards in panic and dread, faster and faster, until all colour had drained from her face and her muscles grew stiff from the chase. At last, she dropped down to the earth, exhausted and beaten, and within seconds she was transformed into a stone.

Stunned and horrified by what had happened, Yü called out to his wife: 'Give me my son, my only precious son.' Immediately, the stone burst open and a small baby tumbled on to the earth. Yü named the child Qi, meaning 'cracked stone', and the story of his unusual birth earned him great fame even before he had grown to manhood.

Other Gods

THE ORDINARY CHINESE PEOPLE seemed to have have had little difficulty amalgamating and absorbing a number of different religious beliefs, resulting in popular superstitions which convey the diverse influences of Confucianism, Taoism and Buddhism. Confucius was a pragmatic man, whose main concern was for the smooth running of the state where individuals took personal responsibility for the creation of a harmonious atmosphere on earth, reflecting that of the Heavens. Taoism argued that there was a natural order in the world determining the behaviour of all things and that even inanimate objects had an existence of their own. Buddhism contributed to society the concept of the transmigration of souls and introduced the notion of an Underworld, presided over by the gatekeeper, Yen Wang.

Overall, Chinese people believed that there was a great deal of communication between heaven and earth. It was widely believed that the Gods lived on earth in the capacity of divine officials, and returned to the heavens regularly to report on the progress of humanity. Even the most humble objects were reputed to possess a guardian spirit, while the elements were considered to be more important Gods, meriting sacrifices and ceremonial worship to keep them in a good temper.

The Kitchen God

THIS IMPORTANT DEITY is said to be a Taoist invention, a God entrusted with the power to punish and reward members of the family under his supervision. In the old days, every Chinese household created a temple for him in a small niche above the kitchen stove where an incense stick burned continuously. From this position, the Kitchen God kept an account of how well the family behaved, compiling his annual report for the attention of the Supreme Being of the Heavens. At New Year, he was destined to return to the firmament to present his report and he was sent on his way with a great deal of ceremony. Firecrackers were lit and a lavish meal prepared to improve his mood. His mouth was smeared with honey, so that only 'sweet' words would escape his lips when he stood before the Supreme Being.

The Door Gods

IT WAS THE IMPORTANT TASK of these Gods to ward off undesirable visitors and evil spirits from Chinese households and often, pictures of ferocious warriors were pinned on either side of the door for this purpose. These pictures represented two war ministers of outstanding ability from the Tang dynasty who were deified after death to become the Door Gods.

The story unfolds that one day the Emperor fell gravely ill with a high fever and during the night he imagined he heard demons in the passageway attempting to gain entry to his chamber. The Emperor grew increasingly delirious and everyone became concerned for his health. Eventually it was decided that two of his finest warriors, Chin Shu-pao and Hu Ching-te, should stand guard overnight outside his door.

For the first time in many weeks, the Emperor slept soundly and peacefully. Next morning, he thanked his men heartily and from that time onwards his health continued to improve. Soon he felt well enough to release his men from their nocturnal duty, but he ordered them to have their portraits painted, looking as fierce as they possibly could, so that he could paste these on his bedroom door to keep evil spirits away in the future.

The Gods of the Elements

THE NUMBER OF SPIRITS and guardians associated with the elements in Chinese legend is vast. Each of these elements is managed by a Ministry in the Heavens, composed of a large number of celestial officials. Members of these ministries are the most powerful of the guardian spirits, since they control the unpredictable forces on earth, such as fire, thunder, lightning, wind and rain.

Natural disasters caused by these forces occur again and again in Chinese mythology. It is always crucial in these stories to maintain a favourable relationship with the God in charge. The Ministry of Thunder, to take but one example, has a complicated infrastructure. It is presided over by the Ancestor of Thunder, Lei Kung, followed by other officials in order of seniority: Lei Kung, the Duke of Thunder, Tien Mu, the mother of Lightning, Feng Po, the Count of Wind, Yü Shih, the Master of Rain and a string of other lesser Gods.

The Duke of Thunder, Lei Kung, is represented in Chinese legend as an ugly black creature with clawed feet and a monkey's head. In his hand he holds a chisel which he uses to beat on a drum, producing the ferocious noise of thunder. A popular story about him recalls how one day, a youth who had been chopping firewood high in the mountains noticed a thunderstorm approaching and took shelter under a large tree. Suddenly a great fork of lightning struck the tree, trapping the Duke of Thunder underneath its great weight as it fell to the ground. Lei Kung begged the youth to release him, promising to reward him handsomely, until finally the terrified youth agreed to his request. In return for his help, the Duke of Thunder presented him with a book which would teach him to conjure up storms and tempests.

'When you need rain,' the God told him, 'call on one of my four brothers and they will come to your aid. But don't call on me unless it is really necessary because my mood is often unpredictable.'

After he had said this, Lei Kung disappeared and the youth headed back to his village.

Within no time he had become a popular figure among the people who regularly took the opportunity to celebrate his great powers in the local inn. One night, however, the youth became so drunk and disorderly he was arrested and carried off by the police. The following morning, as he was led to court, he called upon the God of Thunder to save him from imprisonment. The God responded immediately and thundered through the air so loudly that the windows of the courthouse were shattered by the noise. Cowering to the floor in terror, the magistrate ordered the youth to be released and dismissed him from the court without imposing any sentence.

From this day onwards, the youth used his power to save many people. For whenever he saw that there was danger of the land becoming dried out, he ordered a great storm to appear overhead and the rains to saturate the soil below.

The Goddess of Mercy

THE MOST POPULAR GODDESS of the Buddhist faith is the beautiful Kuan Yin, a deity originally represented as a man, an image completely eclipsed by that of a madonna figure with child in her arms after the mid-seventh century. According to the ancient legend, Kuan Yin was about to enter Heaven when she heard a cry of anguish from the earth beneath her and could not prevent herself from investigating its source. Hence her name translates as 'one who hears the cries of the world'.

Kuan Yin is the patron saint of Tibetan Buddhism, the patron Goddess of mothers, the guardian of the storm-tossed fisherman and the overall protector of mankind. If, in the midst of a fire she is called upon, the fire ceases to burn. If during a battle her name is called, the sword and spear of the enemy prove harmless. If prone to evil thoughts, the heart is immediately purified when she is summoned. All over China this Goddess is revered and her image appears not only in temples of worship but in households and other public places.

The Eight Immortals

DURING THE MONGOL or Yüan Dynasty in the thirteenth century, a group of Taoist deities who were known as the 'Eight Immortals', or Pa Hsien, became the new focus of a whole catalogue of Chinese legends, achieving a rapid and widespread popularity. Partly historical and partly mythical figures, [*Please refer to the Glossary for historical dates where relevant.*] the Eight Immortals were said to share a home together in the Eastern Paradise on the isles of Peng-lai. Characters similar to these Gods were celebrated in earlier Taoist tales, but now for the first time they appeared as a group, whose different personalities were intended to represent the whole spectrum of society ranging from young to old, rich to poor, whether male or female in gender. The Chinese were very fond of these characters and their numerous eccentricities, and increasingly they became a favourite subject for artists. They appeared together frequently in paintings, or on pottery and elaborate tapestries, or as statuettes and larger sculptures.

The most famous of the Eight Immortals was known as Li Tiehkuai, a name which means 'Li of the Iron Crutch'. Among the group, he was perhaps the most gifted disciple of Taoism, an immortal reputed to have acquired his great wisdom from the spirit of Lao Tzu himself. After the course of instruction had been completed, it was said that the Great Master summoned Li to the Heavens to assess his ability more closely. Li willingly answered the call and his soul left his body and journeyed upwards towards the firmament.

But before Li departed the earth, he placed one of his own pupils, known as Lang Ling, in charge of his body, ordering him to guard it well for a period of seven days until he returned to reclaim it. After only six days had elapsed, however, the student was called to his mother's deathbed, and because he was reluctant to leave the body exposed to scavengers, he decided to cremate it before he departed.

When Li returned to earth he found only a mound of ashes where his body once lay and his spirit was forced to wander about in search of another host. Fortunately, however, a beggar had just died of starvation in the nearby woods, and Li entered the body without any further delay. But as soon as he had done so, he began to regret his decision, for the deceased beggar had only had one leg, his head was ugly and pointed, and the hair around his face was long and dishevelled. Li wished to leave the vile body he had entered, but Lao Tzu advised him that this would not be wise. So instead, the Great Master of the Heavens sent him a gold band to keep his matted hair in place and an iron crutch to help him move about more easily.

And one of the first benevolent acts Li performed in this human body was to visit the home of his negligent pupil, where he poured the contents of his gourd into the mouth of Lang Ling's dead mother, bringing her back to life instantly. For two hundred years Li roamed the earth in this way, converting people to Taoism and healing them with his medicine. He represents the sick and his emblems are an iron stick and a gourd.

The second of the Eight Immortals was called Han Chung-li, a powerful military figure, who in his younger days rose to become Marshal of the Empire. After Han became converted to Taoism, however, he chose to live the life of a hermit in Yang-chio Mountain. Here, he studied the ways of immortality and stored whatever secrets he discovered in a large jade casket within his cave. Some say that Han Chung-li was highly skilled in the ways of alchemy and that during the great famine he changed base metals, such as copper and pewter, into silver which he then distributed to the poor, saving thousands of lives. A fan of feathers, or the peach of immortality are his emblems, and he is associated with military affairs.

During a visit to Yang-chio Mountain, Lü Tung-pin, the son of a high-ranking government official and a clever young scholar, met with Han Chung-li, who invited him into his cave to share some rice wine with him. Tired from his journey, Lü Tung-pin readily accepted the invitation, but as soon as he tasted the wine he fell into a deep sleep. And while he slept, he had an unpleasant dream which altered the course of his life.

He dreamt that he had married well, fathered several healthy children, and that he had risen to a position of great prominence in his work before his fiftieth year. After this time, he looked forward to a peaceful retirement, but for some reason, he was exiled in disgrace and his family put to death for his misdemeanours. For the rest of his days, he was condemned to a futile and lonely existence from which he could find no escape. Lü awoke from his dream with a start and began to interpret its meaning. At length, he became convinced of the vanity of worldly dignities and begged Han Chung-li to accept him as a disciple in order that he might train to be one of the Eight Immortals. He is commonly associated with scholars and is always portrayed carrying a sword.

The fourth Immortal, Chang-kuo Lao, was also a famous hermit who lived in the Heng Chou Mountains. He usually appeared seated on a white donkey which he was able to fold up like a piece of paper and which would resume its former shape once he had sprinkled water on it. Chang-kuo Lao claimed that he was a descendant of Emperor Yao and his special magical powers enabled him to bring fertility to young couples. His emblem is a white mule, or a phoenix feather, and he represents the old.

Tsao Kuo-chiu, who is associated with the nobility and whose emblem is a scribe's tablet, became an Immortal after he renounced the wickedness of his worldly life. Tsao was the eldest of two brothers whose sister was married to the Emperor, Jen Tsung. One day the Empress invited a young graduate and his wife to dine with her at the palace, but disaster struck when the younger brother, Ching-chih, who was notorious for his bad behaviour, allowed himself to become besotted by the lady and decided to murder her husband. After he had committed this crime, the soul of the husband demanded justice from the God Pao and Ching-chih was immediately thrown in prison. Knowing his brother would inevitably face the death penalty, Tsao Kuo-chiu encouraged him to kill the graduate's wife so that no evidence of his crime would remain. But the wife escaped to inform Pao of this second attack and Tsao Kuo-chiu was also thrown in prison to face execution.

Eventually, the Empress intervened on her brothers' behalf and begged the Emperor to grant them both an amnesty. As soon as this happened, Tsao was so grateful he decided to abandon his life of luxury and to live by the doctrines of Taoism. For the remainder of his days Tsao Kuo-chiu lived as a hermit devoting himself to the practice of perfection.

The sixth and seventh Immortals were very young men. Han Hsiang Tzu was the grand-nephew of one of the greatest poets of the Tang Dynasty, and from an early age he was schooled by his uncle in the ways of poetry until eventually his ability far surpassed that of the older man.

Shortly afterwards, the youth became a disciple of Lü Tung-pin and at the end of his instruction he was required to climb to the top of the Immortalizing Peach Tree. As he did so, he lost his balance and fell dead to the ground. Miraculously, however, he came to life once more, for he had attained the gift of immortality during the descent. Han Hsiang Tzu is always depicted carrying either a flower-basket or a peach and he represents cultured society.

Lan Tsai-ho, a strolling actor and singer of about sixteen years of age, dressed himself in a tattered blue gown and a black wooden belt, and always wore only one shoe. His life was spent urging people to convert to Taoism and he denounced the material comforts of mortals. When given money, he either strung it on a cord and used it as an instrument to beat time as he sang, or scattered it to the ground for the poor to pick up. His emblem is a lute and he represents the poor.

Only one of the Eight Immortals, Ho Hsien-Ku was a woman and she was always depicted holding a lotus flower or the peach of immortality, presented to her by Lü Tung-pin after she had lost her way through the mountains. While still very young, she chose to live a simple life of celibacy and prayer on Yünmu Ling Mountain. Here, she found a stone known as the Yünmu Shih, 'mother-of-pearl', and was told in a dream to powder the stone and to swallow its dust should she wish to become an Immortal. Ho

Hsien-Ku followed this instruction and spent the rest of her days floating around the mountains, picking wild berries which she carried to her mother. Her emblem is a lotus and she represents young, unmarried girls.

The Crane Maiden and Other Fables

THE TALES THAT FOLLOW demonstrate the mixture of beliefs and religions that were a part of ancient China. In many of the stories the immortal Gods and human beings interact, not exactly as equals, but not within the rigid hierarchy one might expect; it is perfectly feasible, even customary, for the daughter of a God to marry a human, and for such marriages to be successful. Often, we are also transported into a world of spirits and demons, capable of inhabiting animals with malicious intent. Similarly, humans can become transformed into animals or birds, either as a punishment, through grief, or through the will of the Gods.

The image which we perhaps associate most with Chinese myth is that of the dragon. The Chinese dragon breathes cloud, not fire, and is a creature of awesome beauty. Although quick to anger and terrible in its fury, the dragon was mostly a force for good, representing the male principle, the yang, just as the phoenix represents the female, the yin. Similarly, the monkey represents the irrepressibility of the human spirit, as well as its tendency to mischief and evil.

Most of the tales told here do not have such a formal meaning. Some may try to explain the creation of particular stars, others how various animals came into being; they might be parables illustrating foolishness, or steadfastness, or wisdom. But above all they are for entertainment and enjoyment, telling of a mythical time when Gods and dragons walked the earth, and when human destiny was determined by magic spirits.

How Monkey Became Immortal

MONKEY HAD BEEN BORN from a stone egg on top of the Mountain of Fruit and Flowers, and had received many special powers from the stone. He had led his tribe of monkeys to a safe home behind a waterfall on top of the mountain of his birth, and become their beloved king, ruling wisely for hundreds of years. Their way of life was extremely pleasant, they had all they needed to eat and drink, and were safe from enemies. Yet Monkey was not content.

'However happy we are here,' he told his followers, 'we still have Death to fear. One day Lord Yama of the Underworld will send for us, and we will have to obey. I have heard of Lord Buddha and the other Gods who cannot die, and I intend to find them and learn the secret of immortality.'

Monkey set off for the world of men, and soon learned the whereabouts of a holy man, Master Subhodi, who knew the way to eternal life. Subhodi knew in advance of Monkey's coming, and realizing this was no ordinary animal, accepted him as a pupil, and gave him a new name: Sun, the Enlightened One. Monkey spent twenty years with Master Subhodi, learning of the road to eternal life, and many other skills. He learned to change his shape as he pleased, and to travel thousands of miles in a single leap. And armed with this knowledge he returned to his home.

There he found that a demon had taken control of his tribe, and although he conquered the demon, Monkey realized he needed a proper weapon for the future. He seized upon the iron pillar of the Dragon King of the Eastern Sea.This could be changed at will, from an eight-foot staff for fighting, to a tiny needle that Monkey could carry behind his ear, and he kept it with him at all times.

One day two men came for him with a warrant of death from Lord Yama, and tried to drag his soul to the Underworld. Monkey cried out in vain that he knew the way to eternal life, for the men only tied him more tightly. With a desperate struggle, Monkey freed himself, and taking the needle from behind his ear, turned it into a staff, and knocked the men to the ground. Then, incensed with rage, Monkey charged into the Underworld itself, beating anyone in his way with his cudgel.

'Bring out the register of the dead,' he demanded. The book was brought to him by the terrified judges, whereupon he found the page with his name on, and the names of all his tribe, and ripped it from the register, tearing it into a thousand pieces. 'Now I am free from your power,' he cried, and charged back out of the Underworld to his own land. The other monkeys assured him he had been asleep, and must have dreamt all this, but Monkey knew in his heart that it had really happened, and that death held no more sway over them.

Appalled by the trouble Monkey was causing, the Jade Emperor, the most powerful God, offered him high office in Heaven, so that the Gods could secretly keep him under their control. Monkey gladly accepted and was made Master of the Heavenly Stables, but he soon realized this was a derisory post, created only to tame him, and he stormed out of Heaven and returned home. The Jade Emperor sent guards to recapture him, but Monkey defeated them, and the Gods sent to seize him. Eventually the Jade Emperor appeased him by offering him a magnificent palace in Heaven, and a proper position as Superintendent of the Heavenly Peach Garden.

Now Monkey knew that the peaches in this garden, which ripened only once every six thousand years, conferred immortality on anyone who ate them, and so he ignored the order not to touch any of them, and devoured a huge number. Unstoppable now, and furious too that he had not been invited to the great Feast of Peaches, given to the Gods by Wang-Mu, Goddess of the Immortals, Monkey was intent on revenge. So, when the preparations were complete, he put all the servants under a spell, and ate and drank all the food and wine prepared for the guests. Dizzy with drink, Monkey staggered into the deserted palace of Lao Chun, where he stumbled across the five gourds in which were kept the seeds of immortality, and, ever inquisitive, he ate them all. Assured doubly of immortality, Monkey returned home.

The Jade Emperor and all the Gods and Goddesses were furious with monkey, but none could defeat him in battle. Until, that is, the Jade Emperor's nephew, Erlang, aided by Lao Chun and the celestial dog Tien-Kou, managed to chain him, and bring him, securely bound, back to Heaven. Monkey was sentenced to death, and placed in Lao Chun's furnace, in which the seeds of immortality were made. But Monkey was now so powerful that he burst free from the crucible, stronger than ever, and proclaimed himself ruler of the Universe.

At this, Buddha appeared, and demanded of Monkey what powers he had that entitled him to make such a claim. Monkey replied that he was immortal, invulnerable, that he could change shape at will, and could travel thousands of miles in a single leap. Buddha smiled, and taking Monkey in the palm of his hand, said, 'If you can jump from out of my hand, I will make you ruler of the Universe and all it contains.'

Monkey laughed at this, and in two mighty leaps found himself opposite the five red pillars that mark the edge of the Universe. Delighted, he wrote his name on one of them as proof that he had been there, and returned to the Buddha.

'I have been to the ends of the Universe in two bounds,' he bragged. 'And now I seek my reward.'

'The ends of the Universe?' asked the Buddha, 'You never left the palm of my hand.' And Buddha showed Monkey his fingers, on one of which was Monkey's name in his own writing. Monkey realized the five pillars were merely the five fingers of the Buddha, and that the whole Universe was contained in his hand, and that he could never be defeated. Afraid for the first time in his life, Monkey tried to run away, but Buddha closed his hand over him, and changing his fingers into the five elements of earth, air, fire, water and wood, created a great mountain in which he imprisoned Monkey.

'There you must stay until you have fully repented and are free of your sins,' Buddha told him. 'At that time someone will come and intercede for you, and then you may be free.' And crushed under the mountains the dejected Monkey was forced to stay.

The Pair of Fools

ONCE, A POOR VILLAGER called Lin unexpectedly found ten pieces of silver, riches beyond anything he had ever owned before. After his first flush of exhilaration at finding such wealth, Lin realized that he must hide the money, as he worked in the fields all day, and it could so easily be stolen from him. He looked despairingly around his sparse, mud-walled hut for a hiding place for the silver, but there was no furniture, no secret cupboards, nothing. Then suddenly he thought of the wall itself, and pausing only

to check through the door that no one was coming, he hollowed out a cavity in the mud wall, and poured the silver pieces into it. He quickly covered the hole with fresh mud, and guarded his door against all visitors until the mud had dried and there was no sign of the hiding place.

However, the next morning, before he left for the fields, Lin had another attack of nerves. If someone did come into his hut looking for money, there was only one place it could be hidden. There was no furniture, no secret cupboards, only the wall itself. It would be the first place any thief would look.Then Lin had a flash of inspiration, and picking up his brush and ink, he wrote on the wall: 'There are no silver pieces hidden in this wall.' Reassured, he went off to the fields for his day's work.

A few hours later Lin's neighbour, Wan, came to look for him. Seeing no sign of Lin, his eyes were drawn to the writing on the wall, and he chuckled to himself: 'Of course there are no silver pieces hidden in the wall, why should there be?' Then a second thought struck him: Why would Lin say there weren't any, unless there actually were?

Pausing only to check through the door that no one was coming, Wan attacked the wall with vigour and found the ten pieces of silver almost immediately. Delighted, he ran home with them to his own hut, where he was struck by an attack of nerves. What if they searched his hut and found the money, and he was taken before the Judge and tortured until he confessed, and then sentenced to death? He must stop anyone from suspecting his guilt. Suddenly, Wan had a flash of inspiration, and picking up his brush and ink, he wrote on the front of his door: 'I, Wan, an honest man, did not steal the ten silver pieces from the hole in the wall of Lin's hut.'

The Silkworm

MANY CENTURIES AGO a certain man was called up to fight for his Emperor, in the war that was raging on the Chinese borders far, far from his home. The man was distraught at leaving his wife and family, but, being a loyal subject he promptly went away to fulfil his duty. As he left, he instructed the family to look after their farm as best they could, and not to worry unduly as to his fate in the battles that were to come, as all life is in the hands of the Gods.

Try though they might to obey his parting instructions, the family missed him terribly, none more so than his daughter. In her loneliness, the young girl took solace in tending the family's horse, a creature that had been her father's for many years, and one that he loved dearly. Every day she would tenderly groom its fine coat, brush its silky mane, and make sure it had clean hay and enough oats to eat, talking to it all the while about how much she missed her father, and how she prayed nightly for his return. However, what little news reached them from the borders became more and more alarming, and the family began to doubt in their hearts if they would ever see their husband and father again.

One day, the daughter was in the stable tending the old horse and thinking of her father, barely able to hold back her tears in her fear for his safety. 'If only you could gallop from here to the wars and rescue him from his peril,' she murmured. 'If anyone could do that, I swear that I would gladly marry him at once, and serve him joyfully all my days, whatever his state or situation in life.'

Immediately the horse reared up violently, and with a loud whinny, tore at the leash that held him, breaking it in two, although it was made of the strongest leather. With a mighty kick of its powerful front legs, it splintered the stable door and galloped across the courtyard and out of sight before the startled girl could stop it, or even call out to the servants. When it became clear that the horse was not going to return, she made her way sadly to the house to tell of its disappearance, not mentioning the oath she had sworn in front of the animal.

Many days later, the runaway horse reached the Chinese borders, and despite the confusion and destruction caused by the war, managed to find its owner in the camp where he was billeted. The man was astonished to see his old horse, and even more surprised when he could find no message from his family on the animal. Immediately, he feared the worst, and became convinced that some disaster had befallen them, and although he was a brave and true subject, his fears for his family overcame his loyalty.

He secretly saddled up the horse, and under cover of darkness he eluded the guards and galloped as fast as possible back to his homeland, and to his farm.

His family were amazed and delighted to find him home again; tears of joy rolled down their cheeks seeing him alive and unharmed by the horrors of war. Only his daughter seemed less than overwhelmed by his return, and avoided his gaze whenever he looked at her, and answered his questions briefly, without emotion. The man was surprised to find nothing amiss in the household, after all his fears and misgivings, but presumed that the horse had come to fetch him out of devotion, and an understanding that his family missed him so much. In gratitude he lavished attention on the faithful beast, gave it the best oats and hay and the finest stable, and groomed it himself. The horse, however, refused all food and kindness, and just moped in the corner of its stall, making no sound at all. Only when the daughter of the house came near, which she did as rarely as possible, did the animal seem to come alive; then it would rear up, and whinny and froth at the mouth, so that it took several servants to restrain it.

The father became increasingly worried about the horse, which was becoming distressingly thin. Noticing the effect his daughter had on the beast, he asked her one day if she knew why the animal was behaving in so peculiar a fashion. At first the young girl lied, and said she has no idea of the cause of the problem, but eventually, because she was an honest girl, she told her father of the promise she had made in the stable to marry whomsoever would return her father to her, whatever his state or station in life. The father became extremely angry at her lack of sense and modesty, and confined the girl to her room in the house. He forbade her to so much as peep out of the door if the horse was in the courtyard, so as not to disturb it further; for although the man was very grateful to the horse for its years of service, and its intelligence in finding him in the front lines, he still could not imagine allowing a dumb animal to marry his daughter.

The horse continued to pine and mope, and deprived of even a glimpse of the girl, wasted away more and more, day by day. Eventually the father realized there was only one thing he could do, and sadly he took up his bow and arrow and shot the horse to put it out of its misery. The animal gave a piteous whimper, and died, still looking at the house in which it knew the daughter was imprisoned. The man took off the horse's skin, and placed it in the sun to dry, and then went to tell his daughter what he had been compelled to do. She was thrilled to hear that her problem was solved, and that she would not have to marry a horse, and ran into the courtyard to greet the sun for the first time in days. As she passed the dead creature's hide, it suddenly lifted as if on a gust of wind, and wrapped itself tightly around the girl's shoulders, and then her whole body, and started to spin her round like a top. Whirling faster and faster, the girl cried out, but no one could stop her, and she disappeared out of the farm and into the countryside, carried away on the wind, her cries growing ever fainter.

Appalled, her father ran after the whirlwind his daughter had become, and followed it for many days, although it appeared to get smaller and smaller the further it travelled, until it was barely visible to the naked eye. At last, the whirlwind stopped by a mulberry bush, and breathlessly, the exhausted father rushed up to it. There, on a mulberry bough, he found a small worm feeding on the leaf, and seeing that this was all that was left of his daughter, he took it home, grieving in his heart. He and his wife cared for the worm with tenderness, feeding it thick mulberry leaves every day, and after a week the worm produced a fine thread that glistened and shone, and was soft and cool when woven, and more beautiful to look at than any cloth they had ever seen. They called it silk, and bred more and more of the worms, which became famous throughout the land. And in time silk became one of China's most acclaimed and desired products, and many people profited through its sale, so that in years to come silk weavers throughout the country worshipped thankfully the silkworm girl who had given them such a great treasure through her love for her father.

The Crane Maiden

TIAN KUNLUN WAS A BACHELOR, who lived alone with his elderly mother whose one desire in life was to see her son happily married before she died. It was a desire that Tian keenly shared, but they had little money, and he had little chance of finding a suitable bride.

Not far from their home was a beautiful pool of clear, fresh water, shaded by willows, and fringed with rushes. One day, as Tian was on his way to the fields, he heard the sound of girls' laughter coming from the pool, and creeping as silently as he could through the rushes, Tian edged nearer to the water to see whose voice sounded so sweet. Before him he saw three of the most lovely maidens he had ever set eyes on, playing and splashing in the pool, their clothes piled on the bank near him. Entranced, Tian watched for a while, gazing at their beauty, when suddenly he sneezed loudly. Instantly the three young women turned into three white cranes, and beating their fine wings, they flew from the water. Two of them swooped and picked up their clothes and soared away, up and up into the clear sky, but the third was not fast enough, and Tian managed to reach her clothes before her. The bird circled him for a moment, and then returned to the water, again taking on the form of the beautiful maiden Tian had seen first. Bashfully, she begged him to return her clothes, but first he insisted on knowing who she was.

'I am a daughter of the High God, and those were two of my sisters,' the girl answered. 'Our father gave us the clothes to pass between Heaven and earth; without them I cannot return to our home.' Again the girl pleaded with Tian to return them, adding, 'If you do give them back I shall gladly become your wife.'

Tian accepted the offer, thinking what a perfect wife the daughter of the High God would make any man, but he feared that if he returned her clothes, she would simply fly away, and he would never see her again. Instead, he gave her his own coat and leggings, and carried her clothes home with him; the crane maiden unwillingly following behind him.

Tian's mother was thrilled that her son was to marry such a beautiful and high-born girl, and their wedding feast was long and lavish, all their friends and neighbours sharing in their joy. The couple lived together, and learned to love each other, and after a time they had a son, whom they called Tian Zhang, and on whom they both doted.

Some years later, Tian was called away to fight in the wars on the borders of China, many many miles from his home. Before he left, he called his mother to him and showed her his wife's celestial clothes and begged her to keep them well hidden, so that she could never put them on and fly away to Heaven. She promised she would, and found a safe hiding place. Tian then said a tearful farewell to his wife and son, and set off for the wars.

After his departure, the young wife asked her mother-in-law every day for a look at her old clothes, just one quick look.

'If you will let me see them only the once I shall be happy,' she told the old lady. Seeing how desperate the girl was to see them, and fearing for her health if she continued as she was, the woman relented. She fetched the clothes from the bottom of a large chest in her own room, and showed them to her. The crane maiden wept with joy to see them and hugged them to her breast. Then, in a flash, she threw off her human clothes, put on the celestial garments, and, instantly was transformed into a beautiful white crane. Then she flew out the window before the old lady could stop her, up, up into the clear sky.

When Tian returned from the wars, his mother told him the news of the crane maiden's flight, but both knew that there was nothing they could do to bring her back. Tian readily forgave his mother, but his little son was inconsolable, always crying out her name, and looking longingly out of the window, hoping she would return. He wandered the fields looking for her, weeping, and would accept no comfort from his father or grandmother. One day his cries were heard by a wise old man who sat beneath a willow, and who knew the cause of the boy's grief.

'Go to the pool near your home,' he told the child, 'and you will see three ladies all dressed in white; the one that ignores you will be your mother.'

Tian Zhang did as he was told, and sure enough, there were three girls all in white silk, as the wise man had said. There was the crane maiden, who had so missed her little son, that she had begged her sisters to accompany her back to earth to see that he was happy and well cared for, and to look once more at his face. Tian Zhang boldly walked up to the women, and two of them cried out, 'Sister, here is your child to see you,' but the crane maiden looked away, her eyes wet with tears of guilt and joy intermingled. The boy then knew that this was his mother, and ran to her, and seeing this, the girl broke down and took him in her arms, embracing him as if she would never let him go, weeping, and crying, 'My son, my son.'

After some time, one of the sisters said, 'Sister, it is time for us to go. If you cannot bear to be parted from the child, we will take him back to Heaven with us.'

Between them they lifted the child and flew up, up into the clear sky, all the way to the palace of the High God. He was delighted his daughter was no longer unhappy, and also greatly taken with his grandson, whom he taught personally, telling him of all the things of Heaven and earth. The child was quick to learn, and after a few days the High God gave him eight books, and sent him back to earth with these words: 'Study well, my son, for all knowledge is in these, and you may use them to give great benefit to the earth.'

So Tian Zhang returned to earth, where he found that not a few days, but twenty years had passed on earth, and that he was a young man. He tried to find his earthly family, but his grandmother had died, and his father left for the mountains of the West in grief for having lost mother, wife and child. So Tian Zhang devoted his life to studying the eight books, and armed with the knowledge the High God had given him, he became a renowned scholar and judge. He was granted a high place at the Emperor's court, and was famed throughout the land for his wisdom and his desire to help mankind.

And thousands of miles away, in the mountains of the West, the aged Tian heard of his son's fame, and was content.

The Cuckoo

THERE WAS ONCE A GOD called Wang, who lived in Heaven, but whose love for the earth and its people was so great that he used to visit it regularly, using his powers to help struggling humanity, and to right wrongs. On one such visit he met a woman, like him an immortal, who had been forced from her original home at the bottom of a deep well, and was now living in the kingdom of Shu, which we would now call Sichuan. The two immortals fell instantly in love with each other, and were soon married; Wang left his home in Heaven and came to live in Shu with his new bride, where they reigned together as king and queen.

Wang and his wife were excellent rulers, kind and caring. Wang taught the farmers how to get the most from their land, which crops would grow best, and how to observe the seasons, so that soon the whole kingdom prospered. Amid all this peace and happiness, only one thing still troubled Wang, the one thing over which he had no power to help his people. Every year the mighty Yangtze river would flood, breaking its banks and destroying vast tracts of farming land, sweeping across all before it, crops, livestock, and people alike. Try as he might, with all the powers of an immortal, Wang could do nothing to control this force of nature, and he bitterly grieved over his impotence.

One day a messenger came to Wang's palace to report a miracle: a corpse had been found floating in the great Yangtze, but floating upstream against the current. Moreover, as soon as the body had been pulled out of the river, it had revived and asked to see the king. Amazed at this report, Wang had the stranger brought before him, and asked him his story. The man said that he came from Chu, several thousand miles downstream from where they now stood, and that he had tripped over a log and fallen into the river. He was unable to explain why he had drifted upstream, but he impressed Wang enormously with his knowledge and understanding of the river and its ways, and he talked of the methods they used in Chu to control the floods, and the damage they could cause. Wang immediately asked the stranger if he could help with their problem, and when the man agreed to try, Wang made him Minister of the River, and accorded him much honour at court.

Not many weeks had passed before the river came into flood again, and the new Minister journeyed far along its banks to try and determine the cause. It did not take him long to find his answer: in the higher country the river ran through a series of ravines too narrow to take the flood waters caused by melting snow on the mountain peaks. This made the river break its banks. He instructed engineers to bore drainage channels through the rock from the main channel, allowing the water to disperse safely, and so preventing flooding further downstream in the valuable farmlands.

Wang was so ashamed that he had not thought of this himself, and so impressed by the stranger's abilities as an engineer, that he decided the stranger would make a better king for his people than himself. Accordingly, he gave over the kingship to the Minister and secretly left the court to go and live in isolation in the mountains of the West. He had been there a very short time, however, when rumours reached him of a disturbing nature. It was said that while the man from Chu had been in the mountains, Wang had seduced his wife, who had come to court only recently, and that the stranger, on his return, had found the two of them together. The rumour told that Wang had handed over the throne in shame and guilt, in return for the man's silence, and had been banished to a life in exile.

So stricken was Wang on hearing this vile and ungrateful gossip, and so regretful of his act of generosity in handing over the throne for the good of his people, that he wasted away in his mountain retreat, and died broken-hearted. The Gods turned his spirit into a cuckoo, whose mournful cry in Chinese calls out 'Better return', reminding people for all time, and especially in the Spring at the time of planting, of Wang's grief at leaving his people, and the land of Shu that he loved.

The Wooden Bridge Inn

THERE WAS ONCE a travelling merchant called Chao, whose trade took him all over China, and who prided himself on knowing all the roads, and all the inns on those roads, throughout the country. One day, however, finding himself in a strange district with his donkey tiring by the mile, he had to admit his ignorance of the area, so he stopped to ask a farmer where he could find accommodation for the night, and, if possible, purchase a new donkey as he had much further to travel.

The farmer replied that travellers always stayed at the Wooden Bridge Inn, run by a woman called Third Lady.

'And does this Third Lady sell donkeys?' Chao asked the man. 'Oh, yes. Best donkeys in the district,' the man replied. But when Chao asked where these fine animals came from, the man looked uneasy, and would not look Chao in the eye. 'Better ask her that,' he said, 'I have absolutely no idea, I'm afraid.' And without further comment, he returned quickly to his field, and did not look back.

Chao walked his weary animal the mile or so to the Wooden Bridge Inn, which was an inviting and comfortable building, presided over by a young woman who greeted Chao warmly. She introduced herself as Third Lady, and invited him to join the six or seven other guests, who were already drinking cups of wine. Chao stabled his donkey around the back, and joined the others for a delicious dinner of fish, vegetables and rice. While chatting to the other merchants, he admired their capable hostess's ability to make them all welcome, plying her guests with wine until they were quite drunk. Chao, however, was not a drinking man, and left the wine alone, preferring to drink only tea.

As midnight approached, the other guests soon fell into a drunken slumber, and Chao was given a clean and comfortable bed alongside a rush partition, where he lay for a while, musing on his fortune in finding such a pleasant resting place. Just as he was about to drift into sleep, he was startled by a low rumble on the other side of the partition, and fearful that someone might be doing harm to his hostess, he peered through a chink in the rush matting. There was Third Lady, alone, dragging a large trunk across the floor of her room, and Chao watched as she knelt before it, opened the lid, and took out a little wooden man. Intrigued, Chao watched as she next brought out a little wooden ox and a little wooden plough, hitched them together and set the man behind the plough. Then, from a small phial, she sprinkled water over the figures, and to Chao's utter amazement, they began to move, and in no time at all had ploughed up the floor of the room.

Third Lady then gave a tiny seed basket to the little man, who proceeded to sow the field that the floor had become, and immediately green shoots of wheat sprang from the soil, ripened, and were harvested by the tiny farmer, who gave the crop to his mistress. Third Lady quickly ground the corn into flour, and under Chao's astonished gaze, made cakes from it, which she put into the oven to bake. She returned the now lifeless figures to the trunk, and pushed it back to the corner of the room. She then retired for the night, leaving Chao to lie alone in the darkness, wondering at what he had witnessed.

When dawn broke, the guests arose, and Third Lady courteously offered them a breakfast of tea and freshly baked wheat cakes. Chao thanked her profusely, but was determined not to eat his cake, hiding it up his sleeve instead. He then went to fetch his donkey from the stable, ready for the next stage of his journey. As he left the Wooden Bridge Inn, he happened to glance through the door, and he froze in astonishment. The other guests, finishing off their cakes, all suddenly became frenzied, their clothes turning into rough animal hair, their ears growing absurdly long, their voices changing to a grating bray. Within minutes the room was filled with six or seven donkeys, which Third Lady promptly herded with a stick out of the back of the Inn, towards the stables.

Chao hurried his donkey on its way, grateful to have escaped such a terrible fate; he went on to the capital where his business was, saying not a word to anyone about what he had seen. And when he had concluded his trade, he prepared to return home, stopping off only to buy some wheat cakes identical to the ones Third Lady had made for her guests.

On his return journey, he again stayed at the Wooden Bridge Inn, where the hostess welcomed him warmly. This time Chao was the only guest, and Third Lady cooked him an excellent dinner, and bade him drink the wine freely, which he again declined. At midnight, he retired to the same comfortable bed, and was roused again some time later by the same low, rumbling noise of the trunk being pulled into position. Chao did not even bother to look through the partition, he just allowed himself to drift away into a deep sleep.

The next morning, Third Lady again offered him tea and wheat cakes, but Chao, bringing out those he had bought in the city, said, 'Gracious Lady, please try one of these, they are from the capital, and are said to be particularly fine,' and he handed her the cake of her own making that he had taken a few days before. Third Lady had little option but to thank him, and eat the cake. She took only one bite and immediately her hair grew rough, her ears grew absurdly long, and she turned into a donkey. Chao examined the beast, and was delighted to find it was a strong, powerful beast, infinitely superior to his own decrepit animal, which he promptly set free. Staying only long enough to open the trunk, take out the figures and burn them, so they could do no more harm, Chao then spurred his new mount homewards.

For five years Chao had excellent service from his strange donkey, until one day he was riding through Changan. An old man came up to him, and looking at the donkey, cried 'Third Lady of the Wooden Bridge Inn! I would hardly have recognized you. How you have changed!'

Then turning to Chao, he said, 'I congratulate you on preventing her from causing more grief, but she has served her penance now. Please let her go free.' Chao dismounted, and unloaded the beast, which brayed loudly in gratitude. The old man took his sword, and split the creature's stomach in two, and out sprang Third Lady. With a cry of shame, and without looking at Chao or the old man, she ran into the wilderness, and no living person ever saw or heard from her again.

The Three Precious Packets

IN THE FREEZING DEPTHS of a particularly severe winter, a poor student called Niu was travelling to the capital to take his law examinations, so that he could start on the ladder of success that might eventually lead to him becoming a magistrate. As the snow fell, and night darkened around him, Niu stopped at a small inn for some food and shelter. His meagre finances allowed him a bowl of noodles, and some hot rice-wine, and he sat contentedly warming himself in front of the fire.

Suddenly, the door of the inn was thrown open, and in a flurry of snow, an old man staggered into the room. He was dressed in rags, had no shoes on his feet, and was clearly half-frozen, his teeth chattering too much to allow him to speak. Without waiting to be asked, Niu leapt from his seat and offered the man his place in front of the fire, which the wretch took with a grateful nod. Soon he began to recover, but when the landlord asked him what he wanted, he replied, 'I only have money for a bowl of tea, and then I will be off again.' The landlord grunted and went off to get the tea, but Niu, poor though he was, could not bear to think of the man having to face the freezing weather again that night without food. He insisted that the man share his noodles, and when they were rapidly eaten, he ordered more, and then more still, until the stranger had eaten five full bowls. He then stood to go, but Niu insisted he share his bedding and get a good night's rest before facing the winter's anger in the morning. Once again, the man gratefully accepted, and fell asleep almost immediately.

In the morning, Niu settled up with the landlord, using up almost all his money in the process, and was about to leave, when the stranger woke and said, 'Please wait, I have something to give you.' He took Niu outside the inn, and said, 'Although I am in beggar's rags, I am actually a messenger from the Underworld; for your kindness to me last night, when you could ill afford it, I would like to give you these in return,' and from his pocket he took three small, folded packets. 'When you are faced with impossible difficulties, you must burn incense and open one of these; it will help you, but only when your circumstances seem hopeless.' Niu took the packets, and all at once the stranger disappeared on the wind.

Niu continued on his way to the capital, not really believing what the man had said. There he continued his studies and waited for the examinations, but the city was terribly expensive, and he was soon forced to cut down on food to the point where he was close to starvation, his studies suffering badly as a consequence. He was about to return to his village in despair, when he remembered the three packets and, lighting a stick of incense, he opened the first of them. Inside was a slip of paper which read, 'Go and sit outside the Bodhi Temple at noon.' The Bodhi Temple was some miles distant, but Niu went there through the cold, and sat in the freezing snow outside the building, all the while thinking that he must be wasting his time. After a time a monk came out and asked him what he wanted. Niu replied that he just wanted to sit there for a while, and taking pity on this strange man, the monk brought him some tea, and started talking to him. He asked Niu his name, and when Niu told him, the monk reeled backwards in astonishment.

'Are you related to the late Magistrate Niu of Chin-Yang?' he asked, and Niu replied that he was the man's nephew. After asking a few further questions, to assure himself that Niu really was the dead man's relative, the monk said, 'Your uncle was a great benefactor of this temple, but he also left three thousand strings of coins with me for safe keeping. When he died, I was at a loss as to what to do with them, but now that you have miraculously come here, you must take them as his next of kin.'

The astonished Niu was now a very wealthy man, able to live in complete comfort, and concentrate entirely on his studies. However, try as he might, he could not pass the examinations necessary to fulfil his ambition of becoming a Magistrate, and he began to despair. After failing for the third time, Niu was about to give up and return to his village, when he again remembered the three packets, and quickly finding the remaining pair, he lit a stick of incense and opened the second. Inside was a slip of paper which read, 'Go and eat in Shu's restaurant.' Rather baffled, Niu did as he was told. He ordered tea, and sat in the restaurant, wondering what he was doing there. Then, from behind a partition on his right, Niu heard two men in a private room talking, and he could not help overhearing their conversation. 'I am worried,' said one, 'that the questions are too easy. After all, this is an important examination, and we do not want to let standards slip.'

The other replied, 'Tell me the quotations you have set, and I will tell you what I think.' The first man then ran through the list of quotations that were to be set as exam topics, and the astonished Niu realized that he was being told exactly what would be required of him at the next round of examinations. Rushing home, he wrote down all he had heard, and when the time came for the exams he passed with flying colours.

So impressive were his results that he was given an important official post, and very soon became a Magistrate, as he had always wished. He became famous for his fairness and wisdom, and also for his kindness, never turning away any person in need. He always carried with him the last of the three packets, but felt that he would never have to open it, so great was his good fortune. However, when still in middle age, Niu fell ill, and nothing that the doctors or the priests could do seemed able to cure him. At last, with his strength failing, Niu decided to open the last packet. He lit a stick of incense and opened the packet; inside there was a slip of paper which read, 'Make your will.'

Niu knew now that his life was ending. He carefully put all his affairs in order, and said farewell to his family and friends. Then he died, peacefully, and full of contentment at a life well spent, mourned by the whole city, and remembered with love and admiration by the entire population.

The Haunted Pavilion

MANY YEARS AGO a student was walking along a road south of Anyang, heading towards that city. In those days it was common for students to travel the country, seeking knowledge from ancient sites and men of learning throughout China: 'wandering with sword and lute' as it was known.

On this particular night the student arrived at a village some twelve miles short of Anyang, and as night was closing in fast, he asked an old woman if there was an inn nearby. She replied, saying that the nearest inn was some miles distant, whereupon the student remarked that he had just passed a pavilion on the road and that he would rest there. Such pavilions were common in China at that time, used as resting places for weary travellers, and looked after by neighbouring villagers.

The old woman went white at the student's words, and told him he must on no account stay in the shelter, as it was cursed with demons, and no one who had stayed there had ever lived to tell the tale. But the student laughed off the dire warning, saying that he thought he could take care of himself, and brushing aside the protestations of the villagers, he set off for the pavilion.

Night fell, but the student did not sleep; instead he lit a lamp and read aloud to himself from one of his books. Time passed; for a long while nothing stirred, until, on the stroke of midnight, the student heard footsteps on the road outside. Peering out of the door, he saw a man in black. The man stopped and called the master of the pavilion.

'Here I am,' came a voice from just behind him, causing the student to jump in surprise. 'What do you want?'

'Who is in the pavilion?' the man in black asked.

'A scholar is in the pavilion, but he is reading his book and not yet asleep,' the voice replied.

At this the man in black sighed, and turned towards the village, and the scholar returned to his reading. Some while later he again heard footsteps, and this time, as he peered of the door, he saw a man in a red hat stop on the road outside the pavilion.

'Master of the Pavilion!' the man cried.

'Here I am,' came the voice from just behind him.

'Who is in the pavilion?' the man in the red hat asked.

'A scholar is in the pavilion, but he is reading his book and not yet asleep,' the voice replied.

At this the man in the red hat sighed too and turned towards the village. Then the student waited for a few minutes, until he was sure there was no one else coming down the road. He crept out of the door, and standing on the road, called out, 'Master of the Pavilion!'

'Here I am,' came the voice from within.

'Who is in the pavilion?' the student asked.

'A scholar is in the pavilion, but he is reading his book and not yet asleep,' the voice replied.

The scholar sighed, and then asked, 'Who was the man in black?'

'That was the black swine of the North,' the voice answered.

'And who was the man in the red hat?'

'That was the Red Cock of the West.'

'And who are you?' the student asked.

'I am the Old Scorpion,' came the reply. At this, the student slipped back into the pavilion, and stayed awake all night, reading his book undisturbed.

The next morning the villagers rushed to the pavilion to see if the student had survived the night, and were astonished to see him sitting on the verandah, strumming his lute. As they gathered round him, bombarding him with questions, the student held up his hand for silence.

'Follow me,' he said, 'and I will remove the curse from this building.' Then he went back inside the pavilion, followed by the villagers. He pulled aside a rotting screen in one corner of the room, and there behind it was a huge black scorpion, many feet long, and ready to strike. With one sweep of his sword, the student split the creature from head to tail, and it fell lifeless to the floor.

Next he asked the villagers where they kept a black pig. 'In the house north of the pavilion,' they answered, and showed him the place. There was a huge black pig, its eyes glinting with demonic fury. Again the student drew his sword, and in moments the pig lay dead at his feet.

'Now, where do you keep a large red rooster?' he asked.

'In a shed to the west of the pavilion,' they answered, and showed him the place. There was an enormous red cockerel, with a huge red comb, and long, sharp talons. With another swish of the student's sword, the bird was decapitated, and lay dead at his feet.

The scholar explained to the startled villagers how he had discovered the identities of the demons, and from that day on, no traveller's rest was ever against disturbed in the pavilion south of Anyang.

The Dragon's Pearl

MANY HUNDREDS OF YEARS AGO a mother and her son lived together by the banks of the Min river in the province of Shu, which we now call Sichuan. They were extremely poor, and the young boy had to look after his mother, who was very old and very ill. Although he worked long hours cutting and selling grass for animal food; he barely made enough to support them both, and was always afraid that ruin lay just around the next corner.

One summer, as the earth grew brown through lack of rain, and the supply of good grass became even more sparse than usual, the young boy was forced to journey farther and farther from home to make any living at all; higher and higher into the mountains he went in search of pasture. Then one day, tired and thirsty, the boy was just about to set out empty-handed on the long homeward journey, when he came across a patch of the most verdant, tall grass he had ever seen, waving in the breeze, and giving off a pleasing scent of Spring. The boy was so delighted that he cut down the whole patch, and joyfully carried it down the mountain to his village. He sold the grass for more than he often earned in a week, and for once he and his sick mother were able to eat a good meal of fish and rice.

The next day the boy returned to the same area, hoping to find a similar patch of grass nearby, but to his complete amazement, the very spot which he had harvested the day before had grown again fully, as green and luscious as before. Once again, he cut down the whole patch and returned home. This happened day after day, and the boy and his mother were delighted by the upturn in their fortunes. The only disadvantage was the distance the boy had to travel every day, a long, hazardous journey into the mountains, and it occurred to him that if this was a magic patch of grass, it should grow equally well in his village as it did in the mountains.

The very next day he made several journeys to the mountains, and dug up the patch, grass, roots, soil and all, and carried it back to a spot just near his house, where he carefully re-laid the plot of earth. As he was doing so, he found to his wonder and delight, hidden in the roots of the grass, the largest, most beautiful pearl he had ever seen. He rushed to show it to his mother, and even with her failing sight, she realized that it must be of enormous value. They decided to keep it safely hidden until the boy could go to the city to sell it in the market there. The old woman hid it at the bottom of their large rice jar, which contained just enough to cover the stone, and the boy went back to re-laying the magic grass patch.

The next day he rushed out of bed to go and harvest his crop, only to find that, far from luxuriant pasture he had expected, the grass on the patch was withered, brown, and obviously dying. The boy wept for his folly in moving the earth and destroying its magic, and went inside to confess his failure to his mother. As he was going into the house, he heard his mother cry out, and rushing to her, found her standing in amazement over the rice jar. It was full to the brim with rice, and on the top of the jar lay the pearl, glinting in the morning sun. Then they knew that this must be a magic pearl. They placed it in their virtually empty money box, and sure enough, the next morning, they discovered that it too was absolutely full, the pearl sitting on top of the golden pile like a jewel on top of a crown.

Mother and son used their magic pearl wisely, and became quite wealthy; naturally in a small village this fortune did not go unremarked, and the neighbours who had been kind to the mother and son in their times of hardship now found themselves handsomely repaid, and those in need found ready relief for their distress.

However, the villagers were curious as to the source of this new wealth, and it did not take long for the story of the fabulous pearl to become known. One day the boy found himself surrounded by people demanding to see the stone. Foolishly he took it from its hiding place and showed it to the assembled throng. Some of the crowd grew threatening, jostling and pushing, and asking why the boy should be allowed to keep such a lucky find. The son saw that the situation was about to turn ugly, and without thinking, he put the pearl into his mouth to keep it safe. But in the uproar he accidentally swallowed it with a loud gulp.

Immediately, the boy felt as if he was on fire, his throat and then his stomach was consumed with a heat so intense he did not know how to endure it. He ran to his house and threw the contents of the water bucket down his throat, but it had no impact on the searing pain; he dashed to the well, and pulled up bucket after bucket of water, but to no avail. Although he drank gallon after gallon he was still burning up, and in a frenzy of despair he threw himself down on the banks of the Min and began to lap up the river as fast as he could, until eventually he had drunk it absolutely dry. As the last drop of the mighty river disappeared down his throat, there was a huge crack of thunder, and a violent storm erupted. The earth shook, lightning flashed across the sky, rain lashed down from the heavens, and the terrified villagers all fell to the ground in fear. Still the boy was shaking like a leaf, and his frightened mother grabbed hold of his legs, which suddenly started to grow. Horns sprouted on his forehead, scales appeared in place of his skin, and his eyes grew wider, and seemed to spit fire. Racked by convulsions the boy grew bigger and bigger. The horrified mother saw that he was turning into a dragon before her very eyes, and understood that the pearl must have belonged to the dragon guardian of the river. For every water dragon has a magic pearl which is its most treasured possession.

The river was now filling up with all the rain, and the dragon-boy started to slither towards it, his weeping mother still clinging to his scaly legs. With a powerful jerk, he managed to shake her free, but even as he headed for the torrent, he could still hear her despairing cries. Each time she called out, he turned his huge body to look at her, each writhing motion throwing up mud-banks at the side of the river, until, with a last anguished roar, he slid beneath the waves for the last time and disappeared for ever. And to this day the mud banks on the Min river are called the 'Looking Back at Mother' banks, in memory of the dragon-boy and his magic pearl.

The Dragon King's Daughter

THERE WAS ONCE A STUDENT named Liu Yi, who lived in the central region of China, near the great lakes. One day, as he was returning from the capital having successfully taken his examinations, he saw on the road ahead of him a young woman herding a flock of sheep. She was the most beautiful woman Liu had ever seen, but she was deeply distressed, tears coursing down her fair cheeks, her whole body shaking with sobs. Liu's heart went out to the girl, and he got down from his donkey and asked her if there was any way in which he could be of assistance. The girl thanked him through her tears, and explained the cause of her grief.

'My father is the Dragon King of Lake Dongting,' she explained, 'and many months ago he married me to the son of the God of the Jing river, whom I do not love. My husband is cruel to me, and his family torment me, but I cannot complain to my father as Lake Dongting is too far away for me to travel, and the family intercept my messages to him. I know my father would help if he but knew of my grief, but I am so utterly alone and friendless.'

Liu was so touched by the girl's plight that he offered to take the message to her father himself, but he could not see how it could be done.

'Although the shores of Lake Dongting are my home,' he said, 'I am a mere human. How could I ever reach your father's palace in the terrifying depths of the lake?'

The girl replied, 'If you are strong in heart, go to the sacred tangerine tree on the northern shore of the lake. Tie your sash around its trunk, and knock on it three times. From there you will be led to the palace.'

Liu willingly agreed to undertake the journey, and the girl handed him a letter from the folds of her gown. As he remounted his donkey, he called out, 'When you return to Dongting, I sincerely hope that we shall meet again.Then, spurring the animal on, he set off. After a few minutes he looked back, but the girl had disappeared together with her sheep.

Liu went straight to the northern shore of Lake Dongting, and finding the sacred tangerine tree, he tied his sash around its trunk and knocked on it three times as the girl had said. At once the waves of the lake parted, and a man rose up from the depths, and asked Liu what he wanted.

'I must talk to your king,' Liu said. 'It is a matter of the utmost importance.'

The man nodded, and placed a blindfold over Liu's eyes. Liu became aware of a silence engulfing him, and his body became colder and colder, but he did not flinch. After a time, the blindfold was removed, and Liu found he was in a great palace, beautifully decorated with pearl and other precious stones, and all the warmth flooded back into his body. His guide showed him into a vast chamber, and there, on a mighty throne, sat the Dragon King.

Liu bowed low, and humbly proffered the girl's letter, explaining where and how he had met her on the road from the capital. The Dragon King read the letter, and as he did so great tears rolled down his face, and his huge hands shook. Then he instructed a servant to take the letter to the queen, and said to Liu, 'I thank you for all your trouble. You have taken pity on my daughter, while I did nothing to save her from her suffering. I shall never forget your kindness to her, and your bravery in making this journey.'

At that moment he was interrupted by a loud wailing from the queen's chamber, and the sound of weeping. 'Quickly,' ordered the king with a worried frown, 'tell them to be quiet, or they will arouse Chiantang.'

'Who is Chiantang?' asked Liu, surprised that anything should disturb such a mighty ruler.

The Dragon King explained that Chiantang was his younger brother, once ruler of Lake Chiantang. His quick temper had caused such floods and devastation, even threatening the Five Holy Peaks, that the High God had banished him from the lake, and forgiven him on the understanding that his brother guarantee his good behaviour. 'This news would infuriate him, as he is extremely fond of his niece, and would instantly demand revenge.'

As he spoke, there was a tremendous crash, and the chamber filled with smoke. In a tumult of lightning, thunder and rain, a huge red dragon tore through the hall, clouds streaming from his nostrils, and a mighty roar issuing from his throat. Liu fell to the ground in terror, but the dragon left as quickly as it had appeared.

'That was Chiantang,' the Dragon King explained, helping the terrified Liu to his feet. 'I must apologize for his frightening you like that.' He called for wine and food, and graciously set them before Liu, who soon forgot his fear, as they talked about Liu's career, and life in the capital. A short while later, they were cut short by the arrival of the queen and her train, smiling and laughing amongst themselves. And Liu saw to his amazement that the Dragon King's daughter, whom he had met on the road, was in the group. The king embraced her, and he begged her forgiveness for allowing her to marry such a wretch, and she warmly thanked Liu for his help in rescuing her.

At that moment an elegant, dignified young man walked into the chamber and was introduced to Liu as Chiantang. Once he overcame his initial fear, Liu was delighted to find him a charming individual, courteously thanking Liu for his help, and toasting his health. Chiantang explained to his brother that he had fought the Jing River God and his men, and then visited the High God to explain his actions and apologize if he had done wrong. 'He has generously forgiven me,' he said, 'and I now apologize to you, my brother for my fury in your palace, and to you, honoured guest, for scaring you.'

'I am glad the High God has forgiven you,' said the king. 'And I willingly do so too, but you must be less hasty in future. And now tell me of the battle with the God of the Jing river.'

'It was nothing,' said Chiantang. 'I slew six hundred thousand of his men, and destroyed two hundred square miles of his land, and the battle was as good as won.'

'And what of my daughter's erstwhile husband?'

'I ate him,' replied Chiantang casually, and the conversation was over.

The next day a great feast was held in Liu's honour; the Dragon King lavished gifts on him, and Chiantang drank to his health innumerable times. After much delicious food, and even more wine, Chiantang took Liu aside and said to him, 'The king's daughter has been saved thanks to you. She is a fine woman, aware of how much she owes to you, and as it is clear that you are in love with her, I suggest that you marry her straight away.'

Liu did not know what to say; although he was, as Chiantang had guessed, very much in love with the girl, marriage to the daughter of a God was not to be taken lightly. Nor was the suggestion of a rather drunken dragon to be taken too seriously, especially when Liu considered the possibility of Chiantang's anger at his presumption, if the dragon changed his mind when sober. So, regretfully, Liu talked the tipsy Chiantang out of his idea, and the next day left the palace for his home, laden with gifts, and accompanied by many servants. In his heart, though, he still longed for the Dragon Princess.

Months passed, and the now-wealthy Liu, knowing he could not pine for ever, married a local girl, but she was stricken with fever and soon died. To stave off his loneliness, Liu married again, but his second wife too caught the fever, and soon died. Despairing more and more, Liu married a girl from outside the region, who soon bore him a son. As time went by, Liu began to notice that his wife looked more and more like the Dragon Princess, the lost love of his youth, and after his second son had been born, the woman finally admitted that she was indeed the Dragon King's daughter. She had been bitterly disappointed when Liu turned down her uncle's suggestion, and kept remembering his last words to her on the road from the capital: 'When you return to Dongting, I sincerely hope that we shall meet again.' When Liu's second wife had died, she had seized her opportunity to become the third.

The couple lived together in great happiness, and raised a large family. They frequently visited the Dragon King's palace beneath the deep waters of Lake Dongting, and as Liu became older, they stayed there for longer and longer periods. Eventually they left the land of mortal men entirely, and took up residence with the immortal Dragon King and Queen, and Chiantang, in their immortal home beneath the waves.

The Herdsman and the Weaver Girl

MANY, MANY HUNDREDS OF YEARS AGO there lived in the palace of the High God in heaven a little weaver girl who spun and wove the most beautiful garments for the Gods, using colours and patterns more gorgeous than anything anyone had ever seen before. The High God was delighted with her efforts, but worried that she worked too hard, and for such long hours every day, and he decided to reward her diligence by giving her a rest from her labours. He determined to send her down to earth to live among mortals for a short time, to allow her to experience new and different pleasures. To ensure that the girl was well cared for, the High God chose for her a husband for her time on earth, a herdsman called Chen-Li, who lived with his two elder brothers on a farm by a great river.

The brothers had divided up the farm on their parents' death, and Chen-Li, being the youngest, had received nothing but an old ox, and the least fertile, most unproductive, piece of land. Here he built himself a rough home, and toiled day and night to make a living from the barren soil; although his life was hard he never complained, nor harboured a grudge against his brothers, for he was an honest youth of stout heart, which is indeed why the High God chose him for the weaver girl.

One evening Chen-Li was sitting watching the sun set over the distant mountains as his old ox munched the grass near by. A feeling of great loneliness came over him, and he said to himself, 'If only I had someone to share my life with, all my hard work would seem worthwhile.' To his complete astonishment, the ox looked up and answered him, saying, 'Do not be so sad, master. I can help you to find a wife who will bring you great joy.' The ox then explained that it was really the Ox Star, sent to earth by the High God as a punishment, to work out its penance in labouring for mankind. It did not mention that it had also been given specific instructions regarding Chen-Li and the weaver girl, but went on to say: 'If you go upstream you will find a beautiful, clear pool, shaded by willows and rushes. There the Heavenly Maidens bathe each afternoon; if you were to steal the clothes of one of them she would be unable to fly back to Heaven, and would have to, according to custom, become your wife.'

Chen-Li did as the ox suggested, and the next afternoon he followed the river upstream, where he found the clear pool, shaded by willows. As he peered through the rushes, he saw the most beautiful girls he had ever set eyes on, laughing and splashing in the crystal waters. Spying their clothes piled on the banks of the pool, he leapt forward and snatched one of the piles; the noise disturbed the girls, who flew from the pool, took up their clothes, and soared away, up into the sky. Only one girl was left, naked in the pool, the little weaver girl, who looked shyly at Chen-Li and said, 'Good Sir, if you would be generous enough to return my clothes, I will gladly come with you and become your wife.' Chen-Li handed her clothes to her without hesitation, so strongly did he believe her promise. Then the girl dressed and, true to her word, followed him home and became his wife.

The couple were extremely happy in their simple existence, so much so that the weaver girl forgot all about the palace of the High God, and her place among the immortals. And in the fullness of time she bore the herdsman a fine son and a beautiful daughter, whom they loved dearly. However, the High God did not forget her, and grew impatient for her return. Eventually, when it became clear that she had no intention of

leaving Chenh-Li, he sent down to earth his soldiers to bring her back. The weaver girl was distressed beyond all measure at leaving Chen-Li and her two children, but the soldiers were adamant, and carried her away, up into the sky. Chen-Li looked on in horror, unable to prevent this catastrophe, and he cried out in anguish, 'What can I do? What can I do?'

The old ox saw his grief, and taking pity on Chen-Li said, 'Master, my earthly form will die soon so that I can return to my celestial home; when I am dead, take off my hide and wrap it around you, and you will be able to follow your beloved.' Saying this, the creature lay down and died at Chen-Li's feet, and, quickly, he did as the ox had instructed him. He picked up his son in one arm and his daughter in the other, and threw the leather hide around him. Instantly, all three soared up into the sky, and began to chase after the weaver girl, who was fast disappearing into the distance.

The High God watched this pursuit with much displeasure, and when he saw that Chen-Li would soon catch up with the weaver girl, he threw down his white silk scarf, which flowed and shimmered like fire between the lovers, forming a great river. Chen-Li called across the fiery torrent to his beloved, but to no avail, since neither could cross it. Defeated, he returned to his desolate home.

When the High God saw how much the weaver girl missed Chen-Li and her children, and how terribly they missed her, his anger abated, and he decreed that once a year, on the seventh day of the seventh month, all the magpies in the world would fly up into Heaven and form a bridge across the fiery river, so that the lovers could cross to each other and meet face to face. Whenever they met, the weaver girl would weep, and her tears fall to earth as drizzling rain; then all the women on earth would sorrow, and say, 'Our sister is weeping again.'

Chen-Li and the little weaver girl spent so much time in the sky, they eventually turned into stars; that is why, when we look up into the night sky, we can still see them both shining there. The fiery river is the Milky Way, on one side is Vega, the bright star that is the weaver girl, and on the other side shines Aquila, with two small stars beside it; which are Chen-Li and his two children. And if you look closely at the Milky Way on the night of the seventh day of the seventh month you will see these two stars meet as the two lovers are reunited for a few, precious hours, giving courage and hope to parted lovers throughout the world.

The Foolish Old Man and the Mountains

THERE WAS ONCE A VERY OLD MAN, more than ninety years old, called Yu Gong. He lived with his family in the mountains of the West and their house stood right in front of two great peaks, Taihang and Wangwu. Every time the old man went anywhere, he had to cross the two peaks, and he hated them with all his soul for always exhausting him.

Eventually he could stand it no longer, and calling his family together, told them that they were going to move the peaks out of the way.

'Where will you put all the earth?' asked his wife, who thought the whole plan insane.

'We'll just carry it all to the shores of the great lake,' replied Yu Gong. And all the men of the family set to work, right down to his youngest nephew.

They carried bucket after bucket, sack after sack of earth and rock away, all the way to the shores of the great lake, but still the mountains seemed no smaller, the climb in the mornings no less strenuous. The wise old man who lived nearby saw all this and laughed at Yu Gong.

'This is madness,' he cried. 'You are old, Yu Gong, your life is like a candle guttering in the wind; stop this nonsense now.'

'Stop now?' replied Yu Gong. 'Don't be absurd. When I die my sons will carry on the work, and their sons after them. The work will continue on down the generations until the great task is finished. You really are no wiser than my youngest nephew.'

And the wise man kept silent, as he had no answer to this.

Now it so happened that a God overheard this exchange, and he went to the High God to warn him of the old man's ambition, fearing the two peaks might one day actually disappear. But the High God was so impressed by Yu Gong's fortitude and determination that he sent two giants to help the old man, and they took the mountains away, one to Yongnan in the South, and the other to Shuodong in the East. And the old man was able to live out his remaining years without ever again having to climb over the twin peaks.

Classical Greek Myths

Introduction

Each form of worship that hath swayed
The life of man, and given it to grasp
The master-key of knowledge, reverence,
Enfolds some germ of goodness and of right;
Else never had the eager soul which loathes
The slothful down of pampered ignorance
Found in it even a moment's fitful rest.
James Russell Lowell, Rhoecus

THE MYTHS AND LEGENDS of Greece have come to us across thousands of years of alteration and embellishment, communicated by speech, by gestures, by art and music, and eventually by the written word. They are the subjects of poetry and plays, which combine stories, legends, folktales and religious myths, so that the myths and legends as we know them today present a veritable feast of images, associations and meanings.

The Greek people called themselves Hellenes, and their country Hellas. Greek is the name given to them by the Romans. The Greeks lived not only in Greece, as we know it today, but all around the Mediterranean, in what today is called Turkey, their lands stretching as far south as the tip of Spain. Their civilization is the oldest we know of, stretching back to the Bronze Age, around 3000 BC. Our understanding of the Greeks and their civilization was widened by the discovery of the treasures at Mycenae, in the north-west of the Peloponnesus, where a new kingdom was created when Crete fell into decay. Mycenaean Greece, which lasted from about 1400 to 1150 BC, was characterized by massive palaces on rocky coasts, and mountain tops. They were a warring people, fighting for wealth among themselves. They left treasures such as gold daggers and cups, death-masks and weapons, and impressive tributes to the gods which were as detailed as they were magnificent. The Trojan War took place in this glorious age, and Troy was, according to legend, a rich and luxurious city on the Asian side of the sea that separates Europe from Asia. There is no doubt that Troy existed, and the legends of this time are steeped in both fact and fiction, intertwined so as to make the very best stories which cannot fail to intrigue and to suspend all disbelief.

The Greek Dark Ages ensued, from about 1100 to 700 BC, and they were marked by the collapse of the Mycenaean civilization, destroyed by barbarian tribes of the Roman empire. There was violence and looting, war and plundering, providing little inspiration for literature or for art, and while myths and legends were carried through these years, there was little embroidery to what existed. The bards continued the tradition of storytelling, and great comfort was garnered from the exciting tales of Ancient Greece, with its palaces and romances, adventures and intrigue. And then came the advent of classical Greece, from 600 to 300 BC, when city states took the place of kingdoms, ruled by dictators and infantry warfare. This was a sophisticated civilization, developed in the city states of the mainland, and in the islands nearby, but it too was short-lived, and the empire of the Persians, which had expanded towards the Aegean Sea, conquered the Greeks of Asia Minor, taking their political freedom, their wealth and then their great wisdom. From this time, the leadership of the Greeks passed to the mainland, especially to Athens, where it remained until the conquests of Alexander.

But it was many years before the cultural and intellectual development of the Greek civilization that gods and goddesses ruled the imagination, that myths and legends were a vital part of everyday life, when poets and musicians and writers found endless inspiration in the stories of the past, which they embalmed and then allowed to permeate every aspect of their culture, their enlightenment.

For the Greeks had a unique and varied past, riddled with developments which today make them one of the most fascinating civilizations on earth. They were the fathers of democracy, of medicine and political and moral ideals, they were great philosophers and scientists, and much of mythology represents their quest to understand more clearly the nature of the earth and its occupants.

The most ancient Greeks were farmers, tending their land and their flocks, bringing forth wheat, grapes and olives. Olive oil was used in cooking, in bathing, and to provide the fuel for lights, and grapes were harvested for delicious wines that became a staple of the Greek diet. Goats and sheep were raised in rocky mountain pastures, and a Greek shepherd would live a lonely life with his flock. Life was difficult and unpredictable, and it is not surprising that the people were comforted by the myths and legends which gave meaning to the disasters which befell them, to the plagues and disease which robbed them of their crop, to the unruly weather which killed their harvest, to the whispers and mysterious movements of the grasses in the half-light, the babble of the springs which were answered at once by the wind in the trees. The world was alive with magic, and the Greeks drew consolation from naming it, and making it a part of their lives. It was soothing to think that sacrifice, that eternal praise of a god might bring forth good omens; like religion is and has always been, the faith and the belief in the gods of Greece offered hope where there would have been emptiness.

The gods and the goddess of Greece were worshipped by the Greeks as were the heroes and heroines which existed alongside them. The legends which were created around these great figures were a key part of daily life, and their reverential treatment has filtered through to the modern day. A great deal of superstition still surrounds the myths and legends of Greece, and while the stories are more often than not communicated for entertainment, for many, they still hold a grain of truth, a note of caution to mortals.

Myths were woven around historical fact, real people and places and true events. In this form they are legends, exaggerated, surely, and distorted to make them tellable, more exciting, but created in order to convey the basic moral message of an event which has had some significance in the lives of those touched by it. There were folktales, too, which are tales of enchantment, deceit and trickery, in which heroes and heroines live alongside nymphs, talking animals, giants, monsters and witches. Folktales are based on magic, and used to explain phenomena which may otherwise, to a mind uneducated in science, be frightening, and inexplicable. Folktales provide explanations for the wind, the trees, the weather, for echoes, ghosts and seasons.

Religious myths are an essential part of most cultures, and the Greeks are no exception. They are the myths of philosophy, addressing matters which concern all of us. They relate to the conception of the world, to death and to living, to gods and to the state of godliness. They may deal with matters relating to a specific tribe, culture or people, making sense of rituals, superstitions and routines.

The Greeks were craftsmen, and the ritual of praying to gods was as important to them as it was to the lonely shepherd on his rocky outpost. Masons and potters, metal-workers and candle-makers, all prayed to their patron the god Hephaestus. If Hephaestus was not honoured, pots would break, metal would turn brittle, an avalanche would fall upon a hapless stone mason as he worked in the quarry. And so too did travellers pray to Poseidon and to the gods of the wind, who could suddenly produce a storm that would wreck the vessel of even the most devout mortal.

It is easy to see how the myths and legends of Greece could be nurtured, could feed the collective imagination to such an extent that they have been expanded, cosseted and preserved by centuries of genius and artistic endeavour, passing into literature of other cultures and lands, where they are as enriching as they have been enriched. Their paganism had sprouted from some seed of believable notion, and while the stories have passed now into the realms of entertainment, they once held the greatest fascination and importance to their owners.

The myths and legends of Greece have come down to us through their great writers, who based their works on stories which have been told and retold for thousands of years. In Greece, before the advent of archaeology, the primary source of knowledge about their people and civilization was the poems of Homer, to which were attached a series of epics dealing with the Trojan War. *The Iliad*, for example, relates to events which occurred in the tenth year of that war. The journey of the Odysseus, in *The Odyssey*, tells the tale of his return home to Ithaca. Homer describes the part played by Greek gods on the way, who fought on one side or another, depending on who was in favour.

After Homer came Hesiod, who attempted to put together the pieces of the war in a more comprehensive form, in his *Works and Days* and *Homeric Hymns*. These were intended, in the form of poetry, to link Greek families to the gods through their genealogical trees. The *Theogony* is the account of the gods and heroes, and their struggle with the giants at the beginning of time. And then came storytellers, who sought to put in narrative the most evocative of the legends, and those which provided the most significance to daily life. Hecataeus of Miletus is one such story-teller, and it was he who said, 'The stories the Greeks tell are many and, in my opinion, ridiculous. What I write is what I believe to be true.'

Hecataetus attempted to give a reasoned explanation for the creation of the earth, and for ensuing events, and it was this prying into nature which led to the birth of modern philosophy. But the Greeks were not as eager to lose their heritage, and believed firmly in the existence of their gods and heroes, through mythology, long after the death of Hecataeus.

Some areas of Greece were richer sources of legends than others, including Argolis, Boeotia, Thessaly and Attica. Some legends were local, and others extended to encompass the whole of the classical world, eventually translated into Latin by the Romans when they took over the empire. Legends which spread far and wide include the myths of Heracles, Jason and the Argonauts, and Odysseus. Others became the subjects of Greek literature, in particular plays and epic poems which were recited to large audiences by the rhapsodes, the succours of the bard who sang and played at Homeric feasts. Concerts for playwrights and rhapsodes were held at Epidars, a theatre built in the fourth century BC, which seated up to 14,000 people. Authors like Sophocles and Euripides altered the legends, creating endings or diversions that would appeal to a more modern audience.

But for many Greeks, Homer was their bible, and school-children, once education was made possible, grew up using *The Iliad* and *The Odyssey* as their textbooks. And today they hold an important place in the study of history and of literature, and it is impossible, sometimes, to see them as more than that, to understand what they really meant to the Greeks and their civilization. Our knowledge of myths is of course mainly through their literature, which is made more real by their art, and given credibility by architectural discoveries. We know there are many myths which have been lost, referred to in other works, and that many lyrical poets have cut or destroyed whole swathes of their work, for many great narrative poems fail to tell a story in a linear sequence. Great historians, like Euhemerus, in the fourth century, reinterpreted the myths, believing them to be based on great men of the past, not deities.

Apollodorus, in the second century, provided us with an indispensable encyclopaedia of mythology, and his work is a scholarly attempt to make sense of a plethora of gods and kings, all of whom appeared to live simultaneously, or with huge gaps between their reigns. Alexandrian poetry traced myths still further, and poets like Theocritus or Callimachus narrated myths which are new, perhaps to them, or just retold versions of a theme which had not been recorded earlier. Later scholars refused to discard the rich tradition of myths as nonsense, or indeed entirely as fiction. Strabo, for instance, in his introduction to *Geography*, called the study of Greek myths essential to the understanding of history and ultimately philosophy. He felt that myths were a palliative which allowed knowledge to be absorbed and carried on, presenting facts interspersed with clever fiction, almost novel-like in their importance and accuracy. Plutarch, in the second century AD, called mythology a kind of warped religion, 'reflections of some true tale which turns back our thoughts to other matters'.

The Romans leapt upon the pantheon of Greek gods with a vengeance, and they became even further ingrained in the consciousness of the European culture, which eventually spread northwards and across the oceans. Ovid and Virgil gave the myths new meaning and significance, imbibing them with credibility and elevating them to an art form. And with each ensuing generation, writers and readers have been inspired by the myths of the Greeks, and have adopted them as an essential part of their culture, retold, reworked and often redesigned for a new audience, but most importantly continued.

But bearing in mind the importance of the role of myths in the lives of the Greeks, it is essential that their motivation for creating them is understood. The Greeks created myths in order to make a pronouncement, to say something about their experience of the world. The fact that they have passed into ours is indicative of the infallibility of their myths to enchant, to please, and to offer answers to some of the eternal questions, whether or not we choose to believe them.

Many of the earliest legends deal with the concept of chaos, a state which existed before the beginning of the world. This emphasis on religious or philosophical interpretation of the evolution of the earth is not unique to the Greeks – most cultures and civilizations have their own answers to the questions that have plagued mankind from the beginning of time. But the Greeks believed that from chaos was born the goddess Gaea or Ge, called 'Wide blossomed Earth, the sure foundation of all, the eldest of beings who supports creatures and things.' And it is here that the story begins, the consummation of divine forces which conceived everything around us, the birthplace of earth. The beginning of time was created and peopled by gods, and these were the threads of some of the greatest myths and legends of all time. They are a part of our world, a part of our culture, our fundamental beliefs and our understanding of ourselves and each other. The Greek gods and heroes have never failed to captivate, and their importance cannot be overstated.

The Pantheon

AFTER EARTH CAME EROS, who was not the god of love (Cupid) as he became known in later legends, but an immortal being who rose to send passion to earth, which would eventually govern the hearts of men and gods. From chaos came Darkness and Night, called Erebus and Nyx, and these drew together to create Aether, the air, and Hemera, the day. This was light, and the beginning of our world as we know it.

Then Ge, or Gaea spawned Uranus, the starry heaven, who became her partner. Other deities were spat out of chaos, including Doom, Black Fate, Sleep, Death and Woe, then the Hesperides who guard the apples on the edge of the Western world, Destiny and Fate, and then Nemesis, Deceit, Age, Strife and Friendship. From Uranus and Ge, was born the first race of divine children, twelve of them known as the Titans. One of them, Rhea, replaced her mother as Earth goddess, and Cronus would take over the role of his father Uranus. Oceanus was also born of Uranus and Ge, and he was the father of many, including Nereus, the Old Man of the Sea.

These were the forefathers of many great heroes and gods, including Achilles and Iris.

The Titans were despised by Uranus, who jealously believed that they wished to destroy him. They were hidden underground by their mother, from where they were eventually liberated by Cronus, who made his father impotent. One night he took the sickle of Ge, and waited in ambush for his father. He reached out and castrated Uranus, flinging his genitals out to the sea. There they touched the foam and from it sprung the goddess Aphrodite, who rose of the sea to the island of Cythera. There she was joined by Eros and Desire, and the three immortals, and they lived there together, putting together their powers in order to plague the hearts of mortals with their actions. When drops of his blood touched the ground, giants sprang forth, along with nymphs called the Meliai, and the avenging Furies. Cronus took over the rule from his father, and the first generation of gods was now in place.

Cronus and Rhea married, but before their first child could be born, Cronus was told by an Oracle that he would be supplanted by one of his sons. In response, he devoured each child as it was born, eating Poseidon, Demeter and Hera, Hestia and Hades in this way. Rhea was filled with grief, and as each child was snatched from her she grew more rebellious, more angry. She begged her parents for help, and when she was heavy with Zeus, she was spirited off into the night by Ge, who allowed the baby to be born in the safety of Lyktos in Crete. Zeus was hidden in a cave, and Rhea wrapped a large boulder in swaddling clothes, which she presented to her husband instead. The boulder was swallowed whole, and Zeus was saved. He was brought up by Ge, fed on the milk of goats and on nectar and honey, and the nymphs of the mountains guarded over him, taking great pleasure in their important role.

The sands of time slipped by, bringing with them manhood for Zeus, who as he grew vowed revenge on his father. With the help of Metis, the daughter of Oceanus, he presented Cronus with a draught which caused him to vomit up his children. From Tartarus, Zeus also released the giants and Cyclopes born of Ge, and he enlisted their help in overthrowing his father. The Cyclopes were so grateful for their freedom that they presented Zeus with thunderbolts and lightning, with which he could do battle. And so it came to pass that these creatures were gods, and went to live on Mount Olympus, where they enraged the Titans, with the exception of Oceanus, who swore revenge against them.

The Titans lived on Mount Othrys, and from there they launched attacks on Mount Olympus, and so commenced a war that lasted ten bloody years, as the earth was ravished and ravaged by battle. It was won at last by the gods, and the Titans were cast deep into the bowels of the earth.

But in the tumultuous new world, where order had not yet cast a cloak of calm, war followed war, and the next threat to the gods was the attack of the giants who had been born from the blood of Uranus. They attacked Olympus, almost scaling its heights before Zeus, with the aid of Heracles, cast them aside. Then Ge, distraught by the plight of her children, sent a monster, Typhon, to fight Zeus, but it too was beaten by the powerful thunderbolts of the king of gods, and it fled to Mount Etna, where it took refuge in its base.

And the world shook and twisted, all at once turbulence and misfortune. Volcanoes erupted, earthquakes and tornadoes broke and churned the earth's surface. Whirlpools thrust themselves up from the great boiling sea, and then, when the final war was waged, all was quiet. The birds flew tentatively from their nests, animals and trees poked their heads above the earth, which blossomed once more, flowering with peace and new hope. There was tranquillity across the lands, and to the top of Mount Olympus went Zeus and his gods, where they built their thrones. There they lived in luxurious palaces, guardians of the mortals who went about their humble duties on the earth. From their supernatural realm they toyed with the lives of men on earth, occasionally intervening, often falling in love with their playthings, demanding sacrifices and holy worship, sitting back on their opulent thrones drinking nectar, and feeding on ambrosia.

Mount Olympus sits on the border between Macedonia and Thessaly, the towering pinnacle some 9500 feet in height. Its tip is wreathed in cloud, enshrouding the immortals from the prying gazes of men. Their palaces were the stuff of dreams, cast in gold and marble, encrusted with jewels and hung with fine fabrics. Music was piped through heated rooms, where gods and goddesses bathed, and feasted, and lolled in complete comfort. They dabbled in the events on earth beneath them, and although they found themselves victims, instigators and pawns in war, they could not be killed, for instead of true blood, ichor ran through their noble veins.

There were twelve gods on the mountain of Olympus, and they were headed by Zeus, thunderer and lord of the Bright sky. He was the chief of gods, their king, and he was honoured with many names. His brothers were Poseidon and Hades, but the latter did not live on the mountain, but beneath the earth in the Underworld, where he was king. Many years before Zeus came to power, the three godly brothers had drawn straws to divide the ancestral estate of Cronus and Rhea. Poseidon had drawn the sea, Zeus the heavens, and Hades the world below, and although they shared the job of governing the earth and everything above and beneath it, Zeus was the mightiest, and the most divine.

Zeus was a lusty god, and he was not content with just one partner in his bed. He slept with Themis, who gave birth to Eunomia, Dice and Eirene, also known as Government, Justice and Peace. And then Eurynome spawned the Graces. Next Demeter shared his bed, and Persephone was their offspring, who later became her uncle's queen. Mnemosyne and Zeus produced the nine Muses, and Leto bore him the twins Apollo and Artemis. Finally Zeus chose as his wife Hera, and she became the queen of Olympus, but he was not monogamous, and many more children were born to him, including Hermes, the divine messenger, Dionysus, the god of wine, and from Hera herself were produced Ares, Hebe and Eileithyia, the god of war, the goddess of youth, and the goddess of childbirth.

Zeus's brother Poseidon ruled the sea with a will of iron, and he was also master of horses, riding a chariot drawn by splendid steeds. When he travelled by sea, his chariot was pulled by Tritons, who were half men, half fish. His palace lay beneath the fiery sea, a sumptuous castle which glittered through the waves, seen for a splendid instant and then gone again, almost entirely invisible to enquiring eyes. He dictated the currents, the waves and the direction of the rivers and streams, and he was often unpredictable, impetuous, and unkind. He brought fear to the heart of mortals for he was easily upset, and difficult to placate. He married Amphitrite, a jealous and vengeful wife, but he too laid with many others, fathering Pegasus, Arion and the Mysteries.

Hades ruled the Underworld with wisdom, and he grew to love the deep, dark and forbidding place from which no mortal could return. He was called Zeus of the Underworld, and he was a severe and uncompromising leader, who provided the punishments decreed by his brother Zeus. His chariot was drawn by black horses which came to embody anarchy and destruction, controlled only by their tempestuous leader. When he left his kingdom he often travelled in the cloak of invisibility, surprising mortals by his sudden appearance, and thereby becoming a presence to be feared. He was a rich god, owner of all the jewels and metals in the earth, and he had a deep knowledge of the ill deeds of men, which caused him to be called the good counsellor.

Other gods and goddesses on Mount Olympus included Hephaestus, Hermes, Ares, Apollo, Hera, Athene, Artemis, Hestia, Aphrodite and Demeter. There were other deities including Helius (god of the sun), Selene (goddess of the moon), Leto, Dionysus and Themis. Those who waited on the gods lived there as well, and they were the messenger Iris, Hebe, who served them their food and drink, the Graces, the Muses and Ganymedes, the cup-bearer.

For many millennia these gods ruled the earth, until the time came for Dionysius to take over the reins, at which the kingdom of Zeus passed away. And in that time, the world came also to be populated by mortals, of whom there were five ages. The first was the Golden Age, when man was free from toil and illness, described by Hesiod in his *Works and Days*:

Like gods they lived, with calm untroubled mind,
Free from the toil and anguish of our kind:
Nor e'er decrepit age mis-shaped their frame,
The hand's, the foot's proportions, still the same.
Pleased with the earth's unbought feasts, all ills removed,
Wealthy in flocks, and of the bless'd beloved,
Death as a slumber pressed their eyelids down;
All nature's common blessings were their own;
The life-bestowing tilth its fruitage bore,
A full, spontaneous and ungrudging store:
They with abundant goods, mid quiet lands,
All willing shared the gathering of their hands.

The Golden Age was followed by the Age of Silver, when man was less noble, and incurred more often the wrath of the gods. The Bronze Age brought man who insisted on fighting with weapons made of bronze, and this race was, like the one before it, destroyed by the angry gods, who had not been appeased or pandered to. The fourth age brought Iron. It was an age of heroes and demi-gods, many of whom were killed in battle and in war. This was the time of the Trojan War and a time when man as we know it was evolving from the grandeur of his ancestors, many of whom lived on that great mount of Olympus.

And then the fifth age is ours, a time when, as Hesiod says,

Far-seeing Zeus made yet another generation of men, who are upon the bounteous earth ... and men shall never rest from labour and sorrow by day, and from perishing by night, and the gods shall lay sore trouble on them ... Strength will be right and reverence shall cease to be; and the wicked will hurt and ... man, speaking false words against him ...

If his words are prophecy, then our lives are still governed by those passionate gods, high on the mountain of Olympus. The following presents a picture of some of these deities, and these are their stories.

Tales of Troy

THE CITY OF TROY grew on the low hill on the plain near the entrance to the Hellespont, founded by Ilus, a descendant of Zeus, who marked out the boundaries of a city and settled there. Ilus prayed to the gods for good luck and discovered the following morning a large wooden statue, the Palladium, the image that the goddess Athene had made in memory of her friend Pallas. Apollo appeared and begged Ilus to keep sacred the image, to guard and respect it against all invaders. As long as Troy preserved the token of godly esteem, the city would be safe. But men being men, and even then subject to the fates and powers of the gods, events would occur to threaten the sanctity of the beautiful city of Troy. And that city would become the food of legends for aeons to come, the site of a battle which involved the greatest heroes of Greece, the most powerful gods of Olympia, and the most beautiful women in the land. The tales of Troy are the longest and most exciting of all the legends, and they begin with a beautiful woman, and a handsome man, cast from his noble birth ...

The Judgement of Paris

THE GOOD NAME of Troy had been blackened over the years by many of the gods, who had been wronged by her leaders. These gods held a grudge that was relaxed only under the shrewd and swift-footed King Priam, who took over the reins of Troy and allowed her once more to blossom. Now Priam was a superstitious and careful monarch, never erring in order that his command of the lovely land might be released. And when his wise wife Hecuba dreamed that she had borne a firebrand their youngest son was cast away, left to die on the heights of Mount Ida.

This child was Paris, but he did not die. He was suckled by a bear and brought to live with the herdsmen of the mountain, where he grew strong and handsome, proud and respected by his peers. He grew up ignorant of his noble breeding, content to wed and live with an exquisite mountain nymph Oenone in a humble home. He was called Alexander there, the 'helper of men'.

And then one day, as he tended his flocks on the sunlit mountains, surrounded by greenery, and more than content with his simple lot, he was visited by Hermes, messenger of the gods. There had been an altercation he said, looking with awe at the beauty of this mortal, and three of the loveliest goddesses required a judge to ascertain which was the fairest. It had been decreed by Zeus that Paris was a man of great wisdom and fair looks, and that this lowly shepherd should be given the task of judging amongst the goddesses.

'Fear not, Paris,' said Hermes, 'Zeus bids thee judge freely which of the three seems fairest in thine eyes; and the father of gods and men will be thy shield in giving true judgement.'

Paris nodded in amazement, the sanctity of his simple life at once eclipsed by the excitement and shallowness of the deed before him.

The first goddess to appear to him was Hera, Queen of Olympus. She explained to the young shepherd that a wedding had taken place between Peleus and Thetis, to which Eris alone among the immortals had not been included through some oversight. She had appeared nonetheless at the feast, and churning trouble, she threw an apple at the feet of three of the greatest of the goddesses, those who thought themselves the most beautiful in the land – Hera, Athene and Aphrodite. The apple was inscribed with the words: For the Fairest.

And it was to judge that fairest that Paris had been summoned, to put an end to the petty quarrelling. Hera went on to offer him all her queenly gifts, including money and the richest land on earth.

Athene offered him wisdom and success in battle, 'Adjudge the prize to me,' she whispered, 'and thou shall be famed as the wisest and bravest among men.'

The third goddess was Aphrodite, as beautiful certainly as her sisters, but with cunning that matched her looks. 'I am Aphrodite,' she said softly, coyly drawing herself up to the shepherd. 'I can offer thee gifts that are sweeter than any on earth. He who wins my favour needs only love to be loved again. Choose me, and I promise thee the most beautiful daughter of men to be thy wife.'

And although Paris was wed already, he chose Aphrodite without a moment's hesitation, and he gave the golden apple to the goddess of love who thanked him with such a radiant smile that his cheeks were rouged with pleasure.

It was with this glow of gratification that Paris set off the next day to take part in the games arranged each year by King Priam to commemorate the death of his youngest son, Paris. It was his first visit to the city since his birth, and he was anxious to test his strength. He excelled at the games, his strength, his passion and his ambition surpassing even that of his own brothers, the young princes of Troy. And when they, greatly angered by his prowess, took offence, and plotted to have an errant arrow sent in his direction, his sister Cassandra, who had a gift of divination, shouted out, not knowing what she said, 'Do not raise your hand against your brother.'

The princes were aghast, King Priam delighted, and it was with open arms that Paris was reunited with his family and welcomed back to Troy. He was given a great duty to perform for the King, to travel to Greece in order to secure the return of Hesione who had been borne off by Heracles many years before. Cassandra alone was vehemently against this venture, her prophetic vision showing her death and destruction that would lead to a great war against Troy. But her words were ignored, and Paris set off on his voyage, stopping during its course to visit Menelaus, king of Sparta, who was married to Helen, the most beautiful woman in the world.

It was this diversion which led Helen far from her marriage vows, into the arms of another man in an elopement which would excite the world of Greece and begin a battle that would run for ten long, blood-thirsty years.

Helen and Paris

The face that launched a thousand ships,
And burnt the topless towers of Ilium.
Christopher Marlowe, Faustus

HELEN WAS THE DAUGHTER OF LEDA and Tyndareus, King of Sparta, and she was undoubtedly the most beautiful woman in all of Greece.

Her beauty caused her to be carried off to Attica by Theseus, and to be worshipped as a goddess at Sparta. As she grew older, she attracted suitors from around the world who swarmed to her side in order that she might receive their attentions.

Men with impeccable records of bravery, with inordinate riches, vied to become Helen's husband, including the wise and cunning Odysseus, Ajax, Diomedes, Philoctetes and Menestheus. Tyndareus did not wish to offend these great men, and he chose the wealthiest of the princes, Menelaus, brother of Agamemnon, lord of Argos, who was married to Helen's half-sister Clytemnestra. Odysseus suggested to Tyndareus that the suitors who had not been chosen to wed Helen should take a vow, swearing to defend to the death the lucky suitor, should anyone or anything appear to strip him of his good fortune. And so it was that Menelaus became King of Sparta, married to the exquisite Helen, who lived with him in harmony and happiness. He was warmly congratulated by the suitors who had not been chosen, and bound by their vow, they returned to their respective homes. Tyndareus marked the occasion by providing an offering to the gods, but it was ill fortune indeed that he omitted Aphrodite in his address, an oversight that would be long remembered and regretted by mortals and gods alike.

Helen gave birth to three children, and all was well in the luxurious palace, where food and drink were plentiful, where Menelaus ruled fairly and kindly, and where Helen and Menelaus grew to find a mutual respect and adoration for one another.

And then, one cruel day, the Fates chose to send to Sparta the ship of Paris, who decided, from the moment he set eyes on Helen, that he must have her as his wife. His true wife Oenone was forgotten, lonely on the Mount of Ida, and so too were his sense of honour, his mission, and the commands of his long-lost father. He called to Aphrodite to fulfil the promise she had made to him on the hillside, and when honest Menelaus set out on an expedition, he trusted the lovesick Paris to care for his wife in a manner befitting his status. Before he could return, Paris had eloped with Helen leaving behind Hermione, her daughter by Menelaus.

With treasure they had looted from the palace of Menelaus, Paris and Helen sailed idly, deep in love that blossomed as they travelled. It was only after months of tender lovemaking, and a true, rich affection, that Paris returned home to Troy, to show off his prize. On their journey, however, the sea became suddenly calm, no breath of air rippling her surface. An eerie silence fell upon them, threatened to overwhelm them with its sinister threat of ill-fate. And then, from the sea, rose a creature so fearful, that Paris thrust Helen below the deck, and with his sword ready, moved forward to hear its words. The quiet was deafening. The creature spoke not, but laid its dripping trident across the prow of the ship and leant forward, its mighty weight dipping the vessel dangerously close to the edge of the sea. And then it uttered words that chilled the heart of Paris.

'I am Nereus, god of the sea. Ill omens guide thy course, robber of another's goods. The Greeks will come across this sea, vowed to redress the wrong done by thee and to overthrow the towers of Priam. How many men, how many horses I see there, dead for thy misdeed, how many Trojans murdered for thy sins, how many Trojans laid low about the ruin of their city!' And with that he cast his trident high into the sky, and disappeared beneath the mirrored sea.

But the deed was done, and fate had cast the die. Paris had been weak in mind and body, and for those sins he would bring about the disgrace and disintegration of Troy and her people. Head down, he surged across the waves that swelled up to greet them, breathed in the air that began to circulate once more. In the name of love, and on the wings of pride, he continued on to Troy, determined to build a life there with his lady love.

The Seeds of War

THE ELOPEMENT of Paris and Helen sent waves of shock through the land. Menelaus, his trusting soul rent by sadness, gathered together those men who had pledged an oath to aid him in times of trouble. He called upon all the great rulers from other lands, men who would take up their arms to recover his beloved wife, and to punish the violator of his home. He and his brother Agamemnon were the greatest and most powerful lords of the Peloponnese, and together they summoned the finest leaders of the land to bring their ships and their most courageous warriors for war against Troy, and ever respectful of these two great men, all but two answered the call and set out for Troy.

One of these men was Odysseus, a crafty and highly regarded leader of the small island of Ithaca. Odysseus had recently married his great love Penelope, who had given birth to their son Telemachus. He had found great happiness with his family, and was loath to quit it for a war which had been predicted as long and painful. An Oracle had confirmed to him that he risked twenty years of separation from his home and his wife if he travelled to Troy, and he was not inclined to respond to the summons. Instead, he feigned madness, and when he was visited in person by Menelaus and Palamedes, he put on a rustic cap and ploughed salt into the furrows of his rocky land, with an ox and an ass yoked together. But Palamedes was not fooled by this show, and he laid down the infant Telemachus, in the path of the plough, at which Odysseus was forced to admit his deceit, pull up the team, and rescue his son from certain danger. And so it was that Odysseus travelled reluctantly to Troy, where the oracle proved true, but where he made his name as the most distinguished warrior of all time.

Achilles was also summoned, but had defied the call on the advice of his mother Thetis, who had dressed him in the garb of a maiden and hidden him among the daughters of the King of Scyros. He was the son of Peleus, a mortal who had married the goddess Thetis. Achilles was the youngest of many children born to Thetis, but all had died as she attempted to immortalize them by holding them over a fire. When Achilles was born, she wished once more to make him immortal, but cleverly ignored the murderous flames which promised such status and hung him instead over the waters of the River Styx, making him invulnerable by dipping him into the waters. The heel by which she held him remained the one vulnerable part of his body, and he was brought up with other heroes by Cherion, who fed him on the hearts of lions and the marrow of bears. He was a popular boy, endowed with great prowess and skill in war.

His mother knew that the Trojan War would lead to his certain death, and it was she who hatched the plan to hide him from Menelaus and his men. But it was crafty Odysseus who found him, and revealed him by disguising himself as a purveyor of fine fabrics and jewellery, which provided great excitement to the other young women, but which failed to interest the young hero. When cunning Odysseus laid out a dagger and shield they were leapt upon by Achilles, who disclosed himself, and came readily with Odysseus.

When King Priam heard news of Paris's activities at Sparta, he sank back in disbelief. Odysseus had journeyed to Troy with Palamedes and Menelaus, to demand that Priam return Helen, but Paris had not yet returned to the island and Priam was loath to judge a man before he'd had his say. He responded with courtesy to the requests of these great men who had appeared on his shores with such an urgent mission, but he put them off. And when Paris did finally appear with Helen, King Priam and his sons were so besotted by her, so taken by her beauty that they forgave Paris all his weakness and swore that Helen should remain in Troy for ever. Helen confirmed that she had eloped of her own free will, and that her love for Paris was greater than any known to man or god before them.

However, the people of Troy were less kindly disposed to their new mistress, for with her she brought the threat of war, which would draw into action its many men, and rob them of their freedom and good name. And when Paris stalked the streets of Troy, his new bride on his arm, he was followed by muttered curses. The men of Troy gathered together their troops, led by the great Hector, and Priam's son-in-law, Aeneas, prince of the Dardinians and son of Aphrodite herself.

Many years had passed since Menelaus had put out that first call for assistance, but the impressive collection of warriors grouped now at Aulis, a harbour on the Ruipus, where more than a thousand ships were gathered. But as they prepared to set forth for Troy, their sails were met by calm that disallowed even a breath of wind to set them on their course.

And so it transpired that Artemis was behind the deathly stillness, for Agamemnon had unwittingly hurt her pride by slaying one of her sacred hind, and she now demanded the death of Agamemnon's own daughter Iphigenia in return.

Agamemnon was torn by the command and refused to consider it, while the men of Greece became surly and impatient to begin a war which threatened to be long and hard. So the great lord listened to his men, and encouraged by his brother Menelaus, he called his wife to bring Iphigenia to the site, where he promised her Achilles as a husband. And for that reason alone, Iphigenia was brought to the ships, and when she greeted her father with excitement and love, he cast her aside, daring not to meet her glances. Seeing his unhappiness, Menelaus swallowed his own sadness and forbade his brother to kill the young girl, but this sympathy and pity hardened the heart of Agamemnon and he prepared for the sacrifice.

Clytemnestra was Agamemnon's wife, and she grew suspicious when she saw him shirk the embraces of his favourite daughter. She took herself to the tent of Achilles, who professed no knowledge of an impending wedding, and finally admitted the real purpose of Iphigenia's visit to the camp. In a fiery rage and distress, Clytemnestra flew back to her husband, and found her daughter begging for mercy at his feet.

And then, as Agamemnon struggled again to make a decision that would calm his angry men, console his desperate wife, Iphigenia drew herself up, and wiping away her tears, proclaimed, 'Since so it must be, I am willing to die; then shall I be called the honour of Greek maidenhood, who have given my life for the motherland. Let the fall of Troy be my marriage feast, and my monument.' And the brave young woman cast herself down on the sacrificial table at the altar of Artemis, gazing heavenward as her peaceful expression filled her family with woe anew.

The seer Calchas unsheathed the knife, having been given this painful duty, but as he lifted his arm to strike a blow, Iphigenia vanished, taken by Artemis herself who had pitied the lovely maiden, and borne her away to become a priestess of her temple at Tauris, to live in eternal maidenhood. In her place on the table lay a snow-white fawn, sprinkled with virgin blood, and with a great roar of gladness, Calchas proclaimed Artemis to be appeased. His words were carried away on the whisper of wind that grew until it became a mighty gale, pulling at the idle ships and filling her crew with anticipation and joy.

The winds carried them to Lesbos, and then on to the island of Tenedos, from where the distant walls of Troy could be seen glowing in the light of dawn. The war would begin.

The Trojan War

Many a fire before them blazed:
As when in heaven the stars about the moon
Look beautiful, when all the winds are laid
And every height comes out, and jutting peak
And valley, and the immeasurable heavens
Break open to their highest, and all the stars
Shine, and the Shepherd gladdens in his heart:
So many a fire between the ships and stream
Of Xanthus blazed before the towers of Troy,
A thousand on the plain; and close by each
Sat fifty in the blaze of burning fire;
And champing golden grain the horses stood
Hard by their chariots waiting for the dawn.
Alfred, Lord Tennyson, The Iliad

THE WAR BEGAN BADLY, with the death of Tenes, the son of Apollo, before the invaders had reached the shores of Troy. Achilles had been warned never to take the life of any child of Apollo, but when he saw a figure hurling rocks at the ships of the Greeks, who were approaching the walled city of Troy, he struck him down with one swoop of his mighty sword. Tenes was dead before Achilles could be cautioned, and gloom was cast over the ships as they waited warily for Apollo to strike his revenge.

Then the excellent marksman Philtoctetes was bitten by a snake, causing a wound so stagnant with infection that the Greeks had no choice but to leave the warrior on the rocky island off Lemnos, where he was abandoned and forced to live alone for many years. And while the sombre army struggled to come to terms with the loss of one of their greatest men, Protesilaus, a youth of determination and valour, leapt on to the beaches of Troy where he was slain instantly by Troy's champion Hector, Priam's eldest son. The war had begun. It had been decreed by Zeus himself that mankind must be depleted, and so it was that the gods themselves became involved in a war that had been sparked by one single mortal woman.

For nine years the Greeks fought the impenetrable walls of Troy, guarded zealously by fine men of battle, including Hector, who led King Priam's other forty-nine sons in war. Paris joined their ranks, although the fury at this selfish man was ill-concealed by many. Antenor and Aeneas were men of wisdom and justice, and they too fought for Troy, although peace was their ultimate goal. The walls of the city had been built by Apollo and Poseidon themselves, and could not be damaged or scaled, despite the best efforts of Agamemnon's army. So the men of Greece attacked the allies of Troy instead, burning and looting their cities, and ravishing their women. It was at one such rape that a quarrel occurred which would change forever the course of the battle, drawing it to a fiery close that had been nearly a decade in coming.

Achilles and his men had attacked the city of Lyrnessus, taking as their prize two beautiful young women, Cryseis, who was chosen by Agamemnon, and Briseis, who became Achilles's. When it was discovered that the maiden Cryseis was a priestess of Apollo, a plague struck the camp, and Agamemnon was forced to return her to the temple. This he did, but upon his return, he stealthily lured Briseis from the camp of Achilles, and took her as his own. Achilles was so enraged and disgusted by this act that he threw down his armour and swore that he would no longer fight for such men, no better than pigs as they were.

Achilles was a fighter beyond compare and his absence pressed upon the Trojans an unexpected advantage. But the years of war had taken their toll, and the warriors on both sides had grown tired of the hostility. A peaceful end was sought, and Hector appeared, bravely suggesting that Menelaus and Paris fight a dual in order to decide the fate of Helen. This course was considered fair, and the two men engaged in a battle. Swords clashed, and many maidens fainted at the sight of two such glorious men tempting death so readily, so easily. They were well matched, but Menelaus had the power of a grudge that had festered for many years, and with this advantage, he pinned Paris to the walls of his city, determined to take his self-seeking life.

But Aphrodite could stand the battle no longer, and Paris's life was a sacrifice she would not allow. With flowing locks and gowns, she descended on the fighters, her beauty lighting their faces, filling their hearts with surprise and calm. And then she struck, hiding her beloved behind a cloud and pulling him to safety behind the city walls. Menelaus looked on in amazement, so close had he come after all these years to reclaiming his bride, and here the gods took them as their playthings, changing the course of fate, of mortal lives, on a whim. He cried out in rage, a call that was heard by the rest of the gods, and which opened up a wound that would not be healed until the end of the war was in sight.

Thetis screamed for justice for her son Achilles, and Apollo fell in with the defenders, making them strong. Zeus had taken the side of the invaders, who in their eager fury wounded both Ares and Aphrodite, spilling their immortal blood. The Greeks continued to fight, and in a night raid managed to take the life of Rhesus, capturing the white horses which he was taking to the Trojans under the cover of darkness. Apollo swooped down to encourage the Trojan forces, and they repaid this travesty by burning some of the Greek ships, which had been moored in the harbour. And as the fleet burned and threatened the lives of the Greek army, Patroclus, the great friend of Achilles, appeared in his friend's armour, and frightened the Trojans into retreat.

Forgetting himself, and confident in the armour of Greece's greatest warrior, Patroclus leapt to the top of the Trojan walls, sending their army into panic that was calmed only by Apollo. Once more this great god took the side of the Trojans, and knowing that this brave warrior was none other than Patroclus, he winded him, knocking from his body the sword and shield which protected him. Patroclus called out in anguish, begging for mercy, his bravado shorn from him along with the armour, but Hector stepped in and killed Patroclus with one single blow.

The roar of the Greeks wakened the slumbering Achilles, who had thrust from his mind all thought of the battle. Word of the death of his dear friend soon reached him, and he sprang into action, crying out for revenge which struck terror in the hearts of all who heard him. He trembled with rage, his blood coursing through his veins as he flexed his mighty muscles. New armour was summoned and he dressed quickly, making his way to Troy without delay.

And again the gods chose to intervene. As the terrified Trojans retreated into their city, the river god of the Scamander produced a wall of water that held back the murderous aggressor. This act was met by Hephaestus, who immediately stepped in to dry the waters with a flaming torch. And with a lust for revenge more invincible than the brave Achilles himself, he fought on, searching out the unfortunate Hector and slaying all who crossed his path. Sweat gleamed on his brow, which was furrowed with determination. Achilles presented a picture of such manly beauty that many of his opponents were stopped in their tracks, transfixed by this vision of glorious power. And when Hector saw Achilles, he too stopped dead, and bowed down, determined to fight him hand to hand until he saw that fiery gleam in Achilles' eye and knew that this marauder and his army meant his own certain death. He turned on his heels, and tried to run, but Achilles was stronger, more powerful. Three times they ran round the walls of the city, Hector becoming weaker, more frightened as they ran. And then Achilles caught him, and pinning him like a rabbit to the wall with his sword, howled a mighty cry then thrust his sword through Hector and killed him at once.

The Trojans moaned and wailed for their lost leader, stopping the battle briefly to mourn before swearing vengeance and carrying on more furiously than before. Achilles was unstoppable. When Penthesileia brought her Amazon women to help the Trojans, Achilles killed her mercilessly. And then Thersites, the nasty politician was struck down by Achilles' powerful fist. The invincible Achilles fought on and on, never tiring, never losing his composure, his cunning. Then Memnon arrived with a troop of Ethiopians, putting the favour of the gods once more with the Trojans, who allowed their forces to be increased so heavily. But Achilles enraged and irreverent, called upon Zeus to judge between himself and Memnon, to reverse the damage done by these visiting troops.

Memnon was out of favour with the king of gods, and Achilles was presented with a sword with which to slay the Ethiopian. And when he died, his followers turned immediately to birds and followed him to his rocky tomb on the neck of the island.

Achilles continued on, more boastful than ever, never losing a battle, never missing a stroke with his mighty sword. And then the gods lost patience, and irritated by his show of pride, they stepped in once again. Apollo had not yet repaid Achilles for the death of Tenes. Now was his chance. Guiding the hand of Paris, an arrow was directed to the heel of Achilles, the only part on his body which was not invincible. He died immediately.

For a time, the Greeks were weakened by the death of their hero, their determination dwindling their lust for battle dead. But as they mourned their forsaken leader, a new resolve grew in their hearts and after a solemn funeral, at which Achilles was awarded the highest honours of any warrior, they regrouped to plan their revenge. If their heart had been cut from them, their mind still functioned They were supremely competent strategists, extremely confident aggressors. Menelaus appeared to remind them once again of the reason for their battle, and thus inspired they set about deciding whom should take on the arms of Achilles. Agamemnon chose Odysseus, for his intelligence and courage, but Ajax the Greater was steeped in jealousy, knowing his strength was greater than that of Odysseus, beyond all doubt. He swore to avenge himself against Odysseus, but Athene, always a friend to Odysseus, persuaded him in another direction, and thinking he was murdering Odysseus and his troops, he slaughtered instead a flock of sheep. Convinced of his own madness, Ajax took his own life, another untimely and worrying loss to the Greeks.

The war had gone on too long. Zeus had planned it from beginning to end, but now he stopped to appraise, to ensure that the balance was correct. Troy must fall, he decreed but it could not be achieved without the bow and arrows from the quiver of Heracles, and without the presence of Achilles' son, far away in Scyros. The Greeks moved swiftly. And as they set about summoning Neoptolemus, the son of Achilles, from his home, they were warned of one final condition, without which the war could not be won. The Palladium must be removed from the city, for she guarded the gates and protected her from all invaders Odysseus began to plan.

Philoctetes was rescued from his terrible ordeal on Lemnos, his wounds long since cleared He had trained his mind and his muscles while he waited impatiently to be saved, and he was anxious to fight, to use the bow of the great Heracles in battle. He lifted it now, spitting on his palms as he did so, and feeding a poisoned arrow into the string of the bow. With a shriek that released the years of tortuous loneliness and pain, he sent the arrow straight to its mark at the neck of the handsome Paris, who was felled at once. And so Neoptolemus was dressed in his father's armour, a shaking, frightened youth with no knowledge of war, no interest in fighting but he took courage from the dress of his father, and he rose to the challenge, calmly leading his restored army towards the gates of Troy.

Odysseus was busy elsewhere. Dressed as a miserly beggar, with the help of Athene and Diomedes, he talked himself through the gates of the great city, where he fell upon the sleeping guards of the Palladium with such speed and grace that not one person in the entire city knew of his treachery. And on his stomach, he crawled from the city, dragging the Palladium with him, through a vermin-ridden drain where he struggled through sewage and mud to reach his army on the other side, the Palladium drawn triumphantly behind him.

Troy was on the verge of defeat. The Palladium no longer cast its splendid power over the city, and without that advantage, and with the minds of such cunning men as Odysseus to contend, there was no hope. But still she stood firm against the invaders, until Odysseus, with the help of Athene once again, came up with a final plan.

The craftsman Epeius was commissioned to build an enormous wooden horse, the inside of which was hollowed to hold fifty warriors. Agamemnon chose his greatest men to ride in its belly, and then gathering up the remainder of his fleet, he made as if to sail away, leaving the bay at Troy, but travelling only round the bend of the land, where he waited with anticipation and many prayers. Sinon was left behind on land, and as expected, he was taken prisoner by the Trojans, who wondered at their sudden luck. Sinon feigned fury at his colleagues who had left him behind, and taking the side of the Trojans, he wormed his way into their affections, into their grace, so that when he suggested they take into their walls the wooden horse, they did so, marvelling at its inscription:

A thank-offering to Athene for our safe return home.

Again, it was Cassandra who spoke out against the enemy's soldier, proclaiming that the horse brought nothing but death and final disaster for the city. The prophet Laocoon agreed with her, but as he made his way to the palace to warn the king, he was strangled by two serpents who leapt from the sea, and disappeared once they had finished their deadly task. And the great horse was dragged into the city, into the temple of Athene, where it was wreathed with ribbons and festooned with garlands of herbs.

The Trojans feasted that night, revelling and celebrating the end of a war that had taken quite small toll, despite its very long duration. Inside the wooden horse, the men of Greece laid quietly, waiting for darkness to fall, for their opportunity to strike. Helen alone remained suspicious, knowing that the Greeks were too clever, too ambitious to give in before the bitter end, and she held a grudging admiration for their daring, whatever it may be. She suspected the horse, and late in the evening, she slipped into the darkened temple and called out in the voices of the wives of the men inside, tempting them to come out and be reunited. Only the shrewd Odysseus guessed her trick, and holding his hand over the mouth of each hero who was addressed in false voice, he kept them quiet and soon Helen went away.

The Trojan men were drunk and sleepy when the men slid from the horse on ropes they had prepared earlier. And it was by moonlight, when the city was glowing with a numbing slumber, that the massacre of the Trojans began. King Priam was murdered as he crossed his courtyard, Menelaus went straight to the chambers of his errant wife, who bowed her head and spoke words of such regret, such honest remorse, that the determination in Menelaus was stilled, and he reached out to her and held her again in his arms, transfixed by her beauty, a slave to her love once more.

All was forgiven, and he carried Helen to his ship where she was welcomed into the arms of the Greeks, her fair face disarming them.

The plundering of Troy continued. Women were taken as prizes by the men of Greece who had for so long been starved of female companionship. Cassandra was taken by Agamemnon, and Neoptolemus who had grown in his weeks with the army to become a noble youth, took Hector's widow Andromache. Polyxena was sacrificed at the tomb of Achilles, to appease his ghost. Aeneas was wounded fatally, but the gods swooped to him and healed him. Apollo urged him to challenge the marauders, but Poseidon spoke softly to him, prophesying a day when he would rule Troy. And so Aeneas left the burning city, losing his wife in the escape, his subsequent travels becoming the subject of Roman legends, and Vergil's flawless *Aeneid*.

Queen Hecabe sat in her tower window watching the massacre, the deaths of her family, her colleagues, her servants and their children. And when Odysseus took her as his own, her howls of pure despair reached to the heavens and she was transformed magically into a dog, whose barks could be heard on the shores of Troy for all eternity.

Troy was broken, its streets steeped in the blood of generations of warriors, its walls finally scaled and broken, pouring out the good will and good luck that had been held in her embrace since the very beginning. She was set alight by zealous Greeks, a blazing beacon to all who knew her, her heart beating no longer.

So it was that Helen returned to Sparta with Menelaus, where they were reunited. Other great heroes went their separate ways, many returning to glory, carrying the spoils of their victory in treasure-laden ships. Still others met with disaster on their voyage home, but those are other stories, legends which were spawned by the war of Troy. And the great city of Troy was dead, her fires glowing for all to see, a warning to lovers and to the men of war which would live in their memories for the rest of time.

The Wanderings of Odysseus
The Journey

FLUSHED WITH THE GLORY of his victory at Troy, the brave and clever Odysseus gathered together the men of Ithaca into twelve ships, and headed across the perilous seas to their homeland. Odysseus was the grandson of the Autolycus, a thief of great artfulness and notoriety. That same cunning lay deep within the breast of Odysseus and it would, said the Oracle before Odysseus set off for Troy, bring about his solitary survival. For Odysseus alone would return from Troy, beaten and infinitely weary, having battled the great gods of the sea and sky and winds, having faced temptations and fears which would bring about the certain death of a lesser man. The journey would take ten years, and its cost would be Odysseus's men and very nearly his soul.

The Cicones

The fate of every chief beside
Who fought at Troy is known:
It is the will of Jove to hide
His untold death alone.

And how he fell can no man tell;
We know not was he slain
In fight on land by hostile hand,
Or plunged beneath the man.
William Maginn, Homeric Ballads

TEN YEARS HAD PASSED since brave Odysseus had last set eyes on his faithful wife Penelope, and their son Telemachus. The victory at Troy had been a sweet one, and sated by the triumph, the lean and weathered warrior made plans to return his men to their homeland. Twelve ships were prepared for the voyage, laden with the spoils of their warfare and leaving the wretched and burning city of Troy a blazing beacon behind them.

Odysseus and his men were filled with rumbustuous excitement at the prospect of seeing home once more; they leapt and frolicked aboard the mighty vessels, unable to leave behind the boisterous energy nurtured in them by ten years' war. The sea lay calm and welcoming. The journey had begun, and the ships groaned with booty.

But greed is a fatal human trait, and not content with the plunder they had foraged at Troy, Odysseus and his men sought new bounty, landing first on the island of the Cicones. A mass of carousing warriors, they swept onshore, taking the city of Ismarus, sending its inhabitants to their deaths, and feasting on the carcasses of their sheep and cattle. Only the priest of Apollo was spared from the carnage.

This priest was a clever man, and he sank to his knees in gratitude, bowing his head in respectful silence as he supplied the marauders with skins of powerful wine. While the men feasted and celebrated the newest of their victories, Odysseus grew increasingly uneasy. Although he shared the piratical spirit of his men, he had an ingrown prudence which argued against the excesses of their plundering. He implored his men to return to their ships, doubting now the wisdom of their attack. Soon enough his worries were confirmed.

As the men of Ithaca lay spent and drunk on wine and rich foods, the Cicones appeared on the hilltops, eager for revenge and accompanied by troops they had rallied from the islands around their country. Odysseus tried to rouse his men, but his efforts were futile. The Cicones attacked, driving the disoriented travellers back to their ship, mercilessly slaying those who lagged behind. The carnage took tremendous toll on the crews of each ship, and lamed by defeat they limped out of the harbour and back to sea. Back aboard ship, the surviving men worked quietly, bewildered by the proof of their humanity, their weakness. Home lay just round the Cape at the point of the Peloponnese. But as anticipation rose within them, so did the savage gales of the north-east winds. Zeus, king of the gods, would wreak his vengeance.

The Lotus-Eaters

Branches they bore of that enchanted stem,
Laden with flower and fruit, whereof they gave
To each, but whoso did receive of them,
And taste, to him the gushing of the wave
Far, far away did seem to mourn and rave
On alien shores; and if his fellow spake,
His voice was thin, as voices from the grave;
And deep-asleep he seem'd, yet all awake,
And music in his ears his beating heart did make.
Alfred, Lord Tennyson, The Odyssey

THE POWERFUL WINDS wrenched and buffeted the wretched ships, carrying them and their dispirited crew far from the point of the Cape, ever further from the welcoming shores of Ithaca. The sails were torn, and desperation clung to the men as they struggled against the most powerful of enemies – the sea and the winds themselves. And then, on the tenth day, there was peace. Just beyond the curve of the gentle waves lay land, a southern island from which a pervading and sweet perfume rose languorously into the air.

Ever watchful, Odysseus dared send ashore only three men from his depleted crew, and the men prepared the boat, their hearts beating. As their oars cut softly through the waves, an eerie and disquieting lassitude overwhelmed the men. Their trembling hands were warmed and stilled, their hearts were calmed in their breasts. And there, in front of them, appeared a remarkable being, whose serenity and stillness relaxed the anxious sailors, With a smile the creature beckoned them forth, holding out to them as he signalled, a large and purple flower.

The perfume of the flower snaked around the men, entrancing them and drawing them forth.

'The lotus flower,' the creature whispered softly. 'Sip its nectar. It is our food and drink here on the island of the lotus-eaters. It brings peace.' With that the lotus-eater raised the flower to the mouths of the men, who one by one drank deeply from its cup. Expressions of pure joy crossed their faces and their minds and memories were cleared of all but the rich and overwhelming pleasures of the nectar.

'It is the food of forgetfulness,' smiled the lotus-eater. 'Come, join us in the land of indolence. We have no worries here.'

Odysseus stood on the prow of his ship, a shadow of concern crossing his noble brow. 'Remain here,' he ordered his men, his voice unusually curt. His senses were buzzing with anticipation. He could feel an uneasy melancholy touching at the corners of his mind, and he angrily shrugged it away. All was not well on the island. He could sense no violence here, but danger lurked in a different cloak. He made his way to shore.

There was no sign of his sailors, and he strode purposefully in the direction he'd seen them take. He fought the growing ease which threatened to fill his mind, the strength of his character, his cunning forcefully keeping the invading sensations at bay. His men lolled by the fire of a group of beautiful beings. There was no anger or fear among them. They smiled a beatific welcome and signalled that he was to join them.

A lotus flower was held up for him to drink, and as he softened, a bell of fear rang in his brain. He curled back his lips and with renewed resolve, thrust the flower away. He drew from his pocket a length of rope, and hastily tied it to the scabbards of his men. He ignored their weak protests, and with his sword in their bags, forced them back to shore, and to the ship.

Their eyes were vague, their smiles bloodless. Odysseus and his men were as strangers to them, but they went aboard ship where they were lashed to the masts until the ship could sail on. The enchantment raised the heads of every man aboard Odysseus's ships. He roared at them to keep their heads down, to pierce their longing with good clean thoughts.

'Think of home, men,' he shouted. 'Forget it not, for it is what fires us onwards.'

And so they were to escape the fruit of the lotus-eaters, and the life of ease that threatened to overcome them. Odysseus and his men, weakened but still alive, sailed on.

The Cyclopes

So till the sun fell we did drink and eat,
And all night long beside the billows lay,
Till blush'd the hills 'neath morning's rosy feet;
Then did I bid my friends, with break of day,
Loosen the hawsers, and each bark array;
Who take the benches, and the whitening main
Cleave with the sounding oars, and sail away.
So from the isle we part, not void of pain,
Right glad of our own lives, but grieving for the slain.

Philip Stanhope Worsley, The Odyssey

ODYSSEUS AND HIS MEN sailed until they were forced to stop for food and fresh water. A small island appeared in the distance, and as they drew nigh, they saw that it was inhabited only by goats, who fed on the succulent, sweet grass which grew plentifully across the terrain. Fresh water cascaded from moss-carpeted rocks, and tumbled through the leafy country. The men's lips grew wet in anticipation of its cold purity.

As they clambered aboard shore, the fresh air filling their lungs, the men felt whole once more, and when they discovered, in their travels, an inviting cave filled with goats' milk and cheese, they settled down to feast. Their bellies groaning, and faces pink with pleasure, Odysseus and his men settled back to sleep on the smooth face of the cave, warmed by the hot spring that pooled in its centre, and sated by their sumptuous meal.

They were woken abruptly by heavy footfall, which shook the ground with each step. Eyeing one another warily, the tired men stayed silent, barely alert, but overwhelmingly fearful. Into the cave burst a flock of snow-white sheep and behind them the frightful giant Polyphemus, a Cyclops with one eye in the centre of his face. Polyphemus was the son of Poseidon, and he lived on the island with his fellow Cyclopes, existing peacefully in seclusion. He had not seen man for many years, and his single eyebrow raised in anticipation when he came upon his visitors. Odysseus took charge.

'Sire, in the name of Zeus, I beg your hospitality for the night. I've weary men who ...'

His words were cut off. The Cyclops laughed with outrage and reaching over, plucked up several of Odysseus's men and ate them whole. The others cowered in fear, but Odysseus stood firm, his stance betraying none of the fear that surged through his noble blood.

'I ask you again,' he began. But Polyphemus merely grunted and turned to roll a boulder across the opening to the cave. He settled down to sleep, his snores lifting the men from the stone floor of the cave, and forbidding them sleep. They huddled round Odysseus, who pondered their plight.

When he woke, Polyphemus ate two more men, and with his sheep, left the cave, carefully closing the door on the anxious men. They moved around their prison with agitation, wretched with fear. It was many hours before the Cyclops returned, but the men could not sleep. They waited for the sound of footsteps, they sickened at the thought of their inescapable death.

But the brave Odysseus feared not. His cunning led him through the maze of their predicament, and carefully and calmly he formed a plan. He was waiting when Polyphemus returned, and sidled up to the weary Cyclops with his goatskin of wine.

'Have a drink, ease your fatigue,' he said quietly, and with surprise the giant accepted. Unused to wine, he fell quickly into confusion, and laid himself unsteadily on the floor of the cave.

'Who are you, generous benefactor,' he slurred, clutching at the goatskin.

'My name is No one,' said Odysseus, a satisfied smile fleeting across his face.

'No one ...' the giant repeated the name and slipped into a deep slumber, his snores jolting the men once more.

Odysseus leapt into action. Reaching for a heavy bough of olive-wood, he plunged in into the fire and moulded its end to a barbed point. He lifted it from the fire, and with every ounce of strength and versatility left in his depleted body, he thrust it into Polyphemus' single eye, and stepped back, out of harm's way.

The Cyclops' roar propelled him through the air, momentarily deafening him. The men shuddered in the corner, shrieking with terror as the giant fumbled wildly for his torturers, grunting and shrieking with the intense pain. Soon his friends came running, and when they enquired the nature of his troubles, he could only cry, 'No one has blinded me' at which they returned, perplexed to their homes.

The morning came, cool and inviting, and hearing his sheep scrabbling at the door to get out to pasture, Polyphemus rose, and feeling along the walls, he found his boulder, and moved it. A smug look crossed his tortured features, and he stood outside the cave, his hands moving across the sheep as they left.

'You cannot leave this cave,' he taunted. 'You cannot escape me now.' He giggled with mirth at his cleverness, but his smile faded to confusion and then anger when he realized that the sheep had exited, and the cave was now empty. The men were gone.

Odysseus and his men laughed out loud as they unstrapped themselves from the bellies of the sheep, and racing towards their ships, Odysseus called out, 'Cyclops. It was not No one who blinded you. It was Odysseus of Ithaca,' and with that he lifted their mooring and set out for sea.

The torment of the giant rose in a deluge of sound and fury, echoing across the island and wakening his friends. Tearing off slabs of the mountainside, Polyphemus hurled them towards the escaping voice, which continued to taunt him. He roared a prayer to his father Poseidon, begging for vengeance, and struggled across the grass towards the sea.

But Odysseus had left, his ship surging across the sea to join with the rest of the fleet. Odysseus had escaped once more, and the sea opened up to him and his men, and they continued homewards, unaware that Poseidon had heard the cries of his son, and had answered them. Vengeance would be his.

The Island of Aeolus

ODYSSEUS AND THE REST OF HIS FLEET were carried out to sea by the swell of water which spread from the rocks which Polyphemus had plunged into the waters. His cries echoed across the waters, growing louder as he realized the full measure of Odysseus's treachery, for as he and his men left they had robbed him of most of his flock, which they now cooked on spits over roaring fires in the galley.

They sailed to the Island of Aeolus, the guardian of winds, who lived with his six sons and six daughters in great comfort. Here, Odysseus and his men were entertained and feted, fed with sumptuous buffets which boasted unusual delicacies, their thirst slaked by fine wines and exotic nectars. They remained there for thirty days, convincing Aeolus that the gods must detest these men for unfounded reasons., for they were perfect guests, and Odysseus was a fair man, and an eloquent spokesman and orator.

But at last Odysseus grew restless, eager once more to set sail for Ithaca. The generosity of Aeolus had calmed his men, and well-nourished they were ready to do battle with the elements which were bound to hamper their return. But Aeolus had a gift for Odysseus, which he presented as the men prepared to leave the island. With great solemnity he passed to the warrior a bag, carefully bound with golden lace, and knotted many times over. In it were secured all the winds, except the gentle winds of the west, which would blow them to Ithaca. It was a sacred gift, and a token of Aeolus's regard for his visitor.

The men set off at last, their bellies filled, their minds alert, all maladies relieved. They sailed, blown by the west wind, for nine days, until the bright shores of Ithaca shone, a brilliant beacon in the distance. And so it was that Odysseus, greatly fatigued by the journey, and by the excitement of reaching his native shores once more, allowed himself to rest, to fall into a deep slumber that would prepare him for the festivities about to greet him.

But several of the men who sailed under his command begrudged their gracious leader, and envious of his favour with Aeolus, decided to take for themselves some of the gift presented to Odysseus. It must contain treasure, they thought, so large and unwieldy a parcel it was, and the men encouraged one another, fantasizing about what that bag might contain.

And so it was that the men tiptoed to Odysseus's chambers, and eased the bag from his side, careful not to disturb his slumber. And it was with greedy smiles, and anxious, fumbling hands that the bag was opened and the fierce winds released. They swirled around them, tossing and plunging the ships into waves higher than the mountains of the gods. In no time they were returned to the Island of Aeolus, helpless and frightened by nature's angry howls.

Odysseus was roughly awakened, and pushed forward to greet the displeased Aeolus.

Aeolus cursed himself for humouring such foolish men, and understood at last the antipathy felt towards them by the great powers of Greece.

'Be gone, ill-starred wretch,' he snarled, and turned away from the unhappy seamen, towards the confines of his palace.

And so there was nothing for it but to return to the merciless seas, where the winds played havoc in their renewed freedom, where Poseidon waited for his chance to strike.

The Laestrygonians

THE SHIPS OF ODYSSEUS and his men were buffeted for many days before the winds exhausted their breath. And so they abandoned the ill-fated travellers, and left them in a dreadful calm. The ships sat still, mired in the stagnant waters, sunburnt and parched by the fiery sun. For a week they struggled with the heavy oars, seeming to move no further across the waveless sea. And then, on the eighth day, their ships limped into the rocky harbour of the Laestrygonians, where they moored themselves in an untidy row and made their way to shore. Odysseus was more cautious. Their travels had made him wiser than ever, and he tied his boat beyond the others, to a rocky outcrop in the open water. He signalled the men aboard to hold back, and climbed up the mast to get a better view.

Three of his men had rowed ashore, and Odysseus watched them as they spoke to two lovely young maidens, drawing water from a clear spring. The men stopped to take a drink before pressing on in the direction pointed out to them by the maidens. They looked calm and assured. Odysseus felt no such conviction, and he remained where he was, chewing his lower lip with concern. His men could see the others, and pestered Odysseus to allow them ashore, to drink of the cool fresh water, but he bade them to be silent and returned to his look-out.

The three men were easily visible from his post and Odysseus could see them reaching the walls of a magnificent castle, gilded and festooned with jewels. They hesitated at the gates. And it was then that the Laestrygonians attacked. Great, heaving giants plummeted through the gates on to the hapless men, racing towards shore and wailing a terrible cry, a battle song that tweaked at Odysseus's memory. These were the the evil cannibals who brought overwhelming fear to the heart of every traveller. Their shores were the most dangerous in Greece, their fearsome appetite for violence and unwitting seamen legendary.

They stampeded to shore, flocking in crowds to crush the ships under a deluge of rocks and spears. The sailors were skewered like lambs, and plucked from the waters, swallowed whole or sectioned and dipped into a bath of melted sheep's fat which lay bubbling in a cauldron beside the shores. The Laestrygonians had received word of Odysseus's ships and were prepared for the feast. They splashed and howled, laughing and eating until every one of Odysseus's comrade's ships was destroyed, emptied of its human cargo which presented such a cruel breakfast.

Odysseus had long since cut the ropes which anchored him to the rocks, and he and his crew raced for the deep sea, rowing faster than any mortal before them. Flushed with fear, their hearts pounding, they rowed for two days, one single crew saved from the tortures of the Laestrygonians by the wit of their captain. They rowed until they reached the shores of another island, where they collapsed, unable to lift their weary heads, caring not if in their refuge they courted danger.

Circe and the Island of Aeaea

On his bloomy face
Youth smil'd celestial, with each opening grace.
He seiz'd my hand and gracious thus began:
'Ah! whither roam'st thou, much enduring man?
O blind to fate! What led thy steps to rove
The horrid mazes of this magic grove?
Each friend you seek in yon inclosure lies,
All lost their form, and habitants of sties.
Think'st thou by wit to model their escape?
Sooner shalt thou, a stranger to thy shape,
Fall prone their equal: first they danger know:
Then take the antidote the gods bestow ...
Alexander Pope, The Odyssey

FOR NEARLY TWO DAYS the men slept on the shores of the unknown island, drinking in the peacefulness which covered them like a blanket, coming to terms with the loss of their comrades in their dreams. They woke freshened, but wary, eager to explore the land, but made prudent by their misadventures. In the distance, smoke curled lethargically into the windless sky. The island was inhabited, but by whom?

Odysseus divided the group into two camps, one taken by himself, the other led by his lieutenant, the courageous and loyal warrior Eurylochus. They drew lots from a helmet, and so it was decreed that Eurylochus would lead his party into the forest, towards the signs of life. His men gathered themselves up, and brushed off their clothes, trembling with anticipation and fear. They moved off.

The path wound its way through the tree-clad island, drawing the men into the bosom of the hills. There, at its centre, was a roughly hewn cottage, chimney smoking, and no sign of danger. Its fine stone walls were guarded by wolves and lions, but they leapt playfully towards the explorers, licking them and wagging their tails. Confused but comforted by the welcome, the men drew forward, and soon were enticed by the exquisite melody which drifted from the cottage. A woman's voice rang out, pure and sweet, calming their hearts, and drying the sweat on their brows. They moved forward confidently, only Eurylochus hanging back in caution.

They were greeted by the figure of a beautiful woman, whose hair tumbled to her heels, whose eyes were two green jewels in an ivory facade. Her smile was benevolent, welcoming, her arms outstretched. The men stumbled over one another to greet her, and were led into the cavernous depths of the cottage, where tables groaned with luxurious morsels of food – candied fruits, roasted spiced meats, plump vegetables and glazed breads, tumbling from platters of silver and gold. Wines and juices glistened in frosted glasses, and a barrel of fine brandy dripped into platinum goblets. It was a feast beyond compare, and the aroma enveloped the men, drawing them forward. They ate and drank while Eurylochus waited uncomfortably, outside the gates. And after many hours, when the men had taken their fill, they sat back with smiles of contentment, of satisfied gluttony, and raised their eyes in gratitude to their hostess.

'Who are you, fine woman?' slurred one of the crewman, made bold by the spirits.

'I am Circe,' she whispered back. And with a broad sweep of her hand, and a cry of laughter which startled her guests, drawing them from their stupor, she shouted, ' And you are but swine, like all men.'

Circe was a great and beautiful enchantress, living alone on this magical island where all visitors were pampered and fed with a charmed repast until Circe grew bored with them. And then, stroking their stupid heads, Circe would make them beasts. Now, she raised her mighty hands and laid them down upon the heads of Eurylochus's men and turned them to swine, corralling them snuffling and grunting through the door. Eurylochus peered round a tree in dismay. Ten men had entered, and now ten pigs left. The enchantress followed them, penning them in sties and stopping to speak gently to the other beasts, who had once been men. Happily she returned to her cottage and took up her loom once more.

Eurylochus sprinted through the forest, breathless with fear and disbelief as he rejoined Odysseus and the crew. Odysseus drew himself up, and a determined look transformed his distinguished features. He reached for his sword, and thrusting a dagger in his belt he set off to rescue his men, turning his head heavenwards and praying for assistance from the very gods who had spurned him. Odysseus had suffered the insults of war, and the tortures of their perilous journey. He would fight for his men, for his depleted crew. No woman, enchantress or not, would outwit him, would take from him his few remaining men.

As he struggled through the forest, a youth stumbled across his path.

'Here,' he whispered. 'Take this.' And he thrust into the hands of Odysseus a divine herb known as Moly, a plant with black roots and a snow white flower so beautiful that only those with celestial hands had the strength to pluck it. Moly was an antidote against the spells of Circe, and with this in his possession, Odysseus would be safe. The boy, who was really the god Hermes, sent by the goddess Athene, warned Odysseus of Circe's magical powers, and offered him a plan.

And so it was that Odysseus reached the cottage of Circe, and entered its welcoming gates. There the same feast greeted him, and he partook of the food until he lay sleepy and sated. Circe could hardly disguise her glee at the ease with which she had trapped this new traveller, and as she waved her wand to change him into a pig, Odysseus rose and spoke.

'Your magic has no power over me,' he said, and he thrust her to the ground at the point of his sword. She trembled with fear, and with longing.

'You,' she breathed, 'you must be the brave Odysseus, come from far to be my loving friend.' And she threw down her wand and took the soldier into her warm embrace. They lay together for a night of love, and in the morning, spent yet invigorated by their carnal feast they rose to set free Odysseus's men.

And there, on the enchanted island of Circe, Odysseus and his men spent days which stretched into golden weeks and then years, fed from the platters laden with food, their glasses poured over with drink, resting and growing fat, until they had forgotten the tortures of their journey. Odysseus was charmed by the lovely Circe, and all thoughts of Penelope and Telemachus were chased from his mind. His body was numbed by the pleasures inflicted upon it.

But the great Odysseus was a supreme leader, and even pure indulgence could not blunt his keen mind forever. As his senses gradually cleared, as Circe's powers over his body, over his soul began to wane, he felt the first rush of homesickness, of longing for Ithaca and his family. And in his heart he began to feel the weight of his responsibilities, the burden of his obligations to his country, to his men and to the gods.

With that, he made secret plans for their escape, and as the enchantment began also to wear at the sanity of his men, as they grew tired of the hedonism which filled their every waking hour, they became party to his strategy. With that, he went in search of Circe.

The House of Hades

ODYSSEUS FOUND THE ENCHANTRESS Circe in a calm and equable mood. She loved Odysseus, who had warmed her heart and her bed, but she had known since first setting eyes on the great warrior that he could never be completely hers. This day had been long in coming, but now that it was upon her, she gave him her blessing.

There were, however, tasks to be undertaken before Odysseus could be freed. He and his men could not voyage to Ithaca until they had met with the ghost of the blind prophet Tiresias, wiser than any dead or alive. They must travel to him at Hades, bringing gifts to sacrifice to the powers of the Underworld. Whitened by fear the men agreed to journey with Odysseus, to learn their fate and to receive instructions for their return to Ithaca.

All his men, spare one, prepared themselves for the voyage, but Elpenor, the youngest of the crew, lay sleeping on the roof of the cottage, where he'd stumbled in a drunken stupor the previous night. He woke to see the ship and his comrades setting sail from the island of Circe, and forgetting himself, he tumbled to the ground where he met an instant and silent death.

The men pressed on, unaware that one of their lot was missing. They sailed through a fair wind, raised by Circe, and as darkness drew itself around them, they entered the deep waters of Oceanus, where the Cimmerians lived in eternal night. There the rivers Phlegethon, Cocytus and Styx converged beneath a great rock, and Odysseus and his men drew aground. Following Circe's instructions, they dug a deep well in the earth beside the rock, then they cut the throats of a ram and a ewe, allowing their virgin blood to fill the trough.

The ghosts of the departed began to gather round the blood, some in battle-stained garb, others lost and confused; they struggled up to the pit and fought for a drink. Odysseus drew his sword to hold back the swelling crowd, startled as Elpenor, pale and blood-spattered, greeted his former master. He pressed forward, moaning and reaching greedily for the mortals.

'I have no grave,' he uttered. 'I cannot rest.' He clung to Odysseus whose cold stare belied the anxiety that pressed down on his heart. He was too close to the wretched creatures of the Underworld, near enough to be dragged down with them. He shook Elpenor loose.

'I will build you a grave,' he said gruffly. 'A fine grave with a tomb. There your ashes will lay and you shall have peace.'

Elpenor pulled back at once, a bemused expression crossing his pale face. He slid away, as reaching arms grappled into the space he left. Faces blended together in a grotesque dance of the macabre, writhing bodies struggling to catch a glimpse of mortals, of the other side. Familiar features appeared and then disappeared, as Odysseus fought to keep control of his senses.

'Odysseus,' the voice was soft, crooning. How often he'd heard it, sheltered in the tender arms of its bearer, rocked, adored. Mother.

Anticleia had been alive when he'd sailed for Troy and until this moment he knew not of her death. He longed to reach out for her, to take her pale and withered body against his own, to provide her with the comfort she had so tenderly invested in him.

But his duties prodded at his conscience, and he pricked his sword at her, edging her away from him, searching the tumultuous mass for Tiresias. At last he appeared from the shadowy depths, stopping to drink deeply from the bloody sacrifice. He leaned against his golden staff, and spoke slowly, in a language mellowed with age.

'Odysseus,' Tiresias said. 'Thy homecoming will not be easy. Poseidon bears spite against thee for blinding his Cyclops son Polyphemus. Yet you have guardians, and all may go well still, if, when you reach the hallowed shores of Trinacrian, ye harm not the herds of the Sun that pasture there. Control thy men, Odysseus. Allow not the greed that has tainted their hearts, that has led you astray, to shadow your journey.'

He paused, drinking again from the trenches and shrugging aside the groping arms of his comrades. He spat into the pool of blood.

'If you slay them, Odysseus, you will bring death upon your men, wreckage to your ships, and if you do escape, you will find thy house in trouble, no glory in your homecoming. And in the end, death will come to thee from the sea, from the great Poseidon.' With that, Tiresias leaned heavily on his staff and stumbled away, calling out as he left, 'Mark my words, brave Odysseus. My sight is not hampered by the darkness.'

Odysseus sat down and pondered the blindman's words. Anticleia appeared once again and he beckoned her closer, coaxed her to drink, and with the power invested in her by the blood, she drew a deep breath and spoke. She asked eagerly of his news, and told of her own, how she had died of grief thinking him dead at Troy. But his father, Laertes, she said, was still alive, though weakened by despair and feeble in his old age. Penelope his wife waited for him, loyal despite the attentions of many suitors. And Telemachus had become a man, grown tall and strong like his father.

Odysseus was torn by the sight of his mother, knowing not when he would set eyes on her again. He reached out to touch her, but she shrank from his embrace, a vision only, no substance, no warm blood coursing through her veins. He stood abruptly and was thronged by the clambering dead, as his mother drifted from his sight. He called after her, but she had gone.

Many of his comrades from Troy appeared now, eager to see the fine Odysseus, curious about his presence in Hades without having suffered the indignity of death. There was Agamemnon, and again, Achilles, whose stature was diminished, whose glory had tarnished. Ajax was there, and Tantalus and Sisyphus reached out to him, howling with anguish. And then there was Minos, and Orion, and Heracles, great men once, ghostly spectres now. They circled him and he felt chilled by their emptiness, by their singleness, by their determination to possess him. He turned away and strode from the group, shaking with the effort.

And his men joined him there, as they rowed away from that perilous island, down the Ocean river and back to the open sea. The friendly winds tossed them back to Circe's island, where the enchantress awaited them. Their belongings were ready, and she had resigned herself to the loss of her great love. She pulled Odysseus to one side, stroking him until he stiffened with pleasure, tempted as always to remain with her, enjoyed and enjoying. She whispered in his ear, warning him of the hazards which stood between Aeaea and Ithaca, the perils of his course. And he kissed her deeply and with a great surge of confidence, pushed her aside and went to meet his men.

Together they uncovered the body of poor Elpenor, and burned it with great ceremony, placing his ashes in a grand and sturdy tomb. Their duty done, they looked towards home.

And so it was that Odysseus escaped the fires of Hades, and the clutches of the shrewd Circe, and found himself heading once more towards Ithaca and home, the warnings of Circe and Tiresias echoing in his ears. As chance would have it, the first of the dangers lay just across the shimmering sea.

The Sirens

Come, pride of Achaia, Odysseus, draw night us!
Come, list to our chant, rest the oar from its rowing:
Never yet was there any whose galley fled by us,
But, sweet as the drops from the honeycomb flowing,
Our voices enthralled him, and stayed his ongoing,
And he passed from that rapture more wise than aforetime:
For we know all the toil that in Troyland befell,
When the will of the Gods was wrought out in the war-time:
Yea, all that is done on the earth can we tell.

A.S. Way, The Odyssey

THE AIR WAS HOT and heavy around the vessel; the sunlight glinted on her bow as she cut through the silent sea. The men were restless. The silence held the threat of ill fate and they looked to Odysseus with wary eyes, seeking his wisdom, begging him wordlessly for comfort.

Odysseus stood tall alongside the mast, his noble profile chiselled against the airless horizon. He looked troubled, his head cocked to one side as he heard the first whispers of a beautiful melody.

It stung and tore at his sanity, dredging up a memory, a warning, but lulling him somehow away from his men, from his responsibilities, from the course of his voyage. He struggled against the growing sound, alert to the knowledge that his men had not yet heard its seductive strains but every fibre of his being ached to find its source, to touch its creator.

The Sirens. The words leapt to his troubled mind, and with great effort he drew himself from the reverie.

'Lash me to the mast,' he cried suddenly. Something in his voice caused his astonished men to obey.

'But captain, sir ...' one of the younger seamen ventured to express his amazement.

'Now!' Odysseus felt the bewildered hurt of his men. He also heard the growing symphony of the Sirens. He felt himself being drawn back, their melody licking at his mind like the hottest of fires, burning his resolve and his sanity.

'The candles,' he mouthed groggily. 'Melt the candles.' He could barely choke out the words. 'The wax ... in your ears.'

A startled silence was filled by the roaring of Odysseus's first mate: 'Do as he says, men. We have never had cause to question the wisdom of Odysseus. He has the strength and the cunning of ten men. He sees what we cannot see. We must put our faith in him.'

The ears of each man were carefully plugged by the wax of forty candles. As the last man turned his head, a swell of sound filled the air. Odysseus gave himself to it, wrestling with the lashings that restrained his strong frame. The sweet song of death called him, beckoned him from his lofty post.

The Sirens. The birds of death, temptresses of darkness – their sensuous melody played on the chords of his mind, calling him to a blackness which would envelope him forever. They appeared around him, luxuriant hair tumbling about angelic faces. He was trapped in a swarm of soaring wings and resplendent feathers. Women of the birds, with voices to lull even the hardiest warrior to certain death.

The deafened crew of his ship watched in amazement as the elegant creatures swooped among them, their eyes gleaming with secret knowledge, their voices capturing Odysseus in a cloud of passionate yearning.

Befuddled by the play on his senses, Odysseus signalled to his men to begin to row, then he sank back against the mast, spent and sickened by longing. The mighty vessel collected speed, ploughing through the sea that rippled with the thrust of the Sirens and the power of their music.

The sound increased, their music tortuously alluring as the Sirens fought for the spirit of Odysseus. The men battled with their oars, churning the water aside, sensing the danger that had hewn such fear on the face of their leader.

The music of the Sirens took on a rising note of mirth, and then, as the ship surged away from their grips, they laughed aloud.

'You will be ours again,' they sang together, laughing and diving around the fallen man. 'Ours to the end.'

They rose in a cluster of discord and light and disappeared, a painful silence filling the cacophony of sound that was no more. Odysseus rose again. He looked to the east, to the island of the Sirens, and he signalled to his men to clear their ears. He'd had to hear it. Circe had warned him of the Sirens, and although he trusted not the weak natures of his men, he had relished the chance to tempt his own resolve. But it was a bitter triumph, for he'd very nearly been lost to them, tugged so close to the edge of his mind, to madness and the darkness beneath.

A sweet wind caught the main sail and the ship plunged forward. Their small victory raised a smile on the weather-beaten faces of the seamen, and then they turned their faces to waters new.

Scylla and Charybdis

CIRCE HAD WARNED ODYSSEUS of the dangers that would beset him and his crew should they choose to ignore the words of wise Tiresias. The next part of their journey would take them though a narrow strait, peopled by some of the most fearsome monsters in all the lands. Odysseus was to guide the ship through the narrow passage, through fierce and rolling waters, looking neither up nor down, embodying all humility.

But the pride of Odysseus was more deeply rooted than his fear, and ignoring Circe's words, he took a stand on the prow of his ship, heavily armoured and emboldened by the support of his men. Here he stood as they passed the rocks of Charybdis, the hateful daughter of Poseidon who came to the surface three times each day in order to belch out a powerful whirlpool drawing into her frothing gut all that came back with it. There was no sign of her now, the waters suspiciously stilled. Ahead lay an island, drenched in warm sunlight, beckoning to the weary sailors. They must just make it through.

Odysseus had kept the details of this fearsome strait from his men. They had been weakened by battle, and by the horrific sights which had met their eyes since leaving Troy. They were so close to Ithaca, he dared not cast their hopes and anticipation into shadow. And so it was that only Odysseus knew of the next monster who was to be thrust upon them in that dangerous channel, only Odysseus who knew that she was capable of tasks more gruesome than any of them had seen in all their travels.

For Scylla was a gluttonous and evil creature that haunted the strait, making her home in a gore-splattered den where she feasted on the remains of luckless sailors. She was, they said, a nymph who had been the object of Glaucus's attentions. Glaucus was a sea-god who had been turned into a merman by a strange herb he had unwittingly swallowed. And as much as he adored Scylla, so he was loved by Circe who, in a jealous rage, had turned Scylla into a terrible sea-monster with six dog's heads around her waist. She lived there in the cliff face in the straits of Messina, and devoured sailors who passed. She moved silently. Odysseus was loath to admit it, but the silent danger she represented placed more fear in his heart than the bravest of enemies.

Odysseus and his men passed further into the quiet strait, their mouths dry with fear. A silence hung over them like a shroud. And then it was broken by a tiny splash, and tinkle of water dripping, and up, with a mighty roar, came Scylla, the mouths on each head gaping open, their lethal jaws sprung for one purpose alone. Smoothly she leaned forward and in a flash of colour, of torn clothing and hellish screams, six of his best men were plucked from their posts aboard ship and drawn into the mouth of her cave. Their cries rent at the heart, at the conscience of Odysseus, and he turned helplessly to his remaining crew who looked at him with genuine fear, distrust and anger. A mutinous fever bubbled at the edges of their loyalty, and Odysseus knew he had lost them. He looked back at the cave where Scylla had silenced his hapless men, and signalled the others to row faster. A repeat of her attack would leave him with too few men to carry on. They rowed towards the shores of the great three-cornered island, Thrinacie, where the herds of the Sun-god Helius grazed peacefully on the hilltops.

The Flock of Helius

SHAKEN BY THE TORTURE of his men, Odysseus proclaimed that they would make no further stops until they reached the shores of Ithaca. But the mutiny that had been brooding was thrust forward in the form of an insolent Eurylochus, who insisted that they set down their anchors, and have a night of rest. Tiresias and Circe had warned him of this flock of sheep, and Odysseus ordered his men to touch them not, to ignore their bleatings, their succulent fat which spoke of years of grazing on tender grasses, nurtured

by Helius himself. The sailors took a solemn oath and Odysseus grudgingly allowed them to moor the ship to the rocky coast. They set about preparing a fire, and after a silent meal, fell into a deep sleep.

When morning broke, the skyline was littered with heavy clouds, tugging on the reins of a prevailing wind. And with it came a tempest which blew over the island for thirty days, prohibiting the safe voyage of the men, trapping them on an island that was empty of nourishment. And so it was that for thirty days the crew dined meagrely on corn and wine which the lovely Circe had provided, and when that was devoured, they took up their harpoons and fished the swirling waters for sustenance. And as hunger grew wild within their bodies, so did their minds wander a seditious path, along which their loyalty was cast and their oaths forgotten.

One night as Odysseus slept, weakened by hunger like his men, the errant sailors slaughtered several of Helius's sacred cows, dedicating some to the god, but gorging themselves on the carcasses of many more, till they sat, fattened and slovenly, rebelliously content. The cows were enchanted, and lowed while impaled on a spit over the fire, their empty carcasses rising to trample the ground around the men, but they repented not and continued to eat until soon their treachery was brought to the attention of Helius himself. Odysseus woke to discover the travesty and corralled his men aboard ship, urging them to escape before vengeance could be sprung upon them. But it was too late.

As Helius cried out to Zeus, imploring the king of gods to take divine retribution, Poseidon reached up his powerful staff and stirred up a tempest so violent that the ship was immediately cast to pieces in the furious waters. And Zeus sent storms and thunderbolts which broke the ship and its men into tiny pieces, crashing down the mast upon the sailors and killing them all. Only Odysseus who had remained true to the gods, was saved, and he clung to the wreckage, which formed a makeshift raft. For nine days he tumbled across waves that were larger than the fist of Poseidon himself, but his resolve was strong, his will to live was greater than the anger of the gods.

His men were drowned. Thoughts of Penelope and Telemachus kept him afloat as he fought the turbulent seas, escaping the grasp of an angry Poseidon. He was battered by the storm which drove him back to Charybdis, and as her great whirlpool was spat out, his raft was sucked into the waters that were drawn into her greedy belly. Faint with hunger, with fear, he reached out and held on to the spreading branches of a great fig tree and there he hung, perilously close to the vortex of water, until his raft was thrown out again. And Odysseus dropped into the sea, and paddled and drifted until he spied land once again. And only then did he allow himself to lay down his head, secure in the knowledge that help was at hand. So the noble Odysseus slept, and was washed towards the shores of this secluded island of Ogygia.

Calypso's Island

Around, thick groves their summer-dress
Wore in luxuriant loveliness —
Alder and poplar quivered there,
And fragrant cypress tower's in air.
And there broad-pinion'd birds were seen,

Nesting amid the foliage green;
Birds, which the marge of ocean hunt —
Gull, prating daw, and cormorant;
And there, the deep mouth of the cave
Fringing, the cluster'd vine-bough wave.
Francis Wrangham, The Odyssey

ODYSSEUS COULD SEE LAND and in the distance a beautiful nymph, the most beautiful woman on whom he had ever laid eyes. Her milk-white skin was gleaming in the moonlight, and the wrathful winds tossed her silken hair. Her voice was soft, inviting above the raging storms.

'Come to me, Odysseus,' she whispered. 'Here you will find love, and eternal life.'

Odysseus struggled for breath, filled with longing and wonder. She reached a slender hand towards him, across the expanse of water, and lifted him from its depths, the strength of her grip, the length of her reach inhuman. He shuddered at her touch.

'You have come to join me,' she said calmly, as Odysseus laid restless and dripping beneath her.

Odysseus nodded, his passion spent. He was alive. The others had been clutched by the revengeful Poseidon. He was grateful to this nymph. He would plan his escape later.

'I have asked for you, and you have come,' she intoned quietly, settling herself at his side. Odysseus felt the first stirring of fear, but dismissed it as the lovely maiden smiled down on him.

She was Calypso, the lovely daughter of Thetis, and like Circe she was an enchantress. She lived alone on the island, in a comfortable cavern overhung by vines and fragrant foliage. She was gentle, and quiet, tending to Odysseus's every need, feeding him with morsels of delicious foods, warming him with handspun garments which clung to his body like a new skin, and she welcomed him in her bed, running his body over with hot hands that explored and relaxed the beaten hero until he grew to love her, and to build his life with her on the idyllic island.

For seven years he lived with Calypso, drunk with luxury and love. She was more beautiful than any he had seen before, and her island was dripping with pleasures. And as his happiness grew deeper, his fire and fervour spent to become a peaceful equilibrium, he felt the jab of conscience, of something untoward eating at the corners of his idyll, and he realized that he was living in a numb oblivion, that his passion to return home, to see his family, to take up the responsibilities of his leadership, were as strong in him as they had ever been and that he must allow them to surge forth, to fill him again with fiery ambition.

And in that seventh year he spent more and more time seated on the banks of the island, gazing towards his own land where time did not stand still and where his wife's suitors were threatening to take over his country, his rule. He came eventually to the notice of Athene, whose favour he had kept despite the outrage of the other gods, and she went at once to Zeus on his behalf. Zeus was fair and kind, and he balanced the sins of Odysseus against his innate good will, and the struggles to keep in check his unruly crews, all of which were lost to him now. Poseidon was away from Olympus and the time seemed right to set Odysseus free, for he had lived long enough in an enchanted purgatory.

Calypso reluctantly agreed to allow him his freedom, and she provided him with the tools to create a sturdy boat, and with provisions of food and drink enough to last the entire journey. She bathed him, dressed him in fine silks and jewels, as befitted a returning warrior, and kissing him gently but with all the fire of her love for him, she bade him go, with a tear-stained farewell. She had provided him with instructions which would see him round the dangers, across the perils that could beset him. He set sail for Ithaca.

Nausicaa and the Phaeacians

Resplendent as the moon, or solar light,
Alcinous' palace awed the o'erdazzled sight.
On to its last recess, a brazen wall
That from the threshold stretch'd, illumined all;
Round it of azure steel a cornice roll'd,
And every gate, that closed the palace, gold.
The brazen threshold golden pillars bore,
A golden ringlet glitter'd on the door,
The lintel silver, and to guard his gate,
Dogs in a row, each side, were seen to wait,
In gold and silver wrought, by Vulcan made,
Immortal as the god, and undecay'd.
William Sotheby, The Odyssey

WITH THE STARS of the Great Bear twinkling on his left, Odysseus sailed for eighteen days, tossed gently on a calm sea with a favourable wind breathing on the sails which were pulled tight. And then Poseidon, returning to Olympus, noticed this solitary sailor, and filled with all the fury of a wronged god, produced a calamitous wave which struck out at Odysseus and thrust him overboard. And there ensued a storm of gigantic proportions which stirred the sea into a feverish pitch which threatened with each motion to drown the terrified sailor.

But despite his many wrongs, his well-publicized shortcomings, Odysseus had made friends, and inspired awe and respect among many in Greece. And so it was that the sea-goddess Ino-Leucothea took pity on him, and swimming easily to him in the tempestuous sea, cast off his clothes and hung around his waist a magic veil, which would carry him safely to shore. She lingered before swimming away, her eyes lighting on his strong body which splashed powerfully in the waters, and she laid her hand briefly on his skin, warming him through and filling him with a deep and new energy.

Odysseus swam on, the sea calmed by Athene, and landed, exhausted on the shores of the island of the Phaeacians, where he fell into a profound slumber. Athene moved inland, into the chamber of Nausicaa, the lovely daughter of King Alcinous, and into her dreams, urging her to visit the shores of the island, to wash her clothes in the stream that tumbled by the body of the sleeping warrior. And when she woke, Nausicaa encouraged her friends to come with her to the stream, to play there, and to make clean her soiled garments.

Their cries of frivolity woke the sleepy Odysseus and he crawled from under a bush, naked and unruly. His wild appearance sent the friends of Nausicaa running for help, but she stood still, her virgin heart beating with anticipation. His untamed beauty inspired a carnal longing that was new to her, and from that moment she was devoted to him. She listened carefully to his words and taking his hand, led him to see her father.

Now Athene knew that King Alcinous would be less affected by Odysseus's beauty than his daughter, and prepared a healing mist which enshrouded Odysseus, who had been hastily dressed by Nausicaa.

Alcinous lived in a splendid palace, filled with glittering treasures and elegant furnishings. His table was renowned across the lands, delicious fruits soaked in fine liquors, breads veined with rich nuts, succulent meats which swirled in fine juices, glazed vegetables and herbs from the most remote gardens across the world. There were jellies and sweets, baked goods, cheeses and pâtes, fresh figs and luscious olives, all available every day to whomever visited the kind and generous leader. His women were well-versed in the vocabulary of caring for their men, and the palace gleamed with every luxury, with every necessity, to make an intelligent man content.

He listened to Odysseus now, and was struck by the power of his words. Odysseus had the appearance of a stray, but the demeanour of greatness. Alcinous wondered curiously if he was a god in disguise, so eloquent and masterful was their unknown visitor. But Odysseus kept from them his identity knowing not the reception he would receive, and careful not to destroy his chances of borrowing a ship and some men to take him to Ithaca.

And Odysseus was warmly welcomed in the palace, and fed such marvellous foods and drinks, living in such comfortable splendour, that he considered at length the request by King Alcinous and his lovely wife that he stay on to take Nausicaa as his bride. But he was too close to home to give up, and Alcinous, too polite and kind to keep Odysseus against his will, agreed to let him pass on, aided by the Phaeacian ships and hardy sailors.

So it was that on the final night of his stay with the Phaeacians he was made the guest of honour at a luxuriant feast, where the conversation turned to travels, and to war, and finally, to the victory of Troy. Inspired by their talk, a minstrel took up his lute and began to sing of the wars, of the clear skies of Ithaca, the valour of Achilles, and the skill of Odysseus and Epius. So loudly did he extol the virtues of the brave son of Laertes that Odysseus was forced to lower his head in despair, and the tears fell freely to his plate where they glinted and caught the attention of the king and his men.

'Why do you suffer such dismay?' asked Alcinous gently, for he had grown fond of the elegant stranger in their midst.

Odysseus' reply was choked. The burden of the last ten years now threatened to envelope him. He had never pondered long the nature of the trials that had faced him, but as he ordered them in his mind, preparing his story to tell the King, their enormity swamped him, frightened him, made him weak.

'I am Odysseus,' he said quietly, 'son of Laertes.'

The room filled with excited joy – glasses were lifted, toasts offered, Odysseus was carried to the king where he received a long and honourable blessing. Then silence overcame them and they listened to the tales of the illustrious Odysseus who had suffered such misadventure, and overcome all with his cunning and mastery. They gazed in wonderment on the hero. He had long been thought dead, but everyone knew of the devotion, the loyalty of his wife Penelope, who refused to contemplate the idea. They encouraged him to return home. And if the unknown castaway received such glory in their generous household, a warrior of such note received the very bounty of the gods.

Ships were prepared and laden with gifts. The strongest and bravest of the Phaeacians were chosen to set sail with him, and warmed by the love and admiration of his new friends, Odysseus was placed in fine robes at the helm of a new ship, and sent towards home.

Odysseus, worn by troubles, and the relief of reaching his shores, slept deeply on board the ship, and loathe to wake him, the awe-struck sailors lifted him gently to the sands of Ithaca, where they piled his body with all the glorious gifts provided by the King, and then they retreated through the bay of Phorcys. Poseidon had been smouldering with rage at the disloyalty of Athene and Zeus, but realizing that Odysseus had been charmed, and had friends who would not allow his destruction, he allowed the hero to be placed on the sands, turning his wrath instead on the sailors. As they passed from the harbour into the seas, he struck a blow with his mighty staff and turned them all to stone, their ship frozen forever on the silent waters that led to Ithaca. It remained there as a warning to all who thought they could betray Poseidon and his mighty powers.

And so the mighty Odysseus lay once again on the shores of Ithaca, knowing not that ten years' journey had brought him at last to his promised land, or that the glory predicted by the Phaeacians would not yet be his. Battles new lined themselves on the horizon, but Odysseus was home, and from that secure base, could take on all.

The Wanderings of Odysseus
The Homecoming

WHEN BRAVE ODYSSEUS was laid, deep in slumber, on the shores of Ithaca, he knew nothing of the dangers which faced his country. Loyal Penelope was ensconced in their palace, at the mercy of over a hundred suitors, rulers from neighbouring islands who wished to annex Ithaca. Telemachus had left the island in search of his father, and many of the suitors were involved in a plot to murder him upon his return. Laertes was alive, but old and troubled. When Odysseus woke, he knew not where he was. He was visited by Athene, who briefed him on the ills of his homeland, and who dressed him in the guise of a beggar, and led him to the hut of the faithful swineherd Eumaeus. Here Odysseus could plot, and plan, prepare the tools of battle to make Ithaca his once more.

Penelope and Telemachus

We wooed the wife of Odysseus, the lord so long away,
And unto that loathly wedding said she neither yea nor nay,
But the black doom and the deathday devised for us the while;
Yea in our heart she devised us moreover this same guide;
With a web that was great and mighty her loom in the house did she gear,
A fine web, full of measure, and thus bespake us there.
William Morris, The Odyssey

WHEN ODYSSEUS AWOKE on the sands of Ithaca, a mist had fallen over the majestic land and he knew not where he was. The Phaeacians had vanished from his sight, and he had only a groggy but pleasant memory of his visit to them. He should be at Ithaca now, he thought, but he could see nothing in the steamy air that enshrouded him. From the mists he heard a soft voice – familiar to Odysseus, but he no longer trusted in anything, and he sat back cautiously.

'You are in the land of the great warrior and traveller Odysseus,' said the voice, which belonged to a young and comely shepherd. 'How do you not know it?'

Odysseus lied glibly about his reasons for being there, inventing a fantastic story that was quite different from his actual voyage. At this the shepherd laughed, and changing shape, became Athene.

'So, crafty Odysseus,' she smiled. 'What a rogue you are. The greatest gods would have trouble inventing such tricks.' With that she held out a hand to the weary traveller, and led him across the sands.

'I've hidden you from your countrymen,' she explained, indicating the mists which surrounded them. 'Things are not as you would have hoped. It is not safe for you now. You must tread slowly.'

She helped Odysseus to hide away his treasures, and sat him down to explain to him the matters of his homeland. Penelope was still faithful to him, but time was running out, and she knew that if he did not appear to her within the next months, Penelope would have little recourse but to join herself with another. Telemachus was greatly angered by the insolent suitors who banded themselves at the palace, taking as their own everything that had belonged to his father, and gorging themselves on the food meant for the people of Ithaca. It was an untidy situation, and Telemachus struggled to believe that his father was still alive.

He had left the island for the mainland, desperate for news of Odysseus, never believing that his father could be dead. He'd vowed to allow one year for news, failing which he would agree to the wishes of a stepfather and stand aside.

In Greece Telemachus was greeted with little interest, and his attempts to uncover the whereabouts of his father were useless. Old Nestor, who knew everything about the war at Troy, and had followed the lives of the great men who had made the victory there, had heard nothing of Odysseus. He had disappeared, he said sadly, shaking his head. Determined, Telemachus pressed on to Sparta where Helen welcomed the son of Odysseus, but had little news to impart. Telemachus began to feel the first stirrings of despair, and sat with his head pressed into his hands. When Menelaus returned to his home that evening, he found Telemachus like this, and leaning over the youth, whispered words of comfort.

'I too have wandered,' he said gently.' And news of your father has reached me through the minions of Poseidon.' He went on to warn Telemachus of Poseidon's rage, explaining how Odysseus had blinded his one-eyed son Polyphemus. Menelaus told how Odysseus had been cast upon the shores of Calypso, where he lived a life that was half enchantment and half longing for his past.

Telemachus moved swiftly. His father was alive. A rescue must be planned at once, but most importantly he must warn his mother. The suitors had moved in too closely. They must be disposed of immediately.

At home in Ithaca, Penelope was also filled with a despair that threatened to destroy her. Her loyalty to Odysseus had kept her sane, and filled her with a kind of clever glee which made possible the machinations of keeping the suitors at bay. She'd held her head low with humility, and explained to the suitors who continued to arrive, to take roost in her home, that she must complete work on a cloth she was weaving, before she could contemplate giving herself to another. She worked hours on end in the days, performing for the suitors at her loom, giving them every belief in her excuses for not receiving their attentions. And yet at night she returned to her lonely bedroom and there she sat by torchlight, unpicking the work of the day. And as the years went by, it became established knowledge that Penelope was not free to marry until she had finished her web.

But Penelope was aware that her excuse was wearing thin, that the seeds of suspicion had been sown in the minds of her suitors, and that they were paying inordinate interest in the mechanics of the loom itself. It was only a question of time before they would insist on her hand and she would be forced to make a choice. Her property was being wasted, her lands falling to ruin, her stocks emptied by their marauding parties. She longed for the firm hand of Odysseus to oust them from their adopted home, to renew the sense of vigour that was required by her workers to make things right again. Most importantly, however, she longed for the warm embrace of her husband, the nights of passion, of sweet love. She had resisted the attentions of her suitors, but her body was afire with longing, and she burned at a single look, at a fleeting touch. Penelope was ready for her husband's return. Soon it would be too late.

At the cottage of Eumaeus, Odysseus had been presented with a fine feast of suckling pig by the swineherd, who spoke sadly of his master's absence. He bemoaned the state of the island and explained to Odysseus in his disguise that the suitors visited his cottage regularly, taking their pick of the pigs so that his herd was sorely depleted. He said kindly that a beggarman was as entitled to a feast as were these inappropriate suitors, and he gave Odysseus his own cloak in which to warm himself by the fire. Odysseus told the loyal subject a wild story, but did say that he had heard news of Odysseus and that the great warrior would return to set his house in order within the next year. At this, the swineherd was filled with joy, and produced more food and wine for this bearer of good news. Odysseus settled in for the night.

By this time Telemachus had returned to the island, aided by Athene who had set out to greet him. He was taken to the cottage in darkness, so as not to arouse the suspicions of the suitors, who were plotting his death. Here a tearful reunion was made, away from the eyes of the swineherd who had been sent to the palace for more drink. Odysseus was transformed once more into his old self by Athene, and Telemachus drank in the sight of his father, who he'd hardly known as a child.

They sat together, heads touching, occasionally reaching over to reassure themselves of the other's presence, and the plans were made to restore Ithaca to her former glory, to rid it of the unruly suitors, to reinstate Odysseus and Telemachus at their rightful places at her helm.

The Battle for Ithaca

Then fierce the hero o'er the threshold strode;
Stripped of his rags, he blazed out like a god.
Full in their face the lifted bow he bore
And quivered deaths, a formidable store.
Before his feet the rattling shower he threw,
And thus terrific to the suitor-crew:
'One venturous game this hand has won today,
Another, princes, yet remains to play!'
Alexander Pope, The Odyssey

ODYSSEUS AND TELEMACHUS were ready to set their plans into action. Just before Eumaeus returned to his cottage, Odysseus resumed the form of a beggarman and Telemachus slipped away into the night. The following morning dawned cool and clear, and Odysseus felt a renewed vigour coursing through his veins. He longed to appear in his battle garb, the strong and mighty Odysseus returned from the dead to reclaim his palace, but there was too much at stake to set a wrong foot and he knew the plans he had fixed with Telemachus must be followed to the tiniest detail.

Eumaeus accompanied Odysseus to the palace, to see if there was any work available for a willing but poverty-stricken beggar. He was greeted first by the rude and arrogant Antinous, the leader of Penelope's suitors, who had long considered himself the rightful heir to Odysseus's position within Ithaca. He gazed scathingly at Odysseus as he entered the room where the suitors lolled about on cushions, calling out to the over-burdened servants for refreshment and ever greater feasts of food.

'Who dares to trouble us?' he said lazily.

Odysseus introduced himself as a poor traveller, down on his luck after a long voyage in which his crew members had been struck down by Poseidon. To test them, Odysseus begged them for alms, but he was met by a barrage of rotten fruit, after which several of the younger suitors took turns beating him. Bruised and angry, Odysseus stood his ground, requesting menial work of any nature. And it was then that the young local beggar Irus stepped into the fray. Resenting the competition offered by Odysseus, he challenged him to a fight, at which the lazy suitors leapt to their feet, roaring at the impending carnage. For Odysseus had taken the form of an old man, and Irus was young and strong, a beggar only because of his slothful nature.

But the roars turned to silence as Odysseus lifted his robes to show legs as muscular and powerful as the greatest of warriors, and a prowess with a sword that belonged only to the master of the house. He slayed Irus with one fell of his sword. Odysseus was cheered not by the suitors, who suspected a rival for the attentions of Penelope, and they cast him out, kicking and beating him until he howled with pain and restrained anger. He could not show his true colours yet. The time was not ripe for battle. Odysseus made his way from the waiting rooms, into the kitchen where word of his ill-treatment reached Penelope. Knowing well that gods often travelled in disguise, she sent a message that she wished this sailor to be fed and made comfortable for the night. Penelope herself wished to speak to him, for a traveller might have word of the long-lost Odysseus and she yearned for news of him.

But Odysseus claimed to be too weak to see the mistress of the house, and it was agreed that they would speak later that evening. And so it was that Odysseus slipped from his bed in the kitchen and met with his son in the great hall. Quietly they removed the armour and weapons that the suitors had idly laid to one side, piling them outside the palace gates where they were snatched away by village boys. And now, in the darkened hall, Odysseus agreed to see Penelope, who felt a surge of excitement at their meeting which startled and concerned her. Odysseus had been gone too long, she was losing control.

They met by candlelight, and safe in his disguise, Odysseus wove for Penelope a fanciful story about his travels, which had little in common with the true nature of his voyages, but left her with no doubt that the brave Odysseus was on his way home, and would soon return to set things to right. And then Odysseus heard from Penelope the trials of the last twenty years, and hung his head in shame at the thought of his many years with Calypso, and the time lost through the greed and indolence of his men.

Penelope told of the suitors who had been first quietened by her insistence that the Oracle had promised Odysseus's return, but as the years had passed, they had grown insolent and arrogant, demanding her attentions, her hand in marriage. She had fought them off, she said, by claiming to weave the cloth that would shroud Laertes upon his death, and each night she had spent many hours unpicking the day's work. And then, when this trick had been discovered, she could delay her decision no longer and had feigned illness for many months. The next day was the Feast of Apollo and it was on this day that she had agreed to choose a husband. Penelope wept with misery, her fair face more beautiful with age and distress. Odysseus longed to take her in his arms, to warm her body and to ease her pain, but he held himself back from her, knowing that he must use his anger to feed his resolve, to rid his home of these suitors once and for all.

Penelope was grateful for the reassurance and calm understanding of this stranger, and she urged him to take a chamber for the night, sending the aged nurse Eurycleia to bathe his feet and weary legs. Eurycleia had been Odysseus's own nurse as a child, and when she saw his familiar scar, received in a youthful skirmish with a wild boar, she cried out. Odysseus grabbed her throat.

'Speak not, wise woman,' he whispered harshly, 'all will be set right at the dawn of the feast.' Eurycleia nodded, her eyes bulging with fear and concern and she gathered her skirts around her, heading for the servant's quarters.

The next day was the Feast, and the household was abuzz with activity and preparations. Odysseus took a seat amongst the suitors, strategically placed by the door, but he was jeered at and heckled until he was forced to move to a small stool. Penelope eventually appeared in their midst. Then Agelaus gave her an ultimatum. Today a choice must be made. Penelope turned pleadingly to Telemachus, but he nodded his grudging consent, and she announced that a competition would take place. With that she fled to a table, and shut her eyes in despair.

Telemachus took over, producing Odysseus's great bow, and gently explaining that his mother could only consider marriage to someone the equal of his father, someone who could string the bow and shoot an arrow through the rings of twelve axes set in a row. And one by one, the suitors failed to bend the stiff bow, and disgruntled, cast it aside and sat sullenly along the walls of the hall. So it was that the beggarman was the only remaining man, and he begged a chance to test his strength against the bow. He was taunted, and insults fired at him, but he stood his ground and with the permission of Penelope, who nodded a sympathetic assent, he took the bow.

Like a man born to the act, he deftly wired the bow, and taking an arrow, he fired it straight through the rings of the axes. The room was silent. Telemachus rose and strode across to stand by his father.

'The die is cast,' said Odysseus, thrusting aside his disguise. 'And another target presents itself. Prepare to pay for your treachery.' With that he lifted his arrow and shot Antinous clear through the neck. The suitors searched with amazement for their arms and armour, and finding them gone, tried to make due with the short daggers in their belts. They launched themselves on Odysseus and his son, but the two great men fought valiantly, sending arrow after arrow, spear after spear, to their fatal mark. And when Odysseus and Telemachus grew tired, Athene flew across them in the shape of a swallow and filled them with a surge of energy, a new life that saw them through the battle to victory.

The battle won, the suitors dead, the household was now scourged for those who had befriended the suitors, maids who had shared their beds, porters and shepherds who had made available the stocks and stores of Odysseus's palace. And these maids and men were beheaded and burnt in a fire that was seen for many miles.

Finally Odysseus could pause, and greet properly his long-lost wife, who sat wearily by his side, hardly daring to believe that he had returned. And yet, one look at his time and journey-lined face told her it was all true, and she was overwhelmed once again by her love for this brave man who was so long apart from her. With tears of joy they clutched one another, and their union was sweet and tender. And soon afterwards came Laertes, the veil of madness lifted by news of his son's return.

The courageous Odysseus was home at last, his cunning a match for all that the fates had set in his path. There would be more skirmishes before he could call Ithaca his own once more, and Poseidon must be appeased before he could live fearlessly surrounded by that great god's kingdom, but in time all was undertaken. Some say that Odysseus lived to a ripe old age, dying eventually and suitably on the sea. Others say that he died at the hand of his own son, Telegonus, by the enchantress Circe. All agree that Odysseus was beloved by his subjects, the tales of his journey becoming the food for legends which spread around the world.

Jason and the Argonauts

IT IS FORETOLD, 'Beware of a man with one sandal.' At first glance, hardly the most chilling of prophecies. Yet in an age circumscribed by gods and heroes, when the divine and human intertwined, any such prediction had to be viewed with respect. In this case doubly so, for the prophecy referred to none other than the hero Jason, son of Aeson of Iolcus, whose deeds in pursuit of the famous Golden Fleece would ripple throughout time and legend.

The Quest Begins

Now therefore with ungrudging heart choose the bravest to be our leader, who shall be careful for everything, to take upon him our quarrels and covenants with strangers.
R.C. Seaton, Argonautica

WHEN CRETHEUS, THE KING OF IOLCUS, died, Jason's father Aeson was next in line to the throne. However Aeson's brother Pelias sought power for himself and usurped the throne. Pelias set about his rule with blood-soaked purpose, cutting down all possible contenders for his crown. To protect the newborn Jason from the sword, his mother Alcimede pretended that he was stillborn. The deception stood firm, and with Aeson held prisoner Jason was moved from the city to reside in the country under the tutelage of the centaur Chiron. Unlike many of the centaurs, Chiron was very cultured, and Jason grew up strong and sharp under his protection. Pelias, suffering under the foreboding that often accompanies unlawful power, consulted an oracle about possible threats to his reign. It was then that he received the caution that he should beware the man with one sandal, a prophesy which continued to haunt Pelias.

The years passed, and Jason grew to be an educated and courageous man. His destiny was set, so the time came for his inevitable return to Iolcus. The goddess Hera, slighted by Pelias's supplication to all the gods but her, had already made plans for vengeance. Posing as a helpless old woman, she had Jason carry her through the leg-snatching torrents of the river Anauros. During the crossing, the river took away one of his sandals...

Jason finally reached Pelias's palace, where the one-sandaled man challenged the stunned king for the rightful kingship. With a sly appraisal of Jason's character, Pelias offered his throne in return for Jason's fulfilment of a quest. The challenge was this – he must find and return the Golden Fleece, that of the magical golden-haired winged ram which once carried the children of Nephele, the cloud nymph, to safety from a sacrificial fate. The ram was sacrificed by Nephele's son Phrixus, and the golden fleece was given to the man who had received him, King Aeëtes, ruler of Colchis on the Black Sea. Aeëtes hung the fleece on an oak tree in a grove sacred to Ares, guarded by a huge dragon.

To retrieve such a garment demanded a perilous voyage to the edge of the known world, but Jason embraced the challenge. His first requirement was for a ship of unprecedented seagoing resilience. Here the goddess Athene intervened, inspiring the shipwright Argus to create a fast-running galley called the Argo ('Swift'); Athene formed the bow of the ship from the oak of Zeus's oracle at Dodona, imbuing the very ship itself with the powers of speech and prophecy.

The journey to Colchis was bound to be dangerous, taking all aboard through the jaws of death. Monsters, treacherous seas, violent tribes, demented gods – the voyage was a map of the most primeval fears. Jason therefore assembled a crew equal to the task, heroes all, with a reckless desire for glory. Fifty-men strong, the crew included Heracles, son of Zeus and gifted with extraordinary strength and intelligence; brothers Peleus and Telamon, natural-born warriors who manned the oars at the ship's bow; Euphemus, gifted by his father Poseidon with the ability to run across water; Periclymenus, also son of Poseidon, who could shapeshift into animal form; and the great Orpheus himself beat the rhythm for the oarsmen. Other magisterial names included Philoctetes, Castor and Pollux and the virgin huntress Atalanta.

Thus assembled, the 'Argonauts' represented muscle, mind and magic, a gathering of martial spirit and fearless defiance of fate. As the Argo set sail, the bow foaming the salted blue waters of the Aegean, their vision was closed to the horrors that awaited them.

The Wanderings

...no fair renown shall we win by thus tarrying so long with stranger women; nor will some god seize and give us at our prayer a fleece that moves of itself.'

R.C. Seaton, Argonautica

THE FIRST STOP on Jason's voyage was the island of Lemnos, off the coast of Asia Minor. Lemnos was an island blighted by the gods. Aphrodite, annoyed by the womenfolk's lack of veneration, punished them by imbuing their bodies with a nauseating smell that repelled their husbands. The Lemnian men therefore started to turn to other women, stoking the fury of their neglected wives. Maddened with yearning and anger, the women of Lemnos killed all the male inhabitants of the islands, and lived on under the rule of their queen, Hypsipyle.

The Argonauts' stay at Lemnos would not be a short one. In return for the right to land, Hypsipyle made Jason promise that they would stay for some duration before departing. In the end, Lemnos was home to the warrior crew for a full year – all except Heracles and a small contingent of more disciplined men, who stayed on the Argo. The women, grateful for the male company, lauded the men with pageant and dance, fragrant sacrifices and exquisite foods. Days rolled into weeks, and weeks into months. Some of the warriors even had children with these women; Jason himself had two children with the queen. The Argo sat listlessly at its anchorage under an impassive sun, until Heracles expressed his wrath, and awakened the sense of purpose once more. Jason made his farewells to Hypsipyle, and soon the Argo was on its way east once more.

The experience on Lemnos had lapped at the Argonauts' moral strength. A test of physical and martial strength would face them at their next port of call, the Cyzicus peninsula. Here King Cyzicus of the Doliones welcomed them enthusiastically, but with his own hidden purpose. The Doliones were being terrorized by a tribe of fearsome six-armed giants, the Gegeines, who lived in the land beyond Bear Mountain. King Cyzicus evoked the physical delights of this land, while omitting to mention its earth-shaking inhabitants. Meanwhile, the Gegeines themselves – spurred by greed – had spotted the Argo at anchorage and plotted to raid her. At the moment when most of the crew were ashore, the Gegeines rushed down from the hillside, expecting easy plunder. What they found was the iron resistance and swift muscle of Heracles and a small group of other warriors, who fought the giants with no thought of the struggle being unequal. The Gegeines suffered grievously, many of them killed before the return of the rest of the Argo's crew put the survivors into rout.

Tragedy followed, however. Once the celebrations of victory had died down, Jason put his ship to sea once more, but night-time, smarting rain and capricious winds drove them back to Cyzicus. As they landed, the Doliones confused them with Pelasgian raiders, and fierce battle ensued. Their eyes seeing only a muted world of half shapes, Jason and the king fought a battle, in which Cyzicus was slain. When morning revealed a horror of sword-hewn bodies, and a dead king, the lamentations were compounded by the suicide of the king's daughter, who hanged herself in grief.

Angry storms kept the Argo at anchor until the gods were appeased, then the ship set sail once again, still far from Colchis. Fate then dealt another adverse hand, when Heracles broke an oar, his muscles greater in strength than the oak he gripped. The ship landed at Cius to find a replacement. Heracles' beloved servant Hylas here wandered off on his own, hoping to find water for the evening meal. He happened upon a pool which gave up no reflection when he faced its haunting surface. Instead, he saw the sensuous, floating grace of the water nymphs, creatures with a magnetizing beauty, bodies curving ceaselessly and effortlessly in the water. Hylas was never seen again, drawn down into the nymph's depthless world. Heracles, when he discovered the loss, was distraught, and left the Argo for good to search for Hylas. Jason had lost one of his stalwart warriors.

The events of the recent past focused Jason's thoughts on what might be to come. Thus he took the ship to Salmydessus in Thrace, seeking out the counsel of Phineus, king of Thrace and a seer of unmatched vision. Phineus had been blinded by an offended Zeus, and his misery was multiplied tenfold by the shrill visitations of the Harpies, winged monsters with the head of a haggard woman and the body of a decrepit, razor-clawed bird. Sickening, stinking creatures, the Harpies would prey on Phineus every time he tried to eat, snatching or defiling his food. Half-starved, Phineus pleaded with the Argonauts to help, and they succeeding in freeing him from this torture. Phineus, in his gratitude, told Jason how to pass through the Symplegades ('Clashing Rocks').

The Symplegades were, since the foundation of the Earth, granite guardians at the entrance to the Black Sea. To prevent passage through the straits, these towering rocks, opposing one another, would snap shut in a split second rush, accompanied by a sonorous crack and a tsunami-like displacement of water. Even swift-swimming sea creatures such as dolphins could not always escape the vice-like rocks, and many ships were splintered to destruction. Phineus suggested that Jason release a dove as he approached the rocks; the Symplegades would snap shut on the bird, then the Argo could pass through as they reopened.

It remained to be seen whether Phineus's vision would work in practice. The crew sat in cold fear under the shadow of the rocks as the dove was released. With explosive force, the Symplegades smashed their faces together, just nipping out the tail feathers of the dove as it passed through. Now was the Argo's chance, yet the swelling waves pushed the ship back, delaying its movement forward for crucial seconds. As the Argo moved into the kill zone, the Symplegades towered above them like hammers of death, and a rumbling signalled their imminent crushing movement. Seeing disaster unfold, the goddess Athene herself intervened, holding back one of the rocks with her left hand, while pushing the Argo through the straits. Even the strength of a goddess eventually gave way to the clashing rocks; they smashed together with a roar that seemed to shatter heaven, clipping off the tip of the Argo's stern – but the ship was safe.

The now-weary crew pushed on towards Colchis, enduring further challenges. On the way, their spirits were chilled by the screams of Prometheus, the Titan sentenced to punishment by

Zeus. His agony was to be tied to a rock, and each day a mighty eagle would swoop in to tear open his belly and feast on his liver. Prometheus, body arched in torment, back scraped on the sun-bleached coastal rock, did not die; his liver reformed after each ordeal, only to be gouged from him again the next day, and every day thereafter. Near the Caucasian mountains, the Argonauts saw the rush of wind from the eagle's wings billow the sails, and heard its wing beat disturb the air above the clouds. Then came the dire screams of Prometheus, as he experienced his daily torture. Slowly the cries faded into the distance, and the Argo eventually came to its destination. Colchis drew into view and the anchor thumped into the still coastal waters. The Golden Fleece was now the goal.

Medea and the Golden Fleece

Come now, Erato, stand by my side, and say next how Jason brought back the fleece to Iolcus aided by the love of Medea.

R.C. Seaton, Argonautica

AT COLCHIS Jason met Medea, the daughter of King Aeëtes and a priestess of Hecate, who had all the ambiguous powers of sorcery and magic that that position bestowed. Medea quickly fell in love with Jason, the intensity of her feeling heightened by a love charm which the goddesses Hera and Aphrodite gave to Jason. When presented to Medea, it made her helpless against falling for him. King Aeëtes himself was less taken with the young hero – a prophecy had foretold him that Jason would engineer the fall of his reign. Thus when Jason explained the purpose of his quest – to retrieve the Golden Fleece – Aeëtes saw the means by which to defy his fate. He gave Jason two challenges to claim the fleece, both of which had the certain expectation of death. Despite the difficulty of the tasks, Jason accepted them.

The first challenge was a clash of man and beast. Jason was to sow a field with dragon teeth, the plough to be pulled by two bronze-hoofed oxen with brutal temperaments and fire-breathing jaws. Few men would have survived such an encounter, but Jason dominated the creatures with his muscle and indomitable attitude, and scattered the dragon's teeth into the ground. Yet no sooner had the teeth sunk into the turned soil, than they transformed into fully armed warriors, intent on killing Jason. With the clear thinking born only in those already familiar with death, Jason crouched down behind his shield, hiding from the earth-born opponents. He threw a huge boulder, itself heavier than four normal men could handle, into the midst of the warriors, who in their surprise turned upon one another and fought to the death. Jason added the cut of his own blade, until all opponents were dead and the first challenge had been fulfilled.

Now came the second challenge – to take the fleece itself from beneath the dragon. Jason and Medea crept into the sacred grove at night. Yet no amount of stealth could avoid the unresting eyes of the dragon, who started to uncoil himself from his slumber with a resonating, chilling hiss that awoke people for miles around. The creature fixed the two in his gaze, its muscles tensing, and Jason drew his sword, ready to fight to an almost certain death. Medea stepped forward, however, and armed with nothing more than a sleep-inducing potion that she cast under the creature's nose, she overcame the dragon. Steadily the creature softened, drifting back into sleep under the power of the charm. Seizing the moment, Jason rushed around the dragon and took the Golden Fleece from the oak.

Jason and Medea were momentarily stunned by the magnificence of the fleece, radiating a shimmering light on the ground around their feet. But there was little time for contemplation. Jason was fully aware of Aeëtes' threatening purpose towards him, and he moved in haste back to the Argo. Medea, in the thrall of love, went with him accompanied by her little brother Apsyrtus.

Here Medea's madness began to reveal itself, in the most unnatural way. Aeëtes was quickly informed of the Argonauts' escape, and set off in pursuit with his naval forces. Medea, breaking all bonds of sibling tenderness, murdered her brother and cut his body into pieces, strewing the bloody parts along the River Phasis, down which Aeëtes was following. The king, overcome by shock, grief and tenderness, stopped to retrieve the parts, giving Medea chance to make good her escape with Jason. Through this unsettling act, the Argo made open waters and began the long journey back to home.

The Journey Home

And the heroes, whether they drifted in Hades or on the waters, knew not one whit; but they committed their return to the sea in helpless doubt whither it was bearing them.

R.C. Seaton, Argonautica

WITH THE GOLDEN FLEECE in his possession, Jason turned the Argo towards Thessaly, in the expectation of claiming the throne that was rightfully his. But the journey back was a danger in itself. The Argonauts faced death once again at the hands of monsters, gods and creatures of sometimes subtler but equally lethal forms of coercion. When passing the rocky islands known as the Sirenum Scopuli, the crew began to fall under the lure of the Sirens, enchanting sea maidens who, through their sensuality and song, drew ships to their destruction on the rocks. Even Jason himself felt the bewitching harmonies wrap themselves around him. Keeping his head, Orpheus grabbed his lyre, playing and singing with such verve and volume that the pull of the Sirens was smothered.

On Crete, the Argonauts encountered the anger and power of the mighty Talos, an island guardian made entirely of bronze apart from an exposed patch of human flesh on his ankle, under which blood ran through a single vulnerable vein. Talos would not be conquered by the Argonauts, but by Medea's sorcery. Summoning shrill underworld spirits and dark beings, she tormented the giant even as he prepared to hurl great rocks at the Argo settled offshore. He slipped, cutting open his ankle on a sharp rock, and he toppled like a once-proud oak.

After a harrowing journey, the Argo finally made it back to Iolchus. The ship was anchored in a hidden cove, and Medea left in advance, to gain the advantage. Deftly imitating a priestess of Artemis, she ingratiated herself with the three daughters of Pelias. The daughters confessed their fears for their elderly father, and a desire to see him youthful again. This gave Medea an idea. One evening, she treated the daughters to a spectacle of death and resurrection. She sacrificed an old ram by slitting its throat, then placed the body in a special cauldron of elixir, herbs and roots. Six stirs of the pot (three to the left, three to the right), and the old ram was retrieved, now a young, living lamb. Medea told the girls that here was the way they could restore their father.

Through best intentions and trusting natures, the daughters prepared to commit patricide. They drew their father to Medea's bedchamber. Once he was inside the room, however, two daughters pinned his limbs down while the third opened his throat with a knife, draining him of blood until his eyes glazed and his chest was still. They forced his corpse into the cauldron. Yet now the cauldron contained nothing but a common soup. There would be no resurrection for Pelias, and as the daughters sobbed in anguish the throne now seemed open for Jason.

With the death of the king, the Argonauts participated in epic funeral games, winning glory with fists, discuss, javelin, chariot, lyre or foot. Once the shouts of the crowds finally subsided, however, Jason was faced with an unwelcome future. The murder of Pelias had brought a curse to Iolcus, which forced Jason to flee the city while Pelias's son Acastus stepped forward and donned the crown. Jason went with Medea and their two children to Corinth. However whilst there, Jason was distracted by the beauty of another woman, Glauce, daughter of Corinth's King Creon. Love took hold between Jason and Glauce, leading to the proposal and acceptance of marriage. Medea concealed her bile, even as she began forming a ghastly revenge, which crystallised on the day of the state wedding.

The wedding day brought pageantry and spectacle, as an entire state woke in celebration. Amongst the wedding gifts were those left by Medea herself: a venerable crown for Creon, and a cloak of exquisite threads for the young bride. The king and daughter donned the crown and robe. Straight away, the cursed objects began their deadly work. Glauce's robe gripped her flesh and began to burn with flesh-boiling intensity. Shrieking, her fingernails breaking on the fabric, she raced to a pool, driven mad by pain. Yet once she was immersed, the water did nothing but hasten her journey to a scalded, agonized death.

Creon's fate was no less appalling. The crown tightened in a crushing band around his skull, the pressure increasing as the man's cries rang off the walls of his court in ever-increasing pitch. Then suddenly his head shattered, scattering bone and brains across the floor.

Medea had now exacted what appeared as the fullest revenge upon Jason. Yet her thirst to see his agony was not yet over. Once again defiling the bonds of familial love, she took her own sons and cut their throats from ear to ear. Then she fled, taken to Athens on a dragon-pulled chariot. Jason was left distraught, the great hero whose epic quest for the Golden Fleece had brought him nothing but poisoned love and mouldering death.

The Twelve Labours of Heracles

SON OF ZEUS, father of the Greek Gods, and Alcmene, a human, Heracles was born a mortal who could feel pain, but was possessed with immense strength, courage and intelligence; a man who bridged the gap between mortals and gods. As such, tales of his extraordinary life are legendary and his twelve labours rank as the most incredible of all. As penance for the murder of his children in a fit of insanity brought on by Hera – Zeus's queen who was jealous of Heracles – Heracles was forced to serve his cousin, the spiteful and cowardly King Eurystheus of Argos, for 12 years, performing any tasks that were asked of him, no matter how deadly and perilous. If Heracles could do this, his soul would be purified and he would earn immortality.

The Nemean Lion

Nemea's dreadful Lion first he sought,
The savage slew and to Eurystheus brought,
From his huge sides his shaggy spoils he tore,
Around him threw, & e'er in triumph wore.
Anon

HERACLES' FIRST TASK was to defeat the ferocious lion of Nemea and bring its skin – invulnerable to weapons – back to Eurystheus. The formidable lion terrorized the village and seized its inhabitants to feast upon at will. Armed with a bow and arrow, sword of bronze and his beloved club, which he had fashioned from an olive tree that he uprooted and tore apart, Heracles threw himself into his first labour with vigour, never one to turn away from a challenge.

Tracking the lion to its cave, Heracles shot at his prey with his bow, but the arrows just bounced off its impenetrable skin. Trying a different tactic, Heracles waited until the lion retreated into its cave, then blocked off one of the entrances, leaving only one. Bravely entering the cave, armed with his club, he felt his way through the darkness, managing to stun the lion with one almighty blow. Heracles then vanquished the powerful lion by throttling it with his bare hands.

But his quest was not yet concluded. Try as he might, Heracles could not remove the precious skin from the lion. His blade proved useless, as did the sharp stones on the cave's floor. It was not until Athene, the goddess of inspiration and invention, told him to use the lion's own claws that he was able to remove the skin.

Heracles returned to Argos to present the lion skin to Eurystheus, who was astonished that Heracles had defeated the beast. Entering the palace with the lion skin slung over his person, its head protecting his own, Heracles struck terror into the timorous heart of Eurystheus. From then on, Eurystheus took care not to underestimate his illustrious cousin, even having a huge bronze jar built, in which to hide from the indomitable hero.

The Lernaean Hydra

On Lerna's pest th' undaunted Hero rushes,
With massy club her hundred heads he crushes,
In vain. One crush'd, two hissing heads arise
Anon

FOR HIS SECOND TASK, Heracles had to defeat the dreaded hydra, a creature made by Hera to rid herself from him once and for all. The multi-headed monster dwelled deep in the swamps of Lerna, from which it would rise up and attack the villagers. Heracles

travelled to Lerna with his nephew and charioteer, Iolaus. He used flaming arrows to lure the monster out into the open, hoping to lessen the effects of its poisonous breath.

Heracles then set about attacking its heads with his mighty club and hacking them off with his sword. But his efforts were to no avail. Every time he succeeded in removing one head, two more would grow in its place. Again and again Heracles attacked, hoping that the hydra's regenerative powers would fail, but even his great strength began to wane. The hydra had wrapped itself around his body, slowly crushing his bones, while its merciless heads kept on attacking him.

But Heracles was not defeated. Summoning up his remaining strength, he called for his nephew's aid, tasking him with cauterizing the bloody stump of every head he could sever. Summoning up his courage, Iolaus did as Heracles commanded and one by one the heads fell, with nothing able to grow in their place. Soon, the hydra was left with only one head; the immortal head. Using the bronze sword given to him by Athene, Heracles lopped off the head in a single vigorous strike. The monster was defeated. Taking no chances, Heracles buried the immortal head under a giant rock.

He then dipped the tips of his arrows into the hydra's venomous blood, making them poisonous. Because Heracles had only defeated the Hydra with Iolaus' assistance, Eurystheus stated that this task did not count.

The Ceryneian Hind

WITH TWO LABOURS COMPLETED, Eurystheus and Hera – who had been scrutinizing Heracles' progress – realized that not even a monster was capable of defeating the warrior. They devised a new undertaking that would be even more onerous. Heracles was tasked with catching the Ceryneian hind, a female deer. Sometimes known as a stag because of its golden antlers, the nimble creature also had bronze hooves and could run faster than an arrow in flight. Eurystheus had made the task even more deadly by choosing the pet creature of Artemis, the goddess of the hunt. Even if Heracles did manage to capture the hind, Artemis would likely take vengeance on him for harming her beloved animal.

Heracles gave chase for one whole year, yet the hind never tired. Along the banks of the river Ladon in Arcadia, as the hind slowed to take drink from the cooling waters, Heracles managed to bring it down with an arrow fired between its forelegs, causing the hind to falter and stumble without drawing blood. This way, Heracles captured the fleet-footed beast without provoking the anger of Artemis.

Heracles bound the animal, then explained to Artemis that he had been forced into this ill-treatment as one of his labours. She graciously forgave his impudence and allowed him to leave unharmed as long as he promised to return the treasured hind.

Taking the prize to Eurystheus, Heracles kept his bargain with Artemis by telling Eurystheus that he needed to take the hind from him with his own hands. Reluctantly, Eurystheus emerged from the safety of his palace to see the fabled Ceryneian hind for himself. Reaching for it eagerly, just before he could grasp her fur, Heracles let go and she raced back to Artemis, escaping with ease.

The Eurymanthian Boar

TRAVELLING THROUGH THE MOUNTAINS to capture the Eurymanthian boar for Eurystheus, Heracles took respite with his old friend Pholus, the centaur. Over a shared meal, Heracles asked for wine. Pholus reluctantly opened a jar, which had been a present from Dionysus, the god of wine, meant for all the centaurs. This attracted the other centaurs – proud and noble creatures – who were angry that their gift had been dishonoured and drank. In a frenzied rage, they attacked Heracles. Heracles defended himself with his bow and arrows, which, coated in the hydra's venom, caused many deaths.

Chiron, a centaur who had tutored Heracles, was wounded in the fray. Pholus, curious as to why the arrows had caused such devastation, picked one up to inspect it. It slipped from his hand and pierced his foot, letting in the deadly venom that killed him.

Heavy at heart at the loss of his friend and the difficult task ahead, Heracles continued his quest. Reaching the mountains, he began tracking and chasing his quarry. Following Chiron's advice about trapping the boar, Heracles drove it into a heavy snow drift. He then trapped the wildly struggling boar in a net, tied it snugly, threw it over his shoulder and carried it back to Eurystheus, freeing the villagers from the constant terror the brutal boar had caused. Eurystheus cowered in fear in the bronze jar, increasingly awed by the resilience and courage of his cousin.

The Augean Stables

To cleanse the Augean Stables now he's sped,
Where thirty years three thousand Oxen fed;
The task for man too great. A river's course
He turn'd, & thro' the stables urged its force,
The tide resistless rolls, and in one day
The gather'd filth of years is swept away.

Anon

CONCOCTING an even more arduous task for Heracles, Eurystheus now determined to defeat and humiliate the hero in one repugnant labour. King Augeas of Elis owned massive stables filled with immortal cattle, which had not been cleaned for over thirty years. It was Heracles' task to clean out the stables and he only had one day to do it. Eurystheus was convinced that even the stupendous strength of Heracles was not up to this insurmountable task.

But he did not reckon with Heracles' wisdom. Heracles went to King Augeas and offered to clean his stables in a single day if Augeas would give him one-tenth of the herd as payment. The king readily agreed, believing the task to be impossible. Heracles then headed for the stables. There, he tore great holes in two facing walls of the stables. Digging trenches leading directly to these holes, he redirected the course of two rivers – the Alpheus and the Peneus – straight through the stable, where the rapid flow of water surged through, washing away all the muck and dirt that had built up over thirty years.

Astounded that Heracles had managed his task, Augeas refused to honour their agreement, saying that he never promised Heracles any reward. Heracles responded in anger and pledged to take what was owed to him. Augeas' son, Phyleus, interceded and settled the matter between them. This was the second task that Eurystheus refused to count, saying that Heracles had used the river to do the work and been well paid for his labours.

The Stymphalian Birds

The Lake Stymphalus by his arm was freed,
From those dire birds on human flesh who feed,
By Pallas' aid the dreadful race subdued,
No more its banks with whitening bones are strew'd.
Anon

FOR HIS SIXTH TASK, Heracles was pitted against the ferocious Stymphalian birds. A huge flock of the diabolical fowl had gathered at a lake near Stymphalos, where they were quickly breeding, causing despair and death to the countryside and population. The birds would devour anything – including human flesh – and were able to attack their prey by shooting razor-sharp brass feathers at them. Their beaks were made of bronze and could easily peck right through flesh. Heracles was vastly outnumbered and, to make matters worse, he could not get near enough to the birds to harm them. The swampy lake would not bear his weight and if he tried to force his way through it, he would sink and drown.

Athene, who watched over Heracles, had been observing him try to reach the vile birds. Pledging her assistance, she gave Heracles a pair of clappers made from bronze. These noisemakers had been forged by Hephaistos and, when Heracles shook them, they created a terrible, deafening din that shocked the birds and made them take flight from their impregnable roost. Taking advantage of their fear and confusion, Heracles began to shoot them down with his trusty bow. He dispatched dozens of the creatures and those remaining bolted in terror, never to return. The town was safe and Heracles was now half way through his labours. The menacing birds would later torment the brave souls accompanying Jason and his Argonauts.

The Cretan Bull

MINOS, THE KING OF CRETE, was a powerful and tyrannical ruler who wanted to secure his throne with the help of the gods. He had made a promise to Poseidon that he would sacrifice anything the god sent him from the sea. However, when Poseidon sent a handsome snow-white bull, Minos killed another in its place because he was awed

by the strength and savagery of Poseidon's bull. Furious that a mere mortal would try to deceive him, Poseidon made Minos' wife, Queen Pasiphae, fall in love with the bull. She later sired the Minotaur, a monster with the head of a bull and the body of a man. This monstrous being had to be trapped within a maze known as the Labyrinth where it could wander forever without finding his way out.

Poseidon's massive bull also needed controlling, rampaging across Crete, leaving a wake of death and destruction wherever it went. When Heracles arrived to capture the bull, Minos was delighted. He even offered help, but Heracles refused, knowing he had to entrap the east alone. This he did quite easily, by tracking the bull, then wrapping his unyielding arms around its gigantic neck and, slowly but surely, squeezing until it surrendered. Heracles then tethered the bull securely around its neck and rode the creature back to Eurystheus. Having no idea what to do with the ferocious beast, Eurystheus released the bull, where it roamed around Greece, continuing to terrorize people until Theseus, another hero and acolyte of Heracles, caught up to the bull in Marathon. He killed the satanic swine, offering it as a sacrifice to the gods and ridding Greece from the chaos it provoked. Theseus – himself a demi-god sired by Poseidon and a human woman – would later prove his own strength when he subdued the Minotaur.

The Mares of Diomedes

WITH HERACLES now on his eighth labour, Eurystheus was concerned that he would never outfox the great warrior. For his next diabolical trial, Heracles was set the task of stealing the mares of Diomedes, the King of Thrace. Diomedes was a savage giant, who ruled a sadistic tribe of warriors called the Bistones. The perverse King kept his four mares chained to a manger of bronze and fed them an unnatural diet of human flesh, from unwitting travellers to the region. The barbarous mares had to be safely tethered, as they had been driven mad by their diet, needing more and more flesh to keep them satiated.

Heracles travelled to Thrace with a band of followers to plunder the mares for Eurystheus. In the midst of dispatching the grooms who fed the horses, Heracles' men were set upon by the Bistones. One of Heracles' followers, a youth named Abderos, was left to watch the mares while Heracles and his men crushed their attackers. But Abderos was no match for the frenzied violence of the horses and, on Heracles' return, he found only pieces of his dear friend remained. Devastated at the loss of Abderos, Heracles sought bloody vengeance. The warrior met and fought Diomedes, who was a powerful warrior and as untamed as his mares. Despite his ferocity, he was no match for Heracles, who annihilated his foe. Still mourning Abderos, Heracles then fed Diomedes to his own mares. The flesh of their master satisfied their blood-lust and Heracles was able to take them back to Argos. Even though they were much calmer, Eurystheus feared the feral horses. Set free, they roamed Greece until reaching Mount Olympus, where they were savaged by wild beasts, Zeus having rejected the sacrifice of their unholy flesh.

Hippolyte's Belt

FOR HIS NINTH TASK, **Heracles was set the challenge of retrieving the belt of Hippolyte, Queen of the Amazons. This race of female warriors, who had invented and perfected the art of fighting on horseback, were renowned for their bravery and fighting skills. Hippolyte was the strongest and bravest of all the Amazons. For this, Ares, the god of war, awarded her with a leather belt, believed to give power to its wearer. Hippolyte wore this belt to carry her weapons. Eurystheus wanted the belt for his daughter, Admete, who had always coveted it.**

Taking his followers – including Theseus – Heracles travelled to the land of the Amazons, deep in the Caucasus mountains, to bring back the fabled belt for Admete. When the ship docked, Hippolyte herself came down the mountain to meet the famous band of champions. Heracles explained why they had come and that he was under oath to complete his tasks. Hippolyte, who had been swayed by many tales of Heracles' strength and prowess in battle, said that she would gladly give her belt to him so that he could complete his tasks.

But the ever-vengeful Hera, who was dismayed that Heracles would not have to do battle for the belt, manipulated the Amazons into believing that the strangers intended to carry off their Queen. Furious at the deception, the Amazons laid siege to Heracles and his men. A mighty battle erupted, ending only when Heracles struck the killing blow to Hippolyte and took her belt. In some versions, it was Theseus who subdued the great Amazon Queen, carrying her off and marrying her just as Hera prophesised. Heracles returned to Argo and gave the enchanted belt to Eurystheus for his daughter, fulfilling yet another of his legendary labours.

The Cattle of Geryon

TO BRING BACK THE CATTLE **of Geryon was Heracles' next endeavour. Geryon was a giant monster with three heads and three sets of arms and legs. He was also a fearsome warrior. His cattle were renowned and Eurystheus thought that he had finally given Heracles an unmanageable task, as stealing them would be hard enough, but herding them all the way back to Argos was nigh on impossible.**

Undaunted, Heracles set off for Erythia, passing through the desert of Libya on the way. It was here, frustrated by the intense, relentless heat, that Heracles discharged an arrow from his bow directly into Helios, the Sun god. Helios was impressed by Heracles' valour and presented him with use of the golden cup in which he sailed every night across the sea to his home in the east. Heracles used this cup to sail to Erythia. As soon as he landed, he was brutally attacked by Orthrus, Geryon's vicious two-headed dog who guarded the famous cattle. With but one glorious swing of his club, Heracles killed Orthrus and then dispatched Eurytion, the herdsman, in the same way.

But the odious Geryon would not be so easily quelled. Roaring with rage, he flew at Heracles. The two fought evenly until Heracles shot Geryon through one of his heads with his venomous arrows. After that, it was relatively easy to take the cattle, and head back to Argos. It was only when the vindictive Hera sent a gadfly to irritate the herd, causing them to scatter in every direction, that Heracles encountered any trouble. So fast and so numerous was the herd that it took Heracles the best part of a year to track them down. Next, Hera caused a flood to overfill a river, meaning that there was no way for the cattle to cross. Again, Heracles bested her, filling the river with stones so that the cattle could walk across without being swept away. In a galling put down to all his efforts, when Heracles successfully brought the herd before Eurystheus, he sacrificed them to the spiteful Hera.

The Apples of the Hesperides

To crown his deeds, so wondrous & so great,
Upon his shoulders vast Olympus' weight
He bore, while Atlas did the apples bring,
Which bridal Juno gave to Heaven's dread King.
Anon

NOW NEARING THE END of his labours, Eurystheus had devised what he felt sure was an impossible task. Heracles was to fetch him the golden apples that Gaia, the earth mother, had given to Hera and Zeus on their wedding day. They were safely hidden in a garden under the guard of a fierce dragon called Ladon and the Hesperides, the nymph daughters of Atlas. One of the last Titans, Atlas, had been condemned by Zeus to forever hold up the heavens on his shoulders.

Heracles headed west in search of the garden, his quest taking him through most of Greece. On the way, he killed the abhorrent eagle that tormented Prometheus by daily tearing out his liver. In gratitude, Prometheus related to Heracles that Atlas was the only person who could successfully retrieve the apples. Heracles eventually found the garden by forcing Nereus, the shape-shifting old man of the sea, to reveal its location by holding him in a vice-like grip, no matter what he turned himself into.

To convince Atlas to help him, Heracles acquiesced to shoulder his burden, of which Atlas had grown deathly weary of carrying. Instantly agreeing to help, Atlas easily retrieved the apples from his daughters. However, on his return, Atlas decided he did not want to take back his burden. Heracles was trapped with the heavens on his shoulders and no way of freeing himself. Just as Atlas was taking his leave, Heracles asked the titan if he would temporarily take back the world while Heracles made himself more comfortable. Agreeing, Atlas set down the apples and took back the heavens, only for Heracles to abandon him to his burden.

Returning to Argos, Heracles presented the stunned King with the apples. Being the property of the gods, Heracles eventually had to return the apples to Athene, who replaced them in the garden. This labour is sometimes known as Heracles' last, but he still had one final challenge to fulfill before gaining immortality and the peace he so dearly craved.

Cerberus

In fetters Heracles fierce Cerberus tied,
And took him trembling from grim Pluto's side,
From realms of darkness drag'd away to light
Anon

FOR HIS FINAL LABOUR, Heracles was set his most hazardous challenge by far, which would send him into the Underworld itself to bring Cerberus, the hound of hell, back to Eurystheus alive. Cerberus was a demonic three-headed dog with writhing, hissing snakes as his tail who guarded the gates of Hades. Even entering the Underworld was a task of extreme bravery, as no one who did so had ever escaped alive. Heracles first went to Eleusis, where he was initiated into the Eleusinian Mysteries. Their sacred ceremonies would enable him to travel safely through – and out of – the afterlife.

Heracles then entered the gates of Hades, escorted by Athene and Hermes, the god of boundaries. Before he could reach Cerberus, Heracles had to cross the River Styx. Charon, the ferryman, demanded payment from every passenger: a coin placed in the dead person's mouth. He would also only carry those who were dead. Heracles could meet neither request, but by the sheer force of his anger, Charon relented and rowed Heracles deep into the Underworld to meet the King, Hades.

Hades agreed that Heracles could take Cerberus to Eurystheus, but only on the condition that he overpowered the massive hound without the use of his weapons. Heracles duly surrendered his trusty bow, sword and club, which had been with him since the start of his labours and, unarmed, headed onwards to claim his prize. When Heracles cornered Cerberus by the River Aucheron, he overpowered the beast by wrestling it until it surrendered. Heracles then bound and dragged Cerberus out of Hades, presenting him to Eurystheus.

Finally outdone, Eurystheus fled in terror at the sight of the monstrous hound, begging Heracles to return Cerberus to the Underworld. In return, Eurystheus released Heracles from his service, earning him immortality and freedom.

Myths of Love and Courage

THE GODS AND GODDESSES OF GREECE were the creators of the earth, makers of the universe and rulers thereafter. In their hectic lives, governed by deep-seated jealousies, petty hatreds, overwhelming passion and love, and desperate bids for revenge, there were other beings, mortals who led lives cast in the shadows of these greater entities. But it was also the acts of these mortals which became tools of understanding for the Greeks, for how could they make sense of the world in which they lived without the interaction of mankind with gods? From where came the echo in the deep valleys of Greece; how do you explain the powerful spirits of the woodland, the waters, the winds? These are the tales of mystery and enchantment which form some of the most exquisite allegories in literature worldwide; they speak of love, desire, deceit and trickery; they explain all.

Eros and Psyche

O brightest! though too late for antique vows,
Too, too late for the fond believing lyre,
When holy were the haunted forest boughs,
Holy the air, the water, and the fire;
Yet even in these days so far retired
From happy pieties, thy lucent fans
Fluttering among the faint Olympians,
I see, and sing, by my own eyes inspired.
So let me be thy choir, and make a moan
Upon the midnight hours;
Thy voice, thy lute, thy pipe, thy incense sweet
From singed censer teeming;
Thy shrine, thy grove, thy oracle, thy heat.
Of pale-mouthed prophet dreaming.
John Keats, Ode to Psyche

ONCE THERE WAS A KING and a queen with three lovely daughters. The youngest daughter, Psyche, was so beautiful, so fair of face that she was revered throughout the land, and the subjects of her father reached out to touch her as she passed. No suitors dared to cross her doorstep, so highly was she worshiped. Psyche was deeply lonely.

Her beauty became legend, far and wide, and it was not long before word of it reached the ears of Aphrodite, the epitome of all beauty, the goddess of love herself. Tales of the young princess enraged the jealous goddess, and she made plans to dispose of her. Aphrodite arranged for Psyche's father to present Psyche as a sacrifice, in order to prevent his kingdom being devoured by a monster, and this he grudgingly did, placing her on a mountaintop, and bidding her a tearful farewell.

Eros, the errant son of Aphrodite, was sent to murder Psyche but he too was entranced by her gentle ways, and implored Zephyr, the West Wind, to lift her and place her down far from the hillside, in a lush and verdant valley. When Psyche opened her eyes, she found herself in front of a sumptuous palace unlike any she had seen before. She called out, and although there was no response, quiet voices simmered just beyond her hearing, comforting her, soothing her, setting her at ease. She stretched and thought briefly of food, at which a platter of succulent morsels was laid, as if by magic, at her disposal. When she grew tired, a soft bed was presented, and she slipped dreamlessly into sleep.

Psyche woke in the night. A presence had stirred her, but she felt no fear. A warmth pervaded the room and she closed her eyes, sinking into its musky perfume. She was joined and embraced by a body so inviting, she gave herself at once, filled by a sense of joy that overwhelmed her.

'Who are you,' she whispered, and a finger was laid firmly to her lips. She said no more, spending the night in tender love. When she woke, she felt gilded, but her bed was empty.

And so the days passed, with Psyche growing ever more peaceful, ever happier. She had clothes and jewels which miraculously appeared – her every comfort was seen to. And the only hole in her happiness was loneliness, for apart from the moonlit visits from her phantom husband, she was entirely alone. She'd tried to learn more about this man who held her each night in passionate embrace, but he'd told her that his identity must remain secret, or their alliance would be no more. She agreed to his wishes because she loved him, because he filled her with a sense of belonging that she had never before experienced.

One day, however, her peaceful idyll was interrupted by the cries of her two sisters. Concerned about her disappearance, they'd spent many weeks searching the hills, and now they stood just beyond the bend of the valley. Shrieking with delight, Psyche raced up the mountain, and drew them back into her new home. And as she toured her sisters around her exquisite palace, she failed to notice their growing silence, their churlish looks. Her sisters were sickened with envy, and they teased their younger sister about her ghostly lover.

'No,' she protested, 'he was real.' She felt him, explored him each night. Held him warm in her arms.

But her sisters taunted and teased until Psyche agreed to seek out his identity. That night, when he came to her once again, she broke her word for the first time, leaning across him to light the oil lamp. As she moved, a drop of the hot liquid fell onto the snow white skin of her lover, and his face was revealed. He was none other than the most beautiful of the gods, Eros, son of Aphrodite. But burned, and bewildered, he rose from her bed and disappeared from her forever.

Psyche's torment was so deep that she tried to take her own life. Eros, still deeply in love with his wife, but now invisible to her, saved her on each occasion, caring for her as she travelled across the kingdom in search of him. He longed to touch her, but the wrath of his mother was more than he could bear. He longed to speak to her, but could use only the trees, the winds, the creatures of the forest, to deliver his words.

Searching far and wide for Eros, Psyche came, by and by, to the home of Aphrodite. Poisoned by her jealousy, Aphrodite resolved to dispose of the young princess, knowing not of her son's attachment, caring only that Psyche was more beautiful than she, and that Psyche had eluded her careful plot to send her to her death. She set the young princess impossible tasks, determined to punish her further.

The first task was to pluck the golden wool from a flock of bloodthirsty sheep. As Psyche stood by the edge of their paddock, she heard the quiet song of the reeds in the wind. As she listened, their words became clear. She was not to pluck the wool from their backs. There, on the gorsebushes which lined their field, was the wool that had been brushed from their hides each time they passed. She crept over and filled her basket. Gleefully she returned to Aphrodite, basket held high, but her mistress's sour expression greeted her, and all hope of freedom vanished.

The goddess sent her out once again, this time to fetch water from the stream which flowed to the Styx, the river of the Underworld. As she neared its banks, Psyche grew frightened. The stream itself cut through a deep gorge, and all her efforts to reach its waters failed. Furthermore, as she caught a glimpse of its shimmering blackness, she became aware of the guard of dragons, who patrolled its shores, boiling the seething waters with their fiery breath. She sank down in despair, her bottle falling to her side.

Suddenly it was snatched up, and into the air, clutched in the grasp of Zeus's Royal Eagle. The winds had told him of Psyche's plight, and enchanted by her loveliness, he vowed to help her. Smoothly he dodged the dragons, filling the flask and returning it to her waiting arms.

Aphrodite was ill pleased by this success. She had imagined Psyche long dead by now, and set all her powers of determination to plot the third task. Psyche was to descend to the Afterworld, and beg Persephone for some of her beauty, which should be returned to Aphrodite. Once again Psyche tried to take her own life, deep in desolation and longing for Eros, and frustrated by the seemingly impossible tasks before her. But yet again, she was plucked from death by Eros, and through his powers realized the way to achieve her task. The tower from which she had attempted to leap confirmed the instructions.

Psyche was to follow the path nearby, which would take her to the Afterworld. She was to take several things along – barley cakes and honey cakes for Cerberus, the three-headed dog who guarded the entry and two coins to pay Charon, the ferryman. She was to ignore the messages of her own kind heart and refuse help to anyone who sought her assistance along the way.

Psyche set off, the words ringing in her ears. As she journeyed she was met by hapless travellers who called out for her help. At every turn lay another trap set by Aphrodite, who was determined for Psyche to remain in the Afterworld once and for all. But Psyche too had determination, fed by love for Eros, to whom she longed to return. She made her way past the pitfalls set out for her, and on to Persephone, who presented her with a box.

As she returned once more to the land of the living, she was struck by curiosity, and opened the box. The box seemed empty. But as she struggled to close it, she felt an overwhelming sleep flower around her, kissing shut her eyes, and drawing from her lungs her final breath. Death clung to the maiden, embracing her lifelessness, waiting for its usurpation to be complete.

Ever vigilant, Eros flew down, brushing the sleep of death from her eyes and placing it back in the box. And so Psyche was revived, fresh and invigorated, and glowing with new life. She returned to Aphrodite, and handed over the deadly box. She waited with anticipation. Surely Aphrodite was finished with her now.

But the goddess had a final task in store for Psyche, and led her to a large shed, full of various grains. Here lay oats, and black beans, millet, lentils, vetch and poppyseeds, wheat and rye, mixed together in an overwhelming pile. Psyche was to sort it, said Aphrodite firmly. And then she could be free.

Psyche crouched down and gingerly picked at the pile. Tears welled in her eyes and she felt the beginnings of despair touching again at her heart. As the first glistening tear fell, a tiny voice woke her from her sorrow. An ant, enchanted by the lovely princess, had moved to her side. He could help, he said, and so it was that hundreds of ants marched to the pile, and within just one hour the pile was sorted.

Aphrodite was enraged, but she was also wise enough to know that Psyche was not going to succumb to her plots. She set her free, and Psyche set off once more in her search for Eros.

Now Eros had been deeply disillusioned by his mother's antics. Her jealousy had sparked in him a rebellion such as he'd never felt before, and with a revelatory burst, he flew at once to Olympus and begged Zeus to offer his advice.

Zeus was the King of gods for many reasons. Throughout his reign, many such sensitive matters were put before him, and his awesome wisdom and sense of justice had always prevailed. On this day, Eros was not disappointed. Zeus examined the goodness of Psyche, her dedication and her exquisite charms. He agreed to allow her marriage to Eros, he agreed to make her immortal. And in return Eros must become reconciled to his mother, and they must share the deep respect of family.

And so it was that Psyche became a daughter to Aphrodite, and entered a union with Eros. She returned once again to her palace in the valley, to a happiness that was enriched by the goodness in her heart and which was, as a result of her tribulations, now complete.

The Rape of Persephone

... that fair field
Of Enna, where Proserpine, gathering flowers,
Herself a fairer flower, by gloomy Dis
Was gathered, which cost Ceres all that pain
To seek her through the world ...
John Milton, Paradise Lost

PERSEPHONE WAS THE DAUGHTER of Zeus and Demeter, a virgin of such remarkable beauty that she was kept hidden from the eyes of wishful suitors for all of her life. She spent her days idyllically, gathering fragrant flowers in the fields which spread as far as the eye could see, and dancing with the wood folk, who doted on the young maiden. Demeter was goddess of the earth, and Persephone whiled away the long summery hours helping her mother to gather seeds, to pollinate, and to sow the fertile earth. She was shielded from the outside world by her doting parents, kept carefully away from the dangers that could befall so fair a creature. They lived in the Vale of Enna, where Persephone blossomed like the flowers which surrounded her sanctuary.

One warm, sun-kissed evening, Persephone lay back in the long grasses by the idle stream which trickled through the paddock at the end of the garden. Bees hummed above the lapping waters, butterflies glided and came to rest beside the serene young woman. An eager toad lapped at the darting dragonflies. Persephone's beauty was accentuated by lush green grass, and by the expression of placid contentment which embraced her exquisite features.

It was no wonder then, that the passionate Hades, king of the Underworld, should stop in his tracks when he spied this graceful vision, should draw back the anarchic horses which lunged and tugged at his fiery chariot. He drew a deep breath. He must have her.

Now Hades and Zeus were brothers, and Hades thought nothing of approaching him to ask for Persephone's hand in marriage. Zeus knew that his daughter would be well cared for by Hades, but he felt saddened by the thought of losing her to the world from which no mortal could return. He wavered, reluctant to displease his brother, but more apprehensive still of the wrath of Demeter, who would never allow such a match to take place. Zeus announced that he could not offer his permission, but neither would he deny it, and encouraged by this response, Hades returned to the peaceful spot where Persephone lay and seized her. A great chasm opened in the earth, and holding Persephone under an arm, Hades and his horses plunged into the dark world beneath.

It was many hours before Demeter realized that Persephone had vanished, and many days before she could come to terms with her loss. She shunned the attentions of Zeus, refused to attend the council of the gods. She dressed herself in the robes of a beggarwoman, and in this disguise, prepared to roam the realm, in search of her missing daughter. The earth grew bare as Demeter ceased to tend it; fruit withered on the vine, plenteous fields grew fallow, the warm western winds ceased to blow. The land grew cold and barren.

Demeter's travels took her across many lands. At each, she stopped, searched, and begged for information. At each she was turned away empty-handed, often snubbed and ill-treated. She grew colder, and famine spread across the earth. At last she came to the land of Eleusis, the kingdom of Celeus and his wife Metaneira. There Demeter, in her disguise, was welcomed and taken in by Queen Metaneira, who instinctively trusted the beggarwoman and asked her to act as nurse to her baby son, the Prince Demaphoon.

Demeter was weakened by her journey, and welcomed the respite. She fell in love with the young prince, and poured out her longing for her daughter in his care. She grew more content, bathing the infant in nectar and holding him daily above the fire in order to burn away his mortality. The greatest gift she could offer him was immortality, and she poured her supreme powers into the process, protecting the child from the flames so that he remained unharmed.

One day, Metaneira paid an unexpected visit to the nursery, and chanced to see this extraordinary sight. She flew into a panic, and the startled Demeter dropped the child in to the fire, where he was burned to death. At once Demeter took on her godly form, and chastised the Queen for causing the death of the child they both loved so deeply. The people of Eleusis paid tribute to the god in their midst, and in return she set up a temple, and showed them how to plant and sow seeds in the arid earth. She blessed them, and as their kindness was repaid by an end to their years of famine, so came the news she had long awaited.

A stranger came to her in her temple one night, as she prepared to retire. He'd been tending his flocks, he said, and he'd seen the ground open up to greet a flaming chariot led by a team of black horses. In the carriage was a screaming girl who'd thrust something into the startled herder's hands, just before the earth closed upon her. He held it out to her now. It was Persephone's girdle.

The wretched Demeter knew at once what had befallen her beloved precious daughter. She returned in haste to Olympus, where she confronted Zeus. And so it was decided that Persephone should be allowed to return to her mother. He sent word to Hades, who reluctantly agreed to part from his young bride. As Persephone prepared to leave, he shyly offered her a pomegranate to eat on the journey, a token of his love, his esteem, he said. Persephone was charmed by the gesture, and breaking the fast she had undertaken while trapped in the Underworld, she nibbled at several seeds.

At once darkness fell upon her. Her mother stood just past the gates to the Underworld, but she was unable to reach her. For any mortal who eats or drinks in the land of Hades has no choice but to remain there forever. A chasm opened between mother and child, one which neither could pass.

But Zeus, ashamed by his part in the matter, and deeply concerned by Demeter's neglect of the land, which refused to flower or bear fruit, stepped in. It was agreed that Persephone would become reunited with her mother, and make her home again on earth. But for three months each year, one month for every seed of the pomegranate she had eaten, she must return to the Underworld, and become Hades' queen.

Their reunion was warmed by the sun, which shone for the first time on the cold land. Birds poked their heads from knotted branches, buds and then leaves thrust their way through the hardened earth. Spring had arrived in all her fecund splendour.

But for the three months each year in which Persephone returns to Hades, Demeter throws her cloak across the earth, bringing sterility and darkness until Persephone breathes once more in the land of the living, bringing Spring.

Orpheus and Eurydice

Heavenly o'er the startled Hell,
Holy, where the Accursed dwell,
O Thracian, went thy silver song!
Grim Minos with unconscious tears,
Melts into mercy as he hears –
The serpents in Megaera's hair
Kiss, as they wreathe enamoured there;
All harmless rests the madding throng;–
From the torn breast the Vulture mute
Flies, scared before the charmed lute–
Lulled into sighing from their roar
The dark waves woo the listening shore–
Listening the Thracian's silver song!–
Love was the Thracian's silver song!

Friedrich von Schiller, The Triumph of Love

THE MUSIC OF ORPHEUS was known across the lands. With his lyre, he played the sweetest strains which lulled even the fiercest beasts into a peaceful rapture. For his music Orpheus was loved, and he travelled far and wide, issuing forth melodies that were pure, sublime.

Orpheus was the son of Apollo and the muse Calliope. He lived in Thrace and spent his days singing, playing the music that spread his fame still further. One day, Orpheus came across a gentle and very beautiful young nymph, who danced to his music as if she was born to do so. She was called Eurydice, and wings seemed to lift her heels, as she played and frolicked to his music. And then, when their eyes caught, it was clear that it was love at first sight and that their destiny was to be shared.

It was only a few days later that they were joined in marriage, and never before had such an angelic couple existed. As they danced on the eve of their wedding, the very trees and flowers, the winds and rushing streams paused and then shouted their congratulations. The world stopped to watch, to approve, to celebrate.

And then that most sinister of animals, a stealthy viper, made its way into the babbling midst and struck at the ankle of Eurydice, sending her to an icy, instant death. Eurydice sank down in the circle, and all efforts to revive her failed. Time seemed to stop. Certainly there was no music, anywhere.

Orpheus was disconsolate with grief. He could not even bring himself to bury her, and he played on his lyre such tunes that even the rocks, the hardened fabric of the caves, shed tears. After several days he came to a decision which seemed at once as clear and as necessary as anything he had ever undertaken.

Orpheus made his way to the Underworld, determined to rescue his great love. His lyre in hand, his heart pounding with emotion, he reached the river Styx, the black waterway which snakes its way into the Underworld, which divides the other world from our own. There he played his lute so tunefully, so eloquently, that Charon, the ferryman, took him across the river at no charge, granted access to a place into which no mortal must go.

As Orpheus was drawn deeper into the Underworld, grisly, frightening sights greeted his eyes, but he continued to play his soulful tune, filling with tears the eyes of those cast in wretched purgatory, the ghosts of beings who had done ill deeds, the spirits of men who had been cursed. He played on and on, his music seeping into the blackness and creating an effortless light which guided the way.

At the end of his journey King Hades and Queen Persephone sat, entranced by his music. They knew of his mission. They would allow him to take Eurydice. His music had unwound the rigours of their rules, of their laws, and momentarily appeased, temporarily relaxed, they permitted Orpheus to take one of their own.

There was a condition, as there is in all such matters. Orpheus could have his bride returned to him; she would follow him as his shadow. But he must not look back on his trip from their world. The music from Orpheus' lyre picked up the timbre of his pleasure and took on a jaunty character which brought a look of surprise to the stony faces of Hades' guards. Orpheus turned and made his way back to the Styx, to his world, to home and Eurydice.

The gate of the Underworld was in sight when Orpheus felt an overwhelming need to confirm that Eurydice was there. Instinctively, he turned towards his great love, and there she stood, shrouded in a dark cape. As he reached for her, just as he felt the warmth of her skin, her breath on his cheek, she vanished, drawn back into death, into the darkened world of the afterlife.

Orpheus left the Underworld alone, and when he returned to his land, he lay broken and wasted on the shores of the Styx. For the rest of his short life he wandered among the hills, carrying a broken lyre which he would not mend and could not play. He cared for nothing. He was attacked, one day, without the powers to play, to appease his enemy. His attackers were a throng of Thracian women who killed him, and tore him to pieces. His lyre was taken to Lesbos, where it became a shrine, and some years later, his head was washed upon the shores of the island. There it was joined with his sacred lyre, its broken strings representing forever the broken heart of Orpheus.

Echo and Narcissus

Pan loved his neighbour Echo – but that child
Of Earth and Air pined for the Satyr leaping;
The Satyr loved with wasting madness wild
The bright nymph Lyda, – and so three went weeping:
As Pan loved Echo, Echo loved the Satyr,
The Satyr, Lyda – and thus love consumed them.
And thus to each – which was a woeful matter –
To bear what they inflicted, justice doom'd them;
For inasmuch as each might hate the lover,
Each loving, so was hated. – Ye that love not
Be warn'd – in thought turn this example over,
That when ye love, the like return ye prove not.

Percy Bysshe Shelley, Mochus

ECHO WAS A WOOD NYMPH who danced and sang in the forest. She told engaging stories to anyone who would listen, and although she was adored by the other nymphs her headstrong ways meant that none of her playmates had the last word. Echo would skip and frolic among the trees, charming the small creatures and befriending the forest folk as she played.

Hera was enchanted by the nubile young nymph, and she came daily to hear Echo's tales of adventure, of fairies and of far-off places, stories that grew ever more complicated with each telling. One day Hera left earlier than usual, inspired to see her husband Zeus by Echo's romantic tales. It was on this day that Hera was presented with evidence of her husband's philanderings, and discovered that Echo had been involved in the subterfuge, receiving a wage from Zeus to occupy his lovely wife.

Hera flew into a rage which resounded through the Kingdom, and the victim of her wrath was Echo, who was stripped of her power of speech, able only to echo the last words spoken by any person. Echo fled deep into the forest, tortured by her speechlessness, drained of her life and vitality.

Now in this same forest lived a handsome young man named Narcissus, a Thespian and the son of the blue nymph Leirope and the River-god Cephisus. When Narcissus was but a child, his mother consulted the seer Tiresias to learn of his fortune. Would he live to old age? she longed to know.

'If he never knows himself,' said the wise man.

Tales of Narcissus' beauty had spread far and wide and it was not long before a he grew conceited and self-satisfied. Lovers came and went, but Narcissus' heart grew colder, frosted by the knowledge that none could match his charm and grace.

Echo had been drawn to the youth for many months, and secretly followed him in the forest, begging him silently to speak so she could make her presence known. One day her wish was granted, and Narcissus, who had lost his companions in the forest, called out, 'Is anyone here?"

'Here,' cried the young nymph with delight.

'Come!' replied Narcissus, his face a haughty mask.

'Come!' repeated Echo.

'Why do you avoid me?' asked Narcissus, a surprised look crossing his face.

'Why do you avoid me?' said Echo.

'Let us come together,' he shouted, with careless confidence. He looked purposefully around, his manly brow furrowed with intrigue.

'Let us come together.' And as the words tumbled from Echo's tender lips, she leapt from her hiding place, and threw herself against the comely young man.

He stepped back in horror, roughly detaching himself from her grasp, and snarling, 'I will die before you ever lay with me!' Summoning up the arrogance of his youth, he cast Echo aside and left the clearing, failing to hear her pleading 'Lay with me ...' as he stalked away.

Echo grew cold with misery, and unable to draw breath, she lay still and pined for her lost love, the vessel for her childish hopes and aspirations. There Echo laid until she was no more than her voice, her tiny body becoming one with the woodland floor.

Narcissus quickly forgot this uneasy encounter, and carried on his relentless search for love. One day, deep in the forest, he stopped his hunting in order to take a drink from a pure, clear stream. As he leant over the crystal waters he was caught by such a sight of beauty that his breath escaped in a stunned gasp. There, in this magical current, was a face of such perfect loveliness that Narcissus was unable to move, to call out.

He whispered to the dazzling illusion, but though the lips of this creature moved, too, no sound was uttered. Narcissus was enchanted.

He reached forwards to the elegant face, the princely features, but alas, with every movement the object of his passion disappeared in a kaleidoscope of colour.

Narcissus had fallen in love with his own reflection, and he was held captive by its magnificence. He reclined by the stream, unable to move, and there he laid without food or water until he too pined away, to become one with the forest. The last words to slip from his aristocratic lips were,

'O youth beloved in vain. Farewell.' To which the spirit of the love-sickened nymph Echo replied, 'Farewell.'

Those who had once swooned for Narcissus prepared his funeral pyre, but his body had disappeared. In its place grew a slim and elegant flower with a blood-red heart, which gazed piteously at its reflection as it dipped over the water. Today, this flower can be found by the waters of certain streams, a flower known for its beauty, which gazes eternally at its own reflection.

The spirit of Echo is often heard, for she fled that forest, and wanders far from the shores of that stream, ever searching for her lost love, and, of course, her voice.

Perseus and the Gorgon

Peaceful grew the land
The while the ivory rod was in his hand,
For robbers fled, and good men still waxed strong,
And in no house was any sound of wrong,
Until the Golden Age there seemed to be,
So steeped the land was in felicity.
William Morris, The Earthly Paradise

THERE ONCE WAS **a troubled king who learned, through an Oracle, that he would reach his death through the hand of his own grandson. This king was Acrisius, king of Argos, and he had only one child, the fair Danae. Acrisius shut her away in a cave in order to keep her unwedded, and there she grew older, and more beautiful, as time passed. No man could reach her, although many tried, and eventually word of her beauty reached the gods, and finally the king of the Gods himself, Zeus.**

He entered her prison in a cascade of light, and planted in her womb the seed of the gods, and from this the infant Perseus was spawned. Acrisius heard the infant's cries, and unable to kill him outright, he released Danae from her prison, and with her child she was placed on a raft, and sent out on the stormy seas to meet their death.

Now Poseidon knew of Zeus's child, and calmed the seas, lifting the mother and child carefully to the island of Seriphos, where they washed onto safe shores. They were discovered there by a kind fisherman, who brought them to his home. It was in this humble and peaceful abode that Perseus grew up, a boy of effortless intelligence, cunning and nobility. He was a sportsman beyond compare, and a hero among his playmates. He was visited in his dreams by Athene, the goddess of war, who filled his head with lusty ambition and inspired him to seek danger and excitement.

The fisherman became a father figure to Perseus, but another schemed to take his place. The fisherman's brother Polydectes, chief of the island, was besotted by the beautiful Danae, and longed to have her for his wife. He showered her with priceless jewels, succulent morsels of food, rich fabrics and furs, but her heart belonged to Perseus, and she refused his attentions. Embittered, he resolved to dispose of the youth, and set Perseus a task at which he could not help but fail, and from which no mortal man could ever return.

The task was to slay the creature Medusa, one of the three Gorgon sisters. Medusa was the only mortal of the Gorgons, with a face so hideous, so repulsive, that any man who laid eyes on her would be turned to stone before he could attack. Her hair was a nest of vipers, which writhed around that flawed and fatal face. Perseus was enthralled by the idea of performing an act of such bravery and that night, as he slept, he summoned again the goddess Athene, who provided him with the tools by which the task could be shouldered.

Athene came to him, a glorious figure of war, and with her she brought Hermes, her brother, who offered the young man powerful charms with which he could make his way. Perseus was provided with Hermes own crooked sword, sturdy enough to cut through even the strongest armour, and Perseus's feet were fitted with winged sandals, by which he could make his escape. From Pluto he received a helmet which had the power to make its wearer invisible. Athene offered her mirrored shield, which would allow Perseus to strike Medusa without seeing her horrible face. Finally, he was given a skin bag, to carry the Gorgon's head from the site.

Perseus set out the next morning, his first assignment to find the half-sisters of the Gorgons, in the icy wilderness of the northern steppes of Graiae. They alone could provide him with the whereabouts of Medusa. With the aid of his winged sandals, Perseus flew north, till he came to the frosted mists of the mountains. There the earth was so cold, a fabulous crack was rent across her surface. The land was barren, icy, empty, and although he felt no fear, Perseus had to struggle to carry on, his breath frozen on his lips. There, on the edge of the Hyperborean sea were the Gray Sisters, witches from another era who had come there to end their days, wreaking a wretched existence from the snow-capped mountains, toothless and haggard with age. They had but one eye between them, and one tooth, without which they would surely have died.

Perseus chose his moment carefully, and lunged into their midst, grasping their single eye, and stepping out of reach.

'I require your assistance,' he said firmly. 'I must know the way to the Gorgons. If you cannot help me I shall take your tooth as well, and you shall starve in this wilderness.'

The Gray Sisters swayed and muttered, lolling upon the snow and fumbling across its icy surface towards the awe-inspiring voice.

A cry rose up when they realized that he had their eye, and they threatened and cursed Perseus, their howls echoing in the blackness of the wasteland. Finally, they succumbed, the fear of blindness in that empty place enlivening their tongues, loosening their resolve. Perseus graciously returned their eye, and on a breath of Arctic air, he rose and headed southwards, out of sight of the sisters, who struggled to see their tormentor.

Back through the mists he flew, where the sea sent spirals of spray that lashed at his heels and tried to drag him down. On he went, and the snows melted away into a sea so blue he seemed enveloped in it. The sky grew bright, the grass of the fields green and inviting, and as he flew he grew hotter, his eyes heavy with exhaustion, his perfect skin dripping with effort. The other end of the world rose up, a land and a sea where no human dared enter, a land of burning heat, of fiery hatred and fear, where none lived but the Gorgons themselves, surrounded by the hapless stone statues of man and beast who had dared to look upon them.

He came across the sisters as they slept in the midday sun. Medusa lay between her sisters, who protectively laid their arms across her mass. Her body was scaled and repellent, her limbs clawed and gnarled. Perseus dared look no further, but from the corner of his eye he saw the coiling vipers, and the serpent's tongue which even in sleep darted from her razor-sharp lips. Her fearsome eyes were shut. He was safe.

With one decisive movement he plunged himself and his sword towards this creature, Athene's shield held high. And Medusa's answering howl pierced the air, ripping the breath from his lungs, and dragging him down towards her. He struggled to maintain his composure, shivering and drawn to look at the source of this violent cry. He fell on her, shaking his head to clear it, fighting the temptation to give in. And then the courage that was deep inside him, born within him, the gift of his father Zeus, redeemed him. He lifted his head, and with shield held high, thrust his sword in one wild swoop that lopped off the head of Medusa.

He packed it hastily in his bag, and leapt up, away from the arms of the Sisters Gorgon who had woken abruptly, and now hissed and struck out at him. The Gorgons were not human, and could not, like Medusa, be slain by humans. They rose on wings, like murderous vultures, yowling and gnashing their teeth, screaming of revenge.

But Perseus had disappeared. His helmet took him from their side, enshrouded him with a curtain that protected him from their eyes. He was safe.

For days on end he flew with his booty, across the desert, where the dripping blood of Medusa hit the sand and bred evil vipers and venomous snakes, ever to populate the sunburnt earth. The Gorgons flew behind him, a whirlwind of hatred and revenge, but Perseus soared above them, until he was safe, at the edge of his world.

He came to rest at the home of Atlas, the giant, who held up with great pillars the weight of the sky. He begged for a place to lay his weary head, for sustenance and water. But the giant refused him. Tired and angry, Perseus thrust his hand into his bag and drew out the monstrous head. To this day, Atlas stands, a stone giant holding up the skies, his head frosted with snow, his face frozen with horror.

And Perseus flew on, although it was several months and many more challenges before he was able to present his trophy. But his travels are another story, involving passion, bravery and an ultimate battle. He would meet Polydectes once again, would defend his hostage mother, and face his long-lost grandfather. He would make his own mark at Olympus, and become, eventually, a bright star, a divine beacon which would guide courageous wanderers, as he had once been.

Icarus and Daedalus

...My boy, take care
To wing your course along the middle air;
If low, the surges wet your flagging plumes;
If high, the sun the meltin wax consumes;
Steer between both...
Samuel Croxall, Metamorphoses

IN THE CITY OF ATHENS lived Daedalus, an inventor and artisan renowned across the world for his skill and genius. He loved nothing more than to create masterpieces of invention and wonder, except the recognition and admiration his talents won him. On fearing that his nephew and apprentice would one day surpass his lofty skills, Daedalus murdered the boy in cold blood. He and his family then fled to Crete. It was here that King Minos requested his service for a very special purpose.

The King had a monster living among his household, one that was cursed with insatiable, unnatural appetites. This miscreation was the Minotaur, the half-bull, half-human progeny of Minos's wife, Pasiphae. Pasiphae had been enchanted to fall in love with the bull of Poseidon. Her blood boiling in lust for the magnificent beast, Pasiphae demanded that Daedalus build her a contraption so that the bull could mount her. The resulting offspring was the atrocity that grew into the uncontrollable Minotaur. Seeking advice from the Delphic oracle, Minos was told to build a creation dense and elaborate enough to house the beast safely. For this, Minos needed Daedalus. Eager to test his skills, Daedalus accepted and, taking his son Icarus, he set off to Minos's palace to begin work on the Labyrinth, which would be his most extraordinary work.

The Labyrinth was an immense maze in the ground of Minos's palace. Daedalus used every method he could think of in the formation of his masterpiece; dead ends, winding passages, shadowy corners and pathways that never seemed to end, driving anyone trapped within to the very edge of insanity and beyond. So cunning was the Labyrinth that Daedalus himself was almost doomed among its dark and convoluted corridors.

The complex twists and perplexing turns successfully trapped the Minotaur, who was kept contented by annual sacrifices of seven youths and seven maidens for him to hunt down and gorge upon at will.

But Minos did not react as Daedalus expected. Instead of showering him with praise and riches, the king was desperate to ensure that no one would ever discover the secret of the great Labyrinth. He trapped Daedalus and his son in a tall tower to ensure that the dark mystery of the Labyrinth would forever be protected. And so the days passed, but Minos would not release his prisoners. He even took the precaution of having the routes out of Crete by both land and sea guarded. But Daedalus was also crafty, as well as resourceful. The time came when he grew desperately weary of his enforced capture. Never forgetting that his beloved son had been imprisoned because of his ambition and love of fame, Daedalus plotted to win their freedom.

Daedalus began collecting the supplies they would need for their escape. Careful not to arouse suspicion in the King, he knew he would have to use natural objects where possible. He also knew that Minos was watching the roads and sea, which left only one way for escape. They would have to fly.

Daedalus set to work making wings for himself and Icarus. Basing them on the natural curve of a bird's wing, he carefully bound together layers and layers of feathers with cord and sealed the binding with wax, without which the feathers would be pulled out of the cords during flight. He took the utmost care in his creation, placing the wings in order of size from smallest to largest. Finally, the instruments of freedom were ready. Trialling them, Daedalus strapped his wings in place and flapped his arms. The movement caught the wind and lifted him up into the air where he was able to hover above the ground.

Ecstatic with joy at the thought of their approaching freedom, Icarus – a tempestuous boy with little of his father's foresight – wanted immediately to set off for home. Tempering his son's eagerness, Daedalus again impressed upon Icarus how to get home safely. They had to avoid both the spray from the sea that would weigh down the wings and the heat from the sun, which would melt the wax securing the wings together.

Father and son took flight, leaving their tower of captivity forever. As they flew, Crete growing smaller behind them, both grew lighter at heart at the thought of home. Passing landmarks, ever hopeful that they would reach the shores of Athens, Daedalus's heart filled with heady pride at his construction. But he was overconfident. His invention – masterful as it was – was imperfect.

Icarus, his reckless boy, had inherited some of his father's ego. Feeling invincible, all warnings about how to fly safely flew from his mind. As the Aegean sea glittered beneath him, Icarus felt like a king up there in the heavens, so he flew higher and higher so as to fly among the gods. However the blazing sun caused the wax holding his precious wings together to melt. Desperately trying to regain control, Icarus swooped downwards to escape the sun's burning rays. But it was too late. Before his father could even make a move to help him, Icarus – with barely time to give his beloved father one final glance – plummeted to his death. Landing heavily in the deep, dark sea, Icarus breathed his last.

Wracked with grief, Daedalus was almost unable to complete his journey home, the sweet sensation of liberty forever tainted by his tragic loss. In homage to his son, and as a permanent reminder of the grief and loss caused by his pride and arrogance, Daedalus named the land nearest to Icarus's place of death Icaria, which it remains to this day.

Theseus and the Minotaur

ten chosen young men of Athens and ten unmarried girls
used to be given together as sacrifice to the Minotaur.
With which evil the narrow walls were troubled until
Theseus chose to offer himself for his dear Athens
A.S. Kline, Catullus 64

THESEUS, warrior hero of Athens, was half human and half divine. His earthly father was Aegeus, king of Athens, and his mother was Aethra, daughter of King Pittheus of Troezen. Yet on her on wedding night, Aethra had slipped away to the island of Sphairia, to make a sacrifice to the god Poseidon. The god of the sea forced himself upon Aethra, and the result of that night was the boy Theseus. He grew through trial and courage, and the salting of divine blood, to be one of Greece's superlative warriors.

Theseus faced his most defining challenge in the aftermath of war. King Minos of Crete – holding Athens responsible for the death of his son Androgeus – subjugated Athens in a short, bloody conflict. He then carefully constructed the punishment to impose upon the city. His choice was a ghastly annual ritual. Every year, the city had to choose fourteen youths (seven male, seven female) from amongst the nobility, and send them to the Cretan palace at Knossos. Beneath the palace was the Labyrinth, a maze of tortuous ingenuity created by the artificer Daedalus. Those who entered the spectral corridors of the Labyrinth became lost souls, weeping in echo-filled disorientation. But they were not alone in there. At its heart the Labyrinth homed the Minotaur, the grotesque offspring of a bull (a present to Minos from Poseidon) and Minos' wife Pasiphae. His bottom half was that of a preternatural man, his top half a ferocious bull. His gaping jaws displayed a chilling armoury, the teeth of a lion. The Minotaur devoured all those who entered, a creature appalling to behold and maddened by the ravenous desire for human meat.

Athens passed through two cycles of this horror before Theseus stepped forward to stop it. The young hero was angered by the subjugation of both his father and his city. He volunteered to take the place of one of the youths, a substitution willingly accepted by Minos. Theseus's intention was nothing less than to slay the Minotaur, freeing Athens from the annual curse. He and the others were taken aboard Minos's flagship, and set sail for their terminal destination. Minos himself was present on the ship, and already the clash of wills sparked between the two men. Minos was unnerved by Theseus's claims to divine origins, claims supported by various displays of godly intervention, such as the thunder of Zeus, splitting the heavens with its roar.

At Knossos itself, Minos's daughter Ariadne was captivated by Theseus from the moment she first caught sight of him, stood with noble bearing on the prow of the king's ship as it made harbour. She later, and furtively, visited him in the prisoner quarters, where he and the others were held for the night. Here she sighed out her love for Theseus, which Theseus willingly returned, being both attracted to Ariadne and also noting her value as an ally. Ariadne, mindful of the fact that all who had entered the Labyrinth were consumed by it, and guided by the prior advice of none other than Daedalus, gave Theseus a ball of silver thread. The principle was simple – begin unwinding the thread from the moment he entered the Labyrinth. The thread, coiled back in, would then show Theseus the way back out. There remained, nonetheless, the hulking matter of the Minotaur.

The day came for the Athenians' journey into a man-made hell. Shouting Cretans watched fourteen souls dissolve into the shadowy interior, Theseus brave and upright at the front, the others hanging on his confidence with desperation. Theseus, who had managed to conceal a sword in his cloak, unwound the thread behind him as they wandered the endless, blind corridors. Their progress was slow and frustrating, but after a few hours the air became soured by the ghastly odour of the Minotaur. As they advanced, a brutal shape came forth from the half-light. The Minotaur, its senses keen from hunger, jumped to its feet and began bellowing with fury and expectation. Its range of movement was restrained by an unbreakable leg chain, so Theseus, his breath accelerating for the fight, told the trembling others to hold back.

Thus hero and beast ran into combat, animal and human muscle stretching to the fight. The Minotaur flung huge boulders at Theseus, which the hero both evaded and returned, then the two locked in a pummelling wrestling match, the corridors thundering to blows and shouts. The contest continued for time, and slowly the Minotaur weakened, mentally and physically stunned by the resilience of his semi-divine opponent. Eventually the beast collapsed, its huge chest rising and failing with a sobbing pace. Seizing the moment, Theseus launched himself forward, grabbed the Minotaur by the horns, and arched its head back. Theseus drew steel and plunged it into the beast's throat, foul blood jetting out into the dank air. The creature went rigid, then bled its life out onto the floor.

The Minotaur was slain. Theseus led the others from the Labyrinth, following the silver thread. When they emerged, Ariadne was waiting for her love. They raced to the harbour, scuttling all Minos's ships but his flagship, which they boarded to make their escape to a celebratory Athens. Theseus, through strength and guile, had freed Athens from its human tribute to the Minotaur.

Indian Myths

Introduction

THE MYTHOLOGY OF INDIA is as vast and varied as her myriad cultures, languages and beliefs, as diverse as her philosophy and religion. Indeed, more than almost any other nation, India has intertwined her religion, literature and philosophy in a comprehensive mythology that encompasses most of her history in its breadth and vision. In India there are many languages spoken, and many religions observed. The largest of these religions is Hindu, and it is the Hindu myths that comprise the greatest proportion of the stories that appear in this book.

The study of myths has grown to gigantic proportions over the last century, and it has become clear in every aspect of cultural study that myth is intrinsic to an understanding of people, for it represents their beliefs, explains their behaviour, and provides a portrait of their customs and morality. A myth can no longer be dismissed as an entertaining bit of nonsense – time has proved that it is the crucial elements of a people's ideology which are fixed in their mythology, and its study is therefore essential to learning. For many cultures, myths touch on religion; in Indian mythology, gods play by far the most important role, presenting an explanation for religious beliefs which can be at the same time profound and difficult to comprehend.

In *Hinduism*, W. O'Flaherty wrote: 'If myths are stories about the gods, it is difficult to find a Hindu story that is not mythical. "Here there are more gods than men," a puzzled European remarked on India centuries ago, and the line between gods and men in Hinduism is as vague and ephemeral as the cloudy trail of a sky-writer. ... Gods in India are no better than men, merely more powerful. Indeed, their extraordinary powers allow them to indulge in vices on an extraordinary scale: divine power corrupts divinely.'

Indian gods are given their identities by their heritage, and their history. They form an extensive pantheon which has included and occasionally dropped names across the centuries, as the religious beliefs are expounded and transformed.

This pantheon has been recorded in many forms and in many languages, but most importantly in the great Sanskrit epic of *Mahabharata*, a poem which is the longest in any language, at 200,000 lines, and written between 400 BC and AD 200. It consists of a huge mass of legendary material which has developed around one key heroic narrative – the struggle for power between two related families, the Pandavas and the Kauravas (Kurus). At the centre of this work is the *Bhagavadgita*, which has become the national gospel of India, and the most significant religious text of Hinduism. The *Bhagavadgita* was written in the first or second century ad and comprises eighteen chapters. It takes the form of a conversation between the prince Arjuna and Krishna, who is a later incarnation of the god Vishnu. There is a philosophical discussion of the nature of God, and a compelling explanation of how he can be seen, and known.

The *Mahabharata* is a fascinating and extraordinarily vivid work, singing with a characterization that is so rare in old testaments. There is an exquisite blend of characters which create a drama that has enveloped thousands of tales, each of which relates a unique perception, lesson or belief. Most importantly, however, the Mahabharata is entertaining, serving to teach and to work the imagination in order to put forth the fundamental beliefs of the Hindu religion.

Other great works include the *Ramayana*, written about 300 BC. This details the story of Rama and his wife Sita – the perfect king and his wife, directly descended from the gods and the earth. This is a romantic work and less important in the development of the Indian mythology than its counterpart the *Mahabharata*, but it has nonetheless become one of the most popular scriptures of Hinduism, and acts as a gospel of purity and despair.

The *Harivamsa* (AD 400) was another important work in the combined religious and mythological structure of the Indian literature, and it was swiftly followed by the Puranas (AD 400 to 1000).

The *Harivamsa* works as an afterword to the *Mahabharata*, explaining the ancestry and the exploits of Krishna, together with other Hindu legend. The *Puranas*, of which eighteen survive, are extensive works examining the mythology of Hinduism, the sagas of heroes, and the legends of saints. The most significant of them, the *Bhagavata-Purana*, celebrates the god Vishnu in his many incarnations, particularly as Krishna. The *Bhagavata-Purana* has had a profound influence on almost every aspect of Indian culture – her religion, art, music and literature, and many scholars consider it the greatest poem ever written.

The Sanskrit interpretation and record of Hindu and subsequent mythology is one of the most imaginative and luxuriant of any culture; indeed, there was a belief for many years that the folktale tradition originated in India. One of the greatest collections is the Pancatantra, a collection of animal fables which are some of the most famous in Europe.

The central part of classical Sanskrit literature is, however, the *Vedas*, which are sacred Hindu writings from about 1400 to 1200 BC. There are also commentaries on the *Vedas* in the *Brahmanas*, the *Aranyakas*, and the *Upanishads* (1000 to 500 BC), and the epic and wisdom literature (400 BC to AD 1000).

The oldest document is the *Rig-Veda*, which is a collection of more than a thousand hymns, composed about 1400 BC. This is the most important part of early Hinduism and later became known as the *Brahmanas*. These texts did not originally take a written form; they were carried across centuries of oral communication and have been preserved with all the embellishments presented by the many translations. Hindu literature both fed and fed from the *Rig-Veda*, and much of early mythology has become synonymous with it.

Most of the myths contained within the *Rig-Veda* deal with creation – heaven and earth and what intervenes. The hymns were addressed to the Vedic gods, who included:

Agni, fire
Indra, thunder
Surya, sun
Vayu, wind
Aditi, firmament
Varuna, rain and sea
Ushas, dawn
Prithivi, earth
the Ashvins (Castor and Pollux)
Dyaus-piter, the father of light
Yama, death
Vritra, drought
Rudra, storm
Maruts, whirlwinds

The gods of the Vedic pantheon remained a part of Hindu mythology for centuries to come, although their importance was diminished by the entrance of a new and more complicated order of gods. O'Flaherty writes:

They become literary and metaphorical fixtures rather than numinous deities. Indra is mocked for its Gargantuan sexual and alcoholic appetites, depicted as womanizer, a coward and a liar. Yama remains king of the dead, though he now functions, like Indra, as a mere pawn of the true gods, Shiva and Vishnu. The myths about these two great gods and other minor divinities of the post-Vedic period are found in Sanskrit texts composed from about 500 BC until well into the medieval period ... and frequently retold ... to the present day.

In addition to the two major divinities, Shiva and Vishnu, there are others who are still worshipped today. Many scholars argue that Vishnu and Shiva are essentially identical, and are indistinguishable from Prhama, or the creator. Shiva, a Sanskrit word meaning 'auspicious one', is a more remote god than Vishnu. Shiva is regarded as both destroyer and restorer, and he is more difficult to understand than Vishnu. Views about Shiva may have become convoluted, merging roles that were once assigned to various earlier gods. But the differences between Vishnu and Shiva lie in their presentation, for as Jan Knappert points out, 'The difference between the gods is not in their function, but in their character, their qualities. Each god, by his special nature, teaches us something about the universe that we had not seen before, because each god highlights a unique aspect of creation and with that, of our own world of dreams, our own deepest souls.'

Many animals and plants are also regarded as holy. Most notable is the cow. All cattle are protected and monkeys, tree squirrels, and some snakes are also considered hallowed. All rivers are considered sacred, but the Ganges in the north of India is the holiest of rivers because it supposedly flows from the head of Shiva.

The Vedic writers believed in a concept of heaven and hell to which the dead pass, depending on the quality of their earthly lives – something slightly akin to current-day Western beliefs. Some time after the sixth century BC, however, the belief in reincarnation was developed. Although at first confined to small groups of holy men, it soon became widely believed across the Indian continent, and explained in the *Upanishads*, a document prepared for the sole purpose of teaching a knowledge which would encourage the student to absorb a mystical knowledge that allows him to escape the rebirth cycle. The *Upanishads* are the last stage of interpretation of the Vedas, expounding the concept of a single supreme being, Brahman, and investigating the nature of all reality.

By the time the Buddha appeared the belief in reincarnation had been accepted and propounded into a cultural doctrine. From that time Hinduism's main concern became release from the cycle of birth and death instead of making offerings to please or pacify the gods. Sacrifice became infrequent because of an unwillingness to destroy living things. Then the primary older gods of the *Vedas* were slowly displaced by newer deities discussed above and to this day they are still the focus of much devotional prayer and dogma in India.

O'Flaherty points out that the Hindu teaching on divine incarnation (gods becoming flesh) made it possible for the older gods to be accepted as incarnate in the newer ones. The religious development of this period is reflected in both the Mahabharata and the Ramayana. This form of Hinduism took on the title asceticism, which was largely unknown to the religion of the *Vedas*. However, more and more young men became ascetic and gave up the trappings of modern life to become hermits and as a result asceticism took on a key part of the Hindu faith.

In the period immediately preceding the sixth century BC, Buddhism and Jainism emerged, religions centred on the monastic life. A strong emphasis on the holy life in these religions had a profound influence on Hinduism.

Buddhist teachings spread throughout their mythology, mainly through the *Pali canon*, which are the texts of early Buddhism, but also the *Jakatas*, which comprise more than 500 episodes which are said to have occurred during incarnations of Buddha, and in this fascinating collection are fairy tales, animal stories and ballads.

Among the heresies of the Kali Age, which was said to have begun when Krishna died, O'Flaherty says that:

Buddhism was regarded by Hindus of the ancient period as the prime thread, and it was as the Buddha that Vishnu became incarnate after the death of Krishna. Later Hindus have seen in this avatar an attempt at rapprochement with Buddhism, but the avatar was originally designed to damn the Buddhists in Hindu eyes; for Vishnu was said to assume the form of Buddha to mislead, corrupt and ultimately destroy dangerous demons, who were indestructible as long as they remained steadfast in the practice of orthodox Buddhism.

A basic understanding of these two religions helps to unravel the complicated philosophy behind the myths and legends outlined in this book. Although Buddhism does make up only about four per cent of all Indians, its place in history and in literature is undoubted, and its traditions continue to flourish today.

Hinduism, which makes up more than eighty per cent of current Indian religious practice is believed to have spawned in a developed civilization in the Indus Valley, about 2300 BC. This civilization had its own religion, which was transformed when they were invaded about 1500 BC. The invading civilization was the Aryans, and the combined religious dogma was the basis for what we now consider to be ancient Hinduism.

W. J. Wilkins, in *Hindu Mythology* points out that it was a religion of the household, of veneration for ancestors, and of devotion to the world spirit (Brahman):

The Aryans had numerous gods, nearly all of whom were male. But the Aryans made no images or pictures of their gods as later Hinduism has done. Aryan worship was centred around the sacrificial fire at home, while later Hinduism worshipped in temples. The complex ceremony of the Aryans involved sacrifice of animals. Hymns were composed for these rituals, and it is in the collections of the hymns, which are, of course, the Vedas, and it was under their influence that the earliest Hinduism developed.

For the first 200 years after the Buddha's death, Buddhism was a local religion. When King Asoka converted to Buddhism in the third century BC, he used his resources to spread the religion. Trade between India, China, and the Roman Empire brought Indian people and their religions to China. By the fifth century AD, there was very little evidence of the religion in India itself, as it was carried further east. By 1200 a Muslim dynasty had come to power in India, and Buddhism virtually disappeared from the land of its origin. Hinduism does, however, still contain many ideas borrowed from Buddhism, which have enhanced and made it one of the richest religions in the world. Their mythology, certainly in the earliest years, has become largely interchangeable.

Although many gods may be worshipped, modern Hindus are generally divided into followers of Vishnu, Shiva, or Shakti. Nearly all Hindus look upon one of these as an expression of the ultimate being, the one in charge of the destiny of the universe.

Each of the followers holds the *Vedas* in high regard, and has its own scriptures. In the *Bhagavadgita*, for example, Vishnu is honoured in his incarnation Krishna. Another incarnation, Rama, is the hero of the *Ramayana*. Vishnu is the protector and preserver of the world, and he is worshipped by many cults in various forms besides Krishna and Rama.

It is the rich and varied tradition of folktales and fables which have illuminated the mythological fabric of the Indian culture; indeed, every great epic is in fact a compilation of didactic stories, legends, fairy tales and ancient narratives from across the continent. Alongside is an extensive and pervading respect for and acceptance of religion and spirituality. Somewhere, down the annals of history, the two have become intertwined, giving Indian mythology a pedigree unlike any other, and Indian religion a series of parables that bring it alive – probably partly explaining its extraordinary popularity today. And now, even the most emancipated of Hindus believe their mythology is a valid and genuine series of events – because, in many ways, it is.

Tales of the Ramayana

THE RAMAYANA WAS an epic poem of about 50,000 lines, which was originally composed by the hermit Valmiki, probably in the third century. Many versions of this great work exist across India where Rama, the seventh incarnation of Vishnu, and hero of the poem, was worshipped. The Ramayana was originally divided into seven books, each of which celebrated a part of Rama's life. Rama was the greatest human hero of Hindu mythology, the son of a king and the avatar of Vishnu. He was the model of every good man, for he was brave, chivalrous, well versed and virtuous. He had but one wife and his name has become synonymous with loyalty and fidelity in many parts of the Indian nation.

It is believed that this epic poem is cleansing – even a reading of the Ramayana will remove the sins of the reader, for the text itself is regarded as charismatic. Many events befell Rama in his earthly form, and he left behind two sons. The following tales represent some of the most fascinating and profound occurrences in the life of Rama, whose name, even today, is in many parts of the Hindu community, the word for 'God'.

The Birth of Rama

King Dasharatha, thus cried they,
Fervent in penance many a day,
The sacrificial steed has slain,
Longing for sons, but all in vain.
Now, at the cry of us forlorn,
Incarnate as his seed be born.
Three queens has he; each lovely dame
Like Beauty, Modesty, or Fame.
Divide thyself in four, and be
His offspring by these noble three;
Man's nature take, and slay in fight
Ravana, who laughs at heavenly might:
This common scourge, this rankling thorn,
Whom the three worlds too long have borne.

R. Griffith, The Ramayana

ONCE, LONG, LONG AGO, in the great city of Ayodhya there lived a king. Ayodhya was a prosperous city, one where its citizens were happy, pure of heart and well educated in the teachings of both man and god. Its king was also a good man and happy in almost every respect, for he had many wise counsellors and sages in his family and he had been blessed with a lovely daughter, Santa. This king was called Dasharatha, and he married his sweet daughter to the great sage Rishyasringa, who became a member of his inner circle, advising him on all matters with great wisdom and foresight. Two fine priests – Vashishtha and Vamadeva – were also part of his family, and they were known to all as the most saintly of men.

But Dasharatha had one hole in his glittering life; he longed for a son to carry on his line, a son who would one day be king. For many years he made offerings to the great powers, but to no avail, until such time as he made the most supreme sacrifice, that of a horse. His three wives were overjoyed by the prospect of having a son and when, after one year, the horse returned from the sacrifice, Rishyasringa and Vashishtha prepared the ceremony. With the greatest of respect and joy Rishyasringa was able to announce to Dasharatha that he would father four sons, and they would carry his name into the future.

When any sacrifice is made by man, all of the deities come together to take their portion of what has been offered, and so it was on this occasion that they had assembled to take from the sacrificial horse. There was, however, a dissenter among their ranks, one who was greedy and oppressive, and who caused in his colleagues such dissension that they came forward to Brahma with a request that he be destroyed. The evil rakshasa was called Ravana, and at an early age he had been granted immunity from death by yakshas, rakshasas or gods. His immunity had led him to become selfish and arrogant, and he took great pleasure in flaunting his exemption from the normal fates. Brahma spoke wisely to the gathered deities.

'Ravana is indeed evil,' he said quietly, ' and he had great foresight in requesting immunity from death by his equals. But,' and here Brahma paused. 'But,' he went on, ' he was not wise enough to seek immunity from death by humans – and it is in this way that he must be slain.'

The deities were relieved to find that Ravana was not invincible, and as they celebrated amongst themselves, they were quietened by a profound presence who entered their midst. It was the great God Vishnu himself, and he appeared in flowing yellow robes, his eyes sparkling. He carried with him mace, and discus and conch, and he appeared on the back of Garuda, the divine bird attendant of Narayana. The deities fell at his feet, and they begged him to be born as Dasharatha's four sons in order to destroy the deceitful Ravana.

And so it was that Vishnu threw himself into Dasharatha's fire and taking the form of a sacred tiger, spoke to the anxious father-to-be, pronouncing himself the ambassador of God himself. He presented Dasharatha with spiritual food, which he was to share with his wives – two portions to Sumitra, one to Kaikeyi, and one to Kaushalya. And soon, four strong, healthy babies were born to Dasharatha's wives and they were named by Vashishtha, the divine priest. They were Rama, born to Kaushalya, Bharata, born to Kaikeyi, and Lakshman and Satrughna born to Sumitra.

Rama and Vashishtha

DASHARATHA'S FOUR SONS grew into robust and healthy young men. They were brave and above all good, and they were revered for their looks and good sense. The greatness of Vishnu was spread amongst them, and each glowed with great worth. The young men travelled in pairs – Satrughna devoting himself to his brother Bharata, and Lakshman dedicating himself to Rama. Rama was very much the favoured son, favourite of both Dasharatha and the people. He was a noble youth, well-versed in arts, sciences and physical applications alike; his spirituality was evident in all he did. By the age of sixteen, Rama was more accomplished than any man on earth, inspiring greatness in all who came into contact with him.

There lived, at this time, a rishi by the name of Vishvamitra who had become a brahma-rishi, an excellent status which had been accorded to him by the gods themselves. He lived in Siddhashrama, but his life there was far from easy. He was a religious man, and took enormous strength from his daily prayers and sacrifices. Each day his sacrificial fires and prayers were interrupted by two wily and evil rakshasas, Maricha and Suvahu, who received their orders from Ravana himself. Knowing that Rama was the incarnation of Vishnu, Vishvamitra approached Dasharatha and begged him to send Rama to rid him of these evil spirits.

Now Dasharatha was against the idea of sending his favourite son to what would surely be a dangerous and perhaps fatal mission, but he knew as well that a great brahma-rishi must be respected. And so it was that Rama and Lakshman travelled to Vishvamitra for ten days, in order to stand by the sacrificial fire. The young men were dressed in the finest of clothes, glittering with jewels and fine cloths. They were adorned with carefully wrought arms, and they glowed with pride and valour. All who witnessed their passing was touched by the glory, and a ray of light entered each of their lives.

They arrived at Siddhashrama in a cloud of radiance, and as the sacrifice began, Rama wounded Maricha and Suvahu, until they fled in dismay. The other evil spirits were banished, and the little hermitage was once again in peace, cleansed of the evil of Ravana.

Rama and the Bow of Janaka

RAMA WAS GREETED with great acclaim after he rid Vishvamitra's hermitage of the evil spirits, and his taste of heroism whetted in him a great appetite for further adventure. He begged Vishvamitra to present him with further tasks, and he was rewarded by the hallowed priest's plans to visit Janaka, the Raja of Mithila.

Janaka was owner of a splendid bow, one which no man was able to string. He had come by this bow through his ancestor, Devarata, who had received it personally from the gods, who had themselves been presented the bow by Shiva. The bow was now worshipped by all who had seen it, for gods, rakshasas and even the finest warriors had been unable to bend its mighty back.

Janaka was planning a marvellous sacrifice, and it was for Mithila that the three men would depart, in order to take part in the festivities, and to see the great bow in person. As they travelled along the Ganges, they were followed by all the birds and animals who inhabited Siddhashrama, and by the monkey protectors who had been presented to the two brothers upon their birth. They arrived in Mithila in a burst of splendid colour and radiance, and Janaka knew at once that the company he was about to keep was godly in every way. He bowed deeply to the men, and set them carefully among the other men of nobility.

The following day, Janaka brought the men to the bow, and explained to them its great significance.

He said to Rama, 'I have a daughter, Sita, who is not the product of man, or of animal, but who burst from a furrow of the earth itself as I ploughed and hallowed my field. She is a woman of supreme beauty and godliness, and she will be presented to any man or god who can bend the bow.'

Rama and his brother bent their heads respectfully, and Rama nodded towards the bow. A chariot pulled by four thousand men moved the bow forward, and he quietly reached towards it. The case sprung open at his touch, and as he strung it, it snapped into two pieces with a bolt of fire. There was a crack so loud that all the men in the room, bar Rama, Vishvamitra, Janaka and Lakshman, fell to the ground, clutching their ears and writhing. And there was silence – a quiet brought on by fear and reverence. The spectators struggled to their knees and bowed to the great Rama, and a jubilant Janaka shouted his blessing and ordered the wedding preparations to begin. Messengers were sent at once to the household of Dasharatha, and upon his arrival, the festivities began.

Sita was presented to Rama, and Urmila, the second daughter of Janaka was promised to Lakshman. Mandavya and Srutakirti, who were daughters of Kushadhwaja, were presented to Bharata and Satrughna. All around the world erupted in a fusion of light and colour – fragrant blossoms were cast down from the heavens upon the radiant brothers and their brides, and a symphony of angelic music wove its way around them. There was happiness like none ever known, and the four young men cast down their heads with deep gratitude. They returned home, in a shower of glory, to Ayodhya, where they would serve their proud and honoured father, Dasharatha.

Kaikeyi and the Heir Apparent

AFTER MANY YEARS of happiness at Ayodhya, Dasharatha decided that the time had come to appoint an heir apparent. Rama was still the most favoured of the brothers, a fine man of sterling integrity and wisdom.

He was known across the land for his unbending sense of justice, and he was friend to any man who was good. His brothers had no envy for their honourable brother for he was so kind and serene that he invited their good intentions and they wished him nothing but good fortune.

Rama was the obvious choice for heir, and Dasharatha took steps to prepare for his ascendance. He drew together all of his counsellors and kings, and he advised them of his plans. He explained how his years had been kind and bounteous, but that they weighed down on him now, and he felt the need to rest. He proposed that his son Rama become heir apparent. The uproar astonished the elderly king. There was happiness and celebration at his proposal, and at once the air grew clear and the skies shone with celestial light. Bemused, he turned to the esteemed parliament of men and he said, 'Why, why do you wish him to be your ruler?'

'By reason of his many virtues, for indeed he towers among men as Sakra among the gods. He speaks the truth and he is a mighty and even bowman. He is ever busied with the welfare of the people, and not given to detraction where he finds one blemish among many virtues. He is skilled in music and his eyes are fair to look upon. Neither his pleasure nor his anger is in vain; he is easily approached, and self-controlled, and goes not forth to war or the protection of a city or province without victorious return. He is beloved of all. Indeed, the Earth desires him for her lord.' And once again the cheers rose and the preparations began.

The finest victuals were ordered – honey and butter, rices and milk and curds. There were golds, silvers and gems of great gleaming weight, and elephants and bulls and tigers ordered. Fine cloths and skins were draped around the palace, and everyone hummed with incessant, bustling excitement. And above it all was Rama, serene and calm, as cool as the winter waters of the Ganges, as pure of heart as the autumn moon. And just before the time when he would stand forward in his father's shoes, he was brought before the great Dasharatha, who greeted his kneeling form with warmth and lifted him up upon the seat of kings. He said to him then:

'Though thou art virtuous by nature, I would advise thee out of love and for thy good: Practise yet greater gentleness and restraint of sense; avoid all lust and anger; maintain thy arsenal and treasury; personally and by means of others make thyself well acquainted with the affairs of state; administer justice freely to all, that the people may rejoice. Gird thee, my son, and undertake thy task.'

Rama, for all his wisdom, found great solace in his father's words, and as the town around him buzzed with the activity of thousands of men preparing for the holy fast, he sat calmly, in worship and in gratitude.

Now throughout this time, all of Dasharatha's household celebrated the choice of Rama for heir apparent – his mother, Kaushalya, and his wife, Sita, were honoured, and his aunts, too, revelled in their relation to this fine young man. There was no room for envy in their hearts, until, that is, the deceitful old nurse, Manthara, took it upon herself to stir up the seeds of discontent. And this she did by the subtle but constant pressures she applied to her mistress, Kaikeyi, the mother of Bharata.

Kaikeyi was by nature a fair woman, easy natured and gentle. It took many months of persuasion before a hole was pierced in her goodness, and the beginnings of evil allowed to enter. It was a misfortune for Rama to become king, said Manthara, for Bharata would be cast out and Kaikeyi would be the subordinate of Kaushalya. Kaikeyi dismissed such nonsense and carried on with her daily work. Several days later, Manthara was back. Bharata would be sent away, she said. Did that not worry his mother? But Kaikeyi was calm. She said, 'Why grieve at Rama's fortune?' she said. 'He is well fitted to be king; and if the kingdom be his, it will also be Bharata's for Rama ever regards his brothers as himself.'

Manthara did not give up. She twisted her sword a little deeper and was rewarded by hitting at Kaikeyi's pride. 'Don't you know, Kaikeyi,' she said, 'that Rama's mother will seek to revenge on thee that slight that thou didst once put on her. Yours will be a sorry lot when Rama rules the earth.'

Kaikeyi's rage burst from within her and she stalked around her chambers.

'Why he will have to be deported at once,' she said furiously. 'But how can I do it? How can I install Bharata as heir?'

The treacherous Manthara was again at her side, needling the pain and fury that she had inspired in her gentle mistress.

'You have two unused gifts from Dasharatha,' she reminded her. 'Have you forgotten that fateful day when you found him near dead on the battlefield? What did he promise you then, my mistress?' she asked her. 'Why he has made you his favourite of wives and he has done everything in his power to keep you happy. This is what you must do.' And the evil witch leaned forward and whispered in Kaikeyi's ear. Her eyes widened, and their glitter dimmed. She bowed her head and she left the room.

Kaikeyi cast off her jewels and fine clothes, and pulled down her hair. She dressed herself in sacks and she laid down on the floor of the anger chamber where she cried with such vigour that Dasharatha could not fail to hear her sobs. Finding her there, stripped of her finery, he laid beside her and spoke gently to his favourite wife.

'What has happened. What is it?' he whispered. 'If you are ill, there are many doctors who can cure what ails you. If someone has wronged you, we can right that wrong. Indeed, whatever you want, my dear Kaikeyi, I will ensure you have. Your desire is mine. You know that I can refuse you nothing.'

Kaikeyi sat up and brushed away her tears. 'You know,' she said, 'that you promised me that day long ago, when I carried you from the battlefield and administered your wounds, when I saved you from the jaws of death, you know, dear husband, that you promised me two gifts, two boons. You told me then that I could have my desire and until this day I have asked you for nothing.'

Dasharatha roared with approval. 'Of course, dear wife,' he said. 'Whatever you wish, it shall be yours. This I swear on Rama himself.'

'I wish,' she said softly, 'I wish, as Heaven and Earth and Day and Night are my witness, I wish that Bharata become heir and that Rama is cast out, clad only in deer-skins, to lead the life of a hermit in the forests of Dandaka, and that he remain there for fourteen years.'

Kaikeyi knew that in fourteen years her own son, who was good and true, could bind himself to the affections of the people and that Rama, upon his return, could not shift him from a well-regarded throne. Her plan was about to unfold and she shivered with anticipation. As expected, her husband let out a mighty roar and sank down to his knees once again. He begged Kaikeyi to change her mind, and he pleaded with her to allow his son to stay with him, but she refused to relent.

And so it was that Rama was summoned to the weeping Dasharatha, and as he travelled, the crowds rose to greet him, feeling their lives changed in some small way by the benefit of his smile, his wave, his celestial presence. And bolstered by the adoration, and glowing with the supreme eloquence of his righteousness, he entered his father's chamber with unwitting happiness and calm. His father's distress wiped the smile from his lips, and the clouds filled the autumn sky.

'What is it father,' he asked, sensing deep grief and misfortune. But his father could only mutter, 'Rama, Rama, I have wronged thee.'

Rama turned to Kaikeyi, 'Mother, mother,' he asked, 'what ill has overcome my father?'

And Kaikeyi uttered with pride and something approaching glee, 'Nothing, Rama, but your imminent downfall. He cannot frame the words that will cause you distress and unhappiness, but you must do as he asks. You must help him to fulfil his promise to me. You see, Rama, long ago he promised me two gifts. If you swear to me now that you will do as he wishes, I will tell you all.'

Rama spluttered with indignation. 'Of course, dear Mother. Anything for my father. I would walk in fire. I would drink poison, or blood, for him. Tell me now, so that I may more quickly set about easing his poor soul.'

Kaikeyi related to him the story of her gifts from Dasharatha, and told him of her father's decision that he should be sent away to dwell as a hermit in Dandaka forest for fourteen years. Bharata, she said, would be installed as heir at once.

Rama smiled warmly and with such sincerity that Kaikeyi was stung with shame. 'Of course,' he said serenely, 'I am only sad for my father, who is suffering so. Send at once for Bharata while I go to the forest. Allow me some time to comfort my mother, and Sita, and I shall do as you wish.'

He saluted Kaikeyi, and he left at once. His mother was grieved by her son's fate, but she lifted her head high and she swore to him that she would follow him. 'My darling,' she said, 'I shall follow you to the forest even as a cow follows her young. I cannot bear to wait here for your return and I will come with thee.'

Lakshman was greatly angered by the decision, and he vowed to fight for his brother who had been so wronged. But Rama calmed them both, and he spoke wisely and confidently.

'Gentle brother, I must obey the order of my father. I will never suffer degradation if I honour the words of my father.' Rama paused and turned to Kaushalya. 'Mother,' he said, taking her hands, 'Kaikeyi has ensnared the king, but if you leave him while I am gone he will surely die. You must remain and serve him. Spend your time in prayer, honouring the gods and the Brahmans and your virtue will be preserved.'

Sita greeted his news with dignity. 'I too will go forth into the forest with my husband,' she said. 'A wife shares in her husband's fate and I shall go before thee, treading upon thorns and prickly grass, and I shall be happy there as in my own father's house, thinking only of thy service.'

And Rama granted Sita her desire, and he said to her, 'Oh, my fair wife, since you do not fear the forest, you shall follow me and share my righteousness. Make haste, for we go at once.'

Rama's Exile

LAKSHMAN COULD NOT BEAR to remain in his father's home without Rama and he too decided to leave with Rama and Sita for the forest, shunning the wealth and entrapments of his lifestyle to take a part of Rama's righteousness. There was hysteria in the household as the three prepared to leave, and a noble Brahman named Sumantra threw himself on the mercy of Kaikeyi to give in, begging her to allow Rama

to remain. But Kaikeyi's will had turned her heart to stone and she refused all requests for clemency. Dasharatha sat dully, numbed by grief and shame at his wife's ill will. He motioned to send all his own wealth, and that of his city, with Rama into the forest, but Kaikeyi stood firm and insisted that Dasharatha stick to his vows and send Rama into the forest as a beggar.

As their new clothes of bark were set out for them, Sita collapsed and wept – fearing for her future and loathe to give up the easiness of her life, to which she had been both born and bred. The loyal subjects of Dasharatha begged him to allow Rama's wife to take the throne in his stead – there is no one, they said, who did not love Rama, and they would honour his wife as deeply as they honoured him. Yet again, Kaikeyi resisted all suggestions.

But then Dasharatha stood tall and he spoke firmly, drawing strength from his conviction. Sita shall not go without her jewels, and her robes, he commanded. So Sita's worldly goods were returned to her, and she shone like the sun in a summer sky, flanked by the bark-clad brothers whose goodness caused them to shine with even greater glory than Sita in her finery. They climbed up onto their chariot and set off for the forest, the citizens of Ayodhya falling in front of the carriage with despair.

And then Dasharatha turned to his wife Kaikeyi, and with all of his kingly disdain he cursed her, and cast her from his bed and his home.

'Take me to Kaushalya,' he said majestically. 'Take me swiftly for it is only there that I will find peace.'

At the same time, Lakshman, Sita and Rama had made their way from the city and had reached the shores of the blessed Ganga, a river as clear as the breath of the god, and inhabited by gods and angels alike. They were greeted there by Guha, the king of Nishadha, who fed their horses and made them comfortable for the night. Rama and his brother requested a paste of grain and water and they formed their hair into the customary locks of the forest hermits. The following night they slept by a great tree on the far bank of the Ganges, and the two brothers spoke quietly to one another, pledging to protect and care for the other, and for Sita. Rama expressed his great grief at leaving his father, and his concern for Ayodhya. He begged Lakshman to return in order to care for Kaushalya, but Lakshman gently rebuked him.

'Oh Rama,' he said softly, 'I can no more live without you than a fish can taken out of water – without you I do not wish to see my father, nor Sumitra, nor Heaven itself.' The two men slept silently, comforted by their love and devotion for one another. There was only one way to get through the years ahead, and that was as a united twosome.

The following day they reached the hermitage of Bharadwaja, where the great rishi told them of a wonderful place on the mountain of Chitrakuta, a place which teemed with trees, and peacocks and elephants, where there were rivers and caves and springs and many fruits and roots on which to feed. It was a place befitting their stature, he said, and they would be safe there. And so the following morning they set off, crossing the Jamna by raft and arriving at Shyama. There they prayed and set about building a house of wood, next to the hermitage of Valmiki.

A deer was slain by Lakshman, and a ritual sacrifice was offered to the divinities. And then they settled in together and allowed the happiness of their new life to enter their souls, banishing their grief for what they had left behind.

Bharata is King

DASHARATHA WAS A BROKEN MAN, and it was not long before his grief stripped him of his life. He died in the arms of Kaushalya, bewildered by his fate and recalling an incident which had occurred once in the forest, when as a youth he had accidentally slain a hermit with an errant arrow. Dasharatha had been spared punishment by a kind rishi, but he had been warned then that he would one day meet his death grieving for his son. That memory now clung to his mind, suffocating it until he gave in to his untimely death.

Ayodhya was in mourning for the loss of their finest son Rama, and the death of their king was a blow they could scarcely fathom. There was no rain and the earth dried up; an arid curse lay over the land and the dead Dasharatha's people could not even find the energy to go about their daily toil without the wisdom and leadership of the great and wise king. An envoy was half-heartedly sent for Bharata, with a message that he must return at once, but the people cared little about his arrival, and he was not told about the fate of his father and his brother Rama.

On the seventh day, Bharata, son of Kaikeyi, arrived at Ayodhya at sunrise, the first rays of morning failing to light the dark silence that the city had become. He entered his father's palace, and finding no one awake, entered the bed chamber, which he too found empty. And then Kaikeyi appeared, glowing with vanity and pride at her new position.

'Your father is gone,' she said crisply, caring little about the man who had once been her great love. Her son had taken her place in her affections, and she lusted now for the power that he was in the position to accord her.

Bharata wept silently for his father, and then, lifting a weary head, asked quietly, 'Where is Rama, I am happy for him. Was he present to perform the death-bed rites? Where is he, mother? I am his servant. I take refuge at his feet. Please inform him that I am here. I wish to know my father's last words.'

'Blessed are they that see Rama and the strong-armed Lakshman returning here with Sita,' said Kaikeyi. 'That is what he said.'

Bharata looked at her for a moment and paused. 'Where, may I ask, are Lakshman, Rama and Sita,' he asked then, his face losing colour.

'Rama has taken Sita and Lakshman and they have been exiled to Dandaka forest,' she said nobly, and then spilling over with the excitement of her conquest, she poured out the whole story to her son, explaining the wishes granted her by Dasharatha and the wonderful honours which would now be his.

'You are a murderer,' cried Bharata and leapt to his feet, casting his mother to one side. 'I loved Rama. I loved my father. It is for their sake alone that I call you mother, that I do not renounce you now. I do not want the kingdom. I want Rama – and I intend to bring him back from the forest! At once!'

Taking only the days necessary to prepare the funeral rites and to mourn his dead father, Bharata prepared to set out to find his brother. His tears were shared for his father and for his dear brother and he resolved to find him as soon as he could. He refused the throne which was offered to him by the ministers and preparing his chariots, he rode quickly towards the forest, following in the footsteps of Rama and the others. He reached him quickly, and was shocked and dismayed to find that Rama had adorned himself in the dress of a hermit – shaggy locks framed his pale face, and he wore the skin of a black deer upon his shoulders. But that pale face was serene, and he gently wiped away his brother's tears.

'Bharata,' he said, 'I cannot return. I have been commanded by both my father and my mother to live in the forest for fourteen years. That I must do. You must rule, as our father would have wished.'

Bharata thought for a moment. 'If it was our father's will for me to have the kingdom in your place, then I have the right to bestow it upon you.'

Rama smiled kindly then, and shook his head. 'The kingdom is yours, Bharata. Rule it wisely. For these fourteen years I shall live here as a hermit.'

Bharata took his brother's sandals and it was agreed that in fourteen years he would be joined by Rama, and that the sandals would be restored to him then – with the government and kingship of Ayodhya herself.

And Rama, Sita and Lakshman waved their farewells to Bharata and his men, and then they turned to leave themselves, no longer content in a house that had been trampled by feet of the outside world. They drew themselves deeper into Dandaka, where the cool darkness of the forest beckoned.

The Golden Deer

FOR TEN YEARS Rama, Sita and Lakshman wandered through the forests of Dandaka, resting and living for spells with hermits and other men of wisdom along their path. They befriended a vulture, Jatayu, who claimed to have been a friend of Dasharatha, and he pledged to guard Sita, and to offer Rama and Lakshman his help. They settled finally at Panchavati, by the river Godaveri, where lush blossoms hung over the rippling waters and the air was filled with the verdant scent of greenery. Sita, Rama and Lakshman lived happily there, in the green, fecund woodland, and lived virtually as gods, and undisturbed, until one day they were set upon by an evil rakshasi, sister of Ravana called Surpanakha. There ensued a terrible battle when this ugly sister sought to seduce Rama and Lakshman chased her away, cutting off her ears and nose in the process.

Surpanakha fled deep into the forest, angered and bleeding and she stumbled upon her brother Khara who flew into such a rage at his sister's plight that he set out for Rama's clearing, taking fourteen thousand rakshasas with him – each of which was great, courageous and more horrible in appearance that any rakshasa before him.

Rama had been warned of their coming by Jatayu and was prepared, sending Lakshman and Sita to a secret cave and fighting the rakshasas alone, slaying each of the fourteen thousand evil spirits until at last he stood face to face with Khara. Their battle was fierce and bloody, but Rama stood his ground. At last Khara was consumed by a fiery arrow. And there was silence.

Now far from this scene Ravana was brought news of his sister's maiming and his brother's death. He was filled with such a rage that he plotted to destroy Rama by secreting away Sita. Ravana sought the advice of his most horrible accomplice, Maricha, who counselled him.

Ravana was insistent that he could slay Rama single-handedly, and he ignored Maricha's advice to avoid meddling with Rama who could, if angered, quite easily destroy Ravana's city of Lanka.

Ravana's plan was put into action and the unwilling Maricha took on the form of a golden deer, with horn-like jewels and ears like two rich blue lotus flowers. He entered the forest clearing, where he flitted between the trees, golden hide glinting. As expected, Sita looked up and cried out with delight. She called to Rama and to Lakshman and she begged them to catch the deer for her pleasure. Rama, too, suspecting nothing, was enchanted by the deer's beauty, and set out to catch her. He began to give chase.

Lakshman stayed behind, suspicious about the extraordinary beauty of the deer, where he kept watch over Sita. There was silence until, from the darkness of the woods, came the cry, 'Sita, Lakshman.'

The words were spoken in Rama's own voice, but they came from the body of the golden deer who had been hit by Rama's arrow. As the deer died he took on the shape of Maricha once again and in a last attempt to lure Lakshman from the forest clearing, he called out as Rama himself. And then he was dead.

Rama moved swiftly, realizing the ruse, but the cry had worked its magic. Lakshman was sent out into the forest by Sita, who feared for Rama's safety, and as that brave one made his way back to Panchavati, Sita was left alone.

Rama and Sita

ALONE IN THE CLEARING of Panchavati, Sita paced restlessly, concern for her husband and his brother growing ever greater as the moments passed. And then she was startled by a movement in the trees. Into the clearing came a wandering yogi, and Sita smiled her welcome. She would not be alone after all.

She offered the yogi food and water, and told him her identity. She kindly asked for information in return and was startled when he called himself Ravana, and asked her to renounce Rama and become his wife. Ravana gazed at the lovely Sita and a deep jealousy and anger filled his soul. He determined to have her and he cared little now for his revenge of Rama.

Now Sita was enraged by the slight afforded her husband, the great Rama, by this insolent Ravana and she lashed out at him:

'I am the servant of Rama alone, lion among men, immovable as any mountain, as vast as the great ocean, radiant as Indra. Would you draw the teeth from a lion's mouth? Or swim in the sea with a heavy stone about your neck? You are as likely to seek the sun or moon as you are me, for Rama is little like thee – he is as different as is the lion from the jackal, the elephant from the cat, the ocean from the tiny stream and gold from silver.' She stopped, fear causing her to tremble.

Ravana roared into the empty clearing, and taking his own shape once again, grabbed the lovely Sita by the hair and made to rise into the air with her. His cry woke the great vulture Jatayu, who had been sleeping in a nearby tree. He rose in outrage and warned the evil spirit of the wrath of Rama, who would certainly let no spirit live who had harmed his most prized possession. But Ravana sprang upon the poor great bird and after a heroic battle, cut away his wings, so that he fell down near death.

Ravana swept Sita into his carriage and rose into the sky. As she left the clearing, Sita cried out to the flowers, and the forest, begging them to pass on her fate to Rama and Lakshman upon their return. And then she cast down her veil and her jewels as a token for her husband.

Ravana returned her to his palace and begged her to become his wife. Her face crumpled in bitter pain and she refused to speak. And as he persisted, she turned to him then and prophesied his certain death at the hands of Rama. And she spoke no more.

Rama returned from the chase of the golden deer with an overwhelming sense of trepidation, and as he met with his brother, far from the clearing, his fears were confirmed. Rama and Lakshman raced towards the hermitage, but Sita had gone. There they found the weapons which had cut down the brave Jatayu, and the dying bird, who raised himself just enough to recount the events of the previous hours. And then, released of his burden, the soul of the great Jatayu rose above the clearing, leaving his body to sag to the ground below.

And so it was that Rama set out with Lakshman to search for Sita, travelling across the country but hearing little news and having no idea where Ravana kept his palace. He met with Sugriva, a king who had been robbed of his wife and his kingdom by his cruel brother Vali, and with the help of Hanuman, chief of the monkeys they continued their search.

Sugriva and Rama formed an alliance and it was agreed that Sugriva would be restored to his throne with the help of Rama. In return Sugriva would put at his disposal the monkey host, to find the poor Sita, already four months lost.

Rama's signet ring was put in Hanuman's possession, to show to Sita as a sign when he found her, but the monkey chief returned with his host, ashamed and saddened that they had been unable to find the beautiful princess. But then, as hope began to fade, there was news. On the coasts of the sea, where the monkeys sat deep in dejection, was a cave in which an old and very wise vulture made his home. He was Sampati, and he was brother to Jatayu. When he heard of his brother's fate he offered to the host his gift of foresight. Ravana, he announced, was with Sita in Lanka.

A brave and monkey, Jambavan, chose Hanuman for the task of retrieving Sita, and Hanuman swelled with pride at the prospect of his task. He sprang easily across the thousands of leagues, and across the sea – carelessly knocking down any foe who stood in his path. And so it was that he arrived on the walls of Lanka, and made his way towards the palace. The moon sat high in the sky, and the occupants of the golden city went about their nightly activities.

Making himself invisible, he entered the private apartments of Ravana, who lay sleeping with his many wives around him. But there was no sign of Sita. Hanuman roamed the city, increasingly anxious for the safety of Rama's wife, but she was not to be found. A deep desolation overtook him and he realized the enormity of his task. If he was unable to find the beautiful Sita then Lakshman and Rama would surely die of grief. And Bharata and Satrughna would die too. And the shame that would be brought on Sugriva, and the monkey host – it was too great to contemplate. Hanuman gritted his teeth, and monkey fashion swung over the palace walls and into the wood.

The wood was cool and shining with gold and gems. In its midst was a marble palace, guarded by the ugliest of rakshasis. In the palace lay the form of a woman, scantily clad in rags and thinner than any living woman.

Hanuman watched as Ravana raised himself and approached the woman, who must surely be Sita. And he watched as the woman scorned him, and ignored his advances. The glitter in her eye betrayed her identity and Hanuman leapt up and down with glee. As Ravana left, the movement of the monkey caught Sita's eye and she looked at him with distrust. Probably Ravana in disguise, she thought tiredly, used to his tricks. But Hanuman whispered to her, and spoke reams of prayers for Rama, extolling his virtues. Sita was bemused and intrigued. She leant forward to hear more. Hanuman leapt down and spoke to Sita of Rama, presenting her with his ring as a token of his continual concern for his dear wife. Sita knew then that Hanuman was friend, not foe, and she poured out stories of Rama, begging Hanuman to return at once to Rama in order that she could be rescued.

Hanuman took with him a jewel from her hair, and departed. His high spirits caused him to frolic on the way, and he could not resist destroying a few of the trees around the palace. His activities drew attention, and he fought at the rakshasas who leapt up to meet him. He wounded or slayed all who approached him until at last he was caught by the enraged Ravana, who promised him instant death.

What could be worse for a monkey, he pronounced, than having his tail set fire? And so it was ordered that Hanuman's tail should be set alight, in order that he should burn to certain death. Now Sita still had powers of her own, and she prayed then, in Rama's name, that the fire should not burn Hanuman, but rage on at the end of his tail, leaving him unscathed. And so it was that Hanuman was able to leap away across Lanka, touching his tail here and there, in order to burn most of that glittering city to the ground. And then, dousing his tail in the wide, curving ocean, he flew across the sea to Rama.

Rama greeted Hanuman which caused the monkey to squirm with delight. He recounted all that had happened in the forest of Lanka, and he told what he had done with his burning tail. The monkey host leapt and cheered for Hanuman for he had brought them great glory with his bravery, and his craftiness.

Sugriva issued orders that all the monkey host should march to the south, in order to lay siege to Lanka. They reached the shores of the sea at Mahendra, and there they made camp. Rama joined them, and the plan to release Sita was formed.

Rama's Bridge

VIBHISHANA WAS BROTHER TO RAVANA, and on the day that Rama set his camp on the shores of the sea, he was pacing around the palace at Lanka. He spoke angrily to his brother, pointing out that if a monkey could lay waste to half the city, what chance did they have against Rama and his monkey host? There could be nothing but death for all.

'From the day that Sita came,' said Vibhishana, 'there have been evil omens – the fire is ever obscured by smoke, serpents are found in kitchens, the milk of kine runs dry, wild beasts howl about the palace. Do restore Sita, lest we all suffer for thy sin.'

But Ravana dismissed his brother and said that Sita would be his. Vibhishana begged his brother to see reason, but Ravana had become blind in his obsession with Sita and he would not allow anything to stand in his path. Vibhishana rose then, and heading over the sea with his four advisers, he said to Ravana, 'The fey refuse advice, as a man on the brink of death refuses medicine.'

And so it was that Vibhishana flew across the sea to Rama's camp and announced himself as an ally to the great Rama. A deal was struck.

The ocean was a formidable obstacle to the rescue of Sita, and Rama laid himself flat on the ground, begging the turbulent waters to open for him, in order that they could cross. After many days, if Rama had received no response, he would dry up the sea, and lay Varuna's home bare. Mighty storms erupted and across the world people trembled with fear. At last the ocean himself rose up and spoke to Rama, his head a mass of jewels pinning the great rivers Ganga and Sindhu to its peak. He spoke gently, his power simmering beneath a gentle exterior.

'Great Rama,' he said, 'you know that every element has its own qualities. Mine is this – to be fathomless and hard to cross. Neither for love nor fear can I stay the waters from their endless movement. But you can pass over me by way of a bridge, and I will suffer it and hold it firm.'

And so Rama was calmed, and plans were made to build a bridge. With the permission of the ocean, Rama dried up the waters of the north, causing the sea there to become a desert. Then he sent a shaft which caused that dry earth to bloom with woods and vines and flowers. The ocean presented to Rama and his men a fine monkey named Nala, Vishvakarma's son, and the monkey set in force a plan to build a bridge like none other. The host of monkeys began to follow his orders, and bit by bit, timber and rocks were thrust on to the sea until a mighty bridge was formed across its girth. And the monkey host and Rama passed over, in order that the siege of Lanka would begin.

The siege of Lanka was a story which took many years to resolve, and it involved the near deaths of Rama and each of his men. Garuda himself came down to heal their wounds, and the men fought on until, finally, Ravana was slain by Rama – with the Brahma weapon given to him by Agastya. Only this weapon had the force to take the life of the evil spirit, and the wind lay on the wings of this weapon, the sun and fire in its head, and in its mass the weight of Meru and Mandara. Rama held a mighty bow and the arrow was sent forth, where it met its mark on the breast of Ravana. The lord of the rakshasas was slain, and all of the gods poured bouquets of blossoms, rainbows of happiness upon Rama and his men. Rama's greatest achievement – the reason for Vishnu ever having taken human form – had been accomplished. Rama ordered Sita to be brought to him at once.

Sita's Second Trial

RAMA KNEW THAT SITA would not be accepted by his people, for she had lived in another man's house and they had no reason to believe that she was not stained by his touch. Rama greeted her coldly, and told her that he had no choice but to renounce her, as he must renounce everything that had been in contact with the greatest of evils. Sita, begged and pleaded – insisting upon her dedication to her glorious husband, and her continual and undying devotion.

'Oh king,' wept Sita, throwing herself at Rama's feet, 'why did you not renounce me when Hanuman came? I could have given up my life at that time, and you need not have laboured to find me, nor laid a burden on your friends. You are angry – like a common man you are seeing nothing in me but womanhood. I am the daughter of Janaka, Rama, and I am also daughter of the earth. I was born of earth and you do not know my true self.'

She turned then to Lakshman, and she said bravely, 'Build me a funeral pyre, for there is my only refuge. I will not live with an undeserved brand.'

And the fire was prepared.

The gods threw themselves upon the mercy of Rama, praying that he should relent. And an elderly Brahma came forward and spoke words that fell on the ears of the gods and all around them like jewels: 'Sita is Lakshmi and you are Vishnu and Krishna. No stain has touched Sita, and although she was tempted in every way, she did not even consider Ravana in her innermost heart. She is spotless.' The fire roared up in approval, and added, 'Take her back.'

And so Sita was returned to Rama's side, where he pledged his undying love for her. He explained then that this test had been for her own safety – that their followers would now respect her once again for she had been proved pure. Together they set out for Ayodhya, and home.

It had been fourteen long years since Rama had left Ayodhya, but the memory of him and his goodness had remained etched in the hearts of every citizen. When they arrived through the gates of the city, they were greeted with uproarious cheers, and celebrations like none other were begun across the land. Bharata bowed to Sita and threw himself at Rama's feet. The kingdom was restored to Rama, and Bharata cried:

'Let the world behold you today, installed, like the radiant sun at midday. No one but you can bear the heavy burden of our empire. Sleep and rise to the sound of music and the tinkle of women's anklets. May you rule the people as long as the sun endures, and as far as the earth extends.'

'So it shall be,' said Rama.

Rama reigned happily in Ayodhya for ten thousand years, and then the day came when Sita conceived a child. Delighted by her news, he begged her to allow him to honour her with any wish, and she expressed a wish to visit the hermitages by the Ganges. Her wish was instantly granted and preparations were made for her travel. Lakshman was to accompany her, but before he left, he took counsel with his brother, the great Rama.

'I am concerned,' said Rama, 'that we know the feelings of our ministers and our people. We must call a conference to ensure that all is well in the kingdom.'

And so a conference was duly called and all of the counsellors and friends of Rama pledged their love for him, and their devotion. There was, however, one unhappiness which stained the otherwise perfect fabric of his rule.

'The people murmur that you have taken back Sita, although she was touched by Ravana and dwelt for many years in Lanka. For all that, they say, you still acknowledge her. That is the talk.' Rama's finest officer uttered these words and as he heard them, Rama's heart was chilled through and through. He sent for Lakshman and pronounced Sita's sorry fate.

'I am crushed by these slanders,' said Rama, 'for Sita was pronounced unstained by gods and fire and wind. But the censure of the people has pierced and this ill-fame can only bring me great disgrace. Take Sita tomorrow and leave her there, brother, and remove yourself now before I can change my mind.'

And so Sita and Lakshman travelled to the Ganges, armed with gifts for the hermits. When they arrived, Lakshman explained Rama's wish. Sita fell into a deep faint from which it took many minutes to recover. When she did, she spoke of her desolation, and her fear at being able to survive in the forest. She could not live there, she feared, and yet she would do so because her master had decreed it. She was faithful. She was unstained. She was prepared to prove it.

The Sons of Rama

THE WORLD ABOUT RAMA was changing, and he was advised by the gods and by his counsellors that the age of Kali had begun. He continued to undertake acts of great kindness and goodness and his fine name sat comfortably on the tongues of subjects across the kingdom. But Rama was lonely. He longed for his great love Sita, and he longed for the day when she would be declared cleansed of all unrighteousness.

And that day came at last, when Rama prepared a horse sacrifice, and invited the hermit Valmiki to the ceremony. He was accompanied by two young boys, Kusha and Lava, and Rama was overjoyed to discover that these were the sons born of Sita, and that she was well and still living with the hermit Valmiki.

His two sons were born in his likeness, with voices as pure as a bird's. They were humble and kind, and when he offered them money for their performance to the people of the kingdom, they refused, saying that they had no need of money in the forest.

Sita was sent for, and Valmiki returned to his hermitage to fetch her. Sita followed Valmiki into a waiting assembly, where the hermit made a pronouncement: 'Oh Rama, Sita is pure and she did follow the path of righteousness but you renounced her because of the censure of your people. Do you now permit her to give testimony of her purity? These twin children are your sons, Rama, and I swear before you that if any sin can be found in Sita I will forgo the fruit of all austerities I have practised for many thousand years.'

And so Sita said quietly, 'I have never loved nor thought of anyone but Rama, even in my innermost heart. This is true. May the goddess of the earth be my protection. I pray now for Vasundhara to receive me.'

And the earth then thrust under the lovely Sita a throne so beautiful that each in the assembly gasped with pleasure. But the earth curled that throne around Sita and drew her back again into itself, home once again and part of the beginning and end of all things.

Rama screamed with despair and fought against the anger that threatened to engulf him. Rama carried on ruling then, for some time, but his heart was no longer in his country. Lakshman travelled to a hermitage and was eventually returned to Indra as part of Vishnu. Bharata no longer wished the kingdom, although Rama begged him to take it back, and eventually it was decreed that Kusha and Lava should rule the kingdom as two cities. But Ayodhya, as it once was, was no longer a kingdom to be ruled, for when Rama left he was followed by all of his people.

Rama joined together with his brothers then, and with the blessing and prayers of the gods and the entire population of his kingdom, he returned to Heaven as Vishnu, in his own form, with his brothers. All of the gods knelt down before him and they rejoiced.

And Brahma appointed places in the heavens for all who had come after Rama, and the animals were given their godly form. Each reached his heavenly state, and in Heaven, all was once again at peace.

On earth it was decreed that the Ramayana should be told far and wide. And to this day, it is.

Legends of Krishna

KRISHNA WAS ORIGINALLY the hero of the Mahabharata, a destructive, evil and immoral warrior who was known for his cunning and martial skills. Later, as Krishna became associated with Vishnu – his third human incarnation – his evil deeds were explained philosophically, and all manner of excuses was devised to explain his previous acts. The murders he had committed were to rid the earth of demons; his forays with women, and their subsequent search for him, have been explained in a metaphor of a worshipper seeking his god. Indeed, he came to represent the doctrine that devotion is a way to salvation. Krishna was a popular god, and the late addition of the Bhagavadgita to the Mahabharata presents him, alongside work and knowledge, as the means by which believers can be saved. But it is his childhood pranks that have come to characterize Krishna, and it is some of these which follow.

Krishna's Birth

THERE ONCE WAS A KING of Mathura, named Ugrasena, who had a beautiful wife. Now his wife was barren, a fact which dismayed them both and caused her to hold her head down in shame. One day, when walking in the wood, she lost her companions and found herself in the company of a demon who assumed her husband's form. Knowing not the difference between this man and the man who was her husband, she allowed him to lie with her and the product of this liaison was a long-awaited son, who they named Kansa.

When Kansa was a child he was cruel and a source of great sorrow to his family and his country. He shunned the religious teachings of the day and taunted his father for his devotion to Rama, the god of his race. His father could only reply, 'Rama is my lord, and the dispeller of my grief. If I do not worship him, how shall I cross over the sea of the world?'

The ruthless Kansa laughed heartily at what he considered to be his father's foolishness and immediately usurped his place on the throne. Immediately a proclamation was issued throughout the kingdom, forbidding men to worship Rama and commanding them to pay their devotions to Siva instead.

This arrogance and tyranny went on for many years, and every man and woman throughout the kingdom prayed for relief from the rule of this truly evil man. Finally, the Earth, assuming the form of a cow, went to Indra and complained. And so it was that Brahma listened to the pleas of the Earth and led them to Siva, and then Vishnu. Vishnu had in the past taken on the incarnation of man and they reminded him of that now, begging him to do so in order to afford the destruction of the seemingly invincible Kansa. Each of the gods and goddesses cheered Vishnu in this mission and promised to leave their heavenly homes in order that they could accompany him on earth. Vishnu arranged that Lakshman, Bharata and Sutraghna would accompany him and that Sita, who would take the name of Rukmini, would be his wife.

One day Kansa was carrying the great Vasudeva and his wife Devaki through the sky when a voice set out the following prophecy:

'Kansa, fool that you are, the eighth child of the damsel you are now driving shall take away your life!' And so Kansa drew his sword and was about to take the life of Devaki when Vasudeva intervened, and said:

'Spare her life and I will deliver to you every child she brings forth.' Kansa laid down his sword, but he placed a guard with her who stayed by her side for her every living hour. And as child after child was given up to him and slain, he continued in his wretched mission.

But Devaki was a woman with a mind as quick as a tree squirrel, and although Kansa had been advised that the children he had destroyed were her own, this was not the case. The children that had been handed over to him were the children of Hiranyakasipu who had been lodged in the womb of Devaki in order that the cruel Kansa might be fooled. Vishnu said to the goddess Yoganindra, who brought the children from the nether regions:

'Go Yoganindra, go and by my command conduct successively six of their princes to be conceived by Devaki. When these shall have been put to death by Kansa, the seventh conception shall be formed of a portion of Sesha, who is part of me; and you shall transfer before the time of birth to Rohini, another wife of Vasudeva, who resides at Gokula. The report shall run that

Devaki miscarries and I will myself become incarnate in her eighth conception; and you shall take a similar character as the embryo offspring of Yasoda, the wife of a herdsman called Nanda. In the night of the eighth of the dark half of the month Nabhas I shall be born, and you will be born on the ninth. Aided by my power, Vasudeva shall bear me to the bed of Yasoda, and you to the bed of Devaki. Kansa shall take you and hold you up to dash you against a stone, but you shall escape into the sky, where Indra shall meet and do homage to you through reverence of me.'

And so it was that when Devaki gave birth to her eighth son, Vasudeva took the child and hurried through the city. When he reached the River Yamuna, which he had to cross, the water rose only to his knees instead of seeking to drown him. And as he reached the house of Nanda, Yasoda had given birth to her child, which Vasudeva seized and, leaving Devaki's child in its place, returned to his wife's bed.

Soon after, the guard heard the cry of a newborn, and summoning himself from the depths of a good sleep, he called for Kansa, who immediately rushed into the home of Devaki and thrust the child against a stone. But as soon as this child touched the ground there was a cry as deep and angry as that of any rakshasa. It rose into the sky and grew into a huge figure with eight arms, each holding a great weapon. It laughed and said to Kansa, 'What avails it thee to have hurled me to the ground? He is born that shall kill thee, the mighty one amongst the gods.'

Kansa collected his ministers and gathered them round. He insisted that every man who was generous in gifts and sacrifices and prayers to the gods must be put to death so that no god shall have subsistence. He said then, 'I know now that the tool of my fate is still living. Let therefore active search be made for whatever young children there may be upon earth, and let every boy in whom there are signs of unusual vigour be slain without remorse.'

Soon after this Vasudeva and Devaki were released from their confinement, and quickly sought out Nanda, who was still unaware of the change in their children. Vasudeva had brought with him another of his child, by Rohini, who was Balarama, and placed him under the care of Nanda to be brought up as his own child. By this means, as Rama and Lakshman were inseparable companions in previous incarnations, Krishna and Balarama were intimately connected.

Nanda and his family had not been settled long at Gokula before efforts were made to destroy the infant Krishna. A female fiend called Putana, whose breast caused instant death when sucked, had taken the child in her arms and offered him a drink. The infant Krishna seized it with such fervour and sucked with such violence that the horrible fiend roared with pain and met with an instant death.

The birth of Krishna had caused great happiness, despite the evil decrees of Kansa, and throughout the land trees blossomed, flowers bloomed and there was music in the souls of all who lived on earth.

The Young Krishna

THE YOUNG KRISHNA was a very mischievous boy and his merry-making became legend throughout the land. One day, as a mere infant lying under the wagon of Nanda, he cried for his mother's breast, and impatient that she did not come to him at once, kicked the wagon over, to the great astonishment of all who witnessed this momentous occurrence.

When Krishna was but five months old, another fiend came in the form of a whirlwind to sweep him away, but at once he grew so heavy that his own surrogate mother could not hold him and had to lay him down. But when the storm became a cyclone, the infant allowed himself to be swept into the sky, and while all the people on the ground wept and bemoaned his sorry fate, he dashed the rakshasa down, killing him and ending the storm.

On another occasion, Krishna and Balarama played with the calves in the fields to such an extent that Yasoda became angry, and tied the errant Krishna to a heavy wooden mortar in which the corn from the farm was threshed. Krishna, trying to free himself, dragged it until it became wedged between two Arjuna trees and then, with a strong pull, uprooted the trees altogether. Again, the people of the surrounding farms were astonished because there had been no storm and yet the trees had fallen, and their roots were exposed. The land must be unlucky, they thought, and they moved away to Vrindavana.

Krishna's tricks were not only for the benefit of himself, for his companions were also defended by his fiery nature, trickery and quick thinking. One day, Brahma came and stole away the calves and the herd-boys, taking them to a cave among the mountains. Krishna quickly made another herd and another group of herd-boys in their likeness and placed them where he had found them. No one but Krishna knew their true identities and he waited impatiently for Brahma to come upon his trick. Now it was nearly a year later before Brahma remembered the herd and the children, and he found the boys and the calves asleep in the cave. But, when he went to Brindaban, he found the boys and the calves there too.

Brahma was puzzled, but he drew back in fear when Krishna, not content with his changelings, drew the herd-boys into the likeness of gods, with four arms and the shape of Brahma, Rudra and Indra. Krishna quickly returned the boys to their shape when he saw Brahma's fright, and Brahma restored them at once. When they awoke they knew nothing of the time that had passed, and Brahma was now in awe of the young Krishna, whose eager mind had caused such devilry.

There are many other tales related of Krishna's youth, for he liked nothing more than to stir a little trouble amongst the local gopis and cow-herds. There is a tale told of the day that Krishna stole the gopi's clothes. The girls had sought out a quiet place to bathe, and laying their clothes on the bank, they frolicked in the fresh water, their lotus eyes glowing with frivolity and the fervour of youth. They sang and played, and Krishna sat in the tree, watching his cows, but drawn to the happy songs of the gopis. Slipping down the bank, he snatched the clothes, and climbed up a kadamb tree which hugged the bank of the water hold.

When the gopis had completed their bath they returned to the banks to retrieve their clothes. They looked everywhere, raising their arms and brows in puzzlement at such a seemingly magical occurrence. Until one of the gopis looked up and saw Krishna sitting in the tree, gently laying out the clothes of each girl. He was wearing a crown and yellow robes and she called out, 'There he is, Krishna, who steals our hearts and our clothes.'

The girls squealed, as all girls across the ages would have done, and plunged into the water to hide themselves. They prayed silently for Krishna to return their clothes but he would not hand them over.

'You must come and fetch them,' he said smartly, grinning from ear to ear.

'We shall tell on you,' said the girls, 'we shall tell your father and ours, and all our friends and you will be punished. Our husbands will protect our honour.'

But Krishna only laughed and said to them then, 'If you are bathing for me, then cast away your shame and come and take your clothes.'

The girls said to each other, 'We must respect him, for he knows our minds and our bodies. There is no shame with Krishna.' And they strolled then from the water, their arms at their sides but their heads lowered in deference to Krishna. At Krishna's encouragement they joined hands and waited for their clothes, which were duly presented. And so the gopis returned home, wiser in some small way that was unknown to them, and more attracted to and confused by the mischievous Krishna than ever.

Krishna and Kaliya

ONE DAY, the cowherds set out early, wandering through the woods and along the banks of the river until they came to a place called Kaliya. There they drank of the river waters, and allowed their cows to drink as well. Suddenly there was blackness and each of the cow-herds and cows laid down, the rich and instant poison of the naga or water snake called Kaliya entering their veins and causing them to die a painful death. Kaliya had come there from Ramanaka Dwipa, where he had once made his home. Garuda, who was the enemy of all serpents, had gone to live at Ramanaka Dwipa and Kaliya had fled immediately, taking refuge in the only place that Garuda was unable to visit, due to an ancient curse. Kaliya was an evil, frothing snake, and for miles around his shimmering form, the river bubbled with the heat of his poison.

Now on this day, Krishna set out to seek the company of the cowherds and their cows, and he came upon their lifeless forms by the banks of the Jamna with some surprise. Krishna's powers were such that it took only a glance to restore the life to their bodies once more, and this he did at once. But Krishna was unhappy about his friends being plagued and he leapt into the water. Now the great Kaliya rose with all one hundred and ten hoods spluttering his poison, and the cowherds wept and wrung their hands at his certain death in that water. But Balarama was calm.

'Krishna will not die,' he said calmly. 'He cannot be slain.'

Now Kaliya had wrapped himself around the body of Krishna, and he tightened his grip with all of his force. But Krishna outwitted him, and making himself so large, he caused the serpent to set him free. Again, Kaliya squeezed his bulk around the youth, but once again Krishna cast him aside by growing in size.

Then, Krishna suddenly leapt onto Kaliya's heads, and taking on the weight of the entire universe, he danced on the serpent's heads until Kaliya began to splutter, and then die. But there was silence and weeping, and the serpent's many wives came forward and begged Krishna to set their husband free. They laid themselves at his feet, and pledged eternal worship.

'Please release him,' they asked, 'or slay us with him. Please, Krishna, know that a serpent is venomous through nature not through will. Please pardon him.'

And so it was that Krishna stepped from Kaliya's head and set the serpent free. Kaliya gasped his gratefulness, and prayed forgiveness for failing to recognize the great Krishna, the Lord, earlier.

Krishna commanded Kaliya to return to Ramanaka Dwipa, but Kaliya lowered his head and explained that he could not return there for Garuda would make a meal of him at first sight. Krishna laughed, and pointed to the mark on Kaliya's head.

'Show him my mark, my friend,' he said to the serpent, 'for when Garuda sees that he will not touch you.'

From that day, the waters were cleared of poisons and the people rejoiced. Krishna was Lord.

Krishna and the Mountain

KRISHNA HAD LONG WISHED to annoy Indra – partly because he was mischievous by nature and partly because he envied the giver of rain for all the gifts he received from the people. And so it was on this day that Krishna spoke to the gopas who were preparing to worship Indra, and he urged them instead to worship the mountain that had supplied their cattle with food, and their cattle that yielded them with milk. And following the wise Krishna's advice, the gopas presented the mountain Govarddhana with curds and milk and flesh, the finest offerings they had.

The crafty Krishna at once transformed himself, appearing on the summit of the mountain saying 'I am the mountain.' There he ate greedily of the offerings while in his own form, as Krishna, he worshipped the mountains with the gopas. Little did they know that Krisha wished only to divert the worship of Indra to himself and that he could appear both as the mountain and in his own form at will.

Now Indra was not pleased that his offerings had all but dried up and pledging to punish the people, he sent down great floods and storms to destroy them and their cattle. An army of clouds swept across the skies and a rain like none had ever seen before was cast down.

'You told us to give up the worship of Indra,' chanted the gopas angrily. 'And now we will lose everything. You told us to worship the mountain and that we did. And so, great Krishna, bring that mountain to us now.'

And so it was that Krishna filled Govarddhana with all of the burning energy that filled his celestial body and he lifted it easily on the tip of one finger. Laying it over the people of Braj and their cows, he sheltered them from the rains and the floods until Indra gave up. Not even a drop of rain had fallen in Braj and Indra knew he had met the Primal Male.

The following day, as Balarama and Krishna laid lazily in the meadows, enjoying the sun and good fortune, Indra arrived and laid himself at Krishna's feet. Krishna was Lord.

Krishna and Radha

ONE DAY, as the cool breeze wafted lazily at the ripples on the river, Krishna and Balarama lay in the grasses under the trees, playing on the flute and joking amongst themselves. As was usually the case they were soon joined by the lovely gopis, who had fallen under the spell of Krishna and who longed for his company. They came towards the music and took up his hands to dance. Now there were too many of these gopis to dance with Krishna and to hold his hands, but as they danced he multiplied himself into as many forms as there were woman so that each woman believed she held the hand of the true Krishna.

It was on this same day that Krishna watched the gopis bathe in the Yamuna river after their dance. He loved them all, of course, but his particular favourite was Radha, the wife of Ayanagosha. Rhada's sister-in-law told her brother of his wife's misconduct with Krishna, and Radha was afraid that she would be murdered as she slept. But when she spoke her fears to Krishna he calmed her, and reassured her easily that when her husband came, he would transform himself into Kali, and instead of finding Radha with her lover, Ayanagosha would find her worshipping a goddess instead.

Krishna took Radha into his embrace, and as he did so, her husband passed. Looking up, he noticed his wife bowing down with Krishna, who appeared at once as the goddess Kali.

The love affair with Radha went on for many years. They walked together in the flowering woods, and she spent many hours worshipping his feet. When Radha made love to Krishna, they made the world, and their love-making was passionate and playful. After their love-making Krishna combed her hair and plaited and pinned it, a servant to his mistress, a servant to his great love. He helped her with her sari. Theirs was a true, divine love – personifying all that is good in the union of man and woman.

There are many more stories of Krishna, who continued his tricks and his love-making, eventually taking on some 16,000 wives, but that is the story of the Mahabharata and other tales.

Legends of Buddha

BUDDHA MEANS 'AWAKENED ONE', or one who has found insight and enlightenment. There are many Buddhas, for he has had many incarnations, but the Buddha to which we refer today is the last incarnation of the great teacher Gautama Buddha, who was born in 563 BC as the son of Suddhodan, the king of Sakya. He is also called Siddhartha and Tathagata, or the one who walks the same path as his predecessors, his earlier incarnations. The myths of Buddha surround the privations and austerity he underwent to attain his enlightenment, and then, the miracles he was able to perform thereafter. When he had attained his awakening, Buddha passed away peacefully, surrounded by his disciples.

There were many stories of Buddha's birth, and it became an accepted belief that others could follow in his path – becoming Buddhist deities and being worshipped themselves. The following tales are some of the richest examples of Buddhist myth, which has, over the years, become embroidered to encompass philosophy of both Hindu and Buddhist religion.

The Life of Buddha

IT WAS IN THE FIFTH CENTURY, when Prince Gautama was born in Kapiavastu, the capital of Shakya. The Raja at this time was Suddhodana and he was married to the two daughters of the Raja of the neighbouring tribe, the Koiyans. There are many myths which set out the birth of Buddha, each subsequent version more splendid and divine. Queen Maya, wife of Suddhodana, recounts a dream in which she saw a white elephant lowered from heaven, and how the moon itself fell into her lap, a ball of pure, white light. And when the birth occurred, Buddha was thrust from her side, like the opening of the letter 'B'.

Now the young prince was born into great luxury, and he was cosseted and adored by the household on all sides. When he learned to walk there were arms outstretched in every direction, but the young prince shunned them all and took seven steps to the north, seven steps to the east, seven steps to the south and seven steps to the west, which signalled to all his spiritual conquest of the earth.

The prince was trained in every sport, becoming an expert in all kinds of martial skills. He was well versed in the arts, and he married, at a very early age, Yasodhara, who he won in a contest at the age of only sixteen. It was not long after this marriage that Yasodhara bore him a son, who he named Rahula.

Gautama lived the life of a normal Indian ruler, eating and drinking plenty, and finding great pleasure in the women the place offered. He had concubines and a chariot that took him far and wide. Although he was a wise man, he thought little about the world around him for it had been his oyster for as long as he could remember and he polished his own little pearl daily, enjoying what he saw in his reflection.

One day, as Gautama was out in his chariot with his respected confidante and charioteer Channa, he spied an old man shuffling along the earth and mumbling to himself. He leant heavily on his stick and clearly had some difficulty moving at all. Channa said wisely, 'Ah, that shall be the fate of all of us one day.'

Several days later Gautama was out once again with Channa, and he saw a man lying poor and ill in the gutter. He expressed some surprise that a man could be in such a state and asked Channa how this had happened.

Channa spoke wisely, 'Ah, this shall be the fate of all of us. Suffering comes to us all.'

It was on their third such trip that Gautama saw the body of a man who had recently died. He looked puzzled for such occurrences were not the common sight of princes. Any ugliness like illness and death had been swept from his sight until now.

Channa spoke wisely, 'Ah, this shall be the fate of us all.'

Now Gautama was deeply affected by his three experiences and it caused him to spend many long hours pondering his condition, and the fate that would eventually befall him – and them all. He found no pleasure in his food or drink. He left his women in peace and he decided that there was nothing lasting or true in his life. And so it was decided that he would leave his palaces and all the trappings of his life to live a life of meditation and solitude.

Later that night, by the glow of the silver moon, he ordered Channa to saddle his favourite horse Kanthaka, and they rode away from the palace, silently escaping from a life that Gautama now knew he could not live. The gods had smiled on him and his enlightenment, and they helped quiet the hooves of his horse so that the sound of their clatter on the flagstones would not waken his family.

Without a whisper, the men left, Channa accompanying Gautama until they reached the edge of the forest. And there, stripping himself of his finery, the prince said good-bye to his dear companion and to his life. At the age of just twenty-nine, Gautama had left it all.

In the wilds of the Indian countryside, the prince lost himself to the world. For many years he sat in meditation. The gods sent him many temptations, including the daughters of Mara, the goddess of seduction, whose wiry bodies writhed and danced, offering him pleasures for which he had at one time hungered. But he resisted them all, for within Gautama was a new calm. He was on the verge of enlightenment.

Gautama fasted for long periods, until he realized the need for food. Reaching out, he plucked the fruit of the fig tree and in its leafy shade he achieved complete bodhi, or enlightenment.

His philosophy had been worked out in his meditations, and all had become clear. He knew now that desire was the root of evil, of anger and violence. He realized that desire made fools of man, chasing money and women and an afterlife. He realized that a person who cannot control desire goes through chains of existences – birth and then death and then birth again, over and over. This was a wheel which could be stopped; this was a chain which could be broken. By suppressing desire, links of the chain can be removed, and instead of there being rebirth after death, there would be the state of nirvana, where there could be no suffering, no more death, no more births.

And so the supreme Buddha took it upon himself to go back into the world, to preach his new wisdom. He could, then, have given himself over to nirvana but his calling drew him to spread the message, to reach out as a teacher to the people who needed deliverance from the unholy waste that their lives had become.

Buddha walked to Varanasi, where he dressed himself in yellow robes – a personification of the sunlight which flowed through his veins and fed his wisdom. He returned to Kapiavastu, and there he appeared to his own people, joined by his son Rahula. For the next forty-five years, Buddha wandered and preached. Animosity and anger were quietened by his gentle words – even the most ferocious of animals bowed to his touch.

Sumedha

To cease from all sin,
To get virtue,
To cleanse one's own heart –
This is the religion of the Buddhas.
Henry S. Olcott, A Buddhist Catechism

IT IS POSSIBLE for any man to take the form of a Buddha, provided he can find enlightenment. There was, however, one case of a man becoming a Buddha-elect while the great Buddha lived. He was called Sumedha, and he lived in the great city of Amara.

Sumedha was a good man who was both wise and wealthy. He had been widely educated and his studies brought to his attention the unhappy lot that was the world around him. He was a Brahman and well-respected, and Sumedha knew he could count on the support of his peers and family in whatever he did. And so it was one day that Sumedha sat down and reflected on the misery that surrounded him. He too saw the unhappy chain of events that followed events – birth, death, rebirth and then death. And in between that unhappy chain fell the links of old age, disease, and for many, the poverty of the elderly.

So Sumedha took himself away then, far away to the Himalayas where he lived as a hermit in a house of leaves. He meditated and strove to attain enlightenment. A day came when the great Buddha would be passing near to Sumedha's hut, and the people of the mountain had come together to prepare a path for his feet. Sumedha joined eagerly in his work, and when the Buddha approached, he laid himself in the muddy rocks and leaves and sought a higher consciousness. And as he laid there, he realized that he could, at that moment, cast all his evil aside and enter into nirvana.

But the good Sumedha paused. How, he said to himself, how can I do this for myself. It would be better for all that I some day achieve complete omniscience and bring with me many people with the doctrines of Buddha.

There appeared at his side Dipankara, the Buddha who was known as One-who-overcame. Dipankara knelt beside Sumedha and rejoiced in his choice. The trees around them blossomed, and their leaves at once became lush. The earth became rich under his body, more fecund and fertile. From the clouds, the gods threw cascades of perfumed flowers.

'You have made the right choice,' said Dipankara. 'Go on and advance. Surely a Buddha thou shalt be, and give many others the chance to do the same.'

Sumedha returned then to the forest, where he practised carefully the conditions of a Buddha. They were perfection in alms, in keeping the precepts in renunciation, in good will and in indifference, and Sumedha learned them all. Beginning to fulfil the conditions of the quest he entered his hut and he stayed there. And then, one day, Sumedha died.

The forms by which he was reborn are countless, and in every one he stayed by his chosen path. Indeed, it has been said that there is not a particle of earth where the Buddha has not sacrificed his life for the sake of the creatures.

The Six-Tusked Elephant

THE JATAKA BOOK outlines the 550 rebirths of the Buddha-elect Sumedha, and this is just one. Once upon a time he was born as the son of an elephant chief, high in the Himalayas on the banks of a great lake. He was born into a royal herd, and they lived happily by the clear waters, enjoying the rich foods that grew on its shores, and finding shelter in the warm caves when the rains came each year. There was a great banyan tree, and the elephants lolled in its cool shade when the heat of the summer burned at their tender hides.

One steamy day, the Buddha-elect took shelter under the tree with his two wives, Chullasubhadda and Mahasubhadda. As the Buddha-elect reached up with his trunk to root out an insect, he accidentally sent down a shower of green leaves and flowers on his wife Mahasubhadda. On the other side, he had dislodged a spray of dry leaves and ants, and these struck Chullasubhadda smartly on the head causing her some pain, and even more jealousy. Later that day, another of the elephants presented the Buddha-elect with a lovely, fresh seven-sprayed lotus, and this he gave to

Mahasubhadda. Chullasubhadda watched from behind the tree, her anger clouding what goodness remained within her.

That night Chullasubhadda laid under the tree and prayed that she might be reborn as the daughter of the king so that she could return as the queen of the king of Benares. She fell into a deep slumber, and her wicked wishes were granted. Chullasubhadda did not awake, and she returned as the favoured wife of the king of Benares. She remembered her wish to come back in this form and she remembered even more clearly the jealousy she had for the Buddha-elect's relationship with Mahasubhadda. She had returned for one reason alone – to destroy him – and that it what she set out to do.

The king of Benares returned to his chamber one evening to find his lovely wife in tears. He begged her to allow him to serve her in some way, and she spoke then of a wish that had been hers since she had been a child. With false innocence lighting her eyes, Chullasubhadda told the king that she had dreamed of a magnificent white elephant with six tusks. She longed for those tusks, she said, and if she could not have them she would surely die.

A hunter was chosen from the palace, and the queen explained to him where he would find the elephant. She promised him great riches and the hunter grudgingly agreed to go. He travelled deep into the Himalayas, far beyond the reaches of ordinary men, and he finally came upon the sweet waters of the lake, by which the herd of royal elephants rested. It was seven years since he had left the palace and he was weary from his travels. The great elephant was beautiful, and the hunter was suddenly saddened by the task ahead of him. Dressing himself in the yellow robes of a hermit who he had met on his travels, he slept for several hours in a hole he had dug near the herd.

When he awoke, he summoned up his courage. Preparing his poisoned arrow, he waited until the great elephant passed, and he shot him straight through the head. Now the Buddha-elect would most certainly have sent this hunter to a sorry death if he had not seen his yellow robes. Intrigued by such poor behaviour on the part of a man of god, he knelt over the hunter and asked why he had performed an act of such violence.

The hunter, frightened by the presence of the elephant, confessed all. The Buddha-elect remembered his wife and he decided then that he would give in to her wishes. He allowed the hunter to saw at his tusks, an act which the poor tired traveller seemed unable to commit. He sawed at the tusks but with such ineffectual action that he caused the great elephant enormous pain and suffering, and filled his mouth with blood. And so it was that the great white elephant took the hunter's saw in his own hands and cut off his tusks himself. He presented them to the hunter, along with magic which would return him to the palace in seven days and seven hours.

As the hunter left, the great elephant laid down and died. That evening he was burned on the pyre by the others in his herd.

When the hunter returned to the queen, she leapt up and down with happiness at her conquest. She clutched the tusks to her breast and took to her bed in order to gloat. But as she looked at them there, saddled in her lap, she felt empty. And then, creeping into the empty hollow that had been her emotions, she felt despair and inconsolable grief. She remembered her life and her husband, and little by little the despair cracked her heart. The queen died.

When she was reborn, it was as Savatthi, a nun. One day she travelled to hear the doctrines of Buddha, and as she sat there, she realized that she had been married to him, and that he had once been the great white elephant. She swooned then, and burst into tears. But the great Buddha only smiled down on her, and when she told her story he only smiled again. Savatthi went on, it is said, to attain the sainthood, and it is her story that was responsible for many men following the great one's path.

Parinirvana

THE GREAT BUDDHA spread the word for forty-five years, and in the final year of his ministry, he suffered a grave illness. He knew then that his nirvana was approaching, and he prepared for the final release, called parinirvana for the great one. Buddha's illness came as he ate with a good smith called Chunda, who had prepared for him the most succulent pork.

It was this meat which brought on the final sickness, for it was tainted and it caused the great one to fall into a fever and a wretched faintness to which his whole body succumbed.

But Buddha felt no anger towards the Chunda, and indeed, as soon as he realized that his illness would, this time, be fatal, he called Chunda to his side.

'Chunda, your offering will bring a great reward. It is your doing which has brought on the attainment of nirvana, and for that I am thankful.'

Buddha made his pleasure clear to all his friends for he feared that Chunda would be blamed for his death when it was a time for rejoicing. Buddha lay himself down on a couch in a grove of sal-trees near Kushinagara. He sent a message to the princes of Malwa to come at once to his side, for he knew they would have a deep regret if they did not witness his final release, if they did not bid him farewell in person. Buddha's couch was soon surrounded by men of the highest order. There were kings and princes, priests and nobles, devas and brahmas of the ten thousand worlds, and they all gathered by his bed to see him pass. There was deep desolation and much weeping, which Buddha was unable to control.

Just before he was to take his last breath, Buddha was approached by a hostile Brahman of Kushinagara, who had not yet reached an understanding or acceptance of Buddha's teachings. Despite the cries of those around his bed to suppress the arrogant Brahman, Buddha was able to raise himself once more, in order to answer the young man's questions, and to argue the points to which he objected. In the end, there was a supreme silence, for the Brahman became a disciple and Buddha had the satisfaction of carrying his work, his teachings to his final rest.

He said to those around him, 'Now my friends I depart to nirvana, leaving you with my ordinances. Do not weep – seek the path to release and you may all reach nirvana. Work on your salvation,' he said quietly, and then he slipped into an unconsciousness which took from him his life.

The body of Buddha was wrapped in the finest cloths and laid in state for six days. And then it was burnt on a pyre in the coronation hall of the princes. The pyre ignited without match, for Buddha's body was ready for the final release, for parinirvana, and it was consumed at once. He left behind his teachings, and the goodness with which he had filled the world.

Tales of the Mahabharata

THE MAHABHARATA IS ONE of the most magnificent epic poems of all time, and the longest in any language. The name Mahabharata probably applies to the Bharatas, who were descendants of King Bharata, the brother of Rama. The poem is unique in Indian literature, for it is driven mainly by the interplay of real people, rather than gods and demons, and it uses a plethora of very lively, dramatic and exciting personalities to present its message. Many believe that the entire philosophy of India is implicit in its romance, and its message is acted out in the great war waged between two ancient families – the Pandavas and the Kauravas, or Kurus.

The poem was finally edited by Krishna Dvaipayana, or Vyasa the Compiler, but since this character is, too, mythical, it is doubtful that his contribution is authentic. There have been many interpretations and many hands turning the text and indeed the pages of the Mahabharata over the centuries – and they have served not to clutter but to make clear the extraordinary vividness of the characterization, and the reasons why this has become the Indian national saga.

The Princes Learn to Shoot

BHISHMA WAS ROYAL GRANDFATHER to the houses of Pandava and Kuru, and he was eager for the princes of these royal houses to have a teacher who could train them in the dignified and royal use of arms. He had put out a search for such a teacher when it happened that the boys themselves were playing ball in the forests outside Hastinapura, when their ball rolled away from them and fell into a well. Although they struggled, and used all of their inventiveness, all efforts to reach it failed, and the ball was lost to them.

The boys sat glumly by the well, gazing with frustration at its walls when suddenly there was a movement from the corner of their eyes. There, thin and dark, sat a Brahman who seemed to be resting after his daily worship.

The boys eagerly surrounded him and begged him to recover their ball.

The Brahman smiled at their boyish jinks and teased them, for what offspring of a royal house could not shoot well enough to retrieve a ball? He promised to do so himself, for the price of a dinner. And then the Brahman threw his ring into the well and promised to bring that up too – using only a few blades of grass.

The boys surrounded the Brahman, intrigued. 'Why that's magic,' said one of the boys. 'We could make you rich for life if you could do as you say.'

The Brahman was true to his word and selecting a piece of grass he threw it as if it were a sword, deep into the heart of the well and there it pierced the ball straight through. He immediately threw another blade, which pierced the first, and then another, which pierced the second, until soon he had a chain of grass with which to draw up the ball.

The boys had by now lost interest in their ball, but their fascination with the Brahman was growing by the moment.

'The ring,' they chorused. 'Show us how you can get the ring.'

And so it was that Drona, which was the name of that Brahman, took up his bow, which had been lying by his side, and choosing an arrow, and then carefully fitting it to the bow, he shot it into the well. Within seconds it had returned, bearing with it the ring. He handed it to the boys who whooped and hollered with glee.

They surrounded Drona again, begging him to allow them to help him, to offer him some gift. Drona grew silent and then with great effort he spoke, carefully choosing his words.

'There is something you can do,' he said quietly. 'You can tell Bhishma your guardian that Drona is here.'

The boys trooped home again and recounted their adventure to Bhishma. Their guardian was at once struck by the good fortune of this visit for he did indeed know of Drona and he would, it seemed, be the perfect teacher for these unruly boys. Bhishma had known Drona as the son of the great sage Gharadwaja, whose ashrama in the mountains had been a centre of higher learning. Many illustrious students had attended as scholars, and most of these had befriended Drona who had been, even then, gifted with divine weapons and the knowledge of how to use them.

Drona had fallen upon hard times when he had pledged his allegiance to Drupada, now king of the Panchalas. Drupada and Drona had been fast friends as scholars, but as regent, Drupada scorned their ancient friendship and set the poor Brahman in the position of a beggar. Hurt by his friend's actions, Drona had left to pursue his studies, and his first task was to find the best pupils to which he could apply his knowledge.

Bhishma did not ask what purpose Drona had for these good pupils, and it was with warmth and genuine delight that he welcomed Drona to his household.

'String your bow, Drona,' he said, 'and you may make the princes of my house accomplished in the use of arms. What we have is yours. Our house is at your disposal.'

The first morning of instruction found Drona lying the boys flat on their backs. He asked them then to promise that when they became skilled in the use of arms they would carry out for him a purpose that he had borne in mind. Ever eager, Arjuna, the third of the Pandavas, jumped up and promised that whatever that purpose might be, he was prepared to accomplish it. Drona drew Arjuna to him and the two men embraced. From that time there would be a special closeness between teacher and student.

The princes came from all the neighbouring kingdoms to learn of Drona and all the Kurus and the Pandavas and the sons of the great nobles were his pupils. There was, among them, a shy and wild-looking boy called Karna who was by reputation the son of a royal charioteer. Arjuna and Karna became rivals, each seeking to outdo the other with his skill and accuracy.

At this time, Arjuna was becoming well versed in the vocabulary of arms. One night while eating, the lantern blew out and he realized that he could still continue to eat in the darkness. It set his mind on to the thought that it would certainly be possible to shoot in darkness, for it surely was habit as much as putting food to one's mouth. Drona applauded Arjuna's crafty mind and declared him to have no equal.

Another of those who travelled to Drona to become a pupil was a low-caste prince known as Ekalavya. Drona refused to take him on because of his caste, and Ekalavya retired to the forest where he made an image of Drona from the earth, which he worshipped and revered as the man himself. He practised often in the forest and soon became so fine a shot that his activities were drawn to the attention of Drona and his pupils.

Drona sought him out and when Ekalavya saw him coming, he fell to the ground. 'Please, Drona,' he cried, 'I am your pupil, struggling here in the woods to learn the skills of military science.'

Drona looked down on the boy. 'If you are,' he said, 'give me my fee.'

Ekalavya leapt to his feet. 'Master, just name your fee and you shall have it. There is nothing I would not do for you.' His face was broken by a wide smile.

'If you mean it,' said Drona coolly, 'cut off your thumb.'

Ekalavya allowed no reaction to cross his proud face and he did as his master bid at once. He laid the thumb of his left hand at the feet of Drona and held up his head.

Drona turned with Arjuna and left, and as Ekalavya bent to collect his bow he realized that he could no longer hold it. His lightness of touch was gone.

And so it was by these means, and others like them that Drona ensured the supremacy of the royal princes, who had, now, no rivals in the use of arms. Each had a speciality and they were all capable of fighting with resourcefulness, strength and perseverance.

The Princes' Trial

DRONA'S PUPILS had now come to the end of their education, and Drona applied to Dhritarashtra the king to hold a tournament in which they could exhibit their skill. Preparations began at once for the great event, and a hall was built for the queens and their ladies.

When the day arrived, the king took his place, surrounded by his ministers and minions, and by Bhishma and the early tutors of the princes. And then Gandharai, the mother of Duryodhana, and Kunti, the mother of the Pandavas, entered the area, beautifully dressed and bejewelled as befitted their stature. Last came Drona, who entered the lists dressed in white, as pure as the heart of Vishnu. Beside him walked his son, Ashvathaman, who held himself with great pride and authority.

In came the princes to a procession, led by Yudhishthira, and there began the most incredible display of expertise seen by any one of the noble spectators of that tournament. Arrow after arrow flew, never missing its mark. Horses pulled chariots and there was much vaulting and careering, but never did the princes lose control or exhibit anything other than the greatest of skill and precision. The princes fought together, and exhibited alone. Their mastery left none in any doubt that he was witnessing the finest example of marksmanship in the land. And then entered Arjuna, and Kunti gave a sigh of delight. Her son was even superior to his splendid cousins and he shot arrows that became water, and then fire, and then mountains, and then an arrow that made them all disappear. He fought with sword, and mace, and then pole and on the breast of his chariot. He met every mark with perfect precision. Here was a champion, and the audience hardly dared expel breath at this show of proficiency.

But the respectful silence that had fallen over the crowd was disturbed by a rustling in the corner. And then a great noise was heard in the direction of the gate. Into the centre of the ring came none other than Karna, grown to manhood and splendid in his arms. Far from the prying eyes of her neighbours, Kunti swooned and shivered with fear. Karna was none other than the son she had given up long ago, the son of the sun itself. He shone as brightly as any summer ray, his good looks matched by his eagerness to fight. He was tall and strong, and his presence caused the crowd to gasp with admiration.

Karna walked towards Arjuna and spoke quietly. 'Oh prince,' he said, 'I have a wish that we should engage in single combat.'

Arjuna could hardly hold back the spittle that multiplied on his tongue. He spluttered and then whispered angrily to Karna, 'The day will come when I will kill you.'

'That is yes, then?' shouted Karna. 'Today I will strike off your head before our master himself.'

The two men stood facing one another, antipathy growing between them like the strongest of armour. They moved into position for single combat, but just as they did so there was a cry from the master of ceremonies. Quietly he made his way across the field and drew the warriors to one side. Until Karna could show noble lineage, he was not by law able to fight with the sons of kings. Princes could not fight with men of inferior birth.

Karna's fury was tangible, but just as he turned to the master he was rewarded by a cry from Duryodhana, who was eager to see Arjuna defeated. 'I'll install him as king of Anga!' he shouted. 'And Arjuna can fight him on the morrow.'

Priests appeared at once, and a throne was brought for Karna, who beamed when he saw his old father Adhiratha, the ancient charioteer.

He embraced his son, pride at his position as king causing him to weep with joy. There was some sniggering amongst the crowd, for how could a king have such a lowly father? But before anyone could speak, Duryodhana leapt forward once again, having pledged eternal support and friendship to Karna.

'We do not know the lineage of all heroes,' he shouted to the crowd. 'Who asks for the source of a river?' And to the cheers of the gathering, he wrapped his arms around Karna's shoulders and helped his aged father to a seat.

The princes and Karna left together. Kunti stared quietly at her sons – princes and now a king. She said nothing and watched them leave, undefeated and grand in every sense. Kunti looked then to the sun ... and smiled.

The Bride of the Pandavas

MANY EVENTS HAD BEFALLEN the Pandavas since the day of the tournament and they had gone into hiding, disguised as Brahmans in the town of Ekachakra. There came to visit them one day an old and fast friend who told them that Drupada, king of the Panchalas, was planning a swayamvara for his daughter Draupadi. They spoke at length about the virtues of the fair princess, and soon the time came for their friend to part.

The princes were silent when their guest had gone and Kunti mourned for her sons who had been cast out. She smiled brightly at them and said, 'Perhaps it is time to depart from Ekachakra – I for one am glad to renew our wanderings.'

The spirits of the princes were lifted at once, and the following day they set off, thanking their gentle host for all his many kindnesses. Before they knew it, they were on the road to Kampilya, the capital of Drupada. As they travelled, they met up with other Brahmans going along the same road in order to witness the great spectacle that was about to take place.

Alone in his castle, Drupada perused the swayamvara that he was about to hold and he wondered aloud at the choice of suitors. He had held for many years a secret wish that Arjuna should wed Draupadi, a wish that he had kept close to his breast over the last years. Arjuna's mastery of the bow was fresh in his memory as he formed the instrument that would be required to shoot an arrow through a ring suspended at great height. It would not be easy to win his princess. In fact, thought Drupada, there was likely only one man who could do it.

The day of the swayamvara dawned bright and clear and the crowds poured in from adjoining kingdoms and lands. Duryodhana came with his dear friend Karna, and the Pandavas arrived in disguise, taking the form of Brahmans once again and living in the hut of a humble potter.

As the festivities began, the lovely Draupadi entered the arena, her stunning robes and jewellery matched only by her shimmering beauty. She held in her hands a wreath and she stood quietly while her twin brother Dhrishtadyumna stepped forward, his booming voice carrying across the crowds, 'Today you are assembled here for one purpose. He who can use this bow' – he gestured down and then up – 'to shoot five arrows through that ring, having birth, good looks and breeding, shall take today my sister for his bride.'

A cheer went up among the crowd and the first name on the list was called forward. Many men reached for that sturdy bow, but none was able even to string it. Karna, sensing the embarrassment of his peers, stood and moved toward the weapon, his head held high, his good looks glowing in the morning sunlight. But as Draupadi caught sight of Karna, her lips curled and she called out with great disdain, 'I will not be married to the son of a charioteer.'

Karna managed a smile and shrugging his shoulders, returned to the crowd. There appeared, then, a movement from its masses, and the gathering parted to let through the strong but bedraggled form of a Brahman. Some of the Brahmans in the crowd cheered aloud as a symbol of sovereignty. Others shook their heads at what was bound to be a disgrace for Brahmans altogether.

Arjuna walked forward in his Brahman disguise and he lifted the bow with ease. Stopping to say a quiet prayer he walked slowly round the weapon until as quick as a flash he drew it up and sent five arrows flying straight through the ring. The cheering was uproarious. Brahman's across the crowd waved their scarves and flowers were sent flying from each direction. The other Pandavas kept down their heads, fearing that Arjuna's victory would draw attention to them all. So far no one had noticed that the Brahman was none other than Arjuna, and Draupadi brought forward a white robe and garland of marriage, which she placed eagerly about his neck.

'I take you as my lord,' she said happily.

Suddenly a roar went up from the crowds, and coming towards them were the other suitors, angered that a Brahman should steal what they thought was rightfully theirs. A great fight broke out and Arjuna and his brother Bhima stood firmly against the masses, proving themselves once again to be excellent fighters. Bhima tore out a tree by its roots and used it to fend off the crowds, a trick he had learned at the hand of Drona. The crowd gasped once again in delight. It was not often that they were treated to such a display.

In the royal gallery, a prince by the name of Krishna stood up.

'Look,' he shouted, pointing out Arjuna and Bhima to his brother, 'I would swear as my name is Krishna that those are the Pandavas.' He watched silently and said no more, waiting for his moment.

On the field the fighting continued until, finally, after much bloodshed, Arjuna was able to extract himself with his brothers and his new bride and return to the home of the potter. Unknown to the brothers, Draupadi's twin brother had been sent by Drupada to hide in next room in order to find out whether it was indeed Arjuna who had strung that bow and sent the arrows so smoothly through their ring.

Kunti greeted the princess warmly and welcomed her to the family, allowing her the honour of cooking for them on that first night. Nearby Dhrishtadyumna lay waiting, his ears pricked for news. If his sister was to marry a Pandava, whatever fate would befall her?

Legends of Shiva

SHIVA IS A SANSKRIT WORD meaning 'auspicious one', and although he is worshipped as profoundly, he is a more remote god than Vishnu. Shiva is the Moon-god and lord of the mountains, with the moon in his hair from which flows Ganga, the sacred River Ganges. He is also god of the yogis, the father of Brahmans who knows and recites the Vedas. Shiva has many other incarnations and as the centuries have passed he has taken on different roles and forms for each new generation of worshippers. Doctrines about Shiva may have merged roles that were once assigned to various earlier gods, for his personifications seem so diverse. Shiva is considered to be both destroyer and restorer.

But the stories which surround Shiva are fascinating and full of allegorical messages. Shiva's dance is one of the most memorable representations in literature – a demon-like god who dances to show the source of all movement in the universe, and most of all his five acts: creation, preservation, destruction, embodiment and release. The stories that follow present a portrait of one of the two great gods of post-Vedic Hinduism, and the very real message they depict.

Shiva

THE THIRD OF THE HINDU TRIAD, Shiva was first known as the destroyer, for his work would balance that of the triumvirate, the two other sides of which were Vishnu the preserver and Brahma the creator. In his early incarnations, he is said to be Rudra, who appears in the Vedas, and his story as Rudra of the Mahabharata and many of the other great Hindu works is this:

On the day that Rudra was born, the earth was lit from within. Into the world came a boy, but he entered crying, and Prajapati said to him, 'Why do you weep when you have been born after toil?'

The boy said then, 'My evil has not been cleansed from me and I have not been given a name. Give one to me now,' he begged. And so Prajapati pronounced: 'Thou art Rudra.'

Now Rudra, or Shiva as he came to be known, was created by Brahma in order to create the world, and in order for him to do so, he required a wife. A goddess is a god's other half, and both of these halves must work together to create the energy necessary for divine acts. Brahma realized that Shiva would need a partner, and so it was arranged that he would have one.

Shiva and Sati

THERE ONCE WAS a chief of gods by the name of Daksha. He was married to Prasuti, the daughter of Manu, and she conceived and bore him sixteen daughters. The youngest of these daughters was Sati, and it was she who would become the wife of the supreme Shiva.

Now Daksha was not happy about marrying his youngest daughter to Shiva, for it had come to his notice, once before at a festival, that he had not offered homage to Daksha. Being a man of small mind, Daksha had held this against him as a grudge, and had pronounced a curse upon Shiva that he would receive none of the offerings made to the gods. A wandering Brahman, however, had been witness to the curse, and had laid down a contrary curse in order that Daksha should have nothing in his life but the wastage of material goods and pleasures.

As Sati grew, she knew her future was with Shiva, and she quietly worshipped him. When she reached an age at which it was suitable to marry, Sati was given a swayamvara, or 'own-choice', to which he invited gods, princes and men of all great ranks from around the country. Sati was handed a wreath and with great excitement, she entered the assembly of men, eagerly searching the crowds for Shiva.

Now Shiva had not been invited to the swayamvara, for Daksha wanted nothing more to do with him, but he had not counted on the deep feelings of his youngest daughter. Her despair crumpled her young face and as she stared out into the crowd she felt nothing but love for Shiva. Calling out his name, she threw her wreath, and made to retreat. But there, in the middle of the court, her prayer had been answered. Summoned by her heart-felt cry, Shiva had responded and he stood there now, her wreath around his noble neck.

Daksha was bound by honour to marry his daughter to Shiva, and it was with great bitternes that he said, 'Though unwilling I will give my daughter to this impure and proud abolisher c rites and demolisher of barriers, like the word of a Veda to a Sudra.'

The happy couple travelled at once to Shiva's home in Kailas. His palace was exquisite, wit every luxury and catered for by all manner of servants and women. But Shiva was not conter with the good things alone, and he spent many hours wandering the hills surrounding Kaila dressed in the robes of a beggar, his bedraggled wife Sati at his side. But Sati and Shiva were one day, dressed well, and out to seek some air in their chariot when Sati received Daksha invitation to take part in a great sacrifice that he was about to make.

Because of the enmity between the two men, Shiva had not been invited. Sati wa broken hearted when Shiva explained to her, 'The former practice of the gods has been tha in all sacrifices no portion should be divided to me. By custom, established by the earlies arrangement, the gods lawfully allot me no share in the sacrifice.'

But Sati was determined to attend the sacrifice, and although Shiva tried to dissuade her, sh set off for her father's home. She was received there without honour, for she rode on the bac of Shiva's bull and she wore the dress of a beggar. Daksha immediately became the victim c her tongue, for she gave him a sharp redressing for his treatment of Shiva the good. But in th middle of her speech, her father broke in, calling Shiva nothing more than a 'goblin', a 'begga and an 'ashman'. Sati, who had found great peace with her husband, announced, 'Shiva is frien to all, Father. No one but you speaks ill of him. All that you are saying his people know, and ye they love those qualities in him for he is a man of peace and goodness.'

Sati paused now, and thought for a moment. Then, with a fire that glinted from her eyes sh made a decision and spoke once more: 'A wife, when her lord is reviled, if she cannot slay th evil speakers, must leave the place and close her ears until she hears no more. Or if she has th power, she must take her own life, and this I will do, for I am deeply shamed to have a body tha was once a part of your own.'

And so it was that Sati released the fire within her and fell at the feet of her father. Sati was deac

The news of his dear wife's death reached Shiva within moments, and he tore at his hair witl a frenzy of despair and fury. His eyes glowed red and then gold, and with all the energy he coulc summon he called forth a demon as terrible as there ever was. This demon kissed the feet o Shiva and pledged to undertake any request he might have.

Shiva spat out the words, hardly able to control his great anger, 'Lead my army agains Daksha and take care that his sacrifice is destroyed.'

And so the demon flew at once to the assembly, and with Shiva's ganas, he broke the vessels polluted the offerings, insulted the holymen and then, with one fell swoop, cut off the head o Daksha and tainted the guests with smears of his fresh blood. Then the demon returned tc Shiva at Kailas but he was deep in meditation and could not be reached. Brahma prayed to hin to pardon Daksha, and to ease the suffering of the injured gods and rishis who had been ir attendance at the sacrifice.

So Shiva lifted himself from his deep dreams and proceeded to Daksha's home, where he permitted his dead wife's father the head of a goat which would allow him to live. Shiva wa invited then to the sacrifice, and allowed to partake of the offerings. Daksha looked upon hin with reverence, and as he did so, Vishnu appeared on the back of Garuda. He spoke then tc Daksha with a gentleness that touched the hearts of all who saw him:

'Only the unlearned deem myself and Shiva indistinct. He and I and Brahma are as one. We have different names for we are creation, preservation and destruction, but we three make up one as a whole. We are the tribune self. We pervade all creatures. The wise therefore regard all others as themselves.'

And then, as the crowds cheered and saluted these most wise and noble gods, the three parts of the universe left and went their separate ways – Shiva to his garden, where he fell once more into the solace of his dreams.

Shiva's Dance

Arise Oh my beloved wife
I am thy husband Shiva-ji
Open thy eyes and look at me!
With thee I can create all things
Without thee I am powerless
I am a corpse, I cannot act
Forsake me not, come back to me!
Oh, let me see thy smile again
Say something sweet into my ear
Dost thou not see me weeping here?
Thy words will be unto my heart
Like summer rain on thirsting land
You used to greet me when we met
With joy and with a smiling face
Why art thou still and without voice?
Cans't thou not hear how I lament?
Oh Mother of the Universe,
Oh Mistress of my very soul, arise!
My beautiful and loving wife,
My faithful spouse, return to me!

SHIVA DANCES TO MARK CHANGE, to show the transition from one stage to another. When the body of his wife Sita was burned, he took her ashes and began to dance, whirling in a flurry of movement that tore at the air around him and sent up a torrid flash of colour. He held a drum as he danced, turning and circling until the entire world began to shake. He moved swiftly, and whirled and turned around the world seven times before he was caught and stopped. The gods were frightened by the violence of his sorrow and they promised then to restore Sita to him. She was returned to him several days later as Uma, or mother. Shiva himself had become Nataraja, or the king of the dance.

There are many other legends of Shiva's dance, and another is recounted here. Shiva heard word that there were, in the forests of Taragam, ten thousand rishis who had become heretics who taught a false religion. Shiva was determined that they should know the truth, and he summoned his brother Vishnu to take the form of a beautiful woman and to accompany him to the forest. Shiva himself dressed as a yogi, and he wore his customary rags and ashes. As they entered the forests, they were immediately set upon by the wild wives of the rishis, women whose lust for men caused them to throw themselves at Shiva in his yogi disguise. The rishis themselves were attracted to Vishnu as well, and so there was pandemonium, as the unholy men and women crowded round the two visitors, clawing at them.

And then there was silence. For all at once it had occurred to the people of Taragam forest that things were not quite right, and gathering together they threw curses at the visitors. A sacrificial fire was built, and then from it was called a mighty tiger, who flung himself upon Shiva in order to eat him whole. Shiva plucked at the tiger and set him to one side, removing his skin whole and causing the heretics to gasp. He wrapped the skin around himself like a shawl, and then, as the rishis produced a serpent more terrible than even Kaliya, he wound it round his neck and began to move. A malevolent dwarf goblin took the centre of the room, swinging his great club with one purpose alone. Shiva dealt with him easily, and with one foot pressed upon its back he began to twirl, and to execute an angry dance.

The heavens opened and the gods lined the walls, anxious to witness the splendid fervour of Shiva in action. The rishis watched in an amazement that fed their diminished belief so that they threw themselves down before Shiva and proclaimed him their most glorious god.

Shiva's dance lived on in their memories and Shiva and his dance were invoked on more than one occasion by every one who had borne witness. Some believe that when devotion is fading, Shiva will appear and dance. For when the faithless see this dance there can be nothing but conviction in their hearts.

Miscellaneous Myths

THERE ARE A HUGE NUMBER of fascinating fables, fairy tales, myths and legends which form the backbone of Indian philosophy explaining ideology that was often complex. Some of these stories had their root in the epics, and in religious works. And later Hindu religious literature calls upon a host of characters and creatures introduced in the Vedas, the Brahamanas, the Puranas and some of the lesser known epics to draw attention to their message, and to exemplify the points they wish to put forth. Many of these stories, plucked from a larger original, and bejewelled with the words of generations, can now stand alone, as individual tales, and lessons. It is often these shorter parables that provide the guidelines for living, which allow new gods to force their way into the pantheon, and which represent some of the most compelling literature of any country in the world. There are thousands of variations of each of these tales, for most of them were not committed to writing for many centuries after their composition – the oral tradition keeping them burning in the consciousness, memories and perceptions of the culture.

The Birth of Ganga

.Thus urged, the saint recounted both
The birth of Ganga and her growth:
R. Griffith, Ramayana

THERE ONCE WAS A KING of Ayodhya named Sagara who was anxious to have son. He provided the saint Bhrigu many penances over the years and finally, the saint was happy to announce that Sagara's worship would be rewarded.

'You shall have a glorious name, and one of your queens shall bear a son to maintain your race and to become your heir. And of the other, there shall be some sixty thousand born to you,' said the saint.

Now the wives of Sagara were most anxious to know which of them would have one son and which would have the vast number predicted. Kesini wished for one child, while Sumati was happy to have sixty thousand. Time passed and Kesini gave birth to a son called Ansuman, who became the heir. And Sumati, the younger of the two wives, gave birth to a gourd whose rind broke to reveal sixty thousand babies.

About this time King Sagara decided to make a horse sacrifice in order to become the reigning Indra, or king of the gods. As the preparations were being made, Ansuman was given the task of following the horse set apart for the sacrifice for according to ritual it was to be set free and allowed to wander for a whole year wherever it would.

Now the present Indra began to fear that such a sacrifice would rid him of his crown, and veiling himself as a demon, he arrived on the appointed day and drove the horse away. King Sagara called at once for his sons to search for the stolen horse, begging them to pursue the demon that had caused it to escape.

And so the sons of Sagara began their search, each digging one league in depth towards the centre of the earth. But still they could not see the horse. The gods were alarmed by the digging of the earth, and they went to Brahma to advise him of the destruction. Brahma was calm, for the earth was protected by Vishnu, and the sons of Sagara would be turned to ashes for their handiwork. The gods returned home to wait for retribution, and as they did so, the sons dug on.

Sixty thousand leagues were dug into the earth without any sight of the horse, and the princes returned to their father requesting guidance. Sagara bid them to dig on, and to continue their search until the horse was found. The sons began to dig once again until there before them stood Vishnu. Thinking that the glitter in his eyes was one of welcome, the sons rushed forward to greet him. Moments later they were but ashes.

King Sagara waited disconsolately for news of his sons, but none arrived. Soon he sent his grandson Ansuman to look for them, but he learned nothing of their fate. Ansuman travelled widely, searching for news but he remained unrewarded, until the day when he reached the very spot of their deaths. Ansuman fell to the ground with dismay when he realized the significance of the ashes. As his tears hit the ashes, his uncle Garuda appeared and offered him consolation holding carefully the harness of the horse that had been lost so long ago.

Prince Ansuman returned to the kingdom. Garuda had given him some advice and he thought carefully about it before he approached his grandfather.

'Garuda has said,' whispered Ansuman, 'that if Ganga would turn her stream below, her waves would wash the ashes of the two princes pure again, and the sixty thousand leagues would be restored while you took Indra's place in the heavens.'

The king thought carefully, thoughts which carried over thirty thousand long years. He had no idea how to induce Ganga to come down from the heavens, and at last he went there himself. After his death, the task became his grandson's and then that grandson's son's. And so it was finally given to Bhagirath to accomplish the work, for he had no son. After many years of austerity, Brahma came to Bhagirath and said to him then:

'You have been blessed, for your austerities have won my grace. What can I do to help you?'

Bhagirath replied, 'I would like Ganga to be let loose with her holy wave, so that the ashes of the heroes shall be washed pure and my kinsmen, Sagara's sons, shall ascend to heavenly bliss for the rest of their days. And please,' he added, 'I wish for a son so that my house shall not end here with me.'

And Brahma said to him then, 'If you pray for this, so it shall be.' Bhagirath stayed in his position of prayer for one year, even as Brahma returned to heaven. Shiva, pleased with the devotion, promised to sustain the shock of the waters. Ganga, however, was not pleased with the command that she descend to earth.

Ganga threatened to wash Bhagirath into hell with her waters and as she made for the earth she was caught by the wily Shiva, who held on to the coils of her hair until her anger abated. Then she fell into the Vindu lake, from which came the seven sacred streams of India. One branch of the stream followed Bhagirath wherever he went. At last Bhagirath reached the ocean and ascended to the depths where Sagara's sons were lying. Ganga followed until her waters touched the ashes. Suddenly their spirits rose and like glittering birds they entered heaven in a burst of light.

The faith in this legend has not died. Indeed, one of the most common places of pilgrimage in India is Sagara Island, where the river Ganges and the ocean meet. Sagara's sons and his son's sons rank high in heaven and will forever more.

The Elephant and the Crocodile

THERE ONCE WAS a royal elephant who made his home with a royal herd on the banks of Triple Peak. They were happy here, for there was plentiful food and drink, and he had many wives who held him dear to their hearts. The day arrived when the royal elephant felt hot and fevered by the oppressive weather, and struggling towards an unknown lake, he plunged in and drank thirstily, stopping to cool his brow with a rush of water from his trunk.

As he reached into the water again to draw water for his wives and his children, he was attacked by a wrathful crocodile whose weight and size made him a very fearful opponent.

Crocodile and elephant fought together in the lake until the old elephant, weakened by the struggle and by his earlier fever, began to fade. His wives and children watched helplessly from the banks, calling out in terror and crying for help. And then, all at once, the elephant closed his eyes and began to pray. He prayed with such devotion to Vishnu, the supreme being, that his ardour was at once rewarded and Vishnu himself appeared on the back of Garuda. With ease he lifted the crocodile from the lake and cut its throat, throwing it back so that its blood stained the waters.

The royal elephant was saved. Now this was not just devotion that had caused Vishnu to come to the elephant's rescue. Every event has another meaning and it soon transpired that this was the culmination of an old curse. The elephant was a gandharva who had, in another life, cursed a rishi who had disturbed him. That rishi was reborn as the crocodile, and by another curse that gandharva had become an elephant.

Vishnu says that the elephant of the story represents the human soul of our age, excited by desires, given over to sensual pleasures which are too great to control. There was no salvation for him until he expressed his devotion to Vishnu, who was the only hope for wicked man.

The King, the Pigeon and the Hawk

THERE ONCE WAS A STORY told by Bhishma to Yudhishthira, and it is a story that, once told, will cleanse the teller and the listener of all sin. This is that tale:

There once was a lovely blue pigeon, hotly pursued by a hawk. The pigeon landed, breathless and terrified on the balcony of the home of King Vrishadarbha of Benares.

The gentle king looked with concern at the bird, and taking it into his care, he asked the cause of his distress.

'I am being chased,' said the pigeon, casting down his eyes.

The king spoke quietly and soothed the bird with his kind words. 'Ah, you are a beautiful bird, blue as the sky on a summer's evening, blue as the lotus that has freshly bloomed. Ah, you have eyes like flowers, like the blossoms of an ashoka tree. I will give you protection here. You have come to a place of safety. Rest, dear bird and take comfort.'

Suddenly there was a rush of wings and there, on his balcony, appeared the hawk, irate and breathing as heavily with indignation as the poor pigeon had with fear.

'That,' he said sternly to the king, 'that is my appointed food and you have no right to interfere.'

'Ah,' said the king, 'leave the poor bird. I'll have a boar and some deer dressed for you at once.'

The hawk sniffed. 'Perhaps, my lord,' he said haughtily, 'perhaps you have control over those who call themselves men, but here in the sky you cannot intervene. This is the law of nature. I am hungry. Without the food that this pigeon offers me, I will starve. Boar and deer are the food of men. I want pigeon. Release him at once.'

The king thought for a moment, and then he shook his head. 'I cannot do that,' he said sadly.

The hawk sniffed again. 'Well, King Vrishadarbha, if you are so intent on saving the life of this pigeon, perhaps you will exchange some of your own flesh for his. Give me flesh from your body equal to the pigeon's weight and I will allow him to go free.'

Vrishadarbha agreed at once, and taking a blade, he began to cut away at the flesh on his arms and legs, weighing it carefully on a scale against the pigeon. He cut away at his body, and piled the flesh on the scales but they refused to budge. All across the kingdom there rose a great wail as Vrishadarbha cut his way to certain death. At last he was no more than a skeleton, and he threw his whole body on the scale against the pigeon.

There was at once a flash of light, and from the sky appeared a convoy of gods, headed by Indra. The sound of celestial music filled the air and lotus blossoms tumbled down from the heavens. King Vrishadarbha was borne away in a magnificent chariot to take his place in heaven.

It can only be true that whosoever protects another shall receive a good end.

The Ashvin Twins

THERE ONCE WERE TWO BROTHERS, divine twins who were the sons of the sky-god Surya. Their names were Dasra and Nasatya and they were the most exquisitely beautiful boys, looks with which they were blessed into adulthood. The Ashvins were bright and friendly, and they attracted only the best attention wherever they flew. They rode in a gilded carriage – gold which appeared tarnished next to the burnished good looks of the Ashvin twins. They flew quickly and travelled widely, for they sought a place among the pantheon of Hindu gods, an honour which had not yet been accorded.

One day, Dasra and Nasatya were stopped in their travels by the sight of the most delicate and elegant woman, who was taking her bath in a stream near her home. This was Sukanya, or 'Fair-Maid', and she was the wife of the aged rishi Chyavana, who had held her hand in marriage for many years and to whom she had pledged her heart and eternal devotion.

The twins were stunned by the sight of her beauty, and they flew to her side, their pearly smiles flashing as they moved forward to greet her.

'You are the most beauteous of all creatures, fair-limbed girl. Who is your father? And how is it that you have been allowed to bathe alone here in these woods?' asked the twins.

'Why I am the wife of Chyavana,' said Sukanya, 'and I bathe here each day.'

The twins shook with laughter. 'How could your father bear for you to give your hand to someone so old and near death. You are the very essence of beauty, fair maiden, and yours should have been the choice of every man.'

'I love Chyavana,' said Sukanya with dignity, preparing to dress.

'Leave your husband,' suggested the Ashvins. 'Come away with us and have a taste of youth. You'll have a life with us and our beauty will be the perfect complement to one another.'

But Sukanya refused their offer and turned to leave her toilet.

But the Ashvins stopped her once again, praying that she should listen to their new request. 'We are medicine men,' they announced, 'and we will make your husband young again, and fair of face. If we do so, fair maiden, will you agree to choose between us a husband for life?'

Sukanya consulted with her husband, who agreed to the plan, and the Ashvins did as they had promised. Within a few moments, Chyavana was at their sides and all three men entered the pool and sank into its depths. There was a pause and then they emerged, all three equal. All three identical.

The three men said in unison, 'Choose among us Sukanya.'

The fair maiden searched carefully for traces of her husband, and when she found them she chose him to be her lord and husband for the remainder of her life.

Chyavana had suffered no indignities, and from this fateful interlude he had had his youth returned to him. He smiled widely, and in gratitude to the Ashvin twins, he promised to win for them the right to sit with the gods, and share in their offerings.

The twins went on their way again, fleet of foot and then high in their gilded chariot. The happy couple lived together in great joy, gods in their own home.

Native American Myths

Introduction

THE WHITE MAN'S first encounter with the native aboriginal population of America dates back to the year 1000 AD, almost five hundred years before the Genoese explorer Christopher Columbus crossed the Atlantic. A group of Norsemen, sailing from Norway to Greenland, was thrown off course in rough weather conditions and soon came in sight of a land of which they had no previous knowledge. The 'Land of Flat Stones', as the adventurers called it, was what came to be called Newfoundland, a barren country whose inhospitable appearance prompted them to sail further south. Soon they approached the low, tree-covered country of what is now Nova Scotia, and named it 'Mark-land'. Sailing still farther south, they came upon a land where the air was warmer, whose soil had produced fields of self-sown wheat and vines laden with ripened grapes. The Norsemen had arrived on the shores of New England and before long they had christened it 'Wine-land'.

Impressed by their welcoming surroundings, they embarked upon a bold attempt to colonize the newly discovered country. But fate decreed that the hostility of several bands of swarthy natives should check this expansion. Soon, the Vikings were subjected to repeated attacks by men they nicknamed 'Skrellings' or 'Chips' owing to their stunted, puny appearance. It was these inhabitants, possessing Eskimo characteristics, who brought about the destruction of the Scandinavian settlements and an end to colonial activity until the arrival of the European settlers in the wake of Columbus's discovery of the West Indian islands.

So who exactly were these strange people the Norsemen encountered, and where had they come from? The name 'Indian', which for many centuries has been used to describe the native aboriginal population of America, is actually a misnomer and owes its origin to Christopher Columbus who believed he had discovered a new route to Asiatic India when he landed in the Caribbean islands in 1492. Once this error had been acknowledged, however, other equally spurious theories on the origin of the race began to emerge. Some theorists traced the native American people back to Egypt, to the South Sea Islands, and even to Wales. Others were intent on proving a connection between the American 'Indian' and the Lost Tribes of Israel.

Most scientists nowadays are agreed that the 'Indians' of the Americas arrived in the New World as immigrants, forced to migrate southwards during the last great ice age over twenty thousand years ago. The physical similarities between the 'Indian' and the Eskimo point to northern Asia as his original home and it is now almost certain that he would have crossed from Alaska to America via the Bering Strait, a land bridge a thousand miles wide once linking Asia and America. When this land bridge became submerged in the melting ice, the 'Indian' found himself stranded in this new homeland and eventually spread out to inhabit all of North, Central and South America.

The first native American people were already competent hunters and gatherers. They were skilled in the making of warm clothing from animal skins and understood the use of fire. Armed with tools of stone, bone, antler and wood, they hunted the great Pleistocene animals, including mammoths, camelops and superbison, surviving almost exclusively on this plentiful supply of meat. Later, when the big game began to disappear, the 'Indian' started to exploit other food sources, learning to cultivate the land to produce fruit and vegetables, seeds and nuts. Many who inhabited areas where soil and climate were good, discovered they no longer needed to move on in search of game and wild food and began to form more permanent communities.

Others continued to maintain their nomadic lifestyle, either hunting or challenging others for whatever they needed to survive. By the time white explorers began arriving in America in the early sixteenth century, the descendants of the original settlers were divided into numerous different tribes, most of them self-sufficient, with their own individual language and customs. It has been estimated, for example, that no less than five hundred languages existed north of Mexico at this time.

Fringing the shores of the Northern Ocean, from the Siberian shore of the Bering Sea in the west to the Gulf of St Lawrence in the east, were the Eskimos, the connecting link between the races of the Old and New Worlds. The name 'Eskimo' means 'raw meat eaters' and these were a carnivorous body of hunters, speaking a distinct language. They differed also in physical appearance from the 'Indian', being of short, stocky build, with a long head, short face and a well-marked Mongol eyefold.

South of the Eskimos, extending in a broad band across the continent from the Hudson Bay to the Pacific, and southwards almost to the Great Lakes, were the Athapascan stock. These tribes spread as far north as the mouth of the Mackenzie River, but also covered a huge area in the opposite direction, migrating south along the Rocky Mountains, where they scattered themselves over the plains of New Mexico under the names of Apaches and Navajos.

The most well-known to us of the native American people, the Algonquins and Iroquois, originally occupied the entire region of what is now Canada and the eastern coast of the United States, extending as far south as Virginia. These two groups are the main focus of this chapter and a selection of their myths and tales, drawn from various tribes, follow in the next two sections.

The Muskhogean Indians, including the Choctaws, Chickasaws, Creeks and Seminoles, originally possessed almost all of Mississippi and Alabama, portions of Tennessee, Florida and South Carolina. Their neighbours to the west were the Dakota Indians, including the Sioux and Winnebagoes. A tall, lithe people, the Dakotas found an agricultural lifestyle uncongenial, but they were recognized as the champion warriors of the native American population. Deeply religious, with a strict moral code, they originally occupied a territory extending from Saskatchewan to Louisiana.

The Caddoan family consisted of a federation of tribes living along the Platte River in what is now the state of Nebraska. They included the Arikara, Pawnee, Caddo, Kichai and Wichita tribes. These peoples were agriculturalists as well as hunters and practised pottery-making and hide tanning.

Living alongside the Caddoan to the west were the Shoshonean, or Snake, family of North American 'Indians', comprising, among others, the Root-diggers, Comanches, Kiowas and Hopi. They originally occupied the great desert region between the Wasatch Mountains and the Sierra Nevada.

The Shoshonean Indians were flanked by the Salishan, Californian and Piman 'Indians'. The Salishan, probably of Algonquian stock, occupied territories of Washington. The Californian, including the Cahrocs, Pericues and Olchones, were a loose conglomeration speaking a variety of different languages, while the Pimans were traditional farmers occupying land in southern Arizona and along the western coast.

Cut off from the rest of the world, the native American did not suffer the dilution of blood and culture which modified the nations of the Old World. This situation no doubt contributed to the fact that as soon as the New World was discovered, its inhabitants became a source of fascination to all classes of Europeans. When these white settlers came, they were generally welcomed by the natives, but soon the 'Indian' discovered that the white man could not be trusted and came to regard the colonizer as the intruder. Treating the natives as savages, the white man took for himself whatever property he considered of value and ruthlessly exploited the natural resources of the land so precious to the native population.

The European invasion brought not only more wars over land and food, but cultural and religious conflict, as well as diseases previously unknown in North America. The changes were dramatic and ultimately disastrous for the 'Indian'. Within a few years of their landing, the whites had freed New England of these 'harmless natives', and as more and more Europeans arrived, the face of native American culture was altered forever. The 'Indian' fought against the invaders as best he could but, step by step, he was driven westwards until he had all but vanished from his ancestral lands. By the late nineteenth century, the United States Government had implemented a policy of housing 'Indian' survivors on tracts of land known as reservations, where many still live today, effectively ending the existence of tribes as independent communities.

The native American people have little to thank the white man for, but among the white traders and missionaries there were at least some with the foresight to attempt to preserve the unique oral heritage they happened upon. Today's native American people have lost many of their customs and beliefs, but a number of the old traditions have been consecrated in their mythology, allowing us a rewarding insight into the way the New World must once have looked and felt to its original inhabitants. It is a world we cannot possibly enter, however, without feeling a profound sense of shame and loss.

The myths and legends retold in this chapter have been selected from among the folklore of the native American tribes of North America and represent only a tiny proportion of the vast number of tales in existence. None the less, it is hoped that the stories included will inspire and encourage the reader to explore further this compelling subject. The chapter focuses on the native Americans as they were, and not as they are. Because of this, the more traditional term 'Indian' is frequently applied, particularly in the stories themselves.

Myths of the Iroquois

THE IROQUOIS, whose name means 'real adders', were perhaps the most resilient and hostile of the native American Indian population, demonstrating a rare political prowess. A race of born warriors, they originally occupied the north-eastern woodlands stretching from the Lake Ontario region as far southwards as Tennessee, Pennsylvania and Virginia. They were leading figures in the early colonial wars against the white settlers, although they eventually made friends with the English and the Dutch, using them to crush their old enemies, the Algonquins.

The League of the Iroquois, which was probably formed around 1570, bonded together five powerful tribes – the Mohawk, Oneida, Onondaga, Cayuga and Seneca. Later the Tuscarora joined this league, allowing the Iroquois to develop a huge sphere of political and cultural influence at the height of their power, unlike the Algonquins whose greatest weakness was a lack of tribal solidity.

Myths and legends of the Iroquois people are of particular interest for their semi-historical portraits. Hiawatha, the great warrior responsible for uniting the feuding tribes, has been immortalized in this manner, alongside Atotarho, the mighty Onondaga chief, who appears in Iroquois legend as a mythical king, clothed in black snakes. In common with other native American races, the Iroquois worshipped a number of deities, including Tahahiawagon – he who comes from the Sky. They held a strong belief in witchcraft and were convinced of the existence of a number of malevolent beings roaming the earth, among them the Stone Giants and the curious creature known as Great Head.

Creation Myth of the Iroquois

AT THE DAWN OF CREATION, before mankind ever existed, the universe comprised two separate worlds. The lower world was a place of eternal darkness, peopled only by creatures of the water, while the upper world, a kingdom of bright light, was inhabited by the Great Ruler and his family. The goddess Atahensic was daughter of the Great Ruler, and at this time she was heavy with child and very close to her time of confinement. As the hour drew near, her relatives persuaded her to lie down on a soft mattress, wrapping her in a ray of light, so that her weary body would gather strength and refreshment for the task ahead. But as soon as she had closed her eyes, the bed on which she lay began to sink without warning through the thick clouds, plunging rapidly towards the lower world beneath her.

Dazzled and alarmed by the descending light, the monsters and creatures of the great water held an emergency council to decide what should be done.

'If the being from above falls on us,' said the Water-hen, 'it will surely destroy us. We must quickly find a place where it can rest.'

'Only the oeh-da, the earth which lies at the very bottom of the water, will be strong enough to hold it,' said the Beaver. 'I will swim down and bring some back with me.' But the Beaver never returned from his search.

Then the Duck volunteered himself for the same duty, but soon his dead body floated up to the surface. Finally, however, the Muskrat came forward:

'I know the way better than anyone,' he told the others, 'but the oeh-da is extremely heavy and will grow very fast. Who is prepared to bear its weight when I appear with it?'

The Turtle, who was by far the most capable among them, readily agreed to suffer the load. Shortly afterwards, the Muskrat returned with a small quantity of the oeh-da in his paw which he smoothed on to the turtle's back. It began to spread rapidly, and as soon as it had reached a satisfactory size for the light to rest on, two birds soared into the air and bore the goddess on their outstretched wings down towards the water and safely on to the turtle's back. From that day onwards, the Turtle became known as the Earth Bearer, and whenever the seas rise up in great waves, the people know that it is the Turtle stirring in his bed.

A considerable island of earth now floated on the waves, providing a timely shelter, for soon Atahensic began to hear two voices within her womb, one soft and soothing, the other loud and aggressive, and she knew that her mission to people the island was close at hand. The conflict continued within, as one of her twin infants sought to pass out under the side of his mother's arm, while the other held him back, attempting to spare his mother this unnecessary pain. Both entered into the world in their own individual way, the first bringing trouble and strife, the second bringing freedom and peace. The goddess wisely accepted that it must be so, and named her children Hahgwehdiyu, meaning Good Mind, and Hahgwehdaetgah, meaning Bad Mind. Each went his way, Hahgwehdiyu anxious to bring beauty to the island, Hahgwehdaetgah determined that darkness and evil should prevail.

Not long after she had given birth, Atahensic passed away and the island grew dim in the dawn of its new life. Knowing the goddess would not have wished it this way, Hahgwehdiyu lifted his palm high into the air and began moulding the sky with his fingers. After he had done this, he took his mother's head from her body and placed it firmly in the centre of the firmament:

'You shall be known as the Sun', he announced, 'and your face shall light up this new world where you shall rule forever.'

But his brother saw all of this good work and set darkness in the west sky, forcing the Sun down behind it. Hahgwehdiyu would not be beaten, however, and removing a portion of his mother's breast, he cast it upwards, creating an orb, inferior to the sun, yet capable of illuminating the darkness. Then he surrounded the orb with numerous spots of light, giving them the name of stars and ordering them to regulate the days, nights, seasons and years. When he had completed this work above, he turned his attention to the soil beneath his feet. To the barren earth he gave the rest of his mother's body from which the seeds of all future life were destined to spring forth.

The Good Mind continued the works of creation, refusing all rest until he had accomplished everything he had set out to do. All over the land he formed creeks and rivers, valleys and hills, luscious pastures and evergreen forests. He created numerous species of animals to inhabit the forests, from the smallest to the greatest, and filled the seas and lakes with fishes and mammals of every variety and colour. He appointed thunder to water the earth and winds to scatter pollen so that, in time, the island became fruitful and productive. But all was not yet complete, for Hahgwehdiyu wisely observed that a greater being was needed to take possession of the Great Island. And so, he began forming two images from the dust of the ground in his own likeness. To these he gave the name of Eagwehowe, meaning the Real People, and by breathing into their nostrils he gave them living souls.

When the earth was created and Hahgwehdiyu had bestowed a protective spirit upon every object of his creation, he went out in search of his brother, hoping to persuade him to abandon his evil and vicious existence. But the Bad Mind was already hard at work, intent on destroying all evidence of Hahgwehdiyu's remarkable labour. Without much effort, he overcame the guardian spirits he encountered and marched throughout the island, bending the rivers, sundering the mountains, gnarling the forests and destroying food crops. He created lethal reptiles to injure mankind, led ferocious monsters into the sea and gathered great hurricanes in the sky. Still dissatisfied with the devastation, however, he began making two images of clay in the form of humans, aiming to create a more superior and destructive race. But he was quickly made to realize that he had not been blessed with the same creative powers as the Good Mind, for as he breathed life into them, his clay figures turned into hideous apes. Infuriated by this discovery, the Bad Mind thundered through the island like a terrible whirlwind, uprooting fruit-trees and wringing the necks of animals and birds. Only one thing would now satisfy his anger, a bloody and ruthless combat to the death, and with this purpose in mind, he hastened towards his twin-brother's dwelling.

Weary of the destruction he had witnessed, the Good Mind willingly submitted himself to the contest that would decide the ruler of the earth. The Bad Mind was keen to discover anything that might help to destroy his brother's temporal life and began to question him rather slyly on the type of weapons they should use.

'Tell me,' he said, 'what particular instrument would cause you the most injury, so that I may avoid its use, as a gesture of goodwill.'

Hahgwehdiyu could see through this evil strategy, however, and falsely informed him that he would certainly be struck down by a lotus arrow.

'There is nothing I fear,' the Bad Mind boasted, but Hahgwehdiyu knew this to be untrue, and wisely remembered that ever since childhood the horns of a stag had always induced feelings of terror in his brother.

The battle began and lasted for two days and two nights, causing panic and disruption throughout the earth as mountains shook violently under the strain of the combat and rivers overflowed with the blood of both brothers. At last, however, the Bad Mind could no longer ignore the temptation to shoot the lotus arrow in his brother's direction. The Good Mind responded by charging at him with the stag-horns, impaling him on their sharp points until he screamed in pain and fell to the ground begging for mercy.

Hahgwehdiyu, the supreme ruler of the earth, immediately banished his evil brother to a dark pit beneath the surface of the world, ordering him never to return. Gathering together as many hideous beasts and monsters as he could find, he flung them below so that they might share with their creator a life of eternal doom. Some escaped his grasp, however, and remained on the earth as Servers, half-human and half-beasts, eager to continue the destructive work of the Bad Mind who had now become known as the Evil Spirit.

Hahgwehdiyu, faithful to the wishes of his grandfather, the Great Ruler, carried on with his good work on the floating island, filling the woodlands with game, slaying the monsters, teaching the Indians to make fires and to raise crops, and instructing them in many of the other arts of life until the time had come for him to retire from the earth to his celestial home.

The Origin of Medicine

IN THE OLD DAYS, there was peace throughout the earth and mankind lived in friendship and harmony with the great beasts of creation. But as time progressed, the human race multiplied rapidly and became so large that the animals were forced to surrender their settlements and seek out new homes in the forests and deserts. Although cramped and unhappy, they did not complain too vociferously, but embraced these changes with an open mind, hoping that mankind would now remain satisfied. Sadly, however, this was not the case, and within a short time, man began to equip himself with a variety of weapons – bows, arrows, axes, spears and hooks – which he used to attack the beasts of the forests, slaughtering them for their flesh and valuable skins.

The animals, at first incredulous, soon became enraged by this show of bloodthirsty contempt and began to consider measures that would guarantee them their survival and safety. The bear tribe was the first to meet in council under Kuwahi mountain, presided over by White Bear, their chief. One after another, members of the tribe stood up and reported the appalling atrocities their families had suffered. Mankind had mutilated their bodies, devoured their flesh, skinned them to make superfluous clothing and displayed their severed heads on wooden stakes as trophies. There was only one way to deal with such hostility, it was unanimously agreed, and it involved wholesale war.

The bears sat down to deliberate their strategy more seriously, but as soon as someone asked about weapons, they all fell silent, knowing that humans had one distinct advantage over them in this respect.

'We should turn man's own instruments upon him,' announced one of the elder bears. 'Let us go and find one of these bows, together with some arrows, and copy their design.'

A messenger returned shortly afterwards with these objects and the group gathered round to examine them carefully. A strong piece of locust wood was called for by the chief and with this he constructed a bow. Then, one of the younger bears provided a piece of his gut for the string and soon the weapon was completed, ready for its first testing.

The strongest, most agile bear volunteered his services. He had little trouble drawing back the bow, but as soon as he attempted to let the arrow fly, his long claws became entangled in the string and the shot was ruined. He quickly realized that he would have to trim his claws, and when he had done this, he let a second arrow fly which hit its target successfully. Delighted with himself, he turned to face the chief, but White Bear did not appear at all pleased by the result.

'We need our claws to climb trees,' he wisely proclaimed. 'If we cut off our claws we will not be able to climb or hunt down prey and soon we would all starve together.' And saying this, he ordered the group to scatter amongst the woods, instructing them to reappear before him when they had found a better solution.

The deer also held a similar council under their chief, Little Deer. After they had aired their grievances and lamented the death of their comrades, they came to a decision that if any human hunter should attempt to slay one of them without first asking suitable pardon, he would be struck down by rheumatism. Notice of this decision was sent out to all the Indian villages nearby and the people were instructed what to do if ever necessity demanded that they kill one of the deer tribe.

So now, whenever a deer is hit by an arrow, Little Deer, who moves faster than the wind and can never be wounded, runs to the spot where the victim has fallen and, bending over the pool of blood, asks the spirit of the deer whether or not he has heard the hunter's plea for pardon. If the reply is 'yes', the hunter remains fit and well, but if the answer is 'no', then Little Deer tracks him to his cabin and strikes him down with rheumatism, transforming him into a helpless cripple.

The fishes and reptiles were the next to gather together to determine an appropriate punishment for their aggressors. They held a council which lasted only a few minutes, where it was quickly decided that those who tortured or killed any of their species would be tormented by nightmarish visions of slimy serpents with foul breath twining around their limbs and throats, very slowly choking them to death. Or else, these brutal attackers would dream, day and night, of eating raw, decaying fish, causing them to refuse all food and to sicken and die as a result.

Finally, the birds, insects and smaller animals held their own meeting, presided over by a grub-worm. Each creature, he announced, should come forward and state his point of view and if the consensus was against mankind, the entire race should be put to death by the most cruel and painful means.

Frog was the first to leap forward and he delivered his tirade in a loud and angry voice:

'Something will have to be done to stop the spread of this human menace,' he thundered. 'See how they have kicked me and beaten me with sticks because they think I'm ugly. Now my back is covered with sores that will never disappear.' And he pointed to the spots on his skin for everyone around him to examine.

Next a group of birds hopped forward and began to condemn mankind for the way in which he ruthlessly set out to burn their feet, impaling them on a stick over a fire as soon as he had trapped them, and turning them slowly until their claws and feathers were singed black.

Others then followed with a string of complaints and criticisms, so that apart from the ground-squirrel, who had seldom been a victim because of his tiny size, there was not one among the gathering who showed any restraint or compassion towards the human species. Hurriedly, they began to devise and name various lethal diseases to be released among the human population. As the list grew longer, the grub-worm shook with laughter and glee, until he suddenly fell over backwards and could not rise to his feet again, but had to wriggle off on his back, as he has done ever since that day.

Only the plants remained friendly towards man, and before long every tree, shrub and herb, down even to the wild grasses and mosses, agreed to provide some remedy for the diseases now hanging thick in the air.

'We will help mankind in his hour of need,' each plant affirmed. 'Every one of us shall assist in the struggle against sickness and disease and hope that in return, the earth will be restored to order.'

Even the weeds in the fields were endowed with healing properties and, in time, every tribe boasted a shaman, a great healer, capable of hearing the spirit-voices of the plants speaking to him whenever he was in doubt about a cure.

It was in this way that the very first medicine came into being, ensuring the survival of a human race which had come so perilously close to destruction.

The Legend of Hiawatha

A GREAT MANY fanciful myths and legends have sprung up around Hiawatha, the famous Iroquois warrior and chief. Such a tradition is demonstrated, for example, by H. W. Longfellow, whose poem, Hiawatha, combines historical fact and mythical invention to produce a highly colourful demi-god figure akin to the Algonquin deity, Michabo. The real Hiawatha, an actual historical figure, lived in the sixteenth century and was renowned for promoting a very down-to-earth policy of tribal union. His greatest achievement was the formation of the original Five Nations Confederacy of the Iroquois people. The legend chosen here, although it too reveres Hiawatha as a man of mystical qualities, is based on that historical accomplishment and has been adapted from a story told by a nineteenth-century Onondaga chief.

Along the banks of Tioto, or Cross Lake as it was often called, there lived an eminent young warrior named Hiawatha. Also known as the Wise Man throughout the district, he exerted a powerful influence over the people. No one knew exactly where Hiawatha had come from. They knew only that he was of a high and mysterious origin and investigated no further than this. He had a canoe, controlled by his will, which could move without the aid of paddles, but he did not use it for any common purpose and pushed it out into the water only when he attended the general council of the tribes.

It was from Hiawatha that the villagers sought advice when they attempted to raise corn and beans. As a direct result of his instruction, their crops flourished; even after they had harvested the corn, food was never in short supply for he taught them how to remove obstructions from watercourses and to clear their fishing grounds. The people listened to Hiawatha with ever-increasing respect, and as he continued to provide them with wise laws and proverbs for their development, they came to believe that he had been sent by the Great Spirit himself, for a short but precious stay amongst them.

After a time, Hiawatha elected to join the Onondagas tribe and it was not long before he had been elevated to a prime position of authority, next in line to its chief. [*History would indicate that this was chief Atotarho.*] The Onondagas enjoyed a long period of peace and prosperity under Hiawatha's guidance, and there was not one among the other tribes of the region that did not yield to their superiority.

But then, one day, a great alarm was suddenly raised among the entire people of the region. From north of the Great Lakes, a ferocious band of warriors advanced towards them [*The Huron, ancient enemies of the Iroquois, although at one time part of the same race.*], destroying whatever property they could lay their hands on and indiscriminately slaughtering men, women and children. Everyone looked to Hiawatha for comfort and advice and, as a first measure, he called together a council of all the tribes from the east to the west and appointed a time for a meeting to take place on the banks of the Onondaga Lake.

By midday, a great body of men, women and children had gathered together in anticipation that they would shortly experience some form of deliverance. But after they had waited several hours they became anxious to know what had become of Hiawatha, for he appeared to be nowhere in sight. Three days elapsed and still Hiawatha did not appear. The crowd, beginning to fear that he was not coming at all, despatched a group of messengers to his home and here they found him sitting on the ground, seized by a terrible misgiving that some form of tragedy would follow his attendance at the meeting. Such fear was hastily overruled by the messengers, whose main concern was to pacify their beleaguered tribesmen. Soon, they had persuaded Hiawatha to follow them and, taking his daughter with him, he pushed his wonderful canoe into the water and set out for the council.

As soon as the people saw him, they sent up shouts of welcome and relief. The venerated warrior climbed ashore and began ascending the steep banks of the lake leading to the place occupied by the council. As he walked, however, he became conscious of a loud, whirring noise overhead. He lifted his eyes upwards and perceived something which looked like a small cloud descending rapidly towards the earth. Filled with terror and alarm, the crowd scattered in confusion, but Hiawatha stood still, instructing his daughter to do the same, for he considered it cowardly to flee, and futile, in any event, to attempt to escape the designs of the Great Spirit. The object approached with greater speed and as it came nearer, it revealed the shape of a gigantic white heron, whose wings, pointed and outstretched, masked all light in the sky. The creature descended with ever-increasing velocity, until, with a mighty crash, it fell upon the girl, instantly crushing her to death.

Hiawatha stared at the spot where the prostrate bird lay and then, in silent anguish, he signalled to a group of warriors nearby to lift the carcass from the earth. They came forward and did as he requested, but when they had moved the bird, not a trace of Hiawatha's daughter was discovered. No word was spoken. The people waited in silence, until at length, Hiawatha stooped to the ground and selected a feather from the snow-white plumage. With this, he decorated his costume, and after he had ensured that other warriors followed his example, he walked in calm dignity to the head of the council. [*Since this event, the plumage of the white heron was used by the Onondagas as a decoration while on the war-path.*] During that first day, he listened gravely and attentively to the different plans of the various tribal chiefs and speakers. But on the second day he arose and with a voice of great authority and strength he began to address his people:

'My friends and brothers, listen to what I say to you. It would be a very foolish thing to challenge these northern invaders in individual tribes. Only by uniting in a common band of brotherhood may we hope to succeed. Let us do this, and we shall swiftly drive the enemy from our land.

'You, the Mohawks, sitting under the shadow of the great tree whose roots sink deep into the earth, you shall be the first nation, because you are warlike and mighty.

'You, the Oneidas, who recline your bodies against the impenetrable stone, you shall be the second nation, because you have never failed to give wise counsel.

'You, the Onondagas, who occupy the land at the foot of the great hills, because you are so gifted in speech, you shall be the third nation.

'You, the Senecas, who reside in the depths of the forest, you shall be the fourth nation, because of your cunning and speed in the hunt.

'And you, the Cayugas, who roam the prairies and possess great wisdom, you shall be the fifth nation, because you understand more than any of us how to raise corn and build lodges.

'Unite ye five nations, for if we form this powerful alliance, the Great Spirit will smile down on us and we shall remain free, prosperous and happy. But if we remain as we are, always at variance with each other, he will frown upon us and we shall be enslaved or left to perish in the war-storm.

'Brothers, these are the words of Hiawatha. I have said all that I have to say.'

On the following day, Hiawatha's great plan was considered and adopted by the council. Once more, he stood up and addressed the people with wise words of counsel, but even as his speech drew to a close he was being summoned back to the skies by the Great Spirit.

Hiawatha went down to the shore and assumed the seat in his canoe, satisfied within that his mission to the Iroquois had been accomplished. Strange music was heard on the air at that moment and while the wondering multitude stood gazing at their beloved chief, he was silently wafted from sight, and they never saw him again.

Ganusquah, Last of the Stone Giants

AS A FINAL desperate measure in the bloody battle to rid themselves of the Stone Giants, the Iroquois called upon the Upholder of the Heavens, Tahahiawagon, to come to their aid. For generations, they had bravely suffered the carnage and destruction alone, but were now so depleted in numbers they agreed they had nowhere else to turn. Tahahiawagon, who had generously provided them with their hunting grounds and fisheries, was already aware of their distress and had waited patiently for the day when he could again demonstrate his loyalty and devotion.

Determined to relieve the Iroquois of these merciless invaders, the great god transformed himself into a stone giant and descended to earth where he placed himself among the most influential of their tribes. Before long, the giants began to marvel at his miraculous strength and fearlessness in battle and soon they reached the unanimous decision that Tahahiawagon should act as their new chief. The great god brandished his club high in the air:

'Now we will destroy the Iroquois,' he roared. 'Come, let us make a feast of these puny warriors and invite all the Stone Giants throughout the earth to celebrate it with us.'

Carrying on with his façade, the new chief marched all the Stone Giants towards a strong fort of the Onondagas where he commanded them to lie low in a deep hollow in the valley until sunrise. At dawn, he told them, they would slaughter and destroy all the unsuspecting Indians while they still lay in their beds.

But during the night, Tahahiawagon scaled a great mountain nearby and began hewing the rock-face with an enormous chisel. When he had produced a great mass of boulders he raised his foot and kicked them over the land below. Only one Stone Giant managed to escape the horrifying avalanche. His name was Ganusquah, and he fled as fast as his legs would carry him through the darkness, all the way to the Allegheny Mountains.

As soon as he had reached this spot, he secreted himself in a cave where he remained until he had grown to a huge size and strength. No human being had ever set eyes on him, for to look upon his face meant instant death. He was vulnerable to attack only at the base of his foot, but it was not within the power of any mortal to wound him. And so, Ganusquah used the whole earth as his path, carving out a massive trail through the forests and mountains where his footprints formed huge caverns that filled with water to make the lakes.

If a river obstructed his path, he would swoop it up in his huge hands and turn it from its course. If a mountain stood in his way, he would push his fists through it to create a great tunnel. If ever he were hungry, he would devour a whole herd of buffalo. If ever he were thirsty, he would drink the ocean dry. Even in the tumult of the storms, he made his presence felt, as his voice rose high above the booming of the clouds, warning the Thunderess to keep away from his cave.

It was during one of these terrific storms that Ganusquah came closer than ever before to one of the human species. A young hunter, blinded and bruised by the hail which hurled itself like sharp pebbles upon him, soon lost his trail and took refuge within the hollow of an enormous rock. Nightfall approached, casting deep shadows on the walls of his temporary shelter and soon the young warrior began to drift off to sleep, pleased to have found a place of warmth and safety. He had no sooner indulged this comforting thought, however, when the rock which housed him began to move, but in the queerest manner, almost as if it was being tilted from side to side with the weight of some vast and heavy burden. The swaying motion intensified and was soon accompanied by the most perplexing jumble of sounds, at one moment as sweet and relaxed as a babbling brook, and the next, as eerie and tormented as a death-cry.

The young warrior stood up in alarm, straining his eyes to find the opening of the cave. But too late, for suddenly he felt a gigantic hand on his shoulder and heard a loud voice rumbling in his ear:

'Young warrior, beware! You are in the cave of the stone giant, Ganusquah. Close your eyes and do not look at me, for no human has yet survived who has gazed upon my face. Many have wandered into this cave, but they have come to hunt me. You alone have come here for shelter and I will not, therefore, turn you away.

'I shall spare your life if you agree to obey my commands for as long as I consider necessary. Although I will remain unseen, you will hear my voice whenever I wish to speak to you, and I will always be there to help you as you roam the earth. From here you must go forth and live freely among the animals, the birds and the fish. All these are your ancestors and it will be your task hereafter to dedicate your life to them.

'You will encounter many of them along your way. Do not pass until you have felled a strong tree and carved their image in the wood grain. When you first strike a tree, if it speaks, know that it is my voice urging you on with your task. Each tree has a voice and you must learn the language of the entire forest.

'Now, go on your way. I will be watching you and guiding you. Teach mankind kindness, the unspoken kindness of nature, and so win your way in life forever.'

The young hunter walked out into the darkness and when he awoke next morning he found himself seated at the base of a basswood tree which gradually transformed itself into a mask and began relating to him the great breadth of its power.

The mask was the supreme being of the forest. It could see behind the stars. It could conjure up storms and summon the sunshine. It knew the remedy for each disease and could overpower death. The venomous reptiles knew its threat and avoided its path. It knew every poisonous root and could repel their evil influence.

'I am Gogonsa,' said the mask. 'My tree is basswood and there is nothing like it in the forest. My wood is soft and will make your task easier. My timber is porous and the sunlight can enter its darkness. Even the wind can whisper to it and it will hear. Ganusquah has called upon me to help you and when he is satisfied with your work, I will lead you back to your people.'

The young hunter listened carefully to every word of advice Gogonsa offered him and then, forearmed with this knowledge, he set about the task of carving the gogonsasooh, the 'false faces' of the forest. On his travels he met many curious animals, birds, reptiles and insects, which he detained until he had carved them in the basswood, inviting them to stay with him until he had learned their language and customs. Guided by the voice of Ganusquah, he moved deeper into the forest and soon he had learned to interpret its many different voices, including the voices of the trees and grasses, mosses and flowers. He learned to love his surroundings and every last creature he encountered, and he knew he would be loathe to leave this world of his ancestors when the time eventually came for him to return to his own home.

A great many years were passed in this way until the hunter, who had entered the cave as a youth, had become an old man, bent in two with the burden of the gogonsasooh he carried with him from place to place. At last, he heard the voice of Ganusquah pronouncing an end to his labour and soon the mask appeared to guide him back to his own people. He wondered if he had the strength to make the journey, but he refused to abandon what he now considered his most precious possessions, the hundreds of gogonsasooh he had carved in basswood.

Wearily, he set off on the track, almost crushed by his heavy load, but after only a short time, he felt a sudden surge of energy. Slowly, his spine began to uncurl, his back began to broaden and strengthen and he felt himself growing taller until he had become a giant in stature, rising high above the trees. He stood up tall and proud and smiled, unaware that in the distance, a great cave had begun to crumble.

Great Head and the Ten Brothers

IN A REMOTE INDIAN VILLAGE at the edge of the forest, an orphaned family of ten boys lived in a small lodge with their uncle. The five elder brothers went out to hunt every day, but the younger ones, not yet ready for so rigorous a life, remained at home with their uncle, never daring to venture too far from their home.

One day, the group of elder brothers, who had been away deer-hunting, failed to return at the usual hour. As the evening wore on, there was still no sign of them, and by nightfall their uncle had become extremely worried for their safety. It was agreed among the remaining family that the eldest boy should go out on the following morning in search of his brothers. He readily accepted the challenge and he set off after sunrise, confident that he would locate them before long. But the boy did not return, and his disappearance caused even greater consternation among the household.

'We must find out what is happening to them,' said the next in line. 'Though I am young and ill-prepared for adventure, I cannot bear to picture any of my family lying wounded in some fearful, hostile place.'

And so, having obtained his uncle's permission, he too set off enthusiastically, though he was not so self-assured as his brother before him. Just like the others, however, the youth failed to reappear, and an identical fate awaited the two more after him who took it upon themselves to go out in search of the lost hunters. At length, only one small brother remained with his uncle at the lodge, and fearing he might lose the last of his young nephews, the old man became very protective of him, turning a deaf ear to his persistent pleas to be allowed take his turn in the search.

The youngest brother was now obliged to accompany his uncle everywhere. He was even forced to walk with the old man the short distance to the wood-pile, and he longed for the day when adventure would come knocking on his door. He had almost resigned himself to the fact that this would never happen when, one morning, as the pair stooped to gather firewood, the young boy imagined he heard a deep groan coming from the earth beneath his feet. He called upon his uncle to listen and the sound, unmistakably a human groan, soon repeated itself. Both were deeply shocked by the discovery and began clawing frantically at the earth with their bare hands. Shortly afterwards, a human face revealed itself and before long, they had uncovered the entire body of a man, caked in mould and scarcely able to breathe.

Carefully, they lifted the unfortunate creature from the soil and carried him into their lodge where they rubbed his skin down with bear oil until he slowly began to revive. It was several hours before the man could bring himself to speak, but then, at last, he began mouthing a few words, informing his hosts that he had been out hunting when his mind had suddenly become entirely blank. He could remember nothing more, he told them, neither his name, nor the village he had come from. The old man and his nephew begged the stranger to stay with them, hoping that soon his memory would be restored and that then, perhaps, he could help them in their own search.

The days passed by, but after only a very short time, the young boy and his uncle began to observe that the person they had rescued was no ordinary mortal like themselves. He did not eat any of the food they served him, but his strength increased daily none the less. He had no need of sleep, and often when it rained he behaved very strangely, tossing restlessly in his chair and calling aloud in a curious language.

One night, a particularly violent storm raged outside. As the rain pelted down and the winds howled fiercely, the boy and his uncle were awoken by the loud cries of their guest:

'Do you hear that noise?' he yelled. 'That is my brother, Great Head, riding on the wind. Can you not hear him wailing?'

'Yes, we can,' said the old man. 'Would you like us to invite him here? Would he come if you sent for him?'

'I would certainly like to see him,' replied the strange guest, 'but he will not come unless I bring him here by magic. You should prepare for him a welcoming meal, ten large blocks of maple-wood, for that is the food he lives on.' And saying this, the stranger departed in search of his brother, taking with him his bow and a selection of arrows, carved from the roots of a hickory-tree.

At about midday, he drew near to Great Head's dwelling and quickly transformed himself into a mole, so that his brother would not notice his approach. Silently, he crept through the grass until he spotted Great Head up ahead, perched on a cliff-face, glowering fiercely at an owl.

'I see you!' shouted Great Head, 'now you shall die.' And he lunged forward, ready to devour the helpless creature.

Just at that moment, the mole stood up, and taking aim with his bow, shot an arrow in Great Head's direction. The arrow became larger and larger as it sped through the air towards the monstrous creature, but then, when it had almost reached its target, it turned back on itself and returned to the mole, regaining its normal size. Great Head was soon in pursuit, puffing and snorting like a hurricane as he trampled through the trees. Once more, the mole shot an arrow and again it returned to him, luring Great Head further and further onwards towards the lodge where the young boy and his uncle nervously awaited their arrival.

As soon as the door to their house burst open, its terrified occupants began attacking Great Head with wooden mallets. But the more vigorously they struck him, the more Great Head broke into peals of laughter, for he was not only impervious to pain, but the sight of his brother standing before him had put him in the best of moods. The two embraced warmly and Great Head sat down to his meal of maple-blocks which he devoured with great relish.

When he had done, he thanked his hosts for their hospitality and enquired of them how he might return their kindness. They began telling him the story of their missing relatives, but had only uttered a few words before Great Head interrupted them:

'You need tell me no more,' he said to them, 'I know precisely what has become of them. They have fallen into the hands of a woodland witch. Now if this boy will accompany me, I will point out her dwelling and show him the bones of his brothers.'

Although reluctant to release him, the uncle perceived how anxious his nephew was to learn the fate of his brothers. Finally, he gave his consent, and the young boy started off with Great Head, smiling broadly at the thought of the adventure which lay ahead.

They did not once pause for rest and after a time they came upon a ramshackle hut, in front of which were strewn dry bones of every size and description. In the doorway sat a crooked old witch, rocking back and forth, singing to herself. When she looked up and saw her visitors, she flew into a rage and began chanting her spell to change the living into dry bones. But her magic had no effect on Great Head, and because his companion stood in his shadow, he too was protected from the charm. The youth sprang forward and began to attack the frail, old witch, beating her with his fists until she fell lifeless to the ground. As soon as she lay dead, a loud shriek pierced the silence, and her flesh was transformed into black-feathered birds that rose squawking into the air.

The young boy now set about the task of selecting the bones of his brothers. It was slow and difficult work, but, at last, he had gathered together nine white mounds. Great Head came forward to examine each of them and when he was satisfied that no bone was missing he spoke to his young companion:

'I am going back to my rock,' he told him. 'But do not despair or think I have abandoned you, for soon you will see me again.'

The boy stood alone, guarding the heaps of bones, trying to decide whether he should make his way back home before daylight faded. Looking upwards, he noticed that a huge storm was gathering and began walking towards the hut for shelter. The hail beat on his back even as he walked the short distance and soon sharp needles of rain pricked his skin all over. The thunder now clashed and lightning struck the ground wherever he attempted to step. The young boy grew fearful and flung himself to the earth, but suddenly he heard a familiar voice calling to him, and lifting his eyes, he saw Great Head riding at the centre of the storm.

'Arise you bones,' Great Head yelled, 'I bid you come to life.' The hurricane passed overhead in an instant, as rapidly as it had first appeared. The young boy felt certain that he must have been dreaming, but then, he observed that the mounds had disappeared. In a moment he was surrounded by his brothers and huge tears of relief and joy flooded down his cheeks.

Sayadio and the Magic Cup

MANY MONTHS HAD PASSED since the young brave, Sayadio, lost his beautiful young sister to a fatal illness. She had been only twelve years old when she died, and her abrupt departure to the Land of Souls had left a deep sadness in the hearts of all who had known her. Sayadio occupied himself as best he could after her death and attempted to carry on a normal life, but often he could not prevent himself falling into the blackest of moods from which it took several long weeks to rouse himself.

Worried that his grief would never be silenced, he decided the time had come to call upon his manitto for help. He found a place of solitude and meditated hard, and soon he heard a voice calling to him:

'Your mourning will only cease', it told him, 'when you have followed the path your sister has taken to the Land of Souls.' Sayadio welcomed the advice of his manitto and in great haste he began making preparations for his journey, resolving to be reunited with his sister before long and to bring her back with him on his return.

But the path ahead was never-ending and the months crept by without offering any sign of improvement. Sayadio began to despair and was just about ready to abandon his quest when, quite unexpectedly, he encountered a stooped old man moving slowly towards him along the same track. The stranger's great white beard trailed the ground and in his right hand he carried a heavy, silver object which, on closer inspection, proved to be a curious type of drinking vessel.

'Can I help you on your way,' Sayadio offered, 'perhaps I can carry something for you.'

'I need go no further,' replied the old man, 'for I have set out to meet you so that I might give you this gourd. If ever you find your sister, use the gourd to catch her spirit and hold it captive until you have returned to your earthly home.'

Delighted to receive such a valuable gift, Sayadio travelled onwards, his mood brighter than it had been for many weeks. It was not long before he approached the outskirts of the Land of Souls and, filled with excitement, he began to call his sister's name over and over again. He received no answer, but he did not feel dejected, for up ahead, in the distance, he suddenly noticed a group of spirits playing in the meadow. Respectfully he advanced towards them, expecting that they would greet him kindly, but to his utter dismay, the spirits fled in horror as soon as they set eyes on him.

At that particular time of year, according to ancient custom, the dead were due to gather together for a great dance ceremony presided over by the Holder of the Heavens, Tarenyawago. Soon the spirit-drum began to beat loudly and the sound of an Indian flute filled the air. The effect of these instruments was almost instantaneous, for the spirits immediately abandoned their hiding places and thronged into a circle anxious to commence their bewildering ritual. Sayadio peered from behind the trees and quickly spotted his sister among the spirits. Without warning, he sprang forward, uncorked his gourd, and attempted to sweep her into the vessel. But she eluded his grasp without any trouble and dissolved into thin air before he knew quite what had happened.

Defeated and despondent, Sayadio made a desperate appeal to the Holder of the Heavens:

'I have come a very long way', he informed the great and powerful spirit, 'because my sister was taken from us before her time. Please will you help me to capture her soul, so that she may be returned to her earthly home and to those who love her.'

Observing the deep perplexity and sadness of the young man, Tarenyawago took pity on him and kindly offered his assistance.

'Take this magic rattle', he told Sayadio, 'and shake it as soon as you catch sight of the spirits gathering again to complete their dance. Be patient, yet swift, and you will succeed in your ambition.'

Shortly before sunset, just as the Holder of the Heavens had promised, the spirits began floating on the air like a thick mist, descending one by one on exactly the same spot as before. Once more, Sayadio saw his sister among the group, stepping lightly, round and round, to the sound of the eerie melody. She appeared to be wholly entranced by the music, and he took this opportunity to step forward cautiously with his magic rattle. As soon as she passed before him again, he shook it delicately in her ear and this time, to his great relief, he found that she came to an abrupt halt, frozen in motion like a graceful statue. Quick as a flash, he swooped her off the ground and into his gourd, securely fastening the lid and ignoring the pitiful cries of the captured soul struggling to regain its liberty.

Retracing his steps homeward, Sayadio soon reached his native village where he summoned his friends and relatives to come and examine the strange gourd housing his precious charge. He called for the body of his sister to be brought forth from its burial-place, for he intended, without further delay, to enact the ceremony that would reunite her spirit with her body. Everything was almost ready for the sacred rite of resurrection when, out of nowhere, the most witless Indian in the village rushed forward and removed the lid of the gourd, no longer able to control his immoderate curiosity.

Without any hesitation, the imprisoned spirit rose up into the air, and failing to look back, glided high up into the sky, disappearing over the horizon. Sayadio gazed helplessly in the direction of its frantic flight, calling upon the departed spirit to return to him, but it made no response to his plea. Overwhelmed with despair, he retreated to his lodge, but soon he heard the familiar voice of his manitto whispering in his ear:

'The spirit of your sister was not destined for this mortal world,' the voice explained. 'She is happy in her new home, so be at peace and cease your mourning.'

Sayadio listened and his grief suddenly abandoned him. And from that day forth, he never again attempted to recall his sister from the dead. [*A legend from the Wyandot tribe of the Iroquois.*]

Myths of the Algonquian People

THE ALGONQUIAN RACE was one of the largest of the north American Indians, comprising well over a hundred different tribes. [*The term 'Algonquian' is used to describe the whole linguistic stock, for example, we would speak of the 'Algonquian race', whereas the term 'Algonquin' is the adjective applied to individuals within this linguistic grouping, e.g., 'Algonquin Indians'.*] From east to west their territory spread from the Atlantic coast as far as the base of the Rocky Mountains and from north to south it extended above the St Lawrence Valley all the way southwards into Illinois and Virginia. The most famous tribes of the Algonquian family included the Blackfeet, Cheyenne and Arapapho in the west; the Abnaki, Delawares, Shawnees, Powhattans and Mohicans in the east; the Chippeways, Crees, Montagnais and Micmacs in the north and north-east, and the Menominees and Kickapoos in the central and southern regions.

The Algonquin Indians were a tall, well-proportioned race, intelligent and obliging, who worked the land or hunted and fished for their survival. Those belonging to the eastern tribes living along the Atlantic were the first native Americans to come into contact with the white settlers. They welcomed the white man and passed on to him the domestic skills they had acquired, even yielding to him many of their most fertile coastal lands. Ultimately, the Algonquins were driven further and further westwards by the settlers, coming into headlong conflict with their old enemies, the Iroquois, and losing almost all of their original territories.

Algonquian myths and legends are some of the most colourful of all native American mythology. A selection of the more well-known tales, introducing the most popular heroic figures, cultural practices, beliefs and general lifestyle of the Algonquin Indians are retold here.

The Great Deeds of Michabo

A VERY POWERFUL manitto once visited the earth and, falling in love with its only inhabitant, a beautiful young maiden, he made her his wife. From this union were born four healthy sons, but in giving birth the mother sadly passed away. The first son was named Michabo and he was destined to become the friend of the human race. Michabo, supreme deity of the Algonquin Indians, is very often represented as an invincible god, endowed with marvellous powers. Sometimes, however, he is given a far more human treatment, and is depicted as a trickster, or troublemaker, as in the story to follow. The second, Chibiabos, took charge of the dead and ruled the Land of Souls. The third, Wabassa, immediately fled to the north, transforming himself into a rabbit-spirit, while the fourth, Chokanipok, who was of a fiery temperament, spent his time arguing, especially with his eldest brother.

Michabo, the strongest and most courageous of the four, had always attributed the death of his mother to Chokanipok, and the repeated combats between the two were often fiercely savage. During one particularly brutal confrontation, Michabo carved huge fragments of flesh from the body of his brother which, as soon as they fell to the ground, were transformed into flintstones. In time, the children of men found a use for these stones and used them to create fire, giving Chokanipok the name of Firestone, or Man of Flint.

After a long and tortuous battle, Chokanipok was finally slain by Michabo who tore out his bowels and changed them into long twining vines from which the earth's vegetation sprung forth. After this, Michabo journeyed far and wide, carrying with him all manner of tools and equipment which he distributed among men. He gave them lances and arrow-points; he taught them how to make axes or agukwats; he devised the art of knitting nets to catch fish; he furnished the hunter with charms and signs to use in his chase, and he taught mankind to lay traps and snares. In the course of his journeys he also killed the ferocious beasts and monsters threatening the human race and cleared the rivers and streams of many of the obstructions which the Evil Spirit had placed there.

When he saw that all this was done, Michabo placed four good spirits at the four cardinal points of the earth, instructing mankind that he should always blow the smoke from his calumet in each of these four directions as a mark of respect during the sacred feasts. The Spirit of the North, he told them, would always provide snow and ice, enabling man to hunt game. The Spirit of the South would give them melons, maize and tobacco. The Spirit he had placed in the West would ensure that rain fell upon the crops, and the Spirit of the East would never fail to bring light in place of darkness.

Then, retreating to an immense slab of ice in the Northern Ocean, Michabo kept a watchful eye on mankind, informing them that if ever the day should arrive when their wickedness forced him to depart the earth, his footprints would catch fire and the end of the world would come; for it was he who directed the sun in his daily walks around the earth.

Michabo Defeats the King of Fishes

ONE MORNING, Michabo went out upon the lake in his canoe to fish. Casting his line into the middle of the water, he began to shout: 'Meshenahmahgwai, King of Fishes, grab hold of my bait, you cannot escape me forever.'

For a full hour he continued to call out these words until, at last, the King of Fishes, who had been attempting to rest at the bottom of the lake, could bear the dreadful commotion no longer.

'Michabo is beginning to irritate me,' he complained. 'Here, trout, take hold of the bait and keep this fellow silent.'

The trout obeyed the request and sunk its jaws into the hook as Michabo commenced drawing in his catch. The line, which was very heavy, caused his canoe to stand almost perpendicular in the water, but he persevered bravely until the fish appeared above the surface. As soon as he saw the trout, however, he began to roar angrily: 'Esa, Esa! Shame! Shame! Why did you take hold of my hook, you ugly creature?'

The trout let go at once and swam back down to the bottom of the lake. Michabo then cast his line into the water once more saying: 'King of Fishes, I am still waiting and I will remain here for as long as it takes.'

This time the King of Fishes caught hold of a giant sunfish and commanded him to do exactly as the trout had done before him. The sunfish obeyed and Michabo again drew up his line, his canoe turning in swift circles with the weight of the monstrous creature. Michabo felt certain he had succeeded and began crying out in excitement:

'Wha-wee-he! Wha-wee-he!' But he was quickly made to realize that he had been deceived once more and his face turned a bright shade of crimson as he screamed into the water:

'Esa! Esa! You hideous fish. You have contaminated my hook by placing it in your big mouth. Let go of it, you filthy brute.' The sunfish dropped the hook and disappeared below the surface of the lake.

'Meshenahmahgwai! I have reached the end of my patience,' Michabo bellowed with increasing fury. 'Do as I have bid you and take hold of my hook.'

By now, the King of Fishes was himself seething with anger and he grabbed hold of the bait, allowing himself to be tugged upwards through the water. He had no sooner reached the surface, however, when he opened his mouth wide, and in one gulp, swallowed Michabo, his fishing rod and his little wooden canoe.

Michabo stumbled about in the belly of the fish wondering, for an instant, who had turned the lights out in the sky. But then, he felt a sudden motion and a tremendous rumbling noise and it dawned on him that the King of Fishes had helped himself to an early supper. Michabo glanced around him and seeing his war-club lying in his canoe, lifted it above his shoulders and brought it down mercilessly wherever he could find a solid wall. He was hurled to and fro as the King of Fishes responded to these blows and complained to those around him:

'I am sick in my stomach for having swallowed that troublemaker, Michabo. He has not provided a satisfying meal.' And as he spoke, Michabo continued with his attack, delivering a number of very severe blows to the fish's heart.

The King of Fishes began to heave violently and, fearing that he would be thrown up into the lake to drown, Michabo quickly rammed his canoe lengthways into the fish's throat. The pain nduced by the obstruction, combined with the repeated beating he suffered internally, caused the King's heart to stop beating, and soon his great body, battered and lifeless, was tossed up by the waves upon the shore.

Michabo sat down in the darkness, faced now with an even greater problem, for he had not paused to consider how he would manage to free himself from the bowels of the King of Fishes once his victim lay dead. Had he been ejected, he might have stood some small chance of survival in spite of the fact that he could not swim, but now, there seemed little or no hope.

He chastized himself for his own folly and had begun to come to terms with his sorry fate when, all of a sudden, his ears were filled with the sound of tapping noises above his head. Certain that the King of Fishes lay dead, he was puzzled by the rhythm, but its source was soon revealed to him, as light began to filter in through an opening in the fleshy roof and the heads of gulls peered into the darkness below.

'What a good thing that you have come, my friends,' cried Michabo. 'Quickly, make the opening larger so that I can get out.' The birds, utterly astonished to discover Michabo in the belly of a fish, chattered excitedly as they obeyed the god's command. In no time at all Michabo found himself at liberty and smiled broadly to find his feet touching firm soil once more.

'I have been foolish,' he told the gulls, 'and you have shown great kindness in releasing me from my confinement. From this day forth, you shall not be looked upon as scavengers, but shall be known as Kayosk, Noble Scratchers, and receive my special blessing.'

Then, walking towards the shores of the lake, Michabo breathed life into the King of Fishes, restoring him to his former glory. The King took up his usual place at the bottom of the water and in this silent world, undisturbed by the cries of a keen fisherman, he carried on with his rest.

The Land of Souls

THE WEDDING CEREMONY of a handsome, young Algonquin chief was fast approaching. He had chosen for his bride a very beautiful woman from a neighbouring tribe. The two had fallen deeply in love and looked forward to a long and happy life together, but sadly this was not to be, for on the eve of their wedding the young woman succumbed to a raging fever and within hours she had passed away, leaving her intended husband grief-stricken and distraught.

The handsome chief, who had once been famous for his courage and heroism throughout the land, now spent all of his time in mourning, making a daily pilgrimage to the burial place of his beloved where he threw himself on the soft mound and sobbed helplessly. Hunting and warfare no longer held any charm for him and he cast aside his bow and arrow, resolving never to use his weapon again. The situation appeared hopeless and even the chief's closest friends began to believe that he would never mend his broken heart or recover his brave reputation.

One day, however, the chief overheard a conversation among the elders of his tribe which, for the first time in many months, prompted him to join the circle and listen attentively. The old men were discussing their loved ones who had died, and they also spoke of a path leading to the spirit-world which, if a man was lucky enough to find it, enabled the living to visit the dead. The grieving young lover eagerly welcomed this unexpected news and, taking up his weapon and a few meagre belongings, set off immediately to discover the path that would lead him to the Land of Souls.

He had no firm idea which direction he should take, but instinct informed him that he must keep travelling southward until he observed some change in the landscape. His journey over the snow-covered fields and hills was both difficult and wearisome, but after fourteen days, he became convinced of a difference in the appearance of the surrounding countryside. Certainly, the thick snow had begun to melt. The sky, too, was of a more radiant blue and the trees had begun to reveal tiny leaf-buds. Moving onwards, as if by enchantment, delicate and colourful flowers emerged from the soil, birds began to chirp sweet melodies and the air grew warm and fragrant. The young chief's heart began to beat with excitement at these changes, for he knew that he must be nearing the Land of Souls.

A rugged path wound its way through the trees of the spreading forest before him and he felt sure that he must follow this path. Passing through a dark grove, he came upon a little lodge set high up on a hill. In the doorway stood an old man, his hair as white as snow and his eyes as bright as sapphires. He wore a robe of swan-skin and in his right hand he carried a long staff with which he beckoned the young chief forward.

'I have been expecting you,' said the old man. 'Come inside the lodge and I will answer all the questions I know you wish to ask me.'

There was no need for the chief to inform the stranger of his quest, since the old man already knew every detail of his misfortune.

'Only a few days ago the beautiful woman you seek rested here within my lodge,' he said to the chief. 'Now she has gone to the Land of Souls and you can follow her there if you do as I say and listen carefully to my counsel.'

'You cannot take your body along with you, nor will your bow and arrow be of any use,' the old man told him. 'Leave them here and they will be returned to you when we meet again. I must warn you that the journey ahead is a perilous one. You now stand at the border of the Land of Souls and you must cross that vast lake beyond to reach the Island of the Blessed where it will be possible for you to visit your loved one again.'

The young chief, who was in no way frightened by the old man's words of caution, grew impatient to be on his way once more. He found, as he travelled onwards, that the forests, rivers and mountains had taken on an almost ethereal quality. Animals bounded along gleefully by his side and as he moved swiftly through thickets and dense woodlands, he realized that he was now a weightless spirit floating effortlessly and fearlessly through the air in the Land of Souls.

It was not long before he reached the broad lake the old man had described to him. Gazing across its waters, he caught sight of a very beautiful island shimmering in the midday sunshine. A canoe of white, shining stone lay tied upon the shore, and the young chief lost no time jumping aboard it and grasping the paddles. He was just about to pull away in the direction of the island when he was struck by a powerful sense that he was no longer alone on the water. Turning to confront his mysterious companion, he was utterly amazed and delighted to see his young bride seated in an identical canoe alongside him, ready to accompany him on his crossing to the Island of the Blessed.

At first, the surface of the silver lake remained as smooth as glass, disturbed only by tiny ripples of frolicking trout anxious to join in the excursion. But then, as the couple approached the half-way mark, the waves of the lake began to swell dramatically in strength and size. The water now changed to a steely-grey colour and as the young chief peered over the side of his canoe, he was shocked to discover several human skulls floating on the spray. He remembered the old man's words, that it would be a hazardous journey, and thought now of those who had attempted it before him, battling on bravely, yet eventually drowning in the furious tempest.

Though he was filled with terror and fear for the safety of both himself and his bride, the young chief did not alter his course but continued to row boldly towards the shore, never once losing sight of his loved one. The Master of Life kept a watchful eye on them from above and, knowing that they were innocent children whose deeds in life had been free of evil, he decreed that they should reach the island unharmed. Suddenly the winds began to ease, the water grew calm and the young couple at last felt their canoes grating on the golden sand.

Leaping on to the island, they embraced each other rapturously, shedding many tears of relief and joy. Then, as they stood hand in hand, they surveyed the perfect world they now occupied where everything seemed designed to bring them the utmost pleasure. The air itself was like an exquisite, mouth-watering food sent to nourish and strengthen them. Walking through the beautiful countryside, they could find no trace of suffering or sadness, no cold or discomfort, no war or destruction, only the sights and sounds of a perfect paradise of nature.

For three days and three nights, the young lovers remained free to enjoy this blissful land, each of them hoping that their happiness would last forever. But on the third evening, the young chief was awoken by a gentle voice calling to him on the breeze:

'Your time has not yet come,' whispered the Master of Life. 'You must return to your own people and fulfil your mortal destiny. Rule them wisely and well, for they need your guidance at this time, and when you have completed your duty to them, you may return here and join forever the bride you must now abandon.'

The young chief rose obediently and, making his way to the old man's lodge on the far side of the lake, re-entered the body he had left behind. Although he was heavy-hearted, he was not resentful of his departure, but felt honoured that the Master of Life had intervened to set him on the correct path.

Returning to his people, the young chief became a just and kindly ruler, winning the admiration and loyalty of all who knew him. Often, at the end of a long hunt, he would call for a great fire to be built and ordering his people to sit around it, he would tell them of the Land of Souls and describe to them the path he knew he would follow once more as soon as he had served his time as father to his people.

The Gift of Corn

But the place was not forgotten
Where he wrestled with Mondamin;
Nor forgotten nor neglected
Was the grave where lay Mondamin,
Sleeping in the rain and sunshine,
Where his scattered plumes and garments
Faded in the rain and sunshine.

Henry Wadsworth Longfellow, The Song of Hiawatha

LONG AGO, there lived a poor Indian who dwelt with his wife and children in a tir lodge in the heart of the forest. The family relied on hunting for their food, an although the father was never lacking in courage and skill, there were often tim when he returned home without provisions, so that his wife and children had only tl leaves on the trees to satisfy their hunger. The eldest son of the family, a boy of fourtee had inherited the same kind and gentle disposition as his father, and as he watched tl old man struggle to take care of them all, he longed only for the time when he would b able to help out in some way.

At last, the young boy reached the age of the great fast, when he was obliged to shut himse away without food, praying night and day to the Great Spirit in preparation for the comir of his spirit-guide and guardian through life. This solemn and sacred event demanded th he empty his mind and heart of every evil thought and he now began to meditate earnest on the generosity of the Great Spirit who never ceased to provide mankind with everythin good and wholesome. As he roamed the fields and mountains during the first few days c his retreat, he was deeply moved by the beauty of his surroundings, the glorious flower the succulent berries, and he felt the strong desire to make his own contribution to th remarkable world.

The young boy was well aware that both he and his family were deeply indebted to the Gre Spirit, but at the same time, he began asking himself why it was that the divine ruler had nc made it easier for them to find enough food to survive on.

'Perhaps if I pray very hard,' the boy thought to himself, 'the Great Spirit will reveal to me i a dream the means by which I can ease the hardship my family now suffers.' And with that h lay down and kept to his bed for a full day and a night.

It was now the fifth day of his fast and the boy lay feeble with hunger, drifting in and ou of sleep and hoping that some sort of vision would soon come to him. Suddenly the room i which he lay became filled with a dazzling light, out of which emerged a beautiful young ma who moved gracefully towards him. The stranger's slender form was draped in a luxuriou satin robe of green and yellow, his complexion was the purest marble-white and on his hea he wore an exotic plume of jade-green feathers. The boy was startled by the apparition, but th stranger's eyes conveyed the gentlest, warmest expression and his voice was as sweet as musi as he spoke.

'The Great Spirit has been listening to your prayers,' he said softly. 'He understands ho deeply you care for your family and he knows that you have always been a loyal and obedier child. For these reasons he has sent me to guide you in your pursuit and to ensure that you desire is fulfilled.'

'Arise young warrior,' added the beautiful stranger, 'and prepare yourself to wrestle with me for such is the wish of the Great Spirit.'

Even though his limbs were weak from fasting, the young boy stood up courageously and di as the stranger commanded him. The struggle which followed was long and punishing and a length the boy began to grow faint. But just at this precise moment, the stranger called a halt t the conflict, promising to return on the following day when the boy had replenished his strength

At exactly the same hour next morning, the celestial visitor reappeared and the two too up the fighting once more. As they battled on, the young boy felt his strength improve and hi courage increase. He threw himself wholeheartedly into the struggle, wrestling fiercely with hi visitor, until the latter was forced to cry out in pain.

'You have certainly proven your worth today,' the stranger declared, 'now it is my turn to rest before we begin our final trial. Tomorrow will be the seventh day of your fast,' he continued, and your father will bring you food to strengthen you. In the evening, you will wrestle with me and easily overcome me, for you have succeeded in winning the favour of the Great Spirit.

'As soon as I have fallen, you must strip me of my garments and bury me in the earth. Once a month, come and cover me with fresh soil and make certain that no weeds or grass are allowed to grow upon my grave. If you do all this, I shall return to life and I promise that you will see me again, splendidly clothed in a garment of green.'

The stranger had no sooner spoken these words than he vanished into thin air, leaving his opponent to fathom the meaning of all that he had been told.

Shortly after dawn on the following day, the young boy's father filled a small basket with nourishing food and set off in search of his son. He was greatly relieved to see the boy again, but noticed that he had grown thin and frail.

'My son, you must eat something,' he urged him. 'You have fasted long enough and I feel certain that the Great Spirit does not require you to sacrifice your own life.'

'Father,' the boy replied, 'please be patient with me until sundown, and at that hour I will happily partake of the meal you have brought me.'

For the young boy was determined to prove his hero's strength without assistance, resolving to rely on his inner strength alone during the trial ahead.

Once again, at the usual hour, the stranger appeared and the contest was renewed as before. Though he had not eaten any of his father's food, or allowed even a drop of water to pass his lips, the boy felt invigorated and irrepressible. Fired by the need to achieve some great purpose, he lunged at his handsome opponent, pushing him violently against a rock in the ground. The stranger did not rise up again to challenge him and, as he bent over to examine him where he lay, the boy could find no trace of life in the handsome youth. A deep sadness and regret suddenly invaded his soul as he began digging the earth to bury the body and he swore to himself that he would tend the grave as lovingly as if it were that of his own mother.

Throughout the spring which followed, the boy never once allowed a day to slip past without visiting the burial place of his friend. He stooped and carefully weeded out the grass and carried fresh soil up the mountain to replace the old, just as he had vowed he would. By summertime, tiny green shoots began to appear in the earth, but because they so reminded the young boy of the feather plume his visitor always wore, he was loathe to remove them and so they continued to rise in height as the months progressed.

The days and weeks passed by and during all of this time, the boy never once revealed to a single soul the purpose of his regular excursions up into the mountains. Then one day, he gingerly approached his father requesting that he follow him on his mysterious ramble. Though he was surprised and a little apprehensive, the old man agreed to accompany his son and soon they had reached the spot where the handsome stranger lay buried.

The sight which now greeted them was truly the most astonishing and gratifying they had ever witnessed. Overnight, the green shoots on the grave had broadened out into beautiful, graceful plants with velvet-soft foliage, each one bearing a generous golden cluster crowned by a majestic plume.

Leaping for joy, the young boy began shouting aloud: 'It is my friend, the friend of my vision who promised he would return to me.'

'It is Mondamin,' [*From the words moedo, meaning 'spirit' and min, meaning 'grain' or 'berry'.*] replied his father, filled with admiration for his son. 'It is the spirit grain the old ones have sometimes spoken of, the Indian corn which the Merciful Master has sent to nourish us because he is greatly pleased with you.'

And the two began to gather the golden ears of corn, tearing away the green husks from the stalks as once the young boy had torn away the garments of his extraordinary wrestling companion.

From that day forward, the people no longer depended entirely on hunting and were blessed with beautiful fields of healthy grain which they harvested every year just as soon as the long hot summer had begun to fade into autumn.

Moowis, the Snow-husband

IN A NORTHERN VILLAGE of the Algonquin tribe there lived a young maiden whose exquisite beauty had won her great fame throughout the region. Every day a whole host of admirers made their way to her father's lodge hoping for an opportunity to feast their eyes on the beautiful young woman. The path to his door was now so well worn, the old man had often considered sending his daughter away but, at the same time, he was fiercely proud of his child and was certain that one day a deserving young warrior would appear and carry her off as his bride.

The young maiden was not so easily satisfied, however, and as the months passed by, she became more and more conscious of her charms, treating her suitors as mere playthings no matter how sincere their intentions towards her. One noble brave, in particular, greatly desired to take the young maiden for his wife. He was of a very kind and sensitive nature, and it was many weeks before he managed to pluck up the courage to visit her at her father's lodge. Kneeling before the beautiful girl, he poured forth from the depths of his soul every agonizing detail of his passion, revealing that he could no longer sleep for love of her, nor partake of any activity without heaviness in his heart. But the young maiden laughed aloud to hear all of this and, failing to consider the appalling cruelty of her response, called to a group of friends nearby and carried on loudly mocking her rejected lover.

By sundown, the entire village had been informed of the morning's events and the noble brave was forced to retire to the solitude of his lodge, overwhelmed by feelings of shame and humiliation. A deep melancholy invaded his spirit and for days on end he remained seated in a fixed position, staring blankly at the walls and refusing to eat, drink or speak. Even when his family and friends began making preparations for the annual migration to their summer camp, he refused to join them, but took to his couch instead, where he lay completely still even as his possessions were packed up for transport around him.

At last, when his family had moved off into the distance and all was silent, the young brave began praying earnestly to his manitto [*Please see glossary note.*], calling for his assistance in a plot to avenge himself on the maiden who had shunned and disgraced him. Before long, his prayer was answered, for his despondency began to ease and he felt impelled to move from lodge to lodge gathering up old scraps of cloth and personal ornaments left behind by his tribe. He took whatever he could find of these items outdoors and began sewing them into a coat and leggings which he trimmed elaborately with beads and feathers. Then he cast around him for any left-over animal bones and, after he had assembled these in the form of a human skeleton, egan coating them with snow, pressing and smoothing it with his fingers until he had moulded ne shape of a tall and handsome man. Again, he called upon his manitto for aid and, breathing pon the image, brought it to life. Next, he placed a bow and arrows in its hands and stood back admire his creation of snow and rags.

'I will call you Moowis,' said the young man, delighted by the figure. 'Come handsome ranger, follow me, and I will explain to you why you have been sent here and how you are estined to help me.'

The two walked forward together in the direction of the tribe's summer camp. Their arrival enerated tremendous excitement, not only because people were pleased to see the young rave returned to health, but also because they all desired to know the identity of his elegant ompanion. The chief of the tribe immediately invited the stranger to feast with his family that vening, while all the maidens of the camp lined up to catch even the slightest glimpse of him.

None was so infatuated by the striking visitor as the beautiful young maiden who had so aughtily refused the noble brave. Confidently, she strode forward and requested the company of er discarded lover and his companion at her lodge early that same afternoon. The two appeared t the appointed time and it seemed as if a transformation had occurred in the maiden, for she ould not do enough to please the handsome stranger, even urging him to take up her father's lace in the most comfortable chair by the fire. Not wishing to run the risk of melting during the isit, Moowis refused her kind offer, but this in itself was interpreted as the most humble and nagnanimous of gestures. The noble brave smiled to see these things, for he knew that his plan vas unfolding nicely and that, before long, the tribe would be celebrating a wedding feast.

On the following day, Moowis announced his intention to marry the beautiful young maiden nd within a week the chief had proclaimed the couple man and wife. They remained very happy ogether for a short time, but then, one morning, Moowis turned to his wife and, gathering up his ow and arrows, declared that he must depart on a long and arduous journey.

'May I not come with you?' his wife pleaded.

But Moowis had been instructed by the young brave not to allow her to accompany him as unishment for her cruel actions towards him.

'The way is too difficult and dangerous,' Moowis told his bride. 'It is far better for you that you emain behind.'

'But there are no dangers I would not fully share with you,' she responded, stirring a wave of ity within her husband's breast. Disturbed and confused, Moowis went to his master's lodge nd related to him his wife's request.

'It is good to see that she is so devoted to you,' the noble brave answered him, 'but she has never listened to the voice of prudence and still she will not listen. It is her own folly that drives er to accompany you and now she must submit to her fate.'

A rough and rugged road lay ahead for the newly wedded pair. The beautiful young wife was naccustomed to hardship of any kind and it was not long before she had fallen behind, her feet orn and bleeding from the severe uphill struggle. Moowis continued his rapid pace, passing hrough thick, shady trees until he reached the broad, open plains. He had been long out of sight vhen the first rays of sun began to disperse the dull, grey clouds overhead, gradually warming he air and causing the snow to melt under his feet. Soon he observed a number of tiny glass eads appear on his white body, gently rolling to the ground through his fingers which had egun wasting away to reveal ivory-coloured bones. Moowis was helpless to prevent himself nelting in the heat and, as he slowly dissolved, his splendid garments began to disintegrate also, lropping piece by piece on to the green grass below.

At length, the young bride arose and resumed her gruelling pursuit, crossing over rocks ar marshland, until eventually she encountered fragments of clothing scattered on the earth. Quick recognizing the tattered garments to be those of her husband, she was thrown into a frenzy concern, but then, believing that some trick had been played on her, she began crying out:

'Moowis! Moowis! Nin ge won e win ig; ne won e wig!' (You have led me astray; I cann find my way.) But the young wife received no reply. Now frantic with fear, she began runnir about wildly, through the forests, among the thickets, over the rocks, in every possible directio hoping to catch sight of her handsome husband walking in the distance.

The years passed and still she roamed the countryside, calling aloud to the air, her face line with exhaustion, her body stooped and twisted in sorrow. On and on she wandered until th day finally arrived for her to be released from her punishment. Falling wearily to the grounc she uttered her husband's name one last time before passing away. In an instant, her spirit ros from her body, ascending high above the spot in the deep recesses of the wood where she ha eventually come to rest. But even to this day, it is said that her unhappy voice is often heard o the breeze, calling through the trees in search of her snow-husband:

'Moowis! Moowis! Nin ge won e win ig; ne won e wig!'

The Beaver Medicine Legend

NOPATSIS, son of a noble Indian chief, dwelt with his younger brother, Akaiyan, i a lodge at the foot of the mountains. Nopatsis was a well-meaning and gentle sou but he did not share his brother's intelligence, and was renowned for the mos impulsive behaviour.

One day he returned home accompanied by a young woman he proceeded to introduce to hi younger brother as his wife. He knew little about her, he told Akaiyan, and was certain onl of one thing, that he had fallen in love with her as soon as he had set eyes on her. Akaiya welcomed the woman into their lodge, respecting his brother's choice, and did all that he coul to make his new sister-in-law as comfortable as possible.

The weeks passed by quite smoothly, and the two brothers remained as close as they ha always been since the day, many years before, when they had been tragically orphaned and lef alone to care for each other. Nopatsis, although now a married man, always set aside time in th evenings to sit with his brother while the two discussed the day's events and watched the su sinking into the clouds. The new wife was not so pleased to see this, however, and it was no long before she began pestering her husband to be rid of Akaiyan.

'He is my only brother,' Nopatsis explained to her, 'and I would not be parted from him fo all the wealth in the world.'

But the young woman would not be put off by these words and decided that she must find more devious way of persuading her husband to do as she wanted.

Her evil mind soon hit upon the perfect solution, and one day shortly afterwards, when sh knew she had been left alone in the lodge with Akaiyan, she removed herself to her bedroon and began tearing at her clothes and clawing at her skin and hair. Nopatsis returned at sundowi to find his wife sobbing and trembling by the door. In a quivering voice, she divulged to him that Akaiyan had treated her brutally, after having first sworn her to a silence she simply could not keep.

Nopatsis, whose misguided perception led him to accept all things at face value, was deeply disturbed by what he heard. Silently he listened, storing up hatred in his heart for his younger brother. Not once did he pause to consider that Akaiyan might be innocent; not once did he allow him an opportunity to defend himself. As his wife had planned it, Nopatsis became consumed by thoughts of revenge, debating in his mind night and day precisely how he would get rid of his brother.

The warmth of summer soon filled the air and with its arrival a large number of wild waterfowl gathered on the island of the great lake where it was customary for them to shed their brightly coloured feathers. Every year, the tribal warriors collected these feathers, using them to decorate their arrows. Nopatsis and Akaiyan now began making the raft that would take them to the island, binding logs together securely with strips of buffalo-hide. When their craft was ready, they set sail, reaching their destination before midday.

The two brothers agreed to separate in their search for feathers and Akaiyan wandered far off along the strand, stooping regularly to salvage the plumes washed up among the pebbles. Raising himself up from his crouched position after an interval of about ten minutes, he was astonished to see Nopatsis aboard their raft sailing back towards the mainland. He called out loudly to him:

'Nopatsis, have you gone mad? What are you doing? Please return at once, I have no way of getting back home.'

But Nopatsis rowed onwards, hurling abuse at his brother for what he had done. Akaiyan protested and swore solemnly that he had not injured his sister-in-law in any way, but his cries were ignored all the more and Nopatsis increased his speed, satisfied that he had served up a proper punishment.

Akaiyan sat down and wept bitterly, knowing that he would certainly perish on the island without food and clean drinking water. As night closed in, he began praying earnestly to the spirits of nature and to the sun and the moon for guidance, after which he felt a little more at ease. He took some branches and built himself a shelter, lining the earth with feathers on which he lay until sleep finally conquered his troubled spirit.

The next morning when he awoke he became aware of a little beaver standing in the doorway of his hut.

'My father would like you to visit him at his dwelling,' said the animal. 'I will lead you there if you care to follow.'

Akaiyan agreed to accept the invitation and promptly arose from his bed. Soon he approached a well-constructed lodge where Great Beaver, attended by his wife and family, waited to receive him. His host was indeed the most ancient and revered of all beavers, a wise old animal with a coat as white as snow and large, curling whiskers trailing the ground. Akaiyan immediately felt that he would be understood in such a place and he began to relate to Great Beaver the story of his ill-treatment.

The wise old animal listened and offered his sympathy and it was soon decided among the community that Akaiyan should spend the winter with them where he would be well cared for and introduced to a great many wonderful things he had never before experienced. Akaiyan was deeply touched by the family's kindness and when the beavers closed up their lodge for the winter he happily took up shelter with them. They kept him warm by placing their thick, fur-coated bodies alongside his and they taught him many secrets, including the art of healing, the planting and smoking of tobacco, and various sacred dances, songs and ceremonial prayers associated with the great mystery of medicine.

Summer returned and Akaiyan appeared above ground once more, hoping to find some way to reach the mainland. As luck would have it, his brother, Nopatsis, had set sail for the island that same morning intent on discovering whether or not his younger brother had survived the winter months. Akaiyan soon recognized the vessel, which now lay unattended, and quickly decided that fate might never again offer him a more favourable opportunity. Racing towards Great Beaver's lodge, he entered one last time and sadly took leave of his friends.

'Choose something to take with you as a parting gift,' Great Beaver urged him, 'some small item you may remember us by.' Gazing around him, Akaiyan's eyes fell upon Great Beaver's youngest child with whom he had formed a very special bond during his stay. At first, the wise old animal would not agree to Akaiyan's request, for he prized his little one above all other things, but finally he surrendered to the wishes of both Akaiyan and his pleading child, counselling Little Beaver to construct a sacred Beaver Bundle as soon as he arrived on the mainland.

Akaiyan was soon walking towards his native village in the company of Little Beaver. Many of the warriors he had hunted with in the past ran forward to greet him, surprised and relieved to see him alive. They longed to hear of his adventures and soon the chief had ordered a great fire to be lit, around which they all sat as Akaiyan told them his story. Little Beaver then stood up and proceeded to explain to the people, as his father had bid him, the mystery of medicine with its accompanying songs and sacred dances. He called for a Beaver Bundle to be made and to this each man contributed a relic conveying good or ill luck, including feathers, animal-skins, bones, rocks and stone-pipes. Long into the evening, they watched Little Beaver as he danced and many chiefs of the animal tribes joined in the ceremony, honoured to receive the Beaver Medicine that had been brought to them from the island.

When he was satisfied that he had accomplished his task of instruction, Little Beaver agreed to be returned to his parents. On the island, Akaiyan found the bones of his vengeful brother and was grateful that he had escaped a fate intended for him. Great Beaver presented the young warrior with a sacred pipe in exchange for his child and taught him the songs and dances that would speed the growth of the tobacco plants on the plains.

Every spring Akaiyan set off on his little raft to visit the beavers, and on each occasion he received some important object to add to his Beaver Medicine Bundle, until it reached a great size, bringing him prosperity and good fortune. Soon afterwards, he married a wholesome woman and together they founded a race of medicine-men who never failed to pass on the traditions and ceremonials of the Beaver Medicine to their own offspring, ensuring that the good works of Akaiyan and Little Beaver have remained with us even to this day.

The Legend of Scar-face

IN A FAR-OFF TIME, there lived an Indian who had a very beautiful daughter. Many young warriors desired to marry her, but at each request, she only shook her head and said she had no need of a husband.

'Why is this?' asked her father. A great many of these young men are rich and handsome, yet still you refuse them.'

'Why should I marry?' replied the girl, 'when I have all that I could possibly want here with you in our lodge.'

'It is a shame for us,' said her mother, 'that we should still have an unmarried daughter. People will begin to believe you keep a secret lover.'

At this, the girl bowed her head and addressed her parents solemnly: 'I have no secret lover, I promise you, but now hear the truth. The Sun-god above has decreed that I cannot marry and he has told me that I will live happily, to a great age, if I preserve myself for him alone.'

'Ah!' replied her father, 'if the Sun-god has spoken thus, then his wishes must be obeyed. It is not for us to question the ways of the gods.'

In a nearby village there dwelt a poor young warrior who had neither parents nor relatives. Left to fend for himself, he had become a mighty hunter with a brave and noble spirit. He would have been a very good-looking young man, but for a long scar on his cheek, left by the claw of a great grizzly bear he had slain in close combat. The other warriors of the village had ostracized the youth because of this disfigurement. They had given him the name of Scar-face and nothing pleased them more than to make a mockery of his appearance. Each of these young men had been unsuccessful in their attempt to win the hand of the beautiful young maiden and now, slightly embittered by failure, they made it an occasion to poke some fun at the poor, deformed youth.

'Why don't you ask that girl to marry you,' they taunted him. 'She could hardly refuse a man like you, so rich and handsome.'

They laughed a great deal to see that they had touched upon a sensitive nerve, for Scar-face blushed from ear to ear at their suggestion and stared longingly in the direction of the young woman's lodge.

'I will go and do as you say,' he suddenly replied and marched off defiantly towards the river to deliver his proposal.

He found the young woman stooping by the banks gathering rushes. Respectfully, he approached her, and as she gazed upon him with bright, enticing eyes, he shyly announced his purpose: 'I know that I am poor and shabbily dressed,' he told her, 'but I have seen you refuse rich men clothed in luxurious fur. I am not handsome either, but you have shunned men of the noblest features. Would you consider having me for your husband? I cannot promise you wealth, but I can promise you love, as much of it as you care to receive from me.'

The young girl lowered her eyes and stared silently into the shallow water. After a time she turned towards Scar-face and spoke softly: 'It little matters to me that you are poor. My father is wealthy and would happily provide for us both. I am glad that a man of courage has finally asked me to marry him. But wait! I cannot accept your offer, for the Sun-god has reserved me for himself and has declared that I may never take a mortal husband. Seek him out, if you truly care for me, and beg him to release me from this covenant. If he agrees to do this, ask him to remove that scar from your face and I will treat it as a sign of his blessing.'

Scar-face was sad at heart to hear these words. He had no idea where to begin his search for the Sun-god and felt that a deity so powerful would almost certainly refuse to surrender to him his intended bride. But the young warrior had never before recoiled from a challenge, no matter how difficult it appeared, and the prospect of such a glorious reward seemed well worth risking his life for.

For many days and many nights he journeyed over the sweeping prairies and on through the dense forests, carrying a small sack of food, a spare pair of moccasins, and a simple bow and arrow.

Every day his sack of food grew lighter, but he saved as much as he could, eating wild berries an roots and sometimes killing a small bird. At length, he came across a bear's cave and paused to as directions to the lodge of the Sun-god.

'I have travelled far and wide,' the bear told him, 'but I have never come across the Sun-god lodge. Stripe-face, who lives beyond in that hole, may be able to assist you. Go and ask him fc his help.'

Scar-face moved towards the hole and stooping over it, called aloud to the animal within: ' generous Stripe-face, O wise old badger, can you tell me the way to the lodge of the Sun-god?'

'I am old and frail and never journey very far,' replied the badger. 'I do not know where he live Over there, through the trees, you will find a wolverine. Go and speak with him.'

Scar-face obeyed the badger's instructions, but having called aloud for several minutes, h could find no trace of the wolverine. Wearily, he sat on the ground and began to examine wh remained of his food: 'Pity me, wolverine,' he cried out despondently, 'my moccasins are wor through, my food is almost gone. Take pity on me, or I shall meet my death here.'

'How can I help you,' said a voice, and turning around, Scar-face came face to face wit the wolverine.

'I have travelled a great distance in search of the Sun-god,' he told the animal, 'but no one ca tell me where he lives.'

'I can show you where he lives,' replied the wolverine, 'but first you must rest, for the journe is long. Tomorrow, as soon as you awake, I will set you on the right path.'

Early the next morning, the wolverine took Scar-face to the edge of the forest and pointed ou the trail he should follow. Scar-face set off and walked many miles until he came upon the shore of a vast lake whose waters stretched as far as the eye could see. His spirits fell at this sight, for th great lake presented him with a problem he could not hope to overcome.

'I cannot cross this black and fearful water,' he said to himself, 'and I do not have the strengt to return home to my own people. The end has come and I must give up the fight.'

But help was not so very far away and soon two beautiful white swans advanced towards hir on the water.

'You are not far from the object of your search,' they called to him. 'Lie on our backs and w will carry you to the other side.'

Scar-face rose up and waded into the water. Before long, he had safely reached dry land where h thanked the swans and began following once more the broad trail leading to the home of the Sun-goc

It was now past midday and still the young warrior had not reached his destination. But h refused to lose hope and before long his optimism was rewarded, for he soon stumbled upon a array of beautiful objects lying in the earth which he knew must be from another world. He ha never seen such splendid, golden-tipped arrows, or a war shield so elaborately decorated wit beads and precious stones. He felt tempted to remove these items from the earth, but decide that would be dishonourable of him, and tried to picture instead what the owner of such fin weapons might look like. He had moved a little further onwards when he observed quite th handsomest youth he had ever seen approaching in the distance. The young man wore clothin of the smoothest animal skin and moccasins sewn with brightly coloured feathers.

'I am searching for my bow and arrows, have you seen them?' the beautiful stranger inquired.

'Yes, I have seen them, back there, lying on the ground,' replied Scar-face.

'And you did not wish to seize these items for yourself?' the young man asked.

'No,' answered Scar-face, 'I felt that would be wrong of me. I knew that the owner woul eventually return for them.'

'I admire your honesty, and you have saved me a tiring search,' said the stranger. 'Where is it you come from? You appear to be a very long way from home.'

'I am looking for the Sun-god,' Scar-face told him, 'and I believe I am not very far from his house.'

'You are right,' replied the handsome youth. 'The Sun-god is my father and I am Apisirahts, the Morning Star. Come, I will take you to my father's lodge. He will be pleased to meet a man of such honest character.'

They set off together and shortly afterwards Morning Star pointed to a great lodge, basked in glorious golden light, whose walls were covered with magnificent paintings of medicine animals and other rare and curious creatures. At the entrance to the lodge stood a beautiful woman, Morning Star's mother, Kikomikis, the Moon-goddess. She embraced her son and welcomed the footsore traveller into their home. Then, the great Sun-god made his appearance and he too greeted Scar-face kindly, inviting him to stay for as long as he needed and urging him to accept the guidance and friendship of his son, Apisirahts.

'He will show you the wonderful sights of our kingdom,' the Sun-god told Scar-face. 'Go with him wherever you please, but never hunt near the Great Water, for that is the home of the savage birds who bear talons as long as spears and bills as sharp as arrows. They have carried off many of our finest warriors and would not hesitate to kill you both.'

Scar-face listened carefully to all that was said and during the months which followed, he lived happily among his celestial friends, learning to love the Sun-god as a father and becoming more and more intimate with Apisirahts whom he came to regard as the brother he had always longed for in his earthly home.

One day, he set off with Apisirahts on a hunting excursion, but the two did not follow their usual route and soon they found themselves by the shores of the Great Water.

'We are the finest hunters in the kingdom,' said Morning Star, 'so let us wait no longer, but go and kill these savage birds that put terror into the hearts of our people.'

'Your father has already told us not to pursue them,' replied Scar-face, 'and I have promised to heed his warning.'

'Then I will go and hunt them alone,' said Morning Star and he jumped into the water, waving his spear and shouting his war-cry. Scar-face was forced to follow, for he did not wish to see his brother come to any harm. Soon he had overtaken Apisirahts and began lashing out boldly with his weapon, slaying the monstrous creatures that swooped down upon him, attempting to sink their barbed claws into his flesh. When he had slaughtered every last one of them, he severed their heads and the two young men carried these back towards the Sun-god's lodge, anxious to relate the details of their heroic conquest.

The Moon-goddess was shocked to see the carcasses of the savage birds and scolded her son for his foolishness. But at the same time, she was relieved that Morning Star had escaped unharmed and ran to inform the Sun-god of his safe return, instinctively aware that she had Scar-face to thank for her son's safe delivery.

'I will not forget what you have done for us this day,' the Sun-god told Scar-face. 'If I can ever repay you, you must let me know at once and whatever you request of me shall be brought to you.'

Scar-face hesitated only a moment and then began to explain to the god the reason for his long journey away from home.

'You have never greedily demanded anything of us,' said the god, 'and you have suffered patiently all these months a great burden of anxiety, knowing that I alone have the power to decide your future with a woman you love and admire so earnestly. Your kindness and your patience have earned the young maiden her freedom. Return home now and make her your wife.

'One thing I will ask of you, however, when you return to your home. Build a lodge in honour of me, shape it like the world, round with thick walls, and paint it red so that every day you will be reminded of your visit here. It shall be a great Medicine Lodge and if your wife remains pure and true I will always be there to help you in times of illness or hardship.'

Then the god explained to Scar-face many of the intricacies of Sun-medicine and rubbed a powerful remedy into the skin on his cheek which caused his unsightly scar to disappear instantly. The young warrior was now ready to return home and the Moon-goddess gave him many beautiful gifts to take to his people. The Sun-god pointed to a short route through the Milky Way and soon he had reached the earth, ready to enter his village in triumph.

It was a very hot day and the sun shone brilliantly in the sky, forcing the people to shed their clothing and sit in the shade. Towards midday, when the heat was at its fiercest, the chief of the village peered through the window of his lodge and caught sight of a figure, wrapped from head to foot in thick animal skins, sitting on a butte nearby.

'Who is that strange person sitting in winter clothing? The heat will certainly kill him, for I see that he has no food or water. Go and invite him to sit indoors with us.'

Some of the villages approached the stranger and called to him: 'Our chief is concerned for you. He wishes you to withdraw to the shade of his lodge.'

But they had no sooner spoken these words when the figure arose and flung his outer garments to the ground. The robe he wore underneath was of the most delicate, embroidered cloth and the weapons he carried were of an extraordinary, gleaming metal. Gazing upon the stranger's face, the villagers recognized in it something familiar, and at last, one of them cried out in surprise: 'It is Scar-face, the poor young warrior we thought had been lost forever. But look, the blemish on his face has disappeared.'

All the people rushed forward to examine the young man for themselves.

'Where have you been?' they asked excitedly. 'Who gave you all these beautiful things?'

But the handsome warrior did not answer. His eyes searched instead through the crowd until they fell upon the beautiful face of the maiden he had returned home to marry.

'The trail was long and tortuous,' he told her as he walked boldly forward, 'but I found the lodge of the Sun-god and I won his favour. He has taken away my scar and given me all these things as proof of his consent. Come with me now and be my wife for that is the Sun-god's greatest wish.'

The maiden ran towards him and fell upon his breast, tears of great joy flowing freely down her cheeks. That same day the young couple were married and before long they had raised a great Medicine Lodge to the Sun-god. During the long years ahead, they were never sick or troubled in any way and were blessed with two fine, strong children, a girl and a boy, whom they named Apisirahts and Kikomikis. [*This legend is attributed to the famous Blackfeet tribe of the western territories.*]

The Sun Ensnared And Other Legends

CHOSEN FROM AMONG the ancient folklore of a number of widely scattered tribes, the stories which follow are a very broad selection of some of the most popular and characteristic of native American legends. These are tales which, centuries ago, occupied a prime position in the tribal story-teller's repertoire, tales that would have been recited to the young and old around the lodge-fires and handed down in an oral form from generation to generation, becoming more exaggerated and colourful with each retelling.

The mythology which evolved in this way is a richly varied one, preserving a striking image of a traditional native American culture before the arrival of European settlers in their homeland. Native American man believed emphatically in the existence of supernatural forces, both good and evil, and sought communion with nature as the most fruitful path to self-fulfilment. Animals had the power to turn into people and people into animals; each individual was protected by a patron guardian spirit; every object of creation, animate and inanimate, possessed life and consciousness.

The nine tales retold here illustrate well many of the popular superstitions of this patient and industrious people who lived happily as caretakers of the earth, promoting the unity and continuity of all life.

The Sun Ensnared

AT THE VERY BEGINNING of time, when chaos and darkness reigned and hordes of bloodthirsty animals roamed the earth devouring mankind, there remained only two survivors of the human race. A young brother and sister, who managed to flee from the jaws of the ferocious beasts, took refuge in a secluded part of the forest where they built for themselves a little wooden lodge. Here, they carved out a meagre existence, relying on nature's kindness for their survival. The young girl, who was strong and hardworking, bravely accepted the responsibility of keeping the household together, for her younger brother had never grown beyond the size of an infant and demanded her constant care. Every morning she would go out in search of firewood, taking her brother with her and seating him on a comfortable bed of leaves while she chopped and stacked the logs they needed to keep a warm fire burning. Then, before heading homeward, she would gather the ripest berries from the surrounding hedgerows and both would sit down together to enjoy their first meal of the day.

They had passed many pleasant years in this way before the young girl began to grow anxious for her brother's future, fearing that she might not always be able to care for him. She had never considered it wise in the past to leave him alone while she went about her chores, but now she felt she must take that risk for his own good.

'Little brother,' she said to him, 'I will leave you behind today while I go out to gather wood, but you need not be afraid and I promise to return shortly.'

And saying this, she handed him a bow and several small arrows.

'Hide yourself behind that bush,' she added, 'and soon you will see a snowbird coming to pick worms from the newly cut logs. When the bird appears, try your skill and see if you can shoot it.'

Delighted at the opportunity to prove himself, the young boy sat down excitedly, ready to draw his bow as soon as the bird alighted on the logs. But the first arrow he shot went astray and before he was able to launch a second, the creature had risen again into the air. The little brother felt defeated and discouraged and bowed his head in shame, fully expecting that his sister would mock his failure. As soon as she returned, however, she began to reassure him, offering him encouragement and insisting that he try again on the following day.

Next morning, the little brother crouched down once more behind the bush and waited for the snowbird to appear. He was now more determined than ever to prove his skill and, on this occasion, his arrow shot swiftly through the air, piercing the bird's breast. Seeing his sister approach in the distance, he ran forward to meet her, his face beaming with pride and joy.

'I have killed a fine, large bird,' he announced triumphantly. 'Please will you skin it for me and stretch the skin out to dry in the sunshine. When I have killed more birds, there will be enough skins to make me a fine, long coat.'

'I would be very happy to do this for you,' his sister smiled. 'But what shall I do with the body when I have skinned it?'

The young boy searched for an answer, and as he stood thinking his stomach groaned with hunger. It seemed wasteful to burn such a plump bird and he now began to wonder what it would be like to taste something other than wild berries and greens: 'We have never before eaten flesh,' he said, 'but let us cut the body in two and cook one half of it in a pot over the fire. Then, if the food is good, we can savour the remaining half later.'

His sister agreed that this was a wise decision and prepared for them their very first dish of game which they both ate with great relish that same evening.

The little brother had passed his very first test of manhood and with each passing day he grew more confident of his ability to survive in the wilderness. Soon he had killed ten birds whose skins were sewn into the coat he had been promised. Fiercely proud of his hunting skills, he wore this new garment both day and night and felt himself ready to meet any challenge life might throw at him.

'Are we really all alone in the world, sister?' he asked one day as he paraded up and down the lodge in his bird-skin coat, 'since I cannot believe that this great broad earth with its fine blue sky was created simply for the pair of us.'

'There may be other people living,' answered his sister, 'but they can only be terrible beings, very unlike us. It would be most unwise to go in search of these people, little brother, and you must never be tempted to stray too far from home.'

But his sister's words only added to the young boy's curiosity, and he grew more impatient than ever to slip away quietly and explore the surrounding forests and countryside for himself.

Before the sun had risen on the following morning, he grabbed his bow and arrows and set off enthusiastically in the direction of the open hills. By midday, he had walked a very great distance, but still he hadn't discovered any other human beings. At length, he decided to rest for a while and lay down on the grass in the warmth of the sun's golden rays. He had happened upon a very beautiful spot, and was soon lulled gently to sleep by the tinkling sound of the waters dancing over the pebbles of a nearby stream. He slept for many hours in the heat of the brilliant sunshine and would have remained in this position a good while longer had he not been disturbed by the sensation that something close to him had begun to shrink and shrivel. At first, he thought he had been dreaming, but as he opened his eyes wider and gazed upon his bird-skin coat, he soon realized that it had tightened itself upon his body, so much so that he was scarcely able to breathe.

The young boy stood up in horror and began to examine his seared and singed coat more closely. The garment he had been so proud of was now totally ruined and he flew into a great passion, vowing to take vengeance on the sun for what it had done.

'Do not imagine that you can escape me because you are so high up in the sky,' he shouted angrily. 'What you have done will not go unpunished. I will pay you back before long.' And after he had sworn this oath, he trudged back home wearily to tell his sister of the dreadful misfortune that had befallen his new coat.

The young girl was now more worried than ever for her little brother. Ever since his return, he had fallen into a deep depression, refusing all food and laying down on his side, as still as a corpse, for a full ten days, at the end of which he turned over and lay on his other side for a further ten days. When he eventually arose, he was pale and drawn, but his voice was firm and resolute as he informed his sister that she must make a snare for him with which he intended to catch the sun.

'Find me some material suitable for making a noose,' he told her, but when his sister returned with a piece of dried deer sinew, he shook his head and said it would not do. Racking her brains, she searched again through their belongings, and came forward with a bird skin, left over from the coat she had made.

'This won't do either, 'her brother declared agitatedly, 'the sun has had enough of my bird skins already. Go and find me something else.'

Finally, his sister thought of her own beautiful long hair, and pulling several glossy strands from her head, she began to weave a thick black cord which she handed to her brother.

'This is exactly what I need,' he said delightedly and began to draw it back and forth through his fingers until it grew rigid and strong. Then, having coiled it round his shoulders, he kissed his sister goodbye and set off to catch the sun, just as the last light began to fade in the sky.

Under cover of darkness, the little brother set his trap, fixing the snare on a spot where he knew the sun would first strike the land as it rose above the earth. He waited patiently, offering up many prayers. These were answered as soon as the sun attempted to rise from its sleepy bed, for it became fastened to the ground by the cord and could not ascend any higher. No light twinkled on the horizon and the land remained in deep shadow, deprived of the sun's warm rays.

Fear and panic erupted among the animals who ruled the earth as they awoke to discover a world totally submerged in darkness. They ran about blindly, calling to each other, desperate to find some explanation for what had happened. The most powerful among them immediately formed a council and it was agreed that someone would have to go forward to the edge of the horizon to investigate why the sun had not risen. This was a very dangerous undertaking, since whoever ventured so close to the sun risked severe burning and possible death. Only the dormouse, at that time the largest animal in the world, taller than any mountain, stood up bravely, offering to risk her life so that the others might be saved.

Hurriedly, she made her way to the place where the sun lay captive and quickly spotted the cord pinning it to the ground. Even now, though the dormouse was not yet close enough to begin gnawing the cord, her back began to smoke and the intense heat was almost overwhelming. Still she persevered, chewing the cord with her two front teeth while at the same time her huge bulk was turned into an enormous heap of ashes. When, at last, the sun was freed, it shot up into the sky as dazzling as it had ever been. But the dormouse, now shrunken to become one of the tiniest creatures in the world, fled in terror from its light and from that day forward she became known as Kug-e-been-gwa-kwa, or Blind Woman.

As soon as he discovered that the sun had escaped his snare, the little brother returned home once more to his sister. But he was now no longer anxious to take revenge, since his adventure had brought him greater wisdom and the knowledge that he had not been born to interfere with the ways of nature. For the rest of his life, he devoted himself to hunting, and within a very short time had shot enough snowbirds to make himself a new coat, even finer than the one which had led him to challenge the sun.

The Serpent-men

AFTER OVER A MONTH on the war-path, an eminent band of Sioux warriors accompanied by their chief, were returning home to their encampment in the hills. When they were still quite a long way off, they were suddenly gripped by a savage hunger and decided amongst themselves to scatter in search of wild game to sustain them on the rest of their journey. Some dispersed to the woodlands while others headed for the plains, agreeing that the first to locate an animal should signal to the others to join in the pursuit, for no great warrior could ever enjoy the flesh of a creature he had not helped to track down.

'hey had been on the hunt for some time without having anything to show for their efforts vhen suddenly one of the braves, placing his ear to the ground, declared that he could hear a erd of buffalo approaching in the distance. The prospect of such an enjoyable chase greatly heered the young warriors and they gathered around their chief, anxious to assist in the plan o intercept the animals.

Closer and closer came the sound of the herd. The chief and his men lay very still in the ndergrowth, their arrows poised and ready to shoot as soon as the buffalo came into view. uddenly, their target appeared, but to their absolute horror the group came face to face, not vith the four-legged animals they had been expecting, but with a gigantic snake, its rattle held nenacingly in the air, as large as a man's head. Although almost paralysed with terror, the chief omehow managed to raise his weapon and shot an arrow through the air which lodged itself n the snake's throat. The huge creature immediately keeled over and lay squirming and hissing n the earth for some minutes until all life had passed out of it.

Even though it lay dead, the Sioux warriors did not dare to approach the snake for quite ome time but remained instead at a safe distance, debating what they should do with the arcass. Hunger beckoned once more and for the first time the chief was struck by the thought hat they had, in fact, provided themselves with a perfectly good, if unusual, meal. He called up iis men and ordered them to build a fire and soon they were helping themselves to a delicious tew, as flavoursome as the tenderest buffalo meat. Only one brave refused to partake of the neal. Even his extreme hunger could not conquer his scruples and he remained adamant that ie would not join the others in tasting the body of a great rattling snake.

When the meal was over, the warriors felt both satisfied and drowsy and lay down beside the amp-fire for a brief rest in preparation for their ongoing journey. It was several hours before he chief awoke, but as he slowly opened his eyes, he imagined he must still be dreaming, for ie observed that all around him, his men had turned to snakes. Then he gazed at his own body nd cried out in alarm, for he himself was already half snake, half man. Hastily, he slithered owards his transformed warriors and observed that only one among them had not suffered the ame fate as the others – the young brave who had earlier refused to try any of the food.

The serpent-men and their chief placed themselves under the protection of the young brave, equesting that he gather them together in a large robe and carry them to the summit of the iigh hill overlooking their village. Terrified by the sight of them and fearing he might soon be ttacked, the boy raced all the way to the hill-top and flung the robe beneath some trees. But he snakes broke free quickly and, moving towards him, coiled themselves around his ankles. They had no wish to harm him, they assured him, and soon he discovered that they treated him very kindly, sharing with him their strange wisdom and their many mysterious charms.

'You must return to the village and visit our families for us,' they said to him. 'Tell the people iot to be afraid, and say to our wives and children that we shall visit them in the summer when hey should come out to greet us.'

The young brave readily agreed to deliver this message and set off homewards without urther delay. Tears filled the eyes of every villager as he informed them of the fate of their chief ind the other great warriors of the tribe, but the people were determined not to let grief destroy hem, and took some comfort in the news that they would at least see their loved ones again.

It was a hot summer's morning when the snakes arrived at the little village, striking up a oud, hissing chorus that immediately attracted the attention of every man, woman and child. Abruptly, the villagers gathered together and walked cautiously in the direction of the snakes, aking with them moccasins, leggings, saddles and weapons that once belonged to the missing warriors. Their hearts were filled with fear as they drew closer to the creatures and they stood still at a safe distance, fully prepared to turn on their heels. But the chief, who sat at the centre of the serpent-men, rose up from the earth and spoke to his people reassuringly: 'Do not be afraid of us,' he called to them. 'Do not flee from us, we mean you no harm.'

From that moment, the people grew in confidence and moving boldly forwards, they formed a circle around the serpent-men and chatted to them long into the evening.

In the winter the snakes vanished altogether, but every summer, for as long as the villagers could remember, they returned, wearing a new and brilliant coat. The villagers always treated them with the greatest respect and taught their children to revere the serpent, so that even today if a snake appears in the pathway of a tribal warrior, he will always stop and talk to it offering it some token of his friendship and regard.

The Sacred Bundle

IN A CERTAIN VILLAGE of the Pawnee tribe, there lived a vain young man who always insisted upon wearing the finest clothes and the richest ornaments, no matter how ordinary and uneventful the day that lay ahead. Although unmarried and extremely handsome, he showed no interest in the maidens of the village, but concentrated exclusively on improving his hunting skills, inviting himself to join whatever party happened to be planning an excursion. Among his most prized possessions, he had the down feather of an eagle which he always wore on his head, believing it possessed strange magical properties.

One morning, while he was out hunting, the young man became separated from his companions and, to pass the time, he began following a herd of buffalo for some considerable distance. The animals eventually scattered, with the exception of a young cow, who had become stuck in a mud-hole. Pleased that fate had presented him with such a favourable target, the young man raised his bow and arrow and was about to take aim when he noticed the cow had disappeared, and in its place stood a beautiful young woman. The hunter remained deeply perplexed, for he could not understand where the animal had disappeared to, nor could he comprehend where the maiden had suddenly sprung from.

Warily, he approached the girl, but was surprised to find that she was most friendly towards him and that her presence filled him with a strange delight he had never before experienced. The two sat down and chatted together for many hours, and so enamoured was the hunter by the end of this time that he asked the young maiden to marry him and return with him to his tribe. Graciously she consented, but only on the condition that they set up home in the precise spot where he had discovered her.

To this, the hunter readily agreed and removed from around his neck a string of blue and white beads which he gave to his new wife as a wedding gift.

The two lived very happily together for many months until the evening the young man returned home after a day's hunting to find his lodge surrounded by the marks of many hooves and not a trace of his wife in sight. For weeks he scoured the woodlands and neighbouring countryside, but still he could not discover any sign of her whereabouts. Defeated and dejected, he resolved that he had no option but to return to his own tribe in an attempt to rebuild something of the life he had left behind.

The years passed by, and even though he had a great many offers of marriage, the handsome young man refused to choose for himself a new bride. Try as he might, he could not remove from his mind an image of the beautiful maiden and he mourned her loss with an ever-increasing passion.

One summer's morning, however, as he stood chatting to a number of his friends, he noticed a young boy walking towards him. The child wore around his neck a string of blue and white beads and his clothing revealed that he had come from a distant village.

'Father,' said the boy, 'mother would like to speak to you.'

Annoyed by the interruption, the young hunter replied curtly: 'I am not your father, go away and do not pester me.'

The boy went away, and the hunter's companions began laughing loudly, amused by the fact that the man whose reputation for spurning women was famous throughout the village should ever have been addressed as 'father'. But at length the boy returned only to repeat exactly the same words. He was again dismissed in an angry fashion, but still he did not give up. On the third occasion when he reappeared, some of the men suggested that it might be a good idea for the hunter to follow the child to see what he wanted. This seemed a sensible suggestion and so he set off on the trail of the boy, keen to get to the bottom of the mystery once and for all.

The blue and white beads he had spotted around the boy's neck had begun to agitate the hunter. He could not place them exactly, but then, up ahead, he saw a buffalo cow with her calf running across the prairie and suddenly he began to remember the clearest details of his former life. Taking his bow and arrows, he followed the buffalo whom he now recognized as his wife and child. But the woman, angry that her husband had not come when he had been repeatedly summoned, made sure that the chase was long and wearisome. She dried up every creek they came to, so that the hunter feared he would die of thirst, and frightened off any deer he attempted to pursue, so that he grew pale and weak with hunger. But for the kindness of his child, the young man might well have perished, but the boy took pity on him and managed to obtain food and drink at intervals, enough to sustain the hunter until they arrived at the home of the buffalo.

The leader of the herd, who was father of the buffalo cow, had never approved of his daughter's marriage and it was he who had kidnapped her from the nuptial home many years before. His resentment was still as strong as it had ever been, and as soon as he laid eyes on the young man, he desired only to kill him. But at last, after lengthy deliberations, the great chief agreed that the hunter would be free to live if he survived a number of rigorous trials designed by the elders of the herd.

To begin with, six cows were placed in a row before the hunter, and he was told that his life would be spared if he could identity his wife among them. It was an impossible feat, since each of the cows was almost identical in appearance to the next, but once again the young child intervened to help his father, and secretly indicated to him where his mother stood in the parade. The old bulls were more than surprised at his success, but very irritated at the same time, and insisted that the hunter surrender himself to a second test. This time, they lined up six buffalo calves and asked him to pick out his son from among them. But the hunter felt certain that his son would give him some small clue to his identity, and so, when one of the calves swished its tail high in the air, the hunter pointed to it and successfully located his own son.

The leader of the herd still remained dissatisfied and was determined to rid himself of the intruder even though he had passed all of their tests. Having promised the young man that he would now bring his wife to him, he asked him to sit on the ground until he had returned with his daughter. The hunter had no sooner complied with this request however, when he heard a noise like thunder approaching, and looking up, he saw the entire buffalo herd rushing towards him. One by one the buffalo charged past the spot, coming to a halt only after they felt satisfied that they had trampled him to pieces. But when they turned around to examine their mighty work, they were astonished to find the young hunter sitting calmly in the centre of the circle, a white feather proudly positioned in his hair.

The chief bull, who had never imagined his son-in-law to possess such magical powers, now moved forward respectfully and lifted him off the ground. He had won back his buffalo-wife and child, the chief told him, but there remained one final thing for him to do before he could be welcomed into the buffalo camp. He must go off and gather together a selection of gifts from his tribe and bring them back to the buffalo herd as a mark of his respect.

The young man set off with his wife and son towards his village making a list in his mind of the fine things he intended to gather together to impress the buffalo chief – corn, maize, the finest fruit and the most succulent deer-flesh. But when he arrived at his home, he was shocked to discover that there was no food to be had, for a great famine had descended upon the people causing many to die of starvation. The buffalo-wife, who was quick to notice the distress her husband suffered, quietly withdrew from his company, and it was not long before she reappeared, pulling from under her robe a great slab of buffalo meat which she presented to the starving people. Every day for a whole month she repeated this act of kindness so that the people soon recovered their strength and began to smile anew. As a way of thanking the young man and his wife, they gathered together the very best of their possessions to present to the buffalo chief and sent the family on its way once more, back to the great camp.

But having returned home, the young son could not rest, knowing his father's people were constantly in want of food. At length, he went and spoke with his grandfather, the chief of the herd, and soon they had worked out a solution to the problem.

Transforming himself into a buffalo, the young boy led the whole herd back towards the village, accompanied by his mother and father in human shape. When they had reached their destination, the father, as his son had commanded him, addressed the people with the following words:

'From this day forward you may hunt the buffalo for food, but you must not kill my son, who is among them, for it is he who generously provides you with the yellow calf.

'The time will come when you will be directed to kill the yellow calf and sacrifice it to the god Tirawa. Then you must tan its hide and form a bundle of its skin, placing within it an ear of corn and other things sacred to your tribe.

'Every year, you must look among the herd for another yellow calf. This too, you should sacrifice and keep a piece of its flesh to add to the bundle. Then, whenever food is scarce and famine threatens, you must gather in council around your sacred bundle and pray to Tirawa who will answer your need, and send another yellow calf to you.'

All this was done as the young boy had instructed, and before long food became plentiful and the father rose to become a chief, greatly respected by the people. He lived for many long and happy years among the villagers with his buffalo-wife and when he died the sacred bundle was long preserved and guarded religiously by the tribe who always used it in times of need as a magic charm to bring the buffalo.

The Origin of the Three Races

HAVING RESOLVED to create a new species, the Great Spirit took himself off to a place of solitude and began the labour that was to last him several days. He toiled long and hard and at length he produced a being, different from anything else he had ever before created. The figure, whose skin was black as the night, enthralled the Great Spirit, and at first he was deeply satisfied with his work. But soon, he felt that a single example of the new species was not enough and he decided to embark upon a second attempt, hopeful that the result would bring him equal pleasure.

On the next occasion, his creation proved to be a being with a red skin colour. Placing him alongside his brother, the Great Spirit smiled. He was even more pleased with the fruits of his labour, but once again, after only a short time, he became anxious to try his hand a third time.

'This will be my last effort,' he told himself, and he wandered off to complete his final creation. The being he produced this time had a white skin colour, far lighter than the other two. It proved to be the Great Spirit's favourite, and so utterly satisfied him that he spent several minutes turning it over in the palm of his hand before releasing it to the company of its two elder brothers.

Calling the three men before him one day soon afterwards, the Great Spirit pointed to three boxes lying in the earth. The first box contained books, papers and quills; the second was filled with bows and arrows, tomahawks and spears; the third held a collection of spades, axes, hoes and hammers. The Great Spirit then addressed his children with these words:

'My sons, what you see before you are the means by which you shall live. Each of you must choose one of the boxes for your future use.' And saying this, he beckoned to his favourite, the white man, instructing him to make the first choice.

The youngest brother passed by the working-tools, the axes, hoes and hammers, without paying them any attention whatsoever and moved towards the weapons of war and hunting. Here, he hesitated, lifting a number of them from the box so that he might examine them more closely. The red-skinned brother trembled, for with his whole heart he longed to take possession of these instruments and feared that he was close to losing them. But the white man deliberated only a moment longer and then passed swiftly on to the box of books and writing tools, signalling to the Great Spirit that he had finally reached his decision.

The red-skinned brother came next, and he sprang forward and immediately seized upon the bows and arrows, the tomahawks and spears, delighted with himself that he was now the owner of so valuable a collection.

Last of all, the black man stepped forward, the Great Spirit's first offspring. Having no choice left, he lifted the remaining box filled with tools of the land and humbly carried it all the way back to his dwelling.

It was in this manner, according to ancient Seminole legend, that the three races came into being.

The First Appearance of Man

A GREAT MANY YEARS AGO the Navajos, Pueblos and the white man all lived beneath the earth's surface as one people at the place known as Cerra Naztarny, on the Rio San Juan. The underground world they lived in had no light, and in those days they survived entirely on the flesh of whatever animal they managed to capture in the darkness. But in spite of every difficulty, their world was a peaceful one. The people shared the same outlook and the same language and even the same dwelling, a large and comfortable cave, where each man lived on equal terms with his neighbour.

Among the Navajos there were two dumb men who were skilled in a great many things, but especially in the art of playing the Indian flute. One evening, the elder of the two, having reached a particularly rousing point in his performance, stood up with his flute, tilting it high in the air. Quite by accident, he cracked the instrument against the roof of the cave, producing a peculiarly hollow sound which excited his curiosity. Determined to discover what lay above their heads, the dumb man called to a raccoon nearby, requesting his assistance. The raccoon ascended to the roof of the cave using the flute as a ladder and began digging furiously. But after a reasonable length of time, when he became convinced he was not making any progress, the raccoon came back down the ladder allowing the moth-worm to ascend in his place.

It was several hours before the moth-worm succeeded in boring through the roof, but his perseverance was rewarded when at last a tiny stream of light filtered into the cave. Wriggling through the opening he had made, he soon found himself upon a mountain, surrounded by water. He was more than pleased at the sight, and began throwing up a little mound on which to rest. As he sat there, looking around him more attentively, he noticed four large white swans, placed at the four cardinal points, each carrying an arrow under either wing.

The swan from the north was the first to spot the little visitor, and as soon as he did so he rushed upon him, thrusting both of his arrows through the body of the moth-worm. When he saw that the arrows had drawn blood, the swan withdrew each of them and examined them closely.

'He is of my race,' he then called aloud to his three brothers, and they, in turn, came forward and subjected the moth-worm to the same peculiar ceremony. After the ordeal was gone through, each of the swans resumed its former station and began tunnelling in the earth until it had created a great ditch into which the water swiftly flowed, leaving behind a mass of soft, sticky mud.

The worm carefully descended to the dumb man and related to him all that had happened. The raccoon was then sent through the hole in the roof to verify the tiny creature's story, but as soon as he leaped to the ground, he became stuck in the mud almost to his thighs, staining his paws and legs so that the black marks have remained to this day. After a struggle, the disgruntled raccoon managed to free himself and made his way back down to the cave where the dumb man called upon the wind to come forth and blow upon the mud until it had dried out.

Once this task had been completed, a throng of men and animals gathered at the opening in the roof, anxious to explore the new world for themselves. The larger beasts poured from the cave in a steady stream and scattered directly to the plains. The birds and smaller animals headed straightaway for the woodlands, while the people, the last to emerge, immediately separated into different groups, each with its own new language. The Navajos, who were the first to appear, commenced a large painting in the sand. The Pueblos cut their hair and began building houses. The white man set off towards the point where the sun rises, and was not heard from again for a great many years. [*A legend told by the Navajos, a tribe of Athapascan stock, who believed that the first men and women came from under the surface of the earth.*]

Osseo, Son of Evening Star

THERE ONCE LIVED a tribal chief who had ten daughters, all of whom turned out to be extremely beautiful young women. None was more captivating, however, than the very youngest daughter, the chief's favourite, who was named Oweenee. Unlike her sisters, Oweenee was both spirited and independent, and nothing delighted her more than to do what was least expected of her. She loved, for instance, to roam the open countryside while the rain pelted down upon her, or to run barefoot through the camp in winter, paying little or no heed to the raw, biting cold.

Her elder sisters had all found husbands for themselves and now they were keen that Oweenee should follow their example and choose for herself a man who might succeed in taming her wild and unpredictable nature. Oweenee had rejected many suitors in the past and seemed deaf to all proposals, until the day she set eyes on Osseo, a feeble old man, scarcely able to walk, whose offer of marriage had been refused by every other single woman of her tribe. Oweenee cared only for the fact that Osseo was a kind, devout man who remained obedient in all things to the Great Spirit. It did not trouble her that his walking stick appeared to be his only material possession, or that he was decrepit and his body almost bent in two. Graciously, she decided to accept him as her husband, resolving to care for him as best she could until the day when death would force them to separate.

The announcement that the couple would soon marry was greeted by a chorus of laughter. The nine remaining sisters, each of whom considered their own husbands fine and handsome young men, made a special mockery of Osseo's walking stick and referred derisively to the old man as 'the great timber-chief'.

'He may not carry an elaborately carved staff of precious wood,' Oweenee challenged them, 'but if his simple stick supports him as he walks, then it is of more value to me than all the forests of the north.'

And she never failed to show her husband the greatest respect, which he always returned, teaching her that real love was above all circumstance of physical beauty.

The time was drawing near for the great annual feast in honour of Evening Star. A large party would soon gather at a chosen lodge for celebrations that were set to continue into the small hours. It was an occasion demanding the stamina of youth, but Oweenee would not be put off by the jibes and sneers of the other guests who maintained that her husband would not even survive the short journey to the festivities. Hand in hand, the two set off together, pausing as often as necessary for Osseo to catch his breath.

Presently, they passed a large hollow log where Osseo began muttering to himself, his eyes raised towards the sky. One of the elder sisters overheard the words, 'pity me, my father' and, turning to her husband, she declared furiously:

'Look at him, the silly old fool, praying to the air. It would be a blessing if he should fall down now and break his puny neck. Then, at least, my sister would have the chance to marry a younger, more deserving man.'

She had scarcely finished her tirade before Osseo gave a loud, piercing cry and as he fell trembling to the earth, he was transformed into a beautiful youth with dark, shining hair and a flawless complexion. He stood up regally, proud and ready to greet his beautiful young wife, but to his horror he discovered that their fate had been reversed and that Oweenee stood old and shrivelled before him, clinging to the simple wooden staff he no longer needed.

It was now Osseo's turn to bestow on his wife the love and devotion she had so generously shown him. Carefully, he guided her along the path towards the feast, gazing fondly into her eyes, not noticing the thousands of creases that surrounded them.

When at length they arrived at the lodge, the celebrations were well under way and they took up their places at the end of the table, filling the last two remaining seats. Although the meat was of the finest quality and the fruit of a most delicious fragrance, Osseo would not be persuaded to sample anything that was placed in front of him. He had fallen into a sombre mood, his heart torn apart with sorrow, and as he looked towards his aged wife, he could not prevent his eyes brimming with tears.

Suddenly, in the distance, the sound of a strange, ethereal voice was heard on the air, becoming louder and plainer until its words were clearly distinguishable.

'My son,' the voice spoke gently, 'I have come to call you away from this life filled with pain and sorrow. I see that you have suffered cruelty and abuse, but you will be a victim no more, for the Power of Evil, which condemned you to this wretched earthly domain has now been overcome.

'Ascend, my son, ascend into the skies, know that it is your father, Evening Star, who beckons you. Bring those you love with you and partake of the feast I have prepared for you in the stars.

'Doubt not and delay not. Eat the food that has been put before you, for it is enchanted and will bring you the gift of immortality. No longer will your kettles be moulded from the earth, no longer will your bowls be made of wood. They shall be made of silver and shine like fire. Your wife and those around you shall take on the radiance of stars and become transformed into magnificent birds of the air. They shall dance and never work, they shall sing and never cry. Come, it is time for you to return to happiness and to your celestial reward.'

The lodge began to shake violently as it rose up into the air. Peering through the windows, Osseo observed that they were already high above the tree-tops, moving swiftly in the direction of the clouds. His parents and brothers, his friends and relatives, even Oweenee's sisters who had treated him so unkindly, now soared through the windows into the night air, their wings extended in ecstatic flight, their bodies covered in the most glorious plumage. Oweenee rose and stood by her husband's side, no longer a fragile old woman, but more beautiful than ever before, dressed in a robe of green silk, with silver feathers plaited into her long, silken tresses.

Evening Star waited patiently to greet his son and beamed brightly to see the couple approach. Everything that would make it easier for them to settle into their new home was speedily provided. Then, when he was certain that their every wish had been attended to, the father called for his son to visit him and began conversing with him earnestly.

'My son,' said the old man, 'hang that cage of birds which you have brought with you at the door for protection and I will tell you why you have been sent for.'

Osseo obeyed his father's command and took a seat next to him in the lodge.

'The Power of Evil which transformed you and your beautiful wife into frail and withered reatures lives in the lodge to the left of mine. He is known as the Small Star, a wicked spirit, vho has always felt envious of our family because of our greater power. I have removed the urse he placed on you, but I cannot guarantee that he will not try to harm you again. A single ay of his light serves as his bow and arrow, and all of you must be careful not to let the light f his beams fall on you while you are here with me, for those beams contain the source of is enchantment.'

Osseo and Oweenee remained faithful to Evening Star's wishes and lived a happy and eaceful life, enriched by the birth of their son who was the very likeness of his father. The oy, always hungry for knowledge and adventure, quickly mastered every celestial skill his randfather taught him, but he wished, more than anything, to learn the art of using a bow nd arrow, for he had heard that it was the favourite pursuit of all men on the earth below. Osseo agreed that his son was now old enough to begin hunting and presented him with he weapon he had himself used as a youth. Then, he began releasing into the air some of he birds from the cage hanging by the lodge, instructing his son to practise his shooting on them.

He little imagined that the child would be successful, but the young boy became quite expert after only a few attempts, and in no time at all one of the birds plummeted to the ground. But when he went to retrieve his catch, to his amazement the boy discovered that it had changed to a beautiful woman, his young aunt, who lay with an arrow he did not recognize as his own protruding from her breast.

As soon as her blood fell upon the surface of the pure and spotless Evening Star, the charm which had allowed Osseo and his family to remain there in safety was immediately dissolved. The boy suddenly found himself sinking through the lower clouds until he landed upon a large, rocky island. Looking upwards, he saw all his aunts and uncles following him in the shape of birds, and in mid-air he caught sight of a silver lodge descending gracefully to the earth in which his mother and father were seated.

The lodge came to rest on the steepest cliff of the island and as soon as each of them touched the soil they resumed their natural shape. They could never now return to the skies, but Evening Star still watched over them and, wishing to help them preserve their immortality, he reduced them all to the size of fairies.

From that day forward they lived quite happily among the rocks, never failing on a summer's evening to join hands and dance upon the summit of the cliff as a mark of respect to Evening Star. Their shimmering silver lodge can always be seen on a starry night when the moon is full and its beams touch the horizon. Fishermen who climb the high cliffs at night say they have heard very clearly the merry voices of Osseo, Oweenee and the other little dancers, and because of this they have christened the island Mish-in-e-nok-inokong, land of Little Spirits.

Opeche, the Robin-redbreast

IADILLA WAS THE ONLY SON of an old man and his wife living in the northern woodlands. The couple had watched the boy grow up to be a fine and strong young warrior and they were fiercely proud of his every achievement. The father, in particular, was extremely ambitious for his son and made no secret of the fact that he fully expected

him to rise to the position of chief one day. To this end, he carefully supervised Iadilla's every activity, determined that he should surpass all others in whatever he set out to do.

It was of the utmost importance to the old man that Iadilla obtain a very powerful guardian spirit when the time arrived for him to undergo the customary ceremony. He insisted that his son prepare himself with great solemnity and gave him the most meticulous instructions for his conduct, urging him, above all, to acquit himself with a manly spirit no matter how relentless the suffering ahead.

On the chosen morning, the old man led his son deep into the forest towards the sweating lodge. Having remained within the lodge for as long as his father deemed necessary, the boy reappeared and plunged into the cold water of the river. This process was repeated twice more until his father was satisfied that his purification had been completed. Then he led Iadilla to another, more isolated lodge expressly prepared for him, and ordered him to lie down upon a straw mat woven by his mother. Soon afterwards, Iadilla heard the sound of his father's retreating footsteps and he lay in silence with his face covered, patiently awaiting the approach of the spirit with the power to decide his good or evil fortune in life.

Every morning his father came to the door of the little lodge and offered his son gentle words of encouragement, never failing to remind him of the honour and renown that would attend him should he reach the end of the twelve days without food or water. For over a week Iadilla managed to fulfil his father's expectations without uttering a single word of complaint, but as nightfall approached on the eighth day, his strength began to fail rapidly, so that when he awoke on the following morning he was unable to move his limbs.

As soon as he could hear his father coming towards the lodge, Iadilla broke his silence and cried out weakly:

'Father, I do not have enough strength to endure my fast any longer. My dreams are not good and the spirits who visit me seem to oppose your wishes. Give me permission to break my fast now and I promise I will continue it another time.'

But the old man would not entertain such a thought and replied rather impatiently: 'My son, have you any idea what you are asking? You have only three days left and you must strive a little longer if only for the sake of your ageing parents.'

Overcome by guilt, Iadilla covered his face again and lay perfectly still, neither moving nor speaking until the eleventh day. But as soon as his father appeared in the morning at the door of the lodge, he could not prevent himself repeating the same request.

'Only a very short time now remains,' the old man answered. 'At dawn tomorrow I will visit you carrying a meal prepared with my own hands. Please do not bring shame upon the family just when you are so close to your goal.'

'I will not shame you, father,' replied Iadilla and he lay his head back wearily, his breathing scarcely audible in the still, dark silence of the lodge.

Before the sun had even risen on the twelfth morning, the old man leaped out of bed excitedly and set off to greet his son, carrying with him the meal he had prepared the evening before. Drawing near to the little lodge, he was surprised to hear voices coming from within and stooped to peer through a small crack in one of the walls. He was astonished to discover his son sitting up, not only talking to himself, but in the act of painting his breast and shoulders a rich vermilion colour.

'My father was set to destroy me,' Iadilla muttered to himself. 'Although I was obedient to him, he pushed me beyond my strength and would not listen to my requests. Now he will have to respect my wishes, for my guardian spirit has been kind and just and has given me the shape I desire. At last, I am free. It is time for me to go.'

Hearing these words, the old man broke into the lodge and began pleading through his tears: 'Ningwis! Ningwis! My son, my son, please do not leave me.'

But even as he spoke, Iadilla was transformed into a bird with a beautiful red breast that flew to the top of the lodge and addressed the old man with these words:

'Do not mourn the change you see in me, father. I could not fulfil your expectations of me as a warrior, but in this form I will always seek to cheer you with my song and strive to lift your spirits whenever you are low. I have been released from the cares and

sufferings of human life. The fields and mountains will furnish me with food. The clean, bright air will serve as my path. I shall be happier in my present shape than I ever was before as a man.'

Then, stretching himself on his toes, Iadilla spread his wings and took his first, glorious flight, disappearing high above the feathered clouds. But he did not forget his promise and soon returned to build his nest in the highest branch of the tree overlooking his father's lodge. Every morning, as soon as the old man awoke, he was heard to call aloud, 'Opeche, Opeche', and his call was answered by the sweetest song, as the red-breasted bird sang to him, soothing his troubled spirit and filling his heart with a lasting joy.

White Feather and the Six Giants

THERE WAS ONCE an old man living in the depths of the great forest with his young grandson whom he had taken charge of when the boy was still an infant. The child had never encountered any other human being apart from his grandfather. He had no parents, brothers or sisters, no friends or relatives, and although he frequently questioned the old man on the subject of his family, he could not get even the smallest scrap of information from him.

His guardian insisted upon this silence for the boy's own protection, for he felt certain that he would attempt to avenge the death of his brothers and sisters before long. They had perished at the hands of six great giants after the villagers had challenged the giants to a race they believed they would win, casually offering their children as the forfeit. All were slain by the victorious giants except for the old man's grandson who, by some miracle, managed to escape through the trees to the safety of the isolated lodge.

Here the boy, who was named Chacopee, grew up relatively content. He learned to fish and he learned to hunt, beginning with smaller animals such as rabbits, until he became so highly accomplished with his bow and arrow that he could bring down deer and larger game almost with his eyes closed. Of course, as he developed into a more expert hunter, he longed to roam even further and his curiosity to know what lay beyond the tiny lodge increased with every passing day.

One day he wandered to the edge of the prairie where he happened upon several mounds of ashes, encircled by lodge-poles left standing in the earth. Returning home, he described to his grandfather what he had seen and asked him to explain the presence of these things. But the old man grew agitated and responded that the boy had surely lost his senses, for nothing of the kind existed except in his imagination.

Another day, however, Chacopee had followed a different path through the forest when suddenly he heard a voice calling to him: 'You do not wear the white feather yet, but the hour is not far off when you will prove yourself worthy of it. Go home now and sleep. Soon you will dream of a pipe, a smoking-sack, and a large white feather. When you awake you will find these items by your side.'

Chacopee turned in the direction of the voice and came face to face with a man, an encounter in itself quite shocking for a boy who had only ever seen his grandfather, but made even worse by the man's very peculiar body which was carved of wood from the breast downwards. 'Put the white feather on your head,' the stranger continued, 'and you will become a great hunter, a great warrior and a great leader. If you need proof of my words, smoke the pipe and soon you will see the smoke turn into pigeons.'

After this, the stranger informed Chacopee of his real identity and told him the story of how his family had perished at the hands of the giants, urging him to avenge the wrongs of his kindred.

'Take this enchanted vine,' he told him, 'you will need it when your enemy challenges you to a race. No giant can see it for it is invisible. You must throw it over your opponent's head while he runs. It will entangle him and bring him crashing to the ground.'

Chacopee listened keenly to all of this advice and then returned homeward, extremely bewildered by the meeting. Everything happened just as the Man of Wood had predicted, however. As soon as he lay down the boy fell into a deep sleep and when he awoke he was surrounded by the promised gifts. The old grandfather was greatly surprised to see a flock of pigeons emerge from his own lodge, followed by his grandson wearing on his head a white feather, but then he remembered the old tribal prophecy, and knowing that the day would soon come when he would be forced to relinquish control of Chacopee, he sat down and began to weep inconsolably.

Next morning the young boy set off in search of his enemies. The giants, he had learned, lived in a very tall lodge at the centre of the woods, but this lodge was surrounded by little spirits who carried news to the giants of Chacopee's arrival. The monstrous creatures hastened out of doors and spotted the young boy approaching in the distance.

'Here comes the little man we are supposed to call White Feather,' they mocked among themselves. 'Haven't we been warned that he is destined to achieve great things. Let us welcome him as a great hero and encourage him to attempt some foolhardy trial of strength.'

But Chacopee paid no heed to the giants' fine speeches, and without awaiting an invitation, marched fearlessly into their lodge where he challenged every one of them to a race. It was eventually agreed that the youngest among the giants would be the first to run against him and without wasting any more time, they set off across the fields in search of an appropriate starting-point.

They had soon mapped out a course which extended from an old, rugged tree as far as the edge of the horizon and back again. A war-club of iron was placed at the foot of the tree, to be used by the winner on his defeated opponent. As soon as they had taken their places, a gong was sounded and each of the runners shot off with as much speed as he could muster. Chacopee knew that his little legs would not carry him to victory over such a great distance and so he waited for the giant to overtake him and cast his vine out in front of him, tugging on it sharply as it wrapped itself around the giant's ankles. The hideous creature fell to the ground and when he attempted to rise again, Chacopee lifted the war-club high in the air, bringing it down on the giant's great skull over and over again until he was certain that the giant lay dead.

The next morning, Chacopee ran against a second giant and killed him in exactly the same manner. For five mornings he managed to conquer his foes in this way, but then, on the sixth morning, as he set off confidently to meet the last of the giants, he was met by his old counsellor, the Man of Wood, who informed him that his last opponent was far more cunning than any of the others.

'He is out to deceive you, White Feather,' he told the boy. 'Before you even reach his lodge you will encounter a very beautiful young woman. Do not pay her any attention, for she is there for your destruction. As soon as you catch her eye, you must transform yourself into an elk. Lower your head and feed on the grass and do not look at the maiden again.'

White Feather thanked his kind adviser and walked on towards the lodge, mindful of the advice he had received. Before long, as had been foretold, he met the most beautiful woman. Quickly he transformed himself into an elk and began rooting in the earth, his eyes lowered as he had been instructed. But the woman only moved closer to him and began weeping softly.

'I have travelled a very long way to meet you,' she sobbed. 'Your great achievements have made you famous throughout the land, and I wanted, more than anything, to offer myself as your bride.'

Filled with compassion and remorse, White Feather raised his eyes towards the woman and wished aloud that he might resume his natural shape. At once, he became a man again and sat down under a tree with the beautiful maiden, wrapping her in his arms to comfort her. Soon her tears and sighs had abated and he lay his head in her lap and fell into a peaceful slumber.

After she had listened awhile to his deep breathing and had satisfied herself that White Feather was not likely to wake up, the beautiful woman transformed herself into the sixth giant and, taking up an axe, struck the young man on his back, changing him into a dog. The white plume immediately fell from his hair unto the earth, but as soon as he noticed it, the giant stooped and picked it up, putting it in his own hair. Now stripped of his powers, Chacopee gave a pitiful whimper, and followed wretchedly in the path of the giant towards the neighbouring village.

There were living in this particular village two sisters, the daughters of a chief, who had been bitter rivals for many years. Having heard the prophecy concerning the wearer of the white feather, each had made up her mind to have him for her husband and each was constantly on the look-out from her lodge door, hoping that White Feather would soon appear. When the day finally arrived and the sisters spotted a stranger wearing a white plume heading towards their home, they were filled with excitement. The eldest sister, who was the more ambitious of the two, dressed herself up in all her finery and ran ahead to meet the giant, inviting him into her lodge. The youngest, who did not possess any flamboyant clothes, remained dressed in her simple shawl and moccasins and invited the poor dog into her home where she prepared for him a good supper and a neat bed. The giant, pleased with the attention lavished upon him by the eldest sister, soon agreed to marry her and together they mocked the younger sister for having landed herself a dishevelled old dog as a life-long companion.

It was not long, however, before the villagers began to demand a demonstration of the skill and courage they had come to associate with the famous name of White Feather. The giant, who readily supposed that whoever wore the white plume would possess all of its virtues, boasted of the fact that he could bring back enough food in one day to supply the entire village and set off with the dog across the plains towards the forest.

Immediately, he began shouting and waving his great hands in the air, calling to the animals to come and be killed. But they fled in terror at the sight of him and he failed to catch a single one of them. The dog, on the other hand, stepped into a nearby river and drew out a stone which instantly changed into a fine, fat beaver. The giant stood staring in amazement, but as soon as he had recovered himself, he waded into the water and successfully performed the same feat. He was delighted with himself and having tied the animal to his belt, he called for the dog to accompany him back home.

When he had been seated a short time, savouring in advance the impact of his great achievement on the villagers, he called to his wife to come and examine his hunting girdle. Obediently, she knelt on the floor, but when she lifted his shirt to reveal his belt, she discovered only a massive stone secured to it. The giant stood up furiously and ordered his wife to keep her silence until he had gone out again and returned with the food he had promised.

Next morning, he took the dog along with him as before and watched its every movement closely. This time, the dog plucked a charred branch from a burned-out tree and threw it to the ground where it instantly transformed itself into a bear. The giant did exactly as the dog had done, and managed to produce a bear in precisely the same fashion. He carried the creature homewards to his wife, but again, as soon as he had called for her to inspect it, the bear disappeared and all the woman found was a black stick tied to her husband's belt.

And so it continued on. Everything the giant attempted failed miserably, while everything the dog undertook was a great success. Every day the youngest sister had more and more reason to be proud of the poor dog she had adopted, while every day the eldest sister received yet another reminder that the man she had married did not possess any of the virtues associated with the white feather. But in spite of this, the eldest sister insisted on keeping up appearances and departed the following morning for her father's lodge to inform him what a skilful hunter her new husband was.

As soon as she had set off, the dog began making signs to the younger sister that he wished to be sweated in the traditional manner of the Indians. Accordingly, his mistress built a little lodge just large enough for him to creep into and placed within it a number of heated stones on which she poured water until a thick vapour rose up into the air. When she imagined the dog had been completely sweated, she stooped down to unblock the entrance and was astonished to find, in place of the dog, a handsome young warrior lying on the earth. But she could not get a word out of him and realizing that he was quite dumb, she decided to lead him to the village where she hoped one of the medicine-people might be able to help restore his voice.

As soon as the chief heard his youngest daughter's story, he assembled all the old and wise heads of the tribe for a general meeting. He was now convinced, he told them, that there was some kind of magic at work and was keener than ever to discover the truth about the giant and the young man. And so he called for a pipe to be brought forward and began passing it among the circle. One after another, the elders puffed on the pipe, handing it around until eventually it was the young man's turn. But the handsome warrior signalled politely that it should be given to the giant first. The giant took the pipe and began smoking, swelling his chest and shaking the white feather on his head. But nothing came of this exhibition except a great cloud of smoke. Then the handsome young warrior took hold of the pipe and made a sign to them to put the white feather upon his head. As he drew the smoke deep into his lungs, his voice suddenly returned, and as he breathed out, the smoke became a flock of white and blue pigeons.

From that moment, the villagers turned on the giant and after the young man had recounted his strange adventures, indignation rose to a fever pitch. The chief then ordered that the giant should be transformed into a dog and stoned to death by the people. The villagers were more than delighted to carry out this instruction and danced in a circle around the dead body, greatly relieved that the six giants would trouble them no longer.

The handsome young warrior now gave them all the proof they needed of his right to wear the white feather. Calling for a buffalo robe to be brought to him, he cut it into thin strips and scattered them on the prairie in every direction. Next day he summoned the braves of the tribe to accompany him on a hunt. When they arrived at the edge of the prairie they found it covered with a great herd of buffalo. The people hunted as many of these buffalo as they pleased and afterwards a great feast was held to celebrate White Feather's triumph over the giant.

The Broken Promise

AT THE HEART of a solitary forest, a hunter had built for himself and his family a small wooden lodge, having decided once and for all to withdraw from the company of his tribe. Their deceit and cruelty had caused him to turn from them and he had chosen the loneliest spot he could find, adamant that his three young children should never fall under their poisonous influence.

The years passed by and the family remained happy and peaceful in their new home until, one day, the father fell gravely ill, and took to his couch with little or no hope of a recovery. Day and night the family lovingly attended the sick man, exhausting all of their simple medicines on him, yet never failing to whisper words of encouragement in his ear. But at last, they resigned themselves to the fact that he would not regain his health and gathered around him in the dimly lit room, awaiting the departure of his spirit.

As death drew near, the sick man called for the skin door of the lodge to be thrown open so that he might witness the sun sinking in the evening sky one last time. Then he motioned to his eldest son to raise him up in the bed and with these words he addressed his grieving family:

'I must leave you very shortly,' he said, 'but I am satisfied that I have been a good father and that I have provided you with ample food and protected you from the storms and cold of our harsh climate.

'You, my partner in life,' he continued, casting his eyes upon his wife, 'you, I can leave behind with an easy conscience, for you do not have much longer here and will soon join me in the Isle of the Blessed. But oh, my children who have only just set off on life's great journey, you have every wickedness before you from which I can no longer offer you protection. The unkindness and ingratitude of men caused me to abandon my tribe, and while we have lived here in peace and harmony, those very men have caused the forests to echo with the cries of war.

'My wish for you is that you remain pure at heart and never follow the evil example of such men. I will go tranquilly to my rest only if I am certain that you will always cherish one other.

'My eldest son, my eldest daughter, promise to obey my dying command and never forsake your younger brother, for he is most in need of your care.'

The sick man then closed his eyes and spoke no more, and after a few minutes' silence, when his family came to his bedside and called him by name, they found that his spirit did not answer, for it was already well on its way to the Land of Souls. After eight months, the mother sadly passed away also, but in her last moments she was careful to to remind the two eldest children of the promise they had made to their father. During the winter that followed her death, they could not have been more attentive to the delicate younger child, but as soon as the winter had passed, the older brother became restless and struggled increasingly to conceal his uneasy mood. Before long, he had reached a decision to break his promise to his father and to search out the village of his father's tribe.

'I am lonely and wretched here,' he told his sister one morning. 'Must I forever pretend that we are the only people in the world and sacrifice my youth to this miserable existence? No! I am determined to seek out the society of our fellow-men and nothing you can say will prevent me leaving.'

'My brother,' replied his sister, 'I do not blame you for harbouring these desires, but we have made a solemn promise to cherish each other always and to protect the youngest of our family from all harm. Neither pleasure nor pain should separate us, for if we follow our own inclinations, he will surely become a victim of our neglect.'

The young man made no reply to this and for some weeks afterwards continued on with his work as normal, every day exerting himself in the hunt to supply the wants of the family. But then, one evening, he failed to return home and when she searched his corner of the lodge, his sister found that all of his possessions had vanished. Turning aside from her little brother, she began to weep silently, knowing in her heart that he might never return and that, from now on, she would carry the burden of responsibility her father had placed upon them.

Five moons had waned, during which the young girl tenderly watched over her younger brother, feeding him, clothing him, and building a great fire every day to protect them both from the bitter winds. But soon the solitude of her life began to weary her unspeakably. She had nobody to converse with save the birds and beasts about her, nothing ever to look forward to and she felt at the bottom of her heart that she was entirely alone. Her younger brother was the only obstacle preventing her enjoying the companionship of others and there were times when she wished him dead so that she might escape and have a new life of her own.

At last, when she felt her patience had been entirely exhausted, she gathered into the lodge a large store of food and firewood and announced to her little brother: 'My child, I must go in search of our older brother, but I have provided for you until my return. Do not leave the lodge until I reappear and you will remain safe.'

Then she embraced the young boy warmly and set off with her bundle in search of the village of her father's tribe. Soon she had arrived at her destination and found her brother nicely settled with a wife of his own and two healthy sons. She had been prepared to chastize him severely, but she discovered quite quickly that there was much about the village that appealed to her own starved curiosity. Within a few weeks she had accepted a proposal of marriage from one of the most handsome warriors of the tribe and abandoned all thought of ever returning to the solitary lodge in the forest.

The poor younger brother had fully expected his sister to return, but the months passed by and soon he discovered he had eaten all of the food she had provided him with. Forced to trudge through the woods in search of food, he began picking whatever berries he could find and digging up roots with his pale, slender hands. These satisfied his hunger as long as the weather remained mild, but winter arrived briskly and now the berries were blighted by frost or hidden from view by a thick carpet of snow.

With each new day he was obliged to wander farther and farther from the lodge, sometimes spending the night in the clefts and hollows of old trees, glad of the opportunity to scavenge any scraps of food the wolves might leave for him.

At first fearful of these animals, in time he grew so desperate for food that he would sit waiting a few feet from their circle watching while they devoured their meat, patiently awaiting his share. The wolves themselves became accustomed to the sight of him, and seeming to understand his plight, developed a habit of leaving something behind for him to eat. In this way the little boy lived on through the savage winter, saved from starvation by the generosity of the wild beasts of the woods.

When spring had come and the ice sheets on the Great Lake began melting slowly, the boy followed the wolf pack to the pebbled shore. It so happened that on the same day he arrived, the older brother, whom he had almost entirely forgotten about, was fishing on the lake in his canoe and, hearing the cry of a child, stood up and listened with all his attention, wondering how any human creature could survive in such a bleak and hostile environment. Again, he heard the cry, but this time it sounded very familiar and so he hastened to the shore to confront its source. Here he came face to face with his little brother who had begun singing a mournful little song:

Nesia, Nesia, shug wuh, gushuh!
Ne mien gun-iew! Ne mien gun-iew!
My brother, my brother,
I am almost a wolf!
I am almost a wolf!

The wailing voice touched him deeply and as the song drew to a close, the young boy howled long and loudly, exactly like a wolf. Approaching closer to the spot, the elder brother was startled to see that the little fellow had indeed half changed into a wolf.

'My brother, my brother, come to me,' he pleaded, but the boy fled, leaving behind paw-prints in the sand while he continued to sing:

Ne mien gun-iew! Ne mien gun-iew!
I am almost a wolf.

The more eagerly the older brother called, the faster his brother fled from him and the more rapidly the change continued, until with a prolonged, mournful howl, his whole body was transformed.

The elder brother, sick with remorse, and hearing again the voice of his dying father, continued to cry out in anguish: 'My brother! my brother!'

But the young boy leaped upon a bank and looking back, his eyes filled with a deep reproach, exclaimed: 'I am a wolf!'

Then he bounded swiftly away into the depths of the forest and was never heard of again.

Norse Myths

Introduction

We shall tread once more that well-known plain
Of Ida, and among the grass shall find
The golden dice with which we play'd of yore;
And that will bring to mind the former life
And pastime of the Gods, the wise discourse
Of Odin, the delights of other days.
Matthew Arnold, Balder Dead

THE VIKINGS (VIKINGAR) were men of the north, the inhabitants of Scandinavia who were best known in Europe for their raids throughout the ninth and eleventh centuries. Across history, Vikings have been portrayed as blood-thirsty, passionate and violent savages who looted and plundered England and the coasts of Europe for their own gain. Indeed, the English monk Alcuin wrote, 'Never before has such a terror appeared in Britain as we have now suffered from a pagan race.' The Vikings were a fierce people, and as well as having an intense desire for wealth, power and adventure, they were encouraged by King Harold I to look for foreign conquests. As 'Norsemen' their impact was particularly profound in Northern France, where they began to sail up French rivers, looting and burning the cities of Rouen and Paris, among others, destroying what navigation and commerce they could find. Their ships were spectacular, the finest ever built, and they were able to travel great distances – in the end their quest for adventure and the overpopulation and internal problems in Scandinavia drove them as far as North America and Greenland, where they raided and then settled, showing little regard for existing cultures and religions.

It was these activities which gave the Vikings their reputation, one which has shifted little since the tenth century. Even in 1911, G. K. Chesterton, wrote:

Their souls were drifting as the sea,
And all good towns and lands
They only saw with heavy eyes,
And broke with heavy hands.

Their gods were sadder than the sea
Gods of a wandering will,
Who cried for blood like beasts at night,
Sadly from hill to hill.

These heavy-handed, great men spoke a strange language and their brutality and lack of regard for Christianity in Europe gave them a reputation as being men of little culture, and certainly men of no religion. Very few Vikings were able to write, and most religious, spiritual and cultural documents were transmitted by word of mouth, or through their art. Because they carried with them little that explained their origins and their beliefs, and because they did not have an obvious pantheon and system of belief and scripture, it was many years before their new countries developed any real understanding of the Viking religions and mythology.

There was no one religion common to all the Scandinavian and Teutonic peoples, but descriptions from Icelandic texts indicate that most had similar polytheistic features. In early times two groups of gods were worshipped, the Aesir and the Vanir; later they were joined to form a single pantheon of twelve principal deities, headed by Woden (Odin) and including Tiw (Tyr), Thor (Donar), Balder, Frey, Freyia, and Frigga. Their home was Asgard. There, in the palace Valhalla, Odin and his warrior maidens (the Valkyries) gave banquets to dead heroes. Unlike the gods of most religions, the ancient Nordic deities were subject to Fate (represented by the Norns), and tradition held that they were doomed to eventual destruction by the forces of evil in the form of giants and demons, led by Loki. After a savage battle at Ragnarok, the universe would end in a great fire. But from the burning wreckage of the universe would spring a new cosmos, and a new generation of gods and humans would live together harmoniously.

There was a host of rituals, most of which have not survived the passage of time, but magic rites and prayer played an important part in most people's daily lives. Christianity was established quite late in Scandinavia. Denmark moved towards this religion in the tenth century, with Norway converting slightly later and Sweden some one hundred years later than that. The Vikings formally adopted Christianity in about 1000, although their invading parties may have become Christians earlier than that. The advent of Christianity naturally changed the ethos and ritual of the Vikings, but it is important to understand that the Viking mythology was not intrinsic to their religion, as it is in many other cultures, and it was perfectly possible to believe in both Frey, who could encourage fertility in their land, as it was to believe in Christ, who had little to do with their daily lives. It has been said that the Vikings were easily converted to Christianity, for their own gods were not infallible, and could be influenced by fate and events beyond their control.

The invincibility of Christ must have seemed very attractive to a people who struggled to put their faith in something or someone that had an ability to overcome the dramatic events that occurred in the North. Some believe that Christian myth may have been incorporated in Norse myth, and because there is little record of early myth, it is difficult to know what the Vikings really believed.

The term mythology means different things in every culture. Broadly speaking mythology is the collective myths of a people and scientific study of these myths, which can be described as traditional stories occurring in a timeless past and involving supernatural elements. In ancient cultures, myths were used to express and explain such serious concerns as the creation of the universe and of humanity, the evolution of society, and the cycle of agricultural fertility. Legends, by contrast with myths, are thought to contain some actual historical elements. Many theories have been advanced to explain myths. Theologians have tended to view myths as foreshadowings or corruptions of Scripture. Sir James Frazer in his *The Golden Bough* (1890) proposed that all myths were originally connected with the idea of fertility in nature, with the birth, death, and resurrection of vegetation as a constantly recurring motif.

But in reality, it is likely that myths were woven around historical fact, real people and events and places that truly existed. In this form they are legends, exaggerated, surely, distorted to make them tellable, more exciting, but created in order to present the moral message of an event which has had some significance in the lives of those touched by it. There were folktales, too, which are tales of enchantment, deceit and trickery, in which gods and goddesses live alongside talking animals, giants, dwarfs and trolls. Folktales are based on magic, and used to explain phenomenon which may otherwise, to a mind uneducated in science, be frightening, and inexplicable. Folktales provide explanations for the wind, the trees, the weather, for echoes, ghosts and seasons. The mythology of the Vikings was never a direct representation of their eligion, and the origin of many beliefs was dismissed in the fabric of their legends. Indeed, n Northern Mythology, Kauffmann writes, 'His eye was fixed on the mountains till the snowy eaks assumed human features, and the giant of the rock or the ice descended with heavy read; or he would gaze at the splendour of the spring, or of the summer fields, till Freyia with he gleaming necklace stepped forth, or Sif with the flowing lock of gold'.

There seems to be an almost wry acceptance that their mythology has been created by hem, and that the events within it have not occurred and been recorded. H. A. Guerber n The Norsemen writes, 'The most distinctive traits of this mythology are a peculiar grim umour, to be found in the religion of no other place, and a dark thread of tragedy which uns throughout the whole woof, and these characteristics, touching both extremes, are writ arge over English literature.'

Some of their myths reflected an uncertain religiosity. There are myths of philosophy, ddressing matters which concern all of us. They relate to the conception of the world, to death nd to living, to gods and to the state of godliness. They may deal with matters relating to a pecific tribe, culture or people, making sense of rituals, superstitions and routines. The Vikings ived in a vast, and extreme land, where Nature conspired to quench them in eternal darkness, r burn them with everlasting day; it is not surprising that their mythology took as its central heme the endless struggle of man against Nature. The landscape was at times a frozen, barren vasteland, glittering in the darkness as sharp mountains thrust their way towards a midnight un, great icy waves crashing icebergs against the violent coastline. And then it was alive, plains nd hills bursting with greenery waving in the summer skies that became intense with heat. 'he contradictions in the climate, in the geography of Scandinavia are reflected in the dramatic nythology of her people. Gwyn Jones, in *The History of the Vikings*, wrote: 'The long, flat, vind-swept wastes of Jultand, the axe-resisting, isolative forests of central Sweden, the sundered 3othnian archipelago, the mountain wildernesses of the Keel, the hostile frozen tundra of the orth, and perhaps most of all the fjords, islands, and skerried waterways of the west Norwegian oast – when we add to these distance, cold and the intimidating darkness of winter, when we dd, too, the drams of power and delusions of grandeur which built and rebuilt and shattered nd reshattered the northern realms from long before the Viking age ... we see that Scandinavia ould never be the nursery of weaklings.' As such, the land and the people share a tragic and rand persona; it is easy to understand why the Vikings believed that the earth was the product f fire and ice, and why gods could be fallible, and at the mercy of others. It is even easier to nderstand why their sense of drama is so refined, and yet its implementation so rugged.

The myths and legends of the Vikings have come down to us from three major sources, lthough what we have is incomplete, and bare of theology, which must have existed in artnership with their mythological beliefs. Jones writes, ' ... [the religion] accounted for the reation of the world, and charted the doom to come. It provided mysteries as transcendent as)din hanging nine nights on a windswept tree as a sacrifice to himself, and objects of veneration s crude as the embalmed penis of a horse. Like other religions it rejoiced the devout with idden truth, and contented mere conformers with its sacral and convivial occasions. There was god for those who lived by wisdom and statecraft, war and plunder, trade and seafaring, or the and's increase. Poet, rune-maker, blacksmith, leech, rye-grower, cattle-breeder, king, brewer, ach had a god with whom he felt secure; warlocks, men on skis, barren women, brides, all had deity to turn to. Best of all the powers, attributes, and functions of the gods overlapped so enerously that Odin's man, Thor's man, Frey's man and the like could expect to be looked after n every aspect of life and death.'

The first main source of Viking myths and legends is the *Poetic Edda*, a work in old Icelandic that constitutes the most valuable collection in old Norse literature. Also called the *'Elder' Edda*, it is made up of thirty-four mythological and heroic lays, of various lengths. It was written in the second half of the thirteenth century, after the Vikings had accepted Christianity, and therefore the mythology may be influenced by other cultures and beliefs. Although the *Poetic Edda* was written after Christianity, it is not as easy to ascertain when the poems that make it up were actually composed. Some are clearly pre Viking, and others relate to the period after Scandinavian civilization moved into the Middle Ages. As the name suggests, the works are all poetic, stanzaic in nature, but other than that there is very little linking the various works that comprise it, and many of the poems included in it are obscure. Guerber writes, 'The religious beliefs of the north are not mirrored with any exactitude in the *Elder Edda*. Indeed, only a travesty of the faith of our ancestors has been preserved in Norse literature. The early poet loved allegory and his imagination rioted among the conceptions of his fertile muse ... We are told nothing as to sacrificial and religious rites, and all else is omitted which does not pride material for artistic treatment ... regarded as a precious relic of the beginning of Northern poetry rather than a representation of the religious beliefs of the Scandinavians, and these literary fragments bear many signs of the transitions stage wherein the confusion of the old and new faiths is easily apparent.'

Many of the poems are narrative, many taking the form of a parable or proverb. There are also works surrounding rite, mysticism and magic, describing chants and spells and healers.

The second great collection of mythological material is the *Prose Edda*, probably written around 1222 by Snorri Sturluson, who was a wealthy farmer in the service of the Norwegian king Hakon Hakonarson. He was also a poet, and a widely educated man, and the Prose Edda forms a treatise on the art of Icelandic poetry and a compendium of Viking mythology. There are four main sections to the book, but it is the last, the 'Hattatal, or 'List of Verse Forms' which has provided such a wealth of information on the mythology, for it explains the mythological allusion common in traditional verse, to help poets who wish to recreate it get the facts straight.

R. I. Page, in *Norse Myths*, writes: ' ... Snorri too was a Christian, and could hardly tell such tales as though they were truth, particularly tales that related adventures of the pagan gods. So he distanced himself from the subject in a number of ways. He composed a prologue full of early anthropological observation: how in primitive times men realized there was order in the universe, and deduced it must have a rule; how the most splendid of early communities was Troy in Turkey, with twelve kingdoms each with a prince of superhuman qualities, and one high king above all ...'

Snorri often quotes from the *Poetic Edda*, and in many cases expands ideas and philosophies introduced but never carried to term in the first book. The major failing of the work is the fact that Snorri never manages to place the mythology of the Vikings in any kind of real religious context, by explaining theology or worship. His accounts are very much tainted by his Christianity, and he often takes an orthodox Christian position, identifying the pagan gods and heroes deified by their pagan and therefore ignorant followers.

But the work is lively, witty and full of splendid details; much of the information takes the form of an inventive narrative, in which a chieftain called Odin leads a conquering army into Sweden, where he is welcomed by a king called Gylfi. Gylfi has a series of questions for the Aesir, as the conquerors were called, and these questions and answers are recounted in the Prose Edda, in the form of a fascinating account of lore, folktale and legend.

The third major source for Viking mythology is the work of the court poets or 'skalds'. Skaldic verse comprise a confusion of contemporary events interspersed with works from the Viking ages into the Middle Ages and the advent of Christianity. Again, because these works were written after the conversion to Christianity, there have undoubtedly been alterations to the fabric of the myths and it is unlikely that the transmission of the oral tradition has been entirely accurate. But there are many mythological tales which form the subject of the skalds' verse, and there are several notable writers; however, the poetry was normally very elaborate and often technically pretentious, making it difficult to follow in parts.

To this day, little is understood about the myth and religion of the North – partly because it was not successfully transcribed, and partly because their patterns of worship were not directed by conventional piety and are therefore more difficult to understand. Theirs was a traditionally pagan culture, religion and ideology, one in which the seasons, the land, the patterns of daily life were bound up in a simple pantheon of gods and goddesses who were in charge of each aspect of it. Most gods were interrelated, most could help with the never-ending battle against the elements and the brutal geography. In the end their mythology vanished into little more than literature, and as Eric Sharpe wrote, '... the old myths failed because they lacked consistency and seriousness. Odin was treacherous, Christ was not. Thor could be hoodwinked. Christ could not ... the old religion had no centre, either in ritual or organizational terms. It was a conglomeration of separate elements and functions, which remain to challenge and sometimes puzzle us. But there is often a certain nostalgia among us ... for the memory of men and women who could, for a time at least, shoulder fate aside and worship Thor, because they believed in their own strength.'

How much is genuine Viking legend is difficult to ascertain; what is certain is that the sagas and myths which exist are dramatic, exciting, darkly humorous and passionate. If the role of myth is to entertain, it has undoubtedly succeeded, whatever its source.

The Creation Myths

It was in distant times
When nothing was;
Neither sand nor sea
Nor chill waves;
No earth at all;
Nor the high heavens;
The great void only
And growth nowhere.
Matthew Arnold, Balder Dead

THE DRAMATIC CONTRADICTIONS of the Viking landscape and the constant battle with the elements; the spectacular backdrop of perpetual darkness and then perpetual light provide a mythology of profound contrasts. The creation myths are no exception. It was believed that cold was malevolent, evil, and that heat was good and light; when the two meet – when fire meets ice – there comes into existence a cosmos from which the universe can be created. The myths are filled with frost and fire; they are allusive and incomplete; the images and events are impossible and unlinked. But the creation myths of the Viking people are supremely beautiful, and explain, in a way that only a people in a wilderness could conceive, how we came to be.

The Creation of the Universe

Under the armpit grew,
'Tis said of Hrim-thurs,
A girl and boy together;
Foot with foot begat,
Of that wise Jotun,
A six-headed son.
Benjamin Thorpe, Saemund

IN THE BEGINNING, before there was anything at all, there was a nothingness that stretched as far as there was space. There was no sand, nor sea, no waves nor earth nor heavens. And that space was a void that called to be filled, for its emptiness echoed vith a deep and frozen silence. So it was that a land sprung up within that silence, and it ook the place of half the universe. It was a land called Filheim, or land of fog, and where ended sprung another land, where the air burned and blazed. This land was called Iuspell. Where the regions met lay a great and profound void, called Ginnungagap, and ere a peaceful river flowed, softly spreading into the frosty depths of the void where froze, layer upon layer, until it formed a fundament. And it was here the heat from Iuspell licked at the cold of Filheim until the energy they created spawned the great rost-giant Ymir. Ymir was the greatest and the first of all frost-giants, and his part in the reation of the universe led the frost-giants to believe that they should reign supreme on vhat he had made.

'ilheim had existed for many ages, long before our own earth was created. In the centre was mighty fountain and it was called Vergelmir, and from that great fountain all the rivers of the niverse bubbled and stormed. There was another fountain called Elivagar (although some believe hat it is the same fountain with a different name), and from this bubbled up a poisonous mass, vhich hardened into black ice. Elivagar is the beginning of evil, for goodness can never be black.

Muspell burned with eternal light and her heat was guarded by the flame giant, Surtr, who ashed at the air with his great sabre, filling it with glittering sparks of pure heat. Surtr was the iercest of the fire giants who would one day make Muspell their home. The word Muspell neans 'home of the destroyers of the world' and that description is both frightening and ccurate because the fire giants were the most terrifying there were.

On the other side of the slowly filling chasm, Filheim lay in perpetual darkness, bathed in nists which circled and spun until all was masked. Here, between these stark contrasts, Ymir grew, the personification of the frozen ocean, the product of chaos. Fire and ice met here, and it vas these profound contrasts that created a phenomenon like no other, and this was life itself. n the chasm another form was created by the frozen river, where the sparks of the Surtr's sabre aused the ice to drip, and to thaw, and then, when they rested, allowed it to freeze once again. This form was Audhumla, a cow who became known as the nourisher. Her udders were swollen vith rich, pure milk, and Ymir drank greedily from the four rivers which formed from them.

Audhumla was a vast creature, spreading across the space where the fire met the ice. Her legs vere columns, and they held up the corners of space.

Audhumla, the cow, also needed sustenance, and so she licked at the rime-stones which ha formed from the crusted ice, and from these stones she drew salt from the depths of the eartl Audhumla licked continuously, and soon there appeared, under her thirsty tongue, the forr of a god. On the first day there appeared hair, and on the second, a head. On the third day th whole god was freed from the ice and he stepped forth as Buri, also called the Producer. Bu was beautiful. He had taken the golden flames of the fire, which gave him a warm, gilded glov and from the frost and ice he had drawn a purity, a freshness that could never be matched.

While Audhumla licked, Ymir slept, sated by the warmth of her milk. Under his arms th perspiration formed a son and a daughter, and his feet produced a giant called Thrudgemir, a evil frost-giant with six heads who went on to bear his own son, the giant Bergelmir. These wer the first of the race of frost-giants.

Buri himself had produced a son, called Borr, which is another word for 'born', and as Bu and Borr became aware of the giants, an eternal battle was begun – one which is to this da waged on all parts of earth and heaven.

For giants represent evil in its many forms, and gods represent all that is good, and on tha fateful day the fundamental conflict between them began – a cosmic battle which would creat the world as we know it.

Buri and Borr fought against the giants, but by the close of each day a stalemate existec And so it was that Borr married the giantess Bestla, who was the daughter of Bolthorn, or th thorn of evil. Bestla was to give him three fine, strong sons: Odin, Vili and Ve and with th combined forces of these brave boys, Borr was able to destroy the great Ymir. As they slaye him, a tremendous flood burst forth from his body, covering the earth and all the evil being who inhabited it with his rich red blood.

The Creation of the Earth

Of Ymir's flesh
Was earth created,
Of his blood the sea,
Of his bones the hills,
Of his hair trees and plants,
Of his skull the heavens,
And of his brows
The gentle powers
Formed Midgard for the sons of men;
But of his brain
The heavy clouds are
All created.

R. B. Anderson

YMIR'S BODY was carried by Odin and his brothers to Ginnungagap, where it wa placed in the centre. His flesh became the earth, and his skeleton the rocky crag which dipped and soared. From the soil sprang dwarfs, spontaneously, and they

would soon be put to work. Ymir's teeth and shards of broken bones became the rocks and pits covering the earth and his blood was cleared to become the seas and waters that flowed across the land. The three men worked hard on the body of Ymir; his vast size meant that even a day's work would alter the corpse only slightly.

Ymir's skull became the sky and at each cardinal point of the compass was placed a dwarf whose supreme job it was to support it. These dwarfs were Nordri, Sudri, Austri and Westri and it was from these brave and sturdy dwarfs that the terms North, South, East and West were born. Ymir's hair created trees and bushes.

The brow of Ymir became walls which would protect the gods from all evil creatures, and in the very centre of these brows was Midgard, or 'middle garden', where humans could live safely.

Now almost all of the giants had fallen with the death of Ymir, drowned by his surging blood – all, that is, except Bergelmir, who escaped in a boat with his wife and sought asylum at the edge of the world. Here he created a new world, Jotunheim, or the home of the giants, where he set about the creation of a whole new breed of giants who would carry on his evil deeds.

Odin and his brothers had not yet completed their work. As the earth took on its present form, they slaved at Ymir's corpse to create greater and finer things. Ymir's brains were thrust into the skies to become clouds, and in order to light this new world, they secured the sparks from Surtr's sabre and dotted them among the clouds. The finest sparks were put to one side and they studded the heavenly vault with them; they became like glittering stars in the darkness. The stars were given positions; some were told to pass forward, and then back again in the heavens. This provided seasons, which were duly recorded.

The brightest of the remaining stars were joined together to become the sun and the moon, and they were sent out into the darkness in gleaming gold chariots. The chariots were drawn by Arvakr (the early waker) and Alsvin (the rapid goer), two magnificent white horses under whom were placed balls of cool air which had been trapped in great skins. A shield was placed before the sun so that her rays would not harm the milky hides of the steeds as they travelled into the darkness.

Although the moon and the sun had now been created, and they were sent out on their chariots, there was still no distinction between day and night, and that is a story of its own.

Night and Day

Forth from the east, up the ascent of heaven.
Day drove his courser with the shining mane.
Matthew Arnold, Balder Dead

THE CHARIOTS WERE READY, and the steeds were bursting at their harnesses to tend to the prestigious task of setting night and day in place. But who would guide them? The horses would need leadership of some sort, and so it was decided that the beautiful children of the giant Mundilfari – Mani (the moon) and Sol (the sun) would be given the direction of the steeds. And at once, they were launched into the heavens.

Next, Nott (night), who was daughter of one of the giants, Norvi, was provided with a rich black chariot which was drawn by a lustrous stallion called Hrim-faxi (frost mane). From his mane, the frost and dew were sent down to the earth in glimmering baubles. Nott was a goddess, and she had produced three children, each with a different father. From Naglfari, she had a son named Aud; Annar, her second husband, gave her Jord (earth), and with her third husband, the god Dellinger, a son was born and he was called Dag (day).

Dag was the most radiant of her children, and his beauty caused all who saw him to bend down in tears of rapture. He was given his own great chariot, drawn by a perfect white horse called Skin-faxi (shining mane), and as they travelled, wondrous beams of light shot out in every direction, brightening every dark corner of the world and providing much happiness to all.

Many believe that the chariots flew so quickly, and continued their journey round and round the world because they were pursued by wolves: Skoll (repulsion) and Hati (hatred). These evil wolves sought a way to create eternal darkness and like the perpetual battle of good and evil, there could be no end to their chase.

Mani brought along in his chariot Hiuki, who represented the waxing moon, and Bil, who was the waning moon. And so it was that Sun, Moon, Day and Night were in place, with Evening, Midnight, Morning, Forenoon, Noon and Afternoon sent to accompany them. Summer and Winter were rulers of all seasons: Summer was a popular and warm god, a descendant of Svasud. Winter, was an enemy for he represented all that contrasted with Summer, including the icy winds which blew cold and unhappiness over the earth. It was believed that the great frost-giant Hraesvelgr sat on the extreme north of the heavens and that he sent the frozen winds across the land, blighting all with their blasts of icy death.

The First Humans

There in the Temple, carved in wood,
The image of great Odin stood.
Henry Wadsworth Longfellow, Saga of King Olaf

ODIN, ALLFATHER, was king of all gods, and he travelled across the newly created earth with his brothers Vili and Ve. Vili was now known as Hoenir, and Ve had become Lothur, or Loki. One morning, the three brothers walked together on the shores of the ocean, looking around with pride at the new world around them. Ymir's body had been well distributed, and his blood now ran clear and pure as the ocean, with the fresh new air sparkling above it all. The winds blew padded clouds across a perfect blue sky, and there was happiness all around. But, and there was no mistaking it, there was silence.

The brothers looked at one another, and then looked out across the crisp sands. There lay on the shore two pieces of driftwood which had been flung onto the coast from the sea, and as their eyes caught sight of them, each brother shared the same thought. They raced towards the wood, and Hoenir stood over the first piece, so that his shadow lay across it and the wood appeared at once to have arms and legs. Loki did the same with the second piece of wood, but he moved rather more animatedly, so that the wood appeared to dance in the sunlight. And then Odin bent down and blew a great divine breath across the first piece of wood. There in front of them, the bark, the water-soaked edges of the log began to peel away, and there the body of a pale, naked woman appeared. She lay there, still and not breathing. Odin moved over to the next piece of wood, and he blew once more. Again, the wood curled back to reveal the body of a naked man. He lay as still as the woman.

Odin had given the gift of life to the man and woman, and they had become entities with a soul and a mind. It was now time for Loki to offer his own gifts. He stood at once over the woman and as he bent over her, he transferred the blush of youth, the power of comprehension, and the five senses of touch, smell, sight, hearing and taste. He was rewarded when the woman rose then and smiled unquestioningly at the three gods. She looked around in wonder, and then down at the lifeless body by her side. And Loki leaned across the body of man this time, and gave to him blood, which began to run through his veins. He too received the gifts of understanding, and of the five senses, and he was able to join woman as she stood on the beach.

Hoenir stepped forward then, and offered to both man and woman the power of speech. At this, the two human beings turned and walked together into the new world, their hands held tightly together.

'Stop,' said Odin, with great authority.

Turning, the two humans looked at him and nodded. 'You are Ash,' said Odin to the man, which represented the tree from which he had been created. 'And you are Elm,' he said to the woman. Then Odin leaned over and draped his cloak around the shoulders of the first human woman and sent her on her way, safe in the care of man, who would continue in that role until the end of time – or so the Vikings said.

Asgard

From the hall of Heaven he rose away
To Lidskialf, and sate upon his throne,
The mount, from whence his eye surveys the world.
And far from Heaven he turned his shining orbs
To look on Midgard, and the earth, and men.
Matthew Arnold, Balder Dead

ASGARD IS ANOTHER WORD for 'enclosure of the gods'. It was a place of great peace, ruled by Odin and built by Odin and his sons on Yggdrasill, above the clouds, and centred over Midgard. Each of the palaces of Asgard was built for pleasure, and only things which were perfect in every way could become part of this wondrous land. The first palace built was Gladsheim, or Joyous home, and it was created to house the twelve thrones of the principal deities. Everything was cast from gold, and it shone in the heavens like the sun itself. A second palace was built for the goddesses, and it was called Vingof, or Friendly Floor. Here, too, everything was made from gold, which is the reason why Asgard's heyday became known as the golden years.

As Asgard was conceived, and built, a council was held, and the rules were set down for gods and goddesses alike. It was decreed at this time that there would be no blood shed within the limits of the realm, and that harmony would reign forever. A forge was built, and all of the weapons and tools required for the construction of the magnificent palaces were made there. The gods held their council at the foot of Yggdrasill, and in order to travel there, a bridge was erected – the rainbow bridge, or Bifrost as it became known. The bridge arched over Midgard, on either side of Filheim, and its colours were so spectacular that one could only gaze in awe upon seeing them for the first time.

The centre of Asgard displayed the plan of Idavale, with hills that dipped and soared with life. Here the great palaces were set in lush green grasses. One was Breibalik, or Broad Gleaming, and there was Glitnir, in which all was made gold and silver. There were palaces clustered in gems, polished and shimmering in the light of the new heavens. And that beauty of Asgard was reflected by the beauteous inhabitants – whose minds and spirits were pure and true. Asgard was the home of all the Aesir, and the setting for most of the legends told here. But there was another family of gods – and they were called the Vanir.

For many years the Vanir lived in their own land, Vanaheim, but the time came when a dispute arose between the two families of gods, and the Aesir waged war against the Vanir. In time, they learned that unity was the only way to move forward, and they put aside their differences and drew strength from their combined forces. In order to ratify their treaty, each side took hostages. So it was that Niord came to dwell in Asgard with Frey and Freyia, and Hoenir went to live in Vanaheim, the ultimate sacrifice by one of the brothers of creation.

Yggdrasill

I know that I hung
On a wind-rocked tree
Nine whole nights,
With a spear wounded,
And to Odin offered
Myself to myself;
On that tree
Of which no one knows
From what root it springs.

Benjamin Thorpe, Odin's Rune Song

YGGDRASILL IS THE WORLD ASH, a tree that has been there for all time, and will always be there. Its branches overhang all nine worlds, and they are linked by the great tree. The roots of the Yggdrasill are tended by the Norns, three powerful sisters who are also called the fates. The roots are nourished by three wells. One root reaches into Asgard, the domain of the gods, and feeds from the well of Wyrd, which is the name of the eldest Norn. The second root leads to Jotunheim, the land of the frost-giants. The well at the end of this root is called Mimir, who was once a god. Only the head of Mimir has survived the creation of the world, and it drinks daily from the well and is kept

alive by the magic herbs which are scattered in it. Mimir represents great wisdom, and even Odin chose to visit him there to find answers to the most profound questions that troubled his people.

The third root winds its way to Filheim, and the well here is the scum-filled fountain of black water called Vergelmir. Here, the root of the tree is poisoned, gnawed upon, and from it rises the scent of death and dying. In Vergelmir is a great winged dragon called Nithog, and he sits at the base of the root and inflicts damage that would have caused another tree to wither away.

And the magnificent tree stands, as it has always stood, as the foundation of each world, and a point of communication between all. The name Yggdrasill has many evil connotations, and translated it means 'Steed of Ygg' or, 'Steed of Odin'. There once was a time when Odin longed to know the secret of runes – the symbols which became writing, as we know it. The understanding of runes was a cherished one, and in order to acquire it, a terrible sacrifice must be undergone by the learner. Odin had longed for many years to have that knowledge, and the day came when he was prepared to make his sacrifice. Odin was told that he must hang himself by the neck from the bough of the World Ash, and he must remain there, swinging in the frozen anarchy of the dark winds, for nine days. The story has been told that Odin, the bravest of the gods, the father of all, screamed with such terror and pain that the gods held their hands to their ears for each of those nine wretched days.

But Odin's strength of character carried him through the tortuous ordeal and so it was that he was at once the master of the magic runes, the only bearer of the secret along the length of the great tree. His knowledge was shared amongst his friends and his wisdom became legendary.

Odin was at the helm of the nine worlds, which stretched from Asgard in the topmost branches, to the world of Hel down below, at the lowest root. In between were the worlds of the Vanir, called Vanaheim, Midgard, where humans lived, as well as the worlds of the light elves, the dark elves, the dwarfs, the frost and hill giants and, at last, the fire-giants of Muspell. The most magnificent, and the world we hear the most about was Asgard, and it is here that our story begins.

Legends of Odin and Asgard

Sokvabek Hight the fourth dwelling;
Over it flow the cool billows;
Glad drink there Odin and Saga
Every day from golden cups.
R. B. Anderson, Norse Mythology

IN THE GOLDEN AGE OF ASGARD, Odin reigned at the head of the nine worlds of Yggdrasill. He was a fair man, well-liked by all, and his kingdom of Asgard was a magnificent place, where time stood still and youth and the pleasures of nature abounded. Odin was also called Allfather, for he was the father of all men and gods. He reigned high on his throne, overlooking each of the worlds, and when the impulse struck him, Odin disguised himself and went among the gods and people of the other worlds, seeking to understand their activities. Odin appeared in many forms, but he was often recognized for he had just one eye, and that eye could see all. Odin had many adventures, and before the war of the gods, before Odin began to prepare for Ragnarok, Asgard was a setting for many of them, as you will see. All of the gods have their stories, and some of the most exciting are recorded here.

Odin and Frigga in Asgard

Easily to be known is,
By those who to Odin come,
The mansion by its aspect.
Its roof with spears is laid,
Its hall with shields is decked,
With corselets are its benches strewed.
Benjamin Thorpe, Lay of Grimnir

ODIN WAS THE SON OF BOR, and the brother of Vili and Ve. He was the most supreme god of the Northern races and he brought great wisdom to his place at the helm of all gods. He was called Allfather, for all gods were said to have descended from him, and his esteemed seat was Asgard itself. He held a throne there, one in an exalted and prestigious position, and it served as a fine watchtower from which he could look over men on earth, and the other gods in Asgard as they went about their daily business.

Odin was a tall, mighty warrior. While not having the brawn of many excellent men, he had wisdom which counted for much more. On his shoulders he carried two ravens, Hugin (thought) and Munin (Memory), and they perched there, as he sat on his throne, and recounted to him the activities in the great wide world. Hugin and Munin were Odin's eyes and his ears when he was in Asgard and he depended on their bright eyes and alert ears for news of everything that transpired down below. In his hand Odin carried a great spear, Gungnir, which had been forged by dwarves, and which was so sacred that it could never be broken. On his finger Odin wore a ring, Draupnir, which represented fertility and fruitfulness and which was more valuable to him, and to his land, than anything in any other god's possession. At the foot of Odin's throne sat two wolves or hunting hounds, Geri and Freki, and these animals were sacred. If one happened upon them while hunting, success was assured.

Odin belonged to a mysterious region, somewhere between life and death. He was more subtle and more dangerous than any of the other gods, and his name in some dialects means 'wind', for he could be both forceful and gentle, and then elusive or absent. On the battlefield, Odin would dress as an old man – indeed, Odin had many disguises, for when things changed in Asgard, and became bad, he had reason to travel on the earth to uncover many secrets – attended by ravens, wolves and the Valkyries, who were the 'choosers of the slain', the maidens who took the souls of fallen warriors to Valhalla.

Valhalla was Odin's palace at Asgard, and its grandeur was breathtaking. Valhalla means 'hall of the chosen slain', and it had five hundred great wooden doors, which were wide enough to allow eight hundred warriors to pass, breastplate to breastplate. The walls were made of glittering spears, polished until they gleamed like silver, and the roof was a sea of golden shields which shone like the sun itself. In Odin's great hall were huge banqueting tables, where the Einheriar, or warriors favoured by Odin, were served. The tables were laden with the finest horns of mead, and platters of roast boar. Like everything else in Asgard, Valhalla was enchanted. Even the boar was divine and Saehrimnir, as he was called, was slain daily by the cook, boiled and roasted and served each night in tender, succulent morsels, and then brought back to life again the following day, for the procedure to take place once again. After the meal, the warriors would retire to the palace forecourt where they would engage in unmatched feats of arms for all to see. Those who were injured would be healed instantly by the enchantment of Valhalla, and those who watched became even finer warriors.

Odin lived in Asgard with Frigga, who was the mother-goddess and his wife. Frigga was daughter of Fiogyn and sister of Jord, and she was greatly beloved on earth and in Asgard. She was goddess of the atmosphere and the clouds, and she wore garments that were as white as the snow-laden mountains that gently touched the land of Asgard. As mother of all, Frigga carried about her a heady scent of the earth – blossoming flowers, ripened fruit, and luscious greenery. There are many stories told about Frigga, as we will discover below.

Life in Asgard was one of profound comfort and grace. Each day dawned new and fresh for the passage of time had not been accorded to Asgard and nothing changed except to be renewed. The sun rose each day, never too hot, and the clouds gently cooled the air as the day waned. Each night the sky was lit with glistening stars, and the fresh, rich white moon rose in the sky and lit all with her milky light. There was no evil in Asgard and the good was as pure as the water, as the air, and as the thoughts of each god and goddess as he and she slept.

In the fields, cows grazed on verdant green grass and in the trees birds caught a melody and tossed it from branch to branch until the whole world sang with their splendid music. The wind wove its way through the trees, across the mountains, and under the sea-blue skies – kissing ripples into the streams and turning a leaf to best advantage. There was a peace and harmony that exists for that magical moment just before spring turns to summer, and it was that moment at which Asgard was suspended for all time.

And so it was that Odin and Frigga brought up their young family here, away from the darkness on the other side, far from the clutches of change and disharmony. There were nine worlds in Yggdrasill, the World Ash, which stretched out from Asgard as far as the eye could see. At the top there was Aesir, and in the bottom was the dead world of Hel, at the Tree's lowest roots. In between were the Vanir, the light elves, the dark elves, men, frost and hill giants, dwarfs and the giants of Muspell.

Frigga kept her own palace in Asgard, called Fensalir, and from his high throne Odin could see her there, hard at her work. Frigga's palace was called the hall of mists, and she sat with her spinning wheel, spinning golden threat or long webs of bright-coloured clouds with a marvellous, jewelled spinning wheel which could be seen as a constellation in the night's sky.

There was a story told once of Frigga, one in which her customary goodness and grace were compromised. Frigga was a slim and elegant goddess, and she took great pride in her appearance – something the later Christians would consider to be a sin, but which the Vikings understood, and indeed encouraged. She had long silky hair and she dressed herself in exquisite finery, and Odin showered her with gifts of gems and finely wrought precious metals. She lived contentedly, for her husband was generous, until the day came when she spied a splendid golden ornament which had been fastened to a statue of her husband. As the seamless darkness of Asgard fell one evening, she slipped out and snatched the ornament, entrusting it to dwarfs whom she asked to forge her the finest of necklaces. When the jewel was complete, it was the most beautiful decoration ever seen on any woman – goddess or humankind – and it made her more attractive to Odin so that he plied her with even more gifts, and more love than ever. Soon, however, he discovered that his decoration had been stolen, and he called together all of the dwarfs and with all the fury of a god demanded that this treacherous act be explained. Now Frigga was beloved both by god and dwarf, and although the dwarfs were at risk of death at the hand of Odin, they remained loyal to Frigga, and would not tell Allfather who had stolen the golden ornament.

Odin's anger knew no bounds. The silence of the dwarfs meant only one thing to him – treason – and he swore to find out the real thief by daybreak. And so it was that on that night Odin commanded that the statue be placed above the gates of the palace, and he began to devise runes which would enable it to talk, and to betray the thief. Frigga's blood turned cold when she heard this commandment, for Odin was a kind and generous god when he was happy and content, but when he was crossed, there was a blackness in his nature that put them all in danger. There was every possibility that Frigga would be cast out of Asgard if he were to know of her deceit, and it was at the expense of everything that she intended to keep it a secret.

Frigga called out to her favourite attendant, Fulla, and begged her to find some way to protect her from Odin. Fulla disappeared and several hours later returned with a dwarf, a hideous and frightening dwarf who insisted that he could prevent the secret from being uncovered, if Frigga would do him the honour of smiling kindly on him. Frigga agreed at once, and that night, instead of revealing all, the statue was smashed to pieces while the unwitting guards slept, drugged by the ugly dwarf.

Odin was so enraged by this new travesty that he left Asgard at once – disappearing into the night and taking with him all of the blessings he had laid upon Asgard. And in his absence, Asgard and the worlds around turned cold. Odin's brothers, it is said, stepped into his place, taking on his appearance in order to persuade the gods and men that all was well, but they had not his power or his great goodness and soon enough the frost-giants invaded the earth and cast across the land a white blanket of snow. The trees were stripped of their finery, the sun-kissed streams froze and forgot how to gurgle their happy song. Birds left the trees and cows huddled together in frosty paddocks. The clouds joined together and became an impenetrable mist and the wind howled and scowled through the barren rock.

For seven months Asgard stood frozen until the hearts of each man within it became frosted with unhappiness, and then Odin returned. When he saw the nature of the evil that had stood in his place, he placed the warmth of his blessings on the land once more, forcing the frost-giants to release them. He had missed Frigga, and he showered her once more with love and gifts, and as mother of all gods, once again she took her place beside him as his queen.

Asgard had many happy days before Frigga's necklace caused the earth to become cold. Frigga and Odin had many children, including Thor, their eldest son, who was the favourite of the gods and the people – a large and boisterous god with a zeal for life. He did everything with great passion, and spirit, and his red hair and red beard made him instantly identifiable, wherever he went. Thor lived in Asgard at Thruthvangar, in his castle hall Bilskirnir (lightning). He was often seen with a sheet of lightning, which he flashed across the land, ripening the harvest and ensuring good crops for all. With his forked lightning in another hand, he travelled to the edges of the kingdoms, fighting trolls and battling giants, the great guardian of Asgard and of men and gods.

Thruthvangar had five hundred and forty rooms, and it was the largest castle ever created. Here he lived with the beautiful Sif, an exquisite goddess with hair made of long, shining strands of gold. Sif was the goddess of the fields, and the mother of the earth, like Frigga. Her long, golden hair was said to represent the golden grass covering the harvest fields, and Thor was very proud of her.

Balder was the second son of Odin and Frigga at Asgar, and he was the fairest of all the gods – indeed, his purity and goodness shone like a moonbeam and he was so pale as to be translucent. Balder was beloved by all, and his innate kindness caused him to love everything around him – evil or good. He lived in Breidablik, with his wife Nanna.

The third son of Odin was Hodur, a blind but happy god who sat quietly, listening and enjoying the sensual experiences of the wind in his hair, the sun on his shoulders, the joyful cries of the birds on the air. While all was good in Asgar, Hodur was content, and although he represented darkness, and was the twin to Balder's light, that darkness had no real place and it was kept in check by the forces of goodness.

Odin's fourth son was Tyr, who was the most courageous and brave of the gods – the god of martial honour and one of the twelve gods of Asgard. He did not have his own palace, for he travelled widely, but he held a throne at Valhalla, and in the great council hall of Gladsheim. Tyr was also the god of the sword, and every sword had his rune carved into its handle. Although Odin was his father, Tyr's mother is said to have been a beautiful unknown giantess.

Heimdall also lived in Asgard, and he was called the white god, although he was not thought to be the son of Odin and Frigga at all. Some said he had been conceived by nine mysterious sisters, who had given birth to him together. His stronghold was a fort on the boundary of Asgard, next to the Bifrost bridge, and he slept there with one eye open, and both ears alert, for the sound of any enemy approaching.

There were many other gods in Asgard, and many who would one day come to live there. But in those early days of creation, the golden years of Asgard, life was simple, and its occupants few and wondrous. The gods and goddesses lived together in their palaces, many of them with children, about whom many stories can be told.

But even the golden years of Asgard held their secrets, and even the best of worlds must have its serpent. There was one inhabitant of Asgard who no one cared to discuss, the very spirit of evil. He was Loki, who some said was the brother of Odin, although there were others who swore he could not be related to Allfather. Loki was the very personification of trickery, and deceit, and his mischief led him into great trouble. But that is another story.

Heimdall in Midgard

To battle the gods are called
By the ancient
Gjaller-horn.
Loud blows Heimdall,
His sound is in the air.
Saemund's Edda

HEIMDALL WAS CALLED THE WATCHMAN of the gods, and he was distinguished by his role at the Bifrost bridge, which he had constructed from fire, air and water which glowed as a rainbow in the sky. The Bifrost bridge was also called the Rainbow bridge, and it connected heaven with earth, ending just under the great tree Yggdrasill.

The golden age of Asgard was one of such happiness that there was never any threat to the peace of the land, and so it was that its watchman became bored. Heimdall was easily spotted, so he could not travel far without being recognized and commended for his fine work. He carried over his shoulder a great bugle, Giallarhorn, the blasts of which could summon help from all nine worlds. One fine day, Odin noticed that Heimdall had been hard at work without any respite for many many years. Odin himself would occasionally slip into a disguise in order to go out into the worlds beneath them, and he decided then that Heimdall should have the same opportunity – after all, Asgard was hardly in need of defence when all was quiet.

Heimdall was delighted, for he had been longing to visit Midgard and to get to know the people there. He carefully laid his bugle and his sword to one side, and dressed in the garb of the people of Midgard, he slipped across the bridge and reached a deserted shore. The first people he clapped eyes upon were Edda and Ai, a poor couple who lived on the bare beaches of Midgard, eking a meagre living from the sands. They lived in a tumble-down shack and had little in their possession, but what they did have they offered gladly to Heimdall. Their shack was sparsely furnished, with only a seaweed bed on which to lay, but it was agreed that Heimdall could sleep there with them, and at night he laid himself between the couple and slept well.

After three nights, Heimdall summoned Ai and Edda as they gathered snails and cockles from the seashore. He had put together several pieces of driftwood, and as they watched, he fashioned a pointed stick from one, and cut out a hole in another. The pointed stick was placed inside the hole, and he turned it quickly, so that sparks, and then a slender stream of smoke was produced. And then there was fire. Ai and Edda flew back against the walls of the shack, astonished by this magical feat. It was then that Heimdall took his leave from them.

Ai and Edda's lives were transformed by fire. Their water was heated; the most inedible nuggets from the beach were softened into tender morsels of food. And most of all, they had warmth. Nine months later a second gift appeared to Edda, for she gave birth to a son who she called Thrall. Thrall was an ugly, wretched-looking boy, with a knotted body and a twisted back, but he was kind and he worked hard. When he came of age, he married one like him – a deformed young woman called Serf. Together they had many children, all of whom worked about the house or on the land with the same diligence as their father and mother. These were the ancestors of the thralls.

Heimdall had left the home of Ai and Edda and travelled on. Soon enough he came to a lovely little house occupied by an older couple Amma and Afi. As he arrived, Afi was hard at work, whittling away at beams with which to improve their house. Heimdall set down his belongings and began to work with Afi. Soon they had built together a wonderful loom, which they presented to Amma, who was seated happily by the fire with her spinning wheel. Heimdall ate well that evening, and when the time came for sleep, he was offered a place between them in the only bed. For three nights Heimdall stayed with Afi and Amma, and then he left them. Sure enough, nine months later, and to the astonishment of the elderly couple, Amma gave birth to a son, who they called Karl the Yeoman. Karl was a thick-set, beautiful boy, with sparkling eyes and cheeks of roses. He loved the land and the fresh air was almost food enough for him, he drew so much goodness from it. When he became of age, he married a whirlwind of a woman who saw to it that their household ran as smoothly as a well-oiled rig, and that their children, their oxen and all the other animals on their farm, were fed and comfortable. They grew very successful, and they are the first of the ancestors of the yeoman farmer.

The third visit in Midgard was to a wealthy couple who lived in a fine castle. The man of the household spent many hours honing his hunting bow and spears, and his wife sat prettily by his side, well-dressed and flushed by the heat of the fire in the hearth. They offered him rich and delicious food, and at night he was given a place between them in their luxurious and comfortable bed. Heimdall stayed there for three nights, although he would happily have stayed there forever, after which time he returned to his post at the Bifrost bridge. And so it was, nine months later, that a son was born to that couple in the castle, and they called him Jarl the Earl. His father taught him well the skills of hunting and living off the land, and his mother passed on her refinement and breeding, so that Jarl became known as 'Regal'. When Regal was but a boy, Heimdall returned again to Midgard, and claimed him as his son. Regal remained in Midgard, but his fine pedigree was soon known about the land and he grew to become a great ruler there. He married Erna, who bore him many sons, one of whom was the ancestor of a line of Kings who would rule the land forever.

Heimdall took up his place once more in Asgard, but he was prone to wandering, as all gods are, and there are many more stories of his travels.

Loki

Odin! dost thou remember
When we in early days
Blended our blood together?
When to taste beer
Thou did'st constantly refuse
Unless to both 'twas offered?
Benjamin Thorpe, Saemund's Edda

LOKI WAS A TRICKSTER, a good-looking rascal of a man whose eyes burned with mischief of the most dangerous kind. His handsome exterior housed a soul that was black and rotten, but for many years he lived happily in Asgard, amusing the gods and causing no real trouble other than that of a clown, or a fool, and so he was tolerated there, and allowed to marry and have children.

Loki was married to Sigyn, and his children were more terrible than him. He had already three children by an ogress called Angurboda – one a wolf called Fenris, another a serpent or dragon, Jormungander, who overtook Midgard as he grew, and the third, a dark but beautiful child called Hel. She was to become the queen of the underworld, and she had control over every man and woman who entered her gates.

Now Loki's trickery was well known in Asgard, and across the nine worlds, and his story is inextricably linked with that of the other gods, for he involved himself in most events in their lives, offering advice, and annoying them. Some of his mischief was amusing; some was dangerous.

One evening, when Freyia had become part of Asgard, Loki spied her marvellous necklace, a golden symbol of the fruitfulness of the earth which she wore about her slender neck at all times. Loki coveted this necklace, and he found he could not sleep until he had it in his possession. So it was that he crept one night into her chamber and bent over as if to remove it. Finding that her position in sleep made this feat impossible, he turned himself into a small flea, and springing under the bedclothes, he bit the lovely goddess so that she turned in her sleep. Loki returned to his shape and undid the clasp of the necklace, which he removed without rousing Freyia.

Not far from Freyia's palace, Heimdall had heard the sound of Loki becoming a flea – a sound so slight that only the great watchman of the gods could have heard it – and he travelled immediately to the palace to investigate. He saw Loki leaving with the necklace, and soon caught up with him, drawing his sword in order to remove the thief's head. Loki immediately changed himself into a thin blue flame, but quick as a flash, Heimdall became a cloud and sent down a sheath of rain in order to douse the flame. Loki quickly became a polar bear and opened his jaws to swallow the water, whereupon Heimdall turned himself into bear and attacked the hapless trickster. In haste, Loki became a seal, and then, once again, Heimdall transformed himself in the same form as Loki and the two fought for many hours, before Heimdall showed his worth and won the necklace from Loki.

There is another story told of Loki, whose tricks were not always used to ill-effect. One day, a giant and a peasant sat together playing a game. There were bets laid on the outcome of the game, and the giant won. The peasant, having little to offer, had pledged his only son, and the giant promised to return the following day to claim his prize. The peasant returned to his wife and admitted his shameful problem, and together they prayed to Odin, who answered their prayers and came down to earth. He changed the peasant's boy into a tiny grain of wheat and hid it in a sheaf of grain in the centre of a large wheatfield. But Skrymsli, the giant, was wiser than Allfather had given him credit for, and when he discovered the boy missing from the peasant's home, he walked straight to the wheatfield, located the shaft of wheat and plucked out the grain which was the boy. He was just about to eat it when Odin heard the child's cry and returned to earth once again. He snatched the grain from the hand of Skrymsli, and transformed the boy to his human form once again. He apologized to the peasants and left them, saying that there was no more he could do for them.

Skrymsli roared and shouted that he had been deceived and he vowed that he would return the following day to claim his prize. Once again the peasants prayed, this time to Hoenir, who graciously came to earth and changed the boy into a soft piece of down, which he hid in the breast of a swan who glided easily across the stream by the peasant's home. It was not long before Skrymsli returned, and he took only a few moments to guess what had happened to the boy. Grasping the swan by the neck, he made as if to bite off its head when Hoenir heard the boy's cries and returned to earth. He returned the boy to his parents, but then he disappeared, explaining that he had done all he could to help and could do no more.

The peasants were in great despair, and the giant promised that he would return the following day to claim his prize. They prayed then to Loki, who came down to them at once, carrying the boy out to sea and hiding him in an egg in the roe of a flounder. The giant spied Loki returning from his task, and he guessed at once where the peasant's boy was being held. He captured a boat, and went at once to sea with his fishing rod in hand, and soon enough he captured the flounder. The fish was opened and the egg extracted, when suddenly, Loki reappeared and plucked the egg from the giant's hand, transforming it once again into the boy, who was sent running home to his parents.

Loki set upon the giant then, cutting off his leg and beating him about the head. But Skrymsli had powers of his own, and he was able to heal himself at once, regaining his form and making for the home of the peasants. He was on the brink of capturing the boy when Loki used a clever ploy. He quickly chopped off the leg of the giant, and threw it away so that it could not be rejoined. He placed a spear of metal where the leg had been, for it was well known that even magic could not cross a metal barrier. The giant was slain at last, and the peasants rejoiced, praising Loki so that he became inflated with pride.

Loki appears many more times in the stories of Asgard, and his name was often on the tongues of its inhabitants.

The Norns

Thence come the maids
Who much do know;
Three from the hall
Beneath the tree;
One they named Was,
And Being next,
The third Shall be.
Ebenezer Henderson, The Voluspa

THE NORNS ARE SPOKEN of with great respect, for they are the sisters who make their home at the base of Yggdrasill and it is they who protect her great roots. Their home is a cave, and in its centre lies a pool as clear as the air in Asgard. Each day, the Norns take water from that pool and mix it with the enchanted clay and gravel on its banks. This they spread across the roots of Yggdrasill, and then they seat themselves in their cave and begin to spin.

It is the spinning of the Norns which most concerns the inhabitants of Asgard, for the Norns spin time on their spindles and it was from this work that they take their names. The oldest sister is Wyrd, or 'Was', the second sister is Verdandi, or 'Being', and the youngest sister is Skuld, or 'Shall be'. The Norns were also called 'The Fates', and they took up their place at the roots of the tree when evil began to enter Asgard.

Once time had reached Asgard, there was nothing to prevent things from ageing, and it was only with the enchanted apples of Idunn that the gods were able to renew their youth each day. The gods knew they were at the mercy of the Norns and for that reason they chose to consult them daily. Even Odin attended their cave on a regular basis to ask for their advice and aid. The Norns spoke little, and many believed that they could not speak the future, that they spun and spun the web of time at the wish of Orlog, the eternal law of the universe, who had bade them weave at his discretion. But Odin was often advised about the fate of his people – although his own future was kept secret from him and from his fellow gods.

The sisters worked quietly, murmuring a chant as they worked, and the two older sisters in particular were considered beneficent. Wyrd and Verdandi worked without purpose, while the youngest sister, Skuld, was much more purposeful, often destroying the hard work of her sisters for no reason at all.

It was the sisters who predicted the great war in heaven, when the Vanir and the Aesir would begin a civil war that would bring down the walls of Asgard – and allow sin to enter.

Idunn and the Apples

Bright Iduna, Maid immortal!
Standing at Valhalla's portal,
In her casket has rich store
Of rare apples gilded o'er;
Those rare apples, not of Earth,
Ageing Aesir give fresh birth.
J. C. Jones, Valhalla

ONE FINE DAY, Odin, Loki and Hoenir wandered throughout the worlds on one of their regular missions to see that all was well. As they travelled, they grew hungry, and finally stopped in order to cook an ox to give them sustenance to carry on. A fine ox was chosen from a herd in a field, and it was duly slain and placed on a spit over roaring flames. After several hours, the ox was removed from the fire, and the three wanderers licked their lips and they prepared for their meal. Hoenir cut into the beef, and stopped. Under the crisp exterior, the beef was raw through and through. Fresh blood dripped on to the fire. Hoenir looked puzzled, but he placed the beef back on the spit and motioned to his friends that they could not eat just yet.

The fire was built up once more and the three men waited for another hour or so before removing the beef from the spit once more. This time Odin cut into the meat, but again it was uncooked – it appeared that the fire had had no effect whatsoever.

Suddenly there was a movement in the trees, and a rush of wings. There, at the top of the tree overlooking their fire sat a great eagle. He sat looking down at them with great satisfaction.

'Our meat is uncooked,' Odin said helplessly, pointing to the fire.

'The meat will remain uncooked,' said the eagle, 'until I ordain it to be cooked.'

The three travellers looked at the eagle with interest. It was not often that gods were challenged, and they waited to hear the reason.

'All right, then,' said Odin fairly, 'please could you allow our meat to cook.'

'I shall do so,' said the eagle, 'if I can eat my fill before you partake from the ox.'

Odin nodded and agreed, for he was famished by hunger now and he was determined to have some of this fine piece of ox. Within five minutes the beef was cooked, and with a flurry of feathers, the eagle landed by the fire and stirring up a great cloud of ashes, began to eat. Moments later there was silence. The eagle had returned to the tree, and the spit was empty.

Now Loki in particular was enraged by this act. He was accustomed to being the trickster, and was not used to having tricks played on him – whatever the reason. 'Who are you,' he called out angrily, to which the eagle only laughed and shrugged.

Loki grabbed a burning log from the fire, and made towards the eagle, who only ducked and dove at Loki until he was quite reddened with fury. Finally, the eagle swooped down and took in his talons the log which Loki held, drawing it up into the air as he flew. Loki struggled to let go of the wood, but he was unable to free himself. His fingers clutched the branch and nothing he could do would loosen them.

'Let me down,' he cried, angrily kicking his feet and shouting. But the eagle flew higher and higher, turning and soaring through the air and terrifying Loki so that he closed his eyes in fear. When at last the eagle sensed that his prisoner could take no more, he spoke.

'I am Thiazzi, the great giant. I will let you loose only if you swear to deliver the goddess Idunn to me. You must lure her beyond the walls of Asgard where I can catch her, and she must bring with her the basket of apples.'

Loki considered this for a moment, and then agreed. Far below him Odin and Hoenir watched, never imagining the treachery of which Loki was capable. In a moment, Loki was set safely on the ground, and for a moment he sat there, stunned. Odin and Hoenir reached his side, and asked him what had passed with the eagle, but Loki told them nothing. The three men returned to Asgard.

Loki knew that the promise he had made to Thiazzi was the worst he could possibly have made, for without the golden apples of Idunn, the ravages of time would take their toll on the occupants of Asgard and he, Loki, alone would be responsible for the ageing and eventual death of each and every one of them.

He paced and paced the gardens where Idunn worked happily, her sweet ways bringing a nuance of spring to all she touched. But as much as Loki realized the trouble he would cause by luring Idunn from Asgard, he knew there would be much more trouble if he did not satisfy his solemn oath to Thiazzi. And so it was on that fateful day that Loki approached Idunn, who was curled up by a bed of flowers.

Idunn smiled innocently at Loki, and began to explain how the flowers responded to her love, and how all growing things could benefit from praise and care.

Loki smiled briefly and interrupted.

'Come, Idunn,' he said carelessly. 'Did you know that yesterday when I walked with Odin and Hoenir I saw a tree bearing enchanted apples just like your own.'

Idunn laughed. 'Why that's not possible,' she said brightly, knowing that her own golden apples were unique. They did not come from any tree, but appeared magically in her basket. When one was eaten, another quickly took its place so that there was an eternal supply of youth.

But Loki talked and talked to Idunn, and he managed to convince her that another source of apples would be a fine thing, for what should transpire if something were to happen to Idunn's basket?

'Bring your basket,' he said slyly, 'and you'll see that the apples are much the same.'

Idunn finally agreed to travel with Loki to see the tree, and they set out for the walls of Asgard. No sooner had Idunn stepped outside when Thiazzi swept down and clutching her in his talons, carried her away. With her went her basket of apples.

Loki skulked back inside the walls of Asgard, and mentioned nothing of what had happened. Soon it was discovered that Idunn was missing, and the Aesir became greatly distressed. Within a few days wrinkles appeared on their youthful cheeks, and their backs became hunched with age. They hardly recognized one another and as the bloom of youth disappeared, so did their happiness. Asgard was a changed place, and everyone called out for the return of Idunn.

Heimdall admitted that he had seen Idunn with Loki, on the fateful day of her disappearance, and at once Odin and his men set out to find the trickster. Loki admitted what had happened and the rage of Odin was so great that Loki volunteered to see about the return of Idunn himself.

Loki sat alone, deeply concerned by the task that lay ahead of him. For how was he to travel to the skies where Thiazzi lived as an eagle? Loki could take many forms when the need arose, but he had not yet mastered the art of flying, and he found himself in a quandary which even his quick wits could not find a way out of. Suddenly it came to him – Freyia's coat! Freyia's coat of feathers!

Freyia agreed at once to the loan of her hawk coat, for she was frightened by the wrinkles which cut deeply into her face and without her legendary beauty she would never be able to attract the souls of the warriors to her domain. And so Loki set out wearing Freyia's coat, and he flew at once over the walls of Asgard until he found the giant's castle.

There, in a pen, sat Idunn, and she was alone. Thiazzi's daughter Skadi had been watching the goddess, but because she was so serene and presented no threat of escape, Skadi had gone off for a walk, leaving Idunn to sit quietly, clutching her basket of apples.

Loki swooped down and spoke quietly to Idunn. 'Idunn, it's me, Loki,' he said quickly. 'Listen carefully: I am here to rescue you. In a moment you must hold your basket to you and I will turn you into a hazelnut and lift you into the sky and back to Asgard.'

Ever trusting, Idunn nodded her head and soon found herself high in the air with Loki the hawk. Just at that moment, Skadi returned and it took her no time at all to realize what had happened. She called out to her father, who was fishing several miles away, and he returned at once, rowing like a crazed person in order to reach his daughter. At once he saw Loki carrying away the nut, and he transformed himself into the giant eagle in order to give chase.

Loki was within reach of the gates of Asgard when the eagle approached. From Asgard the gods watched with horror, and Freyia cried out, 'My hawk will never outfly an eagle.'

And so the gods got to work, and directed by Tyr they put together a great pile of wood shavings which they set alight. Tyr held up the burning shavings and as the eagle flew across, he touched it to him, and the giant bird burst into flames, his feather coat melting off until the giant fell helplessly to the ground, where he was burnt in a rush of flames. There beside him stood Loki, trembling and frightened, but complete, and there was Idunn, mercifully unharmed by the chase, and by the blast of flames. She carefully handed each of the Aesir an apple, and youth was once more restored.

Just as the gods began to settle back into their daily routines, there came a shriek from the walls. There stood Skadi, crying out for her father who was nothing more than two burning embers. She cried out for vengeance, but Odin approached her and settled her down, pointing out that it had been her father who had begun this unhappy episode. It was finally agreed that Skadi would choose a god as her husband, in order that she would have a man to take care of her. She was to choose the one she wanted by looking at his feet.

So a screen was erected and each man in Asgard was bidden to walk past the screen so that she could see their feet. Choosing those that were the cleanest, and purest white, Skadi looked smug, sure that she had picked Balder, for no one else could have such clean white feet.

But when the screen was removed, there was Niord, god of the sea, whose feet were washed clean on the sands of the ocean each day. And so it was that the girl of the mountains married the god of the sea, and the two came together for all eternity. Thiazzi's embers were carried to the sky by Loki in Freyia's coat, and there they sit today, the twin stars of Thiazzi which bear his name and appear each night in the Northern skies.

Sigurd

First wilt thou prince,
Avenge thy father,
And for the wrongs of Eglymi
Wilt retaliate.
Thou wilt the cruel,
The sons of Hunding,
Boldly lay low:
Thou wilt have victory.

Benjamin Thorpe, Lay of Sigurd Fafnicide

ONCE, IN THE HALL OF THE VOLSUNGS, the great line of warriors who are celebrated in the great Scandinavian epic, the Volsung saga, a wedding took place. This was the wedding of Signy, who was to marry the king of Gothland, called Siggeir. Signy was the twin sister of Sigmund, who supported her marriage along with everyone in the kingdom. In the hall of the Volsungs was an unusual sight – built into the hall itself was a huge living oak tree whose branches supported the roof. This oak tree was called Branstock, and it brought good luck to the Volsungs, who tended it carefully.

On this day, the day of the wedding feast, there were great festivities underway. Great platters of food groaned on tables, and mead was passed around in horns as the joyful crowd toasted the health of the new couple. Suddenly there was silence, for in the midst of the crowd appeared a stranger with a wide-brimmed hat. He had only one eye, and his feet were bare and dirtied from his travels. In his hand he carried a spectacular sword, which glinted and shone in the light as if it were made of pure gold. He walked purposefully towards Branstock, and plunged the sword into the trunk of the tree without murmuring a word.

Then he turned, and addressed the crowd:

'Whosoever draws this sword from the tree will have it as a gift from me. Whosoever has as his own my sword will have victory in every battle he fights.' With that the stranger left the room, and there was silence. There was no doubt in any one of their minds that the great Odin had been amongst them.

Each of the men in the group stood up, longing for a chance to pull out the sword. Every great Viking warrior took his turn, while the others chattered excitedly. But one by one they pulled, and tugged and yanked at that sword until there was only one man left amongst them – the small, fair young Sigmund. He stood and walked towards

the sword, the room growing silent. Each of King Volsung's nine sons had failed as had the king himself. No one doubted that this young man would do so as well.

Sigmund laid his hands on the hilt of the sword and with a mighty pull, brought it from the trunk of the tree with ease.

This sword became Sigmund's property and as he grew older, he used it often, becoming the greatest Viking warrior that ever was. And then the day came when Sigmund had reached the final years of his life. He lay dying on a field, the last of the Volsung line, and as he spoke his final words, his beloved wife Hiordis bathed his face and wept over her dear husband.

'I have met with Odin once again,' he whispered to Hiordis. 'I know it was he because my sword could not match the mighty spear he carried. He has come to bring me to Valhalla, and dear one I am ready to go.'

He held out a weary hand and brushed away Hiordis's tears. 'Fear not, little one,' he said quietly, 'for in your womb you carry my son, and he will be the greatest warrior ever known – greater still than any Volsung. He will take my sword, and he shall reign supreme.' And then Sigmund died, as the Valkyrs led him gently to his peace.

Hiordis went on to marry the son of the King of Denmark, a man called Alf, who did not know that the child she carried belonged to Sigmund. When she gave birth there were great festivities, and the boy who was born was called Sigurd.

It is here that this story joins another, for once, just three or four years before Sigurd became a youth, and an apprentice to a smithy, Odin, Hoenir and Loki were walking in Midgard when they came across a burbling stream, rich with salmon and other fine fish. As they prepared to catch one for their meal, they were startled by the movement of an otter, who was just wakening at the side of the stream. Quickly Loki grabbed the otter and killed it, and a fire was quickly built while the otter was skinned. The men dined greedily, and with the pelt of the otter over their backs, they made their way towards a cabin, which was just peeking from between the trees. They knocked at the door and were startled to be met by an angry man who was summoning his thralls to help him tie up the three strangers.

Odin stepped forward. "Do you not know that passers-by are to be treated with kindness, and given a bed for the night? Do you not know that Odin has decreed this?' Odin was in his customary disguise and the angry stranger had no idea who he was dealing with.

The stranger, whose name was Kreidmar, scowled at Odin and said, 'Not when they have murdered my son.'

Kreidmar's son had been a form-shifter, and had just finished a fine meal of salmon, which he had caught in the shape of an otter. He had been murdered before he could become a man again.

Loki and Odin apologized profusely, and offered to do anything in their power to repay Kreidmar.

'There is only one thing you can do,' said Kreidmar, 'and that is to fill my son's otter pelt with gold, and then cover every hair on its back until I cannot see it at all.'

The three men agreed, and set out at once for a waterfall where they knew that a dwarf by the name of Andvari lived as a sharp-toothed pike and guarded a magnificent treasure of gold and jewels. With characteristic cunning, Loki managed to divert the fish, and as Andvari was changed back into a dwarf, to retrieve the treasure.

Loki and Odin gathered together the splendid gold broaches, rings, necklaces and ornaments, and as they made to leave, they saw something glinting from the pocket of the trembling dwarf.

'What's that?' said Loki, ever quick of eye.

'Oh, this ...' said Andvari, ' ... this you cannot have. This ring has a curse on it. Whoever owns it once it leaves my care will have nothing but disaster.'

Loki had little fear curses and enchantment, for he could rival the best with his own, and he snatched the ring from the dwarf and the three men made their way back to the cabin. There they stuffed the pelt of Kreidmar's son, and then covered the body with more gold. Finally they were finished.

Kreidmar came to inspect. 'Ha!' he cried at once. 'I see a whisker still uncovered. You have failed in your task and I will kill you all.'

Loki stepped forward and bent down on his knee. 'Please sir,' he said graciously. 'I have this one ring here which will cover the hair, but it holds an evil curse and I do not wish it upon you or your family.'

'Give me the ring,' snarled Kreidmar, 'and all of you – be off!'

The three travellers continued on their way and soon forgot about Kreidmar and his son, but just moments after they left, the curse began to take effect. Kreidmar had two more sons, one called Fafnir, who also changed shape, and another called Regin. Regin was away, working as a blacksmith in Denmark, and he had as his pupil none other than Sigurd, son of Sigmund. Fafnir, however, lived at home, and on the very day that the curse fell upon his father, Fafnir took on a peculiar glint in his eye and began to covet the treasure that filled his brother's pelt.

A few days later, he murdered his father, and changing shape, he became a monstrous dragon, hiding himself away in a cave and guarding his magnificent treasure.

Now Regin, far away from the treasure had, as part of the curse, begun to covet it himself, and he began to hatch a plan to have it returned. He assessed the young Sigurd, who was working with him, and noticing his bravery and his amazing skill with arms, he decided to approach him to see if he would fight the dragon.

'Sigurd,' he said slyly, ' I notice that you have come of an age that you may want to practise some of your great father's skills. There is a dragon I know of, one who guards a treasure. Perhaps you would like to test those skills?'

Now Sigurd was just young enough to be tempted by the idea of fighting a dragon for treasure, and he went off into the forest the following day to find a horse. As he walked through the trees, where the horses ran free, he met an elderly man, one with just one eye, who suggested that Sigurd test the horses before he made his selection. And so together Sigurd and the old man sent the horses into a nearby river. All of the horses swam easily to the other side, and then galloped off into the distance. Only one horse returned – a lustrous grey stallion with a powerful body and fine, intelligent eyes.

'Take that horse,' said the old man. 'He is a descendant of Odin's own horse, Sleipnir, and he will care for you in times of trouble.'

With that the old man disappeared, leaving Sigurd in no doubt as to who he had just seen. Turning to the horse, he stroked it and was rewarded by a happy snort. 'I'll call you Grani,' he said to the horse, 'and together we shall kill a dragon.'

Sigurd returned to Regin to tell him of his new horse, and to request that the blacksmith make him a great sword with which to kill the dragon. Regin began working, toiling over the hot forge until a sword was brought forth, gleaming. Sigurd lifted it into his hands, and then laid a heavy blow on the anvil. The sword broke into thousands of tiny pieces, and Regin looked at Sigurd in surprise. Back he went to the forge once again, and another sword was made, this one stronger and with a gleam that was even brighter than the first. Again, Sigurd lifted the sword and brought it down on the anvil, and again, it shattered into tiny pieces.

Regin shook his head, and began work on a third. 'Go home, Sigurd, I will have another for you to try tomorrow.'

Sigurd was puzzled by the course of events, and a seed of doubt had entered his mind about the ambitions of his tutor. Regin seemed very keen to have the dragon slain, and Sigurd wondered why. He approached his mother and explained the whole story to her.

Hiordis said, 'My son there is a secret of which you are not aware. You are not the son of the man you think your father. You are the son of King Sigmund, and just before he died, he presented me with the pieces of this sword, which you may have forged to protect you. This sword will slay your dragon, if that is what you wish, and this same sword will protect you from whatever Regin has in store for you.'

The following day, Sigurd returned to the smithy with the sword, and it was placed in the fire by Regin. Suddenly there was a flash of bright light and the sword emerged of its own accord, glittering in the firelight like a crystal. Sigurd reached for the sword and brought it down on the anvil. At once the anvil split in two and the gleam was reflected in the eyes of Regin. He could think of nothing now but the treasure, and so it was that the two gentlemen set off.

When they reached the cave of the dragon, Regin said to Sigurd, 'Go on now, Boy, and slay the dragon. There will be treasure for us both. Whatever you do, don't let his blood touch you for you will burn for certain.'

Sigurd set off in the direction of the dragon, and as he approached, the stranger from the woods appeared to him once again.

'Sigurd, what Regin tells you is wrong. Bathe in the blood of the dragon, for it will make you invincible. Approach him from the back for if you go this way you will surely be burned.' With that the one-eyed man disappeared.

Sigurd did as he was bid, and he struck the great dragon from behind, slaying him at once. He cut a hole in the dragon's neck, and stripping off his clothes, he bathed in the dragon's blood until every part of his body was covered except for a tiny spot between his shoulderblades where a piece of heather had rested.

Gathering up the treasure, he returned to Regin who was delighted to hear of the spoils. 'Do me one more favour, Sigurd,' he asked, 'cut out the heart of the dragon so that I may eat it, and a part of my brother may live on in me.'

Sigurd returned to the dragon and did as he was asked. As he roasted the heart over a fire, a drop of the blood fell on to his hand, where it burned and began to smoke. Suddenly he began to hear voices. Looking around he saw no people, but the voices persisted. And it was at that moment that Sigurd realized that he could hear the birds speaking to one another, and they were discussing him! Sigurd listened while they spoke of Regin's treachery and how foolish he was to have trusted him. And when Sigurd looked up, there was Regin, ready to strike him down. With his mighty sword, Sigurd beheaded the blacksmith with one swing.

And so it as that Sigurd gathered up the treasure. As he put the same cursed ring in his pocket, he heard the birds say, 'He must not take the cursed ring. Does the great Sigurd not know what will happen if he does?'

But shrugging their words aside, Sigurd made off for home. As he travelled, he saw in the distance a fine castle, surrounded by white light. He coaxed Grani up and over the light, and he landed on the marble flagstones of the castle courtyard. Dismounting, Sigurd laid down his sword and entered the castle. There, in the main hallway, lay a knight in shining armour. Sigurd quietly reached towards the knights helmet, and lifted it gently off, curious to see what great warrior lay there in state. But to his great surprise, a tumble of hair fell out from beneath the helmet and there lay an exquisite girl. He prodded her, and as if by magic her armour disappeared, and her eyes opened.

When this girl caught eyes with Sigurd there came between them a feeling that happens most infrequently; it was a love with such intensity that Sigurd knew at once that she was a part of him, and he her. He slipped his hand into his pocket and withdrew the ring, slipping it on her finger. Some say this girl was called Brunhilde, and that she was the daughter of Odin. Other say she was born of Sigurd's need, and therefore was, in truth, a part of himself. Whoever she was, she became a part of Sigurd's life, and a part of the curse that he had just placed on her slender finger. But that, and the other tales of Sigurd and his adventures, is another story.

The Legends of Thor

I am the Thunderer!
Here in my Northland,
My fastness and fortress,
Reign I forever!
Henry Wadsworth Longfellow,
Saga of King Olaf

THOR WAS ONE OF THE TWELVE principal deities of Asgard, and he lived in the splendid realm of Thrudvang, where he built a palace called Bilskirnir. Here he lived as god of thunder, and his name was invoked more than any other in the age of the Vikings. For Thor was the protector of the land, a fine figure of a man with glowing eyes, firm muscles, and a red beard that made him instantly recognizable. He became known across the worlds for his great hammer, Miolnir (the crusher), which had been forged by the dark elves. This hammer, together with Thor's strength and his terrible temper, made him the fiercest god of Asgard, and the personification of brute force. Thor was also god of might and war, and because of his popularity, he soon grew to embody the forces of agriculture, and became a symbol of the earth itself. He is remembered throughout the world on the fourth day of every week – Thursday, or Thor's day.

How Thor Got His Hammer

First, Thor with the bent brow,
In red beard muttering low,
Darting fierce lightnings from eyeballs that blow,
Comes, while each chariot wheel
Echoes in thunder peal,
As his dread hammer shock
Makes Earth and Heaven rock,
Clouds rifting above, while Earth quakes below.
J. C. Jones, Valhalla

THOR WAS MARRIED TO SIF, whose long golden hair was her one great pride. It fell to her feet like a ray of sunlight, and it was the colour of ripe cornsilk in the summer fields. As she brushed it, it glinted in the light and became a symbol of great beauty across Asgard. One day, the glistening cascade of hair caught the eye of Loki, and he wondered then how he ever could have imagined living without it. He thought about that hair all day, and all through the night. And then, just as the moon reached her pinnacle in the midnight sky, Loki leapt to his feet and made for Sif's bedchamber, where he knew he would find her sleeping. The moon cast long shadows into the sleeping goddess's delicately furnished room, and it was easy for the fleet-footed Loki to steal in and set to work.

Loki crept to the side of Sif's bed and very gently, so that he did not disturb her, he withdrew a pair of great shears from his cloak and cut her long veil of hair from her head. Winding the tresses around his arm, he darted from the room once again, and there was silence. Until, that s, Sif awoke to discover the travesty that had occurred.

Her shrieks brought everyone in the kingdom running to her side, and Thor howled with such outrage that the entire kingdom of Asgard shook. It was not long before Loki was ferreted out and brought before the irate god. Thunder boomed in the sky as the shaking trickster fell to his knees before Thor.

'I beg you, Thor,' he cried, 'let me free and I will find a new head of hair for Sif – one that is even more beautiful than the one she has now. I'll go to the dark elves. They'll fashion one!' Loki's head bobbed up and down with fright and eventually Thor gave in.

'You have twenty hours to come forward with the tresses, and if you fail, Loki, you will be removed from Asgard forever.' Thor banged down a thunderbolt at Loki's feet, and the traitor scampered hastily away, hardly daring to breathe at his good fortune.

Loki travelled at once to the centre of the earth, down into the Svart-alfa-heim, where the wily dwarf Dvalin had his home. He threw himself on the mercy of the dwarf, and requested as well two gifts with which he could win the favour of Odin and Frey, who were bound to hear of the news and wish to punish him themselves.

Dvalin worked over the heat of his forge for many hours, and as he worked he chanted the words which would make all he forged the finest there was – for there are no arms as powerful nor as invincible as those fashioned by dwarfs. First he finished the spear Gungnir, which would always hit its mark. Next, he formed the ship Skiblanir, which would always find wind, on even

the most silent of seas, and which could sail through the air as well as on water. The ship wa
folded carefully and placed in a tiny compass. Loki's eyes shone at its undoubted worth.

Finally Dvalin spun the most graceful of golden threads, and these he wove into a head c
hair so lustrous and shining that all the dark elves gasped at its beauty. Dvalin handed it carefully t
Loki, wrapped in the softest of tissues, and said, 'As soon as this touches your princess's head, it sha
grow there and become as her own.'

Loki took all the gifts from Dvalin, who he thanked profusely, and feeling very pleased with himse
he set off for Asgard with a skip in his step. His jauntiness attracted the attention of two dwarfs who s
by the side of a small cottage.

'Why do you smile so?' asked the first – for Loki's reputation had preceded him and the dwarfs wer
certain that his happiness could have no virtuous cause.

'Dvaldi,' boasted Loki, 'is the most clever of smiths – both here and in all the nine worlds.' And wit
that he held up his prizes for the dwarfs to examine.

'Pish,' said the first dwarf, who was called Brokki, 'my brother Sindri can fashion gifts that are far mor
beautiful than those – and sturdier too.' He paused, and then continued, leaning towards Loki who bega
to look rather put out. 'Our gifts would hold the magic of the very centre of the earth,' he whispered.

Loki choked, and then, recovering himself, immediately challenged the dwarf to prove his word
So confident was he of the gifts he held now that he placed a wager on his own head.

And so it was that Brokki and Sindri made their way into their smithy and began work on the hottes
of forges. Sindri agreed to fashion the goods, on the condition that Brokki blew the bellows – a tas
which would prove difficult over the great heat that was necessary for Sindri to win the wager.

Sindri at once threw some gold into the fire, and left the room, eager to invoke the powers whic
would be invested in a great wild boar, which he had decided upon for Frey. Alone with the roaring fire
Brokki worked hard at the bellows, never pausing despite the tremendous heat. Loki watched from th
window and as he observed the determination and strength of the dwarf he began to grow uneasy. A
once, he decided that he must intervene and as quick as a flash of light he turned himself into a gadfl
and alighted on the hand of Brokki, where he set in a stinger so deep that a rush of blood rose to th
surface immediately.

Brokki cried out in pain, but he continued the bellowing, never missing a beat. Sindri returne
to the room and drew from the fire an enormous boar, who they called Gulinbursti for its radian
gold bristles. This boar would have the strength of all other boars there were, but he would have th
additional ability to shine a rich and powerful light into any part of the world in which he travelle
He was the perfect gift for the sungod Frey and nothing could match the brilliance of its light but th
sungod himself.

So Sindri flung more gold into the fire, and instructed Brokki to continue to blow. Once again, h
left the room to seek the necessary enchantment, and once again Loki took on the form of a gadfly. I
an instant he had landed on Brokki's cheek and stung through the weathered skin until Brokki crie
out and turned white with pain. But still he worked on, pumping the bellows until Sindri returne
once more. And triumphant, Sindri drew from the fire a ring which he called Draupnir, which woul
become the very symbol of fertility – for on every ninth night, eight identical rings would drop fro
Draupnir, with powers to match.

The final gift was yet to be prepared, and this time Sindri threw iron on to the fire, leaving Brokk
hard at work as he left to call upon the final spirits. Brokki's strength was beginning to flag, but his
will was as strong as ever. He pumped away as the fire burned brighter and brighter until, suddenly
a horsefly lit on his neck and stung him with a ferocity that caused him to leap into the air, but still he
did not miss even one pump of the bellows. Loki was becoming desperate. He arranged himself on

the forehead of the hapless dwarf and he stung straight into a vein on his forehead that throbbed with effort. He was rewarded by a gush of blood that streamed out into the fire and into the Brokki's eyes. The dwarf raised his hand for a split second to wipe aside the blood, but that moment caused damage that could not be erased. When Sindri returned and drew out the great hammer, its handle was short and ungainly.

Brokki hung his head in disappointment, but Sindri pointed out that the powers of the great hammer would more than make up for its small size. Indeed, he thought it might be an advantage, in that it could be neatly hidden in a man's tunic.

So Brokki gathered up the gifts and carried them outside to Loki, who accompanied the dwarf back to Asgard with his booty. Odin was given the ring Draupnir, Frey was given the boar Gulinbursti, and Thor was given the hammer, which they had named Miolnir – meaning invincible power.

Loki then presented Sif with her golden hair, and when she placed it upon her shorn head it latched itself there and began to grow in swirls and waves until it reached her feet once more – a shining veil of hair that shone more brightly than ever. Gungnir, the spear, was given to Odin, and the ship Skidbladnir to Frey. Each god was delighted with his gift, and there was much camaraderie as they slapped the backs of the dwarfs and the redeemed Loki. It was Brokki who put a stop to the celebrations when he stepped forward and explained the wager that had been made by Loki.

The gods looked at one another, and eyed their magnificent gifts. Although it was agreed that Sif's hair could not be more lustrous, or more beautiful, the gods announced that Brokki's gifts were the finest and the most magical – for the sole reason that Thor's great hammer was of such a magnificent size that it could be hidden away and used against the frost-giants at a moment's notice.

Loki's games had backfired, and he turned on his heels and fled before Brokki could undertake his part of the bargain and behead him! Brokki started in outrage and implored Thor to come to his rescue in catching Loki who was making away at all speed. Still smarting from Sif's agony, Thor threw out a lightning bolt and caught Loki by the ankles, returning him to face his fate at the hands of Brokki and his brother.

But when Loki was delivered to the dwarfs, Thor took pity on Loki and insisted to Brokki that he could have Loki's head but that he must not touch his neck – for the neck of Loki belonged to him, Thor. Of course there was no way to remove a head without touching the adjoining neck, and Brokki stomped around in fury before he came up with a plan which would serve him equally. Gathering his brother's great awl for the purpose, he punched holes along Loki's lips and stitched them together with an unbreakable cord.

It was many days before Loki's howls of pain ceased, and many more before he was able to unstitch the cord. Loki did not speak for almost one hundred days, as his torn lips were so painful he could not bear to move them. In time, however, Loki was able to speak once again causing Thor – and everyone in Asgard – to rue the day that the wager was broken.

Thor Goes Fishing

On the dark bottom of the great salt lake,
Imprisoned lay the giant snake,
With naught his sullen sleep to break.

Henry Wadsworth Longfellow, Poets of the North

THOR WAS A GREAT TRAVELLER, and it was in his capacity of war god that he took it upon himself to keep an eye on the activities of the occupants of the other worlds. One day, bored of his battles against the giants, he decided to take on a more dangerous opponent – the world serpent, Jormungander. How he longed to have the horns and head of the great beast on the walls of his palace hall.

And so it was that Thor dressed himself one morning in the attire of a human, trimming and curling his magnificent red beard until he looked the picture of elegance and gentility. He left Midgard and sailed across the sea until he reached Jotunheim. He anchored his ship and with his belongings tied upon his massive back, he set off across the sandy shores. A day or two later, he reached the cabin of the giant Hymir, who was not pleased to see the unexpected visitor.

Hymir knew that customs called for him to welcome the seafarer, but he had lived alone for many years and he disliked company.

'There's no point in resting your head in this household,' he said curtly to Thor, 'for I am up at the crack of the early light to go fishing, and then for the remainder of the day I've to see to my herd.' Hymir was the owner of a magnificent herd of steer, and he tended them zealously, allowing no one to interrupt his duties. He hoped that he would put off the unexpected visitor by being too busy to entertain him, or to provide him with a comfortable bed, but Thor was not to be dissuaded.

Continuing to allow the giant to believe that he was nothing more than a travelling man, Thor laughed and said that he would enjoy very much accompanying the giant on his fishing expedition, in the hopes that he would learn something from his skills. And so it was that Hymir grudgingly allowed Thor into his hut and showed him a room where he could lay his head.

The first light of morning found Hymir preparing to set out for the river, which roared along the bottom of his property towards the sea. He moved quietly so as not to waken the traveller – he had no interest in or intention of taking him fishing and he wanted to be gone before Thor wakened. Slipping silently from the cottage, he moved towards the cattle, which he planned to milk before setting out in his boat. He was dismayed to find Thor waiting for him, patiently stroking one of the cattle.

'You'll be fishing next, I imagine,' said Thor with a wide grin.

'I fish alone,' said Hymir curtly.

'I'd like to join you,' said Thor.

'No room for passengers,' said Hymir again, moving to work on the first cow.

'Not as a passenger,' said Thor with a smile, 'as a fisherman. I'll help you with the rowing.'

Hymir could see that Thor was intent upon joining him and so he nodded grudgingly and pointed towards the manure heap. 'Find yourself some bait then,' he said with a grunt.

Now Thor had seen the giant gesticulating towards the cattle, who lounged over the manure heap. With a mighty blow of his sword, he beheaded one of the finest steer and held it up to show Hymir, blood dripping down his arm. The giant could hardly control his rage – he had intended Thor to dig for grubs, not behead one of his sacred cattle – but he said nothing. I'll lose him at sea, he thought to himself.

Eventually the two men set out in the boat and they began to row. Hymir had noticed Thor's carefully curled beard and assumed he was not the most manly of men, perhaps unaccustomed to the rigours of fishing and farming. He was greatly surprised when Thor took the oars and rowed with splendid ease for hours without showing any sign of fatigue. At last Hymir begged him to stop, pointing out that the best fishing spots were around them.

But Thor carried on rowing, intent on reaching the place where the Jormungander lived. He rowed for an hour, and then Hymir leaned forward and put a hand on his oar. 'You must stop here,' he said, 'for we have reached the waters where the Jormungander swims. Any further and we will attract his attention and be his first meal of the day.'

Thor brightened at this news, and rowed steadily until he was certain they were in the waters of the evil serpent. Then he carefully chose the strongest of Hymir's rods and reels, and placing a line as thick as his forearm on the rod, he placed his tackle on the great hook and let it fall into the water. It was only moments before there was a stirring of the water, and Thor felt his rod being pulled from his grasp.

In the dark reaches of the sea, Jormungander had spied the head of the slain cattle, and taken it in one bite. Now the sturdy hook was trapped in his throat and he thrashed and shrieked as he tried to dislodge it.

Thor stood firmly in the boat, his determination making him strong. He called upon the divine powers that made him godly, and drew in the writhing beast as if it were no more than a fish on a simple rod. Hymir sat back aghast – he knew now that his passenger could be no man. He had never seen such strength, such resolve, and when the serpent was drawn forth from the water, spitting poison and snarling, he turned yellow and fell into a deep faint. For the Jormungander was a frightening sight to behold – with massive teeth, huge, bulging eyes, and a deathly odour that spoke of all who had fallen at his will. Thor held tightly to his rod, muscles groaning with effort. The huge body of the serpent lashed the water into a frenzied current and the boat tossed and tipped, water filling the bottom, and then emptying once again with each terrible wave that passed.

Hymir came to and could take no more. Swiftly he leant forward and grabbed his sharp knife, sawing through Thor's line with all the force he could muster. And then there was silence. The Jormungander slipped silently into the black depths of the sea and disappeared.

Thor's roar was heard far away in Asgard, and his fury caused a great storm to erupt. He had been just about to draw the beast into the ship when robbed of his quarry. The serpent would not be such easy prey from now on and this trip had been wasted. He snarled at the giant and withdrawing his hammer, gave him a blow that sent him flying into the icy waters, never to be seen again.

Some say it was a blessing that Thor did not catch the world serpent on that day, for a prophecy had been made that if ever the Jormungander's tail were removed from his mouth, the perpetrator would suffer a curse that would hang over him until the rest of his days. Thor rowed steadily until he reached the shore, and within a day he was back in Asgard. He did not speak of the fishing expedition again.

Thor in the Hall of the Giants

The strong-armed Thor
Full oft against Jotunheim did wend,
But spite his belt celestial, spite his gauntlets,
Utgard-Loki still his throne retains;
Evil, itself a force, to force yields never.
R. B. Anderson, Viking Tales of the North

THOR HAD PLANNED one of his regular trips to Jotunheim, and he set out on this occasion with Loki. It had not been many months since Loki had shorn Sif's hair and Thor decided that it was safer for all if Loki was under his own keen eye. So it was that they set out in Thor's chariot, and as night fell, they came upon the hut of a peasant where they requested a bed for the night.

The peasant lived in a small hut with his wife and two children, and although they did not have much food to spare, they offered it all to Thor, who ate greedily. It soon became clear that there was not anywhere near enough food for all, so Thor took his two goats from the stable where he'd put them for the night, and slew them, roasting them over the coals of the peasant's hearth until the succulent meat slipped from the bones. He threw down his cloak on the floor and requested that the bones be placed there.

The peasant and his family were in ecstasy, for it had been many months since they had tasted fresh meat. And so carried away was the peasant himself that when Thor looked away from his meal, he slyly cut into the bone of the goat leg he was eating and tasted the marrow. When the meal was finished, Thor wrapped up the bones and placed them outside the door, and the two gods settled down for the night.

When morning came, Thor opened the door, and pulling aside his cloak, set free the two goats which had been reborn. He noticed, however, that one of his goats was rather lame, and that his front right leg appeared to be damaged in some way so that he found it difficult to walk. Thor was furious that his commands had been so rashly disregarded, and he realized that he would have to leave the goat behind, for it was too lame to travel. He thrust his great hammer into the air and was about to slaughter the entire family, when the peasant crept forward and confessed that he had been the one to eat the bone. He begged Thor to show clemency to his family, and grudgingly Thor agreed to take his two children Thialfi, a strong young boy, and Roskva, a pretty girl, to be his lifelong servants, as repayment.

So the peasant was left with the goats, and the four set out on foot, the chariot left behind until the crippled goat could walk again. The countryside was cold and sparse; what water they could find to drink was tainted by the smell of giants, and Thor became ill-tempered. Eventually, night began to fall and they were forced to find a place in which to sleep. Ahead of them was a great hall, and they approached it thankfully, curling up in its centre to spend the night. They had not been sleeping for long when there was a great banging and the earth began to rock and shake. The peasant's two children moaned with fear, but Thor pressed his hands over their mouths and bid them to follow him into an alcove which lead off to the side of the hall. There they huddled, and at last slept.

When morning dawned, the four weary travellers made their way from the hall and stopped with a start. For there lay sleeping a giant bigger than any they had seen before. His snores laid flat the sparse vegetation, and the peasant's children hurled themselves behind Thor in fright. Eventually the giant opened one sleepy eye and caught sight of Thor and his party. He snorted and then sat up, speaking in a loud rumbling voice, 'So you are the ones who dared to make your camp in my mitten.'

Thor looked around in surprise, and his eyes settled on the great hall in which they had managed to find shelter. The hall was none other than the giant's mitten – the alcove had been the thumb! Thor stepped forward and identified himself, and in return the giant said his name was Vasti. Vasti seemed a friendly giant and he suggested that the two arties put together their provisions and travel on together. Thor agreed, for it would do iem no harm to have the additional assistance of a giant should they encounter trouble n their travels. And so they set off, Thor, Loki and the children scuttling along in the iant's footsteps.

The day was long and difficult. Even the great Thor struggled to keep up with the nmense strides of the giant, and when it came time to eat, and to rest, he was as grateful s the others. Vasti opened his sac and removed a large piece of meat, which he consumed a few moments. He grunted and passed the sac to Thor, and then turned on his side and ell into a deep sleep, his noisy snores disrupting the landscape once again.

Thor reached greedily for the bag. They had had no sustenance all day and all four of iem were weak with hunger. He struggled with the cord, and stamped and shouted, but espite his greatest efforts he was unable to unfasten the knots tied by Vasti. Loki then took ie opportunity to weave his own magic on the knots, but they remained tightly fastened. oki and the children settled down to sleep, too cold and hungry to bother any further, but hor was irate. The giant's snoring made it impossible to sleep, and he was more hungry ian he'd been since the day of his conception. Finally, he lifted up his great hammer and anged it down with all the force he could muster, on the giant's head.

Vasti turned, and muttered, and called out in his sleep that the leaf which had dropped n to him was a nuisance, and then he fell back into a deep sleep and left Thor to gaze at im in astonishment. A few moments later, he tried again, this time invoking a series of nchantments to make his blow even more supremely powerful, and he hit Vasti upon the row – deep enough that the hammer was imbedded in the giant's skull. Thor dragged it ut and waited for the inevitable shriek of pain, but Vasti only turned again in his sleep, and omplained about a bit of bark that must have fallen from the trees overhead.

Thor had never been so infuriated. Everyone knew that he was invincible, that his owers were stronger than any on earth, and yet, with his fine hammer, he was unable to nake the slightest dent on the sleeping giant. He tried one last time, and when Vasti started nly slightly, and suggested that perhaps an acorn had fallen upon his head, Thor gave up, nd tried to settle down to sleep.

He slept not a wink that night, and when Vasti rose, early on the morrow, he was in a fiery nood. Vasti had gone as far as he could with Thor and his men, and he would be travelling n to his own home across the icy mountains. He carefully pointed out the way to the castle f Utgard-loki, King of the Giants. But before he left, Vasti spoke quietly to the travellers nd told them that they would find giants even larger than he was at the palace. Perhaps hey should turn back now, he suggested, for he could not guarantee them any safety if they vent on alone ...

But Thor was too fractious to listen to his warnings, and they went on towards the palace. n a few short hours they had arrived. The tiny size of the gods meant that it was easy for hem to slip between the bars of the fence surrounding the castle, and soon enough they iad made their way to the inner chambers, the sanctuary of Utgard-loki himself.

The king of the gods was, as Vasti had promised, larger than all giants and fierce of ountenance and expression. He laughed uproariously when he saw Thor.

'We have heard tales of you, Thor,' he said, 'and we know who you are by that red beard f yours. We didn't expect you to be ... so ... so ... small.' And with that, he broke out into aughter again, sending Thor into spasms of anger.

'My size is of no importance,' he said stoutly, 'for I am capable of feats that men of all

sizes would find impossible.' Loki, who had also suffered enough on their journey lea
forward in Thor's defence.

'We challenge you to beat our many talents,' he shouted. 'And to begin with, I challeng
you to find someone in your ranks who can eat a meal more quickly than I can.' Now Lo
was more than confident of winning such a feat for he had an appetite that was keener tha
most gods at the best of times – here he was virtually starving after two days without foo

The king nodded his head in assent, and signalled to his cook Logi to join them. Th
table was laden with platters of bones, gravy and huge slices of dripping meat. At the soun
of the horn, Logi and Loki began to eat. Loki ate ravenously, devouring meat and grav
with gusto enhanced by the powers he had called down to help him. At the sound of th
horn he stopped and looked around. The king pointed to the other end of the table, an
Loki stopped in his tracks. For not only had Logi eaten all the meat and gravy at his side
the table, but he had eaten the bones, the platters and the table as well. Utgard-loki smile
contemptuously and with a wave of his hand dismissed Loki, who hung his head in sham

Thor stepped forward next, and held up his hand for silence. 'I hereby challenge an
man or giant to drink a greater draught than me – anyone at all,' he shouted.

A horn was dragged before Thor and Utgard-loki smiled once again. 'Your challeng
Thor, shall be met,' he said. 'You'll see before you a horn which can, by our champion, b
drunk in one or two great swallows. Let us see you match that.'

So Thor placed his mouth around the great vessel, which stretched the entire length
the room, and drawing in a deep breath, he began to drink. He sucked in the liquid an
after many moments without breathing, he stopped, and crept along the length of the hor
to see how deeply he had drunk. The horn was full. The level of the drink had not moved b
even the tiniest percentage. Thor shook his head in amazement. He knew his capacity fo
drinking was greater than anyone's and yet he could not make any real dent in the content
of the horn. He swallowed again, and then spat on the floor. 'Salty,' he muttered to himsel
and sat down.

Utgard-loki just nodded his head and said quietly, 'One would have expected more fro
Thor, would they not?'

Thialfi had enough of the taunting; he had grown to love Thor in the days they ha
been together and he leapt quickly to his defence, volunteering himself for a race with th
quickest of the giants. So Utgard-loki put forward his quickest man, a young giant calle
Hugi. The two boys lined up, and the race began. It seemed that the first race had been
draw, for both men appeared to reach the finish line at the same moment. And so anothe
race was called, and they lined up once again. As the bell went, and as Thialfi lifted his foo
to set off in the direction of the finish, Hugi raced to the line and back. The race was ove
and this time there was no question of who had won.

'Well, well, well,' said Utgard-loki, roaring with laughter. 'There are not many tricks t
your trade, are there Thor?' to which the angry god trembled, but said nothing.

'What do you say,' shouted Utgard-loki, winking furiously at the crowd of giants who ha
arrived to witness the spectacle, 'you try to raise our pretty kitty.' He pointed to a giant ca
who reclined gracefully in the corner of the hall.

Thor's pride had taken a beating and he was determined to prove himself. Surely it coul
not be difficult to lift a cat? He strode purposefully towards the cat, who yawned and licke
her paw before sitting up. He tightened his belt Megingiord, which made him stronger, an
then he tugged and pulled at the cat with all his might. But only one paw was lifted fro

ie ground, and despite his every effort he could not move her. The cat batted him playfully ith the paw he'd managed to lift, and laid back once again, her tail flicking to and fro in ie sunlight.

Thor looked towards Utgard-loki and asked for one final challenge.

'Hmmm,' said the king, 'there is one person in my household who may be suitable to restle with you. May I introduce you to my nurse, the hundred-year-old Elli.' There was eat laughter amongst the crowd as Elli crept forth, hardly able to hold herself upright.

Thor moved quickly towards her, and pulled and shoved until Utgard-loki called for him stop.

Thor swallowed with difficulty. He was bewildered and he was furious; he stared at tgard-loki and said quietly, 'I have been beaten. Until this day I thought there was no one reater than I. You have shown me my place, and for that I must respect you.' Thor signalled Thialfi and Roskva, and with Loki on one arm, they made to leave the hall, defeated and umiliated.

But Utgard-loki called out in a voice that was at once humane and conciliatory. 'You ave come here today against my will,' he said proudly. 'This is our home and you are not elcome here. Your show of strength is not welcome here. I was forced to do something to eep you away forever.'

At that the giant transformed and in an instant he was Vasti. 'Do you recognize me?' e said. 'When I lay sleeping just last night, I took the precaution of placing a mountain ver my head – one which was invisible to you, Thor. And it is just as well, for it seems that hen you were unable to open the magic cord of my sac, you took it upon yourself to hit ie mountain.' There he paused, and casting open a curtain, gesticulated out the window a series of valleys surrounding the mountain on the horizon. 'Those valleys,' he said olemnly, 'are the blows you aimed to my head.'

Thor gasped, but said nothing, waiting for the king to continue. And continue he did. oki's opponent had been none other than wildfire, and Thialfi's racing partner had been he king's thoughts – and there could be none as swift as these. Thor's drinking horn had een dipped at one end into the ocean, and no matter how deeply he had drunk, the ocean ould have remained undrinkable. Utgard-loki commented that the tides of the ocean had een altered by Thor's great swallows, but then he hurriedly went on.

The cat was in reality Jormungander, the world serpent, and had Thor not heard the gasp f terror when it seemed as though Thor may be responsible for removing the serpent's tail rom its mouth? Everyone there knew what chaos would exist when such an occurrence ould happen, for it had been prophesied that the end of the world would be nigh.

Elli was old age itself, and he had nearly unseated her. In all, Thor had been successful n many ways.

'You may hold your head high,' said Utgard-loki proudly. 'But please, Thor, do not return o our shores.'

Thor was only slightly placated by the king's explanations, and he lifted his powerful ammer to bring to an end the sedate lifestyle of Utgard-loki and his men. But as quickly s he could lift his hammer, the castle was enveloped in a sea of mist, and he could see othing. The world of the giants was completely enshrouded and Thor had no recourse ut to return home to Asgard. His mission was incomplete, and Thor had been branded a uny weakling in the eyes of the giant, but he had faced many of nature's most formidable nemies and had left his mark. And for that the god of war could stand tall once again.

The Stealing of Thor's Hammer

Wrath waxed Thor, when his sleep was flown,
And he found his trusty hammer gone;
He smote his brow, his beard he shook,
The son of earth 'gan round him look;
And this the first word that he spoke:
'Now listen what I tell thee, Loke;
Which neither on earth below is known,
Nor in heaven above: my hammer's gone.'
William Herbert, Thrym's Quida

THOR'S HAMMER became a symbol of his energy and power, and the mere mentio of its name, Miolnir, was enough to send the giants of Jotunheim trembling. It neat compact size allowed it to be hidden easily on Thor's person, and he neve was without it – except on those nights that he shared his marriage bed with Sif. On on such occasion, after a long and happy night, Thor woke, and stretching out a lazy hanc reached for Miolnir. It had vanished.

His cry of anger soon had all of the palace attendants at his side, and many fruitless hours wer spent searching for the missing weapon.

Loki was summoned, for matters involving theft – particularly in Thor's household – tende to have his hand in them, but his innocence was undoubted on this occasion, and he pledge to help Thor find the real thief.

Loki asked to borrow Freyia's hawk's coat, and after collecting it from Folkvang, he set off fc Jotunheim, travelling across sea and barren stretches of land until he found what he was lookin for – a giant was sitting alone on a crag. Now this giant's name was Thrym, and as prince of th frost-giants, he had cause to dislike and indeed fear Thor, who had made massive losses in thei numbers with his great hammer. Loki settled himself beside the giant, and mustering up all c his wile, set about asking him questions. At last the truth was divulged – Thrym had stolen th hammer and had buried it in a secret location. He would not return it to Thor, unless ... and her the great giant paused ... unless Freyia was presented to him as his bride.

Loki let out a great guffaw! Freyia was the most beautiful of all goddesses – a prize sough after by gods, men and all other creatures alike. It was certainly unlikely that she would agre to marry this prince of giants. Loki told Thrym these things, but Thrym stood firm. He woul return the hammer when Freyia was made his bride – this was his sole condition.

Loki thought hard for a moment, and then made a quick decision. He'd promise Thrym what h wanted, and then leave the matters in the hands of Thor, who would surely find a way round it al With a smile he rose and indicated that Thrym's conditions had been accepted. The giant's smile wa greedy, and he rubbed his hands together in glee as Loki disappeared into the morning sky.

Now Loki's journey took long enough for him to realize that Freyia was not going to be happ about the bargain he had just arranged, and he immediately regretted his hasty acceptance o the giant's proposal. Surely a man of greater wit could have concocted something more practical he lamented as he flew. When he arrived, he cornered Freyia and spoke as quickly as he could begging her to consider the proposal – for wasn't Thor's hammer important to all of them? Wasn't the very safety of Asgard at risk if he was unable to fight off the attacks of the frost-giants?

But Freyia was outraged at the suggestion that she marry a mere giant, and give up all the splendours of her home. She commanded Loki to leave her, and she shut the door smartly behind him. Loki returned to Thor with his head bowed low in shame. Thor listened carefully to his explanation, and patted the surprised Loki on the shoulder.

'You've done the best thing, ' he said gently, much to Loki's astonishment. 'My hammer is the most important thing here.'

And so it was that Loki and Thor set out to beg Freyia to reconsider. They had underestimated the passion of her feelings, for she commenced a tantrum that lasted for one whole day and night _ one so fierce that the necklace about her neck was splintered in to pieces that flew from one end to the other of Asgard. Thor and Loki realized that their attempts were useless, and returned back to Thrudvang.

There they sat and ruminated for many hours, eventually calling upon Heimdall to provide them with advice. His suggestions were met with outrage as profound as Freyia's own anger – for he believed that the very best way for Thor to retrieve his hammer was to dress himself in Freyia's necklace and wedding garments, and present himself as Freyia herself. Thor refused to consider such a plan, until it became quite clear that there were no alternatives. Grudgingly he agreed to don her clothes, and the necklace was secured from the many parts of Asgard and rebuilt to fit his own brawny neck.

Thor travelled with Loki to Jotunheim and with his eyes averted, and a veil covering the coarse red beard and hair, he was presented to Thrym. Thrym welcomed them at the palace door, and his anticipation of having the lovely Freyia as his bride caused him to lick his lips, and made his eyes water so that his eyesight was compromised. He looked slightly astonished by Freyia's size, but he accepted that gods were larger than humans, and that they were much closer to giants in that respect. He led Loki and Thor to the banqueting hall, where the women of the bridal party were taking a meal.

Thor sat down at the end of the table, and reached greedily for the platters of meat and bread. Within a few moments, he had eaten an ox, eight great salmon, and all of the sweet cakes and viands which had been prepared for the women. And this great meal was washed down with two full barrels of mead. Thrym gaped at the spectacle, and could only be comforted when Loki explained that the lovely Freyia had been unable to eat for nearly eight days in anticipation of their meeting.

Thrym gazed with great admiration at such an appetite, for such things were commended in those times, and caught Freyia's eyes. He started back at once, for there was there such burning fury that he felt as if he had been struck by a bolt of Thor's own lightning. He turned with dismay to Loki, but he was soon soothed by Loki's assurance that Freyia was so deeply in love with him that her passion had consumed her, and her look was one of intense longing.

Thrym gathered together the men and women in his party and called for the great hammer to be brought forth – a symbol of the sacred vows which were to commence. He took Freyia's hand, and was slightly disconcerted to discover that on its back were thick, curling red hairs. As he looked into his loved one's eyes, Thor struck. He grabbed his hammer and with one great burst of energy, he slew every giant in the room, and left the palace in ruins. And then, turning to the destruction, he called out a proclamation which caused Loki to stop in his tracks. Thor claimed the land as his own, and from every corner tender green shoots of grass and greenery began to grow. The barren wasteland was fertile; their journey had been a success.

So Thor removed Freyia's clothing, and returned to present the goddess of love with her necklace. The Aesir rejoiced at the return of Thor's hammer, and all was happy again in Asgard.

Freyia and Other Stories

Freyia, thin robed, about her ankles slim
The grey cats playing.
William Morris, The Lovers of Gudrun

FREYIA CAME TO ASGARD from Vanaheim, and before long she was as beloved as if she had been born one of the Aesir. She married well, and brought forth many fine children. She was known particularly for her fine feathered coat, which allowed her – and those she permitted to borrow it – to soar through the air as a hawk. Freyia's story touches on those of many of the other gods, and there are other myths and legends which must be recorded in order to understand how the golden age of Asgard became what it was, how evil entered, and how it eventually fell. There is Niord, who came with Freyia to bring summer, once the seasons had fallen into place. And Tyr, the god of war, who showed bravery which far surpassed any shown by man or god in the heyday of Asgard. And in the stories that follow we meet the elves, and learn why they abandoned their happy existence deep in the bowels of the earth. For every tale leads towards a single inevitable event – Ragnarok, and it hovers at the edge of all, just as it did in those early days of sunlight, when darkness had not yet touched the world of Asgard, and the gods lived a life of splendour ...

Freyia

And Freyia next came nigh, with golden tears;
The loveliest Goddess she in Heaven, by all
Most honour'd after Frea, Odin's wife.
Matthew Arnold, Balder Dead

FREYIA WAS THE NORTHERN GODDESS of beauty and of love, a maiden so fair and graceful that the gods honoured her with the realm of Folkvang and the great hall Sessrymnir, where she would, in eternity, surround herself with all of those who loved her. Like many Viking goddesses, Freyia was fierce and fiery, her cool demeanour masking a passion which lay burning beneath. She was clever, and masterful in battle, and as Valfreya, she often led the Valkyrs to the battlefields where she would claim many of the slain heroes. She wore a simple, flowing garment, held firmly in place on her torso and arms with the finest shining armour, a helmet and shield.

Slain heroes were taken to Folkvang, where they lived a life such as they had never experienced on earth. Their wives and lovers came to join them and Freyia's reputation spread far and wide among the dead and the living. So luxurious was Folkvang, so exquisite were Freyia's charms that lovers and wives of the slain would often take their own lives in order to meet with their loved ones sooner, and to experience the splendour of her land.

And so it was that Freyia, gold of hair and blue of eyes, came to be a symbol of love and courtship, and through that, the earth – which, of course, represents fecundity and new life. She married Odur who symbolized the sun, and together they had two daughters, Hnoss and Gersemi, beautiful maidens who had inherited their mother's beauty, and their father's charisma and charm. But Odur was a man of wandering eyes, and one who appreciated the inner music of women – and not just that of his wife. He grew tired of her song, and her absorption with their daughters, and he grew restless and reckless. And after many months and then years of growing weary of the smiling face of his lovely wife, he left Freyia and his daughters and set off on travels which would take him to the ends of the earth, and around it.

Freyia sank into a despair that cast a shadow across the earth. Her tears ran across cheeks that no longer bloomed, and as they touched the earth they became golden nuggets, sinking deep into the soil. Even the rocks were softened by her tears which flowed without ceasing as she made her decision. And it was decided by Freyia that she could not live without Odur. As well as being the symbol of the summer sun, Odur represented passion and ardour. Without him, Freyia could no longer find it in her heart to bring love and affection to those around her, and she could not fulfil her duties as goddess of love. It was decided that she should travel to find him, so across the lands she passed, leaving behind her tears which glistened and hardened into the purest gold. She travelled far and wide, and took on disguises as she moved, careful to leave no clue as to her identity in the event that he should hear word of her coming and not wish to see her. She was known as Syr and Skialf, Thrung and Horn, and it was not until she reached the deepest south, where summer clung to the land, that she found Odur.

Her husband lay under the myrtle trees that lined the sunny banks of a stream. Reunited, they lay together there, warm in one another's arms and dusted with the glow of true love. And as the passion drew colour into the cheeks of his wife, Odur knew he had to look no further to find his heart's content. The trees above them cast their scent across this happy couple, endowing them with good fortune. They rose together then, and Odur and Freyia made their way towards their home, and their exquisite daughters. As they walked, the earth rose up to meet them, casting bouquets of fragrant flowers in their path, drawing down the boughs of the flowering trees so they kissed the heads of the lovers. The air was filled with the rosy glow of their love, and everything living joined a chorus of cheers with followed their path. Spring and summer warmed the frozen land which had stood desolate and empty when Odur left.

The loveliest of the new flowers which bloomed were named 'Freyia's hair', and 'Freyia's eyedew' and to this day brides wear myrtle in their hair – a symbol of good fortune and true love.

Niord

Niord, the god of storms, whom fishers know;
Not born in Heaven – he was in Vanheim rear'd,
With men, but lives a hostage with the gods;
He knows each frith, and every rocky creek
Fringed with dark pines, and sands where sea-fowl scream.
Matthew Arnold, Balder Dead

WHEN THE WAR between the Aesir and the Vanir was concluded, and hostages were taken by each side, Niord, with his children, Freyia and Frey, went to live in Asgard. There Niord was made the ruler of the winds and of the sea near the shore, and he was presented with a lush palace on the shores of Asgard, which he called Noatun. Here he took up the role of protecting the Aesir from Aegir, the god of the sea, who had a fiery temper, and who could, at a moment's notice, send waves crashing upon the unprotected shores of Asgard.

Niord was a popular god, and he was as handsome as his children. On his head he wore a circle of shells, and his dress was adorned with fresh, lustrous green seaweed. Niord was the very embodiment of summer, and each spring he was called upon to still the winds and move the clouds so that the sun's bright rays could touch the earth and encourage all to grow.

Niord had been married to Mother Earth, Nerthus, but she had been forced to stay behind when Niord was summoned to become a hostage for the Vanir, so he lived alone in Niord, an arrangement which he did not mind in the least. For from Noatun he could breathe in the fresh salt air, and revel in the flight of the gulls and other seabirds that made their home on the banks. The crashing waves lulled him into a state of serenity, and with the gentle seals, he basked in the sunlight of his new home.

All was well, until Skadi arrived. Skadi had chosen Niord as her husband, because of his clean feet, and he had grudgingly agreed to marry her. There could not have been two more different beings, for Skadi was now goddess of winter, and she dressed in pure white, glittering garments, embroidered with icicles and the fur of the white wolf. Skadi was beautiful, and her skin was like alabaster; her eyes were stormy, and told of a deep passion which burned within her. Niord was happy to take her as his wife, although he longed for the days of solitude that his unmarried days had accorded.

And so it was that Skadi moved her belongings to Noatun, and settled in there. The first night spoke of the nights to come, for from that first instant, Skadi was unable to sleep a wink. The sounds of the waves echoed deep in her head, and the cries of the gulls wakened her every time she drifted into the first ebbs of sleep. So Skadi announced to all that she could not live with Niord in Noatun – he would have to return with her to Thrymheim. Niord was deeply saddened by this arrangement, for the sea was a part of him – food for his soul. He finally agreed to travel with Skadi to Thrymheim, where he would live with her for nine out of every twelve months.

It was many days before Skadi and Niord reached her home, high in the frozen mountains, where frost clung to every surface and the air was filled with the vapour of their breath. The wind howled through the trees, sending showers of ice to the ground below, where it cracked and broke into tiny, glistening shards. The waterfalls roared in the background, sending up spray that glistened in the sunlight. At night the wolves joined the fracas, howling at the icy moon. Niord was quite unable to sleep even one wink.

So an agreement was finally forged between the two – for nine months of the year, Niord would make his home with Skadi in the kingdom of winter. For the other three months they would return to Noatun, where he would invoke summer for everyone in Asgard. This arrangement worked well for many years, but both Niord and Skadi felt saddened by having to vacate their homes for months on end. Finally, despite their affection for one another, it was decided that they should part.

Skadi threw herself into hunting, honing her skills so that she became the finest marksman in the land. She married the historical Odin, and she bore him a son called Saeming. Eventually, she married Uller, the god of winter and the perfect companion for the frigid goddess.

Niord returned to his palace by the sea, and frolicked there with the seals, who basked in the summer sun.

How Tyr Lost His Hand

Tyr: I of a hand am wanting,
But thou of honest fame;
Sad is the lack of either.
Nor is the wolf at ease:
He in bonds must abide
Until the gods' destruction.

Benjamin Thorpe, Saemund's Edda

TYR WAS THE SON OF ODIN and Frigga, queen of the gods. He is the god of martial honour, and one the twelve supreme deities of Asgard. He had no palace of his own, but he spent much time at Valhalla. Along with Thor, Tyr was the god of war and of courage, and he was invoked as patron saint of the sword. Tyr was distinguished by the fact that he had only one hand, and this is how it happened.

When Loki had run away and secretly married the giantess Angurboda, she bore him three horrible children – the wolf Fenris, Hel, and Jormungander, the world serpent. Loki was shocked by the appearance of these creatures, and he hid them carefully within Asgard so that no one knew of their existence. But eventually they grew to a size which made them impossible to confine, and when Odin discovered their presence in his kingdom, he took steps to rid Asgard of them forever.

Hel was flung into the depths of Filheim, where she would reign of the nine worlds of the dead. Jormungander was cast into the sea, where he grew to encircle the earth – biting his own tail to form a complete circle as the world serpent.

Fenris, however, was allowed to remain in Asgard, for Odin believed that an animal as beautiful as this would be capable of being trained, and perhaps growing to protect the inhabitants of his kingdom from attacks. None of the gods dared to go near him, and it looked as though Odin's plans would be impossible – when Tyr stepped forward and volunteered to feed and tend to the angry wolf. A tentative relationship was established between the brave god and the wolf, and Fenris accepted food from Tyr, and allowed him to approach without eating him whole.

But like the world serpent, who grew to encircle the earth in just a few short months, Fenris soon reached a size that made it unsafe for any man or god to approach him. His size and strength had become frightening, even for the courageous Tyr, and so the council of Asgard met to discuss his fate.

The peace treaty which had been signed by all members of the council did not allow any blood to be shed on the shores of Asgard. It was therefore decided that Fenris should be bound by the strongest of cables, and kept as their prisoner until such time as they could work magic strong enough to control him.

The first chains were brought forth, and Fenris laughed out loud when he saw them. He held still as they were woven around his limbs, confident that he could burst them apart with one flex of his mighty muscles. His confidence was justified, for just seconds after the chains were locked, he released himself with ease.

The next chains were the strongest as any ever produced by gods, and they were duly wrapped around the heaving bulk of Fenris. Again, they were burst in one breath, and Fenris sat back and laughed at the sight of the puzzled gods.

And so it was that Loki was sent to the dark elves, where the dwarfs were requested to turn their magic to manufacture a binding that no man or beast could break. It was by magic that the silken rope was woven by dwarfs, formed from the sound of a cat's footsteps, a woman's beard, the spittle of birds and the longing of the bear. When it was complete, it was duly handed to Loki, who brought it to Asgard with a flourish. They named it Gleipnir.

Fenris looked carefully at the silken rope, and then shook his head. He would not allow himself to be wrapped in this cord, for although it seemed slender, and insubstantial, he had a deep instinctive distrust and he could not go against his nature. The gods surrounded him then, pleading that he hold still and test his strength against the slight bond of the cord.

Fenris sat quietly, and then spoke, his words falling like stones around the assembled gods. 'I will lay still for the binding, if I have your pledge that no magic arts have been used in its manufacture. As a symbol of your honour, I would like the arm of one of the gods to be placed in my mouth as you bind me.'

The gods looked at one another, and then at Fenris. There was no question but that magic had been used to produce Gleipnir – for it was the only way they would be able to make something strong enough to control the wolf. They began to draw back, admitting defeat, when the sturdy 'yr strode forward, and confidently placed his arm in the enormous jaws. The gods moved ıuickly, and fastened Gleipnir around Fenris's neck and paws, and when they were finished, and 'enris was quite unable to free himself, they shouted with pleasure. At that moment, the great ıws snapped down, biting the god's hand at the wrist and swallowing it whole.

Tyr took this maiming with dignity, and he learned to use the maimed arm as his shield and ɔ wield his sword with his left hand. Fenris was taken to the boulder Thviti, which was sunk leep into the ground. There he let out such fearful howls that the gods were forced to take et one more measure to silence him. Tyr himself forged a steel sword of intense strength and ɔurpose, and he placed it into the mouth of the great wolf so that the hilt rested in the lower aws, and the point rested in the top of his mouth. Fenris's efforts to dislodge it caused a stream ɔf blood to surge forth, and this became the river Von.

Fenris remained there until the last day, and then he would burst forth to prowl the ːarth forever.

The Passing of the Dwarfs

Away! let not the sun view me –
I dare no longer stay;
An Elfin-child, thou wouldst me see,
To stone turn at his ray.
Friedrich de la Motte-Fouqué

WHEN THE EARTH WAS FORMED, the first dwarfs were bred from the corpse of Ymir. Dwarfs were also called black elves, and they were such ugly creatures that it was decreed that they should not be allowed to show their faces above ground, for fear of frightening gods and men to death. They were dark of skin, which made them nearly invisible in the dark, and they were never seen, for they risked being turned to stone by appearing in the daylight. Dwarfs were fine craftsmen, and although they lacked the size and power of the gods, they were certainly more intelligent than any other form of life in the nine worlds, and they were called upon often by the gods to provide assistance when their own magic failed.

And so it was that the dwarfs became great friends to the gods, helping them out by producing the peerless ship Skidbladnir, the golden locks of Sif, the hammer Miolnir, the golden-skinned pig Gulinbursti, the ring Draupnir, the spear Gungnir, and Freya's exquisite necklace, Brisingamen. Without these aids, the gods would never have had the power to keep at bay their many enemies, and when the old gods finally succumbed, the dwarfs themselves lost interest in the world above, and disappeared. This was the passing of the dwarfs.

When the old gods were no longer worshipped in the north, the dwarfs formed a conference and it was decided that they could no longer offer any help to humankind. For centuries they had made themselves useful in households – appearing to knead bread, or help with the farming, or rock a baby when necessary. But the twilight of the gods had caused a change of heart. One night, the dwarfs hired a ferryman, and for the whole of that night he was kept busy, filling his

boat with his invisible passengers, so that it nearly sank, and transporting them back and fort
across the river. When his night's work was complete, he was rewarded with riches beyond hi
greatest imaginings. The next morning the dwarfs had vanished from the land of the dark elve
a cry of protest against the disbelief of the people. Left to his own resources, no man was capabl
of running a household as smoothly without the helpful dwarfs, and no weapon as wondrous c
as invincible as those formed by the dwarfs was ever produced again. The passing of the dwarf
marked the end of an age, and the end of the camaraderie between the two worlds.

Oberon and Titiana

Every elf and fairy sprite
Hop as light as bird from brier;
And this ditty after me
Sing, and dance it trippingly.
William Shakespeare, A Midsummer Night's Dream

NO DISCUSSION OF THE ELVES, or dwarfs as they were commonly known, is complete without a few words about Oberon. There are stories told far and wide o the fairy king Oberon, and his delicate queen Titiania. Oberon was so exquisitel handsome, that mortals were drawn into his fairy world after just one glance at his elegant profile. In every country across the world, there was a sense of unease on the eve of Midsummer, for this is when the fairies congregate around Oberon and Titiana and dance. Fairy dances are a magical thing, and their music is so compelling that all who hear it find it irresistible. But once a human, or indeed a god, succumbs to the fairy music, and begins to dance, he will be damned to do so until the end of his days, when he will die of an exhaustion like none other.

Oberon was also very powerful, and his tricks above ground became legend throughout many lands. With the passing of the dwarfs, humankind had no help with their work, and the little folk were no longer considered to be a blessed addition to a household. Many believe that Oberon harnessed the powers of Frey when he fell, and used them beneath the earth to set up a kingdom of fairies which was a complex and commanding as Asgard had once been. With his strength, and his overwhelming beauty, he was considered by man to be nothing more than a demon.

The End of the World

We shall see emerge
From the bright Ocean at our feet an earth
More fresh, more verdant than the last, with fruits
Self-springing, and a seed of man preserved,
Who then shall live in peace, as then in war.
Matthew Arnold, Balder Dead

BALDER WAS PURE OF HEART, and he represented goodness in every form. His life in Asgard was one of kindness and generosity, and while he lived the force of his righteousness would allow everyone in Asgard to enjoy peace from evil. But evil comes in many forms and not even the gods could be protected from its sinister influence forever. In Asgard, Loki was the evil that would burst the bauble of their happiness, and it was Loki who would bring about the end to the eternal conflict between virtue and corruption. It was an end that had been predicted since the earth was created, and its reality was as frightening as every prediction had suggested. Ragnarok would rid the world of evil, and leave a trail of ashes that blotted out the sun and all that had once glowed in their gilded world. But it is from ashes that new life springs, and the world of the Viking gods was no exception.

The Death of Balder

So on the floor lay Balder dead; and round
Lay thickly strewn swords, axes, darts, and spears,
Which all the Gods in sport had idly thrown
At Balder, whom no weapon pierced or clove;
But in his breast stood fixed the fatal bough
Of mistletoe, which Lok, the Accuser, gave
To Hoder, and unwitting Hoder threw –
'Gainst that alone had Balder's life no charm.

Matthew Arnold, Balder Dead

BALDER WAS the beautiful, radiant god of light and innocence. Each life that he touched glowed with goodness, and he was loved by all who knew him. His twin brother was Hodur, who was blind, and Balder tended to him with every kindness and consideration. Hodur worshipped Balder, and would do nothing in his power to harm him.

There came a morning when Balder woke with the dawn, his face tightened with fear and foresight. He had dreamed of his own death and he lay there petrified, aware, somehow, that the strength of this dream forecasted sinister things to come. So Balder travelled to see Odin, who listened carefully, and knew at once that the fears of his son were justified – for in his shining eyes there was no longer simply innocence; there was knowledge as well. Odin went at once to his throne at the top of Yggdrasill, and he prayed there for a vision to come to him. At once he saw the head of Vala the Seer come to him, and he knew he must travel to Hel's kingdom, to visit Vala's grave. Only then would he learn the truth of his favourite son's fate.

It was many long days before Odin reached the innermost graves on Hel's estate. He moved quietly so that Hel would not know of his coming, and he was disregarded by most of the workers in her lands, for they were intent on some celebrations, and were preparing the hall for the arrival of an esteemed guest. At last the mound of Vala's grave appeared, and he sat there on it, keeping his head low so that the prophetess would not catch a glimpse of his face. Vala was a seer of all things future, and all things past; there was nothing that escaped her bright eyes, and she could be called upon only by the magic of the runes to tell of her knowledge.

The grave was wreathed in shadows, and a mist hung uneasily over the tombstone. There was silence as Odin whispered to Vala to come forth, and then, at once, there was a grating and steaming that poured forth an odour that caused even the all-powerful Odin to gag and spit.

'Who disturbs me from my sleep,' said Vala with venom. Odin thought carefully before replying. He did not wish her to know that he was Odin, king of gods and men, for she may not wish to tell him of a future that would touch on his own. And so he responded:

'I am Vegtam, son of Valtam, and I wish to learn of the fate of Balder.'

'Balder's brother will slay him,' said Vala, and with that she withdrew into her grave.

Odin leapt up and cried out, 'With the power of the runes, you must tell me more. Tell me, Vala, which esteemed guest does Hel prepare for?'

'Balder,' she muttered from the depths of her grave, 'and I will say no more.'

Odin shook his head with concern. He could not see how it could be possible that Balder's brother would take his life; Balder and Hodur were the closest of brothers, and shared the same thoughts and indeed speech for much of the time. He returned to Asgard with his concerns still intact, and he discussed them there with Frigga, who listened carefully.

'I have a plan,' she announced, 'and I am certain you will agree that this is the best course of action for us all. I plan to travel through all nine lands, and I will seek the pledge of every living creature, every plant, every metal and stone, not to harm Balder.'

And Frigga was as good as her word, for on the morrow she set out and travelled far and wide, everywhere she went extracting with ease the promise of every living creature, and inanimate object, to love Balder, and to see that he was not injured in any way.

And so it was that Balder was immune to injury of any kind, and it became a game among the children of Asgard to aim their spears and arrows at him, and laugh as they bounced off, leaving him unharmed. Balder was adored throughout the worlds, and there was no one who did not smile when he spied him.

No one, that is except Loki, whose jealousy of Balder had reached an unbearable pitch. Each night he ruminated over the ways in which he could murder Balder, but he could think of none. Frigga had taken care to involve all possible dangers in her oath, and there was nothing now that would hurt him. But the scheming Loki was not unwise, and he soon came up with a plan. Transforming himself into a beggarwoman, he knocked on Frigga's door and requested a meal. Frigga was pleased to offer her hospitality, and she sat down to keep the beggar company as she ate.

Loki, in his disguise, chattered on about the handsome Balder, who he'd seen in the hall, and he mentioned his fears that Balder would be killed by one of the spears and arrows he had seen hurled at him. Frigga laughed, and explained that Balder was now invincible.

'Did everything swear an oath to you then?' asked Loki slyly.

'Oh, yes,' said Frigga, but then she paused, 'all, that is, except for a funny little plant which was growing at the base of the oak tree at Valhalla. Why I'd never before set eyes on such a little shoot of greenery and it was far too immature to swear to anything so important as my oath.'

'What's it called?' asked Loki again.

'Hmmm,' said Frigga, still unaware of the dangers her information might invoke, 'mistletoe. Yes, mistletoe.'

Loki thanked Frigga hastily for his meal, and left her palace, transforming at once into his mischievous self, and travelling to Valhalla as quickly as his feet would take him. He carefully plucked the budding mistletoe, and returned to Odin's hall, where Balder played with the younger gods and goddesses, as they shot him unsuccessfully with arms of every shape and size.

Hodur was standing frowning in the corner, and Loki whispered for him to come over.

'What is it, Hodur,' he asked.

'Nothing, really, just that I cannot join their games,' said Hodur quietly.

'Come with me,' said Loki, 'for I can help.' And leading Hodur to a position close to Balder, he placed in his hands a bow and arrow fashioned from the fleetest of fabrics. To the end of the arrow, he tied a small leaf of mistletoe, and topped the razor-sharp tip with a plump white berry. 'Now, shoot now,' he cried to Hodur, who pulled back the bow and let the arrow soar towards its target.

There was a sharp gasp, and then there was silence. Hodur shook his head with surprise – where were the happy shouts, where was the laughter telling him that his own arrow had hit its mark and failed to harm the victim? The silence spoke volumes, for Balder lay dead in a circle of admirers as pale and frightened as if they had seen Hel herself.

The agony spread across Asgard like a great wave. When it was discovered who had shot the fatal blow, Hodur was sent far from his family, and left alone in the wilderness. He had not yet had a moment to utter the name of the god who had encouraged him to perpetrate this grave crime, and his misery kept him silent.

Frigga was disconsolate with grief. She begged Hermod, the swiftest of her sons, to set out at once for Filheim, to beg Hel to release Balder to them all. And so he climbed upon Odin's finest steed, Sleipnir, and set out for the nine worlds of Hel, a task so fearsome that he shook uncontrollably.

In Asgard, Frigga and Odin carried their son's body to the sea, where a funeral pyre was created and lit. Nanna, Balder's wife, could bear it no longer, and before the pyre was set out on the tempestuous sea, she threw herself on the flames, and perished there with her only love. As a token of their great affection and esteem, the gods offered, one by one, their most prized possessions and laid them on the pyre as it set out for the wild seas. Odin produced his magic ring Draupnir, and the greatest gods of Asgard gathered to see the passing of Balder.

And so the blazing ship left the shore, will full sail set. And then darkness swallowed it, and Balder had gone.

Throughout this time, Hermod had been travelling at great speed towards Hel. He rode for nine days and nine nights, and never took a moment to sleep. He galloped on and on, bribing the watchman of each gate to let him past, and invoking the name of Balder as the reason for his journey. At last, he reached the hall of Hel, where he found Balder sitting easily with Nanna, in great comfort and looking quite content. Hel stood by his side, keeping a close watch on her newest visitor. She looked up at Hermod with disdain, for everyone knew that once a spirit had reached Hel it could not be released. But Hermod fell on one knee and begged the icy mistress to reconsider her hold over Balder.

'Please, Queen Hel, without Balder we cannot survive. There can be no future for Asgard without his presence,' he cried.

But Hel would not be moved. She held out for three days and three nights, while Hermod stayed right by her side, begging and pleading and offering every conceivable reason why Balder should be released. And finally the Queen of darkness gave in.

'Return at once to Asgard,' she said harshly, 'and if what you say is true, if everything – living and inanimate – in Asgard loves Balder and cannot live without him, then he will be released. But if there is even one dissenter, if there is even one stone in your land who does not mourn the passing of Balder, then he shall remain here with me.'

Hermod was gladdened by this news, for he knew that everyone – including Hodur who had sent the fatal arrow flying through the air – loved Balder. He agreed to these terms at once, and set off for Asgard, relaying himself and his news with speed that astonished all who saw him arrive.

Immediately, Odin sent messengers to all corners of the universe, asking for tears to be shed for Balder. And as they travelled, everyone and everything began to weep, until a torrent of water rushed across the tree of life. And after everyone had been approached, and each had shed his tears, the messengers made their way back to Odin's palace with glee. Balder would be released, there could be no doubt!

But it was not to be, for as the last messenger travelled back to the palace, he noticed the form of an old beggarwoman, hidden in the darkness of a cave. He approached her then, and bid her to cry for Balder, but she did not. Her eyes remained dry. The uproar was carried across to the palace, and Odin himself came to see 'dry eyes', whose inability to shed tears would cost him the life of his son. He stared into those eyes and he saw then what the messenger had failed to see, what Frigga had failed to see, and what had truly caused the death of Balder. For those eyes belonged to none other than Loki, and it was he who had murdered Balder as surely as if the arrow had left his own hands.

The sacred code of Asgard had been broken, for blood had been spilled by one of their own, in their own land. The end of the world was nigh – but first, Loki would be punished once and for all.

Revenge of the Gods

Thee, on a rock's point,
With the entrails of thy ice-cold son,
The god will bind.
Benjamin Thorpe, Saemund's Edda

THE WRATH OF THE GODS was so great that Asgard shuddered and shook. As Odin looked down upon Loki in the form of the beggarwoman, and made the decision to punish him, Loki transformed himself into a fly and disappeared.

Although he was crafty, even his most supreme efforts to save himself were as nothing in the face of Odin's determination to trace him.

Loki travelled to far distant mountains, and on the peak of the most isolated of them all, he built a cabin, with windows and doors on all sides so that he could see the enemy approaching, and flee from any side before they reached him. By day, he haunted a pool by a rushing waterfall, taking the shape of a salmon. His life was uncomplicated, and although he was forced to live by his wits, and the fear of the god's revenge was great, Loki was not unhappy.

From his throne above the worlds, Odin watched, and waited. And when he saw that Loki had grown complacent, and no longer looked with quite such care from his many windows, he struck.

It was one particular evening that Loki sat weaving. He had just invented what we today call a fish net, and as he worked he hummed to himself, glancing every now and then from his great windows, and then back at his work. The gods were almost upon him when he first noticed them, and they were led by Kvasir, who was known amongst all gods for his wisdom and ability to unravel the tricks of even the most seasoned trickster. And as he saw them arriving, Loki fled from the back door, and transformed himself into a salmon, and leapt into the pond.

The gods stood in the doorway, surveying the room. Kvasir walked over to the fishing net and examined it closely. His keen eyes caught a glimmer of fish scales on the floor, and he nodded sagely.

'It is my assessment,' he said, 'that our Loki has become a fish. And,' he held up the fishing net, 'we will catch him with his own web.'

The gods made their way to the stream, and the pond which lay at the bottom of the waterfall. Throwing the net into the water, they waited for daybreak, when Loki the salmon would enter the waters and be caught in their net. Of course, Loki was too clever to be trapped so easily, and he swam beneath the net and far away from the part of the pond where the gods were fishing. Kvasir soon realized their mistake, and he ordered that rocks be placed at the bottom of the net, so that none could swim beneath it. And they waited.

Loki looked with amusement at the god's trap, and gracefully soared through the air above the net, his eyes glinting in the early morning light. And as his fins were just inches from the water, and when he was so close to escape that he had begun to plan his celebrations, two firm hands were thrust out, and he was lifted into the air.

He hardly dared look at his captor, and he began to tremble when he saw that it was none other than Thor who had moved so swiftly to catch him.

'I command you to take your own form, Loki,' he shouted, holding tight to the smooth scales of the salmon.

Loki knew he was beaten. Quietly he transformed himself once again into Loki, only to find himself hung by the heels over the rippling waters. And as Thor raised his great hammer to beat Loki to death, a hand reached out and stopped him. It was Odin, and he spoke gently, and with enormous purpose.

'Death is too good for this rodent,' he whispered. 'Take him at once to the Hel's worlds and tie him there for good.'

And so it was that Loki was taken to Filheim, where Thor grabbed three massive rocks and formed a platform for the hapless trickster. Then, Loki's two sons, Vali and Nari, were brought forth, and an enchantment was laid upon Vali so that he took the form of a wolf and attacked his brother Nari, tearing him to pieces in front of his anguished father. Gathering up Nari's entrails, which were now endowed with magic properties, he tied Loki's limbs so that he lay across the three rocks, unable to move. The entrails would tighten with every effort he made to escape, and to ensure that he could not use trickery to free himself, Thor placed the rocks on a precipice. One false move and he would be sent crashing to his death in the canyon below.

Finally, Skadi caught a poisonous snake, and trapped it by its tail so that it hung over Loki's face, dripping venom into his mouth so that he screamed with pain and terror. He began to convulse and was such a terrible sight that his wife Sigyn rushed forward and begged to be allowed to stay beside him, holding a bowl with which to collect the poison.

The work of the gods was done. They turned then and left, and Sigyn remained with her husband, ever true to her wedding vows. Every day or so she moved from her position at his side in order to empty her bowl, and Loki's convulsions brought an earthquake to Asgard that lasted just as long as it took her to return with her bowl. They would remain there until the end of time – for the gods, that is. The end of time was nigh, and it was Ragnarok.

Ragnarok

Brothers slay brothers;
Sisters' children
Shed each other's blood.
Hard is the world;
Sensual sin grows huge.
There are sword-ages, axe-ages;
Shields are cleft in twain;
Storm-ages, murder-ages;
Till the world falls dead,
And men no longer spare
Or pity one another.

R. B. Anderson, Norse Mythology

THE END OF THE WORLD had been prophesied from its beginning, and everyone across the world knew what to expect when Ragnarok fell upon them. For Ragnarok was the twilight of the gods, an end to the golden years of Asgard, an end to the palaces of delight, an end to the timeless world where nothing could interfere. It was the death of Balder that set the stage for the end of the world, and it was Loki's crimes which laid in place the main characters. And when the action had begun, there was no stopping it.

When evil entered Asgard, it tainted all nine worlds. Sol and Mani, high in the sky, paled with fright, and their chariots slowed as they moved with effort across the sky. They knew that the wolves would be soon upon them and that it would be only a matter of time before eternal darkness would fall once again. And when Sol and Mani had been devoured, there was no light to shine on the earth, and the terrible cold crept into the warm reaches of summer and drew from the soil what was growing there. Snow began to drift down upon the freezing land, and soon it snowed a little faster, and a little harder, until the earth was covered once again in a dark layer of ice.

Winter was upon them, and it did not cease. For three long, frozen seasons, it was winter, and then, after a thaw that melted only one single layer of ice, it was back for three more. With the cold and the darkness came evil, which rooted itself in the hearts of men. Soon crime was rampant, and all shreds of human kindness disappeared with the spring. At last, the stars were flung from the skies, causing the earth to tremble and shake. Loki and Fenris were freed from their manacles, and together they moved forward to wreak their revenge on the gods and men who had bound them so cruelly.

At the bottom of Yggdrasill, there was a groan that emanated the entire length of the tree, for at that moment, Nithog had gnawed through the root of the world tree, which quivered and shook from bottom to top. Fialar, the red cock who made his home above Valhalla shrieked out his cry, and then flew away from the tree as his call was echoed by Gullinkambi, the rooster in Midgard.

Heimdall knew at once what was upon them, and raising his mighty horn to his lips he blew the call that filled the hearts of all gods and mankind with terror. Ragnarok. The gods sprang from their beds, and thrust aside the finery that hung in their bed chambers. They arme themselves and mounted their horses, ready for the war that had been expected since th beginning of time. They moved quickly over the rainbow bridge and then they reached the fiel of Vigrid, where the last battle would be fought.

The turmoil on earth caused the seas to toss and twist with waves, and soon the worl serpent Jormungander was woken from his deep sleep. The movement of the seas yanked hi tail from his mouth, and it lashed around, sending waves crashing in every direction. And a he crawled out upon land for the first time, a tidal wave swelled across the earth, and set afloa Nagilfar, the ship of the dead, which had been constructed from the nails of the dead whos relatives had failed in their duties, and had neglected to pare the nails of the deceased whe they were laid to rest. As the wind caught the blackened sail, Loki leapt aboard, and took he wheel – the ship of the undead captained by the personification of all evil. Loki called upon th fire-gods from Muspell, and they arrived in a conflagration of terrible glory.

Another ship had set out for Vigrid, and this was steered by Hrym and crewed by the frost giants who had waited many centuries for this battle. Across the raging sea, both vessels mad for the battlefield.

As they travelled, Hel, crept from her underground estate, bringing with her Nithog, and th hellhound Garm. From up above, there was a great crack, and Surtr, with sword blazing, leap with his sons to the Bifrost bridge, and with one swoop they felled it, and sent the shimmerin rainbow crashing to the depths below. Quickly, Odin escaped from the battlefield, and slippe one last time to the Urdar fountain, where the Norns sat quietly, accepting their fate. He lean over Mimir, and requested her wisdom, but for once the head would not talk to him, and he remounted Sleipnir and returned to the field, frightened and aware that he had no powers lef with which to defend his people.

The opposing armies lined themselves on Vigrid field. On one side were the Aesir, the Vani and the Einheriear – on the other, were the fire-giants led by Surtr, the frost-giants, the undead with Hel, and Loki with his children – Fenris and Jormungander. The air was filled with poison and the stench of evil from the opposing army, yet the gods held up their heads and prepared for a battle to end all time.

And so it was that the ancient enemies came to blows. Odin first met with the evil Fenris, and as he charged towards the fierce wolf, Fenris's massive jaws stretched open and Odin was flung deep into the red throat. Thor stopped in his tracks, the death of his father burning deep in his breast, and with renewed fury he lunged at the world serpent, engaging in a combat that would last for many hours. His hammer laid blow after blow on the serpent, and at last there was silence. Thor sat back in exhaustion, Jormungander dying at his side. But as Thor made to move forward, to carry on and support his kin in further battles, the massive serpent exhaled one last time, in a cloud of poison so vile that Thor fell at once, lifeless in the mist of the serpent's breath.

Tyr fought bravely with just one arm, but he, like his father, was swallowed whole, by the hellhound Garm, but as he passed through the gullet of the hound he struck out one last blow with his sword and pierced the heart of his enemy, dying in the knowledge that he had obtained his life's ambition.

Heimdall met Loki hand to hand, and the forces of good and evil engaged in the battle that had been raging for all time. Their flames engulfed one another; there was a flash of light. And then there was nothing.

The silent Vidar came rushing from a distant part of the plain to avenge the death of Odin, and he laid upon the jaw of Fenris a shoe which had been created for this day. With his arms and legs in motion he tore the wolf's head from his body, and then lay back in a pool of blood. Of all the gods, only Frey was left fighting. He battled valiantly, and as he laid down giant after giant, he felt a warmth on the back of his neck that meant only one thing. The heat burned and sizzled his skin, and as he turned he found himself face to face with Surtr. With a cry of rage that howled through the torn land, and shook the massive stem of the world ash, Yggdrasill, Surtr flung down bolts of fire that engulfed the golden palaces of the gods, and each of the worlds which lay beneath it. The heat caused the seas to bubble and to boil, and there came at once a wreath of smoke that blotted out the fire, and then, the world.

At last all was as it had been in the beginning. There was blackness. There was chaos. There was a nothingness that stretched as far as there was space.

The End of the World

All evil
Dies there an endless death, while goodness riseth
From that great world-fire, purified at last,
to a life far higher, better, nobler than the past.
R. B. Anderson, Viking Tales of the North

THE EARTH WAS PURGED by the fire and there was at once a new beginning. The sun rose in the sky, mounted on a chariot driven by the daughter of Sol, born before the wolf had eaten her father and her mother. Fresh green grass sprung up in the crevices, and flowers and fruits burst forth. Two new humans, Lif, a woman, and Lifthrasir, a man, emerged from Mimir's forest, where they had been reincarnated at the end of the world. Vali and Vidar, the forces of nature had survived the fiery battle, and they returned to the plan to be greeted by Thor's sons, Modi and Magni, who carried with them their father's hammer.

Hoenir had escaped from the Vanir, who had vanished forever, and from the deepest depths of the earth came Balder, renewed and as pure as he had ever been. Hodur rose with him, and the two brothers embraced, and greeted the new day. And so this small group of gods turned to face the scenes of destruction and devastation, and to witness the new life that was already curling up from the cloak of death and darkness. The land had become a refuge for the good. They looked up – they all looked way up – and there in front of them, stronger than ever was the world ash, Yggdrasill, which had trembled but not fallen.

There was a civilization to be created, and a small band of gods with whom it could be done. The gods had returned in a blaze of white light – a light as pure and virtuous as the new inhabitants of the earth – and in that light they brought forth our own world.

Scottish Myths

Introduction

Look not thou on beauty's charming,
Sit thou still when kings are arming,
Taste not when the wine-cup glistens,
Speak not when the people listens,
Stop thine ear against the singer,
From the red gold keep thy finger;
Vacant heart and hand, and eye,
Easy live and quiet die.

Sir Walter Scott, The Bride of Lammermoor

HIGH ON THE HILLS of Scotland, where the wind answers the cry of the restless seas, where the land dips and soars, and the trees whisper of days gone by, there is a peat fire. And round that fire, fables are spun, myths are embroidered and legends unravelled. The wood folk dart among the trees. Over that hill is a loch, but the monster is silent once more, awaiting the day when the village charms have been cast aside or forgotten. That grassy knoll houses fairies, to be sure, and now, the storytellers draw closer round the fire, for when night lays her cloak across the land, it comes alive.

And so it was that the rich tradition of Scottish myths and legends, folktales and stories was born and passed on. The teller might be a villager, or he may have come from afar, a traveller or a caird. The story is his own, or it has been drawn from centuries of tales, sewn together and embellished. The legend is local fare – modern, perhaps, or as old as the land upon which their fire is lit.

The mythology of Scotland is varied and dynamic, spilling over with creatures from another realm, with transformations and mysteries, with wisdom and heroic battles, with morality and trickery. The thread that links the heritage of myths and legends in Scotland lacks the continuity of the classical myths, but it is distinguished, nonetheless, by a profound capacity to entertain, to explain, to produce a philosophy for living.

Mythology is a dangerous term to use here, one which has grown increasingly to mean myth in the classical sense, a story about superhuman characters or an earlier age, which usually explains how natural phenomena and customs came into existence. The mythology of Scotland is much more disparate, often closer to being history or literature than character-led adventure. The myths of Scotland express ideas about origins of people and of places – about the world as a whole, and the world that surely must exist under and above us.

The word 'myth' comes from the ancient Greek for 'word', and therefore means anything that is spoken – a story or tale of any kind. It has grown, however, to embrace a large number of genres and stories – those which are based on historical or modern legend, those which have a didacticism that enhances its purpose; fairytales or tales of magic and mystery which serve the purpose of explaining the unknown; fables which were created to explain the nature of the earth, man, animals, the stars or the land; and then those stories which were written with a moral message, for children, or to prop up religious belief.

There is an intense and fundamental superstition which feeds the myths of Scotland, and which produces a kind of pagan religion by which people were forced to live. The stories and folktales of Scotland were as ingrained in everyday life as any later religious dogma. There is a structure to the beliefs, and that is what forms the basis of Scottish mythology which although certainly less lavish and expansive than that of the Greeks and Romans, exists in a comprehensive form.

Scottish mythology was, until very recently, an almost entirely oral tradition, and it was, for this reason, constantly changing shape. There was no Homer in Scotland, so the minutiae of their legends, of their beliefs, were never transcribed, never given credence as a whole, never linked in a comprehensive document. Today, much of Scottish mythology is lost, as a result of a dwindling population of travellers, and the death of the age of the bard, the caird, the village storyteller. And, while some stories have continued to circulate, to become part of the unwritten legacy of the country, many have disappeared, or changed so fundamentally as to lose their initial spirit and purpose.

The two different types of storytelling traditions in Scotland are those in Gaelic and in Scots. The Gaelic tradition, which has its roots in the Highlands, is similar to Irish storytelling, although littered with references to the history, the landscape and the clan structure of Scotland. The Scots tradition was based in the Lowlands, influenced by Gaelic storytelling, but is much more like that of the English, with less ornamentation and briefer texts.

The transcription of Scottish myths was an arduous process for while the theme, the basic motif or the moral remained the same, the setting and character, and often the events varied with every new village. Unfortunately, until this century, the transcription process failed to record intonation, gesture, pace and often atmosphere, so that the myths lack the individuality that was so dependent on the personality of the narrator.

In the ninth century, a monk of Bango called Nennius produced a compilation of tales and legends of Britain, which was entitled Historia Brittonum, or History of the Britains. A number of Scottish myths and legends made their way into his collection, and this is the first major attempt at a written record of the oral tradition. He also outlined the history of the Scots in his book, and it is this document in which legends and myths become indiscernible from known fact. Nennius himself said that he compiled the chronicle of Britain's history and arcane lore because he felt the oral transmission was insufficient for future transmission to later generations. And this was largely the case.

But since that time, there have been many chroniclers, and storytellers with a keen knowledge of myths and an overwhelming interest in maintaining the tradition. The myths that have been recorded are often embroidered, and interspersed with other myths and legends, and local, often modern fact, but the basic premise still exists in these myths and without these early attempts to give them posterity, the heritage of Scotland would be much weaker.

After the ninth century, the nature of myths and legends changed, for these were now based more on true events, chivalry, heroes and great adventure. Heroes of the Scottish independence took precedence at that time, and much of the earlier material was lost. Because stories were passed more easily across the country by this point, and there was a more conscious attempt to produce fiction that was enthralling and evocative, rather than simply a good story drawn from an old legend, there was a radical change in the mythological fabric.

After that, there were other additions to the lore of the country. Witches, for instance, began to appear around the eleventh century, inspired, it is said, by King James VI and I, who was a great believer. Sir Walter Scott and Robert Burns produced material in the eighteenth century that mimicked some legends, reproduced others, and then invented still more. The heroes were based on historical figures in the Middle Ages, many of which were borrowed from England and from Ireland, including the great Fionn MacChumail (anglicized to Finn McCool or Fingal).

The tales were based on a number of men who really existed – their magnificent feats joined together to become the career of one single man. Other heroes were fictional, developed to ensure the Scots some supremacy in the ancient world.

In 1760, a Scottish schoolteacher, James Macpherson, produced a ream of translations of what he claimed were verses from Ossian, son of Fionn. There was enormous controversy about these poems, which many considered to be fakes, as the original Gaelic documents were never produced. Until this time, there had been many tales, songs and poems attributed to Ossian, which preserved the legends surrounding him, but there had never been enough material to give the adventures of this hero epic status. Many consider Macpherson's translations to be dull and uninspired. He wrote in *Temora*:

The blue waves of Erin roll in light.
The mountains are covered with day.
Trees shake their dusky heads in the breeze.
Grey torrents pour their noisy streams.
Two green hills, with aged oaks, surround the narrow plain.
The blue course of a stream is there.

But whatever fraud or deceit existed in this collection, it provided many later poets and authors with enormous inspiration, and gave Scotland a hero when few had been recorded.

In the nineteenth century, John Gregorson Campbell compiled one of the best-known collections of Gaelic folktales and legends, painstakingly transcribing the stories, and attributing them to their teller and his location. His collection included many atmospheric touches, among them striking pictures of the storytellers themselves, which brought a surge of new life to an art which was slowing expiring. He said, in one collection, 'I found them to be men with clear heads and wonderful memories, generally very poor and old, living in remote corners of remote islands and speaking only Gaelic.' Of one of these narrators, Donald MacPhie, from whom Campbell collected many of his tales, he wrote:

He had the manner of a practised narrator, and it is quite evident he is one; he chuckled at the interesting parts, and laid his withered finger on my knee as he gave out the terrible bits with due solemnity. A small boy in a kilt, with large round glittering eyes, was standing mute at his knee, gazing at his wrinkled face, and devouring every word. The boy's mother first boiled, then mashed, potatoes; and his father, a well grown man in tartan breeks, ate them. Ducks and ducklings, a cat and a kitten, some hens and a baby, all tumbled about on a clay floor together, and expressed their delight at the savoury prospect, each in his own fashion; and three wayfarers dropped in and listened for a spell, and passed their remarks till the ford was shallow. The light came streaming down the chimney, and through a single pane of glass, lighting up a tract in the blue mist of the peat smoke, and fell on the white hair and brown withered face of the old man, as he sat on a low stool with his feet to the fire; and the rest of the dwelling, with all its plenishing of boxes and box-beds, dishes and dresser, and gear of all sorts, faded away through shades of deepening brown, to the black darkness of the smoked roof and the 'peat corner'.

The main difference between tales which have been transcribed, and those which have been maintained in the oral tradition, is the use of repetition. In literature, such repetition is wearing, in performance, it is an effective device to engage an audience.

The stories were often peculiar to the region, and certain storytellers had a range of tales upon which they called. Neil Philip, in his Penguin Book of Scottish Fairytales, quotes Campbell:

'Each branch of popular lore has its own special votaries, as branches of literature have amongst the learned; that one man is the peasant historian and tells of the battles of the clans; another, a walking peerage, who knows the descent of most of the families of Scotland, and all about his neighbours and their origins; others are romancers, and tell about the giants; others are moralists, and prefer the sagacious prose tales, which have a meaning, and might have a moral; a few know the history of the Fein, and are antiquarians. Many despise the whole as frivolities; they are practical moderns, and answer to practical men in other ranks of society.'

Many cultures, including the Scottish cairds, believed that all tales have a moral, and were a key part of the education of children and young adults. Therefore, most families nurtured the art of telling stories, and legends, of relating memories in their own homes. Hero tales were entertaining, and they provided Scotland with an elaborate and romantic history.

Unlike the mythology of the Celts, which demands that a myth fulfil a certain purpose, and a legend be based upon specific criteria, Scottish mythology is a tapestry of interwoven fact, fiction, legend, myth, fable, folklore – peopled by ghosts, witches and other supernatural beings, royalty, talking animals, fairies and other immortals, heroes and labourers. There is a spareness of detail in the tales, and an element of wonder in almost every story, which becomes a distinguishing feature of the culture, and the splendid powers of imagination it engenders.

The Scots have always been a fiery, vital people, and Scotland a place of mystery and enchantment, inspired, possibly, by the spectacularly dramatic landscape. According to the blend of fact and fiction that has become Scottish legend, the Scots were born in Greater Scythia. A banished noble was sent to Egypt, it was said, about the time of the Exodus, and he married the daughter of the Pharaoh, Scotta. When the Egyptian army was drowned in the Red Sea, in hot pursuit of the Israelites, Egypt was so weakened that this noble feared for the kingdom, which was left open to invasion by the Scythians. Using the name of his wife, he drew together friends and companions and began what would be a forty-two-year pilgrimage to Spain, travelling through the Mediterranean, and along Africa and Gibraltar. Here, the Scots, as they were now known, lived for many thousands of years, at last giving in to the marauders and savages of the country by leaving its shores for Ireland.

And it was from Ireland that the first Scots made their way to the country that now bears their name, maintaining their fierce reputation although their numbers were somewhat diminished. They settled at Argyll, then called Dalriada, and the Scots of Dalriada produced kings of their own and lived there independently for many years. When they were strong enough, they took on the Picts, who were finally displaced.

There are many variations on this story; many disbelieve that the Scots ever travelled from the Middle East. Some give them mixed Irish and Pictish parentage, others adhere to the belief that they were deported from Assyria as Israelites.

In reality, the Scots can be traced to Ireland, through archaeological findings, and various manuscripts which exist. During the Roman period, the Celtic Irish were called 'Scottis', and it was these Irishmen who raided Britain as the Roman Empire fell. They spread across Britain (this can be traced by various inscriptions which mark the course of their invasion), and finally, some 150 of these colonists settled in Argyll, in the late fifteenth century. The leaders of this group were the three sons of a chief called Erc, which was headed by Fergus.

It was this group which spawned the realm of Dalriada, the kings of which ruled from Dunadd, in the Kintyre peninsula. And although the spirit of the intrepid explorer remained, hese settlers were not distinguished by any great military men. It was St Columba who brought them notoriety, when he founded his monastery of Iona, which was responsible for the spread of Christianity among the Picts. Scotland became a state in 1320, with the Declaration of Arbroath, when Bruce became king of Scotland.

With St Columba came a host of legends which have become a fundamental part of Scotland's history and subsequently her image. Columba, for instance, was said to have travelled one day to see the Pictish King Bridei, the son of the Maelgwn of Gwynedd. The journey was long and arduous, and St Columba was forced to climb the Great Glen and travel across Loch Ness. Here, on the banks of the river that enters the loch at Fort Augustus, Columba asked one of his monks to swim across to collect a boat from the bank opposite. As he swam, the monk was pursued by a fierce monster, who spat and roared at the poor terrified monk. St Columba stepped in and ordered the monster not to harm him, and the monster disappeared. Until this day, although the monster does make an occasional appearance, he has never harmed anyone.

There are other, exquisitely detailed stories which punctuate the career of St Columba in Scotland. His monastery at Iona became hallowed ground, and sixty kings are buried here, Scottish, Irish and Norwegian, including the great MacBeth. This graveyard was dedicated to Columba's brother Oran, who died there voluntarily when it was decreed that someone must be sacrificed in order to consecrate the ground. Legend has been built around this event, for it is said that after twenty days of being buried, when a pit was dug over his grave, he spoke, saying:

Heaven is not what it is said to be;
Hell is not what it is said to be;
The saved are not forever happy;
The damned are not forever lost.

He was buried then for ever more. St Columba died in 597, but Iona had become the centre of Christianity in the north, and would remain so for centuries to come.

By the time Columba died, the Scots had begun their fight for power, which was finally resolved in the ninth century, when Kenneth MacAlpine, a Dalriadic king, created the Scottish realm. He claimed the throne of Pictland, saying that he was born with the blood of the Picts, and he destroyed the most powerful Picts during a banquet at Scone. He was also responsible for bringing the Stone of Destiny there. These places still have a mystique and an intrigue that reeks of legend and the myths built around them, and many places like them still exist in Scotland and her isles.

The minstrels of word are few and far between in Scotland, and while her tradition has now been transcribed, and fragments pieced together to form a coherent mythology, it has ceased to grow further. Scotland's storytelling heritage has lasted far longer than in the rest of Britain, and men and women still gathered round the fire in this century, knitting, mending, preparing ropes for fishing the next day. And the myths, folktales, legends and stories which were told time and again have produced a tapestry which refuses to be unwoven, marking forever the vibrant ideology and vivid imagination of its creators.

The stories in this chapter are drawn from many original sources, including Macpherson's tales of Ossian, Campbell's four volumes of stories, and more recently, Neil Philip's Scottish Folktales, A J. Bruford and D.A. MacDonald's Scottish Traditional Tales, and Geoffrey Ashe's Mythology of the British Isles. The author would like to acknowledge their very real contribution to this work.

Legends of Witchcraft

'Tis now the very witching time of the night,
When churchyards yawn and hell itself breathes out
Contagion to this world: now could I drink hot blood,
And do such bitter business as the day
Would quake to look on.
William Shakespeare, MacBeth

WITCHCRAFT CONSPIRED to manipulate the lives of men and women, across the lands of Scotland, and across the ages. The old woman in the village might have powers that not everyone could understand, and when something went wrong, when illness fell, someone had to be given blame for the misfortune. The witchlore of Scotland was spawned and accentuated under the reign of James VI and I, who had an overwhelming superstition of and belief in them. Ultimately, however, the belief in witches reflects a pagan fear of spirits and creatures of the unknown. Witches could cast spells that enchanted, calmed, killed and controlled, and for that they were dreaded and continually plotted against. All witches were eventually defeated, but until that time, it was only safe to keep charms against unusual knots, or black cats, or strange happenings on the sea, for who really knew their origin?

The Brownie

IN SCOTLAND there's a creature that's not a witch, or a warlock, or even really a fairy. He's a brownie, and he's ugly so he's not often seen by mortal eyes. For brownies are small creatures, with great bulging eyes, and faces that are furred like the backside of a donkey. Their teeth are like battered stones, and when they smile they set fear in the hearts of all men. But a brownie is a helpful soul, and although they are not often wanted round about a house or a farm, they work a kind of magic, and help to clean and to tend the farm or run the mill, for just the price of a bowl of cream, and the odd bit of oatmeal.

There once was a brownie who lived round about a house on a farm in Wester Ross in Kintail. The house on the farm was empty, so the brownie had made himself a happy home there. In this same village, near the house on the farm, lived a young miller, who shared a house with his mother. Now his mother was a greedy woman, and she dabbled in magic of all sorts, not all of it white to be sure, and she had set her sights on the young lassie at the big house on the hill, to be the wife of her young miller son.

The lassie was pretty, and her nature was kind, but the young miller was already in love with another, a servant girl who went by the name of Katie. Now Katie was as fair as the morning sky, and her cheeks were flushed with roses. She was a bonnie lass, and she would work hard with her husband to tend a mill and to make him into something grand.

Now the young miller's mother would have nothing of it: 'Look, ye must marry this farmer's daughter, with a big farm and everything, and it would be yours because her father's getting on.'

But the miller was stubborn, and he cared only for Katie.

'I can't help it mother, I love Katie, and I am gonna marry her,' he said firmly, to which his mother replied, 'You're not gonna marry Katie, because Katie is gonna die.'

But the miller's will was stronger than his love for his mother, and he married Katie in secret and took her to live in a deserted house on a farm. Now there were stories told in those parts about the brownie who had made his home there, but the miller was a friendly sort, and not easily scared, and so he convinced young Katie that it would be safe and together they went to meet with the brownie. Katie was a fair lass, and she could see that an appearance did not make a man, and although the brownie frightened her, she could sense his good nature and agreed to live there.

They settled in happily, in the house on the farm, and the brownie was made a fine bed of straw and bracken, and fed all the best bit of oatmeal and cream. For that he tended their mill, and each day new sacks of grain were laid neatly against the mill walls. He interfered not at all in their lives, but they came to love his quiet presence, his charming ways. For he would slip down the chimney as they slept and lay things just right, so that when they woke, the wee house gleamed from every corner.

As is wont to happen, especially with those who are young and in love, the young lady of the house became heavy with child, and as she grew more and more tired, the brownie would work harder, until he spent many a day in the house of the miller and Katie. He became a friend to Katie, and she became accustomed to his horrible face, warmed by his quiet presence, his charming ways. And when the baby was due to come, it was the brownie who she called to fetch her husband the miller, and he scampered with glee down the path to the mill.

Now the miller too had grown fond of the brownie, but he was more traditional than wee Katie, and he felt that the presence of his mother was necessary for that bairn to be born. And so he left Katie with the brownie, who mopped her brow as she called out with pain, and who stroked her face with his own furred hand. But as soon as the footfall of the miller's mother was heard on the path, he leapt up the chimney and disappeared from the room. For brownies are magic beings themselves and they know the dangers of a witch, especially those who dabble in magic that is not all white.

The miller's mother was friendly and calm, and in her pain and distress, Katie could not help but trust her. She allowed her mother-in-law to braid her hair, and to set her back against pillows that were freshly stuffed. A tiny black kitten was set by her side to keep company with her and the new baby. Then, turning the lassie's bed towards the door, she bid her farewell and left.

Now Katie was soothed by the presence of the witch, but when she left the pains began again in earnest and she moaned and writhed for two whole days before the miller was forced to go for help. He went first to his mother, but she feigned an illness and said she could not come back with him. And so he returned to the farm where he found poor Katie sick with exhaustion and great pain.

'I'll go for the howdie woman,' he said, for the howdie woman delivered most of the babies in the village, having the gift for midwifery. But Katie would not hear of it, so frightened she had become.

'Don't leave me here,' she sobbed. 'Send the brownie.' And that thought stopped them short, for many folk were frightened to visit them at their home because of that same brownie, and they wondered now if the howdie woman would fear to come as well.

But Katie's pain was dragging her deeper into a dreadful state, and the roses had disappeared from her cheeks. There was no sight of the bairn and there was nothing for it but to call the brownie to help.

The brownie was only too glad to help, and in the cover of darkness, with a great cloak wrapped across his hideous face, he rode off across the hills to fetch the howdie woman. And she came at once, for her calling was stronger than her fear, and she sat herself behind the brownie and wrapped her arms about him for warmth and for safety. And she whispered in his ear as they rode, 'Katie will be well again, no doubt, but I hope I don't see that brownie. I am terrified of that brownie!'

But the brownie said, 'No, don't worry, I can assure you for certain that you'll not see anything worse than what you're cuddling now.' And he drove the howdie woman to the door of the house and made off with the horse, into the darkness.

The howdie woman had seen no birth like this, and for four more days she sat with Katie, who was expiring quickly now, torn by pains that wracked her thin frame, and struggling to keep sane as they plunged her into a burning hell with every contraction.

The miller sat brooding in a chair, helpless against this pain he could not understand, and suddenly he sat up and snapped his fingers. 'I'll bet a shilling,' he said then, 'that this is the work of my mother.'

So he rode straight to the house of his mother and shouted at her, 'Take that spell off my Katie. I know you've done something.'

And his mother shook her head, and said, 'I will not. I told you she is gonna die, and you are gonna marry the farmer's daughter.' She stood firm then and would not help his poor Katie.

So poor Katie seemed destined to die in agony, and he ran away then into the night, straight to the wee brownie, for he had no one else to whom he could turn. And the brownie thought for a while, and said, 'I'll tell you what you can do. Take me down to your mother.'

'Oh, no,' said the miller, 'that wouldn't help us at all. God himself couldn't help me against my mother.'

'Ah,' said the brownie, 'but you take me down because I can become invisible, and if you were to rush in and tell your mother, "Oh, mother, mother, you've got a beautiful grandson!" and then run off again, I will stay behind to see what happens. And I'll be invisible.'

And so it was decided that the brownie would come along, and when they reached the house of his mother, the miller ran in and cried, 'Mother, you have got a beautiful grandson.'

And she said, 'What?' her face a mask of alarm and fury.

'Oh yes,' shouted the miller, 'But I can't stop, I must see Katie.' And with that he ran back over the hills to wait for the brownie.

And as he went out the door, the woman stamped her feet and pulled at her hair, cursing all the time, 'Who told him about the witches' knots in Katie's hair? How did he know about the black cat? Who told him about the raven's feathers in those great white pillows? And who told them that I'd turned her feet to the door?'

And then the brownie skipped away, as fast as his legs would carry him, over the hills to greet the miller, and together they ran back to the house on the farm where Katie lay with the howdie woman.

Now the howdie woman had only to set eyes on the grinning brownie when she was up and out the door in a flash, but the brownie set himself to work, stroking the poor lass's cheek and mopping her brow, warming her with his quiet presence and his charming ways. He untied her head, and brushed it down around her shoulders, crooning softly in her ears. Then he took those great new pillows and set them aflame in the hearth until only dust remained of those evil black feathers. And then, with one angry twist, he took the head from the kitten and burnt her too, out of sight, of course, of poor Katie. And so it was, when the brownie moved the bed round, so that her feet faced the door no longer, that the cry of an infant was heard in that house on the farm. Katie slept then, and when she woke, her baby was cleaned and swaddled, and the roses returned to her cheeks once more.

But the brownie had gone, for brownies often do that, just disappear, never to be seen again. They missed the wee man's quiet presence and his charming ways, but he had milled enough grain for twenty odd years, and they lived on that house on the farm with their new baby in comfort and in good fortune.

The Three Knots

THERE ONCE WAS A FAMILY **on the island of Heisker in Ulst. They were farm people and worked hard all the year, but when the harvest was over, and the grain tucked safely away for the frosty months ahead, they took it upon themselves to plan a little trip to Lewis, to visit some friends there.**

It was the same every year, they crossed the sea and got to Lewis where they had a grand time of it, and then they went home again, to cosy themselves away for the long frosty months. And so it was this time, that they gathered an able crew and set off.

At Lewis things seemed much the same as they ever had. The man of the family went to greet the woman of the house they were visiting, and they talked for many hours, of days of old and of good friends and family. And just as he made preparations to get off to bed, a tall lithe woman entered the room, with hair as black as a raven's back. Her eyes were cool and dark, and she whispered something to the woman of the house, and then she left, stopping only to stroke the woman's hair.

'Who's that ugly black thing,' asked the man, curious about the familiarity between the two women.

And the woman sighed and replied, 'Is that what you say? Ugly, is she? Woe betide you, man but you'll be lost in love with her before you leave Lewis; if you can, of course.' And with that she rose and went off to bed.

Now the man scowled with the thought of it, for he had three great strong bairns and a lovely wife, as fair and pink and white as this thing was black. 'Indeed,' he muttered to himself, 'I won't fall in love with her.' He spat a bit of the old tobacco into the iron sink and prepared to retire himself.

Now he rose in the morning and the first thing that ate at his mind was the thought of that tall lithe girl, with hair as black as a raven's back, and he went downstairs, stormy as the North Sea waters. That night the girl came again to the house, though she'd not been out of his mind since her last visit, and he hated her even more, all tall and lithe and black, with those cool dark eyes. But when she left he longed for her like he'd longed for no other, and he grew black himself with rage and with desire.

Now this went on every day for a week, with the man from Heisker growing silent and cold, so his wife felt afraid and begged him to take leave of that house.

'We've had a good visit now, and it's time for us to be making for home,' she said firmly to her husband, and with the last tiny shred of rational thought left in his mind, which longed for the tall, lithe girl, with hair as black as a raven's back, he agreed.

And so it was that their belongings were packed, and their big strong boat made good, and they arrived at the sea to leave. But as the first foot was set inside that big boat, a great black gale was brewed and flung at them, and they could go no further. There was nothing for it but to return to the house from which they'd come, and to that tall, lithe woman.

And again the next morning they set out, but the mists drew around them then, cool and dark, and they could go no further. There was nothing for it but to return to the house from which they'd come, and to the cool dark eyes of that woman.

But as they walked away from the coast, they met a wee old witch, with hair that was whiter than the down of a thistle, and a small wrinkled face that spoke of great wisdom. And she stopped them there, and beckoned them aside.

'Well, my good folks,' she said, 'you've a bit of trouble leaving this dark place.'

They nodded, and listened intently.

'It's no wonder,' said the wee old witch, 'seeing the kind of place you've been staying. What will you give to me for fine weather to go tomorrow?'

'Anything, anything we'll give to you,' said the wife earnestly, and looked to her husband, but his eyes were trained on the hill, on the house with the tall, lithe woman, with the cool dark eyes, and his face was rent by a longing such as she'd never seen before. 'We'll do anything,' she said again firmly.

'A pound of snuff,' said the old witch. 'And I'll need to have a word with the skipper. Send him by this evening.' And with that she showed them to the door.

So later that night the skipper of the big strong boat was sent to see the old witch, and there she handed him a rope with three big knots.

'Here you are,' she said. 'You take this aboard and you'll have a good day for sailing tomorrow. It'll not be long before you're at Lewis harbour. Now if you haven't enough wind, just open one of these knots. And then if that is not enough still, untie the second. But whatever you do, by God, don't untie the third.'

And so it happened that on that next morning, the day dawned clear and bright, with a fresh puff of wind to set them on their course. They loaded the boat, and without a backward glance, they headed to sea. And the man of the family let out a sigh of relief so long and frenzied that the others averted their eyes. His thoughts were once again pure, and the magic of that old witch had set him free. He called to the skipper.

'Untie a knot,' he said grandly, 'let's get us home at once.' And so a knot was untied, and a swift breeze blew up that sent them cutting through the waves.

'And again,' he cried, the wind cold on his body, his soul cleansed and clear. And another knot was untied, so that a great wind was let loose on the tiny ship, and they flew across the water now, the sails stretched to the limit.

And the man of the family settled himself on deck, and with the sea air licking his face, he felt safe from all danger, and perhaps a little too confident. For he called out then, 'Let's test that old woman's magic. What means that third knot?'

And his crew cowered away from him, and his wife shook her head, but he insisted, and being the man of the family, and in charge of his boat and his own fate, he had his way and the knot was untied.

What happened then is a story for the ears of the fearless only, for from the sea rose a sight that clamped shut the mouths of the men, and the wife and their children until their dying day. It was a shape, tall and lithe, with a face of sorts, from which shone cold dark eyes. And a hand was reached down, and the man of the family plucked from amongst them, and into the sea. And then the boat itself was lifted high above the waves, placed on the sands of Heisker from where she'd never move again.

She's still there, a warning to all who think that magic can be tested, and the land there has come to be called Port Eilein na Culaigh, or Port of the Island of the Boat.

The Daughter of Duart

THERE ONCE WAS A MAN, MacLean of Duart, who sent his daughter to become a scholar. Now in those days, an education was a novelty for a lassie, but so highly did he think of his daughter that he found the money, and sent her away. And a long time she was away, too, for it was three or four years before her feet touched the MacLean soil once more.

While she was gone, the man, MacLean of Duart, would sit himself in her room, and look around him. It was a fine room, it was, for so highly did he think of his daughter that he found the money to buy her everything she ever wanted. There were books a plenty, but since MacLean of Duart could not read, they meant nothing to them, with their drawings of cats, and circles, and great long poems. There were pictures, too, on the walls of that room, and a soft cover on the bed, that made it look just so. For she was a clever girl, and she knew how to make a room feel warm.

MacLean of Duart was lonely without his daughter, but he carried on working his land, and the day came again when she returned home to him there. And so it was that he took his daughter on his arm, and led her up into the hills, where the clouds quivered around them and the air shone bright and blue. Then they looked around them, at all the beauty of the land and he turned to her, his eyes alight with pride and joy, and he said to his daughter, 'How much have you learned?'

And his daughter stopped, and she looked about, across the mossy hills to the sea beyond, and there she pointed to a tall ship, which fought a course away from them against the waves.

'There,' she said, 'that ship. I have learned enough to bring it to shore.'

And her father laughed warmly, and taking her arm again, he said, 'Well, then, lass, bring her in.'

The ship turned then, and made its way across the waters towards them. And it kept on coming, as the water grew shallow and the sands rose up to meet it, and then the rocks were there, thrusting their way through the waves as the prow of the ship drew nigh. And that ship kept on coming until it was about to be wrecked on the rocks.

MacLean of Duart looked at his daughter then, and he said with a soft voice, 'Save them now lass. Why don't you save them now.'

And his daughter shrugged her shoulders, and she smiled an easy smile, then said, 'But I can't. I don't know how to do that.'

There was silence then, filled by the crash of the ship upon the rocks. He turned to her then, did MacLean of Duart, and he laid down her arm. He looked at his daughter with new eyes, and he said to her, 'Well, then. If that is the education I have bought you, if that is what you have learned, then I would rather your room than your company.'

He strode home, and built a great fire. And when his daughter came in after him, he cut her to bits and burnt her there, saying, as he poked the flames, 'I will never have your sort in the same place as myself.'

And he went to her room, and gathered together her books, and her pictures, and threw them on the fire. Then he took her soft cover from her bed and put that on, too, till there was no trace of the girl who was his daughter. For MacLean of Duart thought so highly of his daughter that he could not allow her to practise the education she'd gathered, for he would have nothing to do with black magic, and she had mastered the art.

The Cauldron

THE LITTLE ISLAND OF SANDRAY juts firmly through the waves of the Atlantic Ocean, which spits and surges around it. No human lives there, although sheep graze calmly on the succulent green grass, freshened by the moist salt air, and kept company by the fairy folk who live in a verdant knoll. But once upon a time there were men and women on the island of Sandray, and one was a herder's wife, called Mairearad, who kept a tiny cottage on the northernmost tip.

e had in her possession a large copper cauldron, blackened with age and with use. One day, she wiped it clean of the evening meal, she was visited by a Woman of Peace, a fairy woman ho tiptoed quietly into the cottage and asked to take away the cauldron for a short time. Now is was an older fairy, with a nature that was gentle and kind, and she presented little danger to airearad. She had a wizened fairy face, and features as tiny as the markings of a butterfly, and e moved swiftly and silently, advising no one of her coming or going. Mairearad passed her e cauldron, and as the Woman of Peace retreated down the cottage path, towards the twin lls that marked the fairy's Land of Light, she said to the fairy,

A smith is able to make
Cold iron hot with a coal;
The due of the kettle is bones,
And to bring it back again whole.

And so it was that the cauldron was returned that evening, left quietly on the cottage oorstop, filled with juicy bones.

The Woman of Peace came again, later that day, and without saying a word, indicated e cauldron. And as days turned into years, an unspoken relationship developed between e two women, fairy and mortal. Mairearad would loan her cauldron, and in exchange she ould have it filled with delicious bones. She never forgot to whisper, as the fairy drew out f sight,

A smith is able to make
Cold iron hot with a coal;
The due of the kettle is bones,
And to bring it back again whole.

Then one day, Mairearad had to leave her cottage for a day, to travel to Castlebay, across the ea on Barra.

She said to her husband before she left, 'When the Woman of Peace comes to the doorstep, ou must let her take the cauldron, but do not forget to say to her what I always say.'

And so her husband worked his field, as he always did, and as he returned for his nidday meal he met with a curious sight, for scurrying along the path in front of him was wee woman, her face gnarled with age, her eyes bright and shrewd. Suddenly he felt an nexplicable fear, for most men have had fed to them as bairns the tales of fairies and the ruel tricks they play, their enchantments and their evil spells. He remembered them all ow in a rush of tortuous thought, and pushed past the fairy woman to slam the cottage oor. She knocked firmly, but he refused to answer, panting with terror on the other side f the door.

At last there was silence, and then, a weird howl echoed around the cottage walls and there vas a scrambling on the roof. Through the chimney was thrust the long brown arm of the fairy voman, and she reached straight down to the fire upon which the cauldron sat, and pulled it vith a rush of air, through the cottage roof.

Mairearad's husband was still pressed against the door when she returned that evening, and he looked curiously at the empty hearth, remarking, 'The Woman of Peace always returns the auldron before darkness falls.'

Then her husband hung his head in shame and told her how he'd barred the door, and whe the fairy had taken the cauldron, he'd forgotten to ask for its return. Well Mairearad scolded h husband, and putting on her overcoat and boots, she left the cottage, lantern in hand.

Darkness can play tricks as devilish as those of the fairies themselves, and it was not lo before the dancing shadows, and whispering trees sent a shiver along the spine of the fier wife Mairearad, but still she pressed on, safe in the knowledge that the Woman of Peace was h friend. She reached the threshold of the Land of Light and saw on a fire, just inside the do her cauldron, filled as usual with tender bones. And so she grabbed it, and half-fearing whe she was, began to ran, exciting the attention of the black fairy dogs that slept beside an old ma who guarded the entrance.

Up they jumped, and woke the old man, who cried out,

Silent woman, dumb woman,
Who has come to us from the Land of the Dead
Since you have not blessed the brugh –
Unleash Black and let go Fierce.

And he let the dogs free to chase the terrified woman right back to the door of her cottag baying and howling, spitting with determination and hunger. As she ran she dropped the tast bones, buying herself a moment or two's respite from the snarling dogs. For fairy dogs a faster than any dogs on earth, and will devour all human flesh that comes across their path Mairearad fled down the path, finally reaching her door and slamming it shut behind her. The she told her breathless story to her husband, and they held one another's ears against th painful wailing of the hounds. Finally there was silence.

Never again did the fairy Woman of Peace come to Mairearad's cottage, nor did she borro the cauldron. Mairearad and her husband missed the succulent bones, but never again di they trouble the fairy folk. They are long dead now, buried on the grassy verge on the island c Sandray, where the sheep graze calmly on the succulent green grass, freshened by the moist sa air, kept company by the fairy folk who live in a verdant knoll.

Legends of Fairies and Sea-folk

The iron tongue of midnight hath told twelve;
Lovers, to bed; 'tis almost fairy time.
William Shakespeare

WHEN DARKNESS FELL across the land, and the hush of evening brought sounds that belonged to no mortal man, the time was ripe for fairies and other wee folk to leave their realm and enter our own. Anything strange, complex or perhaps a little frightening must have a cause, and it was these creatures who were held responsible for acts for which no one else would take the blame. The mischievous deeds of the fairies and their compatriots were the cause of much illness and heartache, but by the same token, they could make a hero of a man, and bring roses to the face of a sickly baby. Fairies were dangerous, and folk from the sea could be fierce and unfamiliar, but the infinite battle to live with them provided a formula, a structure for daily existence, when life, and death and nature held all the fear of the unknown, and a crying baby, that tapping on the window, the light that glinted over the treetops meant something altogether different.

MacCodrum's Seal Wife

DEEP IN THE COLD SEA, long before men chanced the waves for the first time, there lived a king and his queen, and their lovely sea-children. The children were elegant, graceful creatures, with deep brown eyes and voices that filled the sea with laughter and song. They dwelt deep in that sea, in happiness and in comfort, and spent days chasing one another through the schools of fish, catching a ride on a tail, hiding in a murky cave, frolicking in the waves that caressed their young bodies and made them strong.

And so their days were spent, and they were fed and loved by the kindly queen and her husband, who brushed their hair, and stroked their heads, and gave them a home like none other. Until the sad day when the queen became ill and died, and left her children forlorn and lonely, but still with the sea as their home, and the fish, and the warm waves to comfort them. Their voices were softer now, and their music still sweet, but the king was concerned about their uncombed hair, and their unstroked heads, and he began to search for a mother for the sea-children.

The king found them a mother in a darker part of the sea, where the sun could not light the coral reefs, or dance upon the weeds and the shimmering scales of the fish. The mother was in fact a witch, and she charmed the king with a magic potion that put him under her spell. She came with him to the lighter part of the sea, where the sun kissed the elegant bodies of the sea-children, glowed in their soft brown eyes, and she made her home there, combing their hair, and stroking their heads, but never loving them, and so the friendly waters grew cold, and although the light continued to dance, and the waves lapped at their bodies, the children were sad and downcast.

And so it was that the witch decided to dispose of these sea-children, and from the depths of her wicked being she created a cruel spell that would rid the sea-children of their elegance and their beauty. She turned them to seals, who could live no longer in the marine palace of their father the king, their graceful limbs replaced by heavy bodies and sleek dark fur. They were to live in the sea for all but one day each year when they could find a secluded shore and transform, for just that day, into children once more.

But the witch could not rob the children of everything, and although their bodies were ungainly, and they were beautiful children no longer, they retained their soft brown eyes, and their music was as pure and mellifluous as the wind in the trees, as the birds who flew above the water.

Time went on, and the seals grew used to their shiny coats, and to the sea, where they played once again in the waves, and fished, and sang, but they loved too becoming children again, that one day each year, and it was when they had shed their coats, beautiful children once more, that they were seen for the first time by human eyes, those belonging to a fisherman who lived on an isolated rock, a man called Roderic MacCodrum, of the Clan Donald, in the Outer Hebrides.

On this fateful day he walked to the beach to rig his boat when he heard the sound of exquisite singing, and he hid himself behind some driftwood and watched the delightful dance of the sea-children, who waved arms that were no longer clumsy seal flippers, and who ran with legs that were long and lean. Their soft brown eyes were alight with happiness and never before had Roderic MacCodrum seen such a sight.

His eyes sparkled. He must have one. And so it was that Roderic MacCodrum stole one of the glistening pelts that lay cast to the side of the beach, and put it above the rafters in his barn, safe from the searching eyes of the young seal woman who came to call.

The seal woman was elegant and beautiful, her long hair hiding her comely nakedness. She implored him to return her coat to her, but he feigned concern and told her that he knew not where it was. In despair she sat down on his doorstep, her head in her hands, and it was then that he offered her a life on land, as his wife and lover. Because she had no seal skin like her brothers and sisters, and no place to go, she agreed, and so it was that the seal woman came to live with Roderic MacCodrum, where she lived happily, or so it was thought, and bore him many children.

But the seal woman, or Selkie as she came to be called, had a cold, lonely heart, and although she loved and nurtured her children, and grew to find a kind of peace with her husband, she longed for the waves, for the cold fresh waters of the sea. And she would sit on its shores and she would sing a song that was so haunting, so melancholy that the seals would come to her here and cease their frolicking to return her unhappy song, to sing with her of times gone by when the waves and the water comforted them and made them strong, when the sun in the lighter part of the sea kissed their elegant bodies and made them gleam with light.

And then at night she would return to her cottage, and light the peat in the hearth, and make a home for her family, all the while living her life in her dreams of the sea.

It was her unknowing child who found the beautiful fur coat, fallen from its hiding place in the rafters, where it had remained unseen for all those years, and she brought it to her mother whose eyes glowed with a warmth that none had seen before. Her mother kissed her then, and all her brothers and sisters, and whispered that they must look out for her, for she would be back.

Roderic MacCodrum of the Seals, as he had come to be known, returned to his cottage that night to find it empty and cold, like the heart of the seal woman he had married, and his children were lined on the beaches, bereft and alone, for their mother had left for the chill waters and she had not come back.

Their mother never came back, for she had gone with that lustrous fur coat, that gleamed in the light like her soft brown eyes when she saw it. They heard her, though, for from the sea came those same lilting melodies, happier now, to be sure. And they often saw a graceful seal, who came closer to shore than the others, and who seemed to beckon, and in whose presence they felt a strange comfort, a familiar warmth, especially when the sun caught those soft brown eyes they knew so well.

The Fairies and the Blacksmith

THERE ONCE WAS A BLACKSMITH by the name of Alasdair MacEachern, and he lived in a cottage on the Isle of Islay with his son Neil. They lived alone for the blacksmith's poor wife had breathed no more than once or twice when Neil was born to them, but Alasdair MacEachern, or Alasdair of the Strong Arm, as he came to be known, found great comfort in his son and they lived contentedly, with familiar habits and routines that brought them much happiness.

Neil was a slim youth, with unruly hair and eyes that shone with dreams. He was quiet, but easy and his slight, pale frame gave him the countenance of one weaker than he was. When Neil was but a child the neighbours of Alasdair MacEachern had warned the blacksmith of the fairies who lived just over the knoll, the fairies who would find one so slight and dreamy a perfect prize for their Land of Light. And so it was that each night Alasdair MacEachern hung above the door to his cottage a branch of rowan, a charm against the fairies who might come to steal away his son.

They lived many years this way, until the day came when Alasdair MacEachern had to travel some distance, sleeping the night away from his cottage and his son. Before he left he warned his son about the rowan branch, and Neil agreed to put it in its place above the door that night. Neil loved the green grass of the hills, and to breathe in the crisp, sunlit air of the banks of the streams that trickled through their land, but he loved more his life with his father and his work on the forge. He had no wish for a life of dancing and eternal merriment in the Land of Light.

And so it was that Neil wished his father a fond farewell, swept the cottage, tended to the goats and to the chickens, and made himself a feast of cornbread and oatcakes, and goat's cheese and milk, and took himself to the soft green grass of the hills, and walked there by the sunlit banks of the streams until dark fell upon him. And then Neil returned to his cottage next to the forge, and he swept the crumbs from his pockets, and tended to the goats and to the chickens, and laid himself in his tiny box-bed in the corner of the room, by the roaring hearth, and fell fast asleep. Not once had the thought of the branch of rowan crept across his sleepy mind.

It was late in the afternoon when Alasdair of the Strong Arm returned to his cottage, and he found the hearth quite cold, and the floor unswept, and the goats and the chickens untended. His son was there, for he answered his father's call, but there was no movement from his box-bed in the corner and Alasdair crossed the room with great concern.

'I am ill, Father,' said a small, weak voice, and there laid the body of Neil, yellowed and shrunk, hardly denting his meagre mattress.

'But how ... how could, in just one day ...' Alasdair stared with shock at his son, for he smelled old, of decay, and his skin was like charred paper, folded and crisp and creased. But it was his son, no doubt, for the shape and the face were the same. And Neil laid like this for days on end, changing little, but eating steadily, his appetite strange and fathomless. And it was because of this strange illness that Alasdair MacEachern paid a visit to a wiseman, who came at once to the bedside of Neil, for he was a boy well regarded by his neighbours.

The wiseman looked only once at Neil, and drew the unhappy blacksmith outside the cottage. He asked many questions and then he was quiet. When he finally spoke his words were measured, and his tone quite fearful. The blood of Alasdair MacEachern ran cold.

'This is not your son Neil,' said the man of knowledge. 'He has been carried off by the Little People and they have left a changeling in his place.'

'Alas, then, what can I do?' The great blacksmith was visibly trembling now, for Neil was as central to his life as the fiery heat of the forge itself. And then the wiseman spoke, and he told Alasdair MacEachern how to proceed.

'You must first be sure that is a changeling lying in the bed of Neil, and you must go back to the cottage and collect as many egg shells as you can, filling them with water and carrying them as if they weighed more than ten tons of iron and bricks. And then, arrange them round the side of the fire where the changeling can see you. His words will give him away.'

So Alasdair MacEachern gathered together the shells of twenty eggs and did as he was bidden, and soon a thin voice called out from his son's bed, 'In all of my eight hundred years I have never seen such a sight.' And with a hoot and a cackle, the changeling sank back into the bed.

Alasdair returned to the wiseman and confirmed what had taken place. The old man nodded his head.

'It is indeed a changeling and he must be disposed of, before you can bring back your son. You must follow these steps: light a large, hot fire in the centre of the cottage, where it can be easily seen by the changeling. And then, when he asks you "What's the use of that", you must grab him by the shirtfront, and thrust him deep into the fire. Then he'll fly through the roof of the cottage.'

Alasdair of the Strong Arm did as requested, certain now that that wizened, strange creature was not his son, and as the fire began to roar, the voice called out, reedy and slim, 'What's the use of that?' at which the brave blacksmith seized the body that lay in Neil's bed and placed it firmly in the flames. There was a terrible scream, and the changeling flew straight through the roof, a sour yellow smoke all that remained of him.

And so Alasdair MacEachern cleared away the traces of the fire, and returned once more to the man of knowledge, for it was time to find his son, and he could delay no longer.

The wiseman bade him go to fetch three things: a Bible, a sword, and a crowing cock. He was to follow the stream that trickled through their land to the grassy green knoll where the fairies danced and played eternally. On the night of the next full moon, that hill would open, and it was through this door that Alasdair must go to seek his son.

It was many days before the moon had waned, and then waxed again, but it stood, a gleaming beacon in the sky at last, and Alasdair MacEachern collected together his sword and his Bible and his crowing cock and set out for the green knoll where the fairies danced. And as the moon rose high in the sky, and lit the shadowy land, a door burst open in the hill, spilling out laughter and song and a bright light that blazed like the fire in the hearth of the blacksmith's cottage. And it was into that light and sound that the courageous Alasdair MacEachern stepped, firmly thrusting his sword into the frame of the door to stop it closing, for no fairy can touch the sword of a mortal man.

There, at a steaming forge, stood his son, as small and as wild-looking as the little folk themselves. He worked silently, absorbed in his labours, and started only when he heard the voice of his father.

'Release my son from this enchantment,' shouted Alasdair MacEachern, holding the Bible high in the air, for fairies have no power over mortals who hold the good Lord's book, and they stood back now, cross and foiled.

'Return him to me, to his own land,' bawled the blacksmith, but the fairies began to smirk, and they slowly crept around him in a circle, taunting him, poking at him with blades of honed green grass. They began to dance, a slow and wiry gyration, moving to a weird song that tugged at the mind of the blacksmith, that threatened to overcome him. He struggled to stay upright, and as he stabbed his arms out in front of him, he dropped his cock, who woke with a howl and gave one mighty crow that sent the little fairies shrieking from the doorway to the other side, sent them howling away from the cock and the blacksmith and his son, who they pushed now towards him, sending them all slipping towards the threshold of their world. For daylight was the curfew of the fairies, and it was with true fear that the crow of the red-combed cock was heard, for little people may never see the light of day per chance they turn at once to stone.

They struggled now, prodding the mortals from their world, and begging in an awkward chant for Alasdair MacEachern to release his dirk from their door. And as he drew it from the threshold, and stood once more in the land of mortals with his son, a small and crafty fairy thrust his face from the hillside, and called out a curse that fell upon the son of the hapless blacksmith like the mist of a foggy night.

'May your son not speak until the day he breaks the curse.' The head popped back, and the fairy was gone, never to be seen again.

And so it was that Alasdair MacEachern and his son Neil went to live again in their familiar, cosy cottage next to the forge, and took up their work, their habits and their routines in place once more. Neil's tongue was frozen by the curse of the fairies, but his manner was unchanged, and this father and his son lived contentedly, for speech is not always necessary to those who live simply, with things and people to which they have grown accustomed.

One day, a year and a week from the fairy's fateful full moon, Alasdair set his son the task of forging the new claymore for the Chief of his clan. As his silent son held the metal to the fire, he started, and looked for one instant as wild as he had in the Land of the Light, for suddenly Neil had remembered, and in that flash of memory he recalled the intricate forging of the fairies' swords, how he'd learned to temper the blades of their glowing weapons with words of wisdom and charms, with magic and spells as well as with fire. Now he leapt into action, and worked with a ferocity and speed that set his father, Alasdair of the Strong Arm, reeling with shock and with fear.

And then the motion stopped, and holding up a sword that gleamed like the light of the full moon, he said quietly, 'There is a sword that will never fail the man who grasps it by the hilt.'

From that time onwards Neil spoke again, for unwittingly he had removed the curse of the fairies by fashioning a fairy sword to sever a fairy spell. Never again did he remember his days in the fairy kingdom, never again could he forge a fairy sword, but the Chief of his clan never lost a battle from that day, and the sword remained the greatest of his possessions.

Neil and his father, Alasdair MacEachern, returned to their cottage, the finest blacksmiths in all the land, their forge casting a glow that could be seen from hills all round, almost as far as the Land of Light, where the fairies kick up their heels in fury at the thought of that blacksmith and his clever son.

The Fairy Changeling

THERE ONCE WAS A WOMAN who lived on the sea, where the winds blew cold and damp. By day she combed the sands for seaweed, and by night she lay alone in her bed, weak and lonely, for her husband was a fisherman and by the light of the moon he trawled the rocky coasts, eking a cruel living, but one which kept them fed and warm in a cosy cottage.

The woman longed for a child, but it was many years before she was granted her wish, and when her baby finally came he was small and feeble. Her neighbours said he would die, or worse, be snatched by the fairies who loved a child so fair of complexion, so slight of build. He would be taken, they said, to the Land of Light where the fairies danced and sang and played all day, where they set traps and tricks for mortal folk who crossed their merry paths.

The fisherman's poor wife could not help but think that a life of laughter would bring roses to the cheeks of her white child, and she wished with all her being that he would be stolen by the fairies, and taken to a land where he could become strong. And so it was that the fisherman's wife set her child out on the rocks, on the edge of her land, and watched and waited. She slept for a few moments, but otherwise moved not, and still her baby lay there, swaddled and spiritless, an invitation to the little folk which was not accepted.

At length she berated herself for the foolhardy actions, and brought her baby into the cottage once more. And there he surprised her by pulling himself up and demanding food, attaching himself to her teat with such relish that she drew back. He suckled the woman dry, and then demanded porridge, but still he lay small and wizened, more yellow than before, but so hungry that she could not feed him.

So the fisherman's wife placed her baby at her breast, and went to see the wiseman in the village, anxious about her small but starving baby, frightened by his curious change.

The wiseman listened carefully to her story, silently shaking his head.

'You have not your own bairn, but a fairy changeling,' he said finally.

The wife of the fisherman balked, for there in front of her was the very shape and likeness of her baby, and the cry was as shrill as ever. She refused to believe him.

'Take him, then, to your cottage, and leave him in his cradle. Shut the door, but do not go. Spy upon him there and you will be sure.'

And so the fisherman's wife returned to her cottage, and laid the baby upon his bed, shutting the door firmly behind her, but skulking back to peer in the window. And suddenly her baby sat up and drew from under the mattress a chanter, which he began to play. And instead of her baby there was an old fairy bodach.

She fairly flew back to the wiseman, and implored him to help her get rid of the changeling, sickened at the thought of having suckled that gnarled old creature. Calmly the wiseman told her what to do.

The very next day, the wife of the fisherman took her changeling baby and laid him on a rock by the sea, busying herself by collecting seaweed as she did on every day that passed, and comforted by this routine, the baby, or the fairy bodach as she now knew he was, fell asleep. As he slept the tide drew in, licking at the rock on which he slept, until the waters began to dampen his wrappings, and he woke with a start. When he realized that he could not reach the fisherman's wife without swimming he rose to his full height, and a little fairy man once more he began to stamp his feet and howl, shaking his fist at the fisherman's wife who stood entranced as the waters threatened to engulf the fierce fairy.

And so it was that ten or twelve small fairies appeared to rescue their kin, but since fairies cannot swim, they danced helplessly on the shore while the water grew higher and higher about the rock. The fisherman's wife was smug, and she said, 'I shall leave him there, until you return my baby.'

And the fairies disappeared and returned with her baby, who had grown in his time away from his mother, and whose cheeks were roses, whose white skin held the bloom of good health. And she thanked the fairies, and returned their bodach to them.

So the fisherman's wife, flushed with her good fortune, went back to her cosy cottage, protected from the winds which blew cold and damp from the sea. She lived there with her blossoming baby, by day combing the sands for seaweed, and at night nestling warm in her bed with her son, silently thanking the little people who had made him strong.

The Thirsty Ploughman

IT WAS IN BERNERAY that two men from Brusda walked along a hot and sunburnt field, parched from the fiery sun, from a long day of ploughing. Sweat glistened on their brows and they talked little, saving words for a time when their tongues were moister. Their feet were bare and despite the great heat they moved quickly, thirsting for a drink, for cool refreshment.

They passed across a rocky knoll and then they heard a woman, working at a churn. They looked at one another with relief.

'Ah, Donald,' said Ewan, the slighter of the two men, 'if the milkmaid had my thirst, what a drink of buttermilk she would drink.'

Donald was not sure. 'Ah, it's not buttermilk I would care for,' he said.

As they carried on over the dry brush that lined the hillock, the sound of the fresh milk splashing in the churn grew louder, more enticing, and both men licked their lips at the thought of it. There before them stood a fair maiden, her apron starched crisp white, holding a jug that foamed with pure buttermilk. She offered it to them then, Ewan first because he was the smaller of the two.

Ewan refused to drink because he knew neither the maiden nor the source of the buttermilk. He was afraid of what he did not know and though he thirsted for the cool milk, he would allow none to pass his lips.

Donald, who cared not for buttermilk, drank deeply from the jug, and wiping the frosting of white lather from his lip, he declared it the best he had ever tasted.

'Ah,' said the bonny maiden, whose face was cool with contempt, 'you who asked for the drink and did not accept it will have a short life. And you,' she gestured to Donald, 'you who took the drink, but did not ask for it, a long life and good living.'

She turned on her heel, and apron bright in the sunlight, left the men, one thirsty and one sated.

And so it was that Ewan returned home that night and took to his bed, never to waken, for the fear of God had been put into him that day by the maiden on the hill, who could be none other than a witch. And Donald lived a long and prosperous life, ploughing his field alone, but reaping better crops, and amassing great riches. He looked always across the knoll, listened intently for the sound of milk in the churn, but never again did he see the witch, or fairy, though he blessed her often.

Wee Johnnie in the Cradle

THERE ONCE WAS A MAN and his wife who lived on a farm on the edge of a wood where fairies were known to lay their small hats. They were a young man and wife and they had not been married long before a child was born to them, a child they called Johnnie. Now wee Johnnie was an unhappy baby, and from

the beginning he cried so loudly that the birds ceased their flight over the farmer's cottage, and the creatures of the woodland kept a surly distance. The man's wife longed for the days when she could tend the fields with her husband, and chat to him of things which those who are newly wed have to chat of, and to go to market, where they would share a dram and have a carry-on like they had in the days before wee Johnnie was born.

But Johnnie was there now, and their cosy cottage became messy and damp, and some days the hearth was not lit because the man and his wife were so intent on silencing the squalling boy, and some days they could not even look one another in the eye, so unhappy and disillusioned they had become.

And then, perchance, a kindly neighbour, a tailor by trade, took pity on the man and his wife, who grew ever thinner and ever more hostile as the cries of wee Johnnie grew wilder and lustier as he grew larger and stronger.

'I'll take yer bairn and ye can take yer wife to market,' he said to the farmer one day, and the man and his wife eagerly agreed and set off for the day.

They had not been gone longer than a minute or two, when the kindly tailor, who had placed himself beside the fire and was bracing himself for an afternoon of wailing, was startled from his reverie by a deep voice.

'Fetch me a glass o' that whiskey, there, in the press,' it said. And the tailor looked about him in amazement, the room empty but for the wee Johnnie in the cradle who was mercifully silent.

'I said to ye, fetch me a glass,' and up from the cradle of wee Johnnie popped wee Johnnie's head, and from the mouth on that head came that deep and bossy voice.

The tailor rose and did as he was bidden, and when the baby had drained the glass, and then another, and let out a belch that was very unbabyish indeed, he said to the wee bairn, 'You aren't Johnnie, are ye, ye are a fairy without a doubt.'

'And if I am,' said the fairy changeling, 'what will ye say to them, me mam and da?'

'I, I dunna know,' said the tailor carefully, settling himself back into his chair to watch the fairy more carefully.

'Get me some pipes,' said Johnnie the fairy, 'I like a bit of music with me drink.'

'I haven't any ... and I dunna play,' said the tailor, crossing himself and moving further from the loathsome baby.

'Fetch me a straw then,' he replied. And when the tailor complied, the fairy Johnnie played a song which was so exquisite, so effortlessly beautiful that the tailor was quite calmed. Never before had he heard music so haunting, and he would remember that melody until his dying day, although he could never repeat it himself or pass it on. But he was broken from his reverie, for wee Johnnie was speaking.

'Me mam and da, when will they be back?' he whispered.

The tailor looked startled, for the day had been pulled from under him, and it was time indeed for the farmer and his wife to return. He looked anxiously from the window and as they drew up he heard wee Johnnie begin to howl with all the vigour of a slaughtered beast, and he watched as a deep frown furrowed the brow of the farmer's wife, and a dull shadow cast itself across the face of her husband.

He must tell them, for the cruel fairy was manipulating them, taunting them with his tortuous cries. And their own wee bairn was somewhere lost to them.

He pulled the farmer aside as his wife went to tend to the wailing bairn, and told him of the fairy. A bemused look crossed his face and he struggled to keep his composure. 'My wife, she'll not believe it,' he said finally.

But the tailor had a plan. He told the farmer to pretend to leave for market the following day, and he, the tailor, would step in to look after the bairn once again. But the farmer and his wife were not really to leave, they should hide themselves outside the cottage walls and watch when the wee Johnnie thought them gone.

And so it happened that the next day the man and his wife set out for market again, but drove their horses only round the grassy bend, returning stealthily to look through the windows of their cottage. And there was wee Johnnie, sipping on a glass of their best whiskey, puffing idly on a straw pipe that played a song which was so exquisite, so effortlessly beautiful that they were quite calmed. Never before had they heard music so haunting, and they would remember that melody until their dying day, although they could never repeat it.

But when they heard that wee Johnnie's coarse voice demanding more drink, they were snapped from their reverie, and they flew into the cottage and thrust the changeling intruder on the burning griddle which the tailor had prepared for that purpose.

And the scream that ensued was not that of their own baby, and the puff of sickening smoke which burst from the fairy as he disappeared renewed their determination.

And then there was silence, an empty peace that caused the man and his wife to look at one another in dismay, for what had they done to cause their baby to be stolen from them, and where was their own wee Johnnie now?

Then a gurgle burst forth, and there was a movement in the corner of the room where the tiny cradle lay. They rushed to its side, and there lay Johnnie, brought back from his fairy confinement, smiling and waving tiny fat arms, with cheeks like pink buttons, and a smile so merry that the cottage of the man and his wife was warmed once again.

The tailor left them then, a grin on his face as he whistled to himself a tune which was so exquisite, so effortlessly beautiful that he was quite calmed.

The Fairy Dancers

IT WAS CHRISTMAS EVE and by the Loch Etive sat two farmers, longing for a drink but with an empty barrel between them. And so it was decided, on that icy Christmas Eve, that these two farmers would walk the road to Kingshouse, their nearest inn, and they would buy a barrel of the best whiskey there, a three-gallon jar that would warm them through the frosty months to come.

So they set off along the winding road, and over the hills that glistened with snow, all frosted with ice, and came to the warm wooded inn at Kingshouse. It was there that a cup of tea was shared, and a wee dram or two, and so the two men were quite merry as they set off home again, the three-gallon jar heavy on the back of the youngest man, for they would take turns carrying its weight on the long journey down the winding road and over the hills.

And over the hills they went but they were stopped there, by the need for a taste of that whiskey, and for a smoke. Then the sound of a fantastic reel grew louder and louder, and a light shone brighter over the hills, towards the north.

'Och, it's just a wee star,' said one man, ready for his smoke and his tipple.

'Nah, it's a light, and there's a party there to be sure,' said the other, who was a great dancer and loved a reel more than any other.

So they crossed the brae to the north, towards the light, and the sound of pipes, which played a fine tune. There in front of them were dancers, women in silk dresses, bowing and twirling, and men in highland dress, with pipes playing an enchanted, fine tune that drew them towards the hill.

The younger man, who carried the jar, went first, and as he entered the great door in the hillside, and joined the merry throng, the door was closed. When the other farmer, slower than the first, reached the site, there was nothing to be found. For his friend had disappeared and there was no trace of him.

It was a cold and lonely walk home, and the farmer puzzled over what had occurred on that moonlit hill, with a magical reel playing from a light that shone in the darkness. He went first to the farm of the other man, and he told his wife what had happened, but as he talked, faces closed, and brows became furrowed, and it was clear that he was not believed, that no man could lose his friend on a hill just a few miles from home.

And so it was that the policemen were called from Inveraray, and they took him away and asked him questions that made his head spin, and caused him to slump over in exhaustion, and he wished more than anything for a drop of the whiskey that was hung on the other man's back. They kept him there, the police, and he was sent to trial, but he told them all the same thing, how a magical reel had played from a light that shone in the darkness, and how his friend had disappeared without trace.

He was sent back to that prison, and when they asked him again, he could only tell the truth of that fateful night, so they asked him no more, and sent him home, for he would not budge from his story, and that story never changed.

And it was near twelve months before this man had cause to travel past that hill again, and with him this time were some lads from the village who had set themselves the task of catching some fish for the Christmas feast. And with a basket full of fish, they stopped on their way back to their homes, with the need for a smoke and a taste of the whiskey that the farmer had tucked in his belt. And there again they heard that fantastic music, and saw the light beaming from the darkness of the hills.

But the lads from the village had heard too much of this madness, and they struggled home with the fish, ahead of the farmer who wanted more than anything to find his friend, and that barrel of whiskey. So the farmer climbed over the hills, towards that light, and he heard there the sound of pipes, which played a fine tune. There in front of him were dancers, women in silk dresses, bowing and twirling, and men in highland dress, with pipes playing an enchanted, fine tune that drew him towards the hill.

And he stuck his fishing hook in the threshold of the door, for no fairy can touch the metal of a mortal man, and he entered the room which spun with the music, and threatened to drag him into its midst. But this farmer never liked a dance, preferring instead a good smoke and a dram of whiskey, and he resisted the calls on his soul, and struggled through the crowd to find his friend the farmer, who danced in the middle of the reel like a man possessed.

'Och, lad, we've only just begun,' the dancer protested, as his friend dragged him away.

And since he had danced for near twelve months with that barrel on his back, he carried it home again, along the winding road and over the hills that glistened with snow, all frosted with ice. They came to the farm of the man who'd been dancing, and what a surprise met his poor lonely wife when she opened the door. For there was her husband, just skin and bones to be sure, but there nonetheless with his barrel of whiskey, just twelve months late.

And they sat up that night, the man and his friend, and each of their wives, and what a Christmas Eve they had with that barrel of whiskey, which had mellowed with the warmth of the fairy hill, and they drank it all, just twelve months late.

A Dead Wife Among the Fairies

THERE ONCE WAS A MAN who lived with a wife he loved. They had been married for many years, and they made their home in a lighthouse, on the rocky coast by the sea. The waves threw up a spray but never dampened them, for they were sealed tight in their little world inside that lighthouse, and they lived happily there together, needing little else but the other. And so they lived, working together and talking all the day, lighting their beacon in the mists and fogs which fell over the sea like a woollen blanket.

Then one day, the good wife died, and she was buried in the hillside, under the rocks. And on those rocks the man sat each day, never lighting his beacon when the mists and fogs fell over the sea, staring instead at the rock which marked her grave, which marked the end of his life too. And so it was that he became a little mad, and went to see a witch, a fairy midwife who practised the magic of the earth and who could tell him how to get her back, his wife that he loved so well.

He saw her in her cottage, over the hill and across the brae, and she shook her head, and warned him to leave the dead with the fairies, for after death there can be no real life on earth, where the light would turn into dust any mortal who tried to return. But for the poor widowed man there could be no real life either, and so he begged the fairy witch to tell him her secrets and at last she did.

He was to go, she said, to a cave at the brae of Versabreck, on the night of a full moon, and he should take with him a black cat, and a Bible, and a thick wooden staff. There he must cry for his wife, and read to her from the psalms, and when he heard her voice once more, he must throw in the black cat and wait quietly for her to appear. Now the fairy folk would never let a mortal who had died pass back to his own land, so they would rally round her, and fight to keep her in their dust-webbed cave, which led to the Land of Light. The staff was to beat them with, for they could be sent back into their cave by the force of his will.

The moon waned and then it waxed again, and soon the night of the full moon arrived. The man was shivering with the fear of seeing his wife once more, yet he longed to touch her body, to feel her warmth, to hear her tender voice, so he steeled his quivering nerves and set off for the cave at the brae of Versabreck, and under his arm he held a black cat, and a Bible and a thick wooden staff. There he cried for his wife, and he read to her from the psalms, and when he heard her voice once more, he threw in the black cat and waited quietly for her to appear.

Now the fairy folk fought for their mortal princess, and struggled to keep her in their dust-webbed cave, which led to the Land of Light, but he beat them with his staff, and sent them back into their cave by the force of his will.

And there was his wife, paler to be sure, and nothing more than skin and bones, but she smiled her same familiar smile, and although her body held no warmth and she smelled rather sour, he held her to him once again and heard her tender voice. And together they walked to their lighthouse home, snug in a warm embrace, and they lit their beacon in the mists and fogs which fell over the sea like a woollen blanket. When day broke, his wife was safe in the fairy cave again, for light would turn to dust any mortal who tried to return from the dead. And so her husband would watch carefully as the moon waned and then waxed, when they could meet again.

Legends of Ghosts

From ghoulies and ghosties and long-leggety beasties
And things that go bump in the night,
God Lord, deliver us!
Anon

IN SCOTLAND, stories of ghosts and evil-spirits form a rich and vibrant tradition, as alive today as it was centuries ago. It is one of the oldest genres of Scottish mythology and certainly the most enduring, for as little is known today as it ever was about where we go when we leave this earth. Our spirits may visit the realms of heaven, but we have religion to explain that. What of that time before the soul leaves the body? And what of the body in the ground? The dank, dark earth houses many secrets, and it is there that ghosts and other spirits are bred. The newly dead and the long-dead are the most frightening, for they are most venomous in their attacks on unsuspecting family, or even strangers. Beware of a fleeting glimpse of something unknown; watch out for that unexplained flash of light in a haunted house; take note when a chair moves suddenly in an empty room. And if a body is laid out for burial in a house near to you, sleep elsewhere, for the spirits of the dead can come back, in many strange forms. There's no doubt of that, as these stories will tell.

The Fiddler of Gord

THERE ONCE WAS A MAN who lived in Sandness, near Papa Stour. He was a fisherman by trade, but he was known across the lands for the tunes he played on his fine fiddle. Folk came for miles to hear his music, and he could dance and sing a bit, so making it a real evening for anyone who cared to join in.

Now one cold night he left his cottage home, which was nestled in the base of a knoll, sheltered from the winds which burst over the hills from the sea. He left that night grudgingly, for the fire was warm and the company merry, but the larders were empty and more fish must be got by morning. So out he went into the frosted air, which crisped his breath and crunched under his feet. And on to his cold, dark boat he climbed, then out to sea, where he settled himself under oilskins and drew out his fine fiddle and began to play. And the Fiddler of Gord, as the man was called, played for hours as the fish drew closer to hear the wondrous music, catching themselves in his nets, but fighting not at all, so comforted were they by the strains from his fiddle.

Then the fiddler headed homewards, his basket groaning with fresh fish, tastier for having expired happily. As he passed the grassy knoll that hid his sweet, snug cottage from the fierce winds, he heard a graceful melody, and stopping in his tracks and laying down his basket, he listened. There was a light which glinted and beckoned through the grass and he was drawn towards it, as the music grew louder.

A door had opened in the hill, and from inside came the enchanted music of the fairy folk, a melody so divine and simple that his heart grew larger in his breast and he pulsed with pure pleasure. The Fiddler of Gord entered the door that night, and it was shut firmly behind him.

The cottage, tucked into the base of the knoll, was quiet as the night grew longer and the fiddler had not returned, and finally, when it neared dawn, the youngest son was sent out with a lantern, and when he returned with the fiddler's basket of fish there was no doubt in their minds that he'd been blown down the cliffs into the sea. The family lived there for many years, but the fiddler did not return. Finally, they moved from that place to another, and a new family took over the wee cosy cottage tucked into the base of the knoll, and they made a happy home there, warmed by the hearth and protected from the angry winds by the arm of the hillock.

It was on one windy night, when the sky howled at the thundering clouds, that a knock was heard on the door of this warm cottage, and when the door was opened there appeared an old man, bent and cold, and he thrust his hands at the fire, laying his fiddle to one side. And as he looked around he realized that it was not his family who gazed at him with astonishment, but another, and they wore garments which spoke of ages to come, not those he had come to know.

The children who played at the feet of the chairs came to gawk, and he asked, with all the rage he could muster, 'Where is my family? This is my house' to which the new family all laughed and called him mad and a coot from the whiskey barrel.

But the old grandfather of the family stayed silent, and then, at length, he said quietly to their indignant guest, 'Where do you hail from, man?' And when the Fiddler of Gord explained, the grandfather nodded his head slowly and said, 'Yes, you did live here once, but a man of your name disappeared, gone a hundred years now.'

'Well, where are my folk then?' whispered the Fiddler of Gord, his face a mask of confusior and fear.

'Dead,' came the reply, and the room was quiet once more.

'And so I'll join them,' said the fiddler, and drawing himself up to his full height he left the glow of the hearth, and the warmth of the family, and he headed to the top of the hillock, where the winds blew cold and frosty, crisping his breath and crunching under his feet, and he was followed by the wee lad of the house, who hid behind a bush at the base of the hillock to watch

And there, in a glorious symphony of sound the fiddler played a rich and moving song that tugged at the chords of the wee lad's heart and filled his eyes with burning tears. And those tears burnt the melody into his memory, and it remained there until he died. Then the fiddler looked over at the northern star and played the tune once again, and collapsed, his fiddle flying over the hilltop into the sea.

And when the bairn summoned the courage to creep over to the old man, he found there a body of one who had died near one hundred years earlier. So he crept away home again, all the while humming a song that would haunt him till his dying day, blinded by tears and seeing not the door of a magic kingdom which had opened to welcome him to its timeless light.

MacPhail of Uisinnis

MORE THAN THREE CENTURIES AGO there lived a man in Uisinnis, and his name was MacPhail. He was a big man, strong and silent, and he lived in a great stone house with his wife, his son, his son's wife, and their daughter. Now woe had fallen upon the family some thirteen years earlier when the daughter of MacPhail's son had been born dumb. Never a word had crossed the tongue of the young lass, but she was quiet and kind and well-liked by all.

The sad day came when old MacPhail died, and his body was dressed and laid at the end of their great stone house in preparation for burial. And his son, dressed in the black of mourning, drove off that day, to tend to the arrangements and gather together the old man's friends. He would be gone for a day, leaving the three women alone.

That night, as the moon hung high in the sky, lighting the path to the great stone house, and setting the rooms aglow with its beams, a scuffling was heard from the room with the body, and as the noise grew much louder, there came a shriek.

And from the mouth of the dumb girl who had never before spoken a word, came the cry, 'Granny, Granny. My grandfather is up, and he's coming to get you! He'll eat you, he will, but he won't touch me.'

And the old woman flew from her bed, and sure enough, there, striding down the hall was the man who had laid at the end of the hall, dead and about to be buried. And she slammed her door, and thrust the wardrobe against it, and the boxes and piles of mending. She screamed with fright, but the door was shut tight.

Then, at this, the old MacPhail bent down and began to dig. And he dug there for some time, his great hands heaving earth and rocks from under the doorframe, until a tunnel was bored straight under the door. And as he wedged his way into this space, and thrust his mighty shoulders up the other side, his face a mask of horrible pain and determination, a cock flew down from the rafters, on to the floor. And there he crowed three times, and returned to his loft.

And old MacPhail ceased his digging then, and he fell deep into the trough he had dug, stone dead.

His son returned to Uissinis the following morning, and there he found a wife and a mother who could hardly utter a word, and a daughter who could not stop speaking of the ghost that had come. And thinking them all quite mad, he was stopped short in his tracks by the sight of his father, his hands torn and bloodied, half of him in a hole under his mother's door, and half of him out.

Old MacPhail was buried the next day, but the hole he had dug beneath that doorway is still there, in the ruins of that ancient house, and there's been no one able to fill it. 'MacPhail's Pit' is its name, and the spirit of that man lies within it to this day.

Tarbh Na Leòid

ON THE ISLAND OF HEISKER, just west of Uist, lies an enchanted loch. Here lived a water-horse who was so terrible that everyone feared he would enter the village and destroy them all. And so it was that an old man in the village who knew of such things advised his neighbours to raise a bull, one to each household, and never let it out until it was needed.

For many years, the village was safe. Women washed their clothes at the loch in pairs, for everyone knew that the water-horse would only strike if you ventured to the loch alone. And every household had a bull, never let out in the event that it would be needed. But so it was one year, that the villagers had become a wee bit complacent about the water-horse, and women began to be a little less careful about doing their laundry in pairs. And one day, for whatever the reason, a woman washed alone there, and when she finished, she laid down on the banks of the river and slept there.

The sun was high in the sky, and she was warmed into a deep slumber. When she woke, she saw a magnificent man standing there, the sun glinting on his golden hair, and lighting his clear blue eyes. He spoke to her then, about the fineness of the afternoon, and she spoke back.

'You must be very tired, after all that washing,' he said kindly, and the woman blushed, for the men of Heisker never cared much about a woman's tiredness, or about the washing.

'I am indeed,' she stammered.

'Do you mind if I join you there?' He smiled at her. 'Because I am pretty tired myself.'

'Oh, no,' she said sweetly, and made room beside her.

Now that fine young man sat down beside her, and then spoke again.

'Do you mind if I lay my head in your lap?' he whispered, and the woman flushed again and shook her head.

And so it was that this young woman was sitting by the sunny banks of the loch with the head of a handsome young man in her lap. And as she gazed down, hardly believing her good fortune, she noticed sea-dirt in his hair, and weeds, and bits of water-moss. And only then did she notice his hooves, which lay crossed in slumber.

The water-horse.

And carefully, ever so gently, the woman took from her washing bag a pair of sharp scissors, and cutting a hole in her coat where the water-horse's head lay, she slipped out from under him, leaving a bit of her coat behind.

And then she ran back to the village, and as the fear struck her, she shrieked to the villagers, 'Help, it's the water-horse.'

There was a neighing behind her, and the sound of hooves on gravel, and she ran all the faster, calling for help.

Now the old man heard her first, and he called out to his neighbour, a man named MacLeod, whose bull was the closest. The bull was called Tarbh na Leòid, and he was a fierce creature, all the more so for being kept inside all his life.

'Let loose Tarbh na Leòid,' cried the woman, rushing into the village. 'Turn him loose!'

And so the bull was let loose, and he threw himself at the water-horse and there ensued a fight so horrific that the villagers could hardly watch. And it carried on for hours, and then days, and finally the bull beat that water-horse back to the loch, and they both disappeared.

The woman returned to her home, and she laid down on her bed, never to rise again. Nor did the bull or the water-horse, although it is said that the horn of Tarbh na Leòid rose to the surface of the water one fine day, many years later. It's still there, they say, guarding the path to the loch of the water-horse.

Origin and Didactic Legends

I had rather believe all the fables in the legend,
and the Talmud, and the Alcoran,
than that this universal frame is without a mind.
Francis Bacon, Of Atheism

THE LEGENDS WHICH TELL of the genesis of the earth, of the countryside, and its inhabitants may seem wild and unlikely, but for many centuries they were used to account for landmarks, and the origins of creatures. For man has always longed to make sense of his beginnings, to give a formula to the chaos from which we began, and if a hill resembles the footprint of a giant, there's every reason to believe there was once one there. Didactic legends, too, seem far-fetched at times, but the moral is always clear – if you live by the rules, you are safe from the clutches of witches and fairy-folk; if you eat well, you'll have good luck. The simplicity of the message is engaging, but the strictures they put upon daily life were not, for men lived whole lives in fear because of a dirty deed done in childhood, or a curse flung casually by an unhappy neighbour. But so it was that all good boys ate their porridge, and hung a bit of rowan over a door, and treated their wives with kindness. For no one knew who might visit them next, and what that visit might mean.

Dubh a' Ghiubhais

IT WAS MANY HUNDREDS OF YEARS AGO, long before the days when stories were written down, that Scotland was covered in a great dark forest. This was a forest of fir trees, tall and fine as any to be seen, and there lived there a colony of people who made the trees their friends. Trees can be good friends indeed, for they spread their arms across the land, protecting it from the wind that blows from the stormy coasts, and the rain which is carried on its back. And they make homes for the wee folk, and animals of the forest, and wood for the houses and fires of the men who live there.

Now this fine forest was much admired, and there was one in particular who was very envious of Scotland's great dark trees. He was the king of Lochlann and he wanted more than anything to destroy them. He would pace round his castle, overcast and gloomy as the winter sky, and he would lament his unhappy lot, ridden right through with jealousy as hot as any good peat fire.

It was his daughter, the princess, who had watched this curious pacing for years on end who finally came to find out the cause of his unhappiness. He explained that he wished to find a way to destroy the trees of the Scottish forest; and that wee princess, she was a practical lass, and she said there was nothing for it but to do it herself.

And so it was that she bade her father leave to find a witch to put her in the shape of a bird, and when he'd done that, and when she'd become a beautiful, pure white bird, she set out over the grassy hills of Lochlann to the deep fir forests that carpeted the Scottish land. On the west coast of Scotland she came down, and there she struck a tree with a wand she had under her wing. With that single motion the tree would burst into flames and burn there, and it was not long before this beautiful white bird had burnt a great number of trees in that forest.

Now this beautiful white bird was no longer fair or pure; indeed, the smoke of the pinewood had cast an ugly black shadow across her feathers and she came to be known by the people of the country as the Dubh a' Ghiubhais, or Fir Black. And so it was that this Dubh a' Ghiubhais flew across the land, causing damage that robbed the wee folk of their homes and sent the animals scattering for shelter, and the men had no wood for their homes or their fires, and the trees could no longer spread their comforting arms across the land, protecting it from the wind that blows from the stormy coasts, bringing the rain on its back. And it was for this reason that the men of the land grouped together and decided that this bird must be stopped, for the Dubh a' Ghiubhais had brought sadness and rain to their sheltered lives.

It was not easy to catch the Dubh a' Ghiubhais, but it was heard, somewhere on the west coast of Scotland, that the bird had a soft, sweet heart in that blackened breast, and that a plan could be made to capture it.

And so it was that a man at Loch Broom hatched the plan, and on the very next morning spent a day at work in his barnyard, taking mother from her young all across the barn. For the piglets were taken wailing from their sows, the puppies barked as they were snatched from their mothers' teats, the foals were taken from mares, the lambs from sheep, the calves from the cows, the chickens from the hens, the kittens from the cats, and even the kids from the goats that grazed on the tender shoots of grass on the verge. And the uproar that followed was enough to churn the stomach of any man alive, for there were cries so piteous, so plaintive, so eeding that the men and women for miles around hid themselves under soft down pillows in rder to block out that dreadful sound.

It was not long before it reached the ears of the Dubh a' Ghiubhais, who was passing on er fiery course of devastation. And her soft, sweet heart nearly burst with pity for these poor reatures. She flew at once to the ground, and drawing her wand from beneath her wing she nade as if to set the animals free when a small sharp arrow stung her breast, piercing her heart nd bringing a clean, cold death. And the man at Loch Broom picked up his quiver and slinging over his shoulder, bent over to collect the dead bird.

And so it was that the Dubh a' Ghiubhais was hung from a tree, where folk gathered round o cheer her death. News of what had happened reached her father, the king of Lochlann, and e was torn with grief and guilt. He sent his hardiest crew in a great long boat to bring the body f his dear daughter home. But there were fearful gales which pitched and jolted the ships that arried the funeral pyre, and although the brave sailors tried three times, they could get no urther than the mouth of the Little Loch Broom.

And so it was that the Dubh a' Ghiubhais was buried beneath the tree where she hung, at ildonan, at the bend of the loch at Little Loch Broom. She rests there still, a single fir tree rowing atop her grave, which lies beneath a grassy green hillock.

The Pabbay Mother's Ghost

THERE ONCE WAS A MAN who lived in a cottage in Pabbay, a kindly man who knew a woman's needs and saw to them in the course of every day. And so it was that when this kindly man's wife was in childbed, he made for her a great steaming bowl of porridge with butter. For the oats and butter in the porridge would make her strong, and the baby would be born without a murmur.

This man sat by the fireside that night, stirring the porridge and reaching across occasionally to mop the brow of his sweet, dear wife. And then a woman came in and sat by him on his bench, and she asked quietly for a bowl of the steaming porridge with butter. The man handed her the bowl without a word and carried on stirring, reaching across occasionally to mop the brow of his sweet, dear wife. And when the woman returned her bowl empty he filled it once more, and then again, until the woman had three great pots of porridge with butter. But still the man made no sound, passing another bowl across to his wife now and then, reaching across occasionally to mop her sweet, dear brow.

And then the woman stood up, and she said to the man, as he stirred his porridge, 'There, that's what I should have had when I was in childbed myself, for I am strong now, and my baby would have been born without a murmur. It was hunger that was the cause of my death, but now, as long as a drop of your blood remains, no woman shall ever die in childbed if anyone who tends her with porridge and butter is related to you.'

So the woman left the cottage in Pabbay, and it was not long before the man's baby was born without a murmur, and his sweet, dear wife sat up strong and healthy in the childbed. And from that time on, not a wife or child of his, or a wife or child of his children died, for like their forefather, they knew a woman's needs and saw to them in the course of every day.

Luran

THERE ONCE WAS A CROFTER and his wife, and they lived in a glen far from the prying eyes of neighbours. They were quiet folk, but they lived well, with a herd of cattle to be envied, and a good bit of land. Their house was snug and warm in the coldest months, they had cream and milk and butter, and they wanted for nothing, in that glen, far from the prying eyes of neighbours.

Now that crofter was a healthy man, and he liked nothing more than a good meal, particularly if it was a feast of his favourite oakcakes, smeared with butter and dipped again in cream. And he partook of this kind of meal on most days so he grew rather heavy and clumsy. But their house was safe from any kind of danger, being far from the prying eyes of neighbours, and he grew perhaps a little too satisfied, and a little too complacent in his happy home.

For it was a cold Hallowe'en evening that strange things began to happen on the land of that satisfied crofter, and although everyone living near the fairy folk knows that Hallowe'en evening is their time for mischief, the crofter had not had cause to worry before this particular Hallowe'en night.

It was just as he was settling himself and his wife into their beds that they heard the howling of their guard dog, and a rumpus going on in the henhouse. And then they heard the cattle lowing, and everyone knows that cattle never low in the dead of night, so the crofter and his wife grew alarmed. Then he put back on his outdoor clothes, and he lit a lantern and headed towards the barnyard.

There, an astonishing sight met his eyes, for the barnyard was empty, his cattle gone, his pig sty clean, his henhouse bare. And the crofter sat down and held his head in his hands, and he asked himself how such a thing could happen to a house tucked so neatly in the glen, far from the prying eyes of neighbours. And then he started, for there was the sound of a lowing cow just over the knoll, and when he looked more closely there were tracks heading there too.

And so it was that the crofter plucked up his courage that Hallowe'en night, and went over that knoll, into the realm of the fairies. He crept there silently, until he heard voices. Then he stopped and he listened.

'Luran didn't run,' came a voice.

'Didn't run at all,' said another.

'Couldn't run at all,' giggled the first, and then there was a great deal of scuffling and laughter.

'If only his bread were not so hard,' said the other, 'but if Luran were fed on porridge, Luran would outrun the deer.'

And the crofter heard this conversation, and filled with fear (for everyone knows that fairies who speak English are the most dangerous of all) he peeked over the hilltop. There sat two smug fairies and just beyond them were his cattle, and all the livestock of the barnyard. He sat back again, Luran the satisfied crofter, and he began to think.

And when he returned home to greet his anxious wife, he was still thinking, and again in the morning when she offered him his favourite meal of oatcakes, smeared in butter and dipped again in cream. And so it was that Luran held up his hand and said to his wife, 'You'll have to give me porridge and milk every day.'

As the days shortened and then lengthened again, Luran grew long and lean, and a fine, fit ȝht of a man he was. He worked on his farm and he raised more cattle, and on that house in e glen, far from the prying eyes of neighbours, Luran plotted his revenge.

It was twelve months now, and Luran was ready. Hallowe'en night found the crofter hidden the stable of cattle, peering restlessly across their troughs. He was soon rewarded, for in ɔpped the same two fairies who had visited there before, and as they led the first cattle away ɔm his barn, Luran leapt up and chased those fairies over the knoll. And when he caught em, not far from the top, they gazed at him in surprise, and danced a fairy dance of approval.

So the crofter returned to his cosy house, leading his cattle back to the stable. And never again d those fairies trouble that house, tucked in the glen, far from the prying eyes of neighbours, r the master of that house ate nothing but porridge and milk, as all good men should.

The Hugboy

THERE ONCE WAS A GIANT, a hugboy he was called, and he lived with his wife somewhere near Caithness. Now they fought a great deal, that hugboy and his wife, and when they stamped their feet and howled, the little folk scurried for cover, for was likely that a boulder or two could be thrown in their direction, or a mighty foot laced firmly upon a house or farm. Some say it was at that time that the fairy folk went ɔ live inside the hills, for only then were they safe from the rages of the hugboy and his ife.

Vell, so it happened, one dark day, that the hugboy fell out with his wife, and having had enough f his tempers, and with one of her own to match, she set out from home, never to return.

The hugboy was furious, for he chased her north, stepping through the Pentland Firth, nd when he caught sight of her once more he threw a great stone at her. She was nearly ying now, so furious and fast she was making away from the hugboy, and up Ireland Brae ne ran as he threw another great boulder that missed its mark. But that stone still lies in he field above Ramsquoy, and his great fierce fingermarks are in it still. She ran still further, he wife of the hugboy, for there is another stone he threw at her in the Lylie Banks at Skaill 1 Sandwick.

But that's where he lost her, and the hugboy stopped his chase and set about finding some urf to build himself a new home, so far had he come from his old one. He stomped further orth, scooping up handfuls of turf and placing them in his great straw basket. One handful arved out the Loch of Harry, and another made the Loch of Stenness. And then going back to ıy the foundations of his great new house, he tripped, and stubbed his toe, whereupon a great it of turf fell off that is now Graemsay. His toe fell off, too, and it forms a hillock that is mossed ut cannot hide the fact that it was once a part of the hapless hugboy.

It was here that his great basket gave way, tipping its contents over the land. Now that giant ad never had such a bad day, and in disgust he left the contents of his basket strewn as they lay, nd that is what became the hills of Hoy. He turned towards home now, rubbing his sore head, topping occasionally to adjust a sandal over his sore foot, and lamented his unhappy lot. For vho could be so unlucky as to have lost a wife and a toe in one day.

The Three Questions of King James

THERE ONCE WAS A SCOTTISH PRIEST, **a man adored by his flock, but not the King himself; King James he was, and not an easy man to please. Well, th priest had crossed the path of the King and in the course of doing so had manage to offend him. And so it was decreed that the priest would be hung by his neck at th palace at Scone.**

The poor kind priest had accepted his lot, when word came that there had been a parti reprieve. For if that priest would come along to Scone, and sit there with the King, and answ three questions that the King would put to him, he would be free to go home, to preach amo his flock once more.

Now questions are difficult things, for there are some that have no answers at all, ar some that can be put in a way that even the wisest man on earth could find no answer. Ar although the priest was a clever man, and he knew from the top to the bottom his gre black Bible, he knew there would be traps, for who would let a man free on the back three easy questions.

So he mulled over this dilemma, and he hummed and he hawed, and it was many days th he paced round his country cottage, and tapped his head, and sighed.

And then his brother, who lived with him and who was known to all as the simpleton he wa said, 'What is making you so catty?'

'Och, what use is it telling you, you're a simpleton no doubt.'

'Ahh, but can I not hear your problem? Maybe I can help?'

Now the priest thought little of this offer of help, but he was at the end of his frayed wits an he poured out his story to the simpleton man. He explained he was to be executed, and th there would be three questions put to him which could save his life.

'Hmmm,' said his brother, 'there are, you know, questions that just can't be answered.'

'I know it, I know it,' said the priest, shrugging unhappily. 'What am I to do?'

Now the priest was a good man, and even his simpleton brother could see this. 'I am goin in your place,' he said firmly.

'Oh no. How can a fool like you answer questions that may not have answers?' aske the priest.

'Well it seems to me that if you are killed I will die too, for how can a simpleton live on h own. If I am executed in your place, what is the difference?'

So the priest agreed finally that his brother should go in his place, and so he draped hi habit over the simpleton and handed him his staff. A prayer was said on his head and then th simpleton set off for Scone.

When he arrived, he was greeted by a man in a fine uniform, gold and blue and red, and h gravely ushered the priest's brother into the grand hall, for they had been expecting him, an the King was waiting. So the priest's brother was taken then to the King's room, where he sa on a throne that was more opulent than anything the young man had seen before. The roor was hung with gold and jewels that winked and sparkled as the candles flickered in the breez of his entrance. And the young man was enchanted by this fine sight, and he turned eyes at th stiff-faced King which shone as rich and true as any gem.

Now the king had chosen questions which were designed to trap the priest, for he cared not if he lived or died, and he settled back to watch the holy man's discomfort.

'You know why you are here,' he said gravely.

'Oh, yes,' said the simpleton in the priest's disguise.

'Well, then, let us begin. First question: where is the centre of the world?'

'Why, it's right here!' And the simpleton stamped the floor with his great staff.

'Oh!' The King looked surprised. 'I must let you have that one. Yes, I believe that you are right. For the world is a ball, and anywhere can be its centre. Yes, yes ...' he stroked his great beard, 'I'll let you have that one.' And then he continued, 'Next question: What am I worth sitting here, in all this,' he gestured round the room. 'Just what am I worth in money?'

'Well,' said the simpleton without hesitation, 'you are not worth anything more than thirty pieces of silver.'

'Why do you say that?' said the King with some consternation.

'Because the greatest man ever to enter the world was sold for only thirty shillings,' said the simpleton simply.

'Quite right,' blustered the king. 'I'll give you that one, too. Then the third question – and if you can answer this you'll be a free man ...

Do you know what I am thinking now?'

And with that the King sat back, for there was no way that even a man of the cloth could know the kingly thoughts of a monarch.

But the simpleton blazed on. 'Why yes, I do,' he said.

'What's that, then?' said the King, sitting up with amazement.

'You think you are talking to a priest, and you are talking to a fool, his brother,' he said then.

And so it was that the stony King James rose from his throne to shake the hand of a simpleton, and then he laughed out loud.

'Be free man,' he said. Anyone who has a brother like that, and that brother a simpleton, deserves to be free. Away you go.'

Legends for Children

Between the dark and the daylight,
When the night is beginning to lower,
Comes a pause in the day's occupations,
That is known as the Children's Hour.
Henry Wadsworth Longfellow, The Children's Hour

THE MYTHS AND LEGENDS told to children over the centuries were largely fictional, and they were developed to instil in children the kind of morality and superstition they would need to live a life of good fortune and good will. The legends were often violent, and many of the events that occurred were so frightening that a child would be shocked into a rigid belief, and good behaviour. For what child would not go straight to bed each night when he heard of the old fairy wife who comes with her brownie child? But there is a certain perverse morality there, too, designed to appeal to children. Bad mothers are punished, sometimes with death, and children can reign supreme in the fantasy world of the imagination. For when animals can talk, and a tall tale has a moral, anything is possible, and that magic is as strong today.

The Little Bird

A FAMILY ONCE LIVED **in the woods, a man and a woman with their three small children. Now two of these children were boys, but the third was a wee slight girl with a smile that lit the hearts of all who met her. Her face was fair and her eyes held the promise of many dreams, but her mother, who had no time for those dreams, threw up her hands in despair at her fairylike daughter.**

Their cottage was set deep in the woods, and it was a walk indeed to fetch milk from the farm down the hillock. But that wee slight girl was sent on that walk, with her mother's good jug, every day from the time she could toddle, and so it was that she would make that walk again on this particular day.

Now the girl had just counted five years, and on the table, laid there surely by the wee folk, was a bright shiny skipping rope, with handles as red as the flowers that gazed into the stream. And the girl wanted nothing more than to skip with that new rope, and to hold those red handles, but it was time, as it always was in the middle of the morning, to fetch the milk from the farm down the hillock.

'Can I take my skipping-rope with me?' she asked, her eyes shining with excitement.

But her mother, who had no time for that excitement, threw up her hands in despair at her fairylike daughter. 'No, ye can't,' she said sourly, and turned back to her cooking.

'But I won't spill the milk, Mummy, I promise,' said the wee girl.

And because her mother was not the sort who liked a good chat, or indeed a wee girl with eyes that shone with the promise of dreams, she said tersely, 'Well, then. Ye can take the skipping-rope, but if ye spills so much as a drop of the milk, I'll kill ye.'

And so it was that the little girl took her new skipping-rope, and skipped pertly down the lane, over the hillock to the farm, the milk jug clasped tightly in a hand that also clutched the shiny red handles of the skipping-rope. She stopped at the farm, and her jug was filled, and her skipping-rope admired, and away she went home again, skipping with the jug in one hand.

But things being as they are with matters that involve milk jugs and skipping-ropes, it was not long before that jug was dropped and broken, and the wee girl sat sadly in its midst and sobbed.

Now the girl was a familiar figure down this forest road, and soon enough a woman came along who recognized her, and who knew of the girl's mother, who was a very stern woman indeed, having no time for the dreams that shone in the eyes of her wee lass. So this kindly woman took it upon herself to right the young thing, and she said to her then, 'Now come along with me. I've got a jug just the twin of yours there.'

Then the new jug was filled, and with her skipping rope folded carefully and tucked under an arm, the little girl went home without spilling even a drop of milk.

But her mother, whose eyes shone not with dreams but with spite, said, 'Where did ye get the jug?'

And the little girl said, 'It's our jug, Mummy, just the same as ye gave me.'

But she said, 'No, this one is different. My jug had a blue stripe and this one has a red one.'

And with that she killed the wee girl, wrapping that skipping-rope around her thin neck until she was blue and still, and then she baked her in a pie. And being near to dinnertime, it was not long before her father came in, and he asked for the wee girl, for he had a soft spot for her fairylike ways, and those eyes that shone with the promise of dreams reminded him of another wee child with those same bright eyes, and that child had been himself.

His wife shook her head. 'Och, she's out playing, let her be.'

'Should we not call her for her dinner?' asked her husband, surprised at this sudden leniency.

'Na, let her go then.'

So the man tucked into the pie, with morsels of meat so tender that he ate greedily. And then, as he cut into an even larger piece, he found a finger, with a small silver ring.

He looked at his wife in horror, and he said, 'This is my daughter's ring. Why is she in this pie?'

And his wife said then that she had killed her, for she'd broken their milk jug and spilled the milk.

'Now what have you done?' he cried, and made as if to kill his wife himself. But now that the lass was gone there wouldn't be a woman around the house to keep it spic and span, and to make great succulent pies, so he thought again, and said, 'Och, I'll let ye live.'

When the two sons came in they too were distressed by the death of their wee sister, and none could eat his dinner that day.

Time went by, and nothing changed in the cottage set deep in the woods, except they had a visitor, in the shape of a small brown bird, who peeped into the windows of the house for hours of each day, and who had eyes that shone with the promise of dreams. But with the windows misted with the heat of the fire, the boys and their father couldn't see those eyes, and so they would shoo away the wee bird.

But everyday, there it would be again, peeping into the windows of the house.

By the time Christmas came round, the boys had grown to love the wee bird who sat on the sill, and they fed it with crumbs and bits of seed. They were doing just that, on Christmas Eve when a voice startled them from their play. It boomed down the chimney and when the two boys reached the hearth it grew quieter, almost plaintive.

'Brother, look up and see what I've got,' and so the first brother looked up and was met by a shower of toys and sweets.

And then came the voice once again, 'Brother, look up and see what I've got,' and when the next brother looked up, he too was met by a shower of toys and sweets.

Then, 'Father, Father, look up and see what I've got,' and down the chimney came a fine new suit, and a bag of tobacco, and as he was admiring that suit, a letter dropped down the chimney and on it was written the words, 'Open this letter two hours after Christmas night.'

And into the silence came the voice once more, 'Mother, look up and see what I've got,' and when the mother looked up she dropped upon her head a great stone and killed her dead.

When the two hours had passed, the father opened the letter, which said, 'Dear Father this is your daughter. The spell is broken. Once I have killed my mother, I shall return on New Year's Eve.'

The days to New Year's Eve passed slowly, and the father and his boys were filled with fear of what might greet them, for the wee girl had been long dead, and cut into a pie at that. But on that New Year's Eve there was no sign of her, and they grew more and more worried and frightened. And then, there was a tap tap tap at the window, a pecking sound that was familiar to them all.

'Och, it's only the wee bird,' said a brother to the other, but they opened the window anyhow, and prepared to feed it some crumbs. It was then that the bird hopped into the kitchen, and turning to them with eyes that shone with the promise of dreams, said, 'It's me, I'm home.'

They all stood aghast, the father and his two boys, and then the father spoke tentatively, reaching out to stroke the smooth feathers of the little bird, 'But you're a bird now.'

'Yes,' said the little bird, 'but if you take my mother's pinkie ring and give it to me now, I'll ome back as a girl.'

This they did, though it meant digging up the body of the wicked mother from her newly irned grave. But they returned with the ring, and presented it to the bird, who turned at once ito a little girl.

And the girl drew herself up tall, and took the ring that had belonged to her mother, and the ng that had once been hers, and laid them safely away in a box, a reminder of what can happen girls with skipping ropes, and mothers with no time for fairylike ways or dreams.

The Fox, The Wolf and The Butter

ONG, LONG AGO, when a fox could befriend a wolf without fear of becoming his midday meal, and when all animals and folk in the woods spoke Gaelic, there was a wee den set deep in the forest, and it was the home of a fox and a wolf who lived here together. Now this fox and this wolf were friends, and firm friends they were, but here would always be that shadow of mistrust that hung between them, for a fox is a wily reature, and it was then, too, even in the days when a fox could befriend a wolf without ear of becoming his midday meal.

'he fox and the wolf walked together each day, along the path overhung by fronded green firs, nd over the hills, to the beach. And there they would comb the shores for debris that had lown in from the sea. Often it was, too, that they'd find a choice bit of fish for their dinner, or bit of salt pork that had fallen over the side of a poor seaman's ship.

And so it was one day that they walked together, along the path overhung by fronded green irs, and over the hills to the beach. And there they came across a great cask of pure white butter, old and creamy and freshly churned. And what delight lit their beady eyes, and their tongues airly dripped with anticipation of this creamy treat, all cold and freshly churned. They danced bout it then, and said to the other, 'We'll hide it now, till we get a chance to take it home.'

And so the fox and the wolf struggled with this great cask, up the hill and partway along that ath overhung by fronded green firs, where they dug a great hole and buried it. And then they vent home.

When they woke the next morning, the wolf yawned, and licked his lips, and thought of all hat lovely pure white butter, and he said to the fox, 'Shall we bring it a little further today?'

But the fox shook his head. 'Oh no,' he said, 'not today. I am going away today.'

The wolf looked surprised. 'Where are you going?' he asked.

'I am going,' said the fox, 'to a Christening. And then I'll be back.'

So the fox went off and he was gone for near a whole day. And when he came back he was miling and content, and he laid himself down on a cosy bit of the den as if to sleep.

'So you're back,' said the wolf to the fox.

'Yes,' he said.

'What name was the babe given?' asked the wolf.

'We called him Mu Bheul (About the Mouth),' said the fox, to which the wolf nodded sagely.

The fox and wolf settled down for the night, and the next morning the fox rose and made as if to leave. Now it was one thing for the fox to set out alone of a morning, but quite another for him to do it twice, and the wolf felt a funny kind of suspicion, as the shadow of mistrust that hung between them grew ever so slightly larger.

And he said to the fox, 'Shall we bring it a little further today, the cask of butter?'

But the fox shook his head. 'Oh no,' he said, 'not today. I am going away today.'

The wolf looked wary. 'Where are you going?' he asked.

'I am going,' said the fox, 'to a Christening. And then I'll be back.'

So the fox went off and he was gone for near a whole day. And when he came back he was smiling and content, and he laid himself down on a cosy bit of the den as if to sleep.

'So you're back,' said the wolf to the fox.

'Yes,' he said.

'What name was the babe given today?' asked the wolf.

'We called him Mu Leth (About Half),' said he.

'I see,' said the wolf, although he didn't, and as he settled down for the night he felt that shadow of mistrust growing larger still.

But the wolf wakened fresh and ready for the day, the thought of all that pure, creamy butter making him salivate. And he stood and stretched, and looked for his friend, the fox. But he was not there. So he looked around, outside the den, and the fox was just setting off down the path overhung by fronded green firs, and he called out then, 'Fox, where are you going? Shall we bring it a little further today, the cask of butter?'

But the fox shook his head. 'Oh no,' he said, 'not today. I am going away again today.'

The wolf just looked. 'Where are you going today?' he asked.

'I am going,' said the fox, 'to a Christening. And then I'll be back.'

So the fox went off and he was gone for near a whole day. And when he came back he was smiling and content, licking his chops and smacking his lips. And he laid himself down on a cosy bit of the den as if to sleep.

'So you're back,' said the wolf to the fox.

'Yes,' he said.

'What name was the babe given today?' asked the wolf.

'We called him Sgrìobadgh a' Mhàis (Scraping the Bottom),' said he.

'I see,' said the wolf, although he didn't again, and as he settled down for the night that shadow of mistrust was firmly between them.

But he woke again the next morning fresh and hungry, and the thought of that creamy butter made him nearly swoon with expectation. And he said to the fox, his tongue dripping so that he could hardly speak, 'Shall we get it today, the cask of butter we hid?'

And the fox said, 'Yes indeed.'

And so it was that the fox and the wolf set off down the path, overhung by fronded green firs, almost to the hills whereupon lay the shore. And they reached the spot where the great cask of butter was hidden, cold, creamy and freshly churned. They uncovered it then, and lifting off the lid, eager for a succulent pawful, they discovered it ... empty.

It was awful. They jigged and railed and danced a furious reel round that empty cask. And the fox was so puzzled, and so too was the wolf, for neither knew who had taken their butter.

'Well,' said the fox at last, when they lay down spent from their angry dance, 'this is very queer. For not another creature knew of this cask but you and I, dear wolf. And this terribly queer affair means only one thing to me, and that is this: that it was you or me who took that butter. And that is what I think:

If I ate the butter, and it was I
Chiorram chiotam, chiorram, chatam, chiorram chiù
But if you ate the butter and it was you,
A galling plague on your grey belly in the dust.

There was no great harm in the curse of the fox, for his words were empty, but the curse he ıd laid on the wolf was poison indeed, for his belly was empty and the butter was gone.

The Ainsel

DEEP IN THE HEART **of the Border country, where the wind howls with cold, lived a wee boy called Parcie. He lived with his mother in a small, snug cottage where the fire burned bright and bathed the stone clad walls in a soft, cosy glow. They lived alone ıere for his father was long since gone, but they managed with little, living simply and ıppily among the trees and the wood folk who inhabited them.**

ow like most small boys, Parcie plotted all day in order to avoid being sent to bed each night. e longed to sit by the hearth with his mother, watching the burning embers cast intriguing ıadows which danced and performed a story that seemed to Parcie like it could go on forever. ıt each night it was cut short, as was the sound of his mother's mellifluous voice as she sang to m of fairies and sea-folk, and told of stories and legends of long ago. For it was it at this point ıat Parcie's mother would close up her bag of mending.

'It's time for your bed, Parcie,' she would say, always the same thing, and Parcie would be ıcked neatly into his tiny box-bed where the fairies had laid a nest of golden slumberdust so otent that his eyes were shut and he was fast asleep as soon as his head touched his soft pillow. nd there he'd sleep all the night, until the next morning he struggled to hatch a plan to stay vake all night, to carry on and on the drowsy contentment of the evening.

But one night Parcie's tired mother could argue no further and when the fire began to sink own into black-red embers, and she said,

'It's time for your bed, Parcie' he would not go. And so she picked up her mending, and tidied away, setting a bowl of cool, fresh cream by the doorstep as she went along the corridor to er own bed.

'I hope to God the old fairy wife does not get to you, lad, but it will be your own fault if she oes,' whispered his mother as she disappeared into her room.

And suddenly the warm red room took on a more sinister cast, and the shadows no longer ıld a story but taunted him, warning him, tempting him until he was a jumble of fear and onfusion. And just as he steeled himself to dash to his warm box-bed, filled with golden umberdust, a tiny brownie leapt from the chimney and landed on his foot.

Now brownies were common in the days when Parcie lived in the stone cottage with his ıother, and they came each day to every house that had the courtesy and the foresight to leave bowl of cool, fresh cream by the doorstep. And if some foolish occupant forgot that cream ne night, she would be sure to find a tumultuous mess the next day. For brownies came to tidy verything away, neat and clean, collecting specks of dust and laying things just so, so that in the morning the lucky household gleamed with shining surfaces and possessions all in order

But Parcie knew nothing of the magic that dropped through the chimney each night and h
was surprised and rather pleased to see this tiny fairy. The brownie was not, however, so please
to see Parcie, for he was an efficient wee brownie and he liked to have his work done quickly,
order to get to the lovely bowl of cool, fresh cream which awaited him by the doorstep.

'What's your name?' asked Parcie, grinning.

'Ainsel (own self),' replied the brownie, smiling back despite himself. 'And you?'

'My Ainsel,' said Parcie, joining in the joke.

And so Parcie and the brownie played a little together, and Parcie watched with intere
while the brownie tidied and cleaned their cottage in a whirlwind of activity. And then, as h
neared the grate to sweep away some dust that had come loose from the hearth, Parcie too
an inopportune moment to poke the fire, and what should fly out upon the poor brownie but
red-hot ember which burnt him so badly that he howled with pain.

And then, into the snuffling silence that followed, a deep frightening voice boomed down th
chimney. It was the old fairy wife who Parcie's mother had warned of, and she flew into a rag
when she heard her dear brownie's tears.

'Tell me who hurt ye,' she shouted down the chimney, 'I'll get him, so I will.'

And the brownie called out tearfully, 'It was My Ainsel'. Parcie lost no time in hurling himse
from the room and into his box-bed where the golden slumberdust did not cast its magic ove
the terrified boy, for he laid awake and shaking for a long time after his head touched his so
pillow.

But the old fairy wife was not concerned about Parcie, for she called out, 'What's the fuss,
you did it yer ainsel' and muttering she thrust a long brown arm down the chimney and plucke
the sniffling brownie from the fireside.

Now what do you think Parcie's mother thought the next morning when she found he
cottage spic and span, but the bowl of cream still standing untouched, cool and fresh by th
doorstep. How perplexed she was when the brownie stopped visiting her cottage, althoug
she always left a bowl of cream to tempt him. But in the heart of the Border country, where th
wind howls with cold, bad is almost always balanced by good, and so it was then when from tha
night onwards, Parcie's mother never again had to say to him, 'Parcie, it's time for your bed,' fo
at the first sudden movement of the shadows, when the fire began to sink down into black-re
embers, he was sound asleep in his tiny box-bed, deep in the sleep of the golden slumberdust

Tales of the Great Féinn

Unhappy the land that has no heroes.
Bertolt Brecht, Leben des Galilei

THE GREAT FÉINN, or Fians as they are also called, were a fighting people born to battle. Fionn Mac Chumail was their leader, and they numbered nine thousand warriors, their army called the Host of the Fians. The Féinn belonged both to Eirinn (Ireland) and to Alba (Scotland) and every rolling hill in Scotland bears the scars of one of their deeds.

The Host of the Fians was set up when the Lochlannaich, or the Norwegians, as we know them today, ravaged the coasts of Eirinn and Alba, and the King of Eirinn prayed for a way to dispose of them. It came to him in a dream that he must marry the hundred most powerful men and women in the land, and let their children's children become the greatest army ever seen. These were the Host of the Fians, and Fionn Mac Chumail led them into battle against the Lochlannaich and drove them away forever.

Fionn is known in Scotland as Finn MacCool, and Fingal, depending on the part of the country, and there are many variations of the spelling of his surname. His son Ossian, from the Irish Oisin of the Fenian Cycle, has a different number of brothers in different legends, as well as variations in the spelling of his name The feats of the great Féinn, of the wise warrior Fionn, and his sons, Osgar and Ossian, form the basis of some of the most dazzling Scottish legends, for Scotland is a country of many great heroes, and storytellers like nothing better than to remember their deeds.

The Story of Ossian and the Crow

LONG, LONG AGO, in the days of the great Féinn, there lived three brothers who made their home on the grassy hills of the Highlands. They lived apart, in three stone shelters, but they met often, hunting for deer that roamed wild across their land. These three brothers had not yet married, and women were scarce, in the grassy hills of the Highlands, in the days of the great Féinn, so they were always on the look-out for a good bit of lass.

Now Ossian was the eldest of the three brothers, and he had the wisdom and the kindness of all three, for his brothers were daft and selfish lads, and they lived for themselves.

It was a cold, stormy night, the kind of storm that brews all day on the Highlands, until the winds are fevered, and the thunder roars into the darkness. The rain was pelting against the stones of his brothers' shelters, and they huddled against their hearths for warmth. When suddenly, out of the night flew a great Black Crow, with feathers wet against her scrawny body. She flew to the shelter of the youngest brother, and tapped on the door. The crow spoke Gaelic, for all animals did, in the days of the great Féinn, and she begged sweetly for lodging for the night, and a bite of food.

'Och, be gone, Black Crow, or I'll off your head with my finger,' snarled the youngest brother. And the Black Crow flew off.

She was colder when she tapped on the door of the middle brother, and her feathers hung sadly against her tiny body. Her voice was plaintive, but pure, and she asked once again for lodging for the night, and a bite of food.

'Och, be gone, Black Crow, or I'll off your head with my finger,' snarled the middle brother. And the Black Crow flew off.

And when she arrived at Ossian's house she was so cold that her eyes were wild with pain and she could hardly move. Her feathers were useless now, and she could only hobble towards the door. Light shone from the window, and the Black Crow took heart. There was a warmth, here, she felt, and with that canny instinct of animals, especially those from the days of the great Féinn, she knew that she would be safe. When she finally reached the door, tapped upon it, and asked Ossian if she could have lodgings for the night, he greeted her with a great wide grin, and opened his door.

'Come in,' he said, and offered the poor Black Crow a bowl of food that steamed with goodness. She ate hungrily, and then again, and finally sat back. Ossian, sensing she was tired, carried her gently to his upstairs room, and laid her on the bed. He returned, then, to the fire, where a blanket was warming, and carrying it back to the cold Black Crow, he stopped with a jerk.

For there, on the bed in his own room was the most beautiful woman he had ever seen. And she lay there sleeping, her hair spilling across the sheets, her pale white skin lit by the dew of a good night's rest. And as he neared the bedside to take a closer look, she rose, and opened her eyes – eyes that spoke of days gone by, of wondrous sights and eager dreams. Ossian was entranced.

'How, how do you come to be such a beautiful woman when you were but a moment ago a Black Crow?' he stammered, hardly daring to believe his eyes. He rubbed at them, but she was still there, a glorious vision.

'I've been enchanted,' explained the woman kindly, 'and until now, no one would take me in. Until someone gave me a bed and some food, I would have to live my life as a crow. But now,' and she gestured all around her, 'I am here, and I can live as your wife for as long as you never cast up at me the shape in which I arrived. If you do that,' and now her voice grew quiet, 'I will become a crow once again.'

So Ossian and his wife lived there together, to the envy of his oafish brothers, and the crow woman made his shelter a home like none other. Wee curtains appeared, with a soft cover for the bed, and a bit of flower from the hillside was laid on the table for their meals. And his wife blossomed with the attentions he gave her, and she offered him her rare knowledge and her perfect, sweet love.

Ossian went out most days, and hunted the deer which roamed wild on his land, but he always returned to his dear wife, and there was never a cross word between them, for he had remembered her warning and sought never to cast up at her the shape in which she arrived.

Now it was one cold winter's day, like many others, that Ossian prepared to go out for the hunt.

'That bitch should have puppies today,' he said, stroking the dog who lay curled in the corner. 'Put a string around the neck of the first puppy,' he said, and then he left.

He was not gone long when the first puppy was born, and his wife carefully tied a length of string round his neck. She put him to one side, and helped the bitch as more and more puppies were born. She had just put the last to its breast when there was a knock at the door.

Now this knock surprised Ossian's wife, for she had never, in all her time there, been visited on the grassy hills of the Highlands. For long ago, in the days of the great Féinn, people lived far from one another and it could be many months before they spied another man. But she rose, and swallowing the fear which surged up into her throat, she opened the door.

There stood a man as black as the night, his face a tortured mask.

'I want the first puppy,' he said. And he held out a hand that was grimed with the dirt of the afflicted. She jumped back, and went to fetch the puppy.

Now Ossian's wife was a clever lass, and she knew that her husband had wanted that first-born for himself. So she pulled the string from the puppy's slim neck, and placed it round the neck of another, and it was this dog that she presented to the great dark man at the door. He took the puppy, and lifted its ear. And then tugging on it, and shaking it, he was rewarded by the yelp of the dog.

'No,' he said, handing her back, 'she was not the first puppy.'

Then one by one Ossian's wife brought out the puppies, and with each one he took it in his hand, and lifted its ear, and then tugging on it, and shaking it, he waited for the inevitable yelp. And when the last puppy was given to him, for she had not told him of the tiny first-born she had hidden under the blanket by the hearth, he cast it aside and grabbed at her throat.

'The first puppy, or I'll cut off your head,' he said, his face so close that she could count every blackened pore. She pulled back, and returned with the puppy. And he took hold of it and lifted its ear. And then, tugging on it, and shaking it, and then shaking it again, he smiled, for it had made no sound at all. He tucked that puppy under his arm and left, the great dark man, and he never did return.

Ossian's wife was pale and fearful when he returned home that night, and striding into the cottage as he always did, and taking her by the hands, he cried, 'The puppies, they've been born.' Then kneeling over the litter, he chose the one with the string tied round its neck. And he raised it up, lifting its ear, and then tugging on it and shaking it. When the puppy let out a fine whimper, Ossian turned to his wife with cold eyes.

'You've put the string round the wrong neck,' he said then. To which the wife of Ossian hung her head, and told him the story of the great dark man, and how he had threatened to cut off her head, and Ossian looked at her with such disdain that she was numbed with pain. She hardly felt the next blow, but his words worked their magic:

'What can I expect from a Black Crow,' he said coarsely. And then she was gone.

He called to her, then, did Ossian, who was torn by grief and wretched shame, but she could not come back. She called to him from the sky, 'I can never go back now. I told you on that first day. I gave you my warning.' And with that she thrust her beak at him, and there, suddenly in his hand lay a golden ring.

'Place that ring upon your finger,' she said softly, 'so that you may live forever. For you have given me many fine years, dear Ossian.' And the Black Crow disappeared forever.

That was how Ossian lived to an age beyond all others, for such things could happen, long, long ago, in the days of the great Féinn, when crows could become women, and then just disappear into the night.

Fionn and the Journey to Lochlann

IT WAS MANY YEARS since the Lochlannaich had been driven from the land of the Féinn, and Fionn and his warriors spent most of their time stalking deer on the rolling hills of the Highlands, still glorying in the days of war, but keeping their minds sharp with the hunt.

And it was on such a pursuit that Fionn and his men stumbled upon the form of a young man, a stranger who hailed them from the hill, and asked to be taken as one of their party.

'Who are you lad,' asked Fionn kindly, for he was a man of great knowledge and wisdom and the folk of other countries, (this man spoke in an unfamiliar tongue) interested him greatly.

'I have come from great distance, seeking your company,' he said gravely, 'I need a master.'

'And I need a lad to serve me,' said Fionn. 'But what will you want for your pay, if I take you on for a year and one day?'

'Not much,' said the boy, 'just your company at a feast in the palace of the King of Lochlann, one year and one day from tonight. But you must come alone,' he said then, 'without dog, or man, or calf or child, or indeed any weapon.'

The great Fionn roared with laughter, for he enjoyed a good challenge, and he nodded now furiously, and shook the boy's hand.

'I like your terms,' he said with a great smile, 'for there is a hint of adventure there, something quite intriguing. That's it, then, join me for a year and one day and I shall journey with you to Lochlann.'

And so it was that the stranger became an attendant to Fionn, serving him loyally for a year and one day, learning a great deal about the fine warrior. He would watch Fionn, revel at his agile mind that tore strips from the wisdom of others.

For although Fionn was not the strongest of all warriors, his power lay in his gift for clear-headed sagacity, for fairness and honour, and for generosity and kindness. He travelled far and wide with his hound Bran, the finest hunting-dog ever seen, a huge animal whose loyalty to his master was the envy of every warrior of the great Féinn.

And Fionn was a man of his word, and when that year and one day had passed, quickly as it is wont to do, he stood by his promise to travel with the stranger to Lochlann, to feast at the palace of the king.

Fionn called together his warriors, and he told them of his plan, and although they all protested, and a mighty uproar ensued, he stood firm. But if Fionn liked adventure, and the scent of pure excitement, he was also practical, and he knew, deep down, that it was not a feast he would be attending at the palace in Lochlann, but more likely the funeral of someone he knew very well.

But he faced his men now, and he spoke to all nine thousand of them, gathered there to hear him:

'I will go and honour my word. But if I have not returned, in one year and one day, then you shall know that I have been killed, and my blood spilled across the land. And if this comes to pass, there must be no man amongst you without a quiver of arrows or a sword in your hands. For my death shall be avenged on the strand of Lochlann, and the Host of the Fians shall reign supreme.'

And a great roar of approval broke out across the army as Fionn joined the stranger to fulfil his pledge. The mighty dog Bran was to be left behind, and Fionn stroked his great ears and whispered a fond farewell, but just as he was about to take his leave, the court fool beckoned him to one side.

'Sire, listen, great leader of the Féinn,' he whispered, 'take heed. For the wisdom of a king is often trapped in the mind of a fool, and I have that advice for you now.'

And as the powerful Fionn bent over to listen, he carried on.

'Take this. It's not dog, or man, or calf or child, or even a weapon. Take it.' And with that he thrust something in the pocket of Fionn, and stumbled off.

Fionn plunged his hand deep into his pocket and withdrew the treasure. It was the Bran's chain of gold, a lead which calmed the mighty dog and kept him by his master's side. And if Fionn was puzzled, he showed it not, returning the chain to his pocket and nodding silently.

And so his great journey began, and he departed in the steps of the lad who had been his servant. Their travels were swift, for the boy had wings for feet, and he flew across the rocky terrain, over lochs and rivers, under vast cliffs which threatened to belch rocks on the travellers, and along bracken- and moss-lined valleys. And then, after many days of travelling, they reached their destination: the palace of the King of Lochlann.

There it stood, stark and ugly, thrust up from the grey rocks that veered crazily across the coastline. The spray from the sea spattered it in a rhythm that taunted the visitors, inviting them into the dirty depths of the castle. There was no opulence here, but blackness and evil, and Fionn knew then that he had been right. He would feast not tonight. Unwittingly, he reached into his pocket and touched Bran's golden chain.

He was led into the great hall where the King of Lochlann and his evil chiefs plotted his death. A cry surged forth when he entered, and he was flung against a wall and forced to sit down. With an ironic smile, Fionn Mac Chumail complied.

'Hang him,' shouted a group of black-bearded men.

'No, burn him,' shouted another.

'I say drown him,' shouted a lone voice, to which a rowdy cheer went up.

But then rose a man with a face as dark as the stormy seas, and he fair snarled his words to the eager crowd, 'There is only one death that will shame the noble,' and at this he spat to one side, 'Fionn Mac Chumail. Let us send him to the Great Glen, where he will be torn apart by the terrible Grey Dog. There could not be a death worse for the leader of the great Féinn than to fall at the cur of a dog.'

And so it was decreed that Fionn Mac Chumail would be sent to the Great Glen, a gloomy wilderness of black thorn trees and lichen-covered rocks, and he would meet his death there at the jaws of the most frightful dog on earth, the Grey Dog of Great Glen. This dog had teeth that were taller than most men, and a snarl that curdled the blood of even the bravest warrior.

So Fionn was left there alone that night, with the darkness pricking at his courage, and the baying of the hound, which echoed in the distance, tugging at his mind. And the great Fionn waited there, for to run would be useless. In one direction lay the bloodthirsty Lochlannaich, in the other, the cruel Grey Dog.

So he stood his ground, as it was his nature to do, and he prepared to face his death as the hero he was.

And then at once there was the dog, more terrifying than anything he could have imagined, for this great canine had a dripping tongue that hung over fangs like white spearheads, eyes that were filled with an instinctive hatred of all man, and hackles that stood up on his back like the finest wrought armour.

His breath was poison, and the stench and heat of it scorched the skin of Fionn and he staggered back.

And as he fell, his hand flew instinctively to his pocket, where he grasped Bran's golden chain. And as he drew it out, and waved it before him, the Grey Dog leapt on top of Fionn, who cursed his ill-fortune. But it was not the jaws of Grey Dog that found their mark, but his great thick tongue, which lapped at the breath-burnt warrior, and healed him there and then. And with his huge teeth he tugged gently at Fionn, righting him to his feet, and nudging him forward, and the light that shone from the eyes of that dog was no longer that of hatred, but loyalty, and love.

And it was a bemused Fionn who set out of the Great Glen with Grey Dog at his side. He knew not what had happened, but clasped Bran's golden chain round the great dog's neck, and carried on.

At the bottom of the Glen was a wee stone cottage, a humble sort of place that was home to an old man and his wife. Now the wife was at the stream, tending to her washing, when the strange couple rounded the bend, and she flew back to the cottage, screaming and gnashing her teeth, certain that death was upon her, for had she not just seen a vision of hell itself?

And her husband rose unsteadily, and struggled to comfort her.

'But what have you seen?' he asked, failing to get any sense from her tortured words. But at last she could talk, and as she stumbled through sentences riddled with nonsense her fears became clear.

A great warrior, the most illustrious man she had ever seen, was making his way up their path, and who should be beside him but the Grey Dog himself.

At this the old man began to laugh, and he held himself up with pride.

'There is only one man in the world who could tame the Grey Dog, and that is Fionn Mac Chumail. We are honoured to have him on our land,' he said then.

And so the old man and his wife went out to greet Fionn, who told of his adventures at Lochlann. He was soon settled in their comfortable home, and fed with simple fare that warmed him to the root of his being. He became content there, that restless warrior, and delighted in he rare knowledge and insight of the old man. Night after night they sat by the roaring hearth, oasting their toes and sharing the stories of the past, and so Fionn learned how the Grey Dog had become tamed.

For the Grey Dog was lulled by the sight of Bran's chain because he was his brother, separated from him when the litter was young. And as Bran was loyal to Fionn, so too would be the Grey Dog, who in deference to his brother Bran, acknowledged Fionn as his master.

So it was that a year and one day soon passed in the pleasant company of this cottage in the Glen, and Fionn found a deep peace within himself, one which he would call upon often in the months to come.

But his peaceful stay did come to an end, as all good things do, and he was woken with a start one day, by the rallying cry of nine thousand men. He ran from the cottage, and across the knoll, and there, marching across the verge, was an army led by a strong, fierce man with flowing red locks.

Fionn's eyes pricked with tears. It was his own son Osgar, leading the Host of the Fians, and as he flew over the hill, with Grey Dog at his side, his army swarmed around him, cheering and shouting, hailing the great leader whose death they had come to avenge. And above the rejoicing could be heard the howling of two great dogs, for Grey Dog and Bran had long since given up hope of meeting again. They frolicked together now, licking and biting haunches, and rolling in the grassy green knoll.

'We have come,' say Osgar joyously, 'for it is a year and one day since you have left us, and we thought you dead.'

'I am alive, my dear son,' said Fionn solemnly, 'but only by my wits and the grace of a kind fool. For the Lochlannaich have plotted to kill me.' And with that he described his horrific ordeal.

Already fired for battle, the great Féinn needed little encouragement. They drew their swords and with tempers high, plunged across the land to the castle of the king of Lochlann, and there they began a massacre which turned the grimy foam of the deep grey sea red with blood.

And then they returned home again, the triumphant Féinn, but that is another story.

Fionn's Great Sword

AFTER THE DEATH OF DIAMAID at the hands of Fionn Mac Chumail, the great Féinn travelled far. Fionn himself struggled to put the past behind him, to forget his craven deed. They crossed over from Kintyre and hunted on Islay, and it was here that Fionn met with a strange man, who leapt into his path and stood firm.

'Fionn Mac Chumail,' said the wild little man, 'Come with me. For I am a blacksmith, and I'll forge you a sword like no other.' And with that he disappeared over the hillock, his voice echoing back, 'So catch me if you can.'

Now the great Fionn Mac Chumail liked nothing better than a challenge, and being as fleet of foot as any fairy, he joined in the chase. Over the hills they went, and across valleys, feet hardly touching ground. And as the fairy blacksmith leapt out of sight, the hardy Fionn followed close in his footsteps, catching him up once again. And so the chase went on for many hundreds of miles, the great Scottish warrior never losing his foot, never missing a beat.

And they arrived at last, landing on a hill outside a tiny stone cottage, and here it was that the fairy stopped, turning to congratulate Fionn. With a mischievous laugh, he invited him inside.

'Here is my smithy, great leader,' he said gleefully. 'You have matched me in speed and so together we shall go and forge you a sword worthy of your great stature.'

And they entered the cottage, where the blacksmith's fairy daughter blushed and curtseyed to the grand man who had entered their humble abode. And she plied them with food and drink, while Fionn lit the great fire and the blacksmith prepared his tools.

And so it was that a great bar of iron was held over the fire that roared and crackled, scorching the blacksmith, his daughter and Fionn himself. But they worked away, Fionn at the bellows while sweat poured from his noble brow, and the blacksmith with his tools, forging a sword fit for a hero.

When the sword was nearly finished, the blacksmith's daughter drew Fionn to one side.

'My father will fit the handle now, and he will ask you what else there is to do. Then, my lord, you must answer him, saying "The sword is wanting but one little thing yet" and then you must plunge your sword into his body. If it is tempered with fairy blood, your sword will be the mightiest ever made.'

So Fionn waited while the blacksmith worked, and soon enough he stopped and asked what else there was to do.

And Fionn grabbed the sword from the fairy blacksmith, whose face registered only mild surprise, and he plunged it into his body, through the ribs and out the other side. And as he drew it out again, the sword gleamed with the blood of enchantment. He left the house then, with the daughter tending to her slain father, and he joined his men.

And the great Féinn travelled on again, the powerful fairy sword safe by the side of the mighty Fionn. And his prophecy had been true, for wherever that sword was aimed, it struck its mark.

The name of the sword was Mac an Luinne, and from that day onwards, it never left the side of the great Fionn.

Glossary

Achilles The son of Peleus and the sea-nymph Thetis, who distinguished himself in the Trojan War. He was made almost immortal by his mother, who dipped him in the River Styx and he was invincible except for a portion of his heel which remained out of the water.

Acropolis Citadel in a Greek city.

Aditi Sky goddess and mother of the gods.

Adityas Vishnu, children of Aditi, including Indra, Mitra, Rudra, Tvashtar, Varuna and Vishnu.

Aeneas The son of Anchises and the goddess Aphrodite, reared by a nymph. He led the Dardanian troops in the Trojan War According to legend, he became the founder of Rome.

Aengus Óg Son of Dagda and Boann (a woman said to have given the Boyne river its name), Aengus is the Irish god of love whose stronghold is reputed to have been at New Grange. The famous tale Dream of Aengus tells of how he fell in love with a maiden he had dreamt of. He eventually discovered that she was to be found at the Lake of the Dragon's Mouth in Co. Tipperary, but that she lived every alternate year in the form of a swan. Aengus pursues the woman of his dreams and plunges into the lake transforming himself also into the shape of a swan. Then the two fly back together to his palace on the Boyne where they live out their days as guardians of would-be lovers.

Aesir Northern gods who made their home in Asgard; there are twelve in number.

Agamemnon A famous King of Mycenae. He married Helen of Sparta's sister Clytemnestra. When Paris abducted Helen, beginning the Trojan War, Menelaus called on Agamemnon to raise the Greek troops. He had to sacrifice his daughter Iphigenia in order to get a fair wind to travel to Troy.

Agastya A rishi (sage), leads hermits to Rama.

Aghasur A dragon sent by Kans to destroy Krishna.

Agni The god of fire.

Agora Greek marketplace.

Ajax Ajax the Greater was the bravest, after Achilles, of all warriors at Troy, fighting Hector in single combat and distinguishing himself in the Battle of the Ships. He was not chosen as the bravest warrior and eventually went mad.

Ajax Ajax of Locri was another warrior at Troy. When Troy was captured he committed the ultimate sacrilege by seizing Cassandra from her sanctuary with the Palladium.

Alberich King of the dwarfs.

Alcinous King of the Phaeacians.

Alf-heim Home of the elves, ruled by Frey.

Allfather Another name for Odin; Yggdrasill was created by Allfather.

Alsvider Steed of the moon (Mani) chariot.

Alsvin Steed of the sun (Sol) chariot.

Ambalika Daughter of the king of Benares.

Ambika Daughter of the king of Benares.

Ambrosia Food of the gods.

Ananda Disciple of Buddha.

Ananta Thousand-headed snake that sprang from Balarama's mouth, Vishnu's attendant, serpent of infinite time.

Andhrimnir Cook at Valhalla.

Andvaranaut Ring of Andvari, the King of the dwarfs.

Angada Son of Vali, one of the monkey host.

Anger-Chamber Room designated for an angry queen.

Angurboda Loki's first wife, and the mother of Hel, Fenris and Jormungander.

Aniruddha Son of Pradyumna.

Anjana Mother of Hanuman.

Anshumat A mighty chariot fighter.

Apollo One of the twelve Olympian gods, son of Zeus and Leto. He is attributed with being the god of plague, music, song and prophecy.

Aquila The divine eagle.

Arachne A Lydian woman with great skill in weaving. She was challenged in a competition by the jealous Athene who destroyed her work and when she killed herself, turned her into a spider destined to weave until eternity.

Ares God of War, 'gold-changer of corpses', and the son of Zeus and Hera.

Argonauts Heroes who sailed with Jason on the ship Argo to fetch the golden fleece from Colchis.

Arjuna The third of the Pandavas.

Artemis The virgin goddess of the chase, attributed with being the moon goddess and the primitive mother-goddess. She was daughter of Zeus and Leto.

Arundhati The Northern Crown.

Asamanja Son of Sagara.

Asclepius God of healing who often took the form of a snake. He is the son of Apollo by Coronis.

Asgard Home of the gods, at one root of Yggdrasill.

Ashvatthaman Son of Drona.

Ashvins Twin horsemen, sons of the sun, benevolent gods and related to the divine.

Ashwapati Uncle of Bharata and Satrughna.

Asopus The god of the River Asopus.

Asparas Dancing girls of Indra's court and heavenly nymphs.

Asuras Titans, demons, and enemies of the gods possessing magical powers.

Athene Virgin warrior-goddess, born from the forehead of Zeus when he swallowed his wife Metis. Plays a key role in the travels of Odysseus, and Perseus.

Augeas King of Elis, one of the Argonauts.

Augsburg Tyr's city.

Bairn Little child, also called bairnie.

Balarama Brother of Krishna.

Balder Son of Frigga; his murder causes Ragnarok.

Bali Brother of Sugriva and one of the five great monkeys in the Ramayana.

Balor The evil, one-eyed King of the Fomorians and also grandfather of Lugh of the Long Arm. It was prophesied that Balor would one day be slain by his own grandson so he locked his daughter away on a remote island where he intended that she would never fall pregnant. But Cian, father of Lugh, managed to reach the island disguised as a woman, and Balor's daughter eventually bore him a child. During the second battle of Mag Tured (or Moytura), Balor was killed by Lugh who slung a stone into his giant eye.

Bannock Oat or barley cake.

Basswood Any of several North American linden trees with a soft light-coloured wood.

Beaver Largest rodent in the United States of America, held in high esteem by the native American people. Although a land mammal, it spends a great deal of time in water and has a dense waterproof fur coat to protect it from harsh weather conditions.

Behula Daughter of Saha.

Bere Barley.

Bestla Giant mother of Aesir's mortal element.

Bhadra A mighty elephant.

Bhagavati Shiva's wife, also known as Parvati.

Bhagiratha Son of Dilipa.

Bharadhwaja Father of Drona and a hermit.

Bharata One of Dasharatha's four sons.

Bhaumasur A demon, slain by Krishna.

Bhima The second of the Pandavas.

Bhimasha King of Rajagriha and disciple of Buddha.

Bifrost Rainbow bridge presided over by Heimdall.

Big-Belly One of Ravana's monsters.

Bilskirnir Thor's palace.

Bodach The term means 'old man'. The Highlanders believed that the Bodach crept down chimneys in order to steal naughty children. In other territories, he was a spirit which warned of death.

Brahma Creator of the world, mythical origin of colour (caste).

Brahmadatta King of Benares.

Bran In Scottish legend, Bran is the great hunting hound of Fionn Mac Chumail. In Irish mythology, he is a great hero.

Branstock Giant oak tree in the Volsung's hall; Odin placed a sword in it and challenged the guests of a wedding to withdraw it.

Brave Young warrior of native American descent, sometimes also referred to as a 'buck'.

Breidablik Balder's palace.

Brigit Scottish saint or spirit associated with the coming of spring.

Brisingamen Freyia's necklace.

Britomartis A Cretan goddess, also known as Dictynna.

Brokki Dwarf who makes a deal with Loki, and who makes Miolnir, Draupnir and Gulinbursti.

Brollachan A shapeless spirit of unknown origin. One of the most frightening in Scottish mythology, it spoke only two words, 'Myself' and 'Thyself', taking the shape of whatever it sat upon.

Brownie A household spirit or creature which took the form of a small man (usually hideously ugly) who undertakes household chores, and mill or farm work, in exchange for a bowl of milk.

Brunhilde A Valkyr found by Sigurd.

Buddha Founder of buddhism, Gautama, avatar of Vishnu in Hinduism.

Buddhism Buddhism arrived in China in the first century BC via the silk trading route from India and Central Asia. Its founder was Guatama Siddhartha (the Buddha), a religious teacher in North India. Buddhist doctrine declared that by destroying the causes of all suffering, mankind could attain perfect enlightenment. The religion encouraged a new respect for all living things and brought with it the idea of reincarnation; i.e. that the soul returns to the earth after death in another form, dictated by the individual's behaviour in his previous life. By the fourth century, Buddhism was the dominant religion in China, retaining its powerful influence over the nation until the mid-ninth century.

Buffalo A type of wild ox, once widely scattered over the Great Plains of North America. Also known as a 'bison', the buffalo was an important food source for the Indian tribes and its hide was also used in the construction of tepees and to make clothing. The buffalo was also sometimes revered as a totem animal, i.e. venerated as a direct ancestor of the tribesmen, and its skull used in ceremonial fashion.

Bundles, sacred These bundles contained various venerated objects of the tribe, believed to have supernatural powers. Custody or ownership of the bundle was never lightly entered upon, but involved the learning of endless songs and ritual dances.

Cailleach Bheur A witch with a blue face who represents winter. When she is reborn each autumn, snow falls. She is mother of the god of youth (Angus mac Og).

Calchas The seer of Mycenae who accompanied the Greek fleet to Troy. It was his prophecy which stated that Troy would never be taken without the aid of Achilles.

Calumet Ceremonial pipe used by the north American Indians.

Calypso A nymph who lived on the island of Ogygia.

Caoineag A banshee.

Cat A black cat has great mythological significance, is often the bearer of bad luck, a symbol of black magic, and the familiar of a witch. Cats were also the totem for many tribes.

Cath Sith A fairy cat who was believed to be a witch transformed.

Ceasg A Scottish mermaid with the body of a maiden and the tail of a salmon.

Ceilidgh Party.

Cerberus The three-headed dog who guarded the entrance to the Underworld.

Channa Guatama's charioteer.

Chaos A state from which the universe was created – caused by fire and ice meeting.

Charon The ferryman of the dead who carries souls across the River Styx to Hades.

Charybdis *See* Scylla and Charybdis.

Chitambaram Sacred city of Shiva's dance.

Chrysaor Son of Poseidon and Medusa, born from the severed neck of Medusa when Perseus beheaded her.

Chryseis Daughter of Chryses who was taken by Agamemnon in the battle of Troy.

Chullasubhadda Wife of Buddha-elect (Sumedha).

Chunda A good smith who entertains Buddha.

Circe An enchantress and the daughter of Helius. She lived on the island of Aeaea with the power to change men to beasts.

Cleobis and Biton Two men of Argos who dragged the wagon carrying their mother, priestess of Hera, from Argos to the sanctuary.

Clio Muse of history and prophecy.

Clytemnestra Daughter of Tyndareus, sister of Helen, who married Agamemnon but deserted him when he sacrificed Iphigenia, their daughter, at the beginning of the Trojan War.

Confucius (Kong Fuzi) Regarded as China's greatest sage and ethical teacher, Confucius (551–479 BC) was not especially revered during his lifetime and had a small following of some 3000 people. After the Burning of the Books in 213 BC, interest in his philosophies became widespread. Confucius believed that mankind was essentially good, but argued for a highly structured society, presided over by a strong central government which would set the highest moral standards. The individual's sense of duty and obligation, he argued, would play a vital role in maintaining a well-run state.

Crodhmara Fairy cattle.

Crow Usually associated with battle and death, but many mythological figures take this form.

Cu Sith A great fairy dog, usually green and over-sized.

Cutty Girl.

Cyclopes One-eyed giants who were imprisoned in Tartarus by Uranus and Cronus, but released by Zeus, for whom they made thunderbolts. Also a tribe of pastoralists who live without laws, and on, whenever possible, human flesh.

Daedalus Descendant of the Athenian King Erechtheus and son of Eupalamus. He killed his nephew and apprentice. Famed for constructing the labyrinth to house the Minotaur, in which he was later imprisoned. He constructed wings for himself and his son to make their escape.

Dagda One of the principal gods of the Tuatha De Danann, the father and chief, the Celtic equivalent of Zeus. He was the god reputed to have led the People of Dana in their successful conquest of the Fir Bolg.

Dáksha The chief Prajapati.

Dana Also known as Danu, a goddess worshipped from antiquity by the Celts and considered to be the ancestor of the Tuatha De Danann.

Danae Daughter of Acrisius, King of Argos. Acrisius trapped her in a cave when he was warned that his grandson would be the cause of his ultimate death. Zeus came to her and Perseus was born.

Danaids The fifty daughters of Danaus of Argos, by ten mothers.

Daoine Sidhe The people of the Hollow Hills, or Otherworld.

Druid An ancient order of Celtic priests held in high esteem who flourished in the pre-Christian era. The word druid is derived from an ancient Celtic one meaning 'very knowledgeable'.These individuals were believed to have mystical powers and in ancient Irish literature possess the ability to conjure up magical charms, to create tempests, to curse and debilitate their enemies and to perform as soothsayers to the royal courts.

Dardanus Son of Zeus and Electra, daughter of Atlas.

Dasharatha A Manu amongst men, King of Koshala, father of Santa.

Deianeira Daughter of Oeneus, who married Heracles after he won her in a battle with the River Achelous.

Demeter Goddess of agriculture and nutrition, whose name means earth mother. She is the mother of Persephone.

Demophoon Son of King Celeus of Eleusis, who was nursed by Demeter and then dropped in the fire when she tried to make him immortal.

Desire The god of love.

Deva A god other than the supreme God.

Devadatta Buddha's cousin, plots evil against Buddha.

Dhrishtadyumna Twin brother of Draupadi, slays Drona.

Dilipa Son of Anshumat, father of Bhagiratha.

Dionysus The god of wine, vegetation and the life-force, and of ecstasy. He was considered to be outside the Greek pantheon, and generally thought to have begun life as a mortal.

Dioscuri Castor and Polydeuces, the twin sons of Zeus and Leda, who are important deities.

Dog The dog is a symbol of humanity, and usually has a role helping the hero of the myth or legend. Fionn's Bran and Grey Dog are two examples of wild beasts transformed to become invaluable servants.

Divots Turfs.

Draupadi Daughter of Drupada.

Draupnir Odin's famous ring, fashioned by Brokki.

Drona A Brahma, son of the great sage Bharadwaja.

Drupada King of the Panchalas.

Dryads Nymphs of the trees.

Dun A stronghold or royal abode surrounded by an earthen wall.

Durga Goddess, wife of Shiva.

Durk Knife.

Duryodhana One of Drona's pupils.

Dvalin Dwarf visited by Loki; also the name for the stag on Yggdrasill.

Dwarfs Fairies and black elves are called dwarfs.

Dwarkanath The Lord of Dwaraka; Krishna.

Dyumatsena King of the Shalwas and father of Satyavan.

Each Uisge The mythical water-horse which haunts lochs and appears in various forms.

Echo A nymph who was punished by Hera for her endless stories told to distract Hera from Zeus's infidelity.

Edda Collection of prose and poetic myths and stories from the Norsemen.

Eight Immortals Three of these are reputed to be historical: Han Chung-li, born in Shensi, who rose to become a Marshal of the Empire in 21 BC. Chang-kuo Lao, who lived in the seventh to eighth century ad, and Lü Tung-pin, who was born in ad 755.

Einheriear Odin's guests at Valhalla.

Eisa Loki' daughter.

Ekalavya Son of the king of the Nishadas.

Electra Daughter of Agamemnon and Clytemnestra.

Eleusis A town in which the cult of Demeter is centred.

Elf Sigmund is buried by an elf; there are light and dark elves (the latter called dwarfs).

Elpenor The youngest of Odysseus's crew who fell from the roof of Circe's house on Aeaea and visited with Odysseus at Hades.

Elysium The home of the blessed dead.

Emain Macha The capital of ancient Ulster.

Eos Goddess of the dawn and sister of the sun and moon.

Erichthonius A child born of the semen spilled when Hephaestus tried to rape Athene on the Acropolis.

Eros God of Love, the son of Aphrodite.

Erysichthon A Thessalian who cut down a grove sacred to Demeter, who punished him with eternal hunger.

Eteocles Son of Oedipus.

Eumaeus Swineherd of Odysseus's family at Ithaca.

Euphemus A son of Poseidon who could walk on water. He sailed with the Argonauts.

Europa Daughter of King Agenor of Tyre, who was taken by Zeus to Crete.

Eurydice A Thracian nymph married to Orpheus.

Fafnir Shape-changer who kills his father and becomes a dragon to guard the family jewels. Slain by Sigurd.

Fairy The word is derived from 'Fays' which means Fates. They are immortal, with the gift of prophecy and of music, and their role changes according to the origin of the myth. They were often considered to be little people, with enormous propensity for mischief, but they are central to many myths and legends, with important powers.

Fates In Greek mythology, daughters of Zeus and Themis, who spin the thread of a mortal's life and cut it when his time is due. Called Norns in Viking mythology.

Fenris A wild wolf, who is the son of Loki. He roams the earth after Ragnarok.

Fialar Red cock of Valhalla.

Fianna/Fenians The word 'fianna' was used in early times to describe young warrior-hunters. These youths evolved under the leadership of Finn mac Cumaill as a highly skilled band of military men who took up service with various kings throughout Ireland.

Filheim Land of mist, at the end of one of Yggdrasill's root.

Fingal Another name for Fionn Mac Chumail, used after MacPherson's Ossian in the eighteenth century.

Fionn Mac Chumail Irish and Scottish warrior, with great powers of fairness and wisdom. He is known not for physical strength but for knowledge, sense of justice, generosity and canny instinct. He had two hounds, which were later discovered to be his nephews transformed. He became head of the Fianna, or

Féinn, fighting the enemies of Ireland and Scotland. He was the father of Oisin (also called Ossian, o other derivatives), and father or grandfather of Osgar.

Fir Bolg One of the ancient, pre-Gaelic peoples of Ireland who were reputed to have worshipped the go Bulga, meaning god of lighting. They are thought to have colonized Ireland around 1970 BC, after th death of Nemed and to have reigned for a short period of thirty seven years before their defeat by th Tuatha De Danann.

Fir Chlis Nimble men or merry dancers, which are the souls of fallen angels.

Folkvang Freyia's palace.

Fomorians A race of monstrous beings, popularly conceived as sea-pirates with some supernatura characteristics who opposed the earliest settlers in Ireland, including the Nemedians and the Tuatha De Danann.

Frey Comes to Asgard with Freyia as a hostage following the war between the Aesir and the Vanir.

Freyia Comes to Asgard with Frey as a hostage following the war between the Aesir and the Vanir Goddess of beauty and love.

Frigga Odin's wife and mother of gods; she is goddess of the earth.

Fuath Evil spirits which lived in or near the water.

Fulla Frigga's maidservant.

Furies Creatures born from the blood of Cronus, guarding the greatest sinners of the Underworld. Their power lay in their ability to drive mortals mad. Snakes writhed in their hair and around their waists.

Gae Bolg Cuchulainn alone learned the use of this weapon from the woman-warrior, Scathach and with it he slew his own son Connla and his closest friend, Ferdia. Gae Bolg translates as 'harpoon like javelin' and the deadly weapon was reported to have been created by Bulga, the god of lighting.

Gaea Goddess of Earth, born from Chaos, and the mother of Uranus and Pontus.

Galatea Daughter of Nereus and Doris, a sea-nymph loved by Polyphemus, the Cyclops.

Gandhari Mother of Duryodhana.

Gandharvas Demi-gods and musicians.

Gandjharva Musical ministrants of the upper air.

Ganesha Elephant-headed god of scribes and son of Shiva.

Ganges Sacred river personified by the goddess Ganga, wife of Shiva and daughter of the mount Himalaya.

Garm Hel's hound.

Garuda King of the birds and mount Vishnu, the divine bird, attendant of Narayana.

Gautama Son of Suddhodana, also known as Siddhartha.

Geri Odin's wolf.

Giallar Bridge in Filheim.

Giallarhorn Heimdall's trumpet – the final call signifies Ragnarok.

Giants In Greek mythology, a race of beings born from Gaea, grown from the blood that dropped from the castrated Uranus. Usually represent evil in Viking mythology.

Gin If.

Gladheim Where the twelve deities of Asgard hold their thrones. Also called Gladsheim.

Golden Fleece Fleece of the ram sent by Poseidon to substitute for Phrixus when his father was going to sacrifice him. The Argonauts went in search of the fleece.

Goodman Man of the house.

Goodwife Woman of the house.

Gopis Lovers of the young Krishna and milkmaids.

Gorgon One of the three sisters, including Medusa, whose frightening looks could turn mortals to stone.

Graces Daughters of Aphrodite by Zeus.

Great-Flank One of Ravana's monsters.

Great Head The Iroquois Indians believed in the existence of a curious being known as Great Head, a creature with an enormous head poised on slender legs.

Great Spirit The name given to the Creator of all life, as well as the term used to describe the omnipotent force of the Creator existing in every living thing.

Gruagach A kind of brownie, usually dressed in red or green as opposed to the traditional brown. He has great power to enchant the hapless, or to help mortals who are worthy (usually heroes). He often appears to challenge a boy-hero, during his period of education.

Guha King of Nishadha.

Guidewife Woman.

Gungnir Odin's spear, made of Yggdrasill wood, and the tip fashioned by Dvalin.

Gylfi A wandering king to whom the Eddas are narrated.

Hades One of the three sons of Cronus; brother of Poseidon and Zeus, who is King of the Underworld, known as the House of Hades.

Hanuman General of the monkey people.

Hari-Hara Shiva and Vishnu as one god.

Harmonia Daughter of Ares and Aphrodite, wife of Cadmus.

Hati The wolf who pursues the sun and moon.

Hector Eldest son of King Priam who defended Troy from the Greeks. He was killed by Achilles.

Hecuba The second wife of Priam, King of Troy. She was turned into a dog after Troy was lost.

Heimdall White god who guards the Bifrost bridge.

Hel Goddess of death and Loki's daughter.

Helen Daughter of Leda and Tyndareus, King of Sparta, and the most beautiful woman in the world. She was responsible for starting the Trojan War.

Helius The sun, son of Hyperion and Theia.

Henwife Witch.

Hephaestus or **Hephaistos** The Smith of Heaven.

Hera A Mycenaean palace goddess, married to Zeus.

Heracles An important Greek hero, the son of Zeus and Alcmena. His name means 'Glory of Hera'. He performed twelve labours for King Eurystheus, and later became a god.

Hermes The conductor of souls of the dead to Hades, and god of trickery and of trade. He acts as messenger to the gods.

Hermod Son of Frigga and Odin who travelled to see Hel in order to reclaim Balder for Asgard.

Hero and Leander Hero was a priestess of Aphrodite, loved by Leander, a young man of Abydos. He drowned trying to see her.

Hestia Goddess of the Hearth, daughter of Cronus and Rhea.

Himalaya Great mountain and range, father of Parvati.

Hiordis Wife of Sigmund and mother of Sigurd.

Hodur Balder's blind twin; known as the personification of darkness.

Hoenir Also called Vili; produces the first humans with Odin and Loki, and was one of the triad responsible for the creation of the world.

Houlet Owl.

Hrim-faxi Steed of the night.

Hubris Presumptuous behaviour which causes the wrath of the gods to be brought on to mortals.

Hugin Odin's raven.

Hurley A traditional Irish game played with sticks and balls, quite similar to hockey.

Hurons A tribe of Iroquois stock, originally one people with the Iroquois.

Hymir Giant who fishes with Thor and is drowned by him.

Iambe Daughter of Pan and Echo, servant to King Celeus of Eleusis and Metaeira.

Icarus Son of Daedalus, who plunged to his death after escaping from the labyrinth.

Idunn Guardian of the youth-giving apples.

Indra The King of Heaven.

Indrajit Son of Ravana.

Indrasen Daughter of Nala and Damayanti.

Indrasena Son of Nala and Damayanti.

Iphigenia The eldest daughter of Agamemnon and Clytemnestra who was sacrificed to appease Artemis and obtain a fair wind for Troy.

Iris Messenger of the gods who took the form of a rainbow.

Jade It was believed that jade emerged from the mountains as a liquid which then solidified after ten thousand years to become a precious hard stone, green in colour. If the correct herbs were added to it, it could return to its liquid state and when swallowed increase the individual's chances of immortality.

Jambavan A noble monkey.

Jason Son of Aeson, King of Iolcus and leader of the voyage of the Argonauts.

Jatayu King of all the eagle-tribes.

Jormungander The world serpent; son of Loki. Legends tell that when his tail is removed from his mouth, Ragnarok has arrived.

Jord Daughter of Nott; wife of Odin.

Jotunheim Home of the giants.

Jurasindhu A rakshasa, father-in-law of Kans.

Jyeshtha Goddess of bad luck.

Kaikeyi Mother of Bharata, one of Dasharatha's three wives.

Kal-Purush The Time-man, Bengali name for Orion.

Kali The Black, wife of Shiva.

Kalindi Daughter of the sun, wife of Krishna.

Kaliya A poisonous hydra that lived in the jamna.

Kalki Incarnation of Vishnu yet to come.

Kalnagini Serpent who kills Lakshmindara.

Kaluda A disciple of Buddha.

Kama God of desire.

Kamadeva Desire, the god of love.

Kans King of Mathura, son of Ugrasena and Pavandrekha.

Kanva Father of Shakuntala.

Karna Pupil of Drona.

Kashyapa One of Dasharatha's counsellors.

Kauravas or Kurus Sons of Dhritarashtra, pupils of Drona.

Kaushalya Mother of Rama, one of Dasharatha's three wives.

Kelpie Another word for each uisge, the water-horse.

Ken Know.

Keres Black-winged demons or daughters of the night.

Keshini Wife of Sagara.

Khara Younger brother of Ravana.

Kinnaras Human birds with musical instruments under their wings.

Knowe Knoll or hillock.

Kore 'Maiden', another name for Persephone.

Krishna The Dark one, worshipped as an incarnation of Vishnu.

Kumara Son of Shiva and Paravati, slays demon Taraka.

Kumbha-karna Ravana's brother.

Kunti Mother of the Pandavas.

Kusha or Kusi One of Sita's two sons.

Kvasir Clever warrior and colleague of Odin. He was responsible for finally outwitting Loki.

Labyrinth A prison built at Knossos for the Minotaur by Daedalus.

Laertes King of Ithaca and father of Odysseus.

Laestrygonians Savage giants encountered by Odysseus on his travels.

Lakshmana Brother of Rama and his companion in exile.

Lakshmi Consort of Vishnu and a goddess of beauty and good fortune.

Lakshmindara Son of Chand resurrected by Manasa Devi.

Land of Light One of the names for the realm of the fairies. If a piece of metal welded by human hands is put in the doorway to their land, the door cannot close. The door to this realm is only open at night, and usually at a full moon.

Lang syne The days of old.

Lao Tzu (Laozi) The ancient Taoist philosopher born in 604 BC, a contemporary of Confucius with whom, it is said, he discussed the tenets of Tao. Lao Tzu was an advocate of simple rural existence and looked to the Yellow Emperor and Shun as models of efficient government. His philosophies were recorded in the Ta Teh Ching. Legends surrounding his birth suggest that he emerged from the left hand side of his mother's body, with white hair and a long white beard, after a confinement lasting eighty years.

Laocoon A Trojan wiseman who predicted that the wooden horse contained Greek soldiers.

Laomedon The King of Troy who hired Apollo and Poseidon to build the impregnable walls of Troy.

Lava Son of Sita.

Leda Daughter of the King of Aetolia, who married Tyndareus. Helen and Clytemnestra were her daughters.

Leman Lover.

Lethe One of the four rivers of the Underworld, also called the River of Forgetfulness.

Lif The female survivor of Ragnarok.

Lifthrasir The male survivor of Ragnarok.

Logi Utgard-loki's cook.

Loki God of fire and mischief-maker of Asgard; he eventually brings about Ragnarok.

Lotus-Eaters A race of people who live a dazed, drugged existence the result of eating the lotus flower.

Macha There are thought to be several different Machas who appear in quite a number of ancient Irish stories. For the purposes of this book, however, the Macha referred to is the wife of Crunnchu. The story unfolds that after her husband had boasted of her great athletic ability to the King, she was subsequently forced to run against his horses in spite of the fact that she was heavily pregnant. Macha died giving birth to her twin babies and with her dying breath she cursed Ulster for nine generations, proclaiming that it would suffer the weakness of a woman in childbirth in times of great stress. This curse had its most disastrous effect when Medb of Connacht invaded Ulster with her great army.

Mag Muirthemne Cuchulainn's inheritance. A plain extending from River Boyne to the mountain range of Cualgne, close to Emain Macha in Ulster.

Magni Thor's son.

Mahaparshwa One of Ravana's generals.

Maharaksha Son of Khara, slain at Lanka.

Mahasubhadda Wife of Buddha-select (Sumedha).

Makaras Mythical fish-reptiles of the sea.

Man-Devourer One of Ravana's monsters.

Mani The moon.

Manitto Broad term used to describe the supernatural or a potent spirit among the Algonquins, the Iroquois and the Sioux.

Man-Slayer One of Ravana's counsellors.

Manasa Devi Goddess of snakes, daughter of Shiva by a mortal woman.

Manasha Goddess of snakes.

Mandavya Daughter of Kushadhwaja.

Mandodari Wife of Ravana.

Manthara Kaikeyi's evil nurse, who plots Rama's ruin.

Manu Lawgiver.

Mara The evil one, tempts Gautama.

Markandeya One of Dasharatha's counsellors.

Matali Sakra's charioteer.

Medea Witch and priestess of Hecate, daughter of Aeetes and sister of Circe. She helped Jason in his quest for the Golden Fleece.

Medusa One of the three Gorgons whose head had the power to turn onlookers to stone.

Melpomene One of the muses, and mother of the Sirens.

Menaka One of the most beautiful dancers in Heaven.

Menelaus King of Sparta, brother of Agamemnon. Married Helen and called war against Troy when she eloped with Paris.

Metaneira Wife of Celeus, King of Eleusis, who hired Demeter in disguise as her nurse.

Michabo Also known as Manobozho, or the Great Hare, the principal deity of the Algonquins, maker and preserver of the earth, sun and moon.

Midgard Dwelling place of humans (our earth).

Midsummer A time when fairies dance and claim human victims.

Milesians A group of iron-age invaders led by the sons of Mil, who arrived in Ireland from Spain around 500 BC and overcame the Tuatha De Danann.

Mimir God of the ocean, the head of which guards a well; reincarnated after Ragnarok.

Minos King of Crete, son of Zeus and Europa. He was considered to have been the ruler of a sea empire.

Minotaur A creature born of the union between Pasiphae and a Cretan Bull.

Miolnir Thor's hammer.

Mitra God of light, Mithra in Iran, Mithras in the Roman world.

Moccasins One-piece shoes made of soft leather, especially deerskin.

Modi Thor's son.

Moly A magical plant given to Odysseus by Hermes as protection against Circe's powers.

Mount Kunlun This mountain features in many Chinese legends as the home of the great emperors on earth. It is written in the Shanghaijing, (The Classic of Mountains and Seas) that this towering structure measured no less than 3300 miles in circumference and 4000 miles in height. It acted both as a central pillar to support the heavens, and as a gateway between heaven and earth.

Moytura Translated as the 'Plain of Weeping', Mag Tured, or Moytura was where the Tuatha De Danann fought two of their most significant battles.

Mugalana A disciple of Buddha.

Muilearteach The Cailleach Bheur of the water, who appears as a witch or a sea-serpent. On land she grew larger and stronger by fire.

Munin Odin's raven.

Muses Goddesses of poetry and song, daughters of Zeus and Mnemosyne.

Muskrat North American beaver-like, amphibious rodent.

Muspell Home of fire, and the fire-giants.

Nakula Pandava twin skilled in horsemanship.

Nala One of the monkey host, son of Vishvakarma.

Nandi Shiva's bull.

Nanna Balder's wife.

Narcissus Son of the River Cephisus. He fell in love with himself and died as a result.

Narve Son of Loki.

Nataraja Manifestation of Shiva, Lord of the Dance.

Nausicaa Daughter of Alcinous, King of Phaeacia, who fell in love with Odysseus.

Nectar Drink of the gods.

Nemesis Goddess of retribution and daughter of night.

Neoptolemus Son of Achilles and Deidameia, he came to Troy at the end of the war to wear his father's armour. He sacrificed Polyxena at the tomb of Achilles.

Nereids Sea-nymphs who are the daughters of Nereus and Doris. Thetis, mother of Achilles, was a Nereid.

Nestor Wise King of Pylus, who led the ships to Troy with Agamemnon and Menelaus.

Neta Daughter of Shiva, friend of Manasa.

Night Daughter of Norvi.

Nikumbha One of Ravana's generals.

Nila One of the monkey host, son of Agni.

Niord God of the sea; marries Skadi.

Noatun Niord's home.

Noisy-Throat One of Ravana's counsellors.

Norns The fates and protectors of Yggdrasill. Many believe them to be the same as the Valkyrs.

Norvi Father of the night.

Nott Goddess of night.

Nuada The first king of the Tuatha De Danann in Ireland, who lost an arm in the first battle of Moytura against the Fomorians. He became known as 'Nuada of the Silver Hand' when Diancecht, the great physician of the Tuatha De Danann, replaced his hand with a silver one after the battle.

Nü Wa The Goddess Nü Wa, who in some versions of the Creation Myths is the sole creator of mankind, is in other tales associated with the God Fu Xi, also a great benefactor of the human race. Some accounts represent Fu Xi as the brother of Nü Wa, but others describe the pair as lovers who lie together to create the very first human beings. Fu Xi is also considered to be the first of the Chinese emperors of mythical times who reigned from 2953 to 2838 BC.

Nymphs Minor female deities associated with particular parts of the land and sea.

Oberon Fairy king.

Odin Allfather and king of all gods, he is known for travelling the nine worlds in disguise and recognized only by his single eye; dies at Ragnarok.

Odur Freyia's husband.

Odysseus Greek hero, son of Laertes and Anticleia, who was renowned for his cunning, the master behind the victory at Troy, and known for his long voyage home.

Oedipus Son of Leius, King of Thebes and Jocasta. Became King of Thebes and married his mother.

Ogham One of the earliest known forms of Irish writing, originally used to inscribe upright pillar stones.

Oisin Also called Ossian (particularly by James Macpherson who wrote a set of Gaelic Romances about this character, supposedly garnered from oral tradition). Ossian was the son of Fionn and Sadbh, and had various brothers, according to different legends. He was a man of great wisdom, became immortal for many centuries, but in the end he became mad.

Ojibway Another name for the Chippewa, a tribe of Algonquin stock.

Olympia Zeus's home in Elis.

Olympus The highest mountain in Greece and the ancient home of the gods.

Onygate Anyway.

Oracle The response of a god or priest to a request for advice – also a prophecy.

Orestes Son of Agamemnon and Clytemnestra who escaped following Agamemnon's murder to King Strophius. He later returned to Argos to murder his mother and avenge the death of his father.

Orpheus Thracian singer and poet, son of Oeagrus and a Muse. Married Eurydice and when she died tried to retrieve her from the Underworld.

Otherworld The world of deities and spirits, also known as the Land of Promise, or the Land of Eternal Youth, a place of everlasting life where all earthly dreams come to be fulfilled.

Palamedes Hero of Nauplia, inventor of the alphabet. He tricked Odysseus into joining the fleet setting out for Troy by placing the infant Telemachus in the path of his plough.

Palladium Wooden image of Athene, created by her as a monument to her friend Pallas who she accidentally killed. While in Troy it protected the city from invaders.

Pallas Athene's best friend, whom she killed.

Pan God of Arcadia, half-goat and half-man. Son of Hermes. He is connected with fertility, masturbation and sexual drive. He is also associated with music, particularly his pipes, and with laughter.

Pandareus Cretan King killed by the gods for stealing the shrine of Zeus.

Pandavas Alternative name for sons of Pandu, pupils of Drona.

Pandora The first woman, created by the gods, to punish man for Prometheus's theft of fire. Her dowry was a box full of powerful evil.

Pan Gu Some ancient writers suggest that this God is the offspring of the opposing forces of nature, the yin and the yang. The yin (female) is associated with the cold and darkness of the earth, while the yang (male) is associated with the sun and the warmth of the heavens. 'Pan' means 'shell of an egg' and 'Gu' means 'to secure' or 'to achieve'. Pan Gu came into existence so that he might create order from chaos.

Paramahamsa The supreme swan.

Parashurama Hhuman incarnation of Vishnu, Rama with an axe.

Paris Handsome son of Priam and Hecuba of Troy, who was left for dead on Mount Ida but raised by shepherds. Was reclaimed by his family, then brought them shame and caused the Trojan War by eloping with Helen.

Parvati Consort of Shiva and daughter of Himalaya.

Passion Wife of desire.

Pavanarekha Wife of Ugrasena, mother of Kans.

Pegasus The winged horse born from the severed neck of Medusa.

Peleus Father of Achilles. He married Antigone, caused her death, and then became King of Phthia. Saved from death himself by Jason and the Argonauts. Married Thetis, a sea nymph.

Penelope The long-suffering but equally clever wife of Odysseus who managed to keep at bay suitors who longed for Ithaca while Odysseus was at the Trojan War and on his ten-year voyage home.

Persephone Daughter of Zeus and Demeter who was raped by Hades and forced to live in the Underworld as his queen for three months of every year.

erseus Son of Danae, who was made pregnant by Zeus. He fought the Gorgons and brought home the head of Medusa. He eventually founded the city of Mycenae and married Andromeda.

haeacia The Kingdom of Alcinous on which Odysseus landed after a shipwreck which claimed the last of his men as he left Calypso's island.

hiloctetes Malian hero, son of Poeas, received Heracles's bow and arrows as a gift when he lit the great hero's pyre on Mount Oeta. He was involved in the last part of the Trojan War, killing Paris.

ibroch Bagpipe music.

olyphemus A Cyclopes, but a son of Poseidon. He fell in love with Galatea, but she spurned him. He was blinded by Odysseus.

olyxena Daughter of Priam and Hecuba of Troy. She was sacrificed on the grave of Achilles by Neoptolemus

oseidon God of the sea, and of sweet waters. Also the god of earthquakes. His is brother to Zeus and Hades, who divided the earth between them.

radyumna Son of Krishna and Rukmini.

rahasta (Long-Hand) One of Ravana's generals.

rajapati Creator of the universe, father of the gods, demons and all creatures, later known as Brahma.

riam King of Troy, married to Hecuba, who bore him Hector, Paris, Helenus, Cassandra, Polyxena, Deiphobus and Troilus. He was murdered by Neoptolemus.

ritha Mother of Karna and of the Pandavas.

rithivi Consort of Dyaus and goddess of the earth.

roetus King of Argos, son of Abas.

rometheus A Titan, son of Iapetus and Themus. He was champion of mortal men, which he created from clay. He stole fire from the gods and was universally hated by them.

roteus The old man of the sea who watched Poseidon's seals.

syche A beautiful nymph who was the secret wife of Eros, against the wishes of his mother Aphrodite, who sent Psyche to perform many tasks in hope of causing her death. She eventually married Eros and was allowed to become partly immortal.

uddock Frog.

urusha The cosmic man, he was sacrificed and his dismembered body became all the parts of the cosmos, including the four classes of society.

ushkara Nala's brother.

ushpaka Rama's car.

utana A rakshasi.

Pygmalion A sculptor who was so lonely he carved a statue of a beautiful woman, and eventually fell in love with it. Aphrodite brought the image to life.

Radha The principal mistress of Krishna.

Ragnarok The end of the world.

Rahula Son of Siddhartha and Yashodhara.

Rakshasas Demons and devils.

Rama or **Ramachandra** A prince and hero of the Ramayana, worshipped as an incarnation of Vishnu.

Regin A blacksmith who educated Sigurd.

Reservations Tracts of land allocated to the native American people by the United States Government with the purpose of bringing the many separate tribes under state control.

Rewati Daughter of Raja, marries Balarama.

Rhadha Wife of Adiratha, a gopi of Brindaban and lover of Krishna.

Rhea Mother of the Olympian gods. Cronus ate each of her children but she concealed Zeus and gave Cronus a swaddled rock in its place.

Rishis Sacrificial priests associated with the devas in Swarga.

Rituparna King of Ayodhya.

Rohini Rudra, a name of Shiva.

Rudra Lord of Beasts and disease, later evolved into Shiva.

Rukma Rukmini's eldest brother.

Sabdh Mother of Ossian, or Oisin.

Sagara King of Ayodhya.

Sahadeva Pandava twin skilled in swordsmanship.

Saithe Blessed.

Sakuni Cousin of Duryodhana.

Salmon A symbol of great wisdom, around which many Scottish legends revolve.

Sambu Son of Krishna.

Sampati Elder brother of Jatayu.

Santa Daughter of Dasharatha.

Sarasvati The tongue of Rama.

Sati Daughter of Daksha and Prasuti, first wife of Shiva.

Satrughna One of Dasharatha's four sons.

Satyavan Truth speaker, husband of Savitri.

Satyavati A fisher-maid, wife of Bhishma's father, Shamtanu.

Satyrs Elemental spirits which took great pleasure in chasing nymphs. They had horns, a hairy body an cloven hooves.

Saumanasa A mighty elephant.

Scamander River running across the Trojan plain, and father of Teucer.

Scylla and Charybdis Scylla was a monster who lived on a rock of the same name in the Straits c Messina, devouring sailors. Charybdis was a whirlpool in the Straits which was supposedly inhabited b the hateful daughter of Poseidon.

Seal Often believed that seals were fallen angels. Many families are descended from seals, some of whic had webbed hands or feet. Some seals were the children of sea-kings who had become enchante (selkies).

Seelie-Court The court of the Fairies, which travelled around their realm. They were usually fair t humans, doling out punishment that was morally sound, but they were quick to avenge insults to fairies

Selene Moon-goddess, daughter of Hyperion and Theia. She was seduced by Pan, but loved Endymion.

Selkie Seals with the capacity to become humans, leaving their seal-skins to take human form.

Seriyut A disciple of Buddha.

Sessrymnir Freyia's home.

Sgeulachd Stories.

Shaivas or Shaivites Worshippers of Shiva.

Shakti power or wife of a god and Shiva's consort as his feminine aspect.

Shaman Also known as the 'Medicine Men' of Indian tribes, it was the shaman's role to cultivate communication with the spirit world. They were endowed with knowledge of all healing herbs, and learned to diagnose and cure disease. They could foretell the future, find lost property and had powe over animals, plants and stones.

Shamtanu Father of Bhishma.

Shankara A great magician, friend of Chand Sadagar.

Shashti The Sixth, goddess who protects children and women in childbirth.

Shesh A serpent that takes human birth through Devaki.

Shi-en Fairy dwelling.
Shitala The Cool One and goddess of smallpox.
Shiva One of the two great gods of post-Vedic Hinduism with Vishnu.
Shudra One of the four fundamental colours (caste).
Siddhas Musical ministrants of the upper air.
Sif Thor's wife; known for her beautiful hair.
Sigi Son of Odin.
Sigmund Warrior able to pull the sword from Branstock in the Volsung's hall.
Signy Volsung's daughter.
Sigurd Son of Sigmund, and bearer of his sword. Slays Fafnir the dragon.
Sigyn Loki's faithful wife.
Sindri Dwarf who worked with Brokki to fashion gifts for the gods; commissioned by Loki.
Sirens Sea nymphs who are half-bird, half-woman, whose song lures hapless sailors to their death.
Sisyphus King of Ephrya and a trickster who outwitted Autolycus. He was one of the greatest sinners in Hades.
Sita Daughter of the Earth, adopted by Janaka, wife of Rama.
Skadi Goddess of winter and the wife of Niord for a short time.
Skanda Six-headed son of Shiva and a warrior god.
Skrymir Giant who battled against Thor.
Sleipnir Odin's steed.
Sluagh The host of the dead, seen fighting in the sky and heard by mortals.
Sol The sun-maiden.
Soma A god and a drug, the elixir of life.
Somerled Lord of the Isles, and legendary ancestor of the Clan MacDonald.
Stoorworm A great water monster which frequented lochs. When it thrust its great body from the sea, it could engulf islands and whole ships. Its appearance prophesied devastation.
Squaw North American Indian married woman.
Squint-Eye One of Ramana's monsters.
Srutakirti Daughter of Kushadhwaja.
Stone Giants A malignant race of stone beings whom the Iroquois believed invaded Indian territory, threatening the Confederation of the Five Nations. These fierce and hostile creatures lived off human flesh and were intent on exterminating the human race.
Styx River in Arcadia and one of the four rivers in the Underworld. Charon ferried dead souls across it into Hades, and Achilles was dipped into it to make him immortal.
Subrahmanian Son of Shiva, a mountain deity.
Sugriva The chief of the five great monkeys in the Ramayana.
Sukanya The wife of Chyavana.
Suman Son of Asamanja.
Sumantra A noble Brahman.
Sumati Wife of Sagara.
Sumedha A righteous Brahman who dwelt in the city of Amara.
Sumitra One of Dasharatha's three wives, mother of Lakshmana and Satrughna.
Suniti Mother of Dhruva.
Suparshwa One of Ravana's counsellors.
Supranakha A rakshasi, sister of Ravana.
Surabhi The wish-bestowing cow.

Surtr Fire-giant who eventually destroys the world at Ragnarok.

Surya God of the sun.

Sushena A monkey chief.

Svasud Father of summer.

Swarga An Olympian paradise, where all wishes and desires are gratified.

Sweating A ritual customarily associated with spiritual purification and prayer practised by most tribes throughout North America prior to sacred ceremonies or vision quests. Steam was produced within a 'sweat-lodge', a low, dome-shaped hut, by sprinkling water on heated stones.

Syrinx An Arcadian nymph who was the object of Pan's love.

Tailtiu One of the most famous royal residences of ancient Ireland.

Tall One of Ravana's counsellors.

Tantalus Son of Zeus who told the secrets of the gods to mortals and stole their nectar and ambrosia. He was condemned to eternal torture in Hades, where he was tempted by food and water but allowed to partake of neither.

Tara Sugriva's wife.

Taoism Taoism came into being roughly the same time as Confucianism, although its tenets were radically different and were largely founded on the philosophies of Lao Tzu. While Confucius argued for a system of state discipline, Taoism strongly favoured self-discipline and looked upon nature as the architect of essential laws. A newer form of Taoism evolved after the Burning of the Books, placing great emphasis on spirit worship and pacification of the Gods.

Tara Also known as Temair, the Hill of Tara was the popular seat of the ancient High-Kings of Ireland from the earliest times to the sixth century. Located in Co. Meath, it was also the place where great noblemen and chieftains congregated during wartime, or for significant events.

Tartarus Dark region, below Hades.

Telegonus Son of Odysseus and Circe, who was allegedly responsible for his father's death.

Telemachus Son of Odysseus and Penelope who was aided by Athene in helping his mother to keep away the suitors in Odysseus' absence.

Tepee A conical-shaped Indian dwelling constructed of buffalo hide stretched over lodge-poles. Mostly used by native American tribes living on the plains.

Tereus King of Daulis who married Procne, daughter of Pandion King of Athens. He fell in love with Philomela, raped her and cut out her tongue.

Thalia Muse of pastoral poetry and comedy.

Theia Goddess of many names, and mother of the sun.

Theseus Son of King Aegeus of Athens. A cycle of legends has been woven around his travels and life.

Thetis Chief of the Nereids loved by both Zeus and Poseidon. They married her to a mortal, Peleus, and their child was Achilles. She tried to make him immortal by dipping him in the River Styx.

Thialfi Thor's servant, taken when his peasant father unwittingly damaged Thor's goat.

Thiassi Giant and father of Skadi, he tricked Loki into bringing Idunn to him. Thrymheim is his kingdom.

Thomas the Rhymer Also called 'True Thomas', he was Thomas of Ercledoune, who lived in the thirteenth century. He met with the Queen of Elfland, and visited her country, given clothes and a tongue that can tell no lie. He was also given the gift of prophecy, and many of his predictions were proven true.

Thor God of thunder and of war (with Tyr). Known for his huge size, and red hair and beard. Carries the hammer Miolnir. Slays Jormungander at Ragnarok.

Three-Heads One of Ravana's monsters.

Thrud Thor's daughter.

Thrudheim Thor's realm. Also called Thrudvang.

Thunder-Tooth Leader of the rakshasas at the siege of Lanka.

Tirawa The name given to the Great Creator (*see* Great Spirit) by the Pawnee tribe who believed that four direct paths led from his house in the sky to the four semi-cardinal points: north-east, north-west, south-east and south-west.

Tiresias A Theban who was given the gift of prophecy by Zeus. He was blinded for seeing Athene bathing. He continued to use his prophetic talents after his death, advising Odysseus.

Tisamenus Son of Orestes, who inherited the Kingdom of Argos and Sparta.

Titania Queen of the fairies.

Tomahawk Hatchet with a stone or iron head used in war or hunting.

Triton A sea-god, and son of Poseidon and Amphitrite. He led the Argonauts to the sea from Lake Tritonis.

Trojan War War waged by the Greeks against Troy, in order to reclaim Menelaus's wife Helen, who had eloped with the Trojan prince Paris. Many important heroes took part, and form the basis of many legends and myths.

Tvashtar Craftsman of the gods.

Tyndareus King of Sparta, perhaps the son of Perseus's daughter Grogphone. Expelled from Sparta but restored by Heracles. Married Leda and fathered Helen and Clytemnestra, among others.

Tyr Son of Frigga and the god of war (with Thor). Eventually kills Garm at Ragnarok.

Uisneach A hill formation between Mullingar and Athlone said to mark the centre of Ireland.

Xanthus & Balius Horses of Achilles, immortal offspring of Zephyrus the west wind. A gift to Achilles's father Peleus.

Uller God of winter, whom Skadi eventually marries.

Unseelie Court An unholy court which were a kind of fairy, antagonistic to humans. They took the form of a kind of Sluagh, and shot humans and animals with elf-shots.

Urd One of the Norns.

Urmila Second daughter of Janaka.

Usha Wife of Aniruddha, daughter of Vanasur.

Ushas Goddess of the dawn.

Utgard-loki King of the giants. Tricked Thor.

Vach Goddess of speech.

Vajrahanu One of Ravana's generals.

Vala Another name for Norns.

Valfreya Another name for Freyia.

Valhalla Odin's hall for the celebrated dead warriors chosen by the Valkyrs.

Vali The cruel brother of Sugriva, dethroned by Rama.

Valkyrs Odin's attendants, led by Freyia. Chose dead warriors to live at Valhalla.

Vamadeva One of Dasharatha's priests.

Vanaheim Home of the Vanir.

Vanir Race of gods in conflict with the Aesir; they are gods of the sea and wind.

Varuna Ancient god of the sky and cosmos, later, god of the waters.

Vasishtha One of Dasharatha's priests.

Vasudev Descendant of Yadu, husband of Rohini and Devaki, father of Krishna.

Vasudeva A name of Narayana or Vishnu.

Vedic Mantras, hymns.

Vernandi One of the Norns.

Vichitravirya Bhishma's half-brother.

Vidar Slays Fenris.

Vidura Friend of the Pandavas.

Vigrid The plain where the final battle is held.

Vijaya Karna's bow.

Vikramaditya A king identified with Chandragupta II.

Virabhadra A demon that sprang from Shiva's lock of hair.

Viradha A fierce rakshasa, seizes Sita, slain by Rama.

Virupaksha The elephant who bears the whole world.

Vishnu The Preserver, Vedic sun-god and one of the two great gods of post-Vedic Hinduism.

Vision Quest A sacred ceremony undergone by native Americans to establish communication with the spirit set to direct them in life. The quest lasted up to four days and nights and was preceded by a period of solitary fasting and prayer.

Vivasvat The sun.

Volsung Family of great warriors about whom a great saga was spun.

Vrishadarbha King of Benares.

Vrishasena Son of Karna, slain by Arjuna.

Vyasa Chief of the royal chaplains.

Wolverine Large mammal of the musteline family with a dark, very thick, water-resistant fur, inhabiting the forests of North America and Eurasia.

Wyrd One of the Norns.

Yadu A prince of the Lunar dynasty.

Yakshas Same as rakshasas.

Yama God of Death, king of the dead and son of the sun.

Yasoda Wife of Nand.

Yggdrasill The World Ash, holding up the nine worlds. Does not fall at Ragnarok.

Ymir Giant created from fire and ice; his body created the world.

Yudhishthira The eldest of the Pandavas, a great soldier.

Zeus King of gods, god of sky, weather, thunder, lightning, home, hearth and hospitality. He plays an important role as the voice of justice, arbitrator between man and gods, and among them. Married to Hera, but lover of dozens of others.

Further Reading

African Myths & Legends

Abrahams, R.D., *African Folklore* (Pantheon Books, 1983)
Arnott, K., *African Myths and Legends* (Oxford University Press, 1962)
Barker, W.H. and Sinclair, C., *West African Folk Tales* (George Harrap & Co and Sheldon Press, 1917)
Cardinall, A.W., *Tales Told in Togoland* (Oxford University Press, 1931)
Courlander, H., *A Treasury of African Folklore* (Marlowe & Company, 1996)
Courlander, H., *The Crest and the Hide and Other African Stories* (Victor Gollancz Ltd, 1984)
Dayrell, E., *Folk Stories from Southern Nigeria* (Longmans, Green and Co., 1910)
Finnigan, R., *Oral Literature in Africa* (The Clarendon Press, 1970)
Fox, D.C., and Frobenius, L., *African Genesis* (Stackpole Sons, 1937)
Johnston, H.A.S., *A Selection of Hausa Stories* (The Clarendon Press, 1966)
Knappert, J., *Fables from Africa* (Evans Brothers Ltd, 1980)
Knappert, J., *Myths and Legends of the Swahili* (Heinemann, 1970)
Mbiti, J.S., *Akamba Stories* (The Clarendon Press, 1966)
Parinder, G., *African Mythology* (Paul Hamlyn, 1967)
Torrend, S.J., *Specimens of Bantu Folklore* (Kegan Paul, Trench, Trubner & Co Ltd, 1921)
Werner, A., *African Myths and Legends* (George Harrap & Co, 1933)

Celtic Myths & Legends

Chadwick, N., *The Celts* (Penguin, 1997)
Cross, T.P. and Slover, C.H., *Ancient Irish Tales* (G. G. Harrap, 1936)
Jackson, K.H., *A Celtic Miscellany* (Penguin, 2006)
Kinsella, T., *The Táin: From the Irish Epic Táin Bó Cualinge* (Oxford University Press, 2002)
Mac Cana, P., *Celtic Mythology* (Chancellor Press, 1996)
Macalister, R.A.S., *Lebor Gabála Érenn (The Book of Taking Ireland)* (Irish Texts Society, 1941)
Murphy, G., *Saga and Myth in Ancient Ireland* (Mercier, 1971)
O' Hogain, Dr. D., *Myth, Legend and Romance* (Ryan, 1991)
O' Rahilly, C., *Táin Bó Cúalnge from the Book of Leinster (The Cattle Raid of Cúailnge)* (Dublin Institute for Advanced Studies, 1967)
O'Rahilly, T.F., *Early Irish History and Mythology* (Dublin Institute for Advanced Studies, 1984)
O' Sullivan, S., *Legends from Ireland* (Rowman and Littlefield, 1977)
Raftery, J., *Prehistoric Ireland* (B.T. Batsford, 1951)
Rolleston, T.W., *Celtic Myths and Legends* (Courier Dover Publications, 1990)
Sutcliff, F., *The High Deeds of Finn mac Cool* (Random House, 2013)
Yeats, W.B., *Fairy and Folk Tales of Ireland* (Scribner, 1998)

Chinese Myths & Legends

Birch, C., *Tales from China* (Oxford University Press, 2000)
Birrell, A., *Chinese Myths* (British Museum Press, 2000)
Christie, A., *Chinese Mythology* (Paul Hamlyn, 1968)
Fu, S., *Treasury of Chinese Folk Tales* (Tuttle Publishing, 2008)
Kiu, K. L. (trans.), *100 Ancient Chinese Fables* (The Commercial Press Ltd, 1985)
Lianshan, C., *Chinese Myths and Legends* (Cambridge University Press, 2011)
Liyi, Y. (trans.), *100 Chinese Idioms And Their Stories* (The Commercial Press Ltd, 1987)
Luxing, W., *100 Chinese Gods* (Asiapac Books, 1994)
Macgowan, J., *Chinese Folk-Lore Tales* (Forgotten Books, 2012)
Mackenzie, D.A., *China and Japan: Myths and Legends* (Senate Books, 1994)
Paper, J., *The Spirits are Drunk* (State University of New York Press, 1995)
Pitman, N., *The Chinese Wonder Book* (Tuttle Publishing, 2011)
Roberts, M., *Chinese Fairy Tales and Fantasies* (Pantheon Books, 1984)
Tang, W., *Legends and Tales from History* (China Reconstructs, 1984)
Wangdao, D. (trans.), *100 Chinese Myths And Fantasies* (The Commercial Press Ltd, 1988)
Werner, E.T.C., *Ancient Tales and Folklore of China* (G.G. Harrap & Co. Ltd, 1922)
Yang, L., *Handbook of Chinese Mythology* (OUP USA, 2008)

Classical Greek Myths & Legends

Apollonius of Rhodes, *Jason and the Argonauts* (Penguin, 1995)
Buxton, R., *The Complete World of Greek Mythology* (Thames & Hudson, 2004)
Garnett, L.M.J., *Greek Folk Tales* (Eliot Stock, 1885)
Grant, M., *Myths of the Greeks and Romans* (Michael Grant, 1989)
Graves, R., *The Greek Myths* (Penguin, 1955)
Grimal, P., *The Dictionary of Classical Mythology* (Blackwell, 1986)
Hesiod, *The Homeric Hymns* (Loeb, 1914)
Homer, *The Iliad* (Loeb, 1928)
Homer, *The Odyssey* (Loeb, 1928)
Hope Moncrieff, A.R., *Classical Mythology* (George Harrap, 1907)
Kirk, G.S., *The Nature of Greek Myths* (Penguin, 1974)
Kirk, G.S., *Homer and the Oral Tradition* (Cambridge University Press, 1976)
Kupper, G.H., *The Legends of Greece and Rome* (O.C. Heath & Co., 1910)
Lang, A., *Homeric Hymns* (George Allen, 1899)
Morford, M.P.O., and Lenardon, R.J., *Classical Mythology* (Longman, 1985)
Napoli, D., *Treasury of Greek Mythology* (National Geographic Children's Books, 2011)
Otto, W.F., *The Homeric Gods: The Spiritual Significance of Greek Religion* (Thames and Hudson, 1955)
Petiseus, A.H., *The Gods of Olympus* (Fischer Unwin, 1892)
Seton-Williams, M.V., *Greek Legends and Stories* (Rubicon Press, 1993)
Sharwood Smith, J., and Johnson, M., *The Greeks and Their Myths* (Eurobook Limited, 1992)
Stoneman, R., *An Encyclopaedia of Myth and Legend: Greek Mythology* (Aquarian Press, 1991)
Warner, R., *Men and Gods* (Penguin, 1952)
Wood, M., *In Search of the Trojan War* (BBC Books, 1987)

Indian Myths & Legends

ıncroft, A. and Harrison, P., *The Buddhist World* (Hodder Wayland, 2001)
ıattacharji, S., *The Indian Theology* (Cambridge University Press, 1970)
owson, J., *A Classical Dictionary of Hindu Mythology and Religion* (Routledge and Kegan Paul, 1961)
ıtt, R.C., *Mahabharata and Ramayana condensed into English Verse* (E.P. Dutton, 1910)
win, V., *Myths of Middle India* (Oxford University Press, 1954)
ns, V., *Indian Mythology* (Paul Hamlyn, 1967)
ıpur, K.K., *Ganesha Goes to Lunch* (Mandala Publishing Group, 2007)
osambi, D.D., *Myth and Reality:Studies in the Formation of Indian Culture* (Popular Prakashan, 2005)
osambi, D.D., *The Culture and Civilization of Ancient India* (Vikas, 1994)
nappert, J., *Indian Mythology: An Encyclopedia of Myth and Legend* (Diamond Books, 1995)
ıng, T., *Buddhism and the Mythology of Evil* (Oneworld, 1997)
arasinghe, M.M.J., *Gods in Early Buddhism* (University of Sri Lanka (Ceylon), 1974)
ster Nivedita, and Coomaraswamy, A.K., *Myths of the Hindus and Buddhists* (Dover, 1967)
'Flaherty, W., *Hindu Myths* (Penguin, 1975)
ıttanaik, D., *Indian Mythology* (Inner Traditions Bear and Company, 2003)
oy Chaudhuri, P.C., et al., *Folk Tales of India* (Sterling, 1969)
homas, P., *Epics, Myths and Legends of India* (Taraporevala Sons and Co., 1973)
hastri, H.P. (trans.), *The Ramayana of Valmiki, vol. 1* (Shanti Sadan, 1952)

Native American Myths & Legends

lexander, H.B., *Native American Mythology* (Dover Publications Inc., 2005)
rinton, D.G., *Myths of the New World* (McKay, 1896)
)river, H.E., *Indians of North America* (University of Chicago Press, 1969)
dmonds, M. and Clark, E.E., *Voices of the Winds: Native American Legends* (Castle, 2003)
rodes, R., and Ortiz, A., *American Indian Myths and Legends* (Pantheon Books, 1984)
idley, M., *The Vanishing Race: Selections from Edward S. Curtis's The North American Indian* (University of Washington Press, 1987)
lagan, W.T., *American Indians* (University of Chicago Press, 1979)
enness, D., *The Indians of Canada* (National Museum of Canada, 1960)
osephy, A.M., *The Indian Heritage of America* (Harmondsworth, 1975)
eacock, E.B., and Lurie, N.O. (eds.), *North American Indians in Historical Perspective* (Random House, 1971)
Aarquis, A., *A Guide to American Indians* (University of Oklahoma Press, 1960)
Radin, P., *The Story of the American Indian* (John Murray, 1928)
now, D., *The American Indians: their Archaeology and Prehistory* (London, 1976)
Turner, G., *Indians of North America* (Blandford Press, 1979)
Jnderhill, R.M., *Red Man's America* (University of Chicago Press, 1953)
Washburn, W., (ed.), *The Indian and the White Man* (Doubleday, 1971)
Wood, M., *Spirits, Heroes and Hunters from North American Indian Mythology* (Schocken Books, 1981)

Norse Myths & Legends

Auden, W.H. and Taylor, P.B., *Norse Poems* (Faber and Faber, 1983)

Byock, J.L., *The Prose Edda: Norse Mythology* (Penguin, 2005)

Clover, C.J., and Lindow J., *Old Norse-Icelandic Literature: A Critical Guide* (University Toronto Press, 2005)

Colum, P., *The Children of Odin: the Book of Northern Myths* (Benediction Classics, 2011)

Crossley-Holland, K., *The Penguin Book of Norse Myths* (Penguin, 2011)

Davidson, H.R.E., *Gods and Myths of Northern Europe* (Penguin, 1964)

Foster, M.H., *Asgard Stories: Tales From Norse Mythology* (Forgotten Books, 2012)

Hollander, L.M., *Heimskringla: History of the Kings of Norway* (University of Texas Press, 196

Jones, G., *A History of the Vikings* (Oxford University Press, 2001)

Lindow, J., *Norse Mythology: A Guide to Gods, Heroes, Rituals, and Beliefs* (OUP USA, 2002)

Orchard, A., *The Elder Edda: A Book of Viking Lore* (Penguin, 2011)

Orchard, A., *Cassell's Dictionary of Norse Myth and Legend* (Cassell, 1997)

Page, R.I., *Norse Myths* (British Museum Press, 1990)

Picard, B.L., *Tales of the Norse Gods* (Oxford University Press, 2001)

Turville-Petre, E.O.G., *Myth and Religion in the North* (Greenwood Press, 1975)

Scottish Myths & Legends

Ashe, G., *Mythology of the British Isles* (Methuen, 1990)

Black, G.F., *Country Folk-Lore III, Orkney and Shetland Islands* (BiblioBazaar, 2009)

Bruford, A., and MacDonald, D.A. eds., *Scottish Traditional Tales* (Polygon, 1994)

Bruford, A., *Gaelic Folk-Tales and Mediaeval Romances* (Folklore of Ireland Society, 1969)

Buchan, D., *The Ballad and the Folk* (Routledge and Kegan Paul, 1972)

Chambers, R., *Popular Rhymes of Scotland* (W. Hunter, 1826)

Campbell, J.G., *Clan Traditions and Popular Tales of the Western Highlands and Island* (Kessinger Publishing, 2004)

Campbell, J.G., *Superstitions of the Highlands and Islands of Scotland* (J. Maclehose & Sons, 1900)

Campbell, J.G., *Witchcraft and Second Sight in the Highlands and Islands of Scotland* (Jame MacLehose & Sons, 1902)

Douglas, S., *The King of the Black Art and Other Folk Tales* (Aberdeen University Press, 1987)

MacDougall, J., *Folk Tales and Fairy Lore* (John Grant, 1978)

MacInnes, D. (ed.), *Folk and Hero Tales* (Elibron Classics, 1999)

Marwick, E., *The Folklore of Orkney and Shetland* (Batsford, 1975)

Matthews, C. & J., *An Encyclopaedia of Myth and Legend* (Aquarian Press, 1995)

O'Sullivan, S., *The Folklore of Ireland* (Batsford, 1974)

Philip, N., *The Penguin Book of Scottish Folktales* (Penguin, 1995)

Robinson, M. ed., *The Concise Scots Dictionary* (Edinburgh University Press, 1999)

Thompson, S., *The Folktale* (University of California Press, 1977)

Westwood, J. and Kingshill, S., *The Lore of Scotland: A Guide to Scottish Legends* (Randon House, 2009)

Wilson, B.K., *Scottish Folk-Tales and Legends* (Oxford University Press, 1989)

Index